Citizens as Soldiers
A History of the North Dakota National Guard

Jerry Cooper
with Glenn Smith

UNIVERSITY OF NEBRASKA PRESS
LINCOLN AND LONDON

♾

First Nebraska paperback printing: 2005

Library of Congress Cataloging-in-Publication Data
Cooper, Jerry.
Citizens as soldiers: a history of the North Dakota National Guard / Jerry Cooper with Glenn Smith.
p.   cm.
Originally published: Fargo, N.D.: North Dakota Institute for Regional Studies, 1986.
Includes index.
ISBN 0-8032-6449-6 (pa. : alk. paper)
1. North Dakota. National Guard—History.   I. Smith, Glenn.   II. Title.
UA380.C66   2005
355.3'7'09784—dc22   2005000681

Dedicated to those who served

Contents

List of Illustrations

TABLES

MAPS

Acknowledgments

This book is the consequence of a unique collaboration between private groups and individuals, state government, and scholars. In response to requests from the 164th Infantry Association and the strong recommendation of Major General C. Emerson Murry (U.S. Army, retired), then adjutant general, the Forty-seventh Legislative Assembly of the State of North Dakota enacted a bill and appropriated funds for the research, writing, and publication of a history of the 164th Infantry and the North Dakota National Guard. This began a project which has a significant parallel with the histories of the regular forces.

For forty years, the Army, Navy, and Air Force have maintained historical offices staffed by professional historians. These offices have produced historical studies of the United States Armed Forces which are internationally recognized for their quality, objectivity, and analytical insight, despite their designation as "official" history. The official histories, by their nature, have neglected reserve forces, and in particular the Army and Air Force National Guards. Some states have prepared particular unit histories or general recapitulations of their military history. Militia and National Guard unit histories have been written by individuals for decades. Few of these have approached the quality of the studies produced by the regular services.

General Murry, however, using the legislature's generous appropriation, determined to have North Dakota's military past researched and written in such a manner that it would not only recount the services of the state's soldiers, but also meet the standards of scholarly publication. To that end, he engaged the North Dakota Institute for Regional Studies at North Dakota State University, Fargo, to supervise the project and secure qualified historians.

This book is an official history, in that the National Guard through General Murry initiated the study, required certain topics to be covered, and paid for it. The authors, however, were left free to research and write as their instincts, training, and experience led them. North Dakota's agreement with the authors required them to take suggestions from the adjutant general "about the character and contents" of the book, but were "under no duty to adopt them when" in their judgment "such adoption is unwise." That spirit has guided the writing of this book and has been maintained amicably throughout. General Murry, his successor Major General Alexander P. Macdonald, and their staffs have been unfailingly cooperative. Their suggestions, some of which were accepted and others that were not, were offered with grace and the intention of improving the manuscript. It is our hope that the suggestions were received with the same grace and cooperation, and our thanks go to all at National Guard headquarters, Fraine Barracks, Bismarck, who have assisted us.

It was my responsibility to research and write on all aspects of the North Dakota National Guard's history except for the 164th Infantry's World War II experience. I deeply regret that I cannot extend my personal thanks to

ix

Colonel Raymond Bohn, Deputy Adjutant General, who died before he saw the book in print. From my earliest contact with this project until poor health took him from his office, Ray Bohn was my contact at Fraine Barracks. His only response to every letter, phone call, or personal visit was, "How can I help?" He did not stand on ceremony or hide behind red tape; on the contrary, he always reduced the latter to a minimum. His help in finding material, lining up interviews, providing a work space, and easing the difficulties of long distance research made my work truly enjoyable. He never attempted to direct the research or influence the perspective of my writing. My association with him was a lesson in civil-military relations. Ray Bohn was the epitome of the citizen-soldier tradition, and I shall treasure his memory.

I learned a great deal from another National Guardsman, who became in effect my collaborator. I first encountered Chief Warrant Officer Bryan O. Baldwin as a disembodied voice on the oral interviews of former Guardsmen which came to me halfway through the project. It became quickly evident when listening to the tapes that Bud Baldwin not only knew a great deal about the North Dakota National Guard, but was more than casually informed on American military history. I first turned to him for leads to obscure material, then realized that he was the best person to read the manuscript for authenticity. His more than thirty years in the Guard and his possession of much of the Guard's oral tradition not only made him a first rate interviewer but an ideal critic. Bud and I sometimes disagreed rather strongly on certain interpretations and emphases in the final manuscript, and the author's prerogative prevailed, but there is no doubt in my mind that the end product is much the better for Bud's efforts, freely given, and I thank him.

Major Clifford Keller, staff historian at Fraine Barracks, maintains the Guard's records, which include documents, published material, and photographs. Cliff opened the Guard's library and allowed me access to every item there. Throughout the project, he repeatedly sent me material I had missed or could not find, and searched the State Historical Society for information not on hand at Fraine Barracks. He also searched the photographic collection to find the best pictures to illustrate the book, and read the manuscript with care. His assistance, as my work came to a close, had particular value.

Several others at Fraine Barracks gave of their time to make a stranger feel welcome and help him get his work done. Lieutenant Joan Bentz, in Colonel Bohn's office, rendered many favors, large and small. Sergeant Kathy Mader assisted with photocopying. Command Sergeant Major Raymond Scharnowske and Chief Warrant Officer Richard Schell served as intermediaries in arranging interviews, and not incidentally shared insights from their lengthy Guard careers.

I am grateful to Mrs. Heber L. Edwards for an interview and for sharing material from her husband's lengthy military career. Mrs. Robert Carlson also gave an interview and provided documents relating to her husband's service. Mr. Charles Welch, a member of the 188th Field Artillery Battalion in World War II, consented to an interview. Major General LaClair Melhouse (U.S. Army, retired), a former adjutant general, discussed his career at length and loaned me hard to find documents. All interviews were conducted in Bismarck.

Members of the 164th Infantry Association, the 188th Field Artillery Group Association, and the 957th Field Artillery Battalion Association cooperated in the project. Most of these World War II veterans filled out questionnaires, and many were interviewed by Chief Warrant Officer Baldwin. Others provided military records and photographs. Their assistance enabled the authors to go beyond the official records in depicting the Guard's history in peace and war. Mr. Keith Parsons, historian of the 164th Association, was particularly helpful.

I owe a particular debt to Dr. Archer Jones, Director of the North Dakota Institute for Regional Studies. He served as liaison between the adjutant general's office in Bismarck and the historian in St. Louis. Archer was a tolerant supervisor from the beginning. His advice and counsel at various times was consistently sound. I especially appreciate his tact in explaining to our military employers, men acutely attuned to the necessity of being on time, why a scholar might miss not one but two deadlines!

Ms. Cathy Heiraas of the Institute effectively typed several manuscript versions despite the fact that typist and author were separated by several hundred miles. If I did not always remember which version we were working on, she did. Joanne Jones' keen eye for copy-editing improved the manuscript significantly. Thanks too to my collaborator Glenn Smith for leads and suggestions.

The College of Arts and Sciences, University of Missouri-St. Louis, allowed me to take a year's leave of absence during the 1982-1983 academic year to begin the project, and granted a semester's leave to finish it up. I am most grateful for that time off, more precious than money when one is writing. Ms. Ruth Kling, a graduate student in our Department of History, served as my research assistant for two semesters. She learned far more about the National Guard and North Dakota than she ever thought she would when she first entered our Master's degree program. Thanks, Ruth. My colleague and chairman, Neil Primm, read the first three chapters, wielding his infamous felt-tipped pen with vigor. His editorial instincts are rarely wrong and his standards are high. I benefited from his comments not only in the chapters he read but in those I wrote later. Two other colleagues, Chuck Korr and Jim Roark, patiently listened to my problems, offered advice, but best of all gave me what I needed most, friendly support.

Many others assisted along the way, most notably those indispensable people in libraries and archives. The staff of the Inter-Library Loan department, Thomas Jefferson Library, University of Missouri-St. Louis deserve praise, as do those at the United States Army Military History Institute at Carlisle Barracks, Pennsylvania; the State Historical Society of North Dakota at Bismarck; and the Orin G. Libby Manuscript Collection, Chester Fritz Library, University of North Dakota, Grand Forks. Historians could not do their work without these kind people, and they ought to know we remember their help. Many people assisted me at the National Archives in Washington, but I must thank once again my long-time friend Tim Nenninger, who always has time to listen and talk.

Finally, a word of thanks and love to my wife Ellie and daughter Christine. As that third deadline approached, I slipped upstairs too many evenings and too many Saturdays to bang away on the typewriter. They tolerated my absence from the living-room more often than not, and better than I did. Their support and understanding were the most important of all. What is of value in this book is the consequence of a collaborative effort with family, friends, and those I have thanked here. Errors of fact and misjudgments in interpretation are mine alone.

Jerry Cooper
St. Louis, Missouri

I wholeheartedly concur with my colleague, Dr. Cooper, in his acknowledgement of the cooperation received from the people at the headquarters of the North Dakota National Guard. It was a pleasure to work with them, particularly Colonel Bohn and his staff.

Dr. Archer Jones, former Dean of the College of Humanities and Social Sciences at North Dakota State University and Director of the North Dakota Institute for Regional Studies, offered sage advice without directives and his contribution was quietly but effectively omnipresent. Also, I am particularly indebted to Keith Parsons, historian to the 164th Infantry Regiment Association. He was most generous of his time and allowed me free access to the records of the association. Doug Campbell gathered much information for me in the form of newspaper clippings, diaries, photos and other material. I, too, want to pay special recognition to Bryan (Bud) Baldwin for his excellent work on the oral history project closely connected with this book. Since both of us were former combat infantrymen in the Pacific, we had an exceptional rapport.

Lastly, I must express a special gratitude to the men who served with the 164th and shared their experience with me. They permitted me to attend their annual reunions and extended a warm hospitality. I had the pleasure of formally interviewing many of them and learned much from these informal conversations. They are justifiably proud of their record in World War II, as they should be, and I thank them for searching their memories on my behalf.

Glenn Smith
Grand Forks, North Dakota

Foreword

The National Guard was very much a part of small town life in the thirties. To be sure, there were units in the cities, but they were apt to be less prominent in the community. Most historians who mention the Guard in that decade place it in the context of labor-management conflicts and, more often than not, view it with hostility. As one who grew up in a Kentucky town with a population of ten thousand during the Depression, I remember the Guard as an integral part of our community. Among the officers were a couple of lawyers and a postal clerk, one of the sergeants was a barber, and my brother and his best friend were privates. Perhaps a hundred men were in the three units--a tiny medical detachment, a quartermaster company, and a cavalry troop. Understandably, my town was known as a Guard town. The cavalry starred in the local parades. How we children and evidently a good many adults enjoyed seeing those men in uniform on their handsome horses prancing down the street. The Guard was a natural part of life there and in hundreds of other towns and cities throughout the nation. It was also a basic component of our national tradition.

The militia concept, which originated in England in the twelfth century, was ideally suited to conditions in the American colonies. On the frontier, where men and their families lived on a potential battlefield, the theories of universal military obligation and local responsibility for defense were not abstractions but obvious facts of life. As the frontier advanced and as the colonies evolved into a nation, problems arose in maintaining the militia, not only because in more settled areas hostile threats were no longer evident but also because some political leaders tried to make the militia more of a federal than state force. In the nineteenth century, the militia provided a structure to raise troops in times of emergency. As a means of sustaining trained, effective military units, it was a failure. But then, had it really been otherwise before the War of Independence? Those Founding Fathers who wanted a more effective citizen-soldier organization hoped to change (reform, in their view) the system. What emerged and became particularly popular in the 1850s were volunteer companies. Initially, neither the federal nor state governments paid much attention to these units. There was little reason for them to do so, as these were essentially social clubs. The men had shoulder arms, swords, and colorful uniforms and might be able to perform exhibition drills for entertainment, but for them the camaraderie, dances, and other such activities were as important, if not more so, than any military function.

The Civil War brought a temporary end to such amusements, but within a few years after that war volunteer companies began to spring up again. A greater impetus to the National Guard, as it was beginning to be called in the 1870s, came from the turbulence of that decade, however, when laborers clashed with the establishment. Governors of the eastern states where the disorders initially occurred wanted military forces at their disposal, and the militia system was the logical as well as legal means of obtaining them. The federal government also began to take increased interest in citizen soldiery. This set the scene for the major issue in National Guard affairs in the twentieth century: the struggle for power between the state and federal governments. The latter wanted an effectual reserve for the Army, while the states did not want to give up their control to the extent that was necessary to realize that goal. Over the years the pressures of modern war and the great expansion of federal spending in support of the National Guard brought about the standardization of weapons, equipment, and personnel requirements, so that by the 1960s the Guard became the kind of organization that the federal government desired. Gone were the social clubs. Training had now become the Guard's top priority. In fact, by 1980 many Guardsmen were virtually full-time professional soldiers.

In the mid-1880s, when North Dakota was still a territory, a few citizens began to form militia companies which continued to struggle for existence even after statehood. As was generally characteristic of such organizations of that era, they were clubs whose membership wore uniforms and drilled on occasion. Indeed, the secretary of the company at Valley City referred to it as 'the lodge.' Given North Dakota's small and scattered population and limited state funds, the beginnings of the North Dakota militia were feeble. Fortunately, however, the rural nature of the state enabled it to avoid industrial violence so that the emerging National Guard units did not have to bear the burden of quelling labor unrest.

North Dakotans had their initiation in combat in the Philippines, where the First North Dakota Infantry Regiment performed well in the first months of the Insurrection in 1899. As it happened, this was also the only war in which North Dakotans fought in a state-designated unit made up entirely of men from their home state. The First North Dakota went out again in the Mexican Border call-up in 1916, but it became the 164th Infantry in World War I and received an influx of out-of-state recruits. Those officers and men who saw combat went into action as replacements (most of them helped make the 1st Division famous) since the Army broke their regiment up to reinforce veteran divisions.

During the twenties and thirties, the National Guard revived and even prospered in comparison with the peacetime interval between 1899 and 1917. Increased federal subsidies, particularly for pay, meant a greater regularization of drill periods and summer camps. A Guardsman risked going to jail for an unexcused absence. Besides, during the depression he needed the money too much to miss a drill night.

Three units with North Dakota roots, the 164th Infantry Regiment and the 188th and 957th Field Artillery battalions, fought with distinction in World War II, but again, large numbers of outsiders filled the ranks and many of the officer slots as well. During the cold war, veterans and their younger colleagues kept the National Guard colors flying, even through the drastic reorganization of the 1960s. Meanwhile, the Air Guard unit began to add its laurels to the Guard's history.

Most state National Guard histories are chronicles that concentrate almost exclusively on the wartime achievements of the various state regiments. At best, they are accurate and include important documents; at worst, they are merely book-length hurrahs for 'our boys.' This book, in contrast, is a scholarly yet very readable case study. The research is wide in its scope and impressive in its depth. The authors use not only published and manuscript state and national records but also an ample number of newspapers and personal papers as well as interviews and responses to questionnaires from veterans. Indeed, their skillful blending of comments from those personal sources adds a great deal to the book. Thus the reader sees what war was like for individual soldiers in the Philippines, on Bougainville, and in France in addition to what the units' roles were in particular operations.

Professor Cooper carries this technique into the peacetime years as well. The result is a personalized, more readable, and more balanced study than one usually finds in National Guard historiography. This, I must emphasize, is not done at the neglect of major policy matters or of such notable figures as William Treumann, John Fraine, Heber L. Edwards, Ira Gaulke, and Robert Carlson, who contributed so much to the development of the Guard over the years.

This is a history as it should be written. The authors relate this complex story in a direct and simple narrative style buttressed throughout with perceptive analytical judgments. They place the evolution of the North Dakota National Guard squarely in the context of state, national, and when appropriate, world events as well as in the currents of military developments. Jerry Cooper and Glenn Smith have provided North Dakotans with a solidly researched, well-written history of their Guard and military historians, generally, with a reliable state case study that will stand as a model of its kind.

Edward M. Coffman
University of Wisconsin-Madison

☆ 1 ☆

Origins of the North Dakota National Guard

The North Dakota National Guard originated in the Dakota Territorial Militia of the 1860s, which in turn was a descendant of the colonial militia. In the colonial era, a universal military obligation fell on all eligible males, usually free white men between the ages of eighteen and forty-five. The militia trained irregularly and served as a training system from which colonial leaders raised more permanent units to take the field for a lengthy campaign. British authorities, then American commanders in the Revolution, attempted to raise volunteer units from the militia first and only reluctantly resorted to a draft when volunteering failed. After 1783, and until the end of the nineteenth century, state governments provided most of the troops used to fight the nation's wars. The states relied on their otherwise inactive militia systems to recruit volunteers, and calls on the states for wartime troops helped keep alive the spirit and practice of citizen-soldiers first established in the colonial era.

From its inception, the militia was a decentralized force with a strong local orientation. It served state and local governments in suppressing civil disorder, enforcing the law, and coping with disasters. When the volunteer uniformed companies came to full flower in the 1850s, the militia served the fraternal and political interests of its members as well. Informality governed these units far more than official regulations. Militiamen usually elected their own officers, and even when called to serve the federal government, they displayed a casual contempt for military discipline that endlessly disturbed and angered Regular Army officers. The National Guard would inherit much of this local focus and informality.

Historian Russell Weigley has stressed that America's military history is the history of two armies, the Regular Army and the citizen-soldier army raised for war. Until World War I, the vast majority of the citizen-soldiers came to national military service through the state militia systems as volunteers. From World War I through the Korean War, despite conscription, thousands of state citizen-soldiers entered military service through the National Guard, which developed after the Civil War as a direct descendant of the uniformed militia. A great deal of history has been written on one segment of the military's dual tradition, the Regular Army, but far less on the citizen-soldier army. The Guard's history is inextricably bound up with that of the Army's, but it is more than that. A full history of the state citizen-soldier must include his part in the nation's wars, but it also requires a close examination of his experience in and service to his state, and, perhaps most importantly, a full portrait of who he was and why he served.

1

When Congress created Dakota Territory in March 1861, the universal militia had long since lost its vitality, even on the frontier. The Army preceded settlement in Dakota, establishing garrisons at Forts Pierre and Randall on the Missouri River in the south and at Fort Abercrombie on the Red River in the north during the 1850s. These small garrisons regulated Indian-white relations and sought to keep in check hostile Indian action. The Army's presence reduced the need for a militia, and the vast expanse of the Territory, with a population in 1860 of just under five thousand, spread out from Pembina on the Canadian border to Sioux Falls, Vermillion, and Yankton in the south, hindered effective militia organization.

Regular troops were removed from the Missouri River posts early in the Civil War. Territorial Governor William Jayne issued a proclamation in December 1861 calling for two companies of volunteer cavalry to bolster the depleted garrison at Fort Randall. After a month of recruiting at Yankton, Vermillion, and Bon Homme, Jayne managed to raise one company, which he enrolled into territorial service in late January 1862. This was the first unit of the Dakota Militia. On 29 April 1862, the federal government accepted the outfit as Company A, First Dakota Cavalry, for three years' service in the United States Volunteers. Jayne failed to recruit the second company.

Further stimulus for organizing the Dakota Militia came in late summer, 1862, when Sioux Indians in southwestern Minnesota rose up in anger. The massacre at New Ulm, Minnesota, in mid-August alarmed the scattered Dakota settlers. Company A and a recently arrived battalion of Iowa volunteer cavalry at Fort Randall offered the only protection. Although the Indians in Dakota gave no sign of joining the Minnesota Sioux in the uprising, panic spread in the Territory anyway. Farmers left their homesteads for the small villages in the southeast section and many departed the Territory. Governor Jayne ordered the enrollment of the entire militia, all able-bodied men between the ages of eighteen and fifty, on 30 August 1862, acting as much to calm the people and stop the exodus as to deal with actual Indian violence.

In the oldest of militia traditions, Jayne called for every eligible male to enroll in his local company ''for home defense,'' each to supply his own arms and equipment. Enrollees were then to elect their officers. Although Jayne also sent a request for federal arms, asking for three hundred muskets and ample ammunition, the weapons did not arrive until November, after the worst of the Indian threats had passed. In the meantime, in September he appointed an adjutant general for the territorial militia, Charles P. Booge, a Yankton merchant.

Dakotans built temporary fortifications in the southeast villages and organized six militia companies in the fall of 1862. In early October, the governor issued a second call for volunteers, asking for eight companies, half infantry and half cavalry, willing to enlist for nine months' service as United States Volunteers. He intended to use these outfits in offensive action against the Indians to forestall an uprising. The war scare, for such it was in Dakota, evaporated rapidly, and volunteers for the eight companies failed to appear. At the end of 1862, Jayne had only enough men to organize a second troop of cavalry which became Company B, Dakota Cavalry, United States Volunteers, when it entered federal service on 1 March 1863. By that time, the hastily

2

organized militia companies of September 1862 were inactive. Although General Booge reported 266 officers and men enrolled in the militia in his December 1863 report, the force had not served a day in the field for the entire year.

Because the Army returned to the Territory with the intent of breaking Indian power, the Dakota Militia faded away as rapidly as it had come into being. Minnesota militia units, under Colonel Henry H. Sibley, had pursued and severely punished the Indians responsible for the New Ulm massacre. The surviving Indians fled Sibley's forces into Dakota, going northwest, however, and not threatening the southern settlements. In the summer of 1863, the Army launched a two-pronged attack on the Dakota tribes. While Sibley, now a brigadier general in United States service, led a force west from Minnesota, another contingent under Brigadier General Alfred H. Sully came up the Missouri River. Sully devised and led two punishing campaigns against the Indians during the summers of 1863 and 1864. The only territorial forces to serve in these campaigns were Companies A and B, Dakota Cavalry, United States Volunteers, a nominal battalion commanded by Captain Nelson Miner of Yankton.

Dakota Territory did not directly provide troops for the Civil War; although the two cavalry companies, totaling 182 officers and men, served as three-year volunteers throughout the war, they never left the Territory. Their lot consisted of a great deal of routine but arduous patrol duty, serving only as a battalion during Sully's 1864 campaign. The Dakota Militia never took the field nor fired a shot at a hostile Indian. Its ineffectiveness during the Indian war was due largely to a lack of resources. The male population of military age within Dakota did not suffice to field a sizable force and the Territory lacked funds to equip even the small home-defense force mobilized in 1862.

It appeared soon after the war that vigorous leadership from Governor A. J. Faulk would give the Territory an active, well-equipped militia. When he asked the Secretary of War in March 1867 for sufficient arms, ammunition, uniforms, and accouterments to outfit one thousand men, most of them as cavalry, the War Department granted the request, sending arms and other necessities with a total value of $38,000 under an 1808 law that provided for the partial outfitting of the militia by the United States. The shipment far exceeded the Territory's annual allotment, thus leaving it with a deficit of $27,541 that would not allow it to draw equipment for years to come.

The governor proposed to establish companies "for home protection against a threatened invasion of the hostile Indians." He filled the vacant territorial staff offices, naming J. L. Kelly as adjutant general. By the end of July 1867, 538 officers and men were organized in eight companies located in the southeastern part of the Territory, all but one fully armed and equipped. Despite this promising beginning, Kelly's 1867 report hinted at a lack of substance behind the new militia. Kelly made no mention of a legislative appropriation to sustain the force once the federal government equipped it. He asked the governor to request a small sum from the legislature to be used to rent a building for storing surplus military gear. Kelly revealed that little of the twenty-nine tons of arms, uniforms and accouterments sent to Dakota in 1862 could be found, most being "lost or destroyed for want of some suitable place to store them."

The companies of 1867 disappeared, along with their equipment. For the next fifteen years the Territory made no effort to keep up a militia. The adjutant general of the United States Army, in his annual "Abstract of the Militia" for 1877, for example, reported no organized militia for Dakota but mentioned a territorial debt of $20,957.25 remaining on the arms grant of 1867. In his accounting to the Secretary of the Interior in 1868, Governor William Howard pointed out that "Dakota has no public buildings, no military organizations, and no arms." A year later Howard commented that he would like to see at least three companies of organized militia in the Territory to offer protection for the settled areas of the Red River valley, the southeast section, and the Black Hills. Governor Nehemiah Ordway mentioned the lack of a militia system in his 1880 report, disclosing that the territorial legislature of 1877 had passed a comprehensive militia code but, for want of arms, "the law has remained a dead letter." The governor speculated that the arms Faulk had collected had ended up with "irresponsible persons who lost them, or possibly worse, sold them to the Indians." Until Dakota cleared its debt with the War Department, it could not organize a militia, for it had insufficient revenues to purchase material to equip even a small force.

Dakota's militia system lay dormant in the 1870s for other reasons as well. The Territory's farming population remained too small and dispersed to support volunteer companies. As Governor Howard's 1878 report indicated, until the Territory acquired a capitol building, insane asylum, and penitentiary, it was not likely to expend its limited funds on the militia. In 1867, Governor Faulk justified his request for arms under the necessity to defend hearth and home against the Indians, a need that disappeared rapidly as the Regular Army returned in force to Dakota in the late 1860s, establishing a line of posts up the Missouri River into Montana. The Army eliminated the Indian threat for good when it broke the power of the Sioux in the campaigns following the disaster at Little Big Horn in 1876.

Five years after Governor Ordway's 1880 report lamented the lack of an organized militia in the Territory, the Dakota National Guard totaled one thousand officers and men organized in a brigade of two infantry regiments and an artillery battery. The Dakota National Guard held its first encampment that year, a four-day stint at Fargo where a Regular Army officer inspected the brigade. Beginning with the muster-in of four companies in 1884, the Dakota National Guard blossomed in two years into a force of nineteen companies with a full panoply of brigade and regimental officers. Guard companies were located throughout the Territory, from Fargo in the north to Vermillion in the south.

This substantial growth in the Dakota National Guard reflected the rapid growth of the Territory itself, 1878 to 1890 being the years of "The Great Dakota Boom." Railroad construction in both the northern and southern sections of Dakota brought with it a flood of immigration, causing the number of residents to grow from fewer than 15,000 in 1870 to 135,000 in 1880 and 415,610 in 1885, 152,000 of them in northern Dakota. A growing population and a maturing agricultural economy increased territorial revenues, allowing the development of governmental institutions, including prisons, insane asylums, universities, and the establishment of a permanent seat of government at Bismarck. As the farming frontier moved westward, towns and villages in the eastern part of Dakota expanded in size and number. Banks, newspapers, grain elevators, implement dealers, and other commercial enterprises grew with the population. The development of towns was crucial to the progress of the Dakota National Guard, for towns provided a stable population from which to recruit Guardsmen.

Dakota's success in establishing a territorial National Guard paralleled the rejuvenation of state militias throughout the United States. Heralded by some as "the New National Guard," the organized militia of the states increasingly adopted the name National Guard to distinguish itself from the pre-Civil War volunteer militia. The new Guard differed from the old militia in several ways, the most significant change being the willingness of many states to spend money on their military systems, chiefly to control labor disorders. As industrialization expanded rapidly after 1865, labor and management came into increasing conflict. Angry workers struck with greater frequency, and, all too often, labor disputes degenerated into violence. A major railroad strike in 1877, affecting an area from Pennsylvania to Missouri, overwhelmed state and local law enforcement agencies, compelling President Rutherford B. Hayes to direct the United States Army to give aid in the strike-torn area. Many National Guard units around the country performed ineffectively during the 1877 riots, and many states, most notably Pennsylvania, reorganized their militia systems and increased their military budgets. Labor disorders appeared regularly for the remainder of the nineteenth century, leading to further state military support.

Expanded fiscal support permitted reorganization of the inefficient, prewar militia systems. Reform-minded adjutants general asserted greater control over the once semi-independent, locally oriented companies of the pre-1861 militia. The regiment came to replace the company as the focal point of tactical and administrative organization. Increasingly, Guardsmen looked to the federal government and the Regular Army for assistance and advice. The newly formed National Guard Association (1879) successfully lobbied to increase the annual federal arms distribution to the states from $200,000 to $400,000 in 1887. Regular Army officers, upon state request, visited summer camps to inspect and instruct state soldiers. The annual summer regimental training camp, another post-1865 innovation, became the high-water mark of National Guard reform by the end of the century.

Despite these developments, the National Guard did not become an effective military force. The states spent money for a domestic peace-keeping force, while the War Department sought a potential reserve to bolster the Army in wartime. Guardsmen's loyalty and training were often pulled in competing directions. Increased state and federal funds fell far short of meeting the basic needs of the Guard for modern arms, equipment, training facilities, and armories. Each state equipped its force as it saw fit and as it could afford, and in those without a large urban, industrial population, particularly in the economically weak South and in the new states of the West, the National Guard fared poorly. Guardsmen often had to spend their personal money and organize fund-raising activities to provide essential items.

Because the Guard remained chiefly a state institution, it lacked uniformity. All states set their own standards for enlistment and commissioning, laws regulating the size of tactical units varied widely, and weapons and equipment differed from state to state. Most state laws required their Guard to conform to Regular Army rules and regulations but always with some proviso that allowed modification to meet state and local conditions. Poorly trained and disciplined when compared to the Army, the National Guard stressed the camaraderie of the armory and camp in its recruiting appeals, not the rigors of physical training, drill, and discipline. Armory work was seldom more than close-order drill. At summer camp, Guardsmen attempted to cram battalion, regimental, and brigade drill, plus skirmish work and rifle practice, into a six-day camp. Few states found effective ways to compel attendance at armory drill or summer training.

The institutional and physical aspects of the late nineteenth-century National Guard can be described and analyzed with some precision, but the motivations of the men who joined the Guard and remained in it for a long time are more elusive. The volunteer, unpaid nature of the service made it difficult to recruit and retain privates and lower-ranking noncommissioned officers. Few served more than one enlistment. The turnover in higher-ranking noncommissioned officers and company officers approached fifty percent annually. Long-serving company and field-grade officers, usually middle-class business and professional men, with an occasional skilled worker or artisan, composed the backbone of the National Guard.

These men joined the Guard and persevered for a number of reasons. Some indulged their taste for the military, while others appreciated the fraternal benefits of the wholly male Guard society. Social activity sponsored by companies and regiments appealed to the more convivial men. Americans often professed a dislike for professional soldiers but nevertheless accorded respect and prestige to men with military titles, especially in the years after the Civil War. Officer rank in the Guard opened social, economic, and political doors that might otherwise have remained closed. State military rosters reflected this in their multitude of high-ranking field officers far out of proportion to the number of men in the ranks.

The Guard's informality continually irritated hierarchical, rank-conscious regulars. Election of company officers by the enlisted men was nearly universal. In some states, company officers elected their battalion and regimental superiors. This vestige of the old volunteer militia made Army-style discipline impossible. A majority of companies maintained a social organization paralleling the military one, with bylaws, elected officers, rules for enlistment, dues, and organized social activities. Enlisted men were as likely to serve as club officers as were captains and lieutenants. This social side of the Guard, which undoubtedly weakened the command authority of officers, was essential to recruiting and maintaining interest in the company. Without it, the Guard would have failed, for it needed community support and recruiting appeal that offered more than military service.

Governor Nehemiah Ordway recognized this when he set out to establish the Dakota National Guard in the early 1880s. Once he convinced the War Department to drop Dakota's deficit in weapons and issue sufficient material to organize the Dakota National Guard, Ordway devised a plan under which the Grand Army of the Republic (an organization of veterans of the Union Army) would sponsor companies. A local Grand Army of the Republic post sought men qualified to hold commissions, recruited promising young men, and posted bond to insure the arms and equipment issued to the new units by the Territory. Commanded by William A. Bentley, Grand Army of the Republic Post No. 3 of Bismarck sponsored the first company organized under the plan in late 1883. Bentley informed the governor in November that, "According to your request," Post No. 3 "has taken the proper steps to ensure the organization of Co. A 1st Regiment of Dakota Militia."

Company A organized itself according to existing National Guard practice. It adopted a constitution and bylaws, elected Civil War veteran Orson W. Bennett as its captain, and selected officers for its social organization. The company took instruction in the school of the soldier at weekly drills for three months before petitioning the governor for territorial recognition. One of the Grand Army of the Republic sponsors assured Ordway that Company A "comprises the best young men in Bismarck." Other companies were organized in similar fashion throughout the Territory from late 1883 to the end of 1885.

Thomas S. Free, adjutant general, wrote Ordway's successor, Gilbert A. Pierce, in October of 1884 that organizing the Dakota National Guard "within the pale of the G.A.R. is simply an experiment." Though it paid off, it took time as military affairs moved slowly in Dakota Territory. Only four companies were in territorial service at the end of 1884. Free issued a circular letter in December of that year calling for the formation of more companies, to enlist for two years, but made it clear that the Territory was not yet ready to offer financial aid. Dakota would provide nothing but arms and rifle equipment for as many as forty enlisted men per company. Free and Pierce succeeded in having the 1877 militia law amended in 1885 to give each company an annual armory allotment and uniform allowance, plus funds to allow the adjutant general to conduct his business and appropriations for an annual training camp. Free announced the organization of the two infantry regiments in May 1885 and the brigade formation in June. The Dakota National Guard in 1885 included seven units in northern Dakota--the 1st Regiment had two infantry companies at both Bismarck and Fargo and one at Jamestown. Company F at Valley City was the only unit of the 2nd Regiment and Lisbon was home for the artillery battery. These units would form the basis of the North Dakota National Guard. (See Table 1.1.)

Despite promising beginnings in 1885, the Dakota National Guard and its successors failed to develop into efficient military systems. The Dakota National Guard reached a peak in 1887 with 1,137 officers and men, organized in a brigade of two infantry regiments, a cavalry battalion, and the battery. Two years later, it aggregated only 971. Two of the four northern Dakota companies mustered in 1884, Company C of Bismarck and Company F of Fargo, were mustered out in 1886 owing to insufficient membership. They were replaced in the 1st Regiment by Company C of Grafton and Company F of Grand Forks, but their collapse indicated an instability that would plague the Guard for the rest of the century.

TABLE 1.1

Dakota National Guard Companies Located in
North Dakota, 1884-1889

Company	Home Station	Year Mustered In	Mustered Out
1st Regiment			
A	Bismarck	1884	
B	Fargo	1884	
C	Bismarck	1884	1886
C	Grafton	1886	
F	Fargo	1884	1886
F	Grand Forks	1886	
H	Jamestown	1885	
K	Casselton	1889	1892
Battery A	Lisbon	1885	
Troop A	Dunseith	1887	
Troop B	Bottineau	1887	
2nd Regiment			
F	Valley City	1885	

The Territory attempted to do too much with its National Guard. An extensive military code approved in 1887 authorized not only the existing regiments and the brigade but also gave the governor the power to organize single battalions of artillery and cavalry. The law provided for an adjutant general's department, a supply department, and a full support staff including engineer, ordnance, and medical departments. This grand military system, in effect a small army organization, allowed three brigadier generals: the brigade commander, the adjutant general, and the chief of supply. Other field grade officers included two line colonels to command the regiments and a panoply of lieutenant colonels, majors, and captains to fill out brigade and regimental staffs. Yet at its fullest in 1887, the entire Dakota National Guard enrolled only the equivalent of a Civil War infantry regiment. Since it lacked the population to keep up even a semblance of a brigade, the Territory dropped the brigade after 1887 but organized an artillery battery. It was commonplace during this era to organize elaborate state military systems that had no practical function except to provide generalcies and colonelcies for overly ambitious amateur soldiers. The practice too often led to public ridicule as well as too many undermanned line organizations.

North Dakota's 1891 military code differed little from its territorial provisions. State law called for one infantry regiment of ten companies, although the governor had the discretion to increase the regiment to twelve companies. Companies, troops, and batteries were authorized 3 officers: a captain, first lieutenant, and second lieutenant; 11 noncommissioned officers; and a minimum of 20 to a maximum of 40 privates. With a twelve-company regiment, and a battalion of artillery and cavalry of two companies each, all companies recruited to the maximum of 54 officers and men, the North Dakota National Guard had an authorized strength of 864 for its tactical organizations. It never reached the maximum. No governor was tempted to organize a state brigade or call for a full artillery battalion. The state inherited seven infantry companies, an artillery battery, and the two-troop cavalry battalion from the Territory. Some of these units disbanded and others were added during the 1890s. In April 1898, on the eve of war, the North Dakota National Guard totaled nine infantry companies, the battery, a cavalry troop, and a 25-man regimental band, an aggregate of 552 officers and men, its highest enrollment in the 1890s. In part the Guard failed to grow because the Territory, and then the states of North and South Dakota, created in 1889, developed slowly. "The Great Dakota Boom" of the early 1880s ended late in the decade with a bust. Too much land speculation, the disastrous cattle-killing winter of 1886-1887, and dropping wheat prices left the Dakotas underpopulated and short of tax revenues. The National Guard had inherent problems that hindered its development, not only in the Dakotas but across the United States. The economic and political difficulties of the Dakotas simply made matters worse.

Although a state military system could succeed with vigorous executive direction from a well-informed adjutant general backed by an interested governor, Dakota Territory and North Dakota seldom had either. Caught in the politics of land speculation, railroad construction, and bitter disputes over statehood, Dakota's governors seldom gave attention to militia matters. Even though Governor Ordway expressed concern for the Guard, he did not appoint his first adjutant general until just before leaving office in June 1884. His successor, Gilbert Pierce, was more attentive, as seen in his support for the 1885 amendment to the militia law. Pierce was an exception among the territorial governors, however. State governors, except perhaps Andrew Burke, were so overwhelmed by the twin problems of state financial difficulties and the growing anger of economically strapped farmers that the Guard rarely entered their administrative plans. Governor Roger Allin (1895-1897), for example, routinely wrote no on all National Guard requests, even for small sums.

Rarely did a governor or adjutant general give consideration in their public reports to the purposes for which the Guard existed. Federal, state, and territorial laws, of course, provided for the maintenance of the militia. As a venerable American institution, the militia was omnipresent, as was county government or the state legislature. The militia, however, was evolving in new directions. If the National Guard was to become a viable military service, it needed a sense of purpose. It was incumbent upon governors and adjutants general to define and direct that purpose. The few men who raised the issue of the function of the National Guard simply repeated variations of the federal Constitution's definition of militia responsibilities: to enforce the law, to suppress insurrection, to repel invasion. Governor Ordway echoed these in his 1880 call for an organized militia, with the added mandatory reference to hostile Indians. Ordway also justified maintaining a militia as necessary to "keep alive the martial and patriotic sentiments of the people."

William Devoy, North Dakota's first adjutant general, commented acidly that "The need of a well organized and efficient militia force is apparent to everyone, except, perhaps, a North Dakota legislator," but did not use his barbed wit to explain the need. The only fully developed justification of the Guard came from General William A. Bentley in his 1892 report, wherewith, in eight pages of turgid prose, he reviewed the history of the American militia and the appearance of the new National Guard. Under a section titled "Necessity for a Strong National Militia Organization," Bentley spoke of the Army's inadequate resources and the need for a well-organized citizen soldiery to back up the regulars. Americans had always paid lip service to the desirability of a small army supported by citizen-soldiers in time of war, but they had never tolerated a well-organized, well-trained citizen force. Here, Bentley said, was the place for the National Guard. To meet the three constitutional functions, but especially to support the Army in time of war, the states had to recognize "the especial value of a well-organized force." The possibility that the National Guard could serve as reserve force for the Army was not an idea new to Bentley, but the concept lacked the force of law. Service to the state remained the fundamental function of the National Guard to the end of the nineteenth century.

The Territory and state seldom needed the Guard for constabulary purposes in the late nineteenth century. Dakota had no large industrialized urban areas which might explode into violence, as had happened in Pennsylvania and Illinois in the 1870s and 1890s. Neither did they need to worry about militant, strike-prone hard-rock miners as did the states of Colorado and Idaho. The Dakota National Guard performed civil peace-keeping duties occasionally during the mid-1880s to prevent violence between towns fighting over the location of county seats, most notably at Redfield, Spink County, in 1884. County seat "wars" inevitably ended up in court, however, and the Guard simply prevented hotheads from acting rashly. Indian reservations presented a much greater potential for internal disorder, although the Army was chiefly responsible for keeping the peace on or near reservations. Repeated squabbles between Indians and whites over taxes and land titles near the Winnebago Reservation in the Turtle Mountains led to the organization of two troops of Guard cavalry in 1887, one each in Bottineau and Rolette counties. The Turtle Mountain troubles were essentially a federal problem, in this case the Department of the Interior. Both the Dakota National Guard and North Dakota National Guard made general plans for responding to a governor's call to suppress civil disorder, but Captain William A. Shunk, 8th Cavalry, United States Army, found in his 1896 inspection of the North Dakota National Guard that "it does not appear that these matters have been committed to writing." The absence of written mobilization plans indicated an administrative neglect and a want of direction that permeated the service.

Because the National Guard always functioned on the periphery of territorial and state government, the adjutants general exerted little influence in politics. There was no continuity in the governance of the military, and from 1885 to 1898, nine different men held the adjutant generalcy. (See Table 1.2.) Adjutants general came and went with the governor who appointed them. Elliott S. Miller was the first to remain beyond the term of the governor who selected him. Throughout the territorial years, adjutants general were chosen solely for their political affiliations, not their military background, as it was essential for the governor and adjutant general to be politically compatible. Only after statehood did governors look for men who also had served in the Guard. Governor Eli C. D. Shortridge (1893-1895), a Populist, abandoned the practice when he appointed the perhaps too loyal William H. Topping. Topping, quite simply, needed a job. "I hardly know what I would of done if it had not been for the Governor's kindness in appointing me to this office," he conceded to a friend. The Territory did not maintain an office for the adjutant general and North Dakota did not provide office space in Bismarck until 1897. Consequently, the adjutant general's office was the home of the man who held the post. Although both the Territory and the state paid an annual salary of one thousand dollars to the adjutant general, only a man as desperate as William Topping treated it as regular employment. Neither the salary nor the demands of the post justified full-time work.

TABLE 1.2

Adjutants General, Dakota National Guard
and North Dakota National Guard,
1885-1898

Name	Service	Years in Office
Thomas S. Free	DNG	Aug. 1884-Nov. 1886
Noah N. Tyner	DNG	Nov. 1886-Dec. 1887
James E. Jenkins	DNG	Dec. 1887-Sept. 1888
James W. Harden	DNG	Nov. 1888-April 1889
J. S. Huston	DNG	April 1889-Nov. 1889
William Devoy	NDNG	1890
William A. Bentley	NDNG	1891-1893
William H. Topping	NDNG	1893-1895
Elliott S. Miller	NDNG	1895-1905

Continuity in administration was nearly impossible when the effects of the adjutant general's office, that is, correspondence, unit records, even supplies, moved with regularity to the home of each new appointee. After Thomas Free "reluctantly" accepted the job from Nehemiah Ordway, he was most surprised one day when several cases of rifles arrived at his front door with freight charges due. Free paid the charges out of his own pocket. He reported to Governor Pierce that "everything is in chaos," his successors repeating the lament year after year. Upon becoming adjutant general in November 1886, Noah Tyner found "No descriptive or other roll books or compiliation of reports." William Devoy reported that the material he received from Dakota Territory pertaining to Dakota National Guard units located in North Dakota 'were very meagre indeed,' enabling him only to estimate the number of officers and men actually enrolled. Devoy had no forms for enlistments, commissions, or reports. After assuming the job without "a single scrap of paper, not a line or letter, not even a seal of office," General William A. Bentley repeated the litany in 1892. He "had to create an office, obtain new muster rolls, property returns, seal, etc., necessary for active business."

Administration in the tactical units of the North Dakota National Guard was no better. Colonel H. M. Creel, Inspector General, North Dakota National Guard, found "utter chaos" in his 1891 inspection. "No records, no proper organization, in nearly all of our cos.—and the Regimental Hdqrs. was just as bad." General Topping recommended that the state adopt a standard record book to be issued to companies because "At present each company have their own way of keeping the record of their company." The social nature of companies compounded the records problem since most companies did not enlist a man but voted him into their membership at meetings of their civil organizations. Although they recorded the names of new members in their minute books, they did not always notify the state or even have the man sign formal enlistment papers. Company methods for property accountability were also wretched. Elliott Miller discovered a number of rifles and equipment in the hands of the Grand Army of the Republic in 1895. "The Guard have always been short of these articles," Miller complained, "and we never could account for their disappearance." Even though company commanders consistently neglected to submit monthly returns on drill attendance as required by law, neither the adjutant general nor regimental headquarters made much of an attempt to compel the required reporting.

Military men were notorious for their obsession with red tape and the rendering of frequent and redundant reports, but the efficient operation of any military force, including the National Guard, did demand a minimum of reporting and record keeping. A system that could not account for its membership or equipment was hardly a system at all, which was the general condition of affairs in the 1880s and 1890s.

Guardsmen knew well the inefficiencies of their service. The annual reports of the adjutants general invariably ended with recommendations for changes and improvements, and they regularly published the criticisms and suggestions offered by Army officers who inspected the Dakota National Guard and North Dakota National Guard. Territorial and state laws provided for a Military Advisory Board of three field-grade officers who had as their assignment the codification of the Guard's rules and regulations and the making of recommendations to the governors. The Board was particularly active after 1890 in urging the state to acquire a permanent military campground. The Dakota National Guard and North Dakota National Guard readily accepted the Regular Army practice of promotion by seniority when selecting officers for battalion and regimental assignments. After 1894, the North Dakota National Guard adopted a systematic small arms practice to improve its shooting skills. In 1898, General Miller suggested that the state build armories rather than leave that responsibility to individual companies. Colonel H. M. Creel, Inspector General for most of the 1890s, was the most outspoken advocate of Guard reform. He wanted a $.50 military poll tax on all men of militia age to support the Guard and pushed continually for the examination of newly commissioned and promoted officers, a requirement of the militia law which governors ignored regularly when signing commissions. Creel even called for the organization of a "Military Service Institute," which would hold meetings and publish a journal "to raise the standard, educate the members and bring about closer and better relations in the Guard."

Few of these suggestions dealt directly with the Guard's inefficiencies. The service needed stability and a permanent, though not necessarily large, administrative bureaucracy that could supervise and support the tactical organizations. This required money, and from the outset in 1885, the Guard lacked sufficient financial support to maintain even minimal stability and administration. Dakota Territory appropriated $15,000 per annum in 1885 and 1886, and $18,000 from 1887 to 1889 for the Dakota National Guard. In its first session, the North Dakota legislature suspended most sections of the territorial code that provided funds for the Guard, but it continued the annual armory rent for companies (ten units in 1890) and appropriated $400 per year for the salary and expenses of the adjutant general. The legislature approved a new military code in 1891 that included an annual appropriation of $11,000, a figure that prevailed to the end of the century. (In comparison, Wisconsin spent $100,000 annually after 1893, Minnesota had an 1895 Guard budget of $50,000, and Montana expended $21,000 for a force of 510 men that year. Conversely, the South Dakota Guard struggled on an annual budget of $4,000 from 1890 to 1894, Utah's Guard received only $3,000 in 1894 and 1895, and Washington slashed its biennial appropriation of $80,000 for 1893-1894 to a mere $6,000 for the 1897-1898 biennium.) Both the Territory and the state received an annual allotment from the War Department to assist in arming and equipping the National Guard. The War Department furnished material, not cash, sending arms, ammunition, uniforms, and a variety of quartermaster supplies to the states. The Territory's yearly allotment until 1887 was $1,439.36 and $2,764.98 thereafter. North Dakota's annual share, $2,747, remained unchanged from 1890 to 1898.

From these meager funds the Dakota National Guard and North Dakota National Guard provided the companies' annual armory and clothing allowances, attempted to conduct an annual training camp, and covered administrative costs. Throughout the late nineteenth century, the Guard never had sufficient financial support to do all of these things on a yearly basis. The Dakota National Guard confronted the financial crunch just two years after its full organization when it found it could not pay all of the 1887 armory and clothing allowances after expending $16,000 on separate encampments for the infantry regiments and the cavalry battalion. In the ensuing year, Governor Louis K. Church cancelled summer training in order to pay the allowances and because of "a disinclination to incur an expense in excess of the appropriations."

This dilemma occurred each year. If the state paid armory rents and clothing allotments in full, it could not afford to send Guardsmen to camp, even though state law required an annual encampment. Conversely, holding camp meant little or no aid to the companies. In the years 1890 through 1897, North Dakota held but two summer training camps. The 1894 camp, which cost $13,843, that is, nearly $3,000 more than the annual appropriation, left the state so deeply in debt to its Guardsmen and other creditors that it did not sponsor another camp for the remainder of the century. Fiscal mismanagement and poor planning by Governor Eli C. D. Shortridge and his adjutant general, William H. Topping, forced their successors in the next four years to follow stringent money management simply to pay the deferred armory and clothing allowances of 1893 and 1894. The only answer to this dilemma was a larger appropriation, but the North Dakota legislature acted on Guard funding but once in the 1890s. In 1895 it reduced the adjutant general's salary to $500 per year and cut his expense account in half.

Everyone connected with the National Guard recognized the negative effects of underfunding. James W. Harden, adjutant general, noted that the cancellation of the 1888 camp "produced a very discouraging effect upon the guard, which will require time and encouragement to obliterate." Governor A. C. Mellette was moved to issue a general order to the Dakota National Guard a year later apologizing for the lack of funds. He lamented the state of affairs "which leaves the military organizations without even the pittance provided by law for their maintenance." Some hoped that statehood would lead to greater support, but for North Dakota it brought a temporary reduction in 1890. William Devoy, acerbic as ever, predicted: "I venture to say there will not be a man left in the National Guard of the state, except, perhaps, the Adjutant General, and he, in all human probability, will be too much occupied dodging his creditors to make his annual report."

State military leaders struggled year after year with the question of whether to have a camp or pay the armory and uniform allowances. The chief issue was Guardsmen's morale. General Topping argued for a camp in 1894 because "by doing this we can pay the boys all their dues [per diem] something that has not been done for some time." Soon after recommending a camp to Governor Shortridge, however, Topping wrote that Troop A was on the verge of collapse "on account of not receiving their clothing allowance." He feared if they did not get the allowance "they will not enlist again." Elliott S. Miller favored a camp in 1896 because "not to have one will be very demoralizing to the Guard." Miller thought that since the companies seldom received clothing support they would not miss it anyway.

Neither the Territory nor the state deliberately kept the National Guard in poverty. As General Topping observed in 1893, however, "There is no money to pay the Guard at present...it takes money to do business." The depression of the early 1890s, which hit the agricultural sector of the economy particularly hard and thus affected North Dakota greatly, lowered tax revenues even more. As a consequence, all state institutions and services wanted for adequate funding. Because it was not an essential service as far as most state political leaders were concerned, the National Guard suffered more than most state agencies.

14

Rarely did the Territory or state purchase material for the Guard. Uniforms, arms, and field equipment usually came from the annual federal distribution or were purchased by individual companies. Organization of the Dakota National Guard came at a time of transition, when the National Guard was discarding the gaudy uniforms of antebellum days and adopting the Regular Army fatigue uniform as its standard dress. In the mid-1880s, Dakota National Guard regiments appeared in camp in a variety of uniforms, often designed by Guardsmen. Company H, 2nd Regiment, of Blunt, in southern Dakota, turned out in "long tailed blue coats with red facings, a double row of brass buttons, and red epaulets." This outfit, an old member recalled, "made a combination that would have flagged a railway train a mile off." Several northern Dakota companies of the 1st Regiment sported uniforms in cadet gray with appropriate gold braid and buttons. The shift to the Army fatigue outfit took years to accomplish as companies bought their own or received bits and pieces each year through the federal distribution. Finally, in 1896, the entire North Dakota National Guard appeared in the standard fatigue uniform.

When first organized, the Dakota National Guard was equipped with Civil War issue cap and ball muzzle-loading rifles. It acquired the single-shot, breech-loading Springfield rifle, .45 caliber, model 1884, in 1887 in a special federal issue arranged by Governor Church, which weapons it carried off to war in 1898. Since the Guard lacked the newest rifle equipment, however, it had to use earlier model bayonets, cartridge boxes, and other items into the late 1890s. Each year North Dakota received a few more of these articles from the War Department, dividing them among the companies so that all might have some of the new equipment. The battery at Lisbon drilled without guns until 1889 when the government provided two model 1861 muzzle-loading cannon, but it still lacked caissons, horse harness, and other equipment needed to work the guns properly. Battery members even improvised their own ammunition at camp. The cavalry carried the long Springfield rifle until 1892 when it finally received .45-caliber carbines from the federal government. None of the units had the proper equipment for field duty, lacking knapsacks, canteens, rubber ponchos, and a multitude of other necessary things. North Dakota's adjutants general looked to the federal government to solve the equipment problem, endorsing the National Guard Association's drive to increase the annual national allotment to one million dollars in the 1890s.

Many in the service believed the best means for developing an efficient National Guard was to hold encampments as regularly as fiscal conditions allowed. A week in camp removed companies from their isolation in widely separated towns and gave them a sense of identity, of belonging to a larger organization that existed for a definite purpose. A temporary release from the units' endless struggle for financial survival, the encampment was the only time when the Territory or state spent substantial amounts of money on the Guard. Officers and men received daily pay for their time in camp, and it was fun, a combined social, political, and military event that brought public attention to the Guard. The governor and his staff usually attended the entire proceedings. Civilians came to watch what the boys in uniform were up to, and newspapers suddenly gave front-page attention to the service. Elliott Miller noted the demoralizing effects of not having camp in his 1898 report, emphasizing that the men "all look forward to these as an incentive."

Encampment gave the Guard its only opportunity to function as a military organization. The truncated nature of infrequent armory drills instilled little sense of military duty in most Guardsmen. Going to camp offered company officers a chance to exercise command authority as they readied their units for the trip to camp, then led them in daily military exercises. Staff officers, particularly the adjutant general, inspector general, and chief of supply, had to plan the mobilization of the Guard and arrange transportation and subsistence. On occasion, all three arms of the service, infantry, cavalry, and artillery, drilled together. If at first the entire force marched like an awkward squad, officers and men were always pleased and surprised with the improvements that came in just a few days of continuous drill and field work. The Regular Army officers who attended all the Dakota National Guard and North Dakota National Guard camps in the 1880s and 1890s as inspectors and instructors consistently remarked on the rapid improvement Guardsmen made in the few days they spent in the field.

Unfortunately, the camps also highlighted the underlying problems of the territorial and state National Guard. Since neither the Territory nor the state owned a permanent training ground, camp was always an act of improvisation. The Territory accepted bids from towns competing to be hosts, the bidders offering a prepared camp site, usually a fairgrounds, and a variety of services and financial incentives. Governors selected different towns each year in order to give various sections of the Territory an opportunity to act as hosts. Although some camp sites were better than others, their quality was not the deciding factor. Treating the annual National Guard encampment as traveling circus was common in many states in the late nineteenth century, but adjutants general disliked this and strongly recommended acquiring a permanent military reservation. In 1891, at the suggestion of Colonel H. M. Creel, Inspector General, North Dakota petitioned Congress to cede to the state the recently abandoned Fort Totten military reservation near Devils Lake. Congress turned over 1,200 acres of Fort Totten land in 1894, but the state could not afford to improve the property for camp purposes.

Army inspectors reported a variety of flaws when they inspected the Guard, defects common to all the National Guard at the time. The regulars were consistently unhappy with the informality between officers and men at Guard camps, particularly the neglect of saluting. Inspectors criticized eating arrangements where company officers ate with their men and civilian cooks prepared the meals, a consequence of the improvised nature of the camps. They spent much of their time evaluating the Guard's conduct of routine camp duties. Lieutenant Colonel E. F. Townsend, 11th Infantry, thought guard mount at the 1887 camp "wretchedly done," an observation echoed by Captain W. H. Kell, 22nd Infantry, when he described the North Dakota National Guard's conduct of drills and ceremonies in 1891 as "rather crude affairs." The Guard devoted little time, in the armory or in camp, to target practice. General James W. Harden conceded in his report on the 1887 Dakota National Guard camp that "few if any of the members know anything of the shooting capacity of his gun.'' It was difficult for Dakota Guardsmen to become proficient riflemen when they were given but five rounds to fire in camp.

Camp discipline brought criticisms from both regular and National Guard observers. General Harden disliked encamping the entire Dakota National Guard brigade in one place because brigade camps led to ''too much of the holiday or picnic character'' and caused ''discipline to be lax.'' Colonel Townsend noted the same behavior in 1889, ''many seeming to consider this a grand picnic.'' A picnic atmosphere was nearly unavoidable with the governor and his entourage in camp or when skirmish drill ''was witnessed by several hundred spectators,'' as happened at the 1891 Devils Lake encampment.

While it was not surprising that men who drilled occasionally at the armory and sporadically took active field training for a week did not display great skill at battalion drill or failed to know the intricacies of extended-order drill, it did disturb Army inspectors that the Guard never improved from year to year. Their level of training remained static. At each camp the regulars spent the first day or two explaining the rudiments of guard duty, the basic duties of the officer of the guard, and the elements of company drill. A fundamental weakness was that little instruction took place in the armory. Guard duty, the school of the soldier, simple military courtesy, even the simpler marching maneuvers of the company should have been learned at the armory. As to guard duty, for example, Colonel Townsend reported in 1886, ''I am led to believe that little or no attention is paid to it'' at company drills. Year after year Townsend and other inspectors recommended that companies use weekly drills to learn the fundamentals of squad and company duty so that camp could be devoted to battalion and regimental work. This never happened. Since guardsmen never knew when camp would be held, particularly after statehood, they lacked incentive to prepare for active training.

The perpetual turnover in personnel at the company level, both officers and enlisted men, made inefficient camp performances worse. In 1887, fully sixty percent of the officers and enlisted men were new not only to camp but to National Guard service. Colonel Townsend, who inspected the Dakota National Guard in 1885, 1886, 1887, and again in 1889, reported in the latter year: ''not ten per cent of the enlisted men who were present at former encampments [were] in the ranks, while nearly as great a change had taken place'' among company officers. Only the field officers remained the same. The situation did not alter with the formation of the North Dakota National Guard. At both the 1891 and 1894 camps between sixty and sixty-five percent of the enlisted men were new, as were the company commanders who led them. A well-developed armory training program would benefit the Guard little if companies could not retain experienced men.

Because they focused on the difficulties of the companies, brigade and regimental camps reflected the deeper problems of the Guard. The brigade assembled only for three encampments. The regiments of the Dakota National Guard and North Dakota National Guard met in camp irregularly and were otherwise paper organizations. The men of the regimental staffs did not live in the same towns but came from all over the Territory or state. The companies were the essence of the National Guard, the only element of the service that operated on a continuous basis. Territorial and state law obliged them to hold at least eleven drills, parades, practice marches, or inspections each year, and many drilled more frequently than that. More importantly, companies were the recruiting agencies of the Guard. If they failed to recruit and maintain their membership and organization, then the Guard failed. An army without privates is no army at all, no matter how many generals and colonels it may have.

Since neither the Territory nor the state actively worked to organize local units, the companies were volunteer organizations in the truest sense. A company came into existence when enough men in a particular town organized themselves. Company F, Valley City, 2nd Regiment, Dakota National Guard, organized in this manner in February 1885 when interested citizens met at City Hall, elected officers and noncommissioned officers, and appointed a committee to write a constitution and bylaws to govern the company's activities.[1] They then offered their unit to the Territory to become part of the Dakota National Guard. Colonel N. N. Tyner, aide to Governor Pierce, mustered in the company on 3 March 1885.

Neither the Territory nor the state offered many incentives to men interested in forming a company. The 1885 law required a company to provide its own uniforms, subject to approval, and allotted five dollars per man each year to assist in purchasing and keeping up uniforms, an amount increased by two dollars after 1887. Each company was required to provide at its own expense a room or building, suitable for drill and storage purposes, as an armory. The Territory and state paid each local unit three hundred dollars yearly which, according to the 1885 law, "shall be in full compensation on the part of the Territory for all pay when not called into active service, and for rent of armory." Arms and their equipment also came from the Territory or state. Guardsmen, in return, were obliged to answer the governor's call to enforce the law, suppress insurrection, or repel invasion. Overall, the contractual obligations for both the government and the men were minimal and poorly defined.

It was relatively simple to organize a company but not so easy to maintain it. The burden of territorial and state underfinancing of the National Guard inevitably fell on the individual companies. While government support did not amount to a great deal, it was crucial to company survival. The armory served as a meeting place and storehouse; without one, a company was nothing more than a list of names. A military organization without uniforms was just another lodge or club. In both instances, the annual armory and clothing allowances, small as they were, were essential.

The struggle to keep a company in uniform and in an armory is seen in the minute book of Valley City's company.[2] Financial problems dominated the record of the regular meetings. Company F's first social activity, a dance held in early May 1885, was given "for the purpose of raising funds to purchase uniforms." Using this money as a down payment, the company ordered a full set of uniforms with the intention of using their 1886 allowance to pay the remainder. The Territory failed to pay that year, which forced Company F to take out a sixty-day note for three hundred dollars to meet the balance. When the note came due, the uniform committee requested all members "to pay for their own suits or pay part of the money, to be refunded without interest when the government grant was received." As late as May 1887, Company F still had not fully reimbursed its members.

Company F faced similar problems in obtaining an armory. It failed in attempts to solicit contributions from Valley City citizens and to have the commissioners of Barnes County aid them. Since neither territorial aid nor the members' own resources were sufficient to buy a building, the company moved from place to place as it sought a suitable and affordable building. It used a skating rink during the late 1880s. The company gave up the rink in 1890, suspended drills for most of the year, and simply rented a room to store its equipment. Company G, now North Dakota National Guard, next took up quarters in the Academy of Music for several years, but that place proved to be too expensive in the long run. It finally managed to purchase the old skating rink in 1895 and refit it for use as an armory.

Other companies shared Valley City's armory problems. Most units relied solely on the three-hundred-dollar allotment to acquire a building, which forced them to rent inadequate structures. The adjutant general found Company F, Grand Forks, located in a cellar in 1888, "not a very inviting place." Major William Makee of the Cavalry Battalion reported in his 1889 inspection of Troop B, at Bottineau, that the unit's inadequate housing kept it from training regularly. The troops' armory condition was "greatly owing to not receiving proper encouragement from the Territory." The fiscal crisis of the mid-1890s forced companies to borrow money to keep their armories, and Chief of Supply Colonel C. E. Tuller found the units "in sore distress financially" because of the state's delay in paying armory allowances. North Dakota passed a law in 1897 that allowed current or former Guard members to form corporations that could build, buy, or lease buildings to be used "as a military training school, armory, and place of meeting," land and buildings thus purchased being exempt from taxation. The act made it easier for companies to acquire armory facilities, and by the end of the century several owned their own buildings.

Territorial and state law required an annual armory inspection to assess the condition of the armory, arms, and equipment, and to evaluate the quality of a unit's drill and discipline. The law based the uniform allotment on the percentage of attendance at the inspection. If there was one time each year when the companies needed to perform their very best, this was it. Rarely did performance meet minimal standards. Colonel J. E. Elson, Inspector General, Dakota National Guard, reported an overall armory attendance for the 1st Regiment of sixty-nine percent and sixty-seven percent for the 2nd Regiment in his 1888 inspection. He found the northern Dakota units of the 1st Regiment deficient in drill and discipline. Troops A and B of the Cavalry Battalion held no drills at all during the winter. Company commanders consistently failed to submit necessary returns on drills. Elson reluctantly concluded that "proper discipline and military courtesy does not exist throughout the Guard."

Statehood brought few improvements. Lieutenant F. R. Day, 20th Infantry, United States Army, inspected the North Dakota National Guard in October 1892, a visit intended to evaluate the Guard and also to discover "the causes of the falling off in interest throughout the Guard." His report reviewed the service's financial problems and did not hold the companies responsible for equipment shortages. Nonetheless, he had little good news to report. Only fifty-three percent of the officers and men attended the inspection, with Company A of Bismarck turning out a mere thirty percent. The meager company records available reveal a similar indifference at regularly scheduled drills. Of all the defects Day found, "The lack of prompt and regular attendance [at drill] is the most serious obstacle to good results." Not surprisingly, the companies were poorly trained, showing little knowledge of such fundamentals as squad and company drill, military courtesy, or guard duty. Few units ever held target practice.

Lieutenant Day, however, praised North Dakota National Guard officers as "an excellent lot of men" and thought the enlisted men were "as good material to make soldiers as can be found anywhere." Restraint governed his final comments because, as he admiringly observed, "The existing rather inefficient state of the N.D.N.G. is not surprising. It is more surprising that it exists in anything but name." Neither Day nor any state official suggested disbanding the most inefficient, neglectful companies, as the wealthier, more populous states did, for new units were unlikely to appear to replace them. The North Dakota National Guard never threatened to withhold state aid from deficient units, yet another practice in many states. Such a policy would ring hollow in a system where "Most of the organizations have been forced to keep up their running expenses by self-imposed fines and dues" and the financial support mandated by law appeared so irregularly.

Another factor in the Guard's weakness was the area's boom-and-bust agricultural economy, with the ups and downs of the wheat market directly affecting it. When the weather was good and wheat prices high, immigrants and transient workers came into the Dakotas. When prices fell or crops failed, the younger single men moved on. To Colonel E. Huntington, Inspector General, Dakota National Guard, "the great drawback to a first-class company [was] the shifting population of the Territory." Men came and went with such rapidity that both recruiting and retention suffered. The state faced the same problem throughout the 1890s.

The impact of the wheat economy on the Guard was seen in 1886 when the Territory unwisely scheduled its encampment for the first four days of September. In 1885, over ninety percent of the Dakota National Guard had attended the Territory's first camp, but attendance fell to fifty-two percent at the 1886 meeting. The decline, Colonel Townsend explained, "was due to the encampment taking place in the midst of the harvest season," and thereafter encampments took place in June and July, between spring planting and the fall harvest. Armory work suffered in late summer and through the fall as well, as General Elliott Miller noted the "decided falling off in attendance and drills" during that time. Since both the Dakota National Guard and North Dakota National Guard conducted the Inspector General's visits to the companies in late October and early November, before bad weather set in, it is not surprising that they at times reported low attendance at armory inspections.

Because it so overwhelmingly dominated the economy and society of the Dakotas, agriculture affected the National Guard. Few Guardsmen, however, were farmers, only the units of the 1st Cavalry Battalion, Troop A (Dunseith, Rolette County) and Troop B (Bottineau, Bottineau County) containing a significant number of farmers among its officers and men. In 1889, "with few exceptions," the Dakota National Guard was "composed of students, clerks and professional men." Of the 31 officers of the 1st North Dakota Volunteer Infantry in 1898, only 2 were farmers; among the 127 noncommissioned officers, 12 farmed; and twenty-three percent of the 520 enlisted men came from the farm. Professionals (lawyers, bankers, doctors, engineers), journalists, merchants, and clerks filled the officer corps. Railway workers, machinists, other skilled workers, artisans such as tailors and photographers, and unskilled day workers joined students and clerks in the enlisted ranks of the North Dakota National Guard in the 1890s.

TABLE 1.3

Organization of the North Dakota National Guard in the 1890s, With Population of Home Station and County for 1890

Company	Home Station	County	Year Mustered In	Year Mustered Out
A	Bismarck (2,186)	Burleigh (4,247)	1884	
B	Fargo (5,644)	Cass (19,613)	1884	
C	Grafton (1,594)	Walsh (16,587)	1886	
D	Devils Lake (846)	Ramsey (4,418)	1892	
E	Langdon (291)	Cavalier (6,471)	1892	
F	Grand Forks (4,979)	Grand Forks (18,357)	1886	1897
G	Valley City (1,089)	Barnes (7,045)	1885	
H	Jamestown (2,296)	Stutsman (5,266)	1885	
I	Wahpeton (1,510)	Richland (10,743)	1897	
K	Dickinson (897)	Stark (2,298)	1897	
Battery A and Band	Lisbon (935)	Ransom (5,393)	1885 1890	
Troop A	Dunseith (township 587)	Rolette (2,427)	1887	
Troop B	Bottineau (145)	Bottineau (2,893)	1887	1897

SOURCE: 1890 Cenus Population Statistics

These occupations characterized the towns that developed in the wake of the Dakotas' maturing farm frontier. The economy of the towns followed the rhythms of farm activity and income, however, which is why the North Dakota National Guard was so affected by the harvest season despite the low number of farmers in the service. The towns, nonetheless, provided the key to the Guard's success. Lieutenant F. R. Day, 20th Infantry, stressed in his 1892 inspection report that "In a state having no large towns or cities, it is difficult to find men in sufficient numbers who are imbued with the military spirit...to man military companies." He thought only Fargo and Grand Forks, that is, towns with a population of at least 5,000, could properly support a company. With fifty incorporated towns in 1890, the state had just eight with populations of more than 1,000. Grand Forks and Fargo alone exceeded 2,500. Several of the counties in which Guard companies were located did not have a population of 5,000. (See Table 1.3.) With ninety-four percent of its total population residing in rural areas, North Dakota faced extraordinary difficulties in maintaining adequately manned companies.

North Dakota National Guard companies met another difficulty in recruiting from the state's ethnic composition. One observer noted that men in the Guard came "largely" from the "more active, progressive and adventurous young men of the East." Guardsmen, in other words, were "largely" native-born Americans. This contrasted distinctly with the general population of the state, which, according to the 1890 census, was 43 percent foreign born. Of greater importance, among males of militia age, eighteen to forty-four and the obvious source of recruits, a majority (62 percent) were foreign born. The ratio of native born in the National Guard was the reverse of the ratio among all men of militia age. In the 1st North Dakota Volunteer Infantry of 1898, 71 percent of the officers, 79 percent of the noncommissioned officers, and 71 percent of the enlisted men were native born. While Norwegians made up the single largest group of immigrants in the state (14 percent of the total population in 1890), only three officers (9.5 percent), seven noncommissioned officers (5.5 percent), and twenty-eight privates (5.4 percent) were born in Norway. The largest single group of foreign-born privates (thirty-nine or 7.5 percent) were Canadians, men who shared the English language and British military traditions with native-born Americans.[3]

Immigrants from Norway, Germany, Sweden, and Russia overwhelmingly took up farming, an occupation that had a low participation rate in the Guard regardless of nativity. The urban population of the state, only six percent of the total, had a rate of native-born people nearly ten percent larger than the native-born rate in rural areas. The Guard did not deliberately seek to exclude the foreign born from the service. Many immigrants, especially Germans and German-Russians, had left their homelands in part to escape compulsory military service. As newcomers to America, they were not eager to offer themselves for volunteer military service. (See Table 1.4.)

Denied most of the rural and immigrant population, local units faced a major challenge when recruiting men. The state military code simply read that any able-bodied man "of good character and proper age" might enlist, and it set no physical requirements. This left recruiting decisions to each company. Valley City's company in the 1880s selected men by ballot. At each meeting of its civil organization, unit members considered applications for membership. A recruiting committee investigated candidates' backgrounds, gave a report on each man, then posted the names of applicants on the armory door for a week, presumably for the perusal of current members. The company then voted on the applications. During the 1890s, in order to have more opportunity to observe potential recruits, Company G adopted a bylaw whereby "those wishing to become members of the Co. put in their application and then be put to work during the next 3 months." If the applicant proved to be reliable, the company elected him. Although the man most likely to join the Guard was a town resident in his early to mid-twenties, a few older men, some in their early forties, occasionally appeared in the ranks. The average age of privates in the North Dakota National Guard in 1892 was twenty-four.

TABLE 1.4

The Foreign Born and North Dakota National Guard Companies

County of Home Station	%Foreign Born in County	%Foreign-Born Males of Militia age in County	Company and Home Station	%Foreign Born in NDNG, 1898
Burleigh	27.7	35	Co. A, Bismarck	22
Cass	39.5	57	Co. B, Fargo	28.9
Walsh	51.6	77	Co. C, Grafton	49
Ramsey	41.7	59.6	Co. D, Devils Lake	34
Cavalier	62.6	82	Co. E, Langdon	Not mobilized
Grand Forks	43.4	61.9	Co. F, Grand Forks	Not mobilized
Barnes	39.7	58.3	Co. G, Valley City	27.7
Stutsman	30.8	39.2	Co. H, Jamestown	20
Richland	37.8	59	Co. I, Wahpeton	31
Stark	39.7	49.4	Co. K, Dickinson	26
Ransom	37.7	56	Battery A and Band, Lisbon	Not mobilized
Rolette	57.6	81.7	Troop A, Dunseith	Not mobilized
Bottineau	59.5	79.1	Troop B, Bottineau	Not mobilized

As the complaints of inspecting officers at camp indicated, keeping men in the companies was far more difficult than recruiting them. The Dakota National Guard and North Dakota National Guard followed the pernicious practice, common to the Guard at large, of recruiting heavily in the weeks just before camp, a procedure that guaranteed high enrollment at camp inspection. The lure of a week at camp with pay won many recruits, but the boredom of armory drill in inadequate quarters with outmoded weapons and the endless financial woes of the companies drove them away as the memories of camp faded. Men could legally break their enlistments simply by leaving town, and this they did frequently. Since few companies complied with the law requiring recruits to fill out enlistment papers, the Guard's legal hold on most enlisted men was questionable in any event. A weakness of the companies, Lieutenant Day observed in his 1892 report, was that they "are all managed on the plan of a business organization." They kept accurate records of their business meetings and fund-raising activities, but only Companies A and B retained formal enlistment papers, and those were incomplete.

The few men who re-enlisted after their initial three-year term were assured of reaching noncommissioned rank, with the possibility of becoming a commissioned officer. Territorial and state law dictated the election of company officers, and while the military codes stated that company officers were to appoint their noncommissioned officers, most companies elected them also into the mid-1890s. A full set of officers and noncommissioned officers totaled fourteen per company. During the 1890s, North Dakota National Guard infantry companies averaged forty men, fourteen of them officers and noncommissioned officers and twenty-six privates. With the constant turnover in privates, no man who re-enlisted needed to fear being a private for too long.

The captain's post was the most important, and most coveted, of the positions in a company. The law held the captain responsible for all state property (arms, equipment, state funds) turned over to a company. Given the inadequate financing and indifferent administrative supervision of the Dakota National Guard and North Dakota National Guard, the onus of keeping up an efficient unit fell on the captain. If he had a strong, appealing personality, the combined skills of a teacher and preacher, and some administrative ability, a good captain could make a company work. Effective recruiting depended more on the captain's personality and local reputation than any other factor.

Company members sometimes recognized this when they chose men as their captains who had not even been members of the company. After several years of internal squabbling, Company B of Fargo elected Andrew Burke, then treasurer of Cass County and later governor of North Dakota, their captain in 1888. Burke's political skills, his connections with Fargo businessmen, and his leadership talents gave the company three years of stability. He had not belonged to the unit at the time he was elected. Company G, of Valley City, after losing their popular and effective captain, Amasa P. Peake, on his promotion to major, reached outside the company to elect Frank White as their new leader in May 1891. As was the case with Burke, White's background as a successful businessman and politician, coupled with his innate personal charm and leadership, gave Company G an astute commander. At times, a unit's dependence on or loyalty to its captain was too strong. When Captain William T. Sprake of Company K, Casselton, was called home from the North Dakota National Guard's 1891 encampment due to a death in the family, all of Company K went with him. Despite the pleas of Sprake and Colonel Elliott S. Miller, 1st Regiment commanding officer, the boys of Company K refused to remain in camp. The company lost its uniform allowance that year because it missed the annual inspection, and, a year later, the state disbanded it for inefficiency.

An ineffective captain had just as profound an impact on a company as did a strong leader. While there is no record of captains' errors, their failures in some companies are apparent from the frequency of their departures. The beleaguered Company B of Fargo saw ten different captains come and go in its first fourteen years, 1884 to 1898. Although Andrew Burke (1888-1890) and Gilbert C. Grafton (1892-1894) gave the company sound leadership, both men left the unit to take new jobs in other towns. Captain John D. Black of Valley City's Company F discovered that elected captains could be repudiated. After two years (1885-1887) of uninspiring leadership by Black, the company selected a committee to call on him "and ascertain if it is his desire to remain with the Company and take active part in the welfare of the company." This amounted to a charge of neglect of duty. Black agreed to resign if the company removed the report of the action from the unit's minute book. The company agreed, though the presiding secretary failed to remove the report from the company's minute book. Other Guard companies in the 1880s and 1890s, particularly the Bismarck and Jamestown units, replaced their commanders every two to three years. These repeated turnovers in the most important office in the National Guard contributed substantially to the service's deficiencies.

Company commanders failed so often because the Dakota National Guard's and North Dakota National Guard's problems bore heaviest on them. When the armory and clothing allowances did not come, captains were expected to devise temporary measures to pay the armory rent and keep the uniform fund afloat. Captain Amasa Peake used his own money to make up a deficit in one of Company G's fund-raising efforts in 1890. A captain's recruiting promises of joys to be found at camp turned sour when the Territory or state cancelled yet another one.

The informal operations of the companies' parallel civil organizations, whose bylaws governed their operations more than the law did, generated problems not to be solved by reference to an officer's manual. The most disruptive civil bylaw provided for an annual election of both the civil and military officers of a company. Every year at Valley City, the civil and military officers tendered their resignations to the members. In the years when affairs were in good shape and no significant number of men had been offended, the company unanimously re-elected all incumbents. On occasion, however, when cliques had developed within the unit or some of the officers failed in their responsibilities, the members accepted the resignations. In 1893, Company G refused Captain Frank White's tendered resignation but accepted those of the first and second lieutenants and of all the noncommissioned officers. They then elected a new slate.

Although these rejections led to weeks of bitter argument, White's judicious handling of the upheaval most likely prevented a break-up of the company. He agreed to hold a second election, at which the new officers were elected a second time. Finally, the company wrote a new constitution ending the annual election process and giving the captain the right to appoint all noncommissioned officers (and so made its bylaws compatible with state law). A similar incident in Company F at Grand Forks was solved only after Major William C. Treumann, 1st Regiment, visited the unit and told them to rewrite their bylaws to conform with the military code. "I am informed that there has been much wrangling for positions" just before the yearly election, Treumann reported.

Guard companies did not operate on standard military lines of authority and discipline. The officers were not "book soldiers," indeed it appears that not many company officers owned copies of the Guard's rules and regulations or tactical manuals for company drill. Certainly they were not very familiar with the contents of either book. In the prevailing informality, personality counted far more than did the authority of rank. Since field officers had been promoted from company positions, casual attitudes permeated the service. Armory drill and regimental encampments took on an aura not only of amateurism but of clubbishness. They were social events as much as they were military training activities. In the minutes for an 1893 company meeting, the secretary for Company G recorded that the meeting adjourned, "There being no other business before the *lodge*" (emphasis added).

Under such conditions, the National Guard was unlikely to become a highly trained, well-disciplined, and efficient military system. Increased territorial and state financial support and administrative supervision would have lessened the semi-independence of local companies, but as long as the Guard continued as a volunteer, uncompensated service, its informal social nature would remain. Colonel H. M. Creel, Inspector General, North Dakota National Guard, complained that his fellow Guardsmen were "soldiers for pleasure" and argued that "pleasure must not eliminate a fair and moderate proficiency in their duties." Creel ignored the paradox that, while emphasis on social activities reduced military efficiency, the social side assured a continued interest in the service. Men joined the Guard for social reasons or for the opportunity to use the elective process for advancement in rank. This was especially true in the Dakotas, where the Guard rarely performed constabulary duty and underfinancing limited the opportunities for extended active-duty training.

The companies, then, were the key to the North Dakota National Guard, for all their weaknesses. They attracted a small but important group of men who remained in the Guard for years and gave the service the only stability it possessed. By the end of the century, all of the older companies had a small core of men, sometimes no more than five or six, who had served for ten or more years. Most companies by the mid-1890s had come to respect seniority within the elective process, automatically electing the first sergeant, for example, to the second lieutenancy when it opened up. The regiment promoted by seniority, selecting the senior captain from the line companies as the junior-ranking major when an opportunity for promotion occurred. Promotion by seniority rewarded longevity and offered an important inducement for remaining in the Guard. Company C of Grafton led the North Dakota National Guard in seniority in 1898. Its officers, Captain John H. Fraine, First Lieutenant J. H. Johnson, and Second Lieutenant C. J. Foley, enlisted in Company C as privates in 1887, while First Sergeant Thomas Tharalson had joined the unit as a private in 1889. (See Table 1.5 for entire Guard. The connections to the Dakota National Guard are evident here.)

The National Guard of the late nineteenth century was a state institution, deeply rooted in the social and economic life of the towns and cities. Supporters of the so-called "New National Guard" had not succeeded in the 1890s in articulating a well-defined function for state military systems which would lift the Guard out of its provincialism. Until that new function, serving as a reserve for the Army, relieved the Guard of the obligations of the venerable militia of antebellum years, state and local conditions would continue to shape its stability and efficiency. In the Dakotas, territorial and state fiscal problems, the predominant agricultural, rural nature of the economy and society, and the presence of a large minority of recently arrived foreign-born immigrants imposed additional hardships on the companies not confronted by the National Guard at large.

TABLE 1.5

North Dakota National Guard Roster, 1896, With Terms of Service

---

Name, Rank and Position, Date and Rank when first entered NG,
Original Unit

Elliott S. Miller, Brigadier General and Adjutant General, Lieutenant Colonel,1888, 1st Regiment, DNG

H. M. Creel, Colonel, Inspector and Judge Advocate General, Colonel, 1891, State staff, NDNG

C. E. Tuller, Colonel, Chief of Supply, Colonel, 1892 , State staff, NDNG

1st Regiment of Infantry, NDNG

Amasa P. Peake, Colonel, commanding the Regiment, 1st Sergeant, 1885, Co. F (Valley City), 2nd Regt., DNG

William C. Treumann, Lieutenant Colonel, 2nd Lieutenant, 1887, Co. C (Grafton), 1st Regt., DNG

Frank White, Major, commanding 1st Battalion, Captain, 1892, Co. G (Valley City), NDNG

Harry C. Flint, Major, commanding 2nd Battalion, 2nd Lieutenant, 1889, Co. H (Jamestown), 1st Regt., DNG

Thomas H. Poole, Captain, Regtl. adjutant, Chief trumpeter, Regiment, 1892, Regiment, NDNG

William H. Ryan, 1st Lieutenant, Adj., 1st Battalion, 1st Sergeant, 1886, Co. F (Grand Forks), 1st Regt., DNG

Charles F. Mudgett, 1st Lieutenant, Adj., 2nd Battalion, Private, 1890, Co. G (Valley City), NDNG

W. H. Makee, Major, commanding Cavalry Battalion, Major, 1887, First Cavalry, Bn., DNG

Company Commanders, NDNG, Rank of Captain

R.N. Stevens, Co. A, Captain, 1894, Co. A (Bismarck), NDNG

Frederick Keye, Co. B, 1st Sergeant, 1889, Co. B (Fargo), 1st Regt., DNG

John H. Fraine, Co. C, Private, 1885, Co. C (Grafton), 1st Regt., DNG

Albert Cogswell, Co. D, 2nd Lieutenant, 1892, Co. D (Devils Lake), NDNG

Charles Chisholm, Co. E, Captain, 1892, Co. E (Langdon),NDNG

William Gordon, Co. F, Captain, 1894, Co. F (Grand Forks), NDNG

Frank C. Clark, Co. G, Private, 1885, Co. F (Valley City), 2nd Regt., DNG

William Gleason, Co. H, 1st Sergeant, 1891, Co. H (Jamestown), NDNG

A. J. Hughes, Battery A, Captain, 1890, Battery (Lisbon), NDNG

C.I.F. Wagner, Troop A, 2nd Lieutenant, 1890, Troop A (Dunseith), NDNG

J.C. Stover, Troop B, 2nd Lieutenant, 1888, Troop B (Bottineau), DNG

For varying reasons, a committed few had remained in the National Guard despite difficulties. None of them could devote the time or money to make themselves well-educated amateur soldiers given conditions in the new state of North Dakota. However haphazardly, they had kept alive the spirit of the American citizen-soldier tradition. They created a sense of esprit de corps and comradeship essential to unit integrity in wartime by sustaining the companies in which they would go to war and in choosing the men who would lead them. In light of the many flaws in the North Dakota National Guard, that was a significant achievement.

Notes on Sources

A number of works provide background information for this study. Though mentioned here for Chapter 1, they serve as references to military, political, and social developments for ensuing chapters as well. Two important books that offer both detailed information and larger viewpoints on American military policy are: Walter Millis, *Arms and Men: A Study of American Military History* (New York, 1956), and Russell F. Weigley, *History of the United States Army* (New York, 1967). No single volume effectively tells the National Guard's entire history. The most recent scholarly study is John K. Mahon, *History of the Militia and the National Guard* (New York, 1983), which builds on the work of William H. Riker, *Soldiers of the States* (Washington, D.C., 1957) and Martha Derthick, *The National Guard in Politics* (Cambridge, Mass., 1965). Two less formal studies are Jim Dan Hill, *The Minute Man in Peace and War: A History of the National Guard* (Harrisburg, Pa., 1964), and Elbridge Colby, *The National Guard of the United States : A Half Century of Progress* (Manhattan, Kans., 1977). Hill served in the National Guard for over thirty years, and Colby, who left an unfinished book, was a career regular officer long associated with the National Guard Bureau. For an overview of the history of the militia before the Civil War, see the following: Marcus Cunliffe, *Soldiers and Civilians: The Martial Spirit in America, 1775-1865* (Boston, 1968); John K. Mahon, *The American Militia: Decade of Decision*, 1789-1800 (Gainesville, Fla., 1960); Louis Morton, "The Origins of American Military Policy," *Military Affairs*, Vol. 22 (Summer 1958), pp. 75-82; John Shy, "A New Look at Colonial Militia," *William and Mary Quarterly*, 3rd Series, Vol. 20, No. 2 (April 1963), pp. 175-185; Paul T. Smith, "Militia of the United States from 1846 to 1860," *Indiana Magazine of History*, Vol. 15, No. 1 (March 1919), pp. 20-47; Frederick P. Todd, "Our National Guard: An Introduction to Its History," *Military Affairs*, Vol. 5 (1941), pp. 52-86, 156-170.

Elwyn B. Robinson, *History of North Dakota* (Lincoln, Neb., 1966) was invaluable for providing the social, economic, and political background within which the North Dakota National Guard developed. Robert P. Wilkins and Wynona Wilkins, *North Dakota: A Bicentennial History* (New York, 1977), and D. Jerome Tweton and Theodore B. Jelliff, *North Dakota: The Heritage of a People* (Fargo, N.D., 1983) were useful as well.

For Chapter 1, both unpublished and published sources were used. Information on the territorial militia and National Guard is sparse. The "Dakota Territorial Records, Military Affairs," microfilm edition, from the Orin G. Libby Historical Manuscripts Collection, Chester Fritz Library, University of North Dakota, Grand Forks, were of most value. A minute book for Company F, 2nd Regiment, at Valley City (later Company G, 1st Regiment, North Dakota National Guard), covering 1885 to 1895, allowed insight into the weekly and yearly activities of a single company. The book is part of the Records of the North Dakota National Guard, Adjutant General's Office, Fraine Barracks, Bismarck, North Dakota. The only published annual reports of the adjutant general, Dakota Territory, were those for 1867, 1888, and 1889. Further information came from the "Abstract of the Militia" included in the *Annual Report of the Secretary of War* and "Report of the Governor of Dakota Territory," 1878 to 1889, in the

Annual Report of the Secretary of Interior, both found in the Congressional
Serial Set. Territorial laws, especially Chapter 113, Laws of 1885, and Chapter
100, Laws of 1887, were informative. Wright Tarbell, "History of the South
Dakota National Guard, Including the Territorial Guard from the Year 1862 to
the Present Time," *South Dakota Historical Collection*, Vol. 6 (1912), pp.
363-390, reprints the 1887 adjutant general's report and otherwise unrecorded
data. Useful secondary works included: Richard Cropp, *The Coyotes: A History
of the South Dakota National Guard* (Mitchell, S.D., 1962); Howard R. Lamar,
Dakota Territory, 1861-1889: A Study of Frontier Politics (New Haven, Conn.,
1956); and Herbert S. Schell, *History of South Dakota*, Third Edition, Revised
(Lincoln, Neb., 1975).

Two major sources were used for the statehood years. The Records of the
North Dakota National Guard, particularly reports and correspondence, though
far from complete and not properly inventoried, were essential and invaluable.
The muster-in rolls for the 1st North Dakota Volunteer Infantry, 1898, provided
age, place of birth, residence, and occupation for all officers and enlisted men.
Second, the annual and biennial adjutants general reports for the 1890s offered
details not available elsewhere. Published versions of the state military code
and specific military laws were also consulted. A number of archival collections
at the State Historical Society of North Dakota, Bismarck, indicated by their
scanty materials on military affairs the frequent neglect of the National Guard.
Some material was found in: Series 153, Governor, Administration, Incoming
Letters, 1890s; Series 154, Governor, Administration, Outgoing Letters, 1890s;
and Series 193, Governor, Administration, Military Affairs, 1890s.

Beginning in the 1930s, and throughout the rest of his active service, Colonel
Herman Brocopp, assistant adjutant general from 1933 to 1957, carefully
collected as much material on the North Dakota National Guard as he could
find. Some of it was retained in the Adjutant General's Office, most of it came
to the office after he died, and it contributes substantially here. Colonel Brocopp
issued occasional Historical Bulletins, numbering 1 through 10, between 1954
and 1956, based on his research work. The bulletins deal with such matters
as unit lineage, unit rosters, troop strengths, strengths at mobilization, and other
items of historical information from the 1880s to the 1950s. Brocopp also began
a formal Lineage Book, which traced the history of every unit in the Guard,
with dates of organization, and disbandment where appropriate, and dates of
reorganizations, along with home stations. The Historical Bulletins and the
Lineage Book were essential in following the establishment and development
of units from their origins to the 1960s, in tracing the careers of many officers,
and in providing other items of information as well. They were nearly
indispensable, saved hours of extra work, and are a lasting legacy to the colonel's
deep interest in history. Their value is evident in every chapter.

The Military Information Division, Adjutant General's Office, United States
Army, published yearly reports on the National Guard beginning in the
mid-1890s. These provided some information on the North Dakota National
Guard, but were more useful for comparative purposes and assessing the
condition of the entire National Guard. See Military Information Division Number
7, *The Organized Militia of the United States . . . Covering the Year 1895*
(Washington, D.C.,1896); Military Information Division Publication Number 19,

The Organized Militia of the United States . . . Covering the Year 1897 (Washington, D.C., 1898); Military Information Division Publication Number 29, *The Organized Militia of the United States . . . Up to 20 April 1898* (Washington, D.C., 1900).

Useful secondary works: Jesse A. Tanner, "Foreign Immigration into North Dakota," *Collections of the State Historical Society of North Dakota*, Vol. 1 (1906), pp. 180-200; and Robert I. Vexler and William F. Swindler, *Chronology and Documentary Handbook of the State of North Dakota* (Dobbs Ferry, N.Y., 1978).

Company B (Fargo) Dakota Infantry. Gilbert C. Grafton second from left,
ca. mid 1880s.

Sgt. Ferdinand G. Whitaker in volunteer infantryman's dress uniform, Bismarck, 1884.

Unidentified unit at the first encampment of the Dakota National Guard at Camp Grant, Fargo, Dakota Territory, 22-26 September 1885.

Line Officers, First Infantry, Dakota National Guard, Watertown, Dakota Territory, 1888. (Most of the units of the First Infantry were located in what is now North Dakota.)

☆2☆

The 1st North Dakota Volunteer Infantry:
To the Philippines, 1898

The men who struggled to keep the North Dakota National Guard alive during the difficult 1890s had no idea they would go to war before the decade ended. Despite annual inspections by Army officers, few Guardsmen gave much thought, official or personal, to the possibilities of a call to duty from the War Department. A military institution, however, exists mainly for the purpose of fighting wars. If it cannot meet that function, it has dubious value. Armies not prepared to fight are either expensive, useless appendages to society or potential sources of militarism. Although North Dakota Guardsmen were neither military fops playing at soldier nor incipient militarists, they were woefully untrained and poorly organized for war. With its background of instability and inefficiency, the North Dakota National Guard was required to meet a sudden war call with none of its problems near solution. A decade of neglect in the Dakotas as in other states made mobilization in 1898 slipshod and chaotic.

The National Guard bore much of the responsibility for the military failures of 1898, but it was not the ultimate source of the problems. In 1898, a century of military policy was tested and nearly collapsed in the nation's first overseas war. Nineteenth-century American military practice provided for two armies, a small professional Regular Army for peacetime duties and a large, essentially volunteer citizen-soldier army to fight its wars. Few formal provisions existed for integrating the two in wartime, the main continuities being Army regulations and Regular Army officers. The nation maintained no agencies, civil or military, to coordinate foreign and military policy. It did not give the War Department the authority or resources to plan for war, and so mobilization plans appeared only on the eve of hostilities. The Army lacked a reserve system to use for expansion when war came and was never intended to be large enough to wage war on its own.

When conflicts came, the second American army, the war army, appeared. Recruited as a temporary force to meet the demands of conflict, it greatly overshadowed the peacetime force. The Regular Army did not disappear. Congress invariably enlarged it, at least for the duration, but regular regiments remained separate from the temporary organizations. Experienced regular officers took command of the larger field forces and sometimes led volunteer regiments as well. Nonetheless, the size and number of war army units so overwhelmed the regulars that it was impossible for the Army to provide enough officers to command all of them. The method of recruiting the war army precluded integrating it with the Regular Army in any event. The states, through their militia systems, recruited the war force for the federal government. Political necessity, the desires of the recruits, and state jealousy demanded that volunteer units be commanded by men from the states that organized them.

Volunteering predominated throughout the century as the chief means of recruiting the war army. State government bore the brunt of the volunteer effort, which was always marked by a touch of free enterprise. Since the antebellum uniformed militia lacked structure and centralized state control, ambitious civilians were as likely to organize companies and regiments as were local militia units. And governors were just as likely to accept the tenders of service of civilian-recruited units as they were to take militia organizations, especially if the self-appointed organizers were politically or socially prominent. The military entrepreneurs won commissions and the chance for fame and glory. Their activities relieved the states of many of the burdens of recruiting. Rarely were existing militia units sufficient to meet manpower quotas anyway, as seen at the beginning of the Civil War, for example.

In all wars, the federal government assigned quotas to each state based on its population. When appeals to patriotism and local pride failed to recruit enough men, the states offered bounties. When all else failed, state militia laws gave governors the power to draft men to fill state regiments. During the Civil War the federal government asserted the right to draft militia, but the draft was not very effective. States eager to meet their quotas and get regiments to the front under the state flag as quickly as possible relied chiefly on the eagerness of men to serve as the basis for enlistment. All too often they neglected physical examinations, mental ability, or military experience in their selection process. Volunteer units inevitably reported for federal service without arms, equipment, or uniforms and filled with untrained officers and men.

Given the federal government's lack of a large bureaucracy and a central War Department agency to direct mobilization, the decentralized, state-controlled mobilization system was the logical alternative for raising the war army. The militia systems of the states retained enough vitality to call up the troops effectively, except during the last year and a half of the Civil War, and the nation was fortunate in its nineteenth-century wars to confront opponents who suffered as many, or greater, liabilities as it did. For all its faults, the war-army practice created military organizations capable of preventing defeat, as in the War of 1812, and producing victory in other wars. Given enough time to come to active duty and organize, the state volunteers became effective soldiers.

Nonetheless, the war army practice was inefficient and costly. Mobilization invariably brought chaos, duplication of effort, and often a touch of graft. It took field commanders months to organize and train newly recruited state regiments. State troops usually learned to be soldiers by soldiering, sometimes in the face of the enemy. In the years after the Civil War, Regular Army officers wrote innumerable books and articles calling for a new system. When war threatened in the spring of 1898, Congressmen sympathetic to their view attempted to pass a mobilization bill that would bypass the state system altogether and allow the Army to recruit and provide the officers for the war force. National Guard supporters used their political power to defeat the bill and persuaded Congress to pass legislation giving the Guard first chance to volunteer as entire units.

Adherents of the "New National Guard," through the National Guard Association, had contended for two decades that the service was composed of men intent on serving the nation in time of war. These men deserved first opportunity to supplement the understrength Regular Army when war came. The National Guard Association implied in its arguments that the Guard could provide well-armed, adequately trained units led by knowledgeable officers. The call of 1898 put the Guard to the test.

The mobilization of state volunteers in 1898 differed from previous efforts in that both federal law and President McKinley's call for troops gave preference to existing state militia organizations, the National Guard. To a great extent, this was a test of the governors' will rather than the Guard itself, for neither the law nor McKinley's call obliged governors to use the Guard exclusively. Secretary of War Russell Alger's telegram of 25 April 1898 assigning quotas to the states stated that "It is the *wish* of the President that the regiments of the National Guard . . . shall be used" (emphasis added). Most states respected the President's wishes, Kansas being a notable exception, but governors nonetheless faced considerable political pressure from antebellum-style military entrepreneurs who wished to organize their own units outside of the National Guard. McKinley himself succumbed to this hoary free enterprise military tradition when he allowed Leonard Wood and Theodore Roosevelt to put together the 1st United States Volunteer Cavalry (the Rough Riders).

As relations between the United States and Spain rapidly deteriorated in early April, North Dakotans reacted in much the same manner as had their fellow Americans in 1861, with enthusiasm and a sense of the grandiose. Before Congress enacted mobilization legislation (22 April) or declared war on Spain (25 April), aspiring colonels and captains wrote in haste to Governor Frank Briggs, each hoping to be the first to offer his as-yet unformed regiment or company as part of North Dakota's contingent. Ed Smith of Ellendale asked for a colonel's commission so he could recruit a regiment. Colonel H. M. Creel, Inspector General, announced ostentatiously to the state's newspapers that he was organizing a regiment and that Devils Lake would be "his regimental headquarters . . . until further orders." Offers to raise companies came from small towns all over the state: from Wheatland, Forest River, Lakota, New Rockford, Milnor, towns so small they could not have provided a corporal's guard. The entrepreneurs only asked Governor Briggs for officer's commissions; no one wrote requesting information on how he might enlist as a private.

While Governor Briggs was in California on vacation, his private secretary, George H. Phelps, fielded the flood of requests. With the governor absent and lacking official guidance from Washington, Phelps could do little but promise to file the tenders of service in the order they arrived. He gave particular care to friends of the Briggs administration, informing Smith of Ellendale, for instance, that the desire to control all of the commissions of an entire regiment "really strikes me as being more than you are entitled to." He suggested that Smith try to get authority to recruit a company. After mobilization was ordered on 22 April, Phelps responded to private recruiting efforts that federal law gave preference to the National Guard. He pointed out, furthermore, that the state military code prevented the governor from removing commissioned officers from the Guard without cause and appointing friends and political allies to replace them.

To friends of the administration, Phelps condemned "that infernal military code" which kept him from granting favors. His standard reply to most offers, however, was that the governor intended "to comply with the President's wishes" in allowing the North Dakota National Guard to volunteer first. The War Department quota assigned to the state on 27 April did not take in all the existing Guard units, let alone provide room for the ad hoc organizations so recently organized. Still, the requests continued to come in. Rumors filled the newspapers that North Dakota might have the chance to organize another regiment if McKinley issued a second call for volunteers. Phelps began to react testily to the incessant requests, informing one correspondent that, if there were a second call, then perhaps "The patriotics in your vicinity would have a chance to shed their blood in defense of their honor or any other old thing." Even after the First North Dakota Volunteer Infantry left for San Francisco in late May, and it was obvious the federal government would not ask the state for more troops, queries came into Bismarck. The frustrated Phelps wrote J. A. Johnson of Fargo on 1 June that "thousands" of men were chasing Governor Briggs, and added, "They all want something he *can't give them* because he has no authority. They might as well ask him for a corner lot in the Heavenly City" (emphasis in original).

From 22 April, when Congress passed the mobilization law, the Briggs administration intended to use the North Dakota National Guard to form North Dakota's volunteer unit. It was slow to make the decision known to the public, however, in part because Washington delayed assigning the state its quota but also in order to keep from offending its friends seeking military commissions. Ultimately, the preference for the National Guard served the administration well. Without the Guard's formal claim to volunteer first, Governor Briggs would have had to select eight companies from the twenty-four units that had offered their services. His choice would please eight and offend sixteen would-be captains and their followers. Those were uncomfortable political odds. Phelps obviously delighted in the fact that "there is nothing the Governor can do" in granting commissions outside of the National Guard. When it served his purposes, he defended the Guard's right to go, outlining their suffering and sacrifice during the 1890s. He further explained: "There has never been any money to pay them what was justly due them, and we feel it would not be just to the boys, who have served for years, to muster in any more companies." Neither Phelps nor Briggs evidenced deep concern for military efficiency or training. To them, selection of North Dakota's volunteers was a political problem, a very touchy one, which they could most easily resolve by adhering to federal law and the state military code.

Major problems remained in North Dakota's mobilization effort once the Guard earned the right to form the volunteers. The War Department informed Governor Briggs on 25 April that North Dakota would have a quota of five troops of cavalry. The North Dakota National Guard had only one mounted unit, Troop A of Dunseith, but nine companies of infantry in the 1st Regiment. The request for cavalry units confused and upset state officials. Although the War Department had been collecting information on the National Guard since the early 1880s, it seemed obvious that it did not use that data to guide it in making troop requests to the state. The Fargo *Forum* speculated that Theodore Roosevelt had used his Washington connections in an attempt to organize a mounted regiment of western Guardsmen. It made little sense, the *Forum* argued, to ruin the state's infantry regiment on the whim of a New York City socialite when "Two thirds of the enlisted men never rode a horse in their life."

Because they feared North Dakota troops would lose their state identity when assigned to a full regiment, Brigadier General Elliott S. Miller, adjutant general, and other officials protested the cavalry quota. Miller and Governor Briggs wired Senator Henry C. Hansbrough asking him to get the assignment changed. The senator convinced the War Department to alter the state's quota to two battalions of infantry, or eight companies. This ensured, General Miller reported, "A distinctive organization to represent this state."

The change did not relieve state officials from the need to make more difficult decisions. The North Dakota National Guard's nine infantry companies, Troop A, and the light artillery battery all volunteered. Furthermore, supporters of Company F of Grand Forks, disbanded by the state in 1897 for inefficiency, mounted an effort to reorganize the unit and have it assume its old place in the Guard. Miller and Briggs rejected the Grand Forks claim immediately. Dominated by infantry officers, a conference of Guard officers met at Bismarck on 26 April and decided to allow the infantry companies to volunteer first in order of seniority. If an insufficient number of these volunteered, then the troop and battery could go. The captain of Company E, at Langdon, decided for personal reasons not to volunteer, leaving his unit in disarray and opening the door for Company K of Dickinson to become the eighth company. The other infantry units readily accepted the opportunity. Members of Company E and a few former members of the old Company F deeply resented their exclusion.

Table 2.1

Companies of the 1st North Dakota
Volunteer Infantry

Company A, Bismarck	Company G, Valley City
Company B, Fargo	Company H, Jamestown
Company C, Grafton	Company I, Wahpeton
Company D, Devils Lake	Company K, Dickinson

Selecting the regimental officers of the North Dakota contingent posed an even more delicate problem. The War Department authorized one lieutenant colonel to command the regiment and a major to command each four-company battalion. Since the state was not allotted a full twelve-company regiment, the Department would not allow the complete peacetime complement of regimental officers. If seniority prevailed, Colonel Amasa P. Peake would be reduced to lieutenant colonel, Lieutenant Colonel William C. Treumann to major, with Frank White as the second major. This would leave Harry C. Flint, the junior ranking major, with no place in the unit. The 1st North Dakota also would not be able to take the regimental chaplain, and two captains, who served as regimental quartermaster and adjutant respectively, faced reductions to first lieutenant.

Although the North Dakota National Guard volunteers reported to mobilization camp on 2 May, Governor Briggs delayed his decision on commissioning the regiment's shorter list of officers until 16 May, when it was mustered into United States' service. Briggs hoped the government would solve his problem by allowing the state to furnish twelve companies. While the state and War Department negotiated the issue, rumors on who would win the commissions filled the rendezvous camp at Fargo. None of the principals involved, Peake, Treumann, or Flint, offered to step aside. Some speculated that Flint would resign due to poor health, saving everyone the embarrassment of seeing a long-service Guard officer unceremoniously pushed aside.

To the surprise of many, Briggs on 17 May commissioned Treumann as lieutenant colonel, White as major of the 1st Battalion, and Flint as major of the 2nd Battalion. The Fargo *Forum* reported that many of the company officers disliked Colonel Peake's overemphasis on red tape and dress parade drill. George Phelps denied the report, replying that the governor "decided to let the officers take the same rank and grade in the volunteers, that they held in the N.G." The administration had no desire to eliminate anyone, "there simply was no place . . . for Colonel Peake." Briggs was reluctant to offend the Guard's sensibilities by violating the existing order of rank in the North Dakota National Guard and apparently gave in to the wishes of most of the officers.

Peake was not very popular with the battalion and company officers. Major Flint was mustered in on 16 May 1898 and yet offered his resignation for reasons of health on 20 May, "just to get even with Peake and cause the retirement of that official," according to the Fargo *Forum*. What Flint's complaints against Peake were went unexplained. Thomas Tharalson, first sergeant of Grafton's Company C, mentioned in his personal diary Peake's failure to win the command but expressed little sympathy for the colonel. He simply noted, "Colonel Peake started for home a sad but much wiser man." Governor Briggs, respecting the seniority practice of the Guard, promoted Captain John Fraine of Company C to replace Flint. Captain Thomas Poole, regimental adjutant, also lost his place in the 1st North Dakota when he refused to take a reduction to first lieutenant. Poole apparently hoped he might obtain the majority eventually vacated by Flint. The North Dakota National Guard, however, had long given battalion promotions to line officers in the infantry companies, not staff officers. "Poole's appointment over Captain Fraine," the

Forum noted, "would be one of the most unpopular moves that could be made." The bitterness left over from Peake's and Poole's exclusions would affect affairs in the North Dakota National Guard for years to come.

While the state's newspapers and the governor's office devoted a great deal of time to the politics of selecting units and officers for the 1st North Dakota, the North Dakota National Guard rendezvoused at Fargo. From the outset, the Guard's mobilization was hampered by the past decade's neglect. The failure to develop the Rock Island Military Reservation as a permanent training camp forced the state to set up a temporary mobilization camp as quickly as possible. Because of its railroad connections and because it was large enough to permit the purchase of foodstuffs and other supplies on the open market, the War Department designated Fargo as the concentration point. With the 1st North Dakota under orders to report to Fargo on 2 May, General Miller sent Captain Thomas H. Poole, temporarily acting assistant adjutant general, Captain Invald A. Berg, 1st Regiment quartermaster, and Major Frank White, acting engineer, to Fargo to prepare a camp. The state had the responsibility to transport and feed the volunteers until they were sworn into United States service. The federal government would later reimburse North Dakota for its mobilization expenditures. On hand to advise Poole and his associates was Lieutenant F. H. Albright, United States Army, professor of military science and tactics at the University of North Dakota, Grand Forks. Albright served as United States Mustering Officer.

The North Dakota National Guard had not been to summer camp since 1894, and Poole discovered that the service "was in a sad condition regarding camp equipage, tentage, bedding, etc., for troops to take to the field for active service." The companies had taken home all field kitchens and mess gear after the 1894 camp but now could find little of it. The War Department was unable to make up immediately the North Dakota National Guard's shortage in tents and field equipment as it scrambled to equip the 125,000 volunteers President McKinley had called. General Miller ordered the excluded Company E at Langdon to ship all its arms and equipment to Fargo, a final blow to that disappointed outfit. Poole made up the rest of the shortages by purchasing nonregulation bedding and tents and arranged an effective, although makeshift, messing system to feed the troops. The North Dakota National Guard held arms, equipment, and uniforms for only forty men per company; the men added to bring the regiment to war strength "went into camp in their citizen clothes, civilian shoes, derby or soft felt hats." Like the majority of state units mobilized in 1898, the 1st North Dakota would not be properly outfitted until the Army supplied it.

Company commanders had six days, 26 April to 1 May, to recruit their units to war strength before reporting to Fargo. Enlistment was a two-stage process under the state-centered mobilization system. Recruits first enlisted in their local company, then entered federal service after passing an Army physical examination. Muster-in took place once the companies rendezvoused at the Fargo camp. Nothing in either state or federal law obligated an officer or enlisted man in the Guard to answer the President's call. Many Guardsmen in the late nineteenth century argued that joining the state service was an implicit agreement to volunteer for war. Although the majority accepted the argument, some did not, as the resignation of Captain Charles Chisholm of Company E illustrated.

North Dakota met its quota with ease. First Sergeant Thomas Tharalson of Grafton's Company C noted that Captain John Fraine began recruiting to fill his unit at 9:00 A.M. on 26 April "and at 3 o'clock [P.M.]," he wrote, Fraine "telegraphed the Gov. of N.D. that our Co. was full and awaiting orders to move." Fargo's Company B did not fill up until early May but it had to compete in recruiting with a "free enterprise" outfit for a few days until it was evident that only the Guard held the right to enlist volunteers. Because of enthusiastic support for the war, recruiting posed no problems, but the two-stage enlistment process made mobilization slow and complicated. Throughout the 1890s, North Dakota National Guard infantry companies had been understrength, averaging 45 officers and men, with only 30 privates. The eight companies of the 1st North Dakota had a peace strength of 320 officers and men. Army tables of organization called for a war strength of 685, with 65 privates per company. All officers in the war regiment came from the peacetime Guard, but only 264 (forty percent) of the enlisted men had served in the North Dakota National Guard. The high percentage of untrained enlisted men in volunteer units, coupled with their acute shortage of arms and equipment, greatly weakened the National Guard's performance in 1898.

"The band was there. The girls were there too. They were pinning flags and boutenirs [sic] on the wearers of the blue" when the first companies arrived in Fargo on 2 May 1898. After an honorary dinner, speeches, and a parade through Grafton, Company C left its hometown. "Thousands of people" met the troop train at Grand Forks, and hundreds more watched the train pass through Buxton and Hillsboro. Since field kitchens were not yet ready, Captain Poole fed the arriving troops at Fargo restaurants their first day in camp. Due to a lack of tentage, Companies C and D slept in Company B's armory while men of the Fargo outfit returned home from camp each night to sleep. Sergeant Tharalson and the officers of Company C, along with Lieutenant Colonel Treumann, also of Grafton, spent the night of 2 May at the Webster Hotel. Tharalson did not sleep well because, he wrote, "I think I fully realized what was before me and others." Feeling homesick already, he confided to his diary that "I hardly think that my wife at this time fully realized what it meant and if she did she certainly failed to let me know about it."

Tharalson had little time to worry about his commitment as the officers and noncommissioned officers worked sixteen-hour days to organize the regiment. They had much to do, particularly to familiarize the new recruits with Army routines. Still nominally in command, Colonel Amasa Peake held company and battalion drill mornings and afternoons. All had to pass the dreaded Army physical before they could be mustered into United States service. "The examination is pretty severe," Major Frank White wrote his wife. "Co. A of Bismarck lost 15 of 68 examined. It makes all the boys tremble." Although some companies had mistakenly recruited more than 100 enlisted men and easily replaced those who failed the exam, others had to find new recruits. The arrival of the regiment in Fargo "made the war a reality" to John B. Kinne and his classmates at Fargo's Preparatory College. "Tho discouraged by our professors,'' Kinne wrote, he and two friends joined Company B to replace men who failed the physical. Lieutenant Albright mustered in the companies after they were discharged from state service, between 12 and 16 May. Tharalson found the muster-in ceremony an ''exciting scene.'' Frank White proudly told Mrs. White, ''Well! I am mustered in Major of Volunteers. The only field officer mustered yet.''

The regiment learned on 12 May that it was to be a part of Major General Wesley Merritt's Philippine Island expeditionary force. The assignment generated much excitement in the press and at Camp Briggs. The organization of the 1st North Dakota Volunteer Infantry marked the state's first participation in a major national event since it joined the union less than a decade before. From the opening of Camp Briggs, North Dakota newspapers focused upon the regiment's activities. Civilians came to the camp daily to watch the outfit take shape. On Sunday, 8 May, both the Great Northern and Northern Pacific railways ran special trains to Fargo from the companies' hometowns. Approximately five thousand people visited the camp that day. A much larger conclave took place a week later, stimulated no doubt by the news of the impending move to the Philippines. The regiment turned out to meet the Great Northern special, and nearly ten thousand people flocked to Camp Briggs. In full dress uniform, General Miller led the regiment on horseback in a dress parade through downtown Fargo. Wives and mothers brought cakes, candies, and basket lunches to share with their men. Sergeant Tharalson lost sight of his wife and son in the rush to catch the return train. ''We were kind of lonesome, the next day around camp, but we had plenty of drill and therefore got back into the usual routine business.''

Eager to get off to San Francisco, officers and enlisted men chafed under the dull camp routine. The War Department delayed in setting a departure date. Unaware of the enormous complexities the Department faced in bringing order to the mobilization, the men complained, as soldiers always have, about the Army's inefficiency. When Washington finally set 26 May as departure day, Tharalson recorded, ''there was great cheering among the boys in camp.'' Frank White, too, noted that ''the boys are having a great jollification and are crazy to get off.'' After two murderous world wars, the eagerness and enthusiasm with which the men of the 1st North Dakota embraced the chance to go to war seems naive. This innocence permeated the American response to war in 1898 and was not peculiar to North Dakota soldiers and civilians.

The regiment left Fargo on the morning of the 26th, escorted once again by a large cheering crowd in a parade which ''was one of the finest Fargo had ever seen.'' As Companies B, C, D, and I boarded a Great Northern train, the Northern Pacific transported the other units. The Great Northern paused at Hillsboro, then stopped again at Grand Forks for lunch. A large contingent from Grafton met them, and Sergeant Tharalson reported that at last his wife ''fully realized what it meant and could not stop from showing it. I think,'' he added, ''I held up appearances in good shape but hope never to pass through such an ordeal again.''' The pain of separation struck home as the trains moved out for the Pacific Coast.

The existence of the National Guard in 1898 mitigated some of the worst aspects of the war army practice. For all its liabilities, the Guard gave the state an administrative military structure. Existing companies located throughout the settled portions of North Dakota allowed effective recruiting. The companies offered partially equipped and trained units in which all Guardsmen and raw recruits could be readily moved to the rendezvous camp. The civilians, who so ardently sought to win recognition from Governor Briggs, gave little thought as to how they intended to organize or equip their makeshift units if they were accepted. Most importantly, the Guard provided a group of officers somewhat familiar with military ways and with some experience from the North Dakota National Guard encampments of 1891 and 1894. All of the regimental officers, all of the first sergeants, and fifty percent of the other noncommissioned officers had served in the North Dakota National Guard before 1898. Some, like Lieutenant Colonel William C. Treumann or Captain Frederick Keye of Company B and all of the officers of Company C, had joined the Guard in the 1880s.

The officers lacked detailed knowledge and experience in administration and minor tactics. As had been true throughout the 1890s, most of the company commanders came to the mobilization camp as neophytes. Of the eight company commanders, only the captains of Companies B, C, and D had held the position in 1896. Captain John Fraine of Company C became acting major of the 2nd Battalion (Flint's command) soon after arriving in camp, leaving command of the company to Lieutenant John H. Johnson. The talents of these otherwise inexperienced officers were social, not military. During and after World War II, sociologists and psychologists studying the combat efficiency of Army units discovered that a military organization functions best when it is not only well equipped and trained but bound by social ties developed over months, even years, of familiar association. The better men knew each other, particularly in small primary groups such as the squad and platoon, the more effectively they functioned on the battlefield. The temporary units raised for war in 1898 were certain to be ill-equipped and poorly trained whether put together by the Army, recruited by enterprising civilians, or taken from the National Guard. The challenge in 1898 was to select that method which would most rapidly produce cohesive units from similar raw materials. In the end, the Guard won the privilege, due to political rather than sociological factors.

Nonetheless, the Guard proved a sound choice. The enlisted men of the 1st North Dakota Volunteer Infantry were similar to recruits raised by other states. The vast majority were single (98 percent), and in their twenties (52 percent between 21 and 25; another 21 percent between 26 and 30). They were largely native-born (72 percent), made up of skilled workers (26 percent), farmers (23 percent), and day laborers (36 percent). Their officers were older (39 percent between 26 and 30; 26 percent between 31 and 35; 16 percent over 35), married (58 percent), and from business and professional occupations (68 percent). The social and economic maturity of the officers gave them the moral authority to lead the regiment despite their military inexperience. (See Table 2.2.) The officers' association in the North Dakota National Guard during the 1890s was crucial to the esprit de corps of the 1st North Dakota. Family ties contributed to regimental solidarity as well. Every company had at least one set of brothers; Company H had five. In Company A, a father and son, Ziba B. and William C. Olen, served as privates together, while in Company

K, Captain George Auld, at 54 the oldest man in the regiment, took along his son, Storey E. Auld, as a sergeant. The shared backgrounds provided the social cement that eventually made the 1st North Dakota an effective unit, but it was a regiment in name only in May 1898.

TABLE 2.2

Officers, 1st North Dakota, 1898-1899

Headquarters, 1st North Dakota
Name, Unit/Rank, 1896 Rank, Service Longevity, Age, Occupation

Treumann, W. C., Lt. Col., Regt., Lt. Col., Grafton, 1887-1898, 36, Abstract business

White, Frank, Major/1st Bn., Major, Valley City, 1892-1898, 42, Engineer/farmer

Fraine, John, Major/2nd Bn, Captain, Co. C, Grafton, 1885-1898, 37, Lawyer/real estate

Conklin, Fred , 1st Lt./Regt. Adj., Same, Jamestown, 1892-1898, 21, Clerk

Berg, I.A.*, 1st Lt./Regt. QM, Same, Grand Forks, 1889-1898, 31, Banker

Company Officers and First Sergeants
Name, Rank, Service Longevity, Age, Occupation

Company A, Bismarck

Moffett, William P., Captain, 1890-1898, 32, Editor/publisher

Newcomer, Sherman, 1st Lieutenant, 1891-1898, 31, Reporter

McClean, William J., 2nd Lieutenant, 1891-1898, 23, Printer

Gorsuch, Edward G., 1st Sgt. (promoted to 2nd Lt., Co. K., July 1899), 1892-1898, 32, Machinist

Company B, Fargo

Keye, Fred**, Captain, 1886-1898, 54, Engineer

Gearey, Edward C. 1st Lt.; Capt. (19 Dec 1898), 1890-1898, 26, Clerk

Hildreth, M.A., 2nd Lt.; 1st Lt. (19 Dec. 1898), 1890-1898, 39, Lawyer

Thompson, Robert, 2nd Lt. (from 19 Dec. 1898), 1891-1898, 27, Bookkeeper

Russater, John, 1st Sgt.; 2nd Lt., Co. I (14 July 1899) 1894-1898, 29, Blacksmith

Company C, Grafton

Fraine, John H. Captain (promoted to Maj., 2nd Bn., 20 May 1898), 1887-1898, 37, Lawyer/real estate

Johnson, John H. 1st Lt.; Capt., 21 May 1898, 1887-1898, 39, Deputy treasurer

Foley, C. J. 2nd Lt.; 1st Lt., 21 May 1898, 1887-1898, 29, Railroad worker

Tharalson, Thomas, 1st Sgt.; 2nd Lt., 21 May 1898, 1889-1898, 31, Real estate agent

McLean, John M. 1st Sgt., after 21 May 1898, 1892-1898, 24, Laborer

Company D, Devils Lake

Cogswell, A. W. Captain, 1891-1898, 33, Pharmacist

Redmon, Henry***, 1st Lieutenant, 1891-1898, 32, Machinist

Lonnevik, Thomas, 2nd Lt.; 1st Lt., 2 June 1899, 1892-1898, 31, Teacher

Shortt, Phil, 1st Sergeant, 1896-1898, 28, Publisher

Company G, Valley City

Mudgett, C. F. Captain (resigned, 1 June 1899), 1890-1898, 26, Bookkeeper

Getchell, Charles, 1st Lieutenant, 1890-1898, 25, Bookkeeper

Pray, William H. 2nd Lt. (promoted to 1st Lt., 30 July 1899, and appointed regimental QM), 1894-1898, 28, Farmer

Henry, Frank S. 1st Sergeant, 1894-1898, 22, Pharmacist

Company H, Jamestown

Eddy, Porter W. Captain, 1891-1898, 29, Farmer

Procter, H. G. 1st Lt. (transferred to Co. B,, 22 Oct. 1898), 1891-1898, 26, Clerk

Gruschus, H. J. 1st Lt. (promoted and transferred, from Co. K, Jan. 1899), 1897-1898, 24, Lumberman

Baldwin, Dorman, 2nd Lt. (WIA 1 Apr. 1899; returned, to U.S., 15 June 1899), 1891-1898, 27, Clerk/law student

Mattison, O. T. 1st Sgt.; 2nd Lt., July 1899, 1892-1898, 32, Printer

Company I, Wahpeton

Purdom, William R. Captain, 1897-1898, 33, Merchant

Aspinwall, William, 1st Lieutenant, 1897-1898, 25, Printer

Slattery, Joseph, 2nd Lt. (promoted to 1st Lt. and, transferred to Co. B, 12 July 1899), 1897-1898, 22, Student

McKean, A. E. 1st Sergeant, 1897-1898, 22, Clerk

Company K, Dickinson

Auld, George, Captain, 1897-1898, 54, Register of Deeds

Osborne, A. J. 1st Lieutenant, 1897-1898, 28, Photographer

Gruschus, H. J. 2nd Lt. (promoted to 1st Lt. and, transferred to Co. H, 9 Jan. 1899), 1897-1898, 23, Lumberman

Smith, Fred, 2nd Lt. (was regimental sgt. maj. until promotion and assignment to Co. K, 9 Jan. 1899), 1894-1898, 25, Clerk

Freeman, A. W. 1st Sergeant, 1897-1898, 21, Druggist

---

*Berg was promoted to captain, Company G, July 1899.

**Keye was sent on leave to U.S., 24 October 1898 to 5 December 1898. He resigned for reasons of health, 5 December 1898.

***Redmon was sent on sick leave to U.S., 24 April 1899, and was discharged for disability, June 1899.

The trip to San Francisco did little to dispel the carnival atmosphere surrounding the regiment's departure from Fargo. The Great Northern train carrying the 1st Battalion stopped twice in North Dakota after leaving Grand Forks on the afternoon of 26 May: at Devils Lake, home of Company D, and at Minot late in the evening. A short stop in dreary Saco, Montana, the next day gave some in Company C a chance to visit a saloon where "some of the boys got a little tipsy." Few in the regiment were prepared for the reception the citizens of Washington and Oregon gave them. From Spokane through Walla Walla to The Dalles where the troop train crossed into Oregon, Washingtonians greeted the North Dakotans with food, flowers, and cheers. At Portland, Oregon, on 29 May, "there were thousands of people at the depot waiting for us to come in," Sergeant Tharalson wrote. Teen-aged girls made up the most enthusiastic segment of the crowds, offering the men bouquets and begging for brass buttons from their uniform coats. At the Salem, Oregon, depot, late on the evening of the 29th, girls banging on the window awakened John Kinne and his Company B bunkmate, Bob Thompson. "They had waited for the soldiers and were not going to miss the chance to shake hands even tho we were in bed," Kinne remembered. Yet another large gathering welcomed the unit to San Francisco on 31 May. Red Cross ladies fed the regiment and gave each man a bouquet. Dour Captain John Fraine made Company C throw the flowers away, as he "would not allow" the men "to carry them in the march" to the campgrounds.

Upon their arrival at Camp Merritt, just outside San Francisco, on the afternoon of 31 May, the 1st North Dakota joined other state volunteer regiments to become elements of the Army. The volunteers needed new equipment and at least a month of drill before they were deemed fit for combat. In contrast to Major General William R. Shafter's V Corps, which landed in Cuba, Major General Wesley Merritt's VIII Corps underwent methodical preparation before leaving for the Philippines. Merritt was a better administrator than Shafter, but he also had more time. He dispatched regular troops and the better-trained and equipped volunteers in the first element to leave for the Philippines on 25 May. Other regiments, including the 1st North Dakota, remained at Camp Merritt to learn the rudiments of soldiering. The North Dakota contingent was not as well prepared as such units as the 1st California, the 1st Colorado, the 13th Minnesota, or the 20th Pennsylvania. Neither was it as poorly organized as the 20th Kansas, which Merritt reported was well known "by its want of capacity, so far as officers are concerned," nor as poorly equipped as the 1st Tennessee, an outfit "completely destitute of equipment in any direction."

By general order on 3 June, Lieutenant Colonel Treumann established a training regimen which emphasized squad, company, and battalion drill. Inspections of arms and equipment, and the usual guard mount, filled in the remainder of each day. After two weeks of work on the fundamentals, first the companies, then the battalions, took up extended-order skirmish drill and target practice. "This was pretty hard work," John Kinne recalled, but "these daily hard drills in the different formations brought the regiment into pretty good shape." According to Kinne, by the time the 1st North Dakota left San Francisco on 28 June "it was a much better drilled lot of men than when we arrived nearly a month ago." Just prior to departure for overseas, the regiment received new rifles, uniforms, and a new major when Captain Fraine was finally commissioned to replace Harry Flint.

At midday on 27 June the 1st North Dakota marched to the docks to board the SS *Valencia*. Once again "there was waving of flags, cheering, shooting of cannons and ringing of bells." Red Cross women fed the boys lunch before they boarded ship, and there were more flirtatious girls as well. From their day of muster-in, few could doubt that their countrymen supported them wholeheartedly. The men remained aboard the *Valencia* a full day while the ship took on coal (their first of many experiences with the Army's unavoidable "hurry-up-and-wait" tradition). Just before the *Valencia* left San Francisco Bay late in the afternoon of 28 June 1898, Major Fraine wrote a goodbye letter to Governor Frank Briggs. "We are about to pull out," Fraine said. "We are all well....We hope to so act that the state will not blush for us. We are the only regt. leaving here that has not buried one or more men."

When the Fargo *Forum* first published the news of the Philippines assignment for the 1st North Dakota, it gushed that one of the side benefits for the boys would be "a magnificent ocean voyage." As sons of the great American heartland, few in the regiment found magnificence in ocean travel. Many discovered instead the agony of seasickness. They wrote home about it, commented on it endlessly in their diaries, and recalled its agonies years later. Seasickness brought forth more curses than Army food, or even the miseries of campaigning. An anonymous diarist from Company C combined complaints on seasickness and the *Valencia's* food: "I have been so sick I don't even know my own name....Oh! The smell of the kitchen would kill the oldest man living." Major Frank White graphically recounted to his wife the distress suffered in the officers' mess. Of their first meal at sea, he wrote, "I had hardly seated myself before my stomach gave symptoms of unrest. Lieut. Slattery was the first to go. I was a good second. Capt. Keye and a great crowd on my heels." Eventually they all adjusted to life at sea, and even the worst sufferer, Second Lieutenant Harvey Pray of Company G, improved "and has concluded to live." Black humor helped. A Company C wag observed "that we will be a damned narrow looking outfit when we reach Manila."

A stop at Honolulu helped ease the regiment's initiation to shipboard life. When the convoy arrived in the Hawaiian Islands on 6 July, it stayed for two days, and the North Dakota boys experienced yet another reception of bands, shouting civilians, and Red Cross women. All of the officers and most of the enlisted men went ashore for sightseeing. The unknown Company C writer found the Islands "The most beautiful place I have ever been....to gaze upon it is simply elegant." Twenty-year-old Oscar J. Olson, a resident of Honolulu, thought otherwise. Olson "wanted to see the world," and, after an interview with Captain William Purdom of Company I, enlisted in the 1st North Dakota as his first step in touring the globe. It was some time before he became a complete soldier, as only in November did the Army issue Olson a full uniform.

The trip from Honolulu to Manila Bay lasted from 9 to 31 July. Although not unusually uncomfortable among transports used in the Spanish-American War, the *Valencia* nonetheless earned the enmity of the North Dakota boys. Poorly fitted as a troopship, a consequence of the improvised nature of the American war effort, it lacked proper refrigeration and had an inadequate desalinization plant. As the heat built up below decks, the food rotted, the water became tainted, and the men grew increasingly restless. John Kinne and his friends bartered with the ship's crew for canned fruit and, failing in that, stole the goods. The men fought over gambling games, causing Colonel Treumann to order an end to card playing. Melancholy replaced the heady feelings experienced at the crowded depots and docks. One soldier commented, in Company C "the principle *[sic]* song is 'Just Before the Battle Mother,'" a maudlin camp song of Civil War vintage. Talk of home and regrets over enlisting dominated the outfit's conversation. The thoroughly unpleasant conditions on the *Valencia* provoked some of the discontent. "The next time that they want me to fight anybody they will have to fetch them to me," noted the nameless chronicler. Much of the complaining, however, was stimulated by homesickness and the realization that once the *Valencia* reached Manila, an unknown enemy awaited. New soldiers and veterans alike understandably grumble as they approach a combat zone.

By 17 July, a soldier wrote of Company C: "I tell you if the boys were home you wouldn't get 10 out of the whole bunch...if I had to do it over again I would let some other fellow go in my place." The more mature and enterprising Major White set about learning the semaphore alphabet and leading an officers' school for the 1st Battalion. The latter effort had mixed results because Captain William Moffett, Company A, was too busy. "He was taking pictures, helping the Captain run the ship, reading signals from the other ships, etc.'' White did not call down the overbusy Moffett, for, he wrote, "we will soon be where we will have to attend to business."

The *Valencia* arrived in Manila Bay on 31 July, almost out of drinking water. While eager to get ashore, the North Dakotans spent another five days aboard their hated transport. Though the Americans controlled Manila Bay and the arsenal and garrison on Cavite Peninsula, opposite Manila in the southwest corner of the bay, facilities for off-loading supplies and men were inadequate. Americans did not land on the eastern side of the bay, where they set up Camp Dewey for the seige of Manila, until 15 July. So the 1st North Dakota fretted while Admiral George Dewey and General Merritt discussed when and how to unload them and where to put them. On the night of 1 August, according to John Peterson of Company A, they could hear the Spaniards and Filipino Insurgents exchanging rifle fire. "The boys are feeling good and many are anxious for a fight."

Much of the regiment's baggage and ammunition went ashore on 4 August, but few of the men went over until the 5th. A cumbersome system of tugboats, towing makeshift barges and cascoes (large dugout canoes), shuttled cargo and men to Cavite Peninsula, out of the range of Spanish guns, and then from Cavite to the mainland by the same system. Colonel Treumann assigned Major White to oversee the unloading effort. White complained to his wife that Treumann "says use your own judgment" on how to accomplish the job. "He has a faculty of shifting responsibilities that is amusing," he added. "I can stand it if he can but for the good of the Reg. I wish he had a little more push. All he does is read Dutch novels and write letters." (Treumann, born in Germany, presumably read novels in his native language.) White was frustrated with the lack of news about the siege of Manila. He had heard no war news of either the Philippine or Caribbean campaigns since leaving Honolulu. And he knew little of what was expected of the regiment once ashore, commenting, "As far as we know it is all guess work as to what and where anything will be done." Clausewitz's famous axiom about the fog of war included ignorance about the intentions of one's superiors as well as one's enemy.

The 1st North Dakota got safely ashore on Cavite late on the afternoon of 5 August. White described the rather modern barracks his men occupied, brick with galvanized iron roofing. "You can only imagine what a delighted set of boys there was ashore that night," he penned. The feel of solid land under their feet and the delight of clean quarters restored morale somewhat. John Kinne recalled that that night "The men got hilarious and noisy and with imitation cat calls, lizard calls, etc." It must have seemed for a time like the first night at summer camp. For the next few days the regiment went through light drill. White, for one, worried that they might "forget all they know" before entering combat. He did not worry about the 1st Battalion, for the "officers are in better shape on account of the school" he conducted aboard the *Valencia*. Overall, the men were in good physical condition, he wrote, "better shape than you would expect. They all say we are a pretty husky lot. Too tough to die." They crossed over to the mainland by steamer on the 9th and settled in at Camp Dewey. Orders came two days later to take a twenty-four-hour turn in the trench lines surrounding Manila. "We may have the ring of bullets," White wrote, "but guess not as there hasn't been a shot fired for three days."

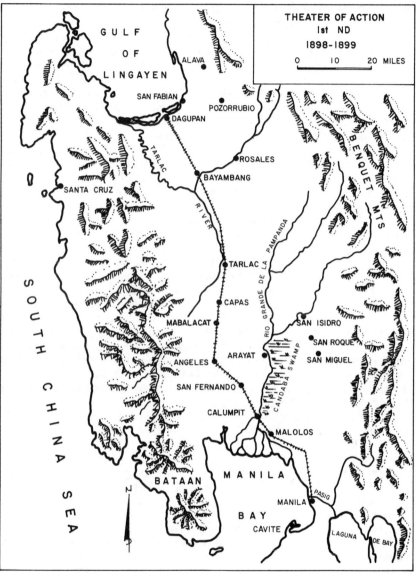

THEATER OF ACTION
Ist ND
1898-1899

0   10   20 MILES

Maps by Michael Fetch

The journey from Fargo to Manila was more than a trip from home to the battle front. It allowed time for the 1st North Dakota to become more than semitrained citizen-soldiers and raw recruits. At Camp Briggs in May, officers and men first learned the rhythms of Army routine. From reveille at 5:30 in the morning, to guard mount three hours later, until taps at 10:00 in the evening, the bugler and military tradition regulated everyone's daily activity. Even aboard the *Valencia* two months later, Major White complained, "We get the same program established...at Fargo. The buglers have kept blowing the same calls." Even White found the routine boring, but it set the men off from civil society and repeatedly reminded them that the Army controlled their lives.

During the month at Camp Merritt the 1st North Dakota learned the rudiments of company and battalion tactics. A major weakness of the National Guard in 1898 was its unfamiliarity with small-unit operations. The Guard was not accountable for its poor arms and equipment, nor for the absence of well-conceived mobilization plans. Those should have been furnished by the War Department. Guard advocates had maintained that the service was a force in being, a ready reserve. This implied that at a minimum, National Guard officers and noncommissioned officers had learned the school of the soldier, company, and battalion at armory drill and summer camp. In fact, few Guardsmen knew these fundamentals, and General Merritt was justified in keeping most volunteer units in camp at least a month before sending them to the Philippines. The enlisted men learned another lesson at San Francisco: the Army was a far harder taskmaster than the National Guard, and breaking its rules led to immediate, and unpleasant, punishment. Under the watchful eyes of Regular officers, Colonel Treumann ordered fines and hard labor under guard to a variety of offenders. Absence from drill, absent without leave, and drunk and disorderly conduct were the most frequent offenses. By the time the regiment reached Manila, it had held twenty-four summary courts-martial.

Even the trip to the Philippines solidified the regiment. The miserable long days on the *Valencia* gave officers and men a shared experience which bound them together. The ocean, the food, the ship itself became common enemies to be outwitted. Key personalities in the outfit emerged. By the time they reached Manila, few could doubt that Major Fraine was a demanding but fair disciplinarian. Major White, conversely, exhibited a flamboyance and self-importance that Fraine did not have. Colonel Treumann read his novels and wrote his letters. The troublemakers gambled and fought, one even earning a drunk and disorderly charge. More thoughtful young men such as John Kinne, John Peterson, and John Russater observed the goings on and recorded them in their diaries. By the time the 1st North Dakota marched up to the trench lines south of Manila on the morning of 12 August, it was a regiment in fact as well as in name.

The regiment was thrown into the lines quickly, in the midst of confusion. The men saw little during their first two weeks in the Islands to generate confidence in their superiors' capacity to wage war. The delay in going ashore and the haphazard landing, for example, showed poor planning. When troops moved from Cavite to the mainland, they left behind most of their baggage and were allowed to take only one change of clothing. With the rainy season at its height, Camp Dewey offered mud and standing water everywhere. The trenches, too, were filled with water. Inevitably, the food was bad.

Conditions around Manila were worse than the usual wartime chaos. The VIII Corps itself was an improvisation, put together and transported to the Philippines in less than three months. Neither the Army nor the Navy had any experience in conducting an overseas war, which demanded interservice cooperation and planning. Logistics suffered the most under these makeshift arrangements. The most complicated aspect of the Manila campaign, however, was the presence of the Filipino Insurgent army in front of the city.

The Insurgent army continued the Filipino rebellion against Spanish rule which first developed in 1896. The rebellion gained new strength in the spring of 1898 and spread rapidly throughout the archipelago with Emilio Aguinaldo's return from exile in May, a return assisted by Admiral George Dewey. In June and July the Filipinos wrested control of the Islands from the Spanish. Aguinaldo declared the Philippines an independent nation on 12 June. By the time the bulk of the VIII Corps arrived, the Insurgents had confined the only effective Spanish military force in the Islands to Manila and its suburbs. The Insurgents' success posed two problems for the Americans, one military, the other diplomatic. Insurgent trenches stood between the American field army at Camp Dewey and the Spanish lines, making it impossible for General Merritt to attack Manila without going through the Filipino forces, unless they agreed to step aside. Merritt and Dewey finally persuaded Aguinaldo to clear some three hundred yards of the line south of Manila for American use just as the 1st North Dakota arrived.

President McKinley had not yet decided what the United States would do with the Islands after the war. If the Insurgents participated in the defeat of the Spanish, it would strengthen their claim for independence. The capture of Manila must be an all-American effort. McKinley consistently reminded his military commanders to minimize all contact with the Insurgents and to make no promises to Aguinaldo. Dewey and Merritt treated Aguinaldo at best as merely an interested bystander, and certainly not as an ally. By mid-July, the Filipinos began to realize that the Americans would not grant them independence and, consequently, they refused to work for the Army, lease draft animals or small boats, or sell them food. This boycott contributed substantially to the VIII Corps' logistical problems.

American forces first occupied a portion of the trenches surrounding Manila on 29 July. After a brief but fierce fire fight there on the 31st, an unofficial ceasefire prevailed for the next twelve days. The Americans wished to take the city before the Insurgents forced a Spanish surrender. Nor did the Spaniards want to surrender to the Filipinos, both for honor's sake and from the fear of reprisals. The Americans sought ways of forcing the Spanish to capitulate. Dewey had the firepower to destroy Manila, but neither he nor Merritt considered a naval bombardment because of the more than 200,000 civilians in Manila. Merritt lacked sufficient territory to mount a ground attack. Aguinaldo finally allowed the VIII Corps to assume nearly a full mile of trench line in early August but refused to pull his forces out of the remaining lines. Neither would he promise to stay out of the battle once Merritt began an attack.

Admiral Dewey's solution was to arrange an agreement with the Spanish providing for a nominal naval bombardment of specified positions, after which the Spanish would surrender. The bombardment would satisfy Spanish honor, which demanded capitulation under fire. In return for minimum resistance, the Americans agreed to keep the Insurgents out of the attack and out of the city. General Merritt took no part in these negotiations but did not oppose them. He prepared to advance on the Spanish lines after Dewey's bombardment. If the Spanish did not resist, some American troops were to move rapidly into Manila to prevent looting while the remainder occupied trenches evacuated by the Spanish. These troops were to keep Insurgents out of the city. Merritt curtly informed Aguinaldo to stay out of the battle and out of the Americans' way.

The general organized the eighty-five hundred combat troops of the VIII Corps into a single tactical division, commanded by Major General Thomas M. Anderson. Anderson's force held a line of approximately a thousand yards on the south side of Manila, running inland from the bay to the Pasay road. Brigadier General Francis V. Greene led the 2nd Brigade on the left, while Major General Arthur MacArthur headed the 1st Brigade on the right. Merritt's plan of attack of 13 August called for Greene's brigade to move out first, with MacArthur to advance soon after. He cautioned his generals to break off the advance if the Spanish displayed any significant resistance. The plan presumed that the enemy would live up to its surrender agreement; if it did not, Merritt intended to call for a massive bombardment. Most of the officers and men of the VIII Corps, unaware of the Dewey-Spanish agreement, anticipated a hot battle.

The men of the 1st North Dakota moved from Camp Dewey on the bay to take twenty-four hours of trench duty early on the morning of 12 August. Assigned to General MacArthur's 1st Brigade on the far right of the American line, the regiment spent an uneventful first day in the face of the enemy. While platoons from each company took turns manning outposts five hundred yards in front of the trenches, the rest of the unit remained in the main line. All buglers, including John Peterson of Company A, stayed at Camp Dewey to guard regimental property, "much against our wishes," he wrote.

The night of 12-13 August proved more exciting. Anticipating the coming combat, Major Frank White recommended doubling the strength of the outposts during the night. Provoked by Insurgent sniping, the Spanish opened fire at 6:30 A.M. "on the outpost" they "had strengthened the night before and scared some of the boys." Company B's outpost, commanded by Lieutenant M. A. Hildreth, also came under fire at the same time. In both cases, Spanish fire did no damage. John Kinne reported on Company B's outpost: "It is said they distinguished themselves....We have only their statement for the noble stand they made." The men were under orders not to fire unless attacked in force, "so the men did not do much shooting," White wrote. "No one was hit but all experienced the whistle of bullets." Relieved from trench duty without further incident at 7:30 A.M., the regiment left the front line and went to reserve in the rear.

Dewey's bombardment began at 9:30 A.M., 13 August 1898, and lasted less than an hour. As promised, the Spanish did not return the fire. Frank White thought it "rather disappointing," as he and his comrades expected a full-fledged fusillade from Dewey's entire fleet of cruisers and monitors. Only four ships actually fired. White correctly assumed, "Guess it wasn't necessary," though he was unaware of the staged nature of the battle. Soon after the bombardment ended, General Greene's brigade advanced against very light resistance. Greene's men suffered few casualties, one man was killed, and they entered Manila before noon. MacArthur's force met greater resistance on the right. The 13th Minnesota led his advance with other units of the brigade, including the 1st North Dakota, in reserve. Insurgent troops hindered MacArthur on his right, ignoring Merritt's command to stay out of the battle and surging on toward Manila. MacArthur moved forward at 11:00 A.M. and faced some resistance until 1:30 P.M.

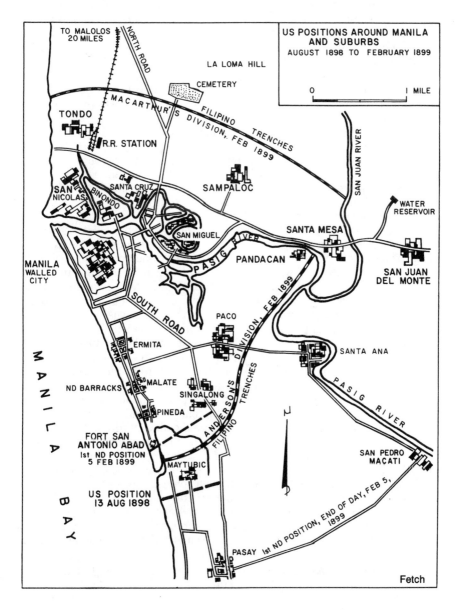

The 1st North Dakota left its trench at noon and passed through two abandoned Spanish lines. They "soon arrived to where the bullets were flying," and the "troops met with little resistance." At about 1:00 P.M. they were ordered to halt and then fall back a few hundred yards. They were ordered forward again at 2:30 P.M., but, according to Private Frank Berg, "Before that time the lines had all been forced and a white flag was flying. We never fired a shot and had but one man hit, a man from Co. A hit in the leg." The regiment marched on unmolested and entered Manila late in the afternoon, where it was "stationed at various points to protect...property and to keep armed natives out of the city." The Spanish surrendered Manila at 5:30 P.M. So ended the "battle" of Manila and the 1st North Dakota's modest role in it.

In the confusion of the fight, the day's affairs affected members of the regiment in different ways. Frank White later wrote praising Captain William P. Moffett, Company A, as "one of the coolest men I had and was under the sharpest fire." The battle, however, disappointed White. "The fight was a very tame affair, there being practically but little resistance." He believed Englishmen or Germans would have held on to Manila for months, but the Spanish, he said, were "cowards" who "would cut and run as soon as our men gave them a volley." White expected, apparently wanted, more fighting and consoled himself by writing to his wife: "but my hide is whole and I suppose should be thankful that it is over with so little action." John Peterson, on the other hand, was disappointed that he missed even the limited action. When a man from his company came to Camp Dewey during the battle to pick up supplies, Peterson noted, he "told me they had been in the warmest part of the fight....How I wish I could have gone...back to the company." In yet another view, John Kinne believed erroneously that the regiment had "orders to retreat" when it fell back for a time, and "most of us were mighty glad to do so." During the withdrawal the men viewed casualties for the first time, seeing "men shot and others drop from exhaustion."

The United States had won the Spanish-American War before the action of 13 August took place, the date on which Spain agreed to cease hostilities and begin negotiations for a final peace treaty. Word of the agreement did not reach the Philippines until the 16th. There would have been no battle without the Insurgents, as Spanish and American commanders maneuvered to keep the Filipinos out of Manila. Although Spaniards fought Americans briefly, both kept a wary eye on this unpredictable third party.

The Americans quickly occupied Manila on the afternoon of the 13th with little rancor and much formality in the formal surrender on the 14th. Units of the VIII Corps fulfilled the American part of the Dewey agreement by keeping Insurgents out of the city, although some of the latter had occupied nearby southside suburbs during the battle. The Filipinos, having fought the Spanish since June, resented their exclusion. Relations between Americans and Insurgents deteriorated in the first days after the Spanish surrender, both at the higher levels of command and in the suburban streets among the rank and file.

From the afternoon of the 13th until 16 August, the 1st North Dakota continued guard duty in Manila. No one could ignore the shared animosity between Insurgents and Americans. Frank White believed the Spanish charge that "the natives expected to get in and loot the town." A display of force by the United States would quiet them down, he thought, then added, "I think we will be able to handle them without killing them." John Peterson was less optimistic, noting in his diary on 14 and 15 August the enlisted men's nervous anticipation of an Insurgent uprising. For the 15th he wrote, "Last night was worse than any we had spent. We all expected a fight, so we had our arms handy...but we were not bothered." He closed the entry by saying, "The soldiers hate the Insurgents as bad as the Spaniards."

Most American troops had gone two to three days with little sleep. When logistical support broke down completely in the confusing days after the battle, the men had to eat what they had carried with them into the fight or buy food from street vendors. While many went hungry, others became sick from eating the native food. Tired, hungry, confused, they took out their anger and frustration on the jostling Filipinos. The majority probably did not yet hate the Insurgents, but they did not trust them either. Relief from guard duty came on the 16th when the regiment marched out of Manila to the southern suburb of Malate on Manila Bay. They were quartered in a bamboo and nipa palm barracks, "which was our headquarters for the rest of our stay in the Islands," wrote one soldier. The regiment retrieved its scattered baggage from Cavite and Camp Dewey, washed up, and rested. That same day the unit lost its first man when Private Joseph Buckley of Company C accidentally shot himself while on guard duty. He died instantly.

Late on the afternoon of 13 August, while Company B manned a street barricade in Manila watching for Insurgent looters, John Kinne and his mates speculated on their chances of going home soon. "I made the statement that I thought we would celebrate Christmas at home, but did not have many supporters," Kinne wrote. He erred in his estimate, his more skeptical comrades proving more realistic. Soon after the 12 August Protocol ending hostilities, the War Department initiated demobilization of many state-recruited units. Most volunteer organizations never left the United States and half of them were civilians again by early November. Many more left the Army in the succeeding three months. Of the nineteen state volunteer units sent to the Philippine Islands, all but the 10th Pennsylvania and 1st Tennessee Infantry regiments came from states west of the Mississippi River. They would spend nearly a full year there before they saw their discharge papers.

The probability of occupation duty had concerned General Wesley Merritt even before he left the United States. Contrary to the recommendations of Admiral Dewey and the Army's Commanding General Nelson A. Miles, Merritt had requested a large contingent of troops (15,000) for the VIII Corps. In mid-May he justified the request to President McKinley when he wrote, "It seems more than probable that we will have the so-called insurgents to fight as well as the Spaniards." The Insurgent presence in some of Manila's suburbs, including Malate where the 1st North Dakota was located, and rapid Insurgent occupation of recently abandoned American trenches put Merritt's force in the same position the Spanish had faced only days earlier. They were now boxed into the city by a sixteen-mile arc of Insurgent lines running from Manila Bay in the north, along the east front of the city, then to the bay again in the south. Insurgent patrols and sentries refused to allow American soldiers to reconnoiter the countryside and attempted to regulate the flow of food and other supplies into the city.

General Merritt and his successor, Major General Elwell S. Otis, who took command of the VIII Corps on 29 August, ordered Aguinaldo to remove his troops from the suburbs and evacuate the trench lines nearest the city. Throughout September and October, relations between the Americans and Filipinos fluctuated. At times they were very tense, as on the occasion of Otis's tactless withdrawal order and when the more militant Filipinos taunted American troops. But when the Insurgents finally agreed to leave the towns of Malate, Paco, and Ermita, in mid-September, good feeling prevailed. While leaving Malate, the Filipinos played American music as they marched out and "cheered the Americans as they passed" the 1st North Dakota barracks. "They yelled 'vivo Americano.'" Another crisis developed in October when General Otis pressed for further Insurgent retreats, but no open conflict occurred.

The Insurgent withdrawals did not eliminate ill-feeling between Filipinos and Americans. Until Spain and the United States agreed to a peace treaty deciding the fate of the Islands, friction would continue. For the Filipinos there were three possibilities: independence, retention by Spain, or annexation by the United States. As long as Otis and his troops remained in Manila, one of the latter two seemed inevitable, with independence denied to a people who had been on the verge of overthrowing their colonial masters. The unsubtle Otis attempted to follow McKinley's orders not to provoke an Insurgent uprising but also not to encourage them to expect an early American departure. Treaty negotiations in Paris dragged on throughout the fall and early winter of 1898. Moderate and cautious Insurgents, led by Aguinaldo, kept the more militant nationalists in check, hoping the final treaty would recognize the Insurgent movement. From September to December 1898, American troops continued an uneasy occupation of Manila and its suburbs.

As Phil Shortt, a sergeant in Company D and later official historian of the regiment, wrote, the ensuing months "were monotonous repetitions, each, of the one just preceding it." Daily drill was prescribed, including bayonet practice and at least a half-hour each afternoon "exclusively devoted to cadence marching in column of fours, platoons or companies." Each company took a regular turn performing outpost and guard duty in the outlying districts where the American and Insurgent lines met. When not at drill or on outpost duty, the men idled away their time in barracks, chafing under the dull routine. "It is a waste of time here with nothing to do that adds a particle to one's advancement," Frank White complained to his wife. "Our life is a daily repetition of garrison duties without an element of danger or change." Some, like Frank Anders of Company B, regretted more and more that they had joined the Army. "I wish I had went into the Navy when the war began. It is the best branch of the service by far," he repined.

The men yearned for a release from duty almost as soon as the Spanish surrendered, filling their diaries and letters with the topic. John Kinne wrote on 20 August, "We heard the first rumors that we were to be sent home." Many were simply homesick, especially the younger men, although even the steady Frank White shared the feeling. Writing to his wife on their fourth wedding anniversary, he expressed surprise that he was now a "soldier 8,000 miles from home taking part in a foreign war." Volunteers, their families, and state officials of all the regiments pressed the War Department for the release of their units. General Otis received hundreds of individual requests for discharge, especially in November and December. To keep his army together until new regular and federal volunteer regiments were organized, Otis rejected all requests. Governor Joseph Devine of North Dakota promised Private Irving Palmer of Company B that his office would do "everything...to get you back here in North Dakota at the earliest possible date." Devine then wrote the War Department in late December, pointing out that Spain and the United States had signed a peace treaty officially ending the war on 10 December. With peace, the men of the 1st North Dakota had fulfilled their enlistment contracts and were eligible for discharge. "In behalf...of the people of the state I urge the early return of the North Dakota volunteers," Devine pleaded.

Volunteer troops had always despised Regular Army routine and discipline. Partly from braggadocio, partly from the fact that the "citizen" side of the American citizen-soldier usually predominated, militia and state volunteers had always expected to go on campaign as soon as they were mobilized. When the Army took too long to train and organize them or assigned them to garrison and guard duty, citizen-soldiers clamored to go home. John Kinne expressed the traditional view when he noted that any soldier found garrison duty "odious" but it was "much more so to volunteer troops." As the occupation dragged on, Kinne and his Company B comrades wondered why they had volunteered and when they would go home. Kinne said he had enlisted to avenge the sinking of the USS Maine. While he was on fatigue duty raking the barracks yard one day, a company wit "called the occupants of his room to the window to see 'Kinne avenge the Maine.' The joke did not appeal to me under the circumstances," Kinne said. Not surprisingly, no one in Company B accepted the Army's offer of a five-hundred-dollar bonus to re-enlist for one year in a regular regiment. Rumors in December that the volunteers would leave Manila in April momentarily cheered Frank Anders. "I hope so any how," he told his mother, "as I am not very much in love with Manila or its surroundings. Those that want the Phillipines [sic] held so, should soldier here awhile."

Frank White consistently told his men and his wife that the regiment would remain in the Islands at least until July 1899. He had noted that throughout the fall ships bringing reinforcements and supplies to Manila invariably were "being sent home empty." His men and other volunteers deeply disliked occupation duty, and, he said, "It is pretty hard to take a philiosofical [sic] view of the matter." White realized, however, that until a peace treaty resolved the issue of Philippine independence, an American military force would remain in Manila. He recognized the volunteer soldiers' rapid shifts in attitudes about military service. By mid-October, he noted, "they have had enough of soldier life...the boys are just as anxious to get back as they were to leave San Francisco."

In part the volunteers grumbled because, however boring, military duties took up only part of their time. "The men have little to do," White reported in September, "and have no money and are kept pretty close to quarters so as to be on hand if needed and chafe under the restraint." Payday at the end of the month happily coincided with the Insurgent withdrawal from the inner suburbs, leading to a reduction in tension and demands for guard duty. Some of the men toured Manila, others rented a boat to tour Manila Bay and visit the big ships of Dewey's fleet. (Throughout their stay in the Philippines, the men from landlocked North Dakota never lost their fascination with the Navy's warships.) A great many of the men, in the way of soldiers, spent their money on gambling, women, and liquor. After payday, John Kinne recorded, "quarters for a few days looked like Monte Carlo on a small scale." The gamblers quickly adopted the Filipino's favorite sporting activity, cockfighting. When asked how soldiers spent their pay, Oscar Olson of Company I replied that "When the Russian women arrived some pay went there." Olson referred to the influx of prostitutes from Russia, Japan, Hong Kong, and other Asian countries soon after the Spanish surrendered. The drinkers took to "a potent native drink" the soldiers called "beno," which was often contaminated. By late August American beer was available, courtesy of United States brewing companies. They had their product "on tap within ten days after our army came into the city," Frank White wrote.

All too quickly, the more rambunctious men spent their small pay ($15.00 a month for privates). Some imaginative soldiers found ways to make extra money, by collecting and selling expended brass cartridge casings, for example. At least two men in Company B sold lumber and hinges taken from Fort San Antonio Abad where the 1st North Dakota stood guard duty. Kinne wrote, "I believe they would have sold the fort if they could have found a buyer." Courts martial, heavy fines, and twenty days in the guardhouse ended that commercial enterprise. Gambling caused so many arguments and fights that company officers prohibited wagering in the barracks.

Many young men in the regiment spurned the wild life. Oscar Olson regularly deposited two-thirds of his pay in a savings account. John Peterson, the Company A bugler, sought out the companionship of musicians in regimental bands of both volunteer and regular organizations. Mail call brought newspapers and books from home as well as letters. The barracks were always quiet for two or three days after mail arrived as the men devoured all new reading material. The officers of the regiment organized a Masonic Lodge, which met two or three times a week. The lodge sponsored a regimental canteen to sell books, pens, paper, and other sundries, but, White noted, it did "not sell any liquors." To break the monotony of garrison duty, the men organized musicals, stag dances, plays, and, above all, baseball teams. Company teams played each other and a regimental team took on squads from other regiments. "It is the most American thing on the Islands," White told his wife, "and makes one feel almost like being at home."

Baseball did not erase memories of home, nor did it make acceptable the seemingly pointless occupation duty. Sometimes an insignificant occurrence rekindled a yearning for civil life. When Frank White met some newly arrived wives of Regular Army officers, it startled him. "It seems very strange to be so out of the social world and female society," he wrote. He had not exchanged "twenty words" with "American ladies since leaving Honolulu." The approach of Christmas strengthened the sense of melancholy. When Christmas boxes arrived from home, the men saved them for the big day. On Christmas Eve, John Russater wrote in his diary, in Company B barracks "there was great festivities....The Insurgents and the war was [sic] forgotten for some time and everybody was talking, laughing and telling each other what he got."

The hot, humid climate of the Philippines and Manila's unsanitary conditions threatened American forces far more than boredom or homesickness. In the Spanish-American War, deaths from disease exceeded combat deaths at a rate of fifteen to one. More appalling, most disease-induced deaths occurred among troops who never left the United States, chiefly state volunteers. Soldiers in the VIII Corps fared better than those in the V Corps who went to Cuba, but they suffered nonetheless. The sick rate in the Philippines soared in the three months following the Battle of Manila, reaching twenty percent in November. A variety of factors contributed to the high illness rate. Approximately one-quarter of the enlisted men on sick report, for example, had venereal disease. Malaria, typhoid fever, and dysentery accounted for most of the others. General Otis, his division commanders, and the Medical Corps issued numerous general orders and circulars to educate the volunteers on field sanitation procedures for the tropics. They warned the men not to eat or drink native foodstuffs. Otis, not the most sympathetic of generals, reported that once the VIII Corps opened a convalescent hospital on Corregidor Island and stopped sending seriously ill soldiers back to the United States, the sick rate declined considerably. A more reasonable explanation suggested that officers and men of the volunteer regiments finally learned proper sanitation practices. By January of 1899, the VIII Corps had stemmed the tide of rampant disease.

In the 1st North Dakota Infantry, Colonel Treumann required company commanders to inspect the barracks daily and to check carefully "the clothing and persons of their men in respect to cleanliness." Through the end of October, the health of the regiment held up fairly well, although Frank White observed, "Our boys have all grown thinner and don't look near as rugged as when we left home." Private John Morgan of Company H was the first to die in late October. Dysentery had killed him, but White thought, "His death is traceable to drinking the native liquor." At the end of October the regiment numbered 677 officers and enlisted men, but only 569 were fit for duty. A month later, there were 531, a sick rate of twenty-one percent ("mostly venereal troubles, dysentery and fever, none seriously sick," according to White). Thereafter, as in the rest of the VIII Corps, the regiment's health improved, with eighty-eight percent of its strength fit for duty at the end of January 1899. It had the lowest sick rate in the 2nd Brigade, 1st Division.

Frank White devoted considerable thought to the health problems of the regiment. He intuitively hit on one explanation for death by disease which sociological study during World War II would eventually confirm. In writing to his wife at the end of November, White noted that three men in the regiment had died of disease. It was "a rather strange coincidence" that all were "men of whom little was known, being men who were picked up to fill out the companies." World War II analysis of combat units indicated that men not socially integrated into primary groups (squads or platoons) suffered higher rates of sickness, wounds, and death. The men to whom White referred, if not loners, nonetheless were not prewar members of the North Dakota National Guard. The major also found a "pretty good index," he wrote, "for discipline and efficiency of our companies and that is the sick report. It shows that where the men are kept under strict discipline and are made to take care of themselves they keep in good health." Effective company officers were the key to the well-being of the regiment.

The rapidly rising sick rate of October and November cannot be attributed to ineffective company officers. Company B lost two of its three officers, Captain Frederick Keye and Lieutenant F. L. Conklin, in September and October, both of whom returned to the United States on extended sick leave. They resigned in December but were not replaced until February 1899 because only the governor had the authority to promote or commission officers in the state volunteers. This anachronistic and pernicious militia tradition denied the regiment two badly needed company officers for over two months.

Another equally detrimental Army practice drew off other regimental and company officers. The Army of 1898-1899 lacked a general staff to perform a wide variety of functions not directly related to combat duties. It had a limited number of logistical and administrative branches, but there were too few of these officers to meet even the Army's peacetime needs. The occupation of Manila and its suburbs increased the strain on VIII Corps staff as General Otis ordered a massive cleanup of the city, reorganization of the municipal government, and a review of the Spanish legal and prison systems, among other things. To meet corps administrative needs and the special occupation activities, Otis had little choice but to detail line officers from the combat units to special duty. These assignments were sometimes temporary. Because of his engineering training, Frank White spent a few days inspecting and repairing the sewer system of Malate District. "The boys call me 'Privy Councillor' because among other things I have to inspect privies," he commented.

Other officers served on detached service for months. Captain William P. Moffett of Company A took charge of the prison in Manila on 25 August and remained there until 23 March 1899, reviewing prison records and releasing all political prisoners as well as cleaning up the prison and administering it. Captain Charles F. Mudgett, Company G, took over as Collector of Internal Revenue for Manila in late October, "a very important and responsible position." In January, Lieutenant M. A. Hildreth, Company B, was detached to lend his legal skills to a board of officers supervising the transfer of Spanish rule of the Islands to the United States.

Detached service hit Major White's 1st Battalion especially hard in the fall of 1898. "My Battalion is getting quite short of officers," he wrote. "I have only one captain left, Capt. Eddy [Co. H], two first lieutenants and three second lieutenants." Second Lieutenant William H. Pray commanded Company G from October through December, its only officer with Captain Mudgett on duty at the Internal Revenue office and Lieutenant Charles W.

Getchell on temporary duty as acting quartermaster for the 2nd Division Hospital. Command of the regiment fell to White in December when Colonel Treumann and Major John Fraine reported to Manila for court martial duty.

Occupation duty strained the ties that bound the regiment. The younger men had volunteered with naive enthusiasm to rush off to smite the nation's enemy. Unexpectedly, they found themselves in the far Pacific Ocean caught up in a complicated and delicate diplomatic quarrel they neither understood nor sympathized with. Subject to tropical diseases and forced to carry on military duties that they thought were fit only for regulars, they demanded to be sent home. Sickness and the Army's need to order line officers to detached service eroded regimental discipline. The regiment's efficiency, sense of identity, and camaraderie established at Camp Briggs and Camp Merritt suffered during the occupation.

In spite of allegations that the American force sent to the Islands "was one of the more undisciplined ever placed in the field by this nation," there has been no comparison of the VIII Corps with other American field forces in other wars. Certainly, however, the behavior of General Otis's men in the fall of 1898, including the 1st North Dakota Infantry, left something to be desired. Few volunteers displayed much interest in maintaining a soldierly appearance. As early as 3 September Major John Fraine had to order the 2nd Battalion's enlisted men to wear shirts and shoes when leaving their barracks. Repeated orders from divisional commanders, Generals Anderson and MacArthur, demanding that the men wear regulation uniforms, cut their hair, and keep clean had little effect, and the VIII Corps would never be known as a spit-and-polish outfit.

More disturbing was the average enlisted man's indifference to guard duty and military decorum. A general order from MacArthur in October reported too many instances of sleeping or appearing drunk on guard duty. He called for harsher punishments for this offense and noted that the death penalty could be imposed. Within two weeks three different men in Company B were charged and eventually convicted for failing to appear for guard duty, sleeping on post, or leaving a guard post without proper relief. Reproofs from corps and division headquarters also failed to stem rampant drunkenness and disorderly conduct in Manila. Because "rowdyism carried on until a late hour at night" was "charged against men" of the 2nd Division, General MacArthur ordered a 10:00 P.M. curfew for enlisted men. In the 1st Division, General Anderson placed "bar rooms, saloons, joints and places of ill-fame" off limits to all officers and men, but the order did not reduce the drinking and raucous behavior. On 10 November, Anderson ordered regimental officers "to prevent drunken soldiers from wandering in the streets." He added, "Complaints have been made that they have insulted respectable ladies in the streets and even invaded houses."

The abuse of liquor plagued the 1st North Dakota. At times, drunkenness represented bored men blowing off steam, as seen, for example, in the trial of four men of Company B in mid-November. The four appeared in barracks extremely drunk and noisy after running along the beach, jumping in the bay while in uniform, boarding a native fishing boat, and harassing Filipino fishermen. After returning to the beach, they "did roll and tumble upon the beach and in the water while dressed and while so intoxicated." Chronic drinkers were more troublesome, for they regularly appeared drunk at roll call and for guard duty, fought with their noncommissioned officers, or went absent without leave while under the influence. Every company in the regiment had two or three men who consistently turned up drunk. A private in Company A set the regimental record with six summary and general courts martial convictions for drunk and disorderly behavior, though Company I had the largest number of offenders. Regular alcohol abusers invariably ended up in the guardhouse or in military prison. Their absence added to the duties of the other enlisted men whose numbers were constantly reduced by a growing sick list.

Men who disliked military service and refused to accept discipline also taxed the regiment's stability. Some of the volunteers failed to distinguish between behavior tolerated in the armory back in North Dakota and the necessity to obey orders in the Philippines. When First Sergeant John Russater, Company B, ordered a private on fatigue duty, the man responded with "'I'll be damned if I will go,' or words to that effect." He lost fifteen days' pay and served two hours' extra duty for five days for his flippant remark. Another private from Company G suffered the same punishment for "contumacious and insulting language to his superior officer." Usually, the false courage generated by alcohol spurred men to defy their superiors. One drunken private in Company B refused to obey Lieutenant E. C. Gearey's order to quiet down and go to bed. Instead the man "did advance upon his commanding officer, thrusting his face close to that of the latter, swinging his arms about and shaking his hand in the face" of Lieutenant Gearey. A summary court sentenced the private to three months in the military prison and the loss of ten dollars pay for each of three months.

Commanders at all levels attempted to enforce discipline, first by general and special orders and then by liberal use of courts-martial. The Corps Judge Advocate reviewed 563 general courts martial convictions (held at corps or division level) and summary courts trials (held at regimental or battalion levels) for 7,090 men between August 1898 and August 1899. The courts kept the officers busy but did not stop the riotous behavior of the troops. Increasingly harsh sentences, including lengthy confinement at Bilibid Prison in Manila, removed repeat offenders from the barracks, but they did not deter indiscipline effectively.

The sorry disciplinary record of the VIII Corps from August 1898 to August 1899 reflected the weakness of the war army system of mobilization. Neither officers nor men in the state regiments understood the discipline necessary for a field army and had to learn that necessity *after* becoming a part of the VIII Corps. The familiarity volunteer officers and noncommissioned officers shared with their men made it initially difficult for the former to demand obedience and even harder for the latter to obey once ordered to do so. Furthermore, the McKinley administration's long delay in deciding the fate of the Philippine Islands kept the volunteers in doubt about their length of stay in the Islands. Sensing a lack of purpose for Otis's army, the men raised hell and shouted to go home. A more attentive commander than Otis would have made some attempt to convince his command of the necessity of their retention in the Pacific.

Most of the discipline problems in the regiment and the VIII Corps occurred between the end of the fighting with the Spanish in August 1898 and the outbreak of the Philippine Insurrection in February 1899. The regiment's court-martial case load followed the same pattern as its sick rate, with a slow build-up in August and September, the peak coming in October and November, and a sharp decline in January of 1899. Discipline improved in part because by January the hard cases were locked up and the officers and noncommissioned officers had learned how to work with their men. Equally important, the corps had found a purpose by January, albeit not one anticipated when the regiment left Fargo back in May.

Throughout the occupation period Americans and Philippine Insurgents approached each other warily. Neither trusted the other, and each expected the other to launch a surprise attack. Soon after the Americans occupied Manila, John Kinne recalled, "we received orders, the first of many, to sleep on our arms with ammunition at hand, to be ready to move at a moment's notice." The orders came from brigade headquarters in reaction to a rumor that Insurgents were about to attack American positions. False alarms and "war scares" occurred with varying frequency in the fall of 1898 as American-Insurgent relations altered from mediocre to bad and back again. John Peterson noted on 8 September that Company A slept with their clothes on and weapons at hand. On September 10, Frank White mentioned "a false alarm from the north part of the city." The September scares ceased when Insurgent forces evacuated the inner suburbs, but in mid-October "war scares renewed," and, according to Kinne, "we were not allowed to leave quarters for a few days." Again, they faded when Insurgents pulled back from American lines as requested by General Otis.

The alarms kept the men uneasy and suspicious of the Filipinos. Americans and Filipinos had never gotten along well, the latter resenting the thwarting of their independence movement. They found the soldiers' contempt for them even harder to take. Many Americans saw the Filipinos as racially inferior to "white men" and ignored orders from General Otis not to refer to them as "niggers." Frank White, although an intelligent and educated man, did not think the Filipinos capable of self-government, and Oscar Olson saw them as "A mixture-- semi-barbaric and those more enlightened. All rulers were grafters--oriental style."

Certainly the off-duty behavior of American troops did little to improve relations with the natives. Two men from Company I were convicted of "striking a native woman while under the influence of liquor." Others were accused of entering native huts while drunk and, although acquitted of that charge, were convicted of drunk and disorderly behavior. Many soldiers refused to pay for food and souvenirs taken from native vendors or paid them in counterfeit money. In an effort to stop cheating and stealing, General Anderson issued a general order condemning actions that could lead "the native people to believe that we are indifferent to their rights or unable to control a lawless element in our army." Still, in mid-January John Russater recorded in his diary that local merchants "are sulky" because in Company B "some of the boys did not pay their bills."

American troops on outpost and patrol duty screened Filipinos as they entered the American sector or visited Manila. According to John Kinne, at the outpost "it was the duty of the one on this post to search all entering the city for firearms, knives, bolos, beno, and other intoxicants." Often, American sentries were neither diplomatic nor gentle in their frisking and sometimes forced women to submit to physical searches. Out where American and Insurgent lines met, troops of both sides exchanged threats and insults. The Insurgents set up their own outposts to prevent armed Americans from entering their lines. Frank White wrote, "This of course will not be tolerated very long and is a constant annoyance requiring a deal of patience on the part of our soldiers."

Strained relations deteriorated further after mid-December when news of the Treaty of Paris, signed by Spain and the United States on 4 December 1898, finally reached the Philippines. Spain ceded the Islands to the United States in the agreement. War scares increased dramatically while the Insurgent leadership waited for word of President McKinley's policy toward their homeland. For the rest of December the 1st North Dakota and other units in the VIII Corps responded to special alerts several times a week. The men hated sleeping in their clothes and turning out in the middle of the night to man their trenches. "Insurgent scares getting to be a chestnut," Russater noted for 28 December. Frank White, while commenting that "the native soldiers are somewhat restless," decided also that he did not "think anything will come of it." But the men remained close to quarters and on expanded guard duty for the rest of the month.

Conflict became nearly unavoidable when General Otis published an edited version of President McKinley's proclamation to the Philippine people on 4 January 1899. Without authorization, Otis modified the language in an effort to remove the sting from McKinley's statement, which informed the Filipinos bluntly that the United States intended to retain and govern the Islands. The Insurgents soon obtained a complete copy of the proclamation. Thereafter, they planned an uprising while meeting with a board of officers representing General Otis in a last-ditch effort to avoid hostilities.

Following Otis's publication of the President's proclamation, both armies went to work improving their trench lines and outposts. Other ominous signs of impending conflict appeared. The American high command replaced Sunday dress parades with extra drill, "the first Sunday duty we had performed for a long time," John Kinne recorded for 8 January. During the second week of January, Filipino civilians began to drift out of Manila and leave the suburbs. The men of the 1st North Dakota were again restricted to barracks and slept once more in their clothes. "I guess the necessity of keeping in quarters and doing duty almost daily is good for our men," White wrote his wife, suggesting a major cause for the reduction of disciplinary problems. Rumors floated about, however, and the repeated alarms created an atmosphere of anxiety. To White, "It seems to be in the air that the fighting will begin very soon. It is just the condition that almost anything would touch it off."

"Almost anything" nearly touched it off in the regiment's sector on 11 January. As Colonel William C. Treumann worked in his office that afternoon, he heard a commotion in the street next to the regimental barracks. Several natives on horseback rode by rapidly and he heard shots in the distance. Treumann promptly reported to brigade headquarters where a staff officer told him an uprising had begun in Manila, and "he ordered me to take my command and occupy the position previously assigned," he wrote. Following the plan, the entire regiment fell in under arms, and the 1st Battalion took its place in nearby trenches. Natives living near the 1st North Dakota quarters quickly deserted their huts in fear of a battle. Colonel Treumann and Major White went up to the front line with the 1st Battalion companies but saw no trouble there. White even talked to Insurgent officers for a short time. Treumann reported, "Seeing no demonstration in our front on the part of the Insurgents," I "ordered that no shot be fired." General Samuel Ovenshine, commander of the 2nd Brigade, 1st Division, soon arrived and ordered the regiment to stand down. It was another false alarm. A similar incident occurred the next day when a nervous, or drunk, bugler from a nearby unit blew "call to arms," and, White wrote, "we again had a great rush to barracks. We took up arms but kept the men in barracks for a time." Neither occasion led to conflict, in large part because regimental and battalion officers like Treumann and White closely supervised outpost and trench positions to prevent nervous soldiers from shooting unnecessarily.

Around 18 January, White noted, "Our war scare seems to have subsided." The possibilities for conflict eased yet another time, but soon the drift toward war resumed. Major White's letter to his wife on 18 January expressed cautious optimism for peace, but when he wrote to her on 1 February he dismissed any chance of an early return to North Dakota "unless," he added, "conditions here go through a very great change." Once again, the men of the regiment slept in their clothes, and day and night rushed to the trenches at any hint of Insurgent activity. Colonel Treumann released all prisoners in the guardhouse in order to increase available manpower in the companies on 1 February. Although the frequent calls to arms prepared the men psychologically for a fight, it began to tell on them physically. Division headquarters suspended daily drills because, according to Kinne, "Our day and night duty was getting too strenuous." White, too, thought "Our men at present are doing more than they should."

Sporadic fighting began during the night of 4-5 February when American sentries fired on an Insurgent patrol. In the morning, General Otis launched a general attack on Insurgent lines surrounding Manila. As White suggested, "Some of these times it will get touched off for sure." No responsible American military or political leader desired a war with the Filipinos, but neither did they pursue policies to avoid a conflict. President McKinley's decision to retain the Islands caused the Insurrection. His refusal to give the Filipinos a substantial role in their government undercut conservatives and moderates who might have accepted a benevolent American stewardship. Furthermore, the President could hardly have selected a more maladroit military representative than General Otis. Imperious, withdrawn, and wholly unsympathetic to the Filipinos, Otis made no effort to lessen the tensions which were evident throughout the fall of 1898 and intensified greatly in January 1899. He was merely following orders in his diplomatic role, but he did so with little finesse.

The questions of imperialism, annexation, and diplomacy were of little interest to the volunteers. Once they had defeated the Spanish, the men wanted to go home. Denied that opportunity, they carped and complained about occupation duty, while many whored and drank. Too often they took out their resentments on the Filipino people by bullying and cheating them, a not insignificant cause of the war. During December and January, exasperation grew in the ranks. Restricted to their barracks, subjected to alternating periods of acute stress followed by unexplained stand downs, the volunteers became uneasy and restless. After describing the frequent alarms of mid-january, Frank White added, ''Altho nothing has come of it they show how our men are strung up.'' John Kinne made light of the war scares, saying, ''we began to think of them as school boys do of fire drills,'' but conceded that ''we were finally anxious to have something real happen.'' The men of the 1st North Dakota Volunteer Infantry now faced six months of hard campaigning in which they could satisfy their bottled-up desires for action. Despite all that had gone before, this would be the real test of the regiment.

Notes on Sources

Archival and manuscript materials provided the major sources on the Spanish-American War. Record Group 94, Records of the Adjutant General's Office, 1890-1917, National Archives and Records Service, contains two valuable entries. Entry 116, Regimental and Company Books, Spanish-American War, 1st North Dakota Volunteer Infantry, includes courts martial records, regimental correspondence, and field returns. Individual personnel files are available in Entry 522, Compiled Military Service Records, Spanish-American War, 1st North Dakota Volunteer Infantry.

The best insight into the 1st North Dakota's organization and mobilization comes from Series 153 (1-1-2), Governor, Administration, Incoming Letters, Governor Frank Briggs, April-August 1898, and Series 154 (1-1-1), Governor, Administration, Outgoing Letters, Governor Frank Briggs, April and May 1898, in the State Historical Society of North Dakota, Archives. The incoming and outgoing correspondence of Governors Joseph Devine and Fred Fancher from the same two series for September 1898 to November 1899 were valuable as well. Useful manuscript holdings at the State Historical Society were the following papers and diaries of members of the 1st North Dakota: William J. McLean Papers, Company A, 1898-1899; William J. Moffett Papers, Company A, 1898-1899; John Peterson Diary, Company A, 1898-1899; John Russater Diary, Company B, 1898-1899.

Records of the North Dakota National Guard include the diary of Thomas Tharalson, Company C, for 1898, and an anonymous diary by a Company C private for 1898. The muster-in and muster-out rolls for the 1st North Dakota, 1898 and 1899, respectively, were useful in identifying regimental members, their backgrounds, and their wartime service. Also available were consolidated military service records on all enlisted men, which contained disciplinary and health records and lists of awards and commendations. Correspondence and unpublished reports from the Adjutant General's Office for 1898 and 1899, as well as the published 1898 Adjutant General's report, revealed information on organization and mobilization and on the regiment's return to the United States. The exchange of letters between Colonel William Treumann and General Elliott Miller were the most interesting and informative.

The Frank White Papers, from the Orin G. Libby Manuscript Collection, Chester Fritz Library, University of North Dakota, contained numerous letters from White to his wife covering April 1898 to July 1899. Some newspaper clippings are also in this collection. White's letters were invaluable. The Frank Anders Papers offered much information on Young's Scouts, a few letters Anders wrote to his mother in 1898, and the immensely entertaining and revealing reminiscences of John Kinne, Company B.

A questionnaire filled out by Oscar Olson, Company I, from the Spanish-American War Survey, United States Army Military History Institute, Carlisle Barracks, Pennsylvania, contained some information.

Phil Shortt, a member of the regiment, wrote the "Official History of the First North Dakota Infantry, U.S.V., in the Campaign in the Philippines," which appeared as an appendix to Karl Irving Faust, *Campaigning in the Philippines* (San Francisco, 1899). Shortt's brief piece had some value. Several government reports and publications were used to trace the mobilization in 1898 and the campaigns in the Islands in 1898 and 1899. See United States Army, Adjutant General's Office, *Correspondence Relating to the War with Spain...Including the Philippine Insurrection...from April 15, 1898 to July 30, 1902* (Washington, D.D., 1902), two volumes; and "Annual Report of Major General Elwell S. Otis, Commanding, Department of the Pacific and Eighth Corps, 31 August 1899," in *Annual Reports of the War Department, 1889.* The latter includes not only Otis's periodic reports to the War Department but those of his subordinate commanders, heads of bureaus, agencies, and departments in the Department of the Pacific and VIII Corps. It also has field correspondence from unit commanders on campaign, including Colonel Treumann and Majors White and Fraine. Some data on the mobilization is in United States Army, Adjutant General's Office, Military Information Division, Publication No. 29, *The Organized Militia of the United States* (Washington, D.C., 1900).

The following is a list of books and articles that contributed to the chapter: Jerry M. Cooper, "National Guard Reforms, the Army, and the Spanish American War," *Military Affairs,* Vol. 42, No. 1 (February 1978), pp. 20-23; Graham A. Cosmas, *An Army for Empire: The United States Army in the Spanish War* (Columbia, Mo., 1971); John M. Gates, *Schoolbooks and Krags: The United States Army in the Philippines, 1989-1902* (Westport, Conn., 1973); Marvin A. Kriedberg and Merton G. Henry, *History of Military Mobilization in the United States Army, 1775-1945* (Washington, D.C., 1955); James E. Leroy, *The Americans in the Philippines,* Reprint (New York, 1970); Stuart C. Miller, *"Benevolent Assimilation": The American Conquest of the Philippines, 1899-1903* (New Haven, Conn., 1982); Lewis O. Saum, "The Western Volunteer and the 'New Empire,'" *Pacific Northwest Quarterly,* Vol. 57, No. 1 (1966), pp. 18-27; William T. Sexton, *Soldiers in the Sun: An*

Adventure in Imperialism, Reprint (Freeport, N.Y., 1971); David F. Trask, *The War with Spain in 1898* (New York, 1981); Leon Wolff, *Little Brown Brother: America's Forgotten Bid for Empire which Cost 250,000 lives*, reprint (New York, 1970).

Captain John H. Fraine (photograph taken in San Francisco, 1898).

Unidentified members of North Dakota Infantry, U.S.V., in Manila,
Philippine Islands, 1899.

Interior view of one of the barracks (located at Malate, Philippine
Islands, used by members of the First North Dakota Infantry while
assigned to guard duty at Fort San Antonio de Abad on the Bay.

☆3☆
The 1st North Dakota in the Philippine Insurrection, February-July 1899

When fighting broke out between General Elwell S. Otis's VIII Corps and the Philippine Insurgents on the evening of 4 February 1899, the Americans found themselves in the same tactical situation the Spanish had faced in August 1898. They were confined to the city of Manila by a sixteen-mile semicircle of Insurgent trench lines arcing from Manila Bay on the north out to the east and back to the bay in the south. Insurgents even occupied the former American trenches on the south side of Manila. Otis's men now defended former Spanish forts and trenches. Although the Insurgent army had between 20,000 and 30,000 men, only half of them carried rifles. Other insurrectionists remained in Manila as potential saboteurs.

General Otis had nearly 21,000 officers and enlisted men in his command at the end of January 1899, but he could not rely on all of these to defend Manila's outer lines. Occupation duties, Insurgent threats on other islands, and the need to keep a 3,000-man provost marshal force to police the city drew off 10,000 troops. The remaining 11,000 effectives defended sixteen miles of trench line, just under 700 men per mile of frontage. The Americans' position was far from hopeless in spite of the Insurgent numbers. Unlike the Spanish, the Americans exuded confidence, even belligerence, in their ability to handle the Insurgents in battle, and the presence of Admiral George Dewey's fleet with its big guns added to that confidence. So too did the organization, equipment, and training of the VIII Corps when compared to Emilio Aguinaldo's amateur army.

General Otis and his commanders prepared detailed plans to meet possible Insurgent attacks. Although Otis made no attempt to man the entire trench line continuously, he did assign a sector to each regiment. The regiments kept a company or two in observation posts in their sector with the remaining companies in reserve but off duty. Telegraph lines connected the regimental sectors to divisional and corps headquarters. These arrangements ensured an immediate defensive response to any Filipino assault. As seen so often in the January war scares, when kept close to quarters the infantry could turn out in full force to man the trenches within a quarter of an hour.

Otis did not intend to remain on the defensive as had the Spanish. If Insurgent harassment developed into full-scale assaults, he planned to take the offensive as soon as possible. He could rely on effective combat command and control in both offensive and defensive operations. The Pasig River, flowing westward from the Laguna de Bay through the city and into Manila

Bay, naturally divided the VIII corps into two parts. North of the river, Otis assigned Major General Arthur MacArthur to command the 2nd Division, divided into two brigades. MacArthur's force included seven infantry regiments, all state volunteer units except the 3rd United States Artillery, serving as infantry, and two batteries of the Utah Light Artillery. Major General Thomas M. Anderson commanded the 1st Division in the south, on the American right. Five volunteer infantry units, including the 1st North Dakota, served under Anderson, along with the 14th United States Infantry, six troops of the 4th United States Cavalry, fighting dismounted, and two batteries of the 6th United States Artillery. Brigadier General Charles King commanded the 1st Brigade, while the 1st North Dakota served in Brigadier General Samuel Ovenshine's 2nd Brigade, on the far right of the American line. The VIII Corps maintained a close liaison with Dewey's fleet to ensure fire support in the event of hostilities. Gunnery officers from the fleet came ashore to chart lines of fire and major targets several days before fighting began.

On the evening of 4 February, a Filipino patrol approaching the 1st Nebraska's observation post refused to answer or obey an order to halt. The regiment was located on the far right of MacArthur's line, on the northeast bank of the Pasig River. As the patrol neared the observation post, a Nebraska sentry fired, killing at least one Filipino. A general fire fight began and firing spread rapidly up MacArthur's line to the bay. To the south, in the 1st North Dakota Infantry sector at Malate and Fort San Antonio de Abad, on the south beach of the bay, the early evening seemed at first to be a repetition of the past few days. A call to arms at 7:30 P.M. brought the men out of quarters and into the trenches. Once again, nothing happened, and as First Sergeant John Russater of Company B recorded in his diary at about 9:30 P.M., "we was ordered back and we are now ready to go to bed." Russater closed his entry for the day with the final comment, "but something is going on further north and a few shots can be heard."

When his regiment returned to quarters that evening, Lieutenant Colonel Treumann went to brigade headquarters for further instructions. He was asked to remain there for the time being. The outbreak of the firing in the north at about 9:15 brought the order, Treumann wrote, "to move my regiment to the front and occupy the position previously assigned." He returned to the 1st North Dakota barracks and ordered out the regiment. Brigade orders detached Company A of the 1st Battalion, under Lieutenant Sherman Newcomer, "to form a part of the inner guard." Company A spent the next five days patrolling in the rear to prevent an Insurgent uprising in Manila. Company I, 2nd Battalion, Captain William Purdon commanding, was ordered to stand in reserve behind the 14th United States Infantry in the center of the 2nd Brigade's section of the line. The rest of the regiment manned the trenches around Fort San Antonio de Abad, remaining there "all night without firing a shot."

The men welcomed the hostilities, according to Company B's John Kinne. "Like thousands of other American soldiers who had gone through these weeks of suspense," he wrote, "we were glad to think that it was over." Company A's bugler, John Peterson, noted that "The boys were all yelling and singing while marching to the trenches.'' Their enthusiasm did not stem the natural nervousness of men unfamiliar with battle. Throughout the night they could hear heavy firing off to their left, in MacArthur's division. Lieutenant Charles Getchell of Valley City's Company G told his mother, "There was one continual rattle," and Kinne described the shooting to the north as "terrific." For the 1st North Dakota, Russater remarked, "everything was still on our front and the boys began to get anxious to take part in the play." Colonel Treumann and Majors Frank White and John Fraine moved about the lines, keeping in check the tendency of nervous troops to fire blindly into the night.

On 5 February, a Sunday, General Otis took the offensive. Hostilities had begun because a Filipino patrol came too close to an American outpost, but the fighting of the night of the 4th could hardly be described as an Insurgent attack. Filipinos and Americans simply fired away at each other in MacArthur's sector from their respective trenches. Otis chose to interpret these events as a *de facto* declaration of war, and, before morning came, he alerted his division commanders to carry out their attack plan when ordered. At daylight, MacArthur's men assaulted the Insurgent lines in their front, routing the Filipinos with comparative ease. General Otis kept Anderson's 1st Division in its trenches until nearly 8:00 A.M. before ordering them to advance.

Once again, the 1st North Dakota waited while others acted. They could hear MacArthur's men on the attack, and when the 1st Division went into action, General Anderson sent Charles King's 1st Brigade forward but kept the 2nd Brigade in place. The 2nd Brigade remained in place until the 1st Brigade, facing the larger number of Insurgents, carried its objectives. General Ovenshine gave Colonel Treumann permission to "open on anything in sight" at about 7:30 A.M. but otherwise to take no action. The regiment opened fire, soon joined by two guns of the 6th United States Artillery in the fort and the batteries of the USS. *Monadnock*, just off shore. The ship's ten- and four-inch naval guns awed the infantrymen. John Russater found that "the roar was terrible. The enormous shells of the monitor exploded with a deafening noise." Later in the afternoon the USS. *Charleston* anchored off Malate To join in the bombardment.

The regiment exchanged fire with Insurgents for the next two hours, but with little effect. "We couldn't see anyone to shoot at," Lieutenant Getchell told his mother, "but every time one of them fired a shot two or three of our fellows would take a shot at the smoke." The Insurgents consistently shot high over the American entrenchments. After two hours, every man in the regiment remained in good health. Colonel Treumann relieved Companies D and C from the trenches when enemy fire from the right let up, sending them back to Fort San Antonio to rest. As anxious as anyone in the outfit to go forward, Treumann requested permission to make a general advance, but General Ovenshine said no. The colonel did order Major White to make a limited attack in their immediate front to stop sniping at the 6th Artillery gunners in Fort San Antonio and to "burn huts" from which came more sniper fire.

At 10:30 A.M., Frank White led Companies G, H, and part of D up out of the trenches in a skirmish line. "To protect the advance as much as possible," Treumann "ordered every rifle on the top of the fort to be brought to bear on the insurgents." The North Dakotans moved rapidly over open ground in extended order, according to Lieutenant Getchell, and "went across that 200 yards like a lot of wild Indians, clear across the insurgent trenches and into the road beyond." As had been the case since MacArthur's first advance early that morning, the Insurgents broke and ran as the Americans charged. Major White believed the constant rifle fire from the fort forced the enemy to keep their heads down, commenting, "we were right on them before they saw us and they fired high, then cut and run." Although the North Dakotans killed between twenty-five and thirty-five Insurgents and took six prisoners, they suffered no casualties, not even a minor wound. According to Private Oscar Amundson of Company G, most of the Insurgents were killed after they left the protection of their trenches. "We got some good shooting at them as they were running down the road," he added.

After clearing the Insurgent's position, White's force rejoined the regiment and awaited orders for a general advance. At 1:30 P.M., General Ovenshine asked Treumann to turn his regiment to the left and advance. The 14th United States Infantry and 4th United States Cavalry (dismounted), in the center of Ovenshine's sector, were engaged in a bitter fight to dislodge Insurgents in a swampy tangle of bamboo and low brush. The regulars had been frustrated all morning in their effort to push the enemy out but were unable to make a charge because of the terrain. The Insurgents fought bravely and effectively here. Once again, White led the movement. "Cos. G&H got into heavy fire here," he wrote, "but before the other cos. could make the swing they had them [Insurgents] agoing and they did not get into it." This brief action in heavy underbrush was confusing, with "the Insurgents...shooting from every direction." Amundson noted, it was "some of the hottest fighting we had. The air seemed full of lead." Taken in the flank by the 1st North Dakota and in front by a battalion of the 14th Infantry, the Insurgents gave up the position and ran off. The 14th Infantry lost five killed and twenty wounded in the charge, and overall for the day it suffered fourteen killed and fifty wounded. "We who were right next to them," White mused, "and acted with them got out practically without a scratch."

When orders for a general advance came at 2:30 P.M., Anderson's entire division moved forward to occupy the trenches abandoned by the Insurgents. By early evening, his troops held a line from San Pedro Macati on the Pasig River, Anderson's left, to the town of Pasay on his right. The 1st North Dakota advanced in a skirmish line to Pasay, searching native huts along the way and burning those that contained arms and ammunition. It then moved up the Pasay-San Pedro Macati road to the latter town and made contact with General King's units. At the end of the day, Major Fraine's 2nd Battalion returned to Pasay and set up outposts to guard the town and the 1st Division's far right flank. White's 1st Battalion lined the road between Pasay and San Pedro Macati for the night. As they had after the battle of Manila, the men went hungry that night, but they took up their vigil that evening with a sense of accomplishment. "Our boys acted finely," Frank White wrote of the day's work, "and we did everything we were called upon to do successfully."

The American military effort on 5 February succeeded everywhere. Otis's troops drove the Insurgents out of their lines and advanced two to three miles all along the front. They achieved this with little effort and at relatively low cost, except in a few places such as the 14th Infantry's front. American losses included fifty-nine killed and just under three hundred wounded, although they had advanced in an open-order skirmish line throughout the attack. Insurgent losses were difficult to determine, due to the terrain, their rapid flight, and their tendency to carry off dead and wounded. General Otis mentioned an estimate of five hundred to a thousand killed and "Lots of prisoners" in a wire to Admiral Dewey at the end of the day. General Anderson's subsequent report claimed two thousand Insurgents killed, wounded, or captured by his division alone. Otis's figure was more likely than Anderson's.

Whatever the final count, the Insurgents suffered heavily that day, in self-confidence as well as casualties. They were wholly unprepared for the vigorous American assault, in part because in their only other experience with conventional war, against the Spanish, they had never seen a well-directed offensive. The Filipinos possessed few artillery pieces, had no knowledge of counterbattery fire, and lacked anything in their arsenal to counter the big guns of Dewey's fleet. While artillery fire hurt them badly, they also suffered from poor training and discipline, especially in rifle marksmanship, as demonstrated by the 1st North Dakota's two unscathed charges across open ground. Worse yet, the Insurgent army lacked a competent military command system that could plan and direct even elementary military operations.

The battle had a positive impact on the morale of the 1st North Dakota Infantry. After weeks of tension and growing animosity toward the Filipinos, the fighting on 5 February gave the men something to boast about. Frank Anders, Company B, wrote home proudly to his mother: "Our regiment done great work along with the 14th Regulars." Lieutenant Getchell described the afternoon advance on Pasay as an opportunity to go "looking for niggers," while Amundson exulted to his girlfriend, "we would plug away at them as they ran." Another member of Company G, Sergeant William H. Lock, wrote to a friend back home, "I tell you the way the insurgents were killed was something awful. There was such a feeling among the boys towards them that they shot them down like they were hunting jack rabbits."

Frank White impressed Getchell a great deal: "Say mother, that man is a crackerjack. I never saw him when he didn't know exactly what to do." Company B's John Kinne also found the major an impressive leader, always giving orders "in his cool way." Kinne "could not refrain from making comparisons" between White and the newly commissioned officers of Company B, all of whom requested enlisted men to serve them as orderlies. "Our Major, we noticed, seldom had an orderly and was always hustling around delivering orders in person," he noted. Colonel Treumann, in his post-battle account to General Ovenshine, proudly described White's morning charge as a "brilliant one." Ovenshine in turn praised the regiment in his report, noting that "The North Dakotans made a dashing charge." Major John Fraine thought the regiment's performance indicated effective fire discipline, commenting that "there was no useless expenditure of ammunition and that the men fired aiming and not carelessly."

The regiment remained in the field another five days. They set to work building new entrenchments around Pasay and on the road to San Pedro Macati and patrolling the rear to consolidate American control of the newly won ground. Patrol and outpost duty in front of the new line absorbed much of their time. After six full days in the field, the regiment returned to its barracks at Malate on 10 February. Here they cleaned up and had their first chance to write home about the exciting events of 4-5 February. Company A at last rejoined the unit from its interior guard duty assignment.

As the tired and dirty men of the VIII Corps took a turn in barracks for a quick cleanup, then reported back to the front, their heady victory in the first battle of the Philippine Insurrection appeared less decisive. The corps remained nearly inert and on the defensive for over a month after the battle. Otis's plan to meet Filipino hostilities with a quick offensive produced immediate results by driving the Insurgents out of their besieging positions. In retrospect, however, the victory of 5 February was only a local tactical success without a decisive follow-up. General Otis had neither the manpower nor a plan to capitalize on his tactical victory.

Frank White wrote his wife on 1 February that his men were overworked and added: "If we should be obliged to make a campaign against them, our force is much too small and will require even more than now on the road" to reinforce the VIII Corps. The manpower shortage became evident in the 1st North Dakota at the call to arms on 4 February. Colonel Treumann released all prisoners from the regimental guardhouse that night to bolster company strengths. The regiment, which now numbered 26 officers and 525 enlisted men, had left Fargo in May 1898 with 31 officers and 651 men. Detached service, men in hospital both in Manila and San Francisco, and prisoners accounted for the losses. Replacements for the sick men never came. A 1st Division general order of 16 February 1899 requested regimental commanders to review disciplinary records of all enlisted men under charges or in confinement and recommend the most reliable for executive clemency. Treumann examined the records of seventeen of his men and recommended clemency for thirteen, several of them "Now on the firing line" and "doing good work." Major White's 1st Battalion gave further evidence of the shortage with lieutenants commanding three of his four companies (A, B, and G).

Shortages also plagued General Otis. He reluctantly withdrew troops from the Provost Marshal in Manila to reinforce MacArthur and Anderson at crucial points during the 5 February advance. Although Insurgent resistance had nearly evaporated in front of General Anderson, Otis had to stop the 1st Division at the Pasay-San Pedro Macati line. A rapid advance would have left his troops unable to protect their flanks or hold the territory already taken. If MacArthur had advanced farther, he would have left the crucial Manila waterworks, a reservoir and pumping station, exposed to enemy sabotage. Short of men, Otis remained on the defensive after 10 February awaiting reinforcements from the United States, while Insurgent forces slowly returned to positions hastily abandoned on 5 February or constructed entrenchments in front of the new American line.

Elwell Otis faced a much larger problem in devising a strategy to defeat the Insurgents and establish American authority in the Islands. He never comprehended the task before him, a difficult one exacerbated by the absence of definite orders from President McKinley. Consequently, he failed to develop an effective plan for victory. Otis needed to meet several objectives of ascending importance and complexity, that is:

1. To control the city of Manila and prevent an internal uprising
2. To prevent a successful Insurgent attack on Manila from without
3. To destroy, capture, or scatter the Insurgent army around Manila, presumably the only substantial Filipino force resisting the Americans
4. To assert United States authority throughout the island of Luzon and establish an American presence on other key islands in the archipelago
5. To quell the insurrection and create conditions under which Filipinos would not only accept American authority but cooperate with it.

The obstacles were many—too many Filipinos and not enough American troops, a harsh terrain and a primitive transportation system, a hostile population and a foe increasingly disinclined to wage conventional warfare. Perhaps a more energetic and imaginative general could have overcome these daunting challenges, but Elwell S. Otis was not that man.

The battle of 4-5 February ended any serious threat to the city of Manila. Otis vigorously quashed a poorly conceived and inept uprising of Insurgent supporters in the Tondo district of Manila on the night of 22 February, leaving some five hundred Filipinos dead and scores of native homes in ashes. These victories gave the VIII Corps a secure base from which it could eliminate the Insurgent army, assert American control on the main islands, and end the insurrection permanently. During the last months of the 1st North Dakota's Philippines service, to the end of July 1899, General Otis struggled to find a way to destroy Aguinaldo's army. It still existed when the North Dakotans sailed for San Francisco.

For two months after 10 February, the regiment served along the Pasay-San Pedro Macati line, though rarely in one position for very long. Regimental returns for February and March summed up the general nature of work. For the rest of February the "regiment performed trench guard duty," and in March "Seven companies...performed trench guard duty on line near Pasay and San Pedro Macati...and one company performed guard duty in district of Malate. Company in Malate being changed each week." The summaries failed to convey the arduous character of the work performed. As they moved from place to place, the men repeatedly dug new trenches or improved old ones. John Russater in late February commented on the construction of a four-foot-thick trench wall, but, he noted, "the ground is as hard as rock and the work is very slow." Two days later he wrote, "The boys has been resting most of the day and they are now at work strengthening our defence." In response to a rumored Filipino attack, Company G prepared "to receive them and threw up intrenchments [sic] all along the front. The boys worked like 'nailers'", Lt. Getchell noted, "and got a pretty good lot of dirt up front." Company A's John Peterson mentioned for 26 February, "Major White had us build our trenches higher so we would be able to stand in them." On 27 March White indicated that little had changed in a month's time. The men, he told his wife, "spend most of their time digging trenches and occupying them."

Trench duty dominated the life of the 1st North Dakota well into March. Company A, for example, provided a guard for a 6th Artillery battery for most of February, during which "The company furnished a squad for outpost duty each day, the entire company sleeping in the trenches at night." Exhausted from a day of digging a new trench, which the 1st Idaho then occupied, the men of Company A were "so tired the last time they moved they didn't build a breast works, but got behind a rice paddy" to sleep, John Peterson wrote on 19 February. Rain came in March and John Russater said, "everything is wet and disagreeable in the trenches." As occurred frequently before the insurrection, rumors of Insurgent attacks meant long nights in the trenches. For 20 February, Peterson noted, "We slept in the trenches last night as we expected an attack." Russater recorded similar expectations on 25 March: "We put all available men on the line" that night.

When given the opportunity to remain in one place for a few weeks, the regiment built shacks for officers' quarters and a cookhouse, and the men contrived bamboo shelters a mile or two behind the front line. The arrangement necessitated lengthy walks each day from the rude quarters to the trenches and often to outposts half a mile or more beyond the main line. These movements often provoked Insurgent sniping, and although no one was hit, nerves suffered. John Peterson on 3 April reported that in Company A "Five of the boys played out on account of the heavy marching every day, so we eat breakfast in camp and take a lunch with us and they bring out supper." When it moved to San Pedro Macati in late March, the regiment set up headquarters in an old Catholic church and quartered the men in native homes. "I think this is the safest place we have been in for some time as there is not a live insurgent within miles of here," Russater wrote. The men now had to man trenches and outposts two to three miles from San Pedro. Treumann and White eased field duty by sending only half a company to the line at one time, the men taking a day's rations with them. "It gives them 24 hours on and 24 hours off duty," White told his wife. "It is pretty stiff work for the men but they stand it all right."

Each company took a turn at a week's guard duty back at their barracks in Malate, near Fort San Antonio de Abad on the bay. Here the men had a chance to clean their bodies and clothes, sleep with their clothes off, write home, and perhaps visit Manila for a few hours. White's letters to his wife appeared at regular seven- or eight-day intervals, written while he was at Malate for his weekly cleanup. Russater's Company B came to Malate on 10 February after a week in the field. The next morning he wrote, "Oh my! how we did sleep last night." Lieutenant Getchell, who had gone two weeks without taking his clothes off, wrote "I haven't shaved in two weeks and look tougher than anybody," before a visit to the barracks finally brought relief. Eventually, guard duty at Malate grated on Russater. "The men will not get much rest. They will soon wish they were in the field again."

Few of Russater's comrades would have agreed with him. Not only did field duty involve digging trenches and putting up with filth, the troops almost always came in contact with Insurgents during this time and frequently were under fire. Sometimes American and Filipino trenches were as close as a thousand yards, more often a mile or two separated them. Although the Insurgents marksmanship was deficient, they fired away at American positions regularly with great abandon, regardless of the distance. Peterson's diary entries mentioned Insurgent firing almost daily. On occasion, as on 4 March, the shooting became widespread. "About 10 o'clock this morning," he penned, "the Insurgents started firing in front of our trenches. Some of the regulars on our left returned fire and soon it became a general fight....Some of the boys in our company also returned fire." Little came of any of the exchanges, but the constant sniping kept nerves taut.

Frank White insisted that his men maintain strict fire discipline. The volunteers were armed with the single-shot Springfield rifle, .45 caliber, using black powder ammunition. Those Insurgents who carried rifles were equipped with smokeless-powder Mauser and Remington repeating rifles, .30 caliber, with higher muzzle velocities and ranges two to three hundred yards greater than that of the old Springfields. Well aware of the greater range of their weapons, they fired at the Americans from beyond the range of the Springfields. Consequently, White told his wife, "I have ordered our men not to do any firing unless we were attacked and so we do not shoot at individuals or squads of soldiers passing along our front." The 1st North Dakota rarely initiated a fire fight and, when White was around, rarely replied to indiscriminate enemy shooting.

White's order frustrated his men. A number of units serving alongside the regiment, most notably the 1st California Infantry, practiced little fire control. "The Californias are firing every night and a good deal in the day time," Russater observed on 15 February. "They must want to be noticed because the Insurgents are out of range." The North Dakotans resented the gun-happy Californians. Their shoot-at-anything policy invariably generated Insurgent volleys, making trench life unpleasant, and White's policy prevented the Dakotans from joining in the fire fight. John Kinne of Company B regularly slipped away from the 1st North Dakota position to visit other regiments so he could take potshots at the enemy. Insurgent shooting at 1:30 in the morning on 6 March provoked American fire up and down the line. "As our officers thought it was general, they ordered us to fire," Peterson wrote. "A most terrible fire was kept up for about twenty minutes, when the order 'cease firing' came, but as it was the boys' first opportunity of blazing away at the enemy, they fired several shots after the order was given. Companies D and C were on the extreme right, and didn't fire, as Major White was with them."

The issue of twelve Krag-Jorgensen rifles to each company of the volunteer regiments on 31 March alleviated some of the frustrations of fighting with the Springfield. Much of the ammunition for the older rifle was defective, and, as Colonel Treumann reported, some of the cartridges issued to his men dated back to 1874. In a test fire on 9 March, regimental shooters fired at an elevation of six hundred yards and "many of the shot struck the ground 300 yards from the firing point." All the volunteers wanted the Krag-Jorgensen, and Treumann preferred it as he thought it was "the more effective gun at any range from 500 or 600 yds. up." All the regular regiments carried the Krag, a .30-caliber, bolt-action repeating rifle with a range equal to the Mausers and Remingtons. The War Department lacked enough Krags to equip all the volunteers, so the VIII Corps supplied enough to each company for scouts and sharpshooters to counter Insurgent superiority in rifle range and rate of fire. "We were mighty glad to give up our "Long Toms,'" Company B's John Kinne recalled.

Kinne, a happy recipient of the new rifle, observed that "The balance of the company were pretty sore that they did not get them." First Sergeant Russater wrote: "The men who got them are very busy cleaning them and taking them apart. Tickled like a small boy over a new toy." The Krags allowed scouts and men on outpost duty to hit unsuspecting Insurgents. Peterson wrote happily on 2 April that "The boys with the 'Craigs' *[sic]* are target practicing, insurgents furnishing the targets." Company B's outpost came under intense enemy fire on 9 April, but the men on duty had Springfields and could not drive them off. "When a detachment armed with Krag-Jorgensens opened up on them they got out of range." Eventually, long-distance firing at Insurgents lost its novelty. When the 1st North Dakota finally left the trench line on 18 April to prepare for active field duty, a regular regiment of mostly new enlistees took their place in the line. The regulars immediately began blazing away at the distant Insurgent trenches. "We had become tired of shooting at them," Kinne wrote, "But it was a new experience for the 'Rookie Regulars' to be shot at."

Surprisingly, despite the dirt, drudgery, occasional danger, and incessant duty in the trenches, morale in the 1st North Dakota remained high. Disciplinary problems, which plagued both the regiment and the entire VIII Corps during the occupation period, practically disappeared. Occasionally, one of the heavy drinkers slipped away from the line for a day or two, then returned, drunk to be sure, but not a deserter. A private in Company B, when told by Sergeant Harold Sorenson to keep quiet on the line, retorted, "Why you...son-of-a bitch what have you got to do with this?" Sorenson put the private under arrest. As his first sergeant, John Russater observed, "Sorenson certainly done right." The majority of the men handled the strain of trench duty without challenging their noncommissioned officers. Humor helped. On one of the nights when the 1st California's pointless shooting brought Insurgent volleys in return, John Peterson of Company A noted, "We had all kinds of fun." One of the company clowns "kept us laughing all night. Every time a bullet sailed over, he would drop, and make all kinds of remarks." Men who laugh and clown around while under enemy fire have few serious morale problems.

On occasion, especially at night, the battlefield offered glimpses of beauty to the more thoughtful men. Peterson commented, after observing the 1st California during one of its midnight firing escapades, "we could see the fire from their guns, which made a beautiful sight." Russater said the nighttime burning of a native village by American troops was "one of the grandest sights I have ever seen of this kind. The dark night is lighted up for miles around and I am writing this by the light from the fire which is at least 4 miles away. I don't believe I blame Nero for burning Rome." On another, quieter night, with the moon in full, Russater could see the lights of Manila and Dewey's ship lit up as well. "The landscape looks peaceful and pretty and everything reminds a person of peace instead of war," he noted.

Morale ran high, largely because everyone believed they would easily beat the Insurgents when General Otis ordered a full offensive. Frank White told his wife in mid-February, the American forces could drive the Insurgents away from Manila anytime they wanted to, but "it would be much better to give them a severe lesson and then agree upon some terms to terminate the war." Frank Anders never doubted American victory, and he could not understand why the Spanish had so much trouble with the Filipinos, commenting, "We have not had any trouble to whip them wherever we meet them." The volunteers waited expectantly for more regular units, not as replacements but to give the VIII Corps the manpower to end the war. "Everybody feeling good," Russater put in his diary for 24 February, "as reenforcements will be coming fast now." When the regulars arrive, White told his wife, "We will soon go after them and close it up." Peterson noted: "It is reported the insurgents want to surrender....Bets have been made that we will be on transports on the way home in two months." Many were eager to engage the Insurgents in open battle. John Kinne recalled seeing elements of Brigadier General Lloyd Wheaton's brigade attack Insurgent positions on 13 March and added, "We who had been in the trenches so long were disappointed in not getting in this attack, having to just lay back and watch the fun."

In mid-March General Otis, bolstered by newly arrived regulars, resumed the offensive. He sent General Wheaton's brigade on a clearing operation down the Pasig River to the Laguna de Bay, a large inland lake fifteen miles east of Manila. Lasting from 10 to 17 March, the movement opened the river for American use and severed communications between Insurgent forces north and south of the river. Wheaton easily brushed aside enemy troops and burned most of the villages lining the river. Otis then called Wheaton back, needing the troops for other operations and fearing that Insurgents might cut off any garrisons left to occupy key river towns. Although Filipinos soon returned to the villages so recently taken by Wheaton, the Americans retained control of the river with armored gunboats armed with light artillery pieces and machine guns.

General Arthur MacArthur directed a much larger American offensive beginning on 24 March. The 2nd Division, with nearly twelve thousand combat troops, faced an enemy force numbering about sixteen thousand. MacArthur planned to take the Insurgents in the flank and thereby trap the entire army and also capture Aguinaldo's capital at Malolos. After offering stiff resistance for two days, the enemy then melted into the interior of Luzon much as they had dispersed on 5 February. MacArthur took Malolos on 31 March. He requested permission from Otis to advance northward to the town of Calumpit in order to seize an important railroad bridge. Fearing an over-extension of the 2nd Division's line, Otis denied the request although Calumpit was only five miles away and no significant enemy force stood in MacArthur's way. The division suffered higher casualties in this effort than in February, losing 139 killed and nearly 900 wounded. Furthermore, MacArthur reported a fifteen-percent sick rate at the end of March. The VIII Corps manpower shortage prevented immediate replacement of the killed, wounded, and sick, a major factor in Otis's decision to keep General MacArthur in place.

A pattern began to emerge in these operations. American attacks regularly achieved immediate tactical success as Insurgents gave way to superior American organization, planning, and firepower, but local victories gained little except an additional few miles of territory. The Insurgents' propensity to run, later adopted as a conscious tactic, usually negated the power of American offensives. When coordinated with an attack on the center, flanking movements failed because the Filipinos abandoned their lines so rapidly. A thrust on an Insurgent flank had the effect of a missed roundhouse punch. Had the Insurgent army stood fast in front of Malolos, for example, MacArthur would surely have taken it in both flanks and either captured it or destroyed it. Filipino resistance evaporated so rapidly that MacArthur's envelopment struck nothing but empty trenches.

Under the conditions of conventional war, an army in flight offered an easy target for destruction. The VIII Corps had followed retreating Insurgents too slowly on 5 February, repeated the failure in March, and again for the rest of 1899. The rugged terrain of Luzon—jungle, swamps, ravines, innumerable streams and rivers, the high country north of Manila—made rapid pursuit of fleeing Insurgents difficult. The absence of decent roads made it impossible. The only railroad on all of Luzon, which ran northwest from Manila to Dugapan on Lingayen Gulf, was under Filipino control from Calumpit to the gulf. Since the VIII Corps had few horses or mules for mounted troops or transportation, Americans conscripted pony carts and water buffalo (carabao) pulling wooden-wheeled carts to carry supplies, thus reducing mobility to the rate of march of the carabao. Also, because the Americans lacked decent maps for Luzon, again and again well-planned operations foundered on the rock of geographic ignorance. Few native guides offered to provide information on geography and topography not available on maps. As the war grew in bitterness, Insurgents used intimidation and murder to deter natives from giving terrain information to Americans.

Increasingly, many of Otis's subordinates, and not a few American newspapermen covering the war, came to think the general himself was the greatest obstacle to VIII Corps mobility. Though he never left Manila to oversee field action, Otis insisted on retaining personal control of operations. He demanded that division commanders submit any plans for a forward movement to headquarters for prior approval. Division commanders had no strategic authority, and even daily tactical movements were subject to Otis's review. The general refused to consider organizing small, mobile units for pursuit purposes to follow up larger tactical victories.[1] Fearful of an Insurgent ambush of a small American force, Otis sent brigades into the countryside to capture a town or break up an Insurgent concentration, but he consistently called those units back to the security of Manila defenses once the expeditionary force achieved its tactical objective. It was difficult to discern any strategic design in Otis's operations throughout 1899. His approach did not destroy the Insurgent army, he made no attempt to occupy permanently territory more than twenty miles from Manila, and he seemed incapable of offering anything to the Filipinos that would induce them to end their support of the Insurgents and accept American rule. Caution guided Otis in his conduct of the war.

The 1st Division remained on the defensive while Wheaton and MacArthur went after the Insurgents. General Otis reduced the number of troops on his right to the minimum needed to defend the sector. Of fifteen thousand combat effectives available, a little over three thousand served in the 1st Division at the end of March, the 1st North Dakota among them. A new commander, Major General Henry W. Lawton, replaced Thomas M. Anderson at the head of the division on 17 March. Lawton transferred the 1st North Dakota to Charles King's 1st Brigade in a divisional reorganization. The regiment moved to San Pedro Macati on the Pasig River, the far left flank of the 1st Division, on 22 March to serve under King. Here the men waited and watched while MacArthur fought the Insurgents.

Not content to leave his troops idly watching the enemy, General King encouraged the men manning outposts to snipe at the enemy with the Krag-Jorgensens. Kinne, Peterson, and Russater noted that King often personally directed sniper fire. He also sent out armed reconnaissances to probe enemy positions or to count enemy troops. Peterson took part in a thirty-man scouting party on 26 March, recalling, "We went three miles beyond our firing line." The party stopped there "while a few advanced about a half mile." The advance party came under heavy Insurgent fire, then "retreated double time, as they were only to locate the enemy and,' he added, "when they reached us we went back to camp."

Major Frank White led a detachment on an attack against an Insurgent outpost on 1 April, an action planned by General King. Of little importance to the final outcome of the war, this small operation illustrated the difficulties of campaigning in the Philippines. What happened to White's force on 1 April occurred frequently to much larger forces during 1899. The 1st North Dakota manned an advanced outpost on a ridge (called King's Bluff) four miles southeast of San Pedro Macati and two and a half miles forward of the main trench line. The Insurgents held an outpost a mile beyond the regiment's lookout, with trenches defending a field camp in its rear. A total of about two hundred Insurgents held the position. King ordered White to take two companies, using the regimental outpost as a starting point, to outflank the enemy outpost, surround it, and capture the Insurgents holding the place. He assumed the camp and defending trenches were far enough in the rear not to bother White.

The plan required the detachment to take a circuitous route from the rear of the American outpost, down through a ravine screened from the enemy by heavy brush, and past the front of the Insurgent position. When White's men arrived at a point beyond the enemy's right, they were to advance as quietly as possible directly toward the enemy. This movement would put them two hundred yards to the right of the outpost but well short of the camp. At this point, King intended to order snipers back at the jump-off point to open fire on the Filipinos and draw their attention. White was then to advance his men on the outpost's flank and rear, surrounding it in one swift movement.

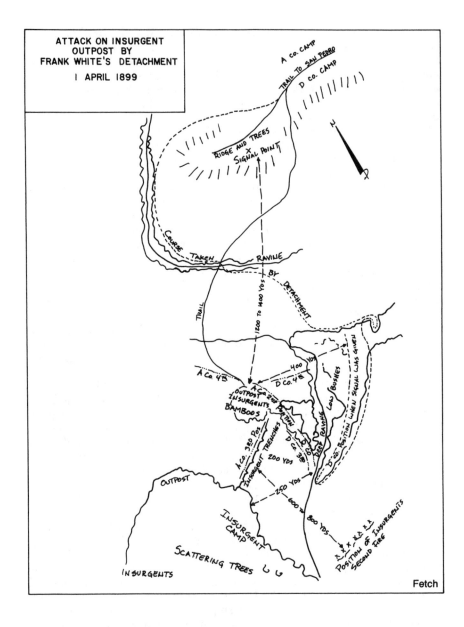

ATTACK ON INSURGENT
OUTPOST BY
FRANK WHITE'S DETACHMENT

I APRIL 1899

A Co. CAMP
TRAIL TO SAN PEDRO
D co. CAMP

RIDGE AND TREES
X
SIGNAL POINT

N

COURSE

TAKEN

RAVINE

BY

DETACHMENT

TRAIL

1200 TO 400 YDS

A Co. 4TH
400 YDS
D Co. 4TH
A Co. 2ND
OUTPOST
INSURGENTS
BAMBOOS
LOW BUSHES
D CO. POSITION WHEN SIGNAL WAS GIVEN
INSURGENT TRENCHES
A Co. 3RD POS.
D Co. 3RD
DEEP RAVINE
200 YDS
OUTPOST
250 YDS
600 TO 800 YDS
INSURGENT
CAMP
X X X X X X
POSITION OF INSURGENTS
SECOND FIRE
SCATTERING TREES
INSURGENTS

Fetch

Companies A and D moved up to King's Bluff on the afternoon of 31 March where White joined them at 3:30 the next morning. After a cold breakfast, the companies left and marched a mile to the ravine. From this point on, things began to go wrong. King and White believed that the ravine followed a northwest to southeast course when in fact it turned directly eastward just in front of the Insurgent outpost. When White finally realized that he had gone beyond the point where he was to move toward the field camp, he retraced his steps until he reached a logical place to advance toward the enemy rear. A large clump of brush lay between him and the Insurgent post. If White went to the right of the brush, he had open ground but would be forced to make a frontal assault. To go to the left necessitated another eastward movement. Fearing discovery if he chose a rightward movement, White took the other course, ''and passing to the eastward after considerable difficulty, succeeded in getting through and well to the rear of the insurgent posts.''

The companies were now in position on the enemy's right flank. ''Forming in line of skirmishers [we] began to feel our way carefully through the brush,'' White noted. The enemy remained ignorant of White's presence when, just at daybreak, King's snipers opened fire. The shooting alerted Insurgent sentries who began firing at White. Company A was on the right of the skirmish line, with open ground in front of it. They ''advanced as fast as the nature of the ground would permit and charged as soon as they got into the clear.'' On the left, Company D was to take the outpost in the rear, but as they moved forward they were ''confronted with a gulley [sic]'' heavy with underbrush and ''its sides of rock three to eight feet high.'' The terrain forced Company D to cross the gully in single files ''and reform on the opposite side.'' As the unit re-formed at the top of the gully, they discovered that the Insurgent camp and trenches lay only two hundred yards to their front and left, not far in the rear as King assumed. Fortunately, Company A's charge had cleared the Insurgent outpost and allowed them to fire on enemy troops in the trenches. In danger of taking fire in his flank, Captain Albert Cogswell turned his Company D to its left to fire on the Insurgent camp ''and poured ten or twelve volleys into them and soon had them going.'' The Insurgents abandoned the camp and trenches, disappearing in the heavy jungle. White ordered John Peterson to blow recall and the battalion reassembled near the abandoned outpost.

As squad leaders counted off their men and White prepared the detachment for an orderly return to King's Bluff, Major Frank Pease, regimental surgeon, tended to Second Lieutenant Dorman Baldwin's wounded knee. While a group of enlisted men ''had unthinkingly been allowed to bunch up around where the surgeon worked,'' some Insurgents had returned to their abandoned trenches and opened fire, wounding two more men. White ''immediately ordered Company A to move back into the trenches in double time and soon silenced their fire.'' During this fire fight, Peterson said, I ''let Major White fire about a dozen shots out of my Springfield.'' Company A remained in the trenches while the wounded men were removed under the guard of men from Company D armed with Krag-Jorgensens. With the wounded safely out of enemy fire, Company A then withdrew, and the detachment returned to its own position at 7:30 A.M. White claimed thirty to forty Insurgents killed or wounded, but John Peterson thought they killed only eight.

John Russater offered the best assessment of the operation. The companies went out ''to try to surround some Insurgent outposts and at day light a sharp fire commenced. The natives ran but could not be surrounded, at least they wasn't,'' he added. A displeased General King criticized Colonel Treumann for the failure of the operation because, in Kinne's words, "one company arrived ten minutes late on the line, allowing to escape eighty 'niggers' that should have been captured." After King ordered White to submit a written explanation, the major described the operation in detail in his 3 April report. "I realize that this movement was not executed with the dash and rush expected and that I hoped to give it," he wrote. He pointed out that a successful " 'rush' " movement "was doubtful of execution," perhaps even "inexpedient." His detachment moved over territory "practically unknown to every person in my command," he explained. The rough country between King's Bluff and the Insurgent outpost made the "time necessary to get into position... entirely problematical." American snipers fired prematurely because King and White underestimated the time needed to reach the enemy position. Finally, "the position of the Insurgent camp, trenches and support was unknown and supposed to be much further from the post." These factors worked against a successful surprise attack. He might have added that the rapid Insurgent retreat also made capture difficult. Colonel Treumann sent a cover letter with White's report supporting his 1st Battalion commander. That ended the matter.

His detachment's behavior on 1 April pleased Frank White. The little operation constituted the first opportunity he had had to take an independent force, however small, into combat. He sent a copy of his report and a map of the action to Colonel Amasa P. Peake, commanding officer of the 1st Regiment, North Dakota National Guard, "Knowing the interests you take in the movements of the boys at the front," he explained. He briefly described the fight to his wife, a more positive description than that in his report to King. "On account of the thick brush we did not succeed in capturing them," he told her, "but did a good deal of damage and got away before their support got up." Mrs. White always wanted to hear about the welfare of the men in White's command. He named the wounded men, all of whom were expected to recover. Unfortunately, Corporal John C. Byron, Company D, died of his wound in late May.

To what end Corporal Byron died remains unclear. The operation was not necessary to clear the regiment's front before a general advance, as none was planned, and King had no intention of holding the Insurgent position. Too small and too far from American lines, the North Dakota detachment could not consider pursuing the retreating Insurgents—the rough country prevented pursuit in any event. The operation's complexity demanded full intelligence of the terrain and precise information on the location of the enemy field camp in the post's rear. Guesswork, including the estimate of time White needed to get into position, determined the outcome of the fight. Given the country they had to move through and the fact that Company D emerged from heavy underbrush at the top of the gully to find an entrenched enemy on its front and left flank, the detachment performed quite well. No one panicked. White and Captain Cogswell handled their men effectively under fire, reacting quickly to both the unexpected flanking fire and the second Insurgent fire fight, while the major directed an orderly withdrawal with proper attention to his wounded men. The skirmish represented Otis's conduct of the war in miniature. White's men successfully attacked an enemy position, killed an unknown number of Insurgents, and drove them off while taking light casualties, but then returned to their own lines. No one could say what they accomplished in doing so.

General Otis had in Major General Henry W. Lawton a subordinate of great energy and considerable reputation. ("They say he is a pusher," Frank White noted.) In order to make use of the restless Lawton, Otis put him in command of a special expedition to the city of Santa Cruz on the southeastern shore of Laguna de Bay. The move was the first American advance into the Philippine countryside, with Santa Cruz thirty-six miles from Manila across Laguna de Bay and sixty miles by land around the south shore of the lake. Otis instructed Lawton to take the water route since Insurgents held the land route and water transport made supply much easier. He also told Lawton to capture Santa Cruz and an Insurgent army "rumored" to be there and to distribute copies of McKinley's proclamation to the Filipinos. Lawton had the option to reconnoiter the country along the east side of the lake and to take the town of Calamba on the lake's south shore if enemy resistance disappeared. Despite Otis's detailed instructions, the strategic purposes of the expedition were poorly defined.

Lawton organized his force from 1st Division units, including elements of the 4th United States Cavalry (dismounted), the 14th United States Infantry, the 1st Idaho Volunteer Infantry, Major John Fraine's 2nd Battalion of the 1st North Dakota, and two mountain guns of the 6th United States Artillery, a total of 1,509 enlisted men. Several gunboats and steam launches went along to support the operation. Lawton directed the expedition but gave tactical command to Brigadier General Charles King. He organized a special four-company battalion of sharpshooters, men armed with Krag-Jorgensen rifles, to serve as scouts. Lieutenant W. J. Gruschius, Company K, led the 2nd Company sharpshooters, made up of forty men from the 1st North Dakota.

The expedition left San Pedro Macati on the afternoon of 8 April, steam launches and tugs pulling cascoes loaded with troops and supplies. Moving down the Pasig River and across the lake during the night, the force arrived off Santa Cruz at mid-morning on the 9th. Lawton intended to land his infantry south of the city with the dismounted 4th Cavalry going ashore north of town. A strong westerly wind hampered the landing, preventing the 4th Cavalry from going in until early the next morning. It took most of the day for the infantry to make the shore, Fraine's battalion finally landing at 3:30 P.M. Fortunately, the Insurgents offered no opposition, for owing to the heavy surf "many of the men were compelled to wade ashore through water at first shoulder deep." Once all the infantry had landed, General King formed a skirmish line, running west to east, with Fraine's battalion on the far left near the lake. The American advance on Santa Cruz began at 5:45 P.M. Major Fraine reported "a desultory fire was commenced by the enemy on my front. It being too dark to see the enemy, no reply was made to its fire." After darkness brought a halt to the attack, the troops slept on the firing line. During the night, King suffered a heart attack and returned to Manila. Lawton gave the tactical command to Major J. J. Weisenberger, 1st Washington Volunteer Infantry, commander of the sharpshooter battalion and senior tactical officer present.

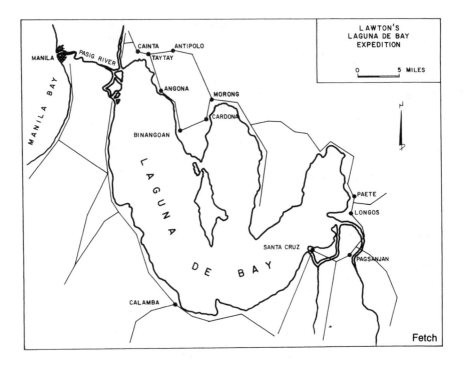

Weisenberger ordered a renewed attack at 7:00 A.M. on the 10th. While the 4th Cavalry charged the town from the north, the infantry moved on it from the south, "meeting little resistance," according to Fraine. As happened frequently, Insurgents defending the city abandoned their trenches and fled into the countryside under machine gun and artillery fire from gunboats on the lake. Lawton's men found the city nearly empty, as civilian Filipinos also ran away. The general estimated an enemy loss of 135 killed and 71 taken prisoner. Seven Americans were wounded. The easy capture of Santa Cruz and hasty Insurgent retreat revealed Otis's strategic vagueness. Since there was no other immediate political or military objective within range of his force, Lawton remained in Santa Cruz for the rest of the 10th, contemplating his next move.

He chose to reconnoiter the countryside. On the morning of 11 April, the Americans marched to the village of Pagsanjan, five miles northeast of Santa Cruz, meeting only scattered resistance along the way. Here, Lawton divided his force. Pagsanjan was located on a navigable river of the same name. The general sent most of his units down the river to the lake shore, clearing the banks of snipers. With Major Clarence R. Edwards, Lawton's divisional adjutant, Major Fraine's battalion went up the west side of the river to search for steam launches reportedly hidden there by Insurgents. The battalion found the boats a mile from the village, moored on the opposite bank. Volunteers, including Captain William Purdon of Company I, swam across the river to attach ropes to the boats. Fraine's force was back in Pagsanjan with four steam launches and a casco by noon without encountering the enemy. The capture of the boats would be the only tangible consequence of the Santa Cruz expedition.

After spending the afternoon and night of 11 April at Pagsanjan, the 2nd Battalion joined Major Weisenberger at midday on the 12th at the village of Longos, seven or eight miles north of Santa Cruz. During lunch, Lawton ordered Fraine to proceed immediately to another small village, Paete, two miles farther north, to look for a suitable place where the expeditionary force could re-embark on the lake boats. The road from Longos to Paete ran through rough country, with the lake lying to the left and screened by thick underbrush lining the west side of the road. To the right, said Fraine, "the road runs along a very steep hill, rising at an angle of from 45 to 70 degrees, and the hill is covered with bamboo, rattan, and other growth, and so cut with dry gullies and bowlders *[sic]* as to be almost impassable." The Americans strongly suspected an Insurgent band was in or near Paete.

Lawton told Fraine "to observe great caution in making his advance." The battalion moved up the road in a column of fours, with a five-man point guard two hundred yards forward and twenty sharpshooters a hundred yards behind them. Because of the rough terrain, Fraine did not put out flank guards, but soon after leaving Longos, "things looked so suspicious" he sent five scouts up the steep hill to his right. As a squad from Company C scrambled up the hill, the point reported finding a trench across the road three hundred yards in front of the column. After halting the battalion, Fraine went up to look over the Insurgent position. He found a "strong breastwork manned by fifteen to twenty Insurgents," and ordered Lieutenant Thomas Tharalson, Company C, to take the sharpshooters to the left of the road and outflank the trench. As Tharalson deployed the sharpshooters, "a very heavy fire from the hillside and trees along the entire command was poured" into them.

Running back to the column, Fraine ordered it off the road, to the left, and under cover. He sent "one platoon from each company into the jungle up the hill to [the] right, the left resting on the road." The platoons formed a firing line "perpendicular to the road" and advanced on the hidden Insurgents, "firing by volleys." Back at Longos, Major Weisenberger heard the heavy firing and rushed forward with a company of sharpshooters from the 1st Washington Volunteer Infantry and the two 6th Artillery mountain guns. Weisenberger sent two more platoons up the hill and ordered the Washington sharpshooters to help Lieutenant Tharalson attack the trench straddling the road. The mountain guns and artillery on the gunboats shelled the trench and the hillside positions. "After about one hour of sharp fighting the entire column advanced," Fraine reported, "and meeting no further resistance, arrived at Paete at 6:15 P.M."

The fight outside Paete on 12 April was the single most costly combat for the 1st North Dakota during their Philippines service. The Company C squad Fraine sent up the hill to scout just before the engagement began walked into an ambush in which three of the five men in the squad died instantly. Private Thomas C. Sletteland, the only man not hit, remained with badly wounded Wagoner Peter Thompkins, who died later that day. "Three separate times the insurgents came over their breastwork to obtain the arms of the killed soldiers and three times alone and unaided Pvt. Sletteland drove them back," Fraine wrote. He then dragged Thompkins down the hill, returning to help remove his dead comrades. Another man, Musician George Schneller, Company K, was shot and killed down on the road. Two men were wounded in the fight. Others killed were Corporal Isadore Driscoll and Privates Alfred Alman and W. C. Lamb.

Later, Fraine rightly praised his men for their behavior under fire. "No trepidation was displayed. Orders were understood and obeyed promptly." As had happened in Frank White's 1 April skirmish, the 2nd Battalion moved through difficult terrain unfamiliar to them. Ignorant of enemy dispositions until fired upon, the inexperienced North Dakotans kept their discipline during the ambush and, as Lawton reported, Fraine "promptly disposed his command to execute a flank movement on the enemy." Fraine, Weisenberger, and Lawton commented on Sletteland's extraordinary bravery. Major Fraine also reported that Private John Wampler, Company D, merited praise, for he "voluntarily took up an advanced post under heavy fire, for the purpose of observing the enemy." Weisenberger commended Fraine "for the very effective work done by him in the trying ordeal." General Lawton recommended Private Sletteland for the Congressional Medal of Honor, which he later received, and Fraine for a brevet lieutenant colonelcy for distinguished service in action. He also gave "special mention in orders" to several 2nd Battalion enlisted men, including Private Wampler.

Lawton's entire command rendezvoused at Paete on 13 April and remained there until the 16th when General Otis ordered it back to Manila. The Santa Cruz expedition revealed the difficulties of campaigning in the countryside. Lawton had taken Santa Cruz easily and the 2nd Battalion had just as easily captured the Insurgent launches. Despite the ambush near Paete, the Americans had moved from village to village as they pleased. Insurgent resistance seldom had lasted beyond the first volley, except at Paete, and even there the enemy had quit after an hour's fire fight. The Insurgents had had no means of countering the small (1.65 inch) mountain guns accompanying Lawton's infantrymen or the lake gunboats with larger caliber artillery and machine guns.

These advantages produced few results. Lawton did not have enough men to occupy Santa Cruz permanently, let alone hold on to the other towns and villages he had taken. Rarely did the Americans' easy tactical victories lead to the capture or destruction of an enemy force. Lawton had little chance to win over Filipino civilians to American authority in what the enlisted men derisively called the "Santa Cruz Bill Poster" expedition. (His men had posted copies of President McKinley's proclamation in every town they passed through.) Lawton hinted in his report that he could have gone on to Calamba on Laguna de Bay's south shore, as originally planned. The physical condition of his men belied that optimism. The general reported to Otis on 13 April that his men were "becoming exhausted" and needed a day or two of rest. After the 2nd Battalion returned, Frank White noted it "was about worn out by their trip up the lake. They saw some very hard work." A nervous Otis called Lawton back to Manila, in part to support a pending offensive under MacArthur, but also because Otis correctly feared the already-exhausted Santa

Cruz force, at the end of the thirty-six-mile supply line, might be cut off from the capital city. Unwittingly, newspaper correspondent Karl Irving Faust, who traveled with Lawton, summed up the expedition's accomplishments. As the launches pulled away from the shoreline to return to Manila, he recalled, "We saw the rebel fires on the hills and discovered that the insurrectos were back in town [Santa Cruz]."

Fraine's men rejoined the regiment at San Pedro Macati on 17 April. The entire 1st North Dakota left the line two days later, marching back to its old barracks at Malate. They had two days to rest and refit, for the North Dakotans were assigned to another expeditionary force under Henry Lawton. He was to take his command northeast of Manila, to the right of the Candaba swamp, to serve as a flank guard for MacArthur's 2nd Division during its new offensive up the Manila-Dagupan railroad. MacArthur had as his first objectives the towns of Calumpit and San Fernando on the swamp's western side. If all went as planned, the two forces would link up at the northeastern edge of the swamp, near the town of San Miguel, in the last days of April. The Americans were then to drive the Insurgent army up the railroad line to Lingayen Gulf.

General Lawton divided his command into two columns. One column, troops from the 2nd Division led by Colonel Owen Summers of the 2nd Oregon Volunteer Infantry, would join him at Norzagaray on 24 April. Lawton accompanied the main force of nearly twenty-five hundred men, including the 1st North Dakota. In order to leave himself free to reconnoiter at will, Lawton gave Lieutenant Colonel Treumann tactical command of the main column. Desperately short of transportation, Lawton ordered that "the command must be equipped in the lightest possible marching order." Each man carried two days' rations, one hundred rounds of ammunition, a canteen, shelter half tent, and rubber poncho. The 1st Division alloted every company two bull carts to carry extra ammunition, rations, and equipment. The men of the 1st North Dakota began the trip in good spirits. Frank White, taking command of the regiment in Treumann's place, wrote his wife on 21 April, "We are not likely to encounter any large force but have some skirmishing. The men...are in very good shape and are glad for a change."

The command left the American lines north of Manila at 5:00 A.M. on 22 April. Lawton's first objective was to join Colonel Summers in the town of Norzagaray on the Quingua River, twenty-five miles from Manila. The 1st North Dakota led the advance. When it encountered enemy outposts after marching six miles, Treumann deployed Major White's 1st Battalion as skirmishers. They met "but feeble resistance" as the Insurgents ran off. A mile down the road, they encountered a larger enemy force. Again, the 1st Battalion formed a firing line, and "the enemy was at once engaged and routed." After driving the Insurgents into dense jungle, "the firing line experienced some difficulty in crossing the Rio de Tulihan." Led by Captain Edward Gearey, Company B jumped into the stream and swam to the far bank. By 10:00 A.M., the 1st North Dakota held the abandoned village of Novaliches, ten miles from the American line. One man suffered heat exhaustion during the fire fight. Treumann's column remained in Novaliches for the rest of the day.

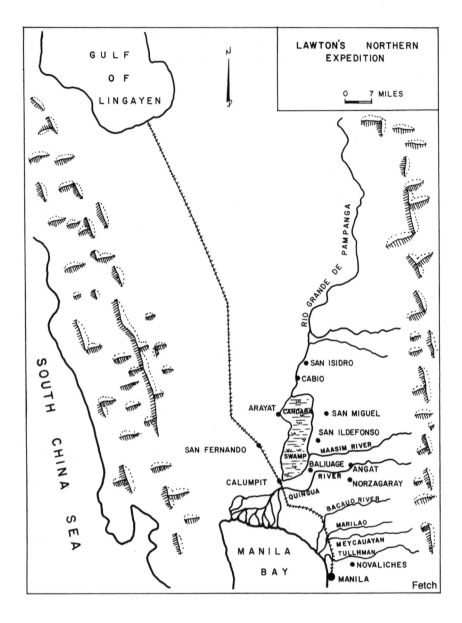

Early on 23 April, the expedition left the village but immediately confronted terrain so difficult the march slowed to a crawl. Lawton planned his operation on information taken from inaccurate Spanish maps—the roads shown on the maps turned out to be mere jungle trails or did not exist. It took the infantry ten and a half hours to cover four and a half miles on the

23rd. They moved only a mile and a half the next day. Although Lawton assumed he would rendezvous with Colonel Summers at Norzagaray on 24 April, he and his personal staff did not get there until the 26th, and his baggage train did not make it until the evening of the 27th. During the entire trip, Colonel Treumann reported, roads were "mere paths over a rough country, crossing numerous ravines."

The 1st North Dakota paid the heaviest physical price during the torturous march from Novaliches to Norzagaray. General Lawton's order of march rotated the previous day's advance guard to the rear as a guard for the wagon train. Protecting the train was assumed to be light duty, but according to the regiment's official historian, "The few days that followed were more full of hardships than any other encountered by the regiment." Beginning on 23 April, the North Dakotans acted as rear guard for four full days. One hundred two-wheeled carts pulled by water buffalo and nine horse-drawn wagons made up the train. The regiment took the train, Lawton reported, "over a succession of hills and through deep valleys. On the former the troops and animals were exposed to the burning rays of the sun and in the latter they labored through jungle and mud holes." Often the roughness of the terrain necessitated, in Treumann's words, "letting down wagons and carts by means of ropes and pulling them up the opposite sides. Rivers were forded in similar manner." The intense heat and lack of water forced the train to stop frequently to rest the carabao. Late that first afternoon the animals began to die. With no way to replace them the men had "to drag along the heavily laden carts." Officers and enlisted men labored endless hours to keep the train moving. John Kinne noted that they made only three miles on the 23rd, falling behind the advancing firing line. That night, according to Company A's Record of Events, they "camped for night on hillside...nameless."

Because of the rough country and the distance between the train and the infantry, Lawton could not relieve the regiment from rear guard duty on the 24th. Throughout that day the regiment struggled to keep moving, pulling some carts by hand. Nine carabao died. Finally, Kinne recalled, "We stopped at sundown thoroughly exhausted." A brief rest followed but the march resumed until near midnight, when, added Kinne, "as soon as we had supper, we lay on the ground to sleep." During the next two days, more and more water buffalo died. The men arduously chopped their way through overgrown trails and built fords across numerous streams. Finally, after passing through Norzagaray, the wagon train joined the rest of the column at Angat on the night of 26-27 April. In his final report on the expedition, General Lawton offered the regiment "special appreciation" for its work. The 1st North Dakota "had orders to leave nothing behind, and literally carried transportation over bad places and put squads of men in the shafts to replace worn out and dead bulls. Every service—even to the use of pick and shovel—was performed by each, from the colonel down to the private, with the same commendable earnestness that has given the regiment its reputation for cheerful and effective accomplishment of every task set it."

Angat lay on the Quingua River, fifteen miles east of Candaba swamp. Lawton had expected to find one or more useful roads leading from the village north to San Miguel. As he reorganized his exhausted command, he sent out scouts to find the roads. There were none. The Spanish maps were wrong again. Up to 27 April, Lawton had accomplished little except to kill a score or more water buffalo, capture several abandoned villages, and tire out one of his best regiments, the 1st North Dakota. On the 29th he decided to resume march down the Quingua toward the swamp. He put Colonel Summers's provisional brigade on the north bank of the Quingua, while Treumann led his column down the south shore, both advancing on the town of San Rafael. When Treumann ran into the enemy two miles out of the town, he deployed elements of the 3rd United States Infantry and White's 1st Battalion and advanced on the Insurgents. As so often happened, 'The enemy made only a short stand.' In the midst of the skirmish, General Lawton abruptly recalled Treumann and Summers back to Angat.

The recall came at the insistence of the always-cautious General Otis. Lawton had had no telegraphic communications with VIII Corps headquarters between Novaliches and Angat. He was short of supplies as well, and there was no feasible way to resupply the expedition over the roadless jungle from Novaliches to Angat. As the expedition moved from village to village, enemy forces disappeared into the jungle and civilian Filipinos also abandoned their towns. Until Lawton had a firm supply line and a permanent wire connection to Manila, and Otis had some idea of where enemy forces were located, the VIII Corps commander wanted the expedition to remain in one place. Angat was that place.

Lawton got under way again on 1 May, retaking San Rafael with little difficulty. His force moved farther down the Quingua the next day, Summers on the north bank, Treumann on the south. After a brief fire fight, Treumann entered the village of Bustos. After swimming the river, some of his scouts ran the Insurgents out of the larger town of Baliuag, which lay astride a good road running north to San Miguel. Baliuag also provided a decent road for supply from Manila and effective telegraphic connections to headquarters. By 3 May, most of Lawton's command was quartered in Baliuag. Otis then put General Lawton on hold a second time, much to the latter's regret. The 2nd Division offensive along the Manila-Dagupan line had quickly bogged down. Innumerable rivers, swamps, the heat, and growing sickness slowed MacArthur's force. The 2nd Division took Calumpit on 27 April and San Fernando on 5 May but moved no farther. There would be no linkup with Lawton at San Miguel. Otis had heard rumors of a large Insurgent army moving on Lawton's right flank from the Laguna de Bay region. Lawton was to remain at Baliuag until the existence of the 'phantom' Insurgent army was disproved.

The energetic Lawton disliked staying put. He wired Otis on 3 May that Insurgent forces and civilian Filipinos ran northward at the first sign of approaching Americans. Reports of enemy strength were "always exaggerated. They have offered no determined or effective resistance. Are greatly demoralized...and disintegrating. With a squadron of mounted men," he suggested, "I could have destroyed the whole outfit here yesterday, but our men on foot cannot stand the extra exertion in this awful heat." Despite the heat, Lawton wanted to press on to San Miguel. Otis said no. Consequently, he remained at Baliuag from 2 to 15 May, although Otis allowed him to send Colonel Summers's brigade five miles up the San Miguel road to the Maasin

River crossing to keep an eye on Insurgent activity. Summers sent out scouting parties "to search for and destroy subsistence stores" as well as Insurgent field forces.

While a quietly angry Lawton chafed under VIII Corps restraint, the men of the 1st North Dakota enjoyed the inactivity at Baliuag. John Kinne said, "[we found the] foraging was very good in this town and we had chicken most of the time." Frank White had a chance to compare the volunteers with new regular regiments, the 3rd and 22nd United States Infantry. He found them mostly raw recruits led by young officers just out of West Point. "So far these regiments have shown themselves to be very much inferior to the volunteers," he said. As to the 1st North Dakota, despite the strenuous march from Novaliches to Baliuag, he reported, "Our boys are standing the trip very well. We have had some hard work but little fighting. Have had three wounded—none fatal." White remained optimistic about the campaign. If the Americans could force the Insurgents to make a stand, he added, "I think we can take care of them," and Lawton's expedition "Will close the hard fighting in the North." The two weeks at Baliuag provided time to watch others work. Kinne described General Lloyd Wheaton's brigade from the 2nd Division as it passed through Baliuag: "It made about as good a parade as I ever saw." Wheaton's boys carried monkeys, goats, parrots, even "a fine coach with two pretty ponies." Mail came on 12 May and, according to Kinne, "we had a noisy jolly crowd in our quarters." The men sang and held a square dance, "and one fellow when calling off among other things said 'Four Scandinavians front and center.'"

Fraine's 2nd Battalion, less Company C, returned to San Rafael to garrison the town and look for the 'phantom' army from Laguna de Bay. They remained there from 6 to 9 May. On the 8th, all was quiet, and Fraine reported, "Returning natives say no insurrectos within 10 miles. Spanish prisoner here says all fighting men have gone to Miguel and San Isidro." Captain John Johnson's Company C escorted a Signal Corps party back to Angat to remove a telegraph wire that ran from Angat to Baliuag. Lawton decided to leave the wire up and have Johnson's men scout for the rumored Laguna de Bay force also. On 7 May, Johnson reported that he had sent a scouting party as far east as Norzagaray, where there was "Nothing in sight except friendly natives moving back." Company C returned to Baliuag with Fraine's battalion on 9 May. The remainder of the regiment performed guard and outpost duties or escorted supply trains.

While at Baliuag, Lawton organized a detachment of scouts, twenty-five "specially qualified enlisted men," to serve as his eyes and ears in the uncharted region east of Candaba swamp. He gave command of the detachment to William H. Young, a civilian. Tall and well built, Young came from Connecticut, a classic soldier of fortune and adventurer who had appeared in Manila in August 1898 to join the Americans in their attack on the Spanish. Something of a legend to the enlisted men by spring 1899 ("he was looked upon by the soldiers as a real hero," John Kinne recalled), Young attached himself to Lawton's force when it moved north in April. He "usually ate with one of the N.D. companies and slept out anywhere like the rest," Kinne wrote. Lawton, an unconventional sort himself, at first was irritated by the civilian's presence on the firing line but came to admire Young's shooting skills and scouting knowledge. He appointed Young Chief of Scouts on 30 April, telling him to select reliable enlisted men for the detachment. Probably because Young frequently ate with the regiment, sixteen of the original twenty-five of Young's Scouts came from the 1st North Dakota.[2]

Most of the scouts had previously been designated as sharpshooters and given Krag-Jorgensen rifles in late March. A few were nonconformists with more than one court-martial on their record. All young and venturesome, they disliked routine military duties and the niceties of military courtesy, such as saluting. Private William Harris, Troop G, 4th United States Cavalry, an original scout, wrote after the war: "I remember the Scouts from the start as a free and easy-going lot, some often taking off on their own to explore the countryside We had no distinguishing marks of any kind to show that we were Scouts, unless it was that about all of us needed shaves or haircuts and in general were not quite as tidy as a soldier should be." Private E. E. Lyon, Company B, 2nd Oregon, complained in later years about officers "green with envy" over the scouts' accomplishments, a complaint seconded by Corporal Frank Anders, Company B, 1st North Dakota, who wrote, "Enlisted men [in the scouts] were not supposed to have any sense or judgment." John Kinne, who joined the scouts on 14 May, remembered that while on the march they ate with a different unit every day and wandered in and out and up and down the column at will. It was not surprising that many regular officers resented Young's scouts.

Lawton intended to have the scouts travel a half day in advance of his main column, reconnoitering the country, mapping the terrain, and locating Insurgent forces. As long as his force remained at Baliuag, he informed General Otis, "I will send these men to look up enemy...storehouses." The scouts ranged the territory east of the swamp and south of the Maasin River under orders to find and destroy Insurgent stockpiles of food and supplies hidden in the jungle. During the so-called "rice burning expedition," which lasted six days, it rained incessantly. The scouts found a number of "food arsenals" and weapons caches, burning most of them. Corporal Anders remembered, "we followed along several streams and thru trackless jungles." It was an arduous week's work. Private Lyons of the 2nd Oregon recalled, we "nearly starved to death before we got back to civilization." The detachment was exhausted when it finally returned to Baliuag on 10 May. "Most of the scouts could not walk," Anders wrote.

The scouts' most striking achievement came in their capture of two key towns on the Baliuag-San Miguel road. With General Otis's approval, Lawton sent Young and his men up to Colonel Summers's position to reconnoiter north of the Maasin River and to find Insurgent dispositions in and around the towns of San Ildefonso and San Miguel. Young led his men out from the Maasin River at 2:00 A.M., 12 May, to scout San Ildefonso. At daybreak, with his men in position to enfilade Insurgent trenches, Young induced the enemy to fire so he could estimate their numbers, later determined to be about four hundred. The fire fight began at 5:00 A.M. "That was a real day's fight," Frank Anders later wrote. "It was a long drawn out affair beginning at daylight south of the town and we gradually worked our way around to the east." The scouts sniped at enemy trenches all day. At 4:00 in the afternoon, when Young led his small band in a flanking charge on an Insurgent trench, the Filipinos abruptly abandoned not only the trench but the entire town. By nightfall, a company each from the 13th Minnesota and the 2nd Oregon regiments came up from Colonel Summers's line to relieve the scouts and occupy the town. Twenty-five men had advanced Lawton's line five miles against an enemy force sixteen times larger. One scout, Private William R. Truelock, Company C, 1st North Dakota, was the only American casualty, with a gunshot wound to the chest.

On 13 May, Young's men, reduced to only eighteen, moved to San Miguel for further reconnaissance, Captain William Birkheimer, a regular officer from Lawton's staff, accompanied them to select artillery positions near the town of twenty thousand. Young and three men from the 1st North Dakota, Corporal Frank Anders and Privates Willis H. Downs and James McIntyre, approached an enemy trench line defending a bridge over the Calumpit River in front of San Miguel. The enemy, perhaps three hundred men, opened fire. Anders recalled, "The scouts, already deployed, at once charged this line." Incredibly, as seven other scouts joined the advance, scores of Insurgents fled the trench and ran across the bridge to San Miguel. After capturing the bridge in a sharp fire fight, the scouts entered the town and took refuge in a church bell tower. From here, they "held the town until about two in the afternoon having in the meantime driven the enemy entirely out of the city." Captain Birkheimer finally brought up two infantry companies to help in securing the place. Mortally wounded at the bridge, Young died a day later in Manila. General Lawton recommended eleven scouts (six from the 1st North Dakota) and Captain Birkheimer for the Congressional Medal of Honor for this feat.[3] The scouts' charge at San Miguel was unquestionably an audacious deed, but as Frank White commented, it actually revealed "the demoralized condition of their army."

Birkheimer, a strait-laced professional who disliked the easy-going ways of the scouts, called them to a meeting at the end of the day. He was unhappy with Mr. Young, despite his wound, because the chief scout had orders to reconnoiter San Miguel, not capture it. Birkheimer now intended to impose order and discipline on the free-wheeling scouts. The meeting was a first for them. Trooper Harris recalled, "I do not remember ever seeing the Scouts in formation." The captain called Corporal Anders, the only noncommissioned officer present, to attention and, Anders related, "he gave me a lecture on saluting." An unpleasant scene followed in which several of the more outspoken privates took issue with Birkheimer's concern for military courtesy and his criticisms of Young's leadership. Birkheimer, Anders, and Private James Harrington, Company G, 2nd Oregon, left the meeting to see General Lawton. The captain requested that Harrington be arrested for insubordination and that the scouts be forced to conform to military regulations. Lawton, according to Anders, told him to leave the scouts alone. "After a few moments silence, Captain Birkheimer turned on his heel," Anders wrote, "and walked out without a further word." Lawton assigned a volunteer officer, Second Lieutenant James Thornton, 2nd Oregon, to command the scouts for the remainder of the expedition.

General Lawton did not rein in the scouts, because their capture of San Ildefonso and San Miguel advanced his position over ten miles despite orders from VIII Corps to stay put. Once the scouts took the towns, Otis could hardly deny Lawton permission to occupy them with infantry units. The obviously peeved Lawton reported the capture of the two towns "as a result of two reconnaissances by less than a score of picked men supported on both occasions by less than a full company of infantry." Meanwhile, his main force remained at Baliuag "waiting for supplies, reenforcements, and what had been most frequently requested, and was most...desired orders to advance." He asked for orders to move his entire force to San Miguel with authority to advance twenty miles farther north to San Isidro, Aguinaldo's current capital, which lay on the Rio Grande de Pampanga, northeast of Candaba swamp. A rapid move there might yet salvage the campaign, as Lawton could then turn west and take the Insurgents facing MacArthur in the rear. Reluctantly, Otis allowed Lawton to move from Baliuag to San Miguel on 15 May and approved the advance to San Isidro for the next day.

With the scouts ranging two miles forward of his infantry, Colonel Summers's brigade left San Miguel for San Isidro on the morning of 16 May. Three miles south of San Isidro, the scouts came upon a swift-flowing stream some forty feet wide, with sheer banks seven to eight feet deep, spanned by a wooden bridge. Insurgents entrenched on the north bank began shooting at the scouts and set fire to the bridge. Twenty scouts quickly set up a firing line on the south bank. "We opened fire on them and advanced to the bank of the river," John Kinne wrote. "The native trenches were just on the opposite bank from us about fifty yards away. We got behind what little protection we could find and began picking off the insurgents as they would show their heads about the trench." Lieutenant Thornton and two enlisted men, one of whom was Corporal William F. Thomas, Company K, 1st North Dakota, ran across the burning bridge. "The floor of the bridge was so badly charred that Thomas...fell through, but crawled out of the creek on the opposite side and joined in the fight," Kinne reported. Thornton and his two companions fired into the flank of the Insurgent trench while the scouts on the south side "sat and shot at them at point blank range for several minutes." The scouts then waded across the river and drove off the Insurgents. After putting out the fire, they held the position until General Lawton and a battalion of the 2nd Oregon arrived. Kinne estimated that "total destruction of the bridge would have meant at least a delay of two days." Thornton recommended twenty-two scouts who fought at the bridge for the Congressional Medal of Honor. Sixteen of the twenty-two came from the 1st North Dakota.[4]

On the morning of 17 May, Lawton's force, the 1st North Dakota, 2nd Oregon, 13th Minnesota, and 22nd United States Infantry, crossed the repaired bridge and moved on San Isidro under the tactical command of Colonel Summers. Summers formed his units into a V-shaped formation "in order to envelop the flanks of the insurgent position." Colonel Treumann commanded the right wing of the V, with Major White's 1st Battalion and a battalion of the 2nd Oregon. White's men "had very difficult ground to pass over, being covered with dense bamboo thickets, thorny hedges, and close underbrush.'' Treumann's wing came under fire for a time, but his men marched forward in a skirmish line ''keeping up a well-directed and effective fire'' while ''the enemy made but a feeble resistance at a few points in small groups.'' Meanwhile, the irrepressible scouts worked their way into San Isidro where, according to John Kinne, they ''advanced right thro the town to the church where we rang the bell as a signal that the Americans were in possession.'' Although under fire from 5:00 to 10:00 A.M., Treumann's command suffered no casualties except a few cases of heat exhaustion.

Since Aguinaldo left San Isidro early on the 17th, just as the attack began, the Americans now held the second capital captured from the Insurgents. With both the government and army of the main Insurrection leader in retreat, Lawton believed he had the opportunity to smash the uprising. However, General Otis stepped in again, informing Lawton he could not pursue Aguinaldo to the north. Instead, he ordered the expedition to move southwest to Arayat on the west side of the swamp and make contact with the 2nd Division. The move to Arayat was not the planned linkup with MacArthur but the first step in a withdrawal of Lawton's force from the territory so recently captured. On 18 May, the 1st North Dakota and 22nd United States Infantry left San Isidro, moving west of the swamp and down the Rio Grande de Pampanga. The rest of Lawton's units followed the next day. They all occupied Arayat on the 21st and the town of Candaba a day later. During the move to Candaba, the Americans encountered only light, scattered resistance. The scouts, roaming on the flanks and in the rear of the column on the lookout for Insurgent forces, came under enemy fire on the morning of 20 May while scouting for a ford across the Rio Grande near Cabaio. For once, they were caught by surprise. John Kinne wrote, when Insurgents opened fire ''I cleared a five-foot fence in one bound....I believe this was the record of the Islands for the high-jump.''

Lawton's men filtered into Calumpit, on the Manila railroad line, from the 24th to the 26th. By then, Otis had ordered a withdrawal of forces left at San Miguel and San Ildefonso. Units of the 3rd United States Infantry departed San Miguel on the 24th, their rear guard coming under Insurgent fire all the way back to Baliuag. Otis established a permanent line from San Fernando, on the railroad west of the swamp, to Baliuag on the right. With the rainy season now in full force, the volunteers overdue for return to the United States, and the supply-transportation problem still unsolved, he did not want American units far out in the countryside. The 1st North Dakota scouts returned to Manila on 25 May, riding on the 2nd Oregon train. ''We crawled on top of the box cars,'' Kinne wrote, ''and it was a merry bunch of scouts that left Calumpit for Manila forty-five miles away.'' They reached the city at 3:00 P.M. and had their picture taken, wrote Kinne, ''just as we were.'' The 1st North Dakota rode the train in the next afternoon and were in their barracks at Malate by early evening. By the time they bedded down that night, the Insurgents had reoccupied every town and village the regiment marched through except Baliuag.

The northern expedition of April-May 1899 failed to achieve the objectives set by Generals Lawton and Otis. When the 2nd Division advance up the west side of Candaba swamp stalled in early May, any hope of a MacArthur-Lawton linkup near San Miguel disappeared. Thereafter, Otis refused to allow Lawton to pursue Aguinaldo and his elusive army beyond San Isidro. Lawton was almost assuredly wrong in his belief that he could easily run down and defeat the Insurgents. At no time during the campaign did they stand and fight. Civilian Filipinos fled their towns whenever Americans approached, sometimes leaving them in flames. The lack of roads, an inadequate American transportation system, and poor intelligence on Insurgent locations prevented Lawton from inflicting serious damage on the enemy. Although his men dispersed Filipino military forces with ease, they did not, as Frank White had so optimistically written to his wife, "disintegrate their force." They could take enemy territory at will, but General Otis did not think Americans could hold that territory until regular units replaced the volunteers.

Despite the physical demands of the expedition, especially the difficulty of traveling through roadless jungles, the 1st North Dakota arrived in Manila in good condition. They had been on the trail for thirty-six days, marching over eighty miles. Rain, heat, and microbes hurt the regiment far more than did the enemy. Of fifty-one cases requiring a medical report, four were gunshot wounds but twenty were malaria cases and eighteen were dysentery. Nonetheless, Colonel Treumann reported that the 1st North Dakota "had more men present for duty" when it returned to Manila "than when it left on the 21st of April." The chief surgeon of the 1st Division singled out the regiment in his report on the expedition. "The First North Dakota Volunteers had less sickness of any kind in proportion than any command" despite their constant hard work.

Few gave thought to the obvious futility of the march, although Frank White said, "we saw much hard marching but not any severe fighting." He took pride in the regiment's performance in the campaign. "Gen. Lawton thinks the North Dak. Reg. as good as any in his command," he wrote Mrs. White. "In our last trip we went through all opposition we met whether it was resistance by the enemy, unfordable rivers or impassable roads, we got there just the same." The North Dakotans provided the majority of men for Young's Scouts, another source of regimental pride, although the detachment disbanded upon their return to Manila. After a week in barracks, White noted in early June, the men "are getting rested up in good shape again," and, he added, we were "congratulating ourselves that we would do no more field duty, but would do interior guard work until sent home."

"We had it all nicely figured out," White continued, "but Gen. Otis thinks different." Otis thought they needed to use the volunteers one last time before returning them to the United States. He organized another special expedition under General Lawton, this time to sweep the Morong Peninsula, which lay directly east of Manila, jutting southward into Laguna de Bay, to trap an army of Insurgents under General Pio del Pilar (the "phantom" army of the northern expedition). Volunteer troops made up most of the expeditionary force, including the 2nd Oregon Volunteer Infantry, which had already boarded transports for the trip home.

Lawton sent one column under Brigadier General Robert Hall southeastward from the Manila waterworks. Hall advanced on a series of towns located along the land side of the peninsula to push the Insurgents southward, beginning his movement early on 3 June. Colonel John Wholley, 1st Washington Volunteer Infantry, made a simultaneous movement with a second column from Pasig. Ignorant of terrain in front of them, Hall's men quickly bogged down in a roadless, bridgeless jungle. As they stumbled toward the village of Antipolo, Wholley's command left Pasig in two columns for Cainta on the northwestern edge of Morong Peninsula with the intent of taking Pilar's retreating forces in flank. While Lieutenant Colonel William C. Treumann led the 1st North Dakota up the western shore of the lake to enter Cainta from the south, Wholley approached the town from the west. They took Cainta with little difficulty late in the afternoon of the 3rd. That evening Wholley left Treumann in command of the column, placed his 1st Washington Infantry on cascoes, and sailed around the peninsula to assault the town of Morong the next morning.

Treumann remained at Cainta until General Lawton ordered him eastward to Taytay, a small village halfway to Antipolo, which he occupied easily. The colonel then moved on toward Antipolo but met General Hall's column before reaching the town. Although Insurgents offered no resistance during the march, "It was a very hot morning and the road was uphill all the way, and the men were much fatigued and suffered greatly for the want of water, and a large number had to fall out." General Hall's men had also experienced extreme heat in the previous two days. Throughout the Morong operation, General Otis later commented, "The Insurgents had scattered, and most of them...had taken the trails into the mountains, where they could not be profitably pursued." Treumann and Hall would not trap the enemy between their two columns, so Lawton ordered Treumann to return to Taytay, proceed south along the lake shore to Angona, then march east across the peninsula to meet the 1st Washington. Treumann took a battalion of the 12th United States Infantry and one platoon, Battery D, 6th United States Artillery, along with the eight companies of the 1st North Dakota. He called together the veterans of Young's Scouts, appointed Private John Killian, Company H, to lead them, and sent them in advance of his column. The march from Taytay to Angona lasted only two hours, with arrival late in the afternoon. "The road was excellent and the command made good progress." Killian's scouts could see Insurgents fleeing into the interior all along the march.

The next morning, 5 June, Treumann's force marched south from Angona to Binangonan along a road moving into high ground. John Kinne, serving with the scouts, thought "this was some of the worst mountain climbing we had struck." After taking Binangonan with no trouble, they ate lunch there and then marched directly east across the peninsula to Cardona. The column traveled over increasingly high country. Several times Insurgent snipers fired on them, "but being well protected by flankers and an efficient advance guard," they "met with no loss." After spending the night at Cardona, which Treumann occupied unopposed, the command moved on to Morong late in the afternoon of 6 June. So ended another failed expedition. Lawton reported that "bad roads and excessive heat" hampered the operation considerably. More disturbing was the tendency of Insurgents to adopt the pose of "amigos," as the Americans called them. Amigos, Otis noted, were "a character of partisan which prevails extensively in this country when first captured by our troops." When American forces approached, Insurgent soldiers "found it expedient to change their uniforms for a white suit, and hiding rifles and ammunition, carried white flags instead," Treumann explained. The increasing appearance of "amigos" marked a coming change in the nature of the war, from conventional methods to guerrilla tactics.

Unlike the strategy he adopted for the Santa Cruz and northern expeditions, General Otis did not evacuate all the towns taken during the foray. When he decided to occupy Morong town in order to keep an eye on Insurgents northeast of the peninsula and on the eastern shore of Laguna de Bay, the 1st North Dakota drew this unpleasant assignment. Morong was the only peninsular town occupied by American troops, the lake serving as the line of communication for resupply from Manila. Although isolated from American positions near the capital, Treumann reported, "I do not fear an attack and can hold my position." He set up outposts north and west of town and regularly sent scouting parties to check the roads to Antipolo and Cardona. Private Killian took the scouts on daily patrols to villages on the east side of the lake. Kinne enjoyed scouting, "it suited me very well," he said, "as scouts were relieved from guard and outpost duty, the rainy season had begun and doing guard and outpost duty was very disagreeable."

On a trip around the lake on 9 June, the scouts attacked an Insurgent outpost. When "Dad" Killian, as the boys called him, was severely wounded, the other scouts put him on a makeshift stretcher and headed back to Morong as rapidly as possible. "The natives were quickly closing in on us," Kinne wrote, "their bullets spattering the mud around us on every side." At one point, the improvised stretcher fell apart, dumping Killian to the ground. "The fellows took position behind rocks and trees and held off the niggers," added Kinne, "while we secured another frame on which to carry him." In the dash back to their lines, the scouts were forced to stop several more times to drive off Insurgents. When Kinne ran ahead to get help, he met Major White who sent a corpsman to meet the party, "but by the time the hospital steward got to him he was dead." Well liked in the regiment, Killian was recommended by Lieutenant Thornton for the Medal of Honor for action at the Tarbon bridge. "He was a valuable man," Treumann wired 1st Division headquarters, "and I deplore his loss."

"This town of Morong was a fierce place," Kinne wrote years later. The regiment had gone off on the Morong expedition assuming they would return soon to Manila for shipment home. Instead, they spent a month occupying the "fierce place" they came to call "More Wrong." In part they detested occupation duty because being there dashed any hopes of an early departure. Every time a boat came out from Manila, they expected to return with it, but usually the boats brought another ten days' rations. And the food was bad. "We starved on sowbelly and hardtack!" Oscar Olson, Company I, later complained. The hard service of the last four months began to tell. Frank White wrote home on 27 June, "Our boys are getting pretty worn down." Volunteer units received no replacements for their dead, wounded, and sick, and the lack of reserve units forced General Otis to keep understrength regiments constantly in the field. "The severe, unremitting, and almost unexampled strain," MacArthur reported, "have told upon whole organizations to such an extent that they are now completely worn out and broken in health.''

TABLE 3.1

Strength, 1st North Dakota, February-August 1899

	Aggregate (officers and enlisted men)	Effectives (total)	Officers	Enlisted
February	659	551	26	525
March	655	584	29	555
April	641	558	26	532
May	637	550	27	523
June	625	487	27	460
July	563*	503	29	474
August	562	505	27	478

Note: In the 1st North Dakota, seven men were killed in battle, two died in accidents, and ten succumbed to disease.

*Sixty-four enlisted men took discharges during this month. Some re-enlisted in United States Volunteer units in the Islands, others wanted to travel in the Far East.

The 1st North Dakota's aggregate and effective strength declined steadily from February through July 1899. (See Table 3.1.) Total strength diminished as the most seriously ill officers and enlisted men returned to the United States for discharge. At the end of June, for example, there were twenty-five men hospitalized in San Francisco awaiting their release, and Captain C. E. Mudgett, 12 Company G, and Lieutenant Henry Redman, Company D, were discharged for disability. Active campaigning from early April onward cut deeply into the regiment's effective strength. The cumulative effects of three months' field duty, plus the climate and contaminated water at Morong, hurt the outfit badly during June. In a 1 July letter to Elliott S. Miller, state adjutant general, Colonel Treumann mentioned his growing sick list, ''mostly of stomach and bowel troubles.'' On that day he had only 369 officers and men fit for duty. ''Most of us are near skeletons and have lost from 15 to 40 pounds,'' Treumann told General Miller. ''The regiment is by no means the rugged and healthy organization that left Camp Briggs over a year ago.''

Morale began to suffer. The usually optimistic Frank White mentioned another expedition under Lawton, which began near the end of June: ''We did not get into the fight...and I am not sorry....from what I can hear [they] had a pretty hot time.'' A bitter John Kinne contended: ''Otis had said when he got through with the volunteers he would be able to send them all home on the same boat, and if our experience at Morong had long continued his prediction would have certainly come true as far as we were concerned.'' The lengthy sick list and recruiting for the newly organized 36th United States

Volunteer Infantry left the 1st North Dakota short of enlisted men. Kinne noted that on 20 June, Company B had only thirty-four of its authorized seventy-six privates on duty. On 24 June he wrote, "That night I was the only well private of Company B in camp." Four days later "Our number was so small that...I stood one post all night." When several recruits left for the 36th Infantry on 2 July, only twenty-four privates were available for duty.

Relief finally came on 6 July with the arrival of two battalions of the 21st United States Infantry. The 1st North Dakota left the miserable place the next day on cascoes, bound for Manila and preparation for going home. As a fitting end to duty at Morong, their convoy ran into a heavy rain storm. "Progress was slow and the last of the companies arrived at their barracks in Malate at midnight." An ironic conclusion to the regiment's entire campaign experience from April to June came when General Otis withdrew the Morong garrison and left the entire peninsula once again in Insurgent hands.

The majority of the North Dakotans were more than ready to go home in July 1899. Few had given much thought to why they were in the Philippines or why they were fighting the Filipinos. Only Frank White occasionally commented on the issue. Back in September, he wrote his wife: "the same impulses that prompted and warranted our interference in Cuba should dominate here." America must free the Filipinos from corrupt and tyrannical Spanish rule. Still, he went on in another letter, "the natives had grown up under the Spanish system and are incapable of any other at present." Unfit for self-government, the Filipinos would have to accept some form of American stewardship.

These vague altruistic impulses, not particularly shared by White's comrades, disappeared with the outbreak of the Insurrection. The men welcomed combat as a relief from the boredom of occupation duty and as a means of striking back at the ungrateful Filipinos, who rejected America's guidance. In the first few days of the Insurrection, the VIII Corps, in order to secure its rear, dealt harshly with Insurgent sympathizers. John Russater noted in his diary for 7 February: "we have orders to burn every house where we find evidence of Insurgents." Kinne, too, commented on the burning of shacks "except those which contained women and children, and were flying white flags." They searched native huts for arms, ammunition, and other signs of Insurgent support. "The numerous columns of black smoke in the neighborhood gives evidence that many such houses has been found," Russater added. Private Oscar Amundson of Company G wrote home that if natives objected to the searches, "we had orders to shoot them. We did not have to do that though."

What originated as a military necessity in early February became an all-too-common practice after that. Americans continued to use fire to punish Filipinos suspected of aiding the Insurgents. John Peterson wrote on 8 March that Idaho troops "burned the shacks of Filipinos" thought to be "amigos." "It was a rather pitiful sight." When Sergeant Russater sent out a scouting party to find a rice cache on 1 April, the party took some of the rice and "destroyed the rest by burning the houses in which it was." Quartered in an old church at San Pedro Macati, Frank White mused on the destruction of so many churches during the Insurrection. Americans and Filipinos used churches as defensive positions, he wrote, and "our soldiers sacked and burned them just the same as other houses whenever shots were fired from them."

On occasion, American troops killed civilians by accident or design. Sergeant William H. Lock of Company B wrote to a friend in Valley City: "most of the boys say as the cowboys of our North American Indian: A dead Philipino [sic] is a good Philipino." This was more than mere bragging. Russater cryptically noted in his diary on 11 February that "They caught a sharpshooter in the act of changing his uniform for a white suit and now he is a *good* Philipino [sic]!" (emphasis in original). Although Russater did not identify "they," the context of his entry leaves little doubt that "they" were from the 1st North Dakota. While Young's Scouts were ranging forward of Lawton's column south and west of San Isidro in mid-May, they accidentally shot and killed a woman. Kinne, as reluctant as Russater to name the shooter, described the incident: "We proceeded inland about a mile and at one place as one of the boys came through a hedge across an opening there were a number of insurgents in a yard with women and children. He called to the insurgents to surrender but they bolted for the woods and he shot. Unfortunately a woman holding a baby was shot through the chest and died instantly. None of the insurgents was hit. This was the saddest thing that occurred to us for some time."

Americans "foraged" regularly on campaign, taking food from the natives. In the days immediately after the outbreak of the insurrection, when VIII Corps supply failed to provide rations for the troops, the men took food wherever they could find it. "The boys are foraging liberally," Russater commented, and the chickens are in a state of despair." Lieutenant Charles Getchell, Company G, told his mother, "we go out and rustle pigs and sweet potatoes and rice and these with government rations make a good meal." Company H's Oscar Olson denied that Americans looted in the Philippines but conceded, "we did look thru shacks and homes' and during the northern expedition 'helped ourselves to chickens as we were starved."

Looting, burning, and intimidating Filipinos marked American behavior throughout the insurrection. Division and VIII Corps commanders repeatedly demanded that regimental officers control their men when in the field. General Lawton in particular always included stern instructions against looting in his expeditions' field orders. The orders failed to take effect. Major C. G. Starr, Inspector General, 1st Division, in his otherwise laudatory comments on the discipline of volunteer troops in June 1899, stressed that they continued to show "a disposition to loot and destroy." Attempts to restrain indiscriminate behavior were important not only for humanitarian reasons but to conform to General Otis's developing policy of pacification. Otis came to believe that only a "benevolent" occupation would win civilian Filipinos over to American control. His approach became the cornerstone of American policy in the Philippines, one too often negated by the men in the field even as it was being developed.

The 1st North Dakota performed as well as any volunteer unit in the Philippine Insurrection. After 4 February, its internal discipline held up well. As seen in the 1 April fire fight of the 1st Battalion under Frank White, at the Paete ambush when five men in Major John Fraine's 2nd Battalion were killed, and in the laborious trek from Novaliches to Angat during the northern expedition, the North Dakotans fought and soldiered with skill and courage. Their morale remained high even after Spain and the United States exchanged treaties on 11 April 1899 formally ending the war. This ended the government's claim on their service, yet the volunteers fought their hardest campaigns after their legal obligation to serve terminated. The regiment's failing, common to all troops in the Islands, was to see the Filipinos as inferior people and to treat them as such. The insurrection lasted until July 1902, prolonged in part by the American soldier's disrespect for civilian Filipino life and property.[5]

Under insistent pressure from the War Department, General Otis finally began dispatching volunteer units to the United States in mid-June. He had kept them beyond their legal tenure in hopes of ending the insurrection before the rainy season began in July. When the April and May offensives failed, Otis released the state soldiers. He retained hopes that many of them would re-enlist in the two United States Volunteer Infantry regiments being organized in Manila. The VIII Corps offered a five-hundred-dollar bonus to any volunteer who re-enlisted and tendered sergeant's stripes to veterans of Young's Scouts. Both offers failed to appeal to most volunteers. Colonel Treumann told Adjutant General Miller, "only a few of our men have signified their intentions to remain." Thirty-three men of the 1st North Dakota re-enlisted, six of whom had served in the Scouts. Two officers, Captain Adelbert Cogswell, Company D, and Second Lieutenant Fred Smith, Company K, took commissions in the United States Volunteers.

After its return to Manila from Morong on 6 July, the regiment idled away the rest of the month while the VIII Corps arranged transport back to the United States. The men were given two months' pay on the 12th. According to Kinne, "The boys from now on put in a great deal of time buying curios and other things to take home." Buying souvenirs soon became boring, and for most of the month "The boys had little to do but eat, sleep, read and write for tedious days, waiting to get orders to get aboard." Captain Edward C. Gearey, Kinne's company commander, held regular drills and dress parades as he wanted Company B to be "the 'Pride of the Regiment,'" but Kinne and his mates "were not anxious to become dress parade soldiers.' Frank White requested leave to visit China and Japan. Although the VIII Corps granted the leave, it came too late for the visit to China. He left Manila on 26 July for Nagasaki, Japan, to rejoin the regiment at Yokohama for the trip to the states. White had resisted his wife's plea that he return early so they could take a vacation after he arrived in San Francisco. He thought "it best to stay with the boys until we get home," he wrote her.

The War Department offered the volunteers the option to muster out in Manila or San Francisco. The 1st North Dakota voted unanimously for the latter because, as Treumann informed General Miller, "it is financially to the best interest of every man in the regiment," Along with the Idaho regiment and Wyoming battalion, they boarded the transport *Grant* on 28 July. Since nothing in the Philippines was done easily or quickly, it took three days to load and coal the ship. The *Grant* left Manila Bay on 31 July, stopping first at Nagasaki for three days, with a three day visit to Yokohama after that. The men enjoyed sightseeing in such an exotic place as Japan. Kinne commented, "the good times we are having made us feel that the government was trying to do something to square itself with the volunteers." On 14 August, the *Grant* departed Yokohama bound for San Francisco. Colonel Treumann praised the troops for their behavior in Nagasaki and Yokohama: "No complaints whatever were made in either port."

At 5:30 P.M., 29 August 1899, the *Grant* approached Oakland Bay, coming to anchor at 10:30 P.M. at Angel Island, but the regiment could not go ashore until it passed a medical inspection for contagious diseases. They spent the 30th at the island, where a delegation from North Dakota boarded the ship to welcome the boys home. The group included General Miller, Senators Henry C. Hansbrough and Porter J. McCumber, and Representative Burleigh F. Spalding. When the ship moved over to the main docks of San Francisco later that day, a much larger group from home came aboard, including Mrs. Treumann, Mrs. White, Mrs. Fraine, and other officers' wives. "There was a great deal of excitement," Kinne wrote. "One woman almost fell in a faint, and another almost threw her boy overboard in her enthusiasm."

The regiment went ashore the next day, 31 August. Major General William R. Shafter, United States Army, welcomed them home. The city of San Francisco provided a parade up Market Street from the docks to the Presidio where the North Dakota, Idaho, and Wyoming units would camp until mustered out. Sirens and foghorns blew and a California National Guard band played military music: "The march over the cobblestones to camp at the Presidio was one continual ovation," Kinne warmly remembered. "Both sides of the street were lined with people all trying to make as much noise as possible." Adjutant General Miller, Colonel Amasa P. Peake, the two senators and Congressman Spalding, the officers' ladies, all preceded the regiment, while "Every volunteer was decked with flowers, at least one bouquet in a rifle barrel." It was an unexpected but exciting welcome home.

While the presence of several North Dakota political figures suggested a conscious effort to gain publicity and share in the regiment's achievements, state officials had come to San Francisco because, in their eyes, the regiment still belonged to them. Indeed, the state had never cut its ties to the unit. Governor Fred B. Fancher ordered General Miller to the West Coast to represent the state and "to render such aid and assistance as may be necessary to the First Infantry North Dakota Volunteers upon their return." (Only an unexpected illness prevented Governor Fancher from welcoming the boys home.) Miller made sure the sick men received proper medical care and helped cut red tape so they would be released from the hospital to return home with the regiment. He also carried commissions for several recently appointed second lieutenants. The state legislature appropriated $2,500 for the health and welfare of the outfit and sent the check to Colonel Treumann. The officers voted to use the money to buy sleeping car accommodations for the enlisted men back to the state, allowing them to save their muster-out pay.

The governor's office retained an active interest in the 1st North Dakota throughout its overseas service. Governors Joseph Devine and Fancher acted as liaisons with the War Department for soldiers and their families with questions or problems. The governors had pressured the War Department to release the volunteers from late 1898 onward. Appointments of new officers and promotions within the regiment remained the governors' prerogative, even though the 1st North Dakota was in federal service. Letters from men in the Philippines, the North Dakota National Guard in the state, local politicians, and parents of boys in the service came to Bismarck, offering candidates for appointment and promotion. Governor Devine followed seniority when he promoted Lieutenant Edward C. Gearey, Jr., and Second Lieutenant M. A. Hildreth to replace Captain Fred Keye in Company B but ignored seniority among the sergeants when he appointed Sergeant Robert A. Thompson as second lieutenant to replace Hildreth. Significantly, Devine took suggestions from North Dakota National Guard members and interested Fargo people but did not ask Colonel Treumann for a recommendation. While Treumann wrote General Miller "The promotions were favorably received by the regiment," he went on to point out that Thompson's promotion was not "in line with the understanding had at Fargo." The officers had agreed with Miller and Colonel Peake before leaving the state in 1898 that all promotions would follow the lineal rank of officers and noncommissioned officers, regardless of company. Governor Fancher promised Treumann he would keep to the agreement, which he did in 1899.

General Miller and Colonel Treumann engaged in an unpleasant argument caused partly by an August 1898 fire which destroyed most of the adjutant general's records. When the 1st North Dakota mustered into the Army, Miller, Lieutenant I. A. Berg, regimental quartermaster, and Lieutenant E. C. Gearey, regimental ordnance officer, failed to complete all the War Department forms transferring state military property to the federal government. Miller argued endlessly with the War Department over property responsibility, but due to the fire, the regiment held the only records available to settle the issue. Miller found it difficult to obtain the necessary information from Treumann, Berg, and Gearey.

The adjutant general turned the issue into a general attack on Colonel Treumann. He wrote Frank White about the problem in April 1899, "with a generous roast for myself, QM Berg and former ordnance officer Capt. Gearey," according to Treumann. Miller accused the colonel of failing to inform him of the regiment's activities and general condition. He criticized Treumann for not commenting on the recent promotions, for neglecting to send the needed property accounts, and for ignoring a War Department general order that required state unit commanders to inform state officials of regimental casualties. Miller's letter to White asserted: "'there is no question but what we could have had him [Treumann] promoted to colonel if he had interested himself in the matter more.'" The adjutant general called the 1st North Dakota "a bobtail, 2 battalion command" which could have been a full regiment except for Treumann, possibly with Miller himself as the full colonel. Miller wrote to other officers in the regiment, a particularly scathing letter going to Lieutenant Berg disparaging Treumann. He never wrote directly to the colonel. Miller's evident jealousy of Treumann, fed in part by an envious Thomas Poole, now private secretary to Governor Fancher, triggered these attacks. The selection of regimental officers in May 1898 left bad feelings within the North Dakota National Guard which festered long after the regiment left.

Treumann did not hesitate to confront General Miller. In reference to the letter to White, he wrote Miller on 14 May, "I prefer to be jacked up direct." He maintained he had made efforts to keep the adjutant general informed but, he added, "You must take into consideration that my regiment has been in the field since the 4th of February and have been in barracks but 24 hours since."[6] His only office was a saddlebag, which made it difficult to keep track of all records and general orders. The failure to correct the property accounts was Miller's fault and could "have been fixed up at Fargo before the regiment left or even during the month that we remained in Frisco and it is no fault of mine that it was not done," Treumann said. Treumann could not resist taking a jibe at Miller's contention that he "had it in your power to promote me to colonel," but added, "Don't lose any sleep General on account of my nonpromotion." The colonel had the distinct psychological advantage of writing from a combat zone, one which he used throughout the unseemly business. "With the great interest that you profess to have in the regiment it may please you to know that on this expedition of General Lawton's I was the ranking officer and since April 21st have been in command of the Brigade." In another letter to Miller on 1 July Treumann again defended himself, adding more references to his campaign work in May and June. Treumann closed with an attempt to soothe the adjutant general and bring the argument to an end. "There is no disposition on the part of any officer to slight you as you seem to suppose," he assured General Miller.

The matter was buried, if not forgotten, in the homecoming celebration at San Francisco. While the Army took its time processing the regiment for muster out, including a final settlement with General Miller on the property accounts, officers and men toured the city. John Kinne attended a speech by William Jennings Bryan. On 9 September, the 1st North Dakota went to the docks to welcome the 1st South Dakota and 13th Minnesota home. "Sept. 25 was the eventful day for the N.D. Vols.," Kinne recalled. "We were mustered for the last time," then marched to headquarters, paid off, and discharged. "We bought our railroad tickets home, paid our debts, and bid farewell to camp and left for the city, free men." Colonel Treumann issued his last regimental general order, congratulating the men "upon the harmony which has at all times prevailed in the regiment," and offering "my most sincere good wishes for your welfare and success in the changed life upon which we will soon enter."

Now civilians, the men boarded a special train the next day and left for North Dakota. "All along the route we were royally treated," Kinne recalled, "especially at Portland, Tacoma, and Spokane." The train pulled into Dickinson on 1 October and dropped off Company K. It stopped at Bismarck, where Company A detrained, then at Jamestown, leaving behind Companies D and H. At Valley City, Company G got off, along with Major Frank White. Spontaneously, according to Kinne, "The boys carried the Major through the streets on their shoulders, and every man shook hands with him before we parted." The train stopped last at Fargo where the remaining companies dispersed to their hometowns. A warm crowd of family and friends met them at each stop from Dickinson to Fargo. President William McKinley came to Fargo on 12 October to speak on the volunteers' service in the Philippines.

Many veterans of the regiment, and all of Company B, shook hands with the President.

The 1st North Dakota Volunteer Infantry, organized eighteen months earlier at Camp Briggs, returned to its point of origin, then disbanded. It left the state amid much public attention and affection. All along its route to San Francisco, the citizens of Idaho, Washington, Oregon, and California turned out to give the regiment a proper send-off. When the 1st North Dakota returned to the United States after a year's hard service in a war not all Americans supported, it received the same popular attention, from the welcome home parade in San Francisco, during the return trip through Oregon and Washington, to the final welcome home at the companies' home stations in North Dakota. The presidential thank you at Fargo capped the return.

Throughout their active duty in 1898 and 1899, the North Dakotans never doubted that their fellow citizens recognized and endorsed their military service. Unit pride reinforced this sense of support. The 1st North Dakota left the state as a unit and returned as the same organization, its personnel reduced by death and disease but the core of the original outfit intact at muster-out. The 1st North Dakota's origins in the North Dakota National Guard, sustained by state support and interest, ensured the regiment's social cohesion, which was the key to its combat effectiveness. Poorly trained, inadequately equipped, led by amateur citizen-soldier officers, the 1st North Dakota learned to function as a viable military organization because the bonds of friendship and mutual respect among officers and men gave it an internal unity sufficient to overcome military ignorance.

The personalities of the three ranking officers in the regiment complimented each other nicely and helped account for its cohesiveness and solid performance. Colonel Treumann, a genial, informal man, represented the old-style volunteer. He dispensed advice and admonishments to the boys like an uncle. His talents were more administrative than tactical in any event. Frank White, surely the most popular of the two majors, off the line joked with his men, lent them money, and worked to keep their spirits high. He generally behaved as though the North Dakota National Guard were simply in summer camp. In the trenches or under fire, White dropped the informality and insisted on strict fire discipline and immediate obedience to orders. If not charismatic, he still exhibited coolness and bravery in battle, as seen during the 1 April ambush.

John Fraine was a "book soldier," far more formal than White. A stern, distant personality, he kept the line between officers and men distinct, on and off the line. Though no martinet, Fraine demanded Regular Army discipline. He lost no respect and generated no resentment for that because of his unscrupulous fairness. His courage and ability, seen clearly on the terrible day at Paete, was sufficiently evident to the men of the 2nd Battalion to allow them to accept Fraine's leadership willingly. Colonel Treumann and Majors White and Fraine gave the 1st North Dakota a style of leadership typical of volunteer units in the nineteenth century. Not learned professional soldiers, they learned how to lead men. In the twentieth century, the nature of war and dramatic changes in American military organization would alter substantially the ways in which National Guard units would go to war.

Notes on Sources

See notes on sources for Chapter 2.

[1]General Anderson's successor in command of the 1st Division, Major General Henry W. Lawton, suggested this approach.

[2]They were: Co. A, Pvts. Michael Glassley and Calvin Wilson; Co. B, Cpl. Frank Anders, Musician Otto M. Luther, Pvt. Edward McBain; Co. C., Pvt. Forest Warren; Co. D, Pvt. Gottfried Jensen; Co. G, Artificer Neil Christianson and Pvt. Sterling Gault; Co. H, Wagoner Willis Downs and Pvt. John Killian; Co. I, Pvts. Otto Boehler and John Desmond; Co. K, Cpl. William F. Thomas and Pvts. Patrick Hussey and John C. Smith. Others who eventually served with the scouts on a regular basis were: Co. A, Pvt. Richard Longfellow; Co. B, Pvts. John McIntyre and John Kinne; Co. C, Pvt. William Truelock; Co. G, Pvt. Charles P. Davis; Co. H, Pvt. Frank Ross; Co. K, Pvts. Frank Summerfield and Thomas W. Sweeney.

[3]The North Dakota scouts were: Anders, McIntyre, Downs, Jensen, Hussey, and Summerfield.

[4]They were: Glassley, Longfellow, McIntyre, Kinne, Jensen, Davis, Gault, Downs, Killian, Ross, Boehler, Desmond, Thomas, Summerfield, Hussey, and Sweeney.

[4]One measure of the regiment's effectiveness was that ten of its men came home with the Congressional Medal of Honor. They were: Corporal Frank L. Anders, Co. B; and Privates Otto Boehler, Co. I; Charles P. Daivs, Co. G; Willis H. Downs, Co. H; Sterling Gault, Co. H: Gottfried Jensen, Co. D; John B. Kinne, Co. B; Richard M. Longfellow, Co. C. All but Pvt. Sletteland served in Young's Scouts.

[6]Treumann wrote to Miller several times on all these matters, as seen in the correspondence records of the Adjutant General's Office, North Dakota National Guard. Mail from the Philippine Islands to the United States was notoriously slow, which probably accounts for this.

Members of an unidentified unit of the First Regiment, First North Dakota Infantry, U.S.V., in the trenches outside Manila, Philippine Islands, 1899.

ung's scouts, members of the First North Dakota Infantry, U.S.V. on
tpost duty near San Pedro Macati, Philippine Islands, 1899.

First Regiment, North Dakota Infantry, U.S.V. upon return from the Philippine Insurrection, The Presidio, San Francisco, 31 August 1899.

☆4☆
The Years of Reform, 1900-1916

When the 1st North Dakota Volunteer Infantry entered federal service in 1898, the state lost most of its National Guard. Companies were organized at Langdon (E), Hillsboro (L), and Ellendale (M), hoping to become a part of the 1st North Dakota, but they remained at home, neglected by the state. The regiment took all the field equipment and the best of the rifles. Units remaining in state service carried Civil War-vintage .50-caliber Springfield rifles and received no armory rent in 1898 and 1899. At the end of 1899 Elliott S. Miller, adjutant general, reported that Companies E, L, and M, Battery A, and Troop A composed the North Dakota National Guard. He 'estimated' their total enrollment at two hundred officers and enlisted men. The adjutant general did not inspect them in 1899 'on account of the many protests received, so many members of the Guard being in business and interested in farming.' General Miller admitted that until the recently returned war companies reorganized themselves, the Guard remained in limbo.

If the condition of the North Dakota National Guard in late 1899 and early 1900 suggested a return to the 1890s policies of neglect and poverty, such was not to be the case. The National Guard in North Dakota and throughout the United States underwent significant and long-lasting change in the years 1900-1916. As a consequence of the Guard's abysmal 1898 mobilization, the War Department, the National Guard Association, and Congress urged changing the nation's military laws. War Department reformers sought to create in the Guard what had been most lacking during the Spanish-American War, a reliable reserve trained, organized, and equipped according to Regular Army standards. In the process, the War Department and Congress fundamentally changed the states' responsibilities and Guardsmen's obligations. Although a majority of National Guard officers supported militia reform, few seemed to realize the long-term effects of reform. Without change, however, Guardsmen feared the War Department would look elsewhere for its reserve. With reform, the federal government offered the National Guard badly needed funds and modern equipment, things the state governments would not or could not provide.

Reform began in 1900 when Congress increased the War Department's annual distribution of military equipment to the states from $400,000 to $1 million. The War Department hoped the increase would allow the states to acquire arms and equipment. The Militia Act of 1903, commonly known as the Dick Act after its chief sponsor, Congressman Charles F. Dick of Ohio, had even more significance. The 1903 act established principles that have governed a shared state and federal control of the National Guard ever since.

State soldiers wanted the federal government to promise the *Guard*, not simply state volunteers in general but the National Guard specifically, a first call in forming a war army. Guardsmen also expected substantial federal aid to arm and equip their service. On the other hand, the War Department insisted on two essentials: the National Guard must be willing to serve when called and state military units must conform to Army regulations on discipline and tables of organization. Federal law governing the National Guard underwent innumerable change after 1903, but these basics prevailed.

The Dick Act offered the Guard recognition for war service and money. Section 13 provided a one-time allotment of $2 million, which the states would share, to re-equip the Guard with modern rifles and equipment. Another section permitted the states to use their portion of the $1 million distribution to support summer camp, including Regular Army pay rates for enlisted Guardsmen when in camp. The law allowed opportunities for Guard units to join Regular outfits in joint training camps and maneuvers and for Guard officers to attend Army post and service schools. All state military systems accepting federal assistance must, within five years, conform to Regular Army organization, equipment, and 'discipline,' the latter term meaning training and instruction. Annual armory inspections by Regular officers would determine progress toward 'conformity.' Additionally, Guard companies, batteries, and troops were to drill at least twenty-four times a year and go into camp or on practice march at least five consecutive days annually. Finally, states had to take proper care of federal property distributed under the Dick Act. Amendments to the law in 1906 and 1908 increased the value of the annual distribution of arms and equipment by another $3 million. The 1908 amendment pushed back the date when the Guard must conform with Army regulations to 21 January 1910.

The Dick Act's full impact would not become evident until 1916, but the flow of federal dollars to the states was readily seen. In the years 1903 to 1917, the federal government disbursed nearly $53 million, twice as much as it had given the states in peacetime for the entire nineteenth century. Annual federal spending on the National Guard occasionally equaled what the states spent collectively. In 1912, for example, the War Department disbursed $5 million and the states spent $5.3 million. The Dick Act and amendments allotted $4 million annually after 1908. Every other year Congress appropriated additional funds to pay for joint Army-National Guard maneuver camps and made periodic special appropriations to purchase expensive arms or equipment the Guard needed. In 1916, for instance, Congress allotted nearly $2 million extra to buy field artillery equipment for state forces.

How federal funds affected a particular state depended largely on the amount that state spent on its National Guard. That depended, in turn, on the state's population, industrial development, political organization, and other factors determining state wealth. Increasingly, more states started to rely upon War Department disbursements. Generally, the older eastern states, with their mature industrial economies and turbulent urban-industrial populations, spent a great deal. So, too, did many Great Lakes and Pacific Coast states. In the old South and the debt-ridden farming states of the Trans-

TABLE 4.1
State and Federal Spending, National Guard,
Selected States, 1913

State	Aggregate Strength, NG	Total NG Budget, and Source		
Connecticut	2,641	Federal State	$ 76,435 193,855 270,290	(28%)
New York	15,957	Federal State	375,000 922,000 1,297,000	(29%)
Illinois	5,914	Federal State	207,000 402,000 609,000	(34%)
California	3,612	Federal State	95,500 237,000 332,500	(29%)
Washington	1,238	Federal State	60,000 108,000 168,000	(36%)
Kentucky	2,013	Federal State	93,800 20,000 113,800	(82%)
South Carolina	1,909	Federal State	53,000 15,000 68,000	(78%)
South Dakota	679	Federal State	49,000 18,200 67,200	(73%)
Nebraska	1,172	Federal State	63,700 38,500 102,200	(62%)

SOURCE: *Division of Militia Affairs Report, 1914,* pp. 318-319.

Mississippi West, however, state military systems received relatively little state support. In these latter cases, including North Dakota, federal spending loomed large. Table 4.1 illustrates the wide disparity in state spending and the relative importance of Dick Act assistance to individual states. In 1913, thirty of the forty-nine states and territories received more federal than state dollars for their military budgets.

The federal government did not take complete control of the National Guard before World War I. Each state force continued to maintain a special flavor based on its history and current political and social conditions. Nonetheless, the Militia Act of 1903, as amended, and a growing number of War Department administrative decisions restricted the ways in which individual National Guards could operate.

It was not the intent of the Dick Act to force states to increase their military budgets, but as state spending in North Dakota revealed, federal reform inevitably led reluctant state legislatures to augment their support for their military systems after years of neglect. North Dakota continued its annual $11,000 military appropriation, maintained during the 1890s, from 1900 to 1903. After the passage of the Dick Act, the legislature raised the yearly budget to $19,000 for 1904 to 1908, then to $25,000 annually from 1909 through 1912. From 1913 to the outbreak of World War I, the state's annual military budget totaled $30,000. These increases were direct responses to the growing costs of complying with federal laws.

Annual armory assistance rose from $300 to $400 in 1904 and to $500 in 1907. In order to continue receiving federal funds, companies had to pass an annual armory inspection and to show proper care of federal property. Each unit needed an armory suitable for drill and storage. Although the annual armory rent helped, local units even then could not provide themselves with decent buildings. To solve this problem, the legislature authorized state assistance for the purchase or construction of armories in 1907. In addition to the regular military budget, North Dakota appropriated $10,000 to $15,000 annually from 1907 to 1912 for armory construction. Special state appropriations, though on a smaller scale, were made periodically to improve the state military reservation at Rock Island, Devils Lake. Federal aid to the National Guard inevitably increased administrative costs for the adjutant general's office and the Chief of Supply, costs that the state had to underwrite.

Despite the growth in state spending, North Dakota failed to support its National Guard adequately. The North Dakota National Guard, of necessity, became more and more dependent on the federal government. In 1906, for example, the War Department sent nearly $16,000 worth of military clothing and equipment to the state and paid another $12,500 for camp purposes, including daily pay for officers and enlisted men. Two years later the federal government allotted over $40,000 to the Guard, again including $12,000 for camp purposes. During the 1909-1910 biennium, the federal government spent over $85,000 on the North Dakota National Guard in regular and special disbursements. Total state spending for the period came to $50,000. North Dakota helped its Guard more effectively than its sister state, South Dakota, which attempted to maintain an infantry regiment on an annual budget of $15,000. Conversely, the state of Washington kept up an eight-hundred-man infantry regiment on an annual state expenditure of $67,000. For North Dakota, federal dollars were essential to maintain its military force from the beginning of the Dick Act. The legislature, with little enthusiasm, occasionally added the state's mite to the military collection plate.

Federal aid solved two major problems of the 1890s, inadequate arms and equipment and infrequent summer camps. Prior to 1903, state and Regular Army inspectors noted the woeful condition of the Guard's arms, uniforms, and field equipment, most of it dating back to the territorial years. Battery A was especially poorly equipped, holding two muzzle-loading rifled cannons which were dangerous to the gun crews. When the battery fired a salute during a Fourth of July celebration at Lisbon in 1902, a premature explosion took off the arm of a private and severely wounded another man. After a similar explosion severed a man's hand at the 1903 summer camp, the guns were then mercifully taken away. The infantry's old single-shot, .50- and .45-caliber Springfield rifles were not dangerous, and, according to state ordnance officer Colonel William H. Brown, "might be said to be effective upon the hypothesis that any enemy with equally poor pieces could be discovered."

Dick Act provisions allowed the state to exchange the Springfields for Krag-Jorgensen rifles in 1903, and five years later the Model 1903 Springfield replaced the Krags. In the ensuing years, new uniforms, tents, and camp equipment also arrived. North Dakota became one of the first states fully outfitted in the new-pattern olive-drab uniforms in 1908, when the War Department absorbed the full twelve-thousand-dollar clothing cost. Federal funds paid for company rifle target ranges and yearly target practice ammunition at home station and summer camp. The Guard was never fully equipped for immediate field service and some Regular Army arms and equipment turned over to it could at best be described as "used." Still, when compared to the meager support of the 1890s, the material provided after 1903 was substantial indeed.

The 1903 Militia Act required state troops to spend a minimum of five consecutive days on bivouac or in camp. The act envisioned bringing local companies into battalion and regimental formation in order to teach them higher unit tactics and how to live in the field. During the first ten years of statehood, the North Dakota Guard went to camp only twice, in 1891 and 1894. From 1902 through 1915, however, it went every year. The early twentieth- century camps were major improvements over those of the 1890s, due partly to better equipment, partly to their regularity, but chiefly to the fact that federal funds underwrote their costs.

Camp requirements generated an immediate benefit, one of lasting significance: the steady betterment of the state military reservation at Rock Island, near Devils Lake. The federal government ceded over fifteen hundred acres to North Dakota in 1894, but the Guard's poverty prevented improvement of the grounds. Throughout the 1890s and into the twentieth century, adjutants general urged the legislature to provide funds to develop a permanent military camp, but the requests went unanswered. The Rock Island reservation was so neglected that farmers used it for pasturage and local residents carried off firewood at will. For a number of years after 1900, the state Military Board, composed of three Guard officers, oversaw the sale of firewood and rental of pasture land. The Military Board used this money, which rarely totaled more than two thousand dollars a year, to make improvements, including fencing in the property, building roads, and clearing off some of the thick underbrush. In 1904, General Miller asked for more money, arguing that ''All improvements from now on should be made looking to the future. They should be permanent.'' He pointed out that he intended to build a rifle range ''with practically no expense to the state,'' as he could use War Department funds and supplies.

Since the legislature did not consider the project very important, improvement came slowly. Year by year, adjutants general and the Military Board cleared more land, drilled wells, built a stone storehouse, and constructed more roads. H. M. Creel, adjutant general, wrote the War Department in 1906 offering the reservation as a place to hold joint National Guard-Army camps of instruction. He hoped the War Department would accept the offer and force the state to build a permanent camp at Devils Lake. Although his bid failed, in 1910 the War Department designated the camp as the concentration point for the North Dakota National Guard in the event of war. In the next three years, the state spent over ten thousand dollars on the reservation, but as late as 1914 it still lacked many necessary permanent buildings, including mess halls and privies. Nonetheless, Devils Lake became the Guard's permanent training grounds. The Guard rendezvoused there regularly when not attending joint camps outside the state. No longer did the state need to offer summer camp to the highest bidder. A permanent camp, isolated to an extent from civil society, gave annual training a seriousness it had lacked in the old days.

The presence of Regular Army officers as instructors and inspectors, paid with Dick Act funds, added to the seriousness of purpose during summer training. As one of its major goals, militia reform aimed to better the instruction of National Guard officers and noncommissioned officers in Army methods and to teach them to think like Regulars as much as possible. Beginning in 1909, all state units had to pass a field inspection in camp, as well as an armory inspection. Regular officers in camp not only inspected but lectured to officers and noncommissioned officers, recommended improvements in drill and training programs, and prepared a detailed report for both the War Department and the state. As part of a larger Division of Militia Affairs program, state officers and senior noncommissioned officers also attended special camps of instruction led by regulars at Fort Lincoln, south of Bismarck, in 1911 and 1912. A number of North Dakota officers, including Colonel J. H. Fraine, First Regiment, and Captain Gilbert C. Grafton, Company B, traveled to San Antonio, Texas, in 1911 to serve two weeks with Regular Army regiments along the Mexican Border. Colonel Fraine thought the trip's greatest benefit was sharing information with National Guard officers from other states. He concluded, ''I am better satisfied that we are on the right track in the training of our Guard.''

The War Department also supported joint Army-National Guard maneuvers and instruction camps. It held the first joint maneuvers in the summer of 1903 at West Point, Kentucky, and Fort Riley, Kansas. Although

North Dakota did not attend, Colonel Amasa P. Peake, 1st Regiment, visited the Fort Riley maneuvers, observing field exercises and attending lectures. North Dakota's first joint camp came in 1906 when two of the three battalions of the 1st Regiment and a detachment of Battery A traveled over one thousand miles to Fort D. A. Russell, Wyoming. In many respects, the camp was a disappointment. The Guardsmen had miserable rail accommodations to and from Fort Russell. Although early August, rain and the cool mountain air made life in the open a trial for the physically soft men. The North Dakota unit was the only Guard outfit in camp, located twenty miles from Fort Russell, and the regulars worked the regiment up to ten hours a day. A mix-up in commissary arrangements forced the Guardsmen to eat field rations (hard biscuits and beans) for two days.

The comments of Major Thomas C. Patterson, regimental surgeon, summed up the experience. Patterson took issue with the twenty-mile march from the depot to the field camp because it subjected "men entirely unaccustomed to such undertakings" to severe physical strain. "In my opinion it will drive more men out of the national guard than anything in the world," Patterson commented, and he ended his report to General Creel by noting, "No objections were ever heard to the maneuvers, but loud denunciations on every hand regarding rations and heavy marching orders." Nearly all the officers, including Lieutenant Colonel William C. Treumann, commanding the regiment, and Colonel Melvin A. Hildreth, Inspector General, questioned the value of the camp. The regiment spent fifteen days away from home, five of them travel days. The War Department paid the entire cost of the trip and Treumann admitted that "This was the first brigade drill in which these battalions had ever participated." Nonetheless, Treumann, Hildreth, and others argued more could be accomplished in less time at Devils Lake if a battalion of regulars joined the North Dakota National Guard there. Major William R. Purdon, regimental ordnance officer, contended: "more people of the state see our guard when they are camped on their own grounds." This stimulated public interest and created "a sentiment in favor of better support of the Guard."

Thomas Poole, when adjutant general, arranged at state expense to have the 2nd Battalion, 6th United States Infantry, from Fort Lincoln, North Dakota, attend the 1907 camp at Devils Lake. The 2nd Battalion, commanded by Major R. R. Steedman, returned to Devils Lake in 1909. Two years later, a battalion of the 14th United States Infantry, which had replaced the 6th Infantry in garrison at Fort Lincoln, attended. No Army units attended state camps after 1911 because they were needed along the Mexican Border in Texas, New Mexico, and Arizona.

Despite the protests after the unhappy 1906 experience at Fort Russell, the North Dakota National Guard continued to attend joint camps. In 1908, the 1st Regiment traveled seventeen hundred miles to Tacoma, Washington, to join Guardsmen from Washington, Oregon, Idaho, and Montana in large-scale maneuvers with regular troops. The state paid only $1,000 of the total $38,500 cost of the trip. Colonel Samuel H. Nuchols, inspector general, believed "That this was in every respect the most profitable encampment in which the regiment ever participated." Lieutenant Colonel John H. Fraine took the regiment to Camp McCoy, Sparta, Wisconsin, for a ten-day camp in August 1910 with South Dakota Guardsmen and regular infantry, cavalry, and artillery units. Fraine, now a full colonel, led the regiment back to Sparta in 1914. He praised the regulars' enthusiasm and value as instructors but again questioned the expense and time involved when regular instructors could just as easily come to North Dakota. The only advantage Fraine could see to going out of state was "a change in terrain from the regular camp at Devils Lake."

Whether held in North Dakota or out of state, the annual training sessions required by the Dick Act were essential to the Guard's development. The camps brought the regiment together once each year, allowing regimental field and staff officers their only opportunity to exercise command and provide logistical support to the full regiment. Camp put enlisted men under the only sustained military discipline they would experience the entire year and provided the one opportunity many men had for extended target practice. As J. M. Amberson remembers, "Summer camp away from home taught us to be self-reliant. It was an adventure also." Annual camps brought state-wide attention to the Guard, particularly on Governor's Day when the commander in chief reviewed his troops and civilian visitors swarmed over the Devils Lake reservation.

National Guard supporters argued that, if given sufficient federal support in material and instruction, state soldiers could create and sustain viable military units capable of reinforcing the Army when war came. Short of war, annual training camps offered the best test of this assertion. The North Dakota experience suggests that before World War I the Guard fell considerably short of this promise. Many of the Guard's weaknesses were inherent in the nature of the system, but others were peculiar to North Dakota or to the personalities of individual Guardsmen.

Regular Army and National Guard field inspections revealed a consistent failure to improve training and readiness. In his 1904 field inspection, Major E. P. Andrus, 3rd United States Infantry, complimented the Guard for enthusiasm and willingness to learn but concluded that "The regiment is at present in no condition to participate in army manoeuvers, being now essentially a parade regiment." Regular inspectors at Fort Russell in 1906 and at the American Lake maneuvers in 1908 reported more favorably on the regiment. Still, in 1912, the Army inspector believed it would take at least a month of training before the regiment would be ready for field duty in case of war. His successor concluded in 1914 that "It is estimated that from 3 to 4 months would be necessary to fit the regiment to take the field as an effective force."

Companies arrived in camp barely able to perform close order drill. From private to captain, few could carry out simple extended order and skirmish drills. Battalion and regimental officers, with rare exceptions, proved ignorant of handling companies in higher-level tactical formations, and noncommissioned officers and privates knew little of the requirements of guard mount or sentry duty. Inevitably, the first few days of the one-week camp were devoted to reviewing the schools of the soldier, squad, and company. Field exercises involved nothing more complicated than a route march, an overnight bivouac, and a simulated trench defense. With the Dick Act just a year in operation, Major Andrus's 1904 observation that "In none of the drills or ceremonies was the proficiency satisfactory" was to be expected. Two years later, however, the Guard's inspector general, Colonel Hildreth, found camp guard duty "disreputable." Lieutenant Colonel Fraine reported that during the regiment's duty at Camp McCoy, Wisconsin, in 1910, far too many of his officers were "at a loss of what to do and how to do it." A year later, the federal inspector noted that "all the companies badly needed instruction" in close and extended order drill.

When Army instructors recommended a more demanding regimen in camp, even the usually strict John Fraine objected. He justified his instruction program for the 1911 camp, which Captain Amos H. Martin, 14th United States Infantry, mildly criticized. Guardsmen, Fraine explained, were amateur soldiers "working without hope of fee or reward and with tools not tempered for the work demanded." Regular soldiers did not understand the difficulties in recruiting Guardsmen, nor the necessity of operating a camp that would appeal to the amateur soldier. "There is no way of making him enlist, re-enlist, or even to stay in the guard unless he is 'pleased.'" A too demanding camp program would not "please" most Guardsmen and would drive them away. Fraine admitted many field problems "were considered of a kindergarten nature" and he intended "not to require too much at first." Because his men were "fresh from civil life," he kept training hours short and avoided close-order drill, the manual of arms, and other routine military duties, since they quickly became monotonous. Dull routine made it "increasingly difficult to secure enlistments or re-enlistments." Colonel Fraine based his camp program on the realities of National Guard service rather than Regular Army ideas. Some Guardsmen enlisted for "pure patriotism and love of the service....while curiosity is perhaps responsible for the balance....Unless the service is either made attractive or profitable," Fraine observed, few would join. "What might be best under other or different conditions would not be best in ours and our conditions and circumstances are the ones to be considered by us."

Army inspectors found National Guard camp discipline, including military courtesy, far too easygoing. For these professional soldiers the casual relations between Guard officers and enlisted men always remained "too familiar." One astonished regular reported that at the 1911 camp he saw men salute officers "with either hand as most convenient to them: also while having pipes, cigars, etc. in their mouths, and some of them while sitting down." Informality between officers and enlisted men had a long history in the militia and was not necessarily a military evil unless officers and men forgot completely the meaning of officers' shoulder boards. In 1906, on the ride to Fort Russell, liquor abounded on the train. "Some of the officers had also indulged," Lieutenant Colonel Treumann regretfully reported, "and the example set was not a good one." Colonel Hildreth's report was not regretful but scathing. "The discipline was bad," he noted, "and never will reach a high state...until a better example is set by the officers." Throughout the camp, too many officers were too "convivial and social with their men." Hildreth recounted a scene where officers and enlisted men passed a bottle around the campfire. Liquor and soldiers were old acquaintances, but shared drinking between officers and enlisted men invariably ruined discipline. Camp discipline and behavior improved considerably after 1906. Hildreth proudly stated that during the 1909 camp "never was there a time when better discipline was maintained in camp." Colonel Fraine quickly squelched drinking during the 1914 trip to Sparta, Wisconsin, by making sure there was "a greater effort on the part of officers...Pto keep the men to a high standard of sobriety and good behavior." The camp discipline of the North Dakota National Guard was, by all reports, as good as or better than other Guard organizations, particularly after Fraine assumed command of the regiment in 1911.

The 1st Regiment failed to evolve into a well-trained military organization largely because many Guardsmen could not or would not participate in the one-week annual camp. Attendance declined steadily in the first fifteen years of the twentieth century. At the 1902 training session, the first since 1894, ninety-one percent of the total strength came to camp. Attendance slowly dropped thereafter, with eighty-five percent present in 1904, seventy-six percent in 1911, and a mere fifty-four percent in 1914. Company B, Fargo, brought three officers, eight noncommissioned officers, and a mere seven privates in 1912. "A company with only seven privates is of no use to me or to the regiment," Fraine complained. He apologized for the poor showing in 1914, observing that the War Department set the dates for the last week of August, a most inconvenient time for North Dakotans. "This is a farming community, where the best efforts of every resident and working man...can take care of the harvest, which in August is at its height." Nonmilitary concerns inevitably intruded on what was a purely voluntary and uncompensated service. The regimental officers' poor attendance at the June 1912 school of instruction, for example, "was due to the fact that the primary elections were held in the state on June 26th, and a great many were candidates for office," instructor Captain Gideon H. Williams, 28th United States Infantry, explained.

North Dakota Guardsmen faced an obstacle to regular camp attendance which was common to the National Guard across the country. Employers were reluctant to give their employees time off for training purposes. A workingman faced the dilemma of losing a week's pay, or hiring a substitute to work for him, or, ultimately, losing his job, in order to attend camp. State law provided means to compel attendance, but Guard leaders were averse to using the authority. Heavy-handed application of the law would simply make it more difficult to recruit. Prior to the 1908 maneuvers at American Lake, regimental and staff officers attempted to persuade employers to release their men so the regiment could make a good showing. Still, one state newspaper noted, the officers "do not wish to get any of the boys into trouble with the employers." Military regulations allowed the adjutant general to grant furloughs from camp, but General Creel did not want the provision made common knowledge "as there are some that would likely go if they thought they had to." Colonel Hildreth proposed that the legislature pass a law "which will permit men who are under employment to attend without danger of being discharged." Railroad companies numbered among the most uncooperative employers, according to Colonel Fraine. He found this "strange," for "in the past all over the country, the railways have been only too eager to call on state troops for protection in time of trouble." Stranger still, Fraine noted, many heads of state agencies in Bismarck refused to release their employees who belonged to the Guard, though "knowing that the National Guard is part of the state government." Fraine heatedly argued that private and public employers needed to be educated in the true meaning of patriotism.

The refusal of mean-spirited employers to give their men time off for summer camp was a symptom of the Guard's inefficiency, not a major cause. Increased federal aid did not eliminate the underlying conditions that had determined the National Guard's performance since the territorial years. Military service remained a voluntary, part-time duty. Men continued to accept commissions or enlist for diverse reasons without much thought for the obligations related to state military service, above all to the time required for study and training at weekly armory drills and yearly field encampments. Since its origins in the 1880s, the North Dakota National Guard's greatest problem had been to recruit and retain enough qualified officers and enlisted men who would carry out the responsibilities of their commissions and enlistment contracts. This remained a problem during the first fifteen years of the twentieth century.

In the short run, the Dick Act actually reduced the number of men in the National Guard and failed to attract the totals anticipated for the long run. At the first federal inspection of the Guard in 1903, the War Department reported a total of 116,547 officers and enlisted men, a number that declined rapidly, reaching a low of 105,693 in 1907. By 1916, the aggregate for all states and territories reached 132,194. Over a period of fourteen years of active recruiting and the expenditure of millions of federal dollars, the states managed to add 15,647 officers and men, much to the War Department's disappointment. North Dakota never quite overcame the decline. Federal inspectors examined 806 Guardsmen in 1903, 703 in 1908, and only 629 in 1913, a decrease of 177 officers and men. The Guard recovered fairly quickly thereafter and for the entire period 1903-1916 lost only 16 men, with 790 inspected by the War Department in the latter year. The greatest loss was in officers, with 72 commissioned officers carried on the roster in 1903 and 55 in 1916.

North Dakota sought to maintain a full twelve-company infantry regiment as its major unit. The state mustered out the remnants of the old 1st Cavalry Battalion, Troop A of Dunseith, in September 1903. Lisbon's Light Battery A, with a history back to the Dakota Territorial Militia, struggled to remain active but failed, and it disbanded in early 1911. Thereafter the 1st Regiment of Infantry and the North Dakota National Guard were virtually synonymous. The companies that formed the 1st North Dakota Volunteers in 1898 comprised the heart of the regiment. Of the eight companies sent to the Philippines, only Company D of Devils Lake could not maintain its peacetime organization and broke up in 1906. The band at Lisbon, also with origins in the territorial Guard, was the only unit with a lineage to match the 1898 volunteer organizations. Companies were added to the 1st Regiment to replace those mustered out or to meet Regular Army organization as required by federal regulations. (See Table 4.2.)

TABLE 4.2

Organization of the North Dakota National Guard, 1900-1916

Unit	Home Station	Mustered In	Mustered Out
First Infantry			
Band	Lisbon	1887	
Machine Gun Co.	Grand Forks	1914	
Company A*	Bismarck	1884	
Company B*	Fargo	1884	
Company C*	Grafton	1886	
Company D*	Devils Lake	1892	1906
	Minot	1907	
Company E	Langdon	1898	1906
	Williston	1907	
Company F	Grand Forks	1900	1904
	Mandan	1907	
Company G*	Valley City	1885	
Company H*	Jamestown	1885b	
Company I*	Wahpeton	1897	
Company K*	Dickinson	1897	
Company L	Hillsboro	1898	
Company M	Ellendale	1898	1907
	Devils Lake	1908	1915
	Grand Forks	1915	
Hospital Corps (Detachment)	Lisbon	1911	
Cavalry			
Troop A	Dunseith	1887	1903
Artillery			
Battery A	Lisbon	1885	1911

*Unit in the 1st North Dakota Volunteer Infantry, 1898-1899.

Company H mustered out in August 1905, reorganized and mustered in, January 1906.

The quality and effectiveness of companies determined the regiment's efficiency. In the twentieth century, as in the 1890s, the companies constituted the focal point of recruitment, retention, and training of enlisted men. Only when they overcame the major nineteenth-century obstacles to stability would the Guard improve significantly. Unfortunately, the Dick Act offered little assistance to local units. Federal support ensured an adequate supply of uniforms, arms, and equipment and underwrote the major costs of yearly instruction camps. At best these served as indirect aids to recruitment. A company commander could now promise a potential recruit a decent uniform and a modern rifle and guarantee him a week in camp at regular army pay, but he could offer little else from the federal government. The ability of a National Guard recruiter to induce a young man to enlist depended upon his personality, the company's social composition, and the few available state benefits.

More than ever, local units needed decent armories. "An organization to be a success, must have a permanent home," Captain Frank Bolles, 6th United States Infantry, stressed in his 1907 inspection report. Each company must have "a place to keep its property, do its work, and to a great extent find recreation." With an attractive, well-equipped armory, the company commander had the opportunity to show an interested man where he would serve his military duty. Bolles supported his contention by noting that Valley City's Company G, the "only company in the state having a proper armory," also made the best showing during inspection. All other organizations rented buildings for armory purposes, "some good and some indifferent," according to General Miller in 1904.

Inspection reports suggested the indifferent greatly outnumbered the adequate. In 1906, H. M. Creel criticized Company K's Captain C. J. Phelan, Dickinson, for using the town's opera house as a part-time drill hall, but Dickinson had no other building fit for a meeting place. According to the federal inspection report for that same year, Bismarck's Company A rented a frame building for one night a week for drill purposes and had only one small room in which to store company property. In Fargo, Company B used a Masonic Temple as an armory. Captain J. C. McArthur, 28th United States Infantry, as inspector, waded through six inches of mud and water to reach Company E's rented armory in Langdon, a frame building twenty by forty feet with a leaky roof. Only the homes of Companies C, D, and G met McArthur's minimum standards. "The only practicable way for companies to get armories is to get either State or National assistance," Captain Bolles wrote. Companies used the state armory aid for rent or mortgage payments and to meet utility and maintenance costs, but the aid never sufficed.

After intense lobbying by National Guardsmen, the legislature passed the armory assistance act of 1907, which provided a five-thousand-dollar allotment to no more than thirteen organizations, with only one grant to any single county. Units receiving the appropriation had to deposit two thousand dollars "as evidence of good faith" and convey a deed for armory land to the state as well. The grant was, in effect, a permanent, interest-free loan not payable unless a unit disbanded. Three organizations would get the allotment in 1908 and two units each year thereafter until all thirteen elements (twelve infantry companies and the battery) benefited from the act. The law authorized the existing Board of Armory Supervisors, composed of the governor, adjutant general, and colonel of the 1st Regiment, to approve armory sites, building plans and specifications, and audit construction costs. The board would designate the order in which the money went to the companies and "take into consideration the proficiency of the military organization asking for aid, and its needs."

In 1908, Companies A, Bismarck; L, Hillsboro; and K, Dickinson, comprised the first units granted assistance. Five new armories were built by early 1909 for Battery A and Companies A, I, K, and L, and another three, for C, D, and H, were completed three years later. Since Company G already owned its building, it used the money to pay off its mortgage. Company M, Devils Lake, was mustered out in 1915 before obtaining state aid. By 1916, all companies were comfortably housed in new armories except Company F, Mandan, and the new Company M in Grand Forks. The *Adjutant General's Report For 1912* proudly printed pictures of nine new armories built since 1908. The next biennial report included a photograph of the finest armory in the state, that belonging to Fargo's Company B. Built at a cost of $110,000, it measured 90 by 140 feet and offered Fargo a fine auditorium as well as a home for Company B. The Fargo building represented best what Guardsmen expected of an armory. Colonel Samuel H. Nuchols, inspector general, explained in his 1908 report that the state wanted buildings that would last for years. First of all, they were to be places of military instruction but also "homes where...young men assemble and healthy, wholesome diversion is had, developing muscle, mind and character, by athletics, reading and writing," Nuchols wrote. He saw the armories, perhaps too grandly, as "dedicated to the universal good," as places of citizenship, as buildings adding to the 'city's architectural embellishment."

Significantly, as the cost of Fargo's armory dramatically suggested, the state's $5,000 contribution did not nearly suffice. Even the modest efforts in Hillsboro, at a cost of $14,000 for the exterior, or the total costs of $26,000 for Company H's armory at Jamestown were not covered by the legislature's largess. Consequently, as in the 1890s, individual units had to find ways to raise money. Most used a combination of public subscription, the sale of stock, and money borrowed from banks or individuals. Through great effort, the men of Company B collected $90,000 in gifts from Fargo citizens to pay for their building. Captain A. J. Osborn, of Dickinson's Company K, explained in detail to General Thomas Poole how his unit raised money in 1908. As soon as Osborn heard of the new law, he "began to talk Armory" to his men and the people of Dickinson. Company K already owned a lot. Osborn assumed that with the state's $5,000 grant and the annual $500 armory maintenance allotment, the unit needed to raise $5,000 by subscription, "not as a donation but as a loan without interest." They planned to repay the subscriptions by renting the armory to civilian groups. Incorporation as a military training school, under an 1897 law, exempted the lot and structure from property taxes.

Company K easily raised the $5,000 subscription, but "here is where the trouble started to come in large chunks." Their contractor estimated total costs for the exterior shell would range from $17,000 to $18,000. Local businessmen convinced Osborn not to reduce the size of the building in order to cut costs but to keep it usable as an auditorium for the town. Total costs, with plumbing, heating, electric lighting, and other amenities, came to $23,000. The company collected $10,000 in subscriptions, to be paid back "as fast as possible," took the state's $5,000, and borrowed $8,000 from the town mayor at eight percent for five years. Osborn told General Poole the company had a guaranteed annual income of $1,130 with which to repay the loan and subscriptions ($500 from the state, $450 rental from the Commercial Club for the upper story, and $180 from Osborn for storage space in the basement). The company planned to rent the hall for dances and other civil functions at $40 a night. Osborn's men agreed to do all janitorial work themselves rather than hire a man, "as the boys are willing," he explained, "to do most anything, now that we have got a nice building in order to get it paid for."

Major efforts to raise building funds illustrated the importance of a new armory to Guardsmen, but the effort often diverted attention from military work, and once they had the new buildings, many companies found it difficult to pay utility bills and maintenance costs. The North Dakota National Guard Association lobbied unsuccessfully for greater state aid, passing a resolution at its 1912 convention advocating an increase in the yearly allotment to a thousand dollars. The current allotment, the convention noted, was "scarcely sufficient to meet the running expenses of the buildings." The unanswered request forced companies to operate under severe budgetary constraint, leaving them financially weak. Although built with state assistance and privately raised local funds, the armories nonetheless indirectly resulted from the Dick Act. The state's refusal to assume greater responsibility for armories forced Guardsmen into fund raising and eroded unit stability and efficiency.

Armory construction only partially solved the companies' efforts to recruit enough men to meet federal requirements. In 1907, the War Department set the minimum company strength at fifty-eight noncommissioned officers and privates. Rarely did North Dakota's companies comply with the regulation. From 1907 through 1915, only in the latter year did a majority, seven of twelve, meet the minimum. Even in that year, Company L, Hillsboro, reported only thirty-nine men, and the Machine Gun Company at Grand Forks a mere twenty-four. The Guard approached compliance in 1915 largely because the Division of Militia Affairs, a section of the Army's General Staff, began to withdraw federal recognition from units not conforming to Division of Militia Affairs regulations. When a company lost recognition, the state forfeited a portion of its federal aid. If the state failed to reorganize or replace the condemned organization within six months, the regiment also was deprived of recognition. Division of Militia Affairs sanctions gave an extra push to recruiting.

Recruiting remained a serious problem in North Dakota for the same reasons as in the 1890s. Captain Frank Bolles, 6th United States Infantry, inspected the North Dakota National Guard in 1907 and informed the War Department that the fifty-eight-man minimum was too high "for a National Guard company of a State so sparsely settled as North Dakota." He could not see how the state could "comply with this requirement" and recommended a forty-man minimum until its population increased. Bolles's figure approximated the average company strength maintained from 1900 through 1914. A stable National Guard system had to have a substantial middle class living in towns and cities from which to recruit, and although the state's population doubled between 1900 and 1920 and its urban population increased nearly four hundred percent, North Dakota remained overwhelmingly rural.

TABLE 4.3

Populations of Towns and Cities (and Their Counties)
Serving as Home Stations for North Dakota National Guard Units, 1900, 1910, 1920

Town/City	Town/City Population			County	County Population			Unit
	1900	1910	1920		1900	1910	1920	
Bismarck	3,319	5,443	7,122	Burleigh	6,081	13,087	15,578	Company A
Devils Lake	1,729	5,157	5,140	Ramsey	9,198	15,199	15,427	Company D, 1900-1906; Company M, 1908-1915
Dickinson	2,076	3,678	4,122	Stark	7,621	12,504	13,542	Company K
Ellendale	750	1,389	1,334	Dickey	6,061	9,839	10,499	Company M, 1900-1907
Fargo	9,589	14,331	21,961	Cass	28,625	33,935	41,477	Company B
Grafton	2,378	2,229	2,512	Walsh	20,288	19,491	19,078	Company C
Grand Forks	7,652	12,478	14,010	Grand Forks	24,459	27,888	28,795	Company F, 1900-1904; Machine Gun Company, 1914-1916; Company M, 1915-1916
Hillsboro	1,172	1,237	1,183	Traill	13,107	12,545	12,210	Company L
Jamestown	2,853	4,358	6,627	Stutsman	9,143	18,189	24,575	Company H
Langdon	1,046	1,214	1,228	Cavalier	12,580	15,659	15,555	Company E, 1900-1906
Lisbon	1,046	1,758	1,855	Ransom	6,919	10,345	11,618	Band; Battery A, 1900-1911
Mandan	1,673	3,873	4,336	Morton	8,069	25,289	18,714	Company F, 1906-1916
Minot	1,277	6,188	10,476	Ward	7,961	25,281	28,811	Company D, 1907-1916
Valley City	2,446	4,606	4,686	Barnes	13,159	18,066	18,678	Company G
Wahpeton	2,228	2,467	3,069	Richland	17,387	19,659	30,887	Company I
Williston	763	3,124	4,178	Williams	1,530	14,234	17,980	Company E, 1907-1916

SOURCE: United States Census Bureau.

In 1900, ninety-three percent of all North Dakotans lived in rural areas. Twenty years later, when the Census Bureau reported for the first time that a majority of Americans lived in urban areas, eighty-six percent of North Dakota citizens still resided in the countryside. (See Table 4.3.)

Sympathetic federal inspectors recognized this constraint on recruiting. Captain J. C. McArthur criticized Company K in 1906 for low enrollment and for enlisting "too many young boys," but, he conceded, Dickinson was "small and suitable material is scarce." McArthur also admitted that Captain Barney C. Boyd, Company L, Hillsboro, was "badly handicapped" in recruiting because of the "size of the town, which is very small." Already at a disadvantage because of a limited manpower pool for recruits, captains encountered further restrictions in the admonitions from adjutants general to enlist only certain kinds of men. In 1907 General Creel advised the captain of Minot's new Company D to "select only young men of good moral character and physical condition whose vocation...will not interfere with their performance of the military duty required as members of the National Guard." A town with less than three thousand did not make it easy to find fifty-eight morally correct young men with stable occupations.

North Dakota's economy, still dominated by wheat farming, continued to hamper recruiting. Railroading was the only "industrial" activity of any significance. Both farming and railroad work offered a great deal of seasonal work and employed many transients. Few semiskilled and unskilled farm and railroad workers had the time or money to indulge in the National Guard. General Creel advised captains not to enlist men whose jobs prevented them "from performing requisite amount of military [work], this will include railroad men." Enlistment offered few benefits beyond exemption from the poll tax and jury duty. The men who enlisted did so because a friend recruited them, or, as J. M. Amberson, who joined Bismarck's Company A in 1913, recalled, because they thought of belonging to the Guard as a "status symbol." Most privates were single, between the ages of eighteen and twenty-five, and worked as laborers, farmers, or clerks, or were students. Although the law permitted young men from eighteen to twenty-one to enlist with parental consent, many boys of sixteen and seventeen signed up. Despite federal and state inspectors' frequent complaints on underage boys in the companies, the adjutant general's office made no effort to stop the enlistments.

Company commanders too often attempted to fill their units just prior to federal inspection or summer camp. Thereafter, many recruits lost interest. New men quickly became "dilatory and negligent about attending the stated drills," S. H. Nuchols, inspector general, complained in 1908, adding that he wanted a law that made failure to attend drill a misdemeanor, punishable "according to the criminal procedure of the state." Many absentees, who were no longer active in their units, had simply left town without notifying their captains. Too often company commanders were "sadly deficient in their official records," to quote General Creel, with many units fifteen to twenty percent under their reported enrollments. A busy captain found it extremely difficult to keep track of the frequent departures made by his less economically stable enlisted men.

TABLE 4.4

Absentee Rate, Federal Armory Inspections,
North Dakota National Guard, 1903-1915

Year	Percent Absent
1903	31.1
1904	15
1905	23
1906	19.4
1907	21.5
1908	16
1909	9.8
1910	16.8
1911	16.3
1912	20.2
1913	Not Available
1914	12
1915	5.8

SOURCES: *Annual Reports Of The War Department*, 1903 through 1908, and *Annual Reports Of The Division of Militia Affairs*, 1909-1916.

Enlisted men often neglected the single most important armory meeting of the year, the federal inspection. Attendance varied greatly between 1903 and 1915. (See Table 4.4.) Individual companies made poorer showings than the Guard as a whole. Company B turned out 53 percent in 1907, and Company D, Minot, reported only 25 of its 52 enlisted men in 1912. Valley City's Company G compiled the best attendance record for federal inspections, but even this stalwart organization had a 24 percent absentee rate that same year. The better captains sought ways to compel reluctant members to attend weekly drill, for example, Captain Harold Sorenson, Company B, threatened to publish absentees' names in Fargo papers, but with little effect. Attendance at inspections and regular drills improved markedly in 1915, chiefly because a new state law permitted the court-martial of officers and enlisted men ''for non-attendance or tardiness at any drill, parade, encampment, inspection...each day being a separate offense.'' It allowed a ten-dollar fine or five days in the county jail for each conviction. Absenteeism at the 1915 inspection fell to 6 percent, the lowest rate since 1903. Companies H and I had 100 percent attendance. The law came too late to give the regiment an experienced rank and file. When called to federal service in 1916, it had only 21 of 832 privates (2.4 percent) with more than two years' service. Noncommissioned officers had more experience than the privates, though far short of what the Regular Army expected of such leaders. The majority of noncommissioned officers, 141 (61.4 percent), had enlisted between 1911 and 1915. Over 20 percent, 50 noncommissioned officers, joined between January and June 1916.

Guardsmen drilled once a week for an hour and a half, a total of seven hours a month or seventy-eight hours a year. Even those who attended regularly were poorly trained, and high absenteeism and a large annual turnover kept companies inefficient. Ten years after the Dick Act took effect, the 1913 federal inspection indicated that the Guard's training remained elementary. The inspector's comments on several companies included these observations: "not well drilled"; "privates did not do their work well"; officers and noncommissioned officers not "well instructed in drill." Leroy Goodwater recalled, "back in 1914-15-16, our training consisted of close order drill." According to J. M. Amberson, Company A spent most of its time on "Squad drills in our Armory. It stressed good team work and precision movement on command." Company training never advanced beyond the parade evolutions. When John Fraine took command of the regiment in 1911, he instituted an annual competition for the "Colonel's Trophy," hoping to stimulate military efficiency through company competition, as the units would be judged on their state and federal inspection performances. "I believe it will be a matter of the greatest company pride," he informed the regiment, "to have been the winner of this trophy at least once." His efforts failed, for in 1916 the federal inspector found four companies and the Machine Gun Company so inefficient he placed them on probation, and the War Department withdrew recognition of Mandan's Company F.

Several companies had collapsed in the previous twelve years. Company F, Grand Forks, went under in 1904 after its armory fund drive failed. It did not drill once from the end of camp in July to the first of December. "As a result," its captain wrote, "Co. F is but little more than a company in name and on paper." The state disbanded units at Langdon (Company E) and Ellendale (Company M) when those small towns could not sustain their memberships. The federal inspector reported that Company E had no drill hall or records and that its captain came to drill irregularly, and, he concluded, the company "is utterly and hopelessly inadequate in every essential." Devils Lake's inability to support a company despite its population of five thousand and proximity to the state military reservation puzzled state and federal inspectors. Company D failed there in 1906 and Company M, mustered in two years later, was disbanded in 1915. In the latter year the federal inspector found that sixteen of the unit's forty-one enlisted men came from the little village of Webster (population three hundred), ten miles north of Devils Lake. "Not a squad in the company could form a skirmish line without hopeless confusion" during the inspection. Battery A, with signs of instability as early as 1906, lasted until 1911 largely because state officials wanted to save one of the old territorial units. It drilled for years without artillery pieces. Captain J. C. McArthur, Regular Army, said it was "remarkable and praiseworthy that so strong an organization has been maintained" without guns or an armory. When the battery did not improve, the federal inspector recommended disbandment in 1910. Governor John Burke reluctantly issued an executive order in February 1911 disbanding Battery A, he said, "with a feeling of sincere regret...but the requirements of the War Department leave no alternative."

Adjutants general blamed company commanders for these failures. Captains too frequently neglected their administrative duties, and "In many cases but little or no attention is paid to directions from this office," General Thomas Poole complained in 1908. His successor, Amasa P. Peake, hoped future adjutants general would not "be hampered by the negligence of company commanders" as he had been. During his tenure, Heber M. Creel sent out a steady stream of letters, often tactless and sarcastic, demanding that captains attend to their duties. He lambasted Company K's captain for failing to submit reports and performing poorly at the federal inspection. "The War Department will not tolerate this condition," Creel warned, a condition which "has materially increased tending to the still further inefficiency of your command." He blasted Captain Thomas H. Tharalson, Company C, "for negligence in military affairs since you have been captain," negligence "so gross" that Creel felt it necessary "to ask for [his] resignation." The general offered little sympathy to Captain Frank Ross on the demise of Langdon's Company E, saying, "I am sorry that you have drifted with the company to its present condition. It is entirely your own fault." Even when dealing with an old acquaintance, whose marriage and company command suffered due to his alcoholism, Creel lacked compassion: "The National Guard cannot succeed with such captains, as you admit yourself...to be utterly unfit for command." He added unnecessarily, "The present condition of Company D is due to you. Further comment is unnecessary."

Creel's self-righteous chiding failed to improve company administration. A graduate of West Point with five years in the Regular Army and a reputation as a political gadfly forever tilting at the windmills of Alexander McKenzie's political machine, Creel was hardly the best man to reform the National Guard. His heavy-handed, by-the-book demands for attention to duty did not conform to the Guard's tradition of informality. Furthermore, Creel ignored the obvious evidence that captains contended with deep-rooted problems, which no amount of attention to administrative detail would overcome. A lack of money contributed greatly, as did the enormous difficulty in recruiting reliable enlisted men. The very nature of Guard service--voluntary, uncompensated, part-time--was the central cause of inefficiency and instability.

Some Guard leaders acknowledged this. Colonel Melvin Hildreth criticized company commanders for their failures but added, "It is hard for captains to take charge of companies for no compensation, and then spend their time looking over matters of detail...but this is what a captain must do if he does his full duty." Colonel Fraine as well understood the demands of Guard service, which fell on men whose first obligations lay with their jobs and families. The only compensation responsible officers received was the "consciousness of having done the best that is in them." Knowing that, Fraine went on, meant no one should accept a commission "who is not fully conscious of the responsibilities" of officership, and "who is not willing *to make any necessary effort* to qualify himself for the proper performance of his duties" (emphasis added). That was asking a great deal of the average businessman or professional with a passing interest in military affairs who took a commission in the National Guard. The weight of command lay with company officers, not field-grade officers at the battalion or regimental levels. Battalion and regimental officers took the field once a year for summer camp and occasionally visited company home stations for inspection purposes. The Guard's decentralized nature put the burden of service on officers of the lower grades, where the men were younger and less experienced.

Company officers' deficiencies went uncorrected because persisting nineteenth- century practices complicated reform. North Dakota's military code continued to permit the election of lieutenants and captains, and no one questioned the need to modify or eliminate this tradition. In a rare public comment on elections, Colonel S. H. Nuchols mused that "The enlisted men of a company do not always use wisdom in selecting their company officers." Curiously, this military system placed the quality of its officers solely in the hands of its enlisted men. The military code also maintained the civil associations so predominant in company affairs before 1900. Civil organizations were vital to recruiting, as they stressed social activities, and crucial to a unit's fiscal health, for they conducted company fund raising. State law allowed companies to expel enlisted men who violated the associations' bylaws upon a majority vote. Not surprisingly, company officers tended to ignore the chain of command and regulations when they so regularly operated in an atmosphere of informality and club rules.

Captain Frank C. Bolles, a federal inspector of the National Guard, unexpectedly offered the most reasonable justification for electing officers. It was, he argued, "the best method...in fact the only method I see that is practicable." Given the casual nature of the Guard, Bolles thought election was "prima facie evidence" that officers had "the confidence and esteem" of their enlisted men. The enlisted men often made sound selections. Those companies that had gone to the Philippines consistently elected veterans as their captains as long as they were active. Most of the companies honored seniority, choosing the incumbent first lieutenant to the captaincy when a vacancy occurred. Much greater continuity existed among captains during the 1900-1916 period than in the 1890s. Captain Barney C. Boyd took command of Company L in 1902 and led it to the Mexican Border in 1916. A number of captains remained in command for ten years, including Gilbert C. Grafton, Company B; Thomas H. Tharalson, Company C; James M. Hanley, Company F (Mandan); and Frank S. Henry, Company G. All but Boyd left their companies to accept promotion to major and command of a battalion.

Company officers impressed federal inspectors during armory inspections. Inspectors expressed their impressions, which amounted to just that and not detailed examinations of the captains' military knowledge and experience, in social terms. They sprinkled their reports with phrases such as: "A young man of excellent standing in the community"; representative of "the best element in town"; and other generalized statements. Captain Bolles summarized the Army officers'' assessment of company officers: "I find they represent most of the professions and some of the trades, and as a general thing, have high standing in the communities in which they reside." Army inspectors rarely spent more than a day with each unit during inspection, seldom having the opportunity to judge the quality of company commanders. Given the nature of the National Guard, it was not incorrect to assess officers on a social basis. Bolles believed that Guard leadership depended upon, "among other qualities, a great amount of tact." Discipline in the Guard, he added, rested "to a great extent upon the application of this quality." He favored enlisted men's election of their officers because they would choose the most tactful men to organize and lead them.

While Bolles, a regular, supported the elective process and an indirect disciplinary approach, many in the Guard called for more formality and stricter discipline. Dick Act mandates and War Department regulations increased pressure on the National Guard for greater efficiency, which in turn made it necessary to improve the officer corps. Inspector general and Colonel M. A. Hildreth, dismayed with the rowdyism during the 1906 Fort Russell trip, complained that the Guard had "never been subjected to the discipline" it needed. He recognized the difficulty in drawing "the line between the social status of an officer and a private" but saw little hope of improvement until officers were selected for reasons other than their "sociability." General Creel wrote Assistant Secretary of War Robert Oliver that until officers received federal pay and were "in some way brought more directly under the immediate control of the War Department...the guard could not pass muster under the militia law."

Two basic issues were involved here. One pertained to managing company affairs. Conditions in the companies would remain the same until the state or federal government provided enough money to make units more than semi-independent, self-supporting social clubs. Sufficient government funding might then be used to modify or end the election system. The second issue concerned officers' military knowledge and leadership skills. State law required each officer to pass an examination "as to his knowledge of military affairs, and general knowledge and physical and other fitness for service" when commissioned or promoted. In practice, the inspector general merely commented on new field officers' qualifications and administered tests only to newly elected lieutenants and captains.

Perfunctory at best, the exams were usually conducted through the mail, making them, in General Creel's words, "in a majority of cases, a mere farce." The inspector general used a great deal of discretion in making his recommendations. For instance, Colonel Hildreth examined a candidate for second lieutenant to serve in Williston's new Company E in the spring of 1907. The young man admitted, Hildreth said, "that he knows little or nothing about military service," but since this was a new unit and "The Captain and First Lieutenant do not know much more," he approved the candidate. Hildreth continually damned the examination-by-mail practice and favored a difficult written exam taken in the inspector general's presence. He accepted the fact that Guard officers lacked the time and opportunity to become as knowledgeable as regular officers but believed "there should be some incentive for officers to study the books." Passing a challenging exam should provide the incentive.

When Hildreth attempted to maintain minimum standards, he provoked anger from all sides. In September 1907, the colonel examined Wayne G. Eddy, Fargo, second lieutenant-elect for Company B. Eddy failed the exam, and, Hildreth said, since "He has never had one hour's military service," he refused to recommend him for a commission. Captain Gilbert C. Grafton, commanding

Company B, and Captain G. Angus Fraser, quartermaster of the 1st Regiment, protested the decision to the adjutant general, Thomas Poole. They argued that despite Eddy's lack of military experience, Company B, "badly run down," needed his enthusiasm, intelligence, and "the necessary standing in the city to help build up the company." When Poole asked Hildreth to reconsider, the latter vehemently rejected the request, taking exception to Poole's interference and calling it a "marked discourtesy," one based on social and political concerns. The inspector general explained he was attempting to "raise the standard, if possible, amongst the officers, non-commissioned officers and privates of the National Guard" and would not succumb to pressure from the adjutant general and two socially ambitious captains. Eddy did not have "the slightest qualifications in the world for a commissioned officer" and would get no recommendation.

Poole asked Governor John Burke to overrule Hildreth. The governor did so, commissioning Eddy. Grafton and Fraser, both long active in the National Guard and veterans of the Philippine Insurrection, remained captives of the old militia style. They particularly disagreed with Hildreth's criticism that Eddy had never served in the ranks of Company B. Grafton noted that his men had reached outside the unit to elect new blood and revive recruiting. Current members, Fraser pointed out, "did not feel they could equip themselves properly" as an officer. Most important, Fraser said, Hildreth's "personal opinion in regard to electing a civilian to the place has nothing to do with the matter, as the law provided that each company shall elect their officers." Curiously, Grafton and Fraser consistently ignored the obvious: Eddy had failed the exam, the fact always uppermost in Hildreth's mind. The incident, involving one of the Guard's oldest, most stable units and two of its best officers, revealed the underlying weakness of the Guard at the level where quality counted the most.[1]

The exam system failed to produce an educated officer corps. Adjutant general Creel declared in his 1906 report that most North Dakota National Guard officers "are ignorant and careless and entirely indifferent to the duties of their profession." Several officers displeased Lieutenant Colonel John Fraine when he took the 1st Regiment to Camp McCoy, Wisconsin, in 1910. These men "hardly come up to my ideas of fitness in either capacity or instruction," he commented. The demands of National Guard service, he declared, made it evident "the time has come to raise the standard of efficiency of the officers." The Guard needed a systematic program of officer instruction, an idea first suggested by Colonel Hildreth in 1907. Most officers were intelligent, capable men who needed guidance and motivation in their military studies. The opportunity came in 1911 when the War Department assigned Regular Army officers as permanent inspector-instructors to each state National Guard. Captain Gideon H. Williams, 28th United States Infantry, served as the North Dakota National Guard's first inspector-instructor. Williams developed a correspondence school in which officers submitted written solutions to map and tactical problems, then took an exam covering the entire course.

139

Table 4.5
Company Officer Participation in Correspondence Schools

Number completing	1911-1912			1912-1913			1913-1914		
	100%	50%	0%	100%	50%	0%	100%	50%	0%
Captains	10	1	4	3	1	11	4	4	8
First lieutenants	8	3	2	1	2	10	4	3	9
Second lieutenants	5	2	4	3	0	11	2	2	7

Captain Williams conducted correspondence schools during the winter of 1911-1912 and 1912-1913, and his successor, Lieutenant F. H. Turner, oversaw a school in the winter 1913-1914. Among the field officers, three of five did all the work for Williams as did four of five under Lieutenant Turner. Company officers were far less attentive to school duties. (See Table 4.5). Understandably, Captain Williams was highly disappointed with the sharp drop in participation during his second school season. Adjutant General William C. Treumann believed this occurred because "it takes too much time away from their business, after attending to their other military duties, giving little time for social enjoyments or recreation." Williams thought he could explain the decline in part because "the novelty has worn off," he said, but largely because the state had no means to force officers to do their work. This well-meaning regular saw little prospect for improvement in the Guard's efficiency until the state adopted a law "whereby the work of the enrolled militia will be compulsory and not voluntary as it is now." Spotty attendance at special camps of instruction in the summers of 1911 and 1912 also suggested that officers did not take seriously the need to spend time on military study.

Guard officials, by dint of lengthy correspondence, occasionally forced an officer to complete schoolwork. Major Thomas H. Tharalson, commanding 2nd Battalion, failed to submit all of his 1911-1912 lessons. After Williams wrote him several unanswered letters, he turned to Colonel Fraine. Fraine then wrote Tharalson a number of times, and when the major ignored these letters, the colonel asked General Treumann to discipline Tharalson. The major finally responded to the adjutant general's threats in a lengthy letter outlining a complex set of work and family obligations that took up all his time. He had little opportunity for National Guard work, pointing out: "I have neither rich parents or pull to get anything for me." The Guard, he complained, was made up of two types of men, "those with means so they do not have to work and the others those that have neither money or jobs to sacrifice." Further, he added, "We are asked to do too much for the allowances we get." Tharalson at last grudgingly submitted his work. Guard officials had few other means to force officers to complete correspondence work. Colonel Fraine and Adjutant General I. A. Berg agreed in 1914 to withhold the annual twenty-dollar clothing allowance from neglectful officers. Even the usually demanding Fraine, however, decided that if a man attended to his company or staff work throughout the year, "the failure to perform the required school work...might very well be overlooked."

Major Tharalson erred in charging that the idle rich and the indolent poor made up the officer corps. North Dakota had precious few of the former and the Guard had none. Poor men rarely served as enlisted men, let alone as officers. Tharalson reflected fairly accurately the average officer's background. Appointed postmaster of Grafton by President Theodore Roosevelt, he held that post for eight years, then served as deputy state treasurer for two years (1912-1914), all the while operating a real estate and insurance business in Grafton. The majority of his colleagues earned their livings meeting the financial, legal, medical, and merchandise needs of farmers in towns scattered across the state. Only five of the fifty-four officers in the 1st Regiment called to federal service in 1916 were farmers. Like Tharalson, many captains and field officers actively participated in politics, holding a variety of part- or full-time county and state positions. Colonel Fraine, a lawyer, served three terms in the House, the last from 1913 to 1915 as speaker, and then as lieutenant governor during Governor Louis B. Hanna's second term. Captain Dana Wright, later a major, worked full time as sheriff of Stutsman County. Tharalson differed from the majority of his peers only in that he had been born in Norway, and not the United States. Even here, other key Guard leaders such as William C. Treumann, John Fraine, and Gilbert C. Grafton were foreign born. The professionals, merchants, and working politicians who composed the North Dakota National Guard's officer corps were, in General Treumann's words, "no leisure class...who might follow the military profession as a pastime."

Many officers were willing to stay in the National Guard a long time. Nearly all the field officers, even in 1916, were Philippine Island veterans. The Guard granted promotion strictly by seniority above the grade of captain. With only five line positions available in the regiment, those who aspired to higher command waited patiently for promotion. (See Table 4.6.) Their lengthy service at the company level before reaching field grade led battalion and regimental officers, perhaps understandably, to be forgiving of company officers' informalities.

These men cared for the Guard, and the majority worked in their own way to improve it. Those in the state legislature introduced and carefully shepherded to passage the few bills an otherwise indifferent body saw fit to pass. The officers, led by General Elliott Miller, formed the North Dakota National Guard Association in 1901 to further service interests. Unlike most state associations, the association accepted enlisted men "to be elected annually by their respective organizations." It also spearheaded most changes in military law, including periodic revision of the code, the armory support law of 1907, and increases in the state's militia appropriation. It lobbied successfully from 1911 on to gain the state congressional delegation's support for a federal militia pay bill.

A willingness to serve for many years did not ensure a well-trained, adequately instructed officer corps. Regular Army inspectors made some attempt to assess the quality of North Dakota National Guard officers in their brief armory and summer camp visits, a few officers earning praise from the regulars. Captain J. C. McArthur, for instance, reported in 1906 that Captain Grafton was "possessed of more than ordinary zeal in military matters." Only

TABLE 4.6

Field Officers, 1st Regiment, Infantry
North Dakota National Guard, 1900-1916

	Years in Grade	Date of Original Appointment
Colonel		
Amasa P. Peake	1900-1908	1885
William. C. Treumann*	1909-1910	1887
John H. Fraine*	1911-1916	1887
Lieutenant-Colonel		
William C. Treumann*	1900-1909	
John H. Fraine*	1909-1910	
Invald A. Berg*	1911-1912	1889
Thomas H. Tharalson*	1913-1914	1889
Gilbert C. Grafton*	1915-1916	1885
Major		
First Battalion		
Frank White*	1900-1901	1892
Frederick Keye*	1902-1906	1886
William R. Purdon*	1907-1912	1897
Frank S. Henry*	1913-1916	1894
Second Battalion		
John Fraine*	1900-1908	
Charles F. Mudgett*	1909-1910	1890
Thomas H. Tharalson*	1911-1912	
Dana Wright*	1913-1916	1898
Third Battalion		
Invald A. Berg*	1900-1910	
Gilbert C. Grafton*	1911-1914	
James Hanley	1915-1916	1906

*Served in the 1st North Dakota Volunteer Infantry, 1898-1899.

one man consistently caught the attention of federal inspectors, however--
John H. Fraine. After the 1904 camp, Major E. P. Andrus, 3rd United States
Cavalry, submitted a confidential report on North Dakota officers to the War
Department, a report not seen in the state. Andrus singled out Major Fraine
as the only officer in the regiment ''well fitted to hold a field officer's
commission'' in United States Volunteers. Fraine regularly warranted the
acclaim of federal inspectors thereafter. Captain Gideon Williams considered
him, in 1912, ''qualified in every way to command a brigade,'' that is, to

hold a brigadier general's commission in the volunteers. Inspectors did not condemn other officers out of hand, but neither did they commend them as they did Fraine. After the 1913 Devils Lake camp, Lieutenant F. H. Turner reported that the colonel "was commanding officer in every respect," with "marked ability" to administer and discipline a military camp. "His ideas along this line are right and he is not afraid to enforce them."

John Fraine was not a charismatic leader. His reserved, austere personality, perhaps reflecting his English nativity, did not encourage backslapping and first-name relations. The colonel's integrity, his insistence on attention to duty and personal responsibility, gave the 1st Regiment a quality it otherwise would not have had. He led by setting a personal example of what a citizen-soldier ought to be, and his fellow officers knew it. When, in 1913, Fraine had the opportunity to go on the retired list with promotion to brigadier general, the regiment unanimously petitioned him to remain on active duty, a request the colonel acceded to. Fraine's influence on the National Guard lasted beyond his years of active service. The officers of the Guard gave him the North Dakota National Guard Medal of Merit in 1938, when the first and second lieutenants of pre-World War I years now served as generals, colonels, and majors. Brigadier General David L. Ritchie, 34th Division, applauded Fraine for the high standards, strict discipline, and stress on efficiency he had set so many years ago. "Truly he is the daddy of us all," General Ritchie toasted, and surely he was.

Although Fraine affected the North Dakota National Guard in many ways, he did not take command of the 1st Regiment until 1911, and only then could he impose his stamp on the organization. Furthermore, one man, a part-time soldier in command of a widely scattered organization that came together infrequently, could achieve only so much. The National Guard needed an adjutant general who was himself more than a part-time Guardsman. This became especially important with the passage of the Militia Law of 1903 and the War Department's growing demands for compliance with its rules and regulations. A full-time administrator with broad authority working from a central office could give the service a unity of purpose. Unfortunately, North Dakota lacked a permanent office for the military department as well as a full-time adjutant general. Until I. A. Berg agreed to move to Bismarck and keep regular office hours during his tenure, 1913-1914, adjutanTts general lived at their own homes. They oversaw routine Guard affairs through the mail, coming to Bismarck only when necessary. Berg moved to the capital in response to a 1912 North Dakota National Guard Association resolution "that it is the sense of this convention that in the future the Adjutant General reside at Bismarck."

Appointees to the adjutant generalcy were not expected to give up their businesses or occupations. The state allocated one thousand dollars in annual salary, plus a nine-hundred-dollar office expense allowance, an amount insufficient to lure most men to Bismarck. Captain George R. Armstrong, a retired military officer, served as the governor's military secretary from May 1908 to February 1908. He was followed by Major R. R. Steedman. These advisers looked after the adjutant general's daily correspondence, advised the governor and adjutant general on military matters, and explained the intricacies of War Department red tape. They did not make policy.

An absentee adjutant general with no permanent staff had little opportunity to develop or implement a long-term improvement program. Adjutants general had little power to demand or force obedience to their plans in any event, as endless struggles with negligent company commanders indicated. During his argument with General Poole over commissioning Wayne Eddy, Colonel Hildreth defiantly told his nominal superior, "You have no authority to order me or any other officer or man in the National Guard of the state. You are *simply* the Adjutant General of the State, the head of a Department" (emphasis added). Poole did not argue the point. State law provided that the colonel commanding the regiment "shall be responsible to the governor for the general efficiency of the National Guard," including drill, instruction, and small arms practice. Effectively, the provision left the adjutant general with little authority over line units.

Heber M. Creel, adjutant general, 1905-1906, attempted to use federal law and War Department regulations as a means, perhaps, more accurately, as a club, to improve the Guard. "The National Guard of this state will comply with the requirements of the War Department as long as I am in charge," he informed one officer. Creel warned Colonel Amasa Peake of the dire consequences "if the superior officers" did "not perform their duty." To staff and line officers alike, he sent the same message: "It is needless to call...attention to the fact that unless there is a marked change in the Guard...our Federal appropriations will be discontinued." General Creel recognized the Guard's weaknesses: it "needs more money and instruction" and strong central direction, he remarked. He suggested that a retired Army officer take the adjutant generalcy, for he could provide military expertise yet remain "untrammeled by local political influence."

Creel's reform efforts failed. A tactless man burdened with too much self-importance, he rarely generated loyalty or cooperativeness in his subordinates because of his heavy-handed letters and blunt criticisms. More importantly, Creel failed because he conceived the Guard in narrow terms. Again and again he justified compliance with War Department regulations solely to obtain federal grants, but annual militia grants rarely put federal dollars in Guardsmen's pockets. The government gave the states military equipment in order to make the National Guard a viable reserve. Neither Creel nor other adjutants general used the reserve function to encourage Guardsmen's cooperation. Guard service had a purpose beyond piling up tents, mess kits, overcoats, and other equipment in the state storehouse. Had the average Guardsman been educated as to his role as a soldier, and appeals made to his obligation to serve, the Guard might have reached a more efficient level.

Even if Creel had articulated a sound reform program, his impact would have been short-lived. Frustrated by the absence of regimental promotion (Amasa Peake and William Treumann had been colonel and lieutenant colonel respectively since 1895), battalion and company officers worked to gain a law in 1905, which greatly affected the adjutant generalcy. The statute provided that all appointments to head the military department, that is, adjutant general, inspector general, chief of supply, must come from field and company officers. It set their terms at two years, after which the incumbent went on the retired list. The 1909 military code stipulated that the governor must offer the adjutant generalcy to the "officer highest in rank [from the line only] who will accept such appointment." Another change made retirement at age sixty-four mandatory for all officers. The men who backed the changes correctly assumed that the regimental colonel would accept the appointment and its concomitant promotion to brigadier general. Only John Fraine spurned the post, in 1913, and it then went to his second in command, Lieutenant Colonel I. A. Berg.

The laws cleared the way for promotion and allowed several long-service captains to gain their majorities. Reform, however, did not improve the adjutant generalcy. Regardless of ability or interest, the regiment's senior officer automatically took the post every two years, unless, as in the case of Colonel Fraine, the eligible candidate passed it up. If the system happened to produce a leader of ability, energy, and foresight, it forced him to retire before achieving significant change. The adjutant general, as the more successful state systems of the era indicated, constituted the key to an effective National Guard. He had to have the time and skills to win support from his governor and legislature and the opportunity to convince Guardsmen to accept a long-term improvement program. Continuity was essential to National Guard leadership at the top but impossible in North Dakota. (See Table 4.7.)

TABLE 4.7
Adjutants General, 1900-1916

Name	Years in Office
Elliott S. Miller	1900-1915
Heber M. Creel	1905-1906
Thomas H. Poole	1907-1908
Amasa P. Peake	1909-1910
William C. Treumann	1911-1912
Invald A. Berg	1913-1914
Thomas H. Tharalson	1915-1916

Thomas Poole challenged the retirement law's constitutionality when his term ended in January 1909. Both the state constitution and military code stated, to quote the 1905 code, "no commissioned officer shall be removed from office except by sentence of court martial." Poole argued the constitution overrode any subsequent law affecting tenure of office or mandatory retirement. When Governor John Burke announced his intention to appoint Amasa Peake to the adjutant generalcy, Poole countered with his own announcement that he refused to vacate the position. Guardsmen complicated the incident when company officers presented Governor Burke a petition requesting Poole's retention. North Dakota National Guard Association actions caused even more confusion. Meeting in Mandan on 6 and 7 January 1909, the association endorsed Poole and resolved that the military code be amended to allow Guard officers to elect the adjutant general. Only John Fraine, a major at the time, publicly dissented from the resolution. Otherwise, these were the same officers who had lobbied for the retirement law in the first place.

Partisan politics had much to do with Poole's actions. Originally elected in 1906, John Burke was the first Democrat to win the governor's chair in North Dakota, with the solid backing of reform minded Republicans. A "stalwart" Republican, Tommy Poole, as the newspapers called him, had a long affiliation with Alexander McKenzie's machine. Governor E. Y. Sarles, also a McKenzie adherent, appointed Poole literally an hour before Burke took office in 1907, noting, on the general's commission, "for a term two years from date." The stalwarts assumed the machine would oust Burke in 1908 and, in the meantime, saddle him with General Poole and save the adjutant generalcy for another Republican in 1909.

The political manipulators underestimated Burke on two counts. First, he won re-election in 1908. Second, when Poole refused to resign and added insult to injury by removing records from the adjutant general's office, Governor Burke ordered him arrested and court-martialed. The adjutant general appealed to the State Supreme Court, alleging that the governor had no power under the Constitution to replace him. The Court sustained Burke. Poole's court-martial met in Bismarck for two weeks in late January and early February 1909, amidst considerable public fanfare and press attention. The court-martial board found him guilty of conduct unbecoming an officer and refusing to obey his commander in chief, and it sentenced him to dismissal from the National Guard.

Poole's actions did little to enhance the Guard's reputation. He had little interest in furthering a reform program and merely sought to keep the adjutant generalcy. As one newspaper observed, "The state guard, in that it has to some extent aided and abetted Poole, has lost prestige with the people of the state and is the object of criticism." Why the officers took a position in the argument remains unclear, although few were Democrats or reform Republicans. Rarely had Guardsmen allowed their purely political affiliations to affect their behavior in National Guard matters. North Dakota's political system was undergoing a major change at this time, as the McKenzie machine slowly dissolved after years of dominance. Guardsmen apparently could not resist entering the fight. Some newspapers hinted that Poole's successor, Colonel Amasa Peake, was generally disliked throughout the Guard, and officers preferred the politically active Poole to the unpopular Peake. The contretemps hurt the service in other ways. Governor Burke's military secretary, Captain George Armstrong, United States Army (retired), got caught up in the case. According to the Bismarck *Tribune*, "instead of being the military adviser of the governor he became the staunch adherent and adviser of General Poole." At the conclusion of the court-martial, Burke wired the War Department requesting Captain Armstrong's immediate relief from duty in North Dakota. The War Department relieved Armstrong and later court-martialed him for his partisan behavior.

Never a man to give up, Tommy Poole appealed his conviction to the Supreme Court, which, in this instance, decided in his favor, ruling that Poole's conviction, based on the Army's Articles of War, was invalid. The state military code placed Guardsmen under the Articles of War, the Court pointed out, only in time of war or public danger. No such condition existed at the time of Poole's conviction. The Court further found the military code too vague on courts-martial procedures and punishments. It ordered Poole restored to the retired list with a brigadier general's rank. The decision amounted to the most lasting and harmful consequence of Poole's defiance of Governor Burke. Captain Gideon Williams lamented, "By that decision all hold on the members of the National Guard was lost." Poole's legacy was not a stronger adjutant general but a weaker National Guard, stripped of the little disciplinary authority it had. Notoriously slow to act on military matters, the legislature finally amended the military code in 1915, precisely defining the powers of courts-martial in time of peace and strengthening the Guard's authority to discipline officers and men.

Militia reform only partially succeeded after 1903. The Dick Act gave the states significant federal assistance for the first time, chiefly in weapons, equipment, and uniforms, but also pay for summer camp and joint maneuvers. Federal grants to North Dakota consistently exceeded state appropriations and became essential to the Guard's existence. Although the National Guard in 1916 was better equipped and trained than it was in 1898, weaknesses remained, especially at the company level, the heart of the decentralized Guard. Recruiting and retaining able enlisted men continued to plague the service throughout 1900-1916. Neither the new law nor the state offered much assistance to companies, and they remained on their own to recruit, maintain their armories, and conduct weekly drills. Harried company officers had to devise useful training programs, even though many lacked a military education, and find time to raise money for their financially weak units. While some urban states gave companies substantial armory support and weekly drill pay, most states did not, as in North Dakota, and the old-style, informal, and socially oriented National Guard persisted.

The Dick Act asked more of Guardsmen than was demanded in the 1890s. Though it required a minimum of twenty-four drills a year and a five-day camp, most companies drilled more frequently, up to forty-eight times yearly. Officers were expected to serve at drill and in camp and give time to tactical study, correspondence courses, and unit administration. Many officers and enlisted men saw few benefits in contrast to the new requirements, and an absence of leadership from adjutants general left Guardsmen with little sense of purpose.

Few discussed the fact that federal law obligated the Guard to support the Army in the event of war. This resulted partly from the longstanding volunteer tradition, where peacetime militia service and service in wartime as volunteers overlapped, but few assumed them to be legally or morally synonymous. Men made the decision to volunteer when war came. They joined the Guard in peace for numerous reasons, only one of which concerned preparation for war. Regardless of the law, in 1903 or 1916, obviously the old ways of thinking persisted. The state certainly approached the matter casually: North Dakota did not make its first effort to align its military code with the Dick Act until 1909. Only steady pressure and threatening letters from the Division of Militia Affairs finally brought the state's military law into conformity with national law in 1915.

147

John Fraine gave thought to the basic obligation of National Guard service. "I have had in my mind," he wrote in 1905, "a dream it might be called, of a day when the National Guard would be a National force in fact, as in name and theory." His dream included expanded federal and state spending and much closer cooperation between the National Guard and the Army. In later years, Fraine advocated compulsory Guard service at age 18 for three years, including a month's field training each summer. With such a policy, he explained, "we will not be worried every time some nation displays animosity to us." A practical man, John Fraine did not expect his dream to come true in the near future. His emphasis on constant study and close attention to detail was aimed at the Guard as it was, and based on the belief it might go to war.

Unlike his brother officers, Fraine regularly commented on that possibility. When he lamented officers' poor performance in camp, he did so, he said, because they "should remember that where they assume responsibilities and do not fit themselves for them by study and work, that in case of war they murder men as directly as if they used a weapon on them individually." He realized the difficulties of part-time study of military tactics and logistics, that an extra hour at the armory took away from business or family life. Few in the service were willing to give the time, as he was. If men in the Guard needed a reason to do extra work, Fraine reminded them that the welfare of their men, their army, and their nation depended on them and, he pointed out, that "should be incentive enough to urge them to make greater sacrifices than they now make." He communicated some of his deep concern to the rest of the regiment, but most Guardsmen did not take the lesson to heart. Reality would soon educate them, if John Fraine could not.

Notes on Sources

The Records of the North Dakota National Guard furnish most of this chapter's information. Of particular value from the many reports and correspondence files were:

1. A letterpress book containing copies of letters sent by Heber M. Creel during his term as adjutant general, 1905-1906.
2. Typescripts of the North Dakota National Guard Association's proceedings, 1900-1914.
3. A scrapbook kept by Captain Barney C. Boyd, Company L, Hillsboro.
4. Muster-in rolls, 1st North Dakota Infantry, 1916, for the Mexican border mobilization. The rolls provide place of residence, place of birth, age, and occupation for every member of the regiment.

The War Department kept some state records while a National Guard unit was in federal service. All the following are from the National Archives. Consequently, RG391, Regular Army Mobile Units, Records of Infantry Regiments, 164th Infantry, box 2837, and RG407, Adjutant General's Office, 1917-1947, World War I Organization Records, National Guard, North Dakota, box 348, give some data. The state's dealings with the War Department and the Division of Militia Affairs, as well as details on federal policy on the National

Guard, were traced in RG94, Entry 25, General Correspondence, and RG168, Records of the National Guard Bureau, Entry 7, Correspondence, 1908-1916, and Entry 12A, General Correspondence, 1916-1923.

Two records series at the State Historical Society of North Dakota, Series 153, Governor, Administration, Incoming Letters, 1900-1916, and Series 155, Governor, Administration, Subject Files, Military Affairs, 1889-1937, offered limited information.

In a major effort to acquire insights and material from former Guardsmen, the Adjutant General's Office sent a seven-page questionnaire compiled by Dr. Jerry Cooper to all active members of the 164th Infantry Association, the 188th Group Association, the 957th Field Artillery Battalion Association, and to retired officers, warrant officers, and enlisted men of the North Dakota Army and Air National Guard. These forms posed a variety of questions pertaining to the reasons men joined the Guard, and their training, social activities, and other aspects of state military service. The following men, with their terms of service, returned questionnaires with material of use for this chapter: J. M. Amberson (1913-1916), Leo H. Dominick (1912-1940), Rolf Glerum (1913-1915, 1917-1919), Leroy W. Goodwater (1914-1919).

Chief Warrant Officer Bryan O. Baldwin interviewed and taped the comments of many of these men to obtain greater detail on their experiences in the North Dakota National Guard. He held interviews for this chapter with Leo H. Dominick, Leroy W. Goodwater, and Harold Serumsgard. Mr. Serumsgard is a long-time resident of Devils Lake, North Dakota, who frequently visited the National Guard training camp at Rock Island Military Reservation between 1912 and 1917, when he was a boy. He worked there as a telephone operator in 1915. Both questionnaire respondents and interviewees are quoted in the text.

Among published sources, the biennial reports of the adjutant general, North Dakota National Guard, from 1900 to 1914 had the greatest value, often containing reports and information not retained in the Guard's original records. The annual reports of the Secretary of War, 1900 to 1916, and yearly reports of the Division of Militia Affairs, 1908 to 1916, either published in the Congressional Serial Set or as separate War Department reports, offered data on the North Dakota National Guard and on overall National Guard policy. The Bismarck *Tribune* and the Fargo *Forum* were read for general knowledge and specific material on the Thomas Poole affair. Published laws pertaining to the National Guard and the state's compiled laws containing the entire military code were perused.

---

[1]Eddy's exam for first lieutenant, taken in May 1908, suggests the problems Hildreth faced. Eddy took and passed the following "exam," written and administered by inspector general S. H. Nuchols, who said the lieutenant was "qualified and fit for such position": 1. What is the date of your commission as second lieutenant? Answer: July 2, 1907. 2. How often have you attended drill? Answer: I have attended all drills of company since my election except when on leave from city. 3. How many times have you been in command of the company since your election as second lieutenant? Answer: Have been in command of the company possibly ten or twelve times. 4. How and for what reasons can commissioned officers in the National Guard of North Dakota be removed from office either by resignation or court martial. 5. How long do you intend to remain in service of the NDNG? Answer: Till the Regiment is mustered out.

First Regiment, First North Dakota Infantry on Dress Parade at Camp
Grafton, 1903.

North Dakota National Guard Commissary Department during a ten-day encampment at Camp McCoy, Sparta, Wisconsin, 1919.

Interior view of Company L (Hillsboro), First North Dakota Infantry Armory, ca. early 1901.

National Guard Armory, Bismarck, built in 1911.

Office of Adjutant General I.A. Berg (1913-14) located in old capitol building. (Note: This was the first permanent office for the First North Dakota National Guard.)

☆5☆

In Federal Service:
The Mexican Border, 1916

The probabilities of a federal call to duty doubtless seemed remote in towns like Wahpeton, Dickinson, or Grafton when a man joined the Guard before 1916. Although the Guard said little about possible extended active duty during its annual recruiting campaigns, the National Guard Association had sought a guaranteed reserve function since 1898. Its lobbying efforts had ensured that President McKinley offer Guard units the opportunity to volunteer first. The Militia Act of 1903 included the 1898 law, though it limited Organized Militia service to nine months following the President's call.[1] Volunteers would most likely be called only for a major overseas war and under these circumstances Guardsmen had no obligation to volunteer their services. The Dick Act did require individual Guardsmen to answer a presidential call to repel invasion, suppress insurrection, or enforce federal law, the traditional constitutional militia uses. Officers and enlisted men refusing to muster in, according to the act, "shall be subject to trial by court-martial and shall be punished as such court-martial may direct." Little noticed at the time, the provision placed Guardsmen under the federal government's legal authority for the first time since the National Guard developed in the 1870s.

Unhappy with the nine-month limit and uneasy with sections that restricted federal use of the Organized Militia to service within the United States, Guardsmen successfully worked to amend the Dick Act. A 1908 amendment allowed the President to set "the period for which such service is required," although no Guardsman had to serve beyond his state enlistment term. More importantly, the 1908 changes gave the President authority to use the Guard "either within or without the territory of the United States." If the demands of war necessitated a large army, the changes provided, "The Organized Militia shall be called into service of the United States in advance of any volunteer force which it may be determined to raise."

While the amended Dick Act seemed to guarantee the National Guard first place behind the Army, professional soldiers on the General Staff thought otherwise. Devising contingency mobilization plans for the first time in the Army's history, War Department planners expressed grave doubts about the Guard's reliability. They based their uncertainty partly on historical example, citing the refusal of militia to cross the international boundary of Canada during the War of 1812 and recalling the defiance of border-state governors to Abraham Lincoln's 1861 militia call. The General Staff displayed a highly selective historical memory in its planning memoranda. Their position papers ignored the obvious fact that Union victory in 1865 settled the question of federal versus state power in the conduct of war. The General Staff conveniently forgot the enthusiastic National Guard response in 1898 and put aside the creditable performance of state units like the 1st North Dakota Volunteer Infantry in the Philippine Insurrection.

More pertinent to the Staff's concern for the value of the National Guard as a ready reserve were the annual armory and field inspection reports of Army inspector-instructors serving with the states. The low efficiency, lack of training, and high turnover of enlisted personnel seen in North Dakota characterized the entire National Guard. The War Department, particularly after Leonard Wood became Chief of Staff in 1910 and Henry Stimson Secretary of War a year later, sought ways to sidestep what it saw as an ineffective National Guard. Staff planners wanted to create a Regular Army Reserve and gain legislation allowing the War Department complete control over any wartime volunteer force.

The political and bureaucratic battle to relegate the National Guard to a home defense force took a new meaning in 1912. Prodded by General Staff memos, Secretary of War Stimson asked United States Attorney General George W. Wickersham to rule on the constitutionality of the 1908 amendment which allowed the President to send the Guard overseas. Wickersham found the section unconstitutional and ruled that the President was restricted to using the Guard, or Organized Militia, for the purposes clearly stated in the Constitution. The War Department then attempted to push a law through Congress that would authorize a federal volunteer war force. It lost. Guard supporters, led by the National Guard Association, successfully amended the bill, sponsored by Representative James Hay (D-Virginia). Again ensuring the Guard's first place in any war army, the Hay Volunteer Act of 1914 stipulated that when three-fourths of the members of any National Guard unit volunteered for United States service, the President was compelled to accept the unit intact.

Legislative success in 1914 spurred the National Guard Association to intensify its campaign for a federal militia pay bill. First appearing in 1910, the idea became a major goal thereafter. Guardsmen argued that the Militia Act of 1903, its amendments, and a growing list of Division of Militia Affairs regulations demanded far more time, money, and effort than had service in the 1890s. They now spent most of their service time meeting federal requirements and preparing themselves for the possibilities of military duty with the United States. Service to the Guardsmen's states took much less time. Federal pay was now essential to encourage recruiting and to compensate officers and men for the added time spent complying with federal law. The National Guard Association contended that, without federal pay, the Guard would find itself unable to keep its best officers and enlisted men.

Although the War Department initially supported the pay bill, it eventually dropped its endorsement due to the many liabilities and deficiencies it saw in the Guard. The pay-bill campaign culminated in the bitter 1915-1916 congressional sessions. When Secretary of War Lindley M. Garrison aggressively led the War Department's efforts to stop the pay bill and replace the Guard with a volunteer federal militia labeled the Continental Army, the National Guard Association countered with an equally strident campaign to win federal pay and defeat what it saw as a cabal of Prussianized staff officers unsympathetic to the American military tradition. Both sides in this complicated controversy indulged in acrimonious name-calling, which embittered War Department-National Guard relations well into the 1920s and left lingering suspicions long after that.

Congress resolved the dispute when it passed the National Defense Act of 1916. A compromise, the act dropped the Continental Army plan, approved federal pay for armory drills, and greatly increased annual appropriations to the states (for fiscal year 1917, Congress appropriated $56,685,000; it approved $6.5 million for fiscal year 1916). The law reaffirmed the Guard's place as second only to the Army in the nation's land forces, but it also significantly expanded War Department control over the Guard. The provisions that allowed the War Department to determine tables of organization and equipment, including unit size and type, for the entire Guard, to set nationwide standards for enlistment terms and physical examinations, and to establish professional standards for National Guard officers had particular importance for the General Staff. The act also tightened considerably the regulations governing the states' care and accountability of federal property.

Section 111 of the law, in the eyes of the chief of the Militia Bureau, constituted "the essential difference between the old Organized Militia and the new National Guard law." This section gave the President the power to "draft into military service of the United States, to serve therein for the period of the war unless sooner discharged, any or all members of the National Guard and National Guard Reserve." When authorized by Congress, the President could call the Guard into federal service with a single order and did not have to ask individual Guardsmen to volunteer or request governors to supply militia for constitutional purposes. Other sections of the law required each officer and enlisted man to take two oaths, one state, another federal.

The National Defense Act of 1916 guaranteed the Guard permanent service as a reserve for the Army as well as substantial appropriations. From the federal perspective, it subjected all Guardsmen to federal duty when the President deemed it necessary, under conditions set by Congress, a momentous change in the Guard's relationship to the federal government. In 1898, for example, North Dakota Guardsmen had only a moral obligation to volunteer. Throughout the nineteenth century, state militia and National Guard units formed the backbone of the first units organized for war, but no specific individual in an organized unit legally had to offer his services at the call for volunteers. Men enlisting in the Guard after 1916 no longer had the option to decline federal service. The act of enlisting was voluntary, of course, but thereafter the government determined active service both at home and abroad.

Most North Dakota National Guardsmen were only vaguely aware of the 1910-1916 political struggles over the Guard's future. The North Dakota National Guard Association regularly endorsed the pay-bill proposals at its annual conventions and in 1912 and 1913 sent resolutions to North Dakota congressmen and senators asking them to vote for the pay bills, which they did. North Dakota routinely sent a small group, usually Colonel John Fraine and the incumbent adjutant general, to the annual National Guard Association meetings where endless discussion examined the pay idea and the growing

War Department animosity toward the Guard. In this general way, North Dakota Guardsmen remained informed on key issues of National Guard interest. Local concerns—keeping the companies financially solvent and up to minimum strength, passing federal inspections, taking the regiment to camp—held their attention. They rarely commented on the national issues and none took a particularly active part in the National Guard Association.

The average Guardsman gave little thought to the ongoing political battle, largely because it was an abstract argument. General Staff planners and National Guard Association spokesmen talked of some future conflict when the nation *might* need a military force larger than the Army. The Guard's right to serve overseas, for example, was a mere theoretical position, even in 1916, despite the onset of war in Europe two years earlier. The obligation to answer the President's call to duty, stated in the 1903 law and given greater force in the 1916 act, remained an abstraction simply because no one, including the General Staff, anticipated an emergency of that magnitude.

A call came in 1916, just two weeks after Congress approved the National Defense Act. Turmoil in Mexico as a consequence of the overthrow of dictator Porfirio Diaz in 1911 continued for nearly a decade afterward, causing revolutionary conflict occasionally to cross the Mexican-American border in those turbulent years. President William Howard Taft ordered American troops to patrol the border, particularly in Texas, throughout 1911. At various times from 1911 to 1916, Regular Army forces numbering ten thousand to over twenty thousand guarded the boundary line between Mexico and the United States to keep the surging Mexican civil war within that country. As relations between the two countries rapidly deteriorated, President Woodrow Wilson directed an American occupation of the city of Vera Cruz, on the Gulf of Mexico, from April through November 1914. The climax of growing conflict came in early March 1916 when guerrilla leader Francisco "Pancho" Villa raided Columbus, New Mexico, shooting up the town and killing several Americans.

After President Wilson ordered Major General Frederick Funston, commanding the Southern Department, to organize a force to pursue Villa's band into Mexico, Funston pieced together a "Punitive Expedition" from units on the border and placed Brigadier General John J. Pershing in command. Pershing left Columbus on 15 March with over six thousand troops. The Punitive Expedition failed to catch Villa in the ensuing months, although it occasionally exchanged gunfire with parts of his band. The presence of a large American military force deep in Mexico offended the government of Venustiano Carranza. In April, and again in June, when elements of Pershing's force engaged in fire fights with regular Mexican troops, both Mexican and American soldiers died in these small combats. Anti-Americanism, already strong in revolution-torn Mexico, grew rapidly in April and May. Armed guerrillas continued to cross the border into the United States. President Wilson stepped up his pressure on the Carranza government to rein in the guerrillas, leading to increasingly hostile Mexican demands that Pershing return to the United States.

When General Funston found himself without enough regular troops to support Pershing and protect the lengthy border, as early as 25 March he recommended that the President call out fifty thousand National Guardsmen to reinforce the regulars along the border. Wilson rejected the advice in March but, as the two countries drifted closer to war, changed his mind. He ordered out the National Guard of Texas, New Mexico, and Arizona on 9 May 1916. Relations worsened markedly in the next month. Finally, responding to another urgent request from General Funston, President Wilson decided to federalize the entire National Guard and send them to the border.

Woodrow Wilson's 18 June 1916 order mobilizing the National Guard caught state officials and Guardsmen unawares. Despite mounting tensions since Villa's raid and newspapers stories recounting Pershing's difficulties in Mexico, Washington had leaked no hints that it might call up the National Guard. Secretary of War Newton D. Baker sent telegrams to forty-four governors (Nevada had no organized militia) late in the afternoon of the 18th, a Sunday, designating the number of units each state must provide and outlining procedures. Governor Louis B. Hanna received Baker's telegram at 10:22 P.M. Neither of the National Guard's two key officers were available to assist Governor Hanna in responding to the call. Thomas H. Tharalson, the adjutant general, had gone to Minneapolis on personal business, and the regimental commander, Colonel John Fraine, was campaigning in Dickinson for the Republican gubernatorial nomination. Major R. R. Steedman, Hanna's military secretary, telegraphed Tharalson just after midnight on 19 June informing him of the call up: "Much data to be attended to from your office. When can we expect you?" Hanna asked Fraine to report to Bismarck immediately.

Reaching the capital early Monday morning, Fraine took charge of mobilization efforts pending Tharalson's return later that day. The colonel prepared General Order Number 9 to go out under the adjutant general's signature. It directed all North Dakota National Guard members to report to "their respective home stations" no later than 9:00 P.M. that day, adding, "Officers and men will habitually wear uniforms." The order gave company commanders authority to purchase food, forage, and other supplies and to commence drill immediately, further stating, "While troops remain at their home stations and where armory facilities do not exist for sleeping, organization commanders are authorized to permit enlisted men...as they may designate to sleep at home." Recruiting was to begin at once "to the maximum practicable ...at home station." Each infantry company needed a minimum of 58 enlisted men, but a war strength of 150 was the ultimate recruiting goal. The order directed commanders to complete recruitment and inventories quickly and notify the adjutant general "as soon as an organization" was "really ready to move to the mobilization camp." At the end of that harried day, General Tharalson's son Paul wired him from Bismarck: "Fraine here all day. Everything attended to except transportation."

The Guard remained at home station for a week. Although infantry companies supposedly maintained a strength of at least fifty-eight enlisted men in order to receive federal allotments, many units fell short of the minimum. At the spring 1915 inspection, Companies F, G, K, and L lacked the proper number, and in June 1916 nearly all companies had to recruit men before reporting to camp. Local organizations opened recruiting offices immediately on 19 June. Company C's Captain Manville N. Sprague sent recruiting parties in automobiles from Grafton to visit surrounding villages.

In Bismarck, Captain A. B. Welch published daily recruiting reports in the Bismarck *Tribune* to stimulate volunteering for Company A and visited the larger businesses, asking employers to promise new Guardsmen they could have their jobs back "without prejudice or discrimination" after demobilization. Many gave that pledge.

Supply and equipment problems also slowed mobilization. Recruiting soon pushed company strengths beyond peacetime levels, but neither local units nor the state maintained reserve stocks of arms, uniforms, or equipment. The War Department needed to ship these items to outfit new men, not only to North Dakota but to all the states. Reporting to mobilization camp before the government corrected the supply problem made little sense. The War Department designated Fort Lincoln, an abandoned Army post two miles south of Bismarck, as the 1st North Dakota Infantry's rendezvous point. General Tharalson needed several days to move the regiment's tents and other field equipment from the Devils Lake reservation to Fort Lincoln, and the Army needed to restore water, electricity, and telephone service to the post. A mustering officer from the Regular Army did not arrive until 24 June.

While state and federal authorities worked to impose order on the mobilization, the companies enjoyed a public attention usually denied them. Local newspapers praised their companies as the best in the state, and the 1st North Dakota as the best regiment in the National Guard. At Grafton, Fargo, Bismarck, and other places, townspeople gave the boys banquets and dances. The people of Grafton raised $653 as a company fund for Company C, with similar amounts collected at Bismarck and Jamestown for Companies A and H. The companies left home station for Fort Lincoln on 24 June, most of them escorted to the troop train by parades and bands. When Company B departed Fargo, the *Forum* solemnly remarked: "Their stay is indefinite; the nature of the trials they will be called upon to face, uncertain." The Walsh County *Record* headlined Company C's move to Fort Lincoln "GRAFTON'S MILITIA LEAVES FOR FRONT." "The militiamen and their friends feel certain," the Bismarck *Tribune* noted when Company A marched off to Fort Lincoln, "that they will see active warfare."

Rather than rapid movement to the battle front, the militiamen encountered at Fort Lincoln the inevitable delays of military mobilization, plenty of "hurry up and wait," and a dose of measles. The regiment assembled at Fort Lincoln on 25 June for inspection and mustering in by a Regular Army officer, a process, not begun until 30 June, that took four days altogether. After 3 July the 1st North Dakota served at the direction of the federal government. Equipment shortages continued to delay full regimental organization. Inexplicably, the War Department transferred Major Max Tyler, the only Regular at Fort Lincoln, and did not replace him for several days. Tyler's departure left the regiment without an officer to muster in new recruits or help cut bureaucratic paperwork in ordering supplies. Before Tyler moved on, he reported the regiment "reasonably ready" for border duty on 7 July. Since no one acted on his report, "Orders were therefore given...to utilize the remaining time for training the regiment." The Southern Department requested that the 1st North Dakota be sent to the border on 15 July, but by then a number of men had contracted measles. Another week passed before the disease ran its course and the regiment could report to General Funston.

The Guard responded rapidly to the mobilization order of 18 June. All but one company had achieved minimum strength by the 21st, and only equipment shortages prevented the regiment from assembling at Fort Lincoln that day. Colonel Fraine efficiently organized the early mobilization efforts, and General Tharalson moved the companies and their gear from home station to rendezvous in one day. Nonetheless, the 1st North Dakota failed in one major area to meet War Department requests and consequently delayed its mobilization. Although state newspapers casually declared that North Dakota could easily provide a war-strength regiment, an assertion repeated by Guard officers frequently, the 1st North Dakota found it difficult to recruit the necessary men. The regiment numbered 641 enlisted men at the President's call, 277 short of prescribed peace strength, and 1,275 below war strength. Twelve men on the rolls never answered the call, and Governor Hanna excused another 48 from their enlistment contracts, illegally as it turned out. The unit lost a total of 60 included on its strength return *before* muster in.

Vigorous recruiting efforts replaced these men and added a large number of new ones. Company I, Wahpeton, enlisted 44 men between 20 June and the end of the month; Company D added 58, Company L, 45, Company M, 44. The regiment as a whole enlisted 575 new men before it left Fort Lincoln. Unfortunately, many recruits and a large number of pre-call members failed the Army's physical examination. Seventy-nine regular enlisted men and 76 new men failed, a total of 155 (or 12.2 percent of all enlisted men presented for muster-in). When the 1st North Dakota left its home state for the border on 22 July, it numbered just over 1,000 officers and men, barely above the peacetime minimum, and only 54 percent of war strength. With fully half its privates raw recruits and 22 percent of its noncommissioned officers with less than a year's service, the 1st North Dakota failed to deliver the partially trained, well-organized regiment Guard supporters had promised since 1903. A high percentage of new recruits (approximately 60 percent) appeared in all National Guard units sent to the border in 1916. The War Department was disappointed, for it had hoped to see a fairly well-trained force quickly mobilized and able to take its place alongside the regulars. "The unfit, and the unwilling who failed to appear, were numerous enough to seriously deplete the strength on the rolls at the date of call," the chief of the Militia Bureau complained. Adding many new men who were "impelled to enlist through the prospect of war has given to the National Guard in the Federal service a good deal of the character of a volunteer force."

War Department planners had worked for a decade to write plans and gain legislation to ensure complete federal control of manpower mobilization. Using the chaotic 1898 call to arms as an example of how not to organize a war army, the General Staff hoped never to see another volunteer army created in the grand nineteenth-century tradition. They wanted a system in which the move from a peace to a war footing proceeded logically, efficiently, and completely planned in advance. To that end, the General Staff developed an organization for the National Guard, placing the forty-seven state systems into twelve tactical divisions, complete with support troops, organized on a geographic basis. (It assigned North Dakota to the 13th Division, along with Wisconsin, Minnesota, South Dakota, and Iowa). For a variety of reasons, the twelve-division plan remained an incomplete, paper arrangement into 1916. The National Defense Act of 1916 seemed to give the War Department the authority it needed to complete the divisional plan and write contingency mobilization plans which it could impose on the National Guard.

President Wilson issued his 18 June call without giving the General Staff time to prepare a well-organized mobilization. Also caught unprepared, National Guardsmen had little opportunity to arrange their personal and business affairs before leaving for camp. Most unfortunate of all, Wilson's call came only two weeks after the passage of the National Defense Act. No single state had yet reorganized its Guard to meet the new requirements, and few Guardsmen had taken the new oath. No state soldier was compelled to take the oath, and in North Dakota and elsewhere some Organized Militiamen refused to enlist in the new National Guard. Because of the Mexican crisis, Secretary of War Baker did not write Governor Hanna until 29 August to explain the new law and North Dakota's obligations under it. Governor and Guardsmen alike felt bewildered. Like other state executives, Hanna excused men from their enlistment contracts when they indicated they would not take the new oath, believing the men were released from any obligation to serve. Eventually, Secretary of War Baker made it clear that Organized Militia, that is, men enlisted under provisions of the 1903 law, and National Guardsmen, those who took the oath, were both legally bound to obey the President's orders. Confusion abounded. The War Department threatened to court-martial all Organized Militiamen who ignored the call or accepted governors' excuses, but it finally dropped the matter when faced with the prospect of prosecuting over seventy-five hundred reluctant militiamen.

As a result of the confusion and misunderstanding, the mobilization assumed aspects both of the old volunteer system and of the new federally controlled arrangement. The average American, including most Guardsmen, saw the call as similar to 1898. Captain A. B. Welch, Company A, announced that few of his men asked to be excused but that in one or two cases men with large families "will be given honorable discharge," he explained. Across the Missouri River, in Mandan, Captain G. I. Solum, Company F, assured all his married men that he would replace them with single men. Neither captain nor anyone else in the Guard had authority to release these men, even under the 1903 law. As in 1898, military entrepreneurs offered to raise companies and regiments for the crisis. General Tharalson told one aspiring military leader, "No place except to enlist in one of the companies." The second lieutenant of Company B wrote Colonel Fraine that his business affairs were so demanding he did "not want to leave unless necessary. If not can I get furlough until I am needed?" General Tharalson bluntly informed the young man, "You are now in the service of the United States and must report to your company commander without delay." Senator Henry C. Hansbrough urged Tharalson to find a place for former Guard officer Thomas Lonnevik: "Appoint Tom captain and you do me a favor. He is entitled to it, he is fit to go anywhere. Don't fail." Even United States senators apparently did not know or understand the military laws. The adjutant general had no authority to appoint officers, particularly after the Guard entered United States service.

If vestiges of the old volunteer system cropped up in 1916, the War Department ultimately controlled the mobilization. Federal officials did not mobilize the entire Guard but called on states to provide units according to the twelve-division plan. Baker's 18 June telegram designated specific units, for example, infantry regiments or battalions, field artillery batteries, or cavalry squadrons, rather than numerical quotas as was the case in the nineteenth century. Each state unit had to conform to Army tables of organization before the government mustered it in. The War Department did not call for National Guard divisions, intending to organize provisional ones on the border once Guard regiments, batteries, and squadrons arrived. This approach left some state units at home. Many Guardsmen believed war with Mexico was imminent. Although those not called resented the lost opportunity for combat and turned to their congressmen and senators to force the War Department to change state assignments, a tactic quite successful in 1898, the plea failed to move the department in 1916. "The call for the militia was based on the twelve division plan which has been recognized since 1914," Adjutant General Henry P. McCain, United States Army, informed disgruntled Florida Guardsmen. "Any departure from this plan would throw the entire mobilization into confusion," he added.

Unlike its actions in 1898, the federal government assumed immediate responsibility for operating the camps. The War Department directed mobilization through the headquarters of the Army's geographic military commands, with North Dakota under the Central Department, headquartered in Chicago. State adjutants general in the Middle West and Plains states reported directly to the Central Department for instructions and took orders from that command in return. The geographic commanders bore the responsibility for examining, mustering, and supplying state units once they assembled at camps. Supply efforts became hopelessly tangled soon after assembly, chiefly because the mobilization was decentralized through the geographic departments, while the Army's supply system was highly centralized. The Quartermaster Department maintained only two supply depots in the entire United States in 1916 from which to supply all Guard units. Inability to equip the Guard promptly was the Army's greatest failure during the Mexican Border incident.

Individual Guardsmen quickly discovered the extent of War Department authority. The Army physician at Fort Lincoln rejected Captain Clarence N. Barker, Company K, owing to a slight hernia. When the mustering officer presented Barker with his discharge, he refused to accept it. With full support from Colonel Fraine, Barker appealed the decision to the Army's adjutant general. In the meantime, the mustering officer called Captain Harold Sorenson from the North Dakota National Guard's supernumerary list to replace Barker, mustering Sorenson in without consulting Governor Hanna, General Tharalson, or Colonel Fraine. State officials regarded this as high-handed treatment of North Dakota's unit. Barker wanted to know why the Army rejected him for a defect "so trifling that I never knew it existed." He simply wanted "a chance to be Captain of the Company," he explained, "to which I have given ten years faithful service." General Tharalson asked Senator P. J. McCumber to clear the way for Barker, but McCumber failed.

Captain D. S. Lewis found the Army just as stubborn when he attempted to resign after the call up. Lewis, 1st Regiment commissary officer, owned a grocery store and a feed and seed store in Fargo. "A continuance of my present absence from attending to the business," he wrote the War Department, "would work irreparable damage and financially ruin me." As with Barker, both Fraine and Tharalson supported Captain Lewis. General Tharalson explained that Lewis volunteered for war in 1898 and served honorably in the Philippines. While overseas, Lewis "sacrificed and lost his business." The adjutant general wrote Major General Thomas H. Barry, commanding Central Department, that Lewis believed "he should not be called on to make such personal sacrifice at this time, when he feels that this service is now only nominal and if war was declared would be glad to join his colors." This solidly adhered to the American volunteer tradition, where the volunteer himself defined the conditions of service. Not accepting such a personal definition, General Barry told Tharalson that Captain Lewis knew the obligations of National Guard service. "He should have resigned from the National Guard as should all officers so situated that they cannot render service when called upon." Senator McCumber again failed to move the War Department in Lewis's case.

Eventually, Barker, who wanted to serve and was ordered out, and Lewis, who sought release but was compelled to stay, both achieved satisfaction. The Army agreed to accept Barker if he had an operation to repair the hernia. Barker's retention made Lewis an extra captain in the regiment, so the War Department finally accepted his resignation. In the past, at least before muster-in, governors settled questions concerning the appointment of volunteer officers; senators and congressmen used their Washington influence to iron out difficulties after muster-in. Governor Hanna, and Senators Hansbrough and McCumber lacked that influence in 1916. The National Guard was no longer a volunteer force in the nineteenth-century sense. Captains Lewis and Barker, even under the 1903 law, were legally bound to answer a call to federal service, and they became subject to military authority once called. State officials had limited power to rearrange the 1st Regiment once the President ordered it to federal duty. General Tharalson managed to save Barker and arrange Lewis's release only by dealing directly with General Barry in Chicago and the Army's adjutant general in Washington.

With all administrative matters finally resolved, and the measles at last under control, the 1st Regiment left Fort Lincoln for the border on 22 July. The men were ready to go, as many found "Life at camp" was "getting monotonous." In some ways the regiment was as raw an organization as the unit that left Fargo in May 1898. Only 38 of the 226 noncommissioned officers had more than five years' service. The 1st North Dakota in 1916, however, was better equipped and trained than the 1898 volunteers. Federal aid since 1903 kept the North Dakota National Guard provided with modern weapons and uniforms. Privates, noncommissioned officers, and junior officers who served before 1916 had gone to summer camp, often under the tutelage of Regular Army officers. Colonel John Fraine and Lieutenant Colonel Gilbert C. Grafton, Majors Frank S. Henry, 1st Battalion, and Dana Wright, 2nd Battalion, Captains Theodore S. Henry, regimental adjutant, and G. Angus

Fraser, regimental quartermaster, all had served in the Philippines. Major James M. Hanley, 3rd Battalion, although a veteran of 1898, was the only field officer without combat service. And the North Dakota National Guard was now old enough to show a family tradition—Grafton's Company C included Second Lieutenant William K. Treumann and Sergeant John Fraine.

"It was a different scene from that when the companies left to mobilize," the Bismarck *Tribune* observed when the 1st North Dakota departed for Texas. "Then there was every indication of an immediate bloody conflict with the southern republic. Peace prospects made yesterday's departure seem more like an enthusiastic send-off to a booster train." North Dakota's regiment of twelve infantry companies, machine gun company, band, and medical detachment took four days to travel to the border. The men no longer expected an immediate march into Mexico to fight Carranza's troops, but neither did they know where they were going or what they would do once they got there.

They reached the border on 26 July, going into camp outside Mercedes, Texas, in a driving rain. "Considerable difficulty was experienced in getting baggage and camp equipment from the train to camp on account of the muddy roads," a Company C boy wrote the Walsh County *Record*. Mercedes, a small town of under a thousand, lay roughly seventy miles west of Brownsville and the Gulf of Mexico and four miles north of the Rio Grande River. The Army had not prepared the camp site, which the locals "had for years used as a dump ground covered with chapparal and mesquite and rubbish," Company A's Herman Brocopp later recalled. It rained regularly for the next six weeks. "The soil of the camp was gumbo, silt, sticky, bottomless when wet." So, the first duty was to clean up the camp and dig a drainage system. "We have been thru the most strenuous work," the Walsh County *Record* correspondent reported two weeks later, "clearing off all of the sod...ditching the whole camp...and clearing off brush ground for a suitable place for drills." As late as the end of August the men continued to dig drainage ditches. The swampy areas near the camp bred mosquitoes, leading to a limited malaria outbreak in early September. Although the regiment lived in tents throughout its border service, eventually "A camp was established which apart from the constant danger of flooding was a very comfortable one," according to Brocopp.

Brigadier General James Parker commanded the Brownsville District within General Funston's Southern Department. Parker's command included all regular and National Guard troops from Mercedes east to the Gulf Coast. Soldiers of the 3rd United States Cavalry, and the 26th and 28th United States Infantry regiments served in the Mercedes region along with Guardsmen from fourteen states. While regulars patrolled the border and guarded key bridges over the Rio Grande, the state soldiers began an intensive six-month training program. Herman Brocopp later argued in the 1930s, "It was apparent, at that time, to anyone who observed the trend of events that these troops would be used in the war in Europe then going on, but nowhere in the program of instructions was any instruction given...in modern military methods such as were being used in Europe."

Brocopp's conclusion, shared by many Guardsmen who later served in France, was logical but erroneous. War between the United States and Germany was neither readily evident nor inevitable in the summer and fall of 1916.

Heeding an uncertain and divided public opinion, Woodrow Wilson had not yet made up his mind about American intervention in the war. Indeed, he was on the verge of conducting his re-election campaign based on the slogan "He kept us out of war" and had recently exacted a German promise to halt unrestricted submarine warfare. The Army's lengthy training program along the border evolved from the necessity to call the National Guard to prevent war with Mexico. Brigadier General William A. Mann, chief, Militia Bureau, thought it necessary to remind Guardsmen that they were the only troops available to meet the emergency, and that was the reason they were called. The crisis with Mexico eased somewhat late that summer, due partly to the mobilization, but tensions remained high enough that the Wilson administration kept the Guard on active duty into 1917.

The War Department adopted the training program, not to prepare for an eventual American intervention in World War I but because it was appalled at the Guard's inefficiency and lack of training. "It was realized from the first that in order to make these troops ready for service in the field," General Parker later reported, "extreme measures were necessary. They contained a large number of recruits and a great many inexperienced officers. Their training had been limited to a small amount of barrack drill, with no field instruction. They required intensive training." Parker believed that only after that training could the Army use the Guard in a possible Mexican conflict. At the same time, the Militia Bureau saw the mobilization as an opportunity to perfect the twelve-division plan. Although the bureau regretted that the call's emergency nature prevented mobilizing the Guard according to the plan, provisional divisions and brigades, plus the formation of Signal Corps, engineer, and other support troops not in the Guard, could now be organized. Here was "an opportunity not to be neglected for proper organization, for the attainment of cohesion, and for the training of higher units," General Mann argued in July 1916. "The 12 divisional organization the Bureau has urged so consistently cannot otherwise be made a practical fact." Seeing border duty as a chance to impress its discipline, organization, and training on the National Guard, the Army made the most of that opportunity.

General Parker developed a uniform training program for the entire Brownsville District. At District Headquarters, he set up an office of militia affairs which coordinated weekly instructional work of inspector-instructors assigned to National Guard units in the district. Parker also established special schools for Guardsmen and posted sergeant instructors with Guard units, instruction covering everything from the school of the soldier to brigade-level field exercises. Overall, the training program was "a combination of garrison and field training" involving "instruction in field and combat exercises... at the same time as preliminary instruction," Parker reported, adding, "Many of these exercises are of the nature of small maneuvers, and in most cases involve contact between two forces."

North Dakota Guardsmen had never experienced such sustained military work. Herman Brocopp remembered "close order drill daily together with early morning marches and other exercises, which kept the men constantly and strenuously employed." Colonel Fraine and the company commanders, in consultation with the regiment's inspector-instructor, prepared weekly training routines which closely followed bulletins and circulars sent from Parker's militia affairs office. In a typical week, 18 to 23 September, for example, Company B took part in a brigade problem on the 18th, underwent a field inspection and held platoon drill the next day, then on the 20th joined the regiment in morning field exercises and afternoon firing drills and extended order work. Camp guard duty followed on Thursday the 21st, and company advance guard drill took place Friday. Parker expected all units to hold a forced march daily and a twelve-mile hike by regiment or brigade each week. The regiment worked on every aspect of military field service, including scouting, advance and rear guard, and the construction, attack, and defense of trenches.

Along with two other regimental junior officers, Second Lieutenant Leo Dominick, Company I, went on detached service with the regulars. Dominick served with Company I, 36th United States Infantry, guarding a bridge over the Rio Grande between Brownsville and Matamoros, Mexico. The Americans manned a machine gun post, with sand bags and live ammunition, facing Mexican troops just seventy-five yards away. They had no problems during this time with the regulars, Dominick recalled, but he was one of the few North Dakota Guardsmen to see "the enemy" while stationed in Texas. Dominick enjoyed his service with the 36th, serving as a platoon leader, and his company commander treated him fairly. After three months of detached service, Dominick met Colonel Fraine accidentally in Brownsville. "I guess I look a little bit hen-pecked and he asked me if I wanted to come back to the regiment," he related. Dominick said yes and returned at the end of October.

The rest of the regiment carried on routine training work week after week under the hot Texas sun. During September, officers from the Southern Department's Inspector General's Office gave the regiment a thorough Regular Army inspection. On 30 September the 1st North Dakota paraded in a large review for General Funston. The 3rd Battalion, Companies C, D, E, and M, escaped the monotony of camp routine for a time in late September and into October when it performed a three-week stint of patrol duty along the Rio Grande. Leroy Goodwater, Company M, remembered that his unit served "out in the mesquite." They guarded water pumps and patrolled the river, but they soon discovered the company had simply exchanged the monotony of camp for the dull routine of patrol duty. The Machine Gun Company moved to Harlingen, Texas, in December to take a two-week machine gun tactics course.

Parker's training program culminated in November with a ten-day maneuver involving twenty-three thousand regular and National Guard troops. Preliminary to the maneuver, the 1st North Dakota, in a brigade with two Nebraska regiments, went on a four-day practice march, 7-11 November. The big field exercise began on 16 November with two forces, the White and Brown armies, operating against each other from Mercedes to Brownsville. All troops engaged in forced marches, reconnaissance, and trench work, with day and night operations. According to Company K field returns, the 1st North Dakota operated with the White army. "This maneuver carried us on the march as far as Brownsville, and return," so noted the returns. The operation concluded when General Parker reviewed the twenty-three thousand troops. Brocopp wrote it was "the largest review of troops that had been seen in the United States since the final review of the Union Army at Washington at the close of the Civil War in 1865."

Leroy Goodwater remembered that "Mercedes wasn't much of a city." Although training activities kept the men busy, work stopped at noon on Saturday and did not resume until Monday morning. The men had most evenings free and could go to Mercedes after supper without a pass, and ten percent could leave camp with a pass, after Saturday inspection, for the remainder of the weekend. Lieutenant Colonel Gilbert C. Grafton assured General Tharalson that the men had many opportunities for "liberty and amusement." The regiment held two field days a month and played "baseball and other athletic sports each week on Saturday afternoon." Despite Grafton's assurances, off-duty hours were nearly as tedious as the training regime. The people of Mercedes and other small border towns took ready advantage of the sudden influx of Guardsmen. "When the troops arrived," a Company C member complained to the Walsh County *Record*, "the border people...grasped time by the forelock and doubled prices on food stuffs, fruit, hardware, merchandise." Price gouging made it difficult for privates, earning just fifty cents a day, to enjoy even the simple pleasure of buying an orange. "We are here to protect these same people from the plundering Mexicans," he protested bitterly.

The dissatisfied tone of this letter, written late in August, hinted at Guardsmen's growing disenchantment with border duty. Young men from many state units wrote similar letters home that summer, grumbling about Army food, the rigorous training, and the apparent lack of purpose for their presence along the Rio Grande. Such complaints typify citizen-soldiers rudely thrust into military life, but enterprising, sometimes unscrupulous, newspapermen covering the mobilization filled their dispatches with Guardsmen's laments, occasionally hinting at near mutiny. Moving quickly to put an end to the negative publicity griping soldiers generated, the War Department unwisely issued a general order in early August forbidding officers and enlisted men from writing "alarming stories, either by private letter or otherwise, concerning conditions" in Texas. Stories or letters "published in a newspaper or other periodical are subject to trial by court martial according to the Articles of War," the order added. This dubious assault on the First Amendment channeled complaining to private areas but did not stop it.

One North Dakota Guardsman, Captain A. B. Welch, Company A, technically violated the order and earned the wrath of General Tharalson. When the Bismarck *Tribune* began a campaign to raise money to purchase a motorized ambulance for the regiment, a *Tribune* reporter asked Welch, as a representative of Bismarck's home company, if the ambulance would help the 1st North Dakota. Welch, in all innocence, said yes. He mentioned that they could use it to carry water during the weekly twelve-mile hikes and to transport heat-exhaustion cases back to camp. The *Tribune* published the interview on 3 September. Tharalson fired off an angry telegram to Colonel Fraine the next day, demanding to know if the regiment took part in marches so severe that men suffered from the heat. He went on, "If these are not the conditions the officer responsible [for the interview] should be mustered out and sent home at once," and requested an immediate report.

Fraine sent the telegram to Captain Welch for comment. Welch at first denied making critical comments, but he altered his position slightly a few days later when he finally saw a copy of the article. He then explained, "There is nothing in this purported interview of a nature which merits censure as it contains no untruths or dissatisfaction with existing conditions." The affair died quietly soon after. Lieutenant Colonel Grafton assured Tharalson that the regiment was not overworked or abused. "Everything possible is done by regimental and higher commanders looking to the health and comfort of the men," Grafton explained. Tharalson remained irked at Welch's interview because, he said, "You cannot expect to get recruits with this kind of story getting into the papers."

The adjutant general had good reason to worry about recruiting. Regimental manpower remained well below war strength, and some companies had failed to reach the peacetime minimum even after muster in. At the end of July, for example, Company F reported only 45 enlisted men. On the other hand, Company D counted 107 men in the same month. The regiment needed a total of 450 to reach war strength and even out the disparity between companies. Because most National Guard units activated in 1916 needed new men, the War Department decided to conduct a nationwide enlistment drive for both the National Guard and the Army, the latter short of war strength also. The campaign used both Regular Army and National Guard teams in their quest for men, both acting under War Department orders. Although the effort lasted from 1 July into early November, it had only a limited success. The War Department enlisted 15,000 men for the two services in four months, barely enough to equal the number lost to expiration of enlistment, discharge for physical disability, and other causes. National Guard enlistments particularly disappointed the War Department. When it became obvious that the Guard was not going to invade Mexico but would patrol the border and take extensive training, enlistments fell off rapidly. General Mann of the Militia Bureau concluded that National Guard "recruiting was most brisk when companies were at their home towns and excitement was high."

North Dakota experienced that phenomenon. Captain G. I. Solum, Company F, led a recruiting party back to the state in early August, accompanied by Lieutenant Ernest S. Hill, Company B, and six enlisted men. For nearly a month, War Department inefficiency left Solum and his men idle, confused, and finally angry. He received conflicting orders from Fort Snelling, Minnesota, and headquarters, Central Department. Recruiting officers at both places claimed authority over the North Dakota contingent, sending the captain contradictory instructions. General Tharalson told Solum to wait. "We waited all right," he wrote Colonel Fraine, "but I must take the liberty to state that we are poor, very poor indeed, at that kind of game." Everyone but Lieutenant Hill "wished they were back at Mercedes." Solum sent his first report to Fraine on 8 September, noting, "Have no blanks or equipment of any kind yet. Greatly delayed and handicapped under present arrangements." After nearly a month at home, his party had not enlisted a single man.

The War Department finally untangled the bureaucratic confusion and placed Solum under the Fort Snelling office. Solum sent Lieutenant Hill and three men to Minot and opened a recruiting office in Bismarck. Still, as he told Fraine on 12 September, "Prospects not good. Reason, no actual fighting nor immediate prospect of any...too much work and everybody busy, and last but not least the firm impression that the troops will all be sent home within thirty days." At the end of the month, Captain Solum reported to Fort Snelling that he had convinced four men to enlist during September. With the harvest season on, he wrote, "no idle men to be found." He wanted to work in smaller towns, naming Edgeley, Ellendale, Oakes, and others, but the Army told him to try Fargo, Grand Forks, and Minot, places that already had companies. Eventually, the Central Department approved making an effort in the smaller towns, as Tharalson wrote Fraine in early November, "but it seems to me that it gave us very little aid." The adjutant general wanted Fraine to replace Solum and Hill. "The men you have here are too slow, especially Hill," he said, "as it seems practically impossible to get him away from the office." At that point, however, the Central Department closed all recruiting offices. Solum, Hill, and the enlisted men returned to Texas at the end of November.

The difficulties obtaining men indicated a strong public perception that border duty was unnecessary and the War Department was keeping Guardsmen there unfairly. Some state soldiers and their families objected to the mobilization from the very beginning. As early as 9 July, a distraught mother wrote Company M's Captain A. G. Wineman that she wanted him "to let Eddie out as he is under age," she explained, "and he joined without our consent so I want you to release that boy at once." Wineman discovered that the boy's father had signed for him, and furthermore, he said, "Private Goodrie himself does not desire a release." He remained with the regiment. When another mother asked Colonel Fraine to release her son because, she wrote, "he is my only son and I do not want him to go," that lad remained also. Yet another upset mother, a widow needing her son's support, requested his discharge. She painted a picture of a desperately unhealthy young man, noting, he "has had one or two attacks of appendicitis, has bad teeth, a year ago last March he broke his ankle and all during last winter the ankle was bandaged." She "was very much surprised that he could pass muster." Some parents simply had concern for their sons' welfare. Captain Thomas Thompsen of Company I assured a worried Wahpeton couple: your boy "is well and working every day with the company. He has not been sick more than the average member of the company." Thompsen told them: do not "worry about your boy for he is in experienced hands as regards to clean living humans."

The Guard's close connection with its home station allowed officers like Captain Thompsen to comfort worried parents. He knew them, and they were familiar with him. The opposite held true as well, however. When a soldier wrote a complaining letter home, it had the potential to upset everyone with a son in the local company. The Walsh County *Record* published a letter from the border in its 8 November 1916 issue headlined "Soldiers Anxious to be Returned Home." Written by a Company C member, the letter contained a list of angry complaints. Calling the border mobilization "The most colossal blunder of the age," the writer maintained, "If I wanted to make soldiering my life work, I would have joined the regular army long ago." He saw his National Guard service as "patriotic" and was "ready and willing to sacrifice my all for a cause," he declared, "but my blood boils when I stop and think that I must be part and parcel to stupid dress parades, grueling marches and military maneuvers for the pleasure and edification of such persons as Secretary of War Baker, et.al. *[sic]* who are toying with the army." He informed the *Record's* editor, "You have no idea what a feeling of discontent prevails here. All these men came down here because they were going to fight Mexicans and they came willingly and gladly. They didn't think they were coming down here to loaf and build roads.'' (Obviously, this soldier ignored the War Department edict regarding critical letters to newspapers. Apparently he went unpunished.)

These bitter sentiments probably exceeded the feelings of many North Dakota soldiers, but resentment at the call-up had been simmering since late June. The number of Guardsmen who sought release from their military obligations at the time of mobilization surprised the War Department. "Reluctance to serve when confronted with the realities of military life was quickly shown,'' General Mann later reported, "in the large number of resignations of officers and applications for discharge by enlisted men." Like Captain Daniel Lewis of the 1st North Dakota, some state soldiers had failed to consider the conflicts between National Guard service and personal or business affairs should a call to arms come. Joining the Guard included accepting a commitment to service, a legal obligation. This did not become apparent until the 1916 Mexican Border incident. In the future, Colonel D. A. Frederick, chief mustering officer, Central Department, recommended, "It should be made plain to all concerned that when the National Guard is called into the service of the United States, which as a rule will be only in case of emergency, applications for discharge will be considered only for the most urgent reasons.''

Along with Lewis, Major James M. Hanley, 3rd Battalion, submitted his resignation soon after the call. Hanley served as judge of North Dakota's Twelfth Judicial District. With four children and a hospitalized wife, he believed family and professional requirements justified leaving the service. The War Department approved Hanley's resignation. By early September, in the face of increasing resignation requests, the government adopted a policy in which "Tenders of resignation for ordinary business or family reasons will be disapproved.'' Fearing a loss of his medical practice and other business interests, Captain Thomas M. MacLachlan, 1st North Dakota surgeon, unsuccessfully tried to resign. He argued poor health also, since, he explained, "with these worries continuously harassing me, I am approaching a state of nervous exhaustion.'' Eventually, the War Department allowed the captain to resign for health reasons after he had spent two months in North Dakota on sick leave. Lieutenant E. W. Jeffrey, Company F, sought release in order to work his large diary farm in Williston, fearing, he said, "if I am unable to return and take the management it will be necessary to sell at sacrifice.'' Again, the Army said no, although Jeffrey received a thirty-day leave to prepare his farm for winter. He gained promotion to captain, Company M, before demobilization.

Enlisted men, particularly married men, faced many of the same family and business responsibilities officers confronted. They did not have the option to resign, and the easy promises company commanders made early in the call-up to release their married men evaporated when the War Department clarified the meaning of the militia laws. Nonetheless, enlisted men with families or dependent relatives quickly submitted applications for discharge on account of dependency. The War Department attempted to accommodate these men for a time. Enlisted men seeking discharges for economic reasons had to submit a form listing their dependents, family wealth, and financial obligations and show that a job awaited them after discharge. Statements on the economic needs of the men from people of local prominence had to accompany all applications. The men of North Dakota's small towns must have found it difficult to open up their private lives, especially financial affairs, to public scrutiny. Although the 1st North Dakota contained relatively few married enlisted men, thirty noncommissioned officers and twenty-eight privates, almost all of them applied for discharge. A number of privates claiming parents who depended on them for support joined them.

As the number of discharge applications rose rapidly in July and August, the War Department took a stronger position, as it had with the growing number of officer resignations, by adopting a policy that allowed only men who had been in the National Guard before 18 June to apply. This approach maintained that those who enlisted after the call-up knew they were going on active duty and therefore knew they had to give up regular employment. Still, discharge applications came in by the thousands. Congress took action in mid-August when it approved a bill alloting fifty dollars a month to enlisted men's dependent relatives. The United States, even in wartime, had never given support to soldiers' families beyond their regular pay. Only the needs of National Guardsmen moved Congress to provide for soldiers' families. North Dakota soldiers and other Guardsmen took ready advantage of this small step forward in the federal government's welfare activities, which thereafter became standard practice in wartime or extended active duty. The dependents' allowance ended discharges for enlisted men. As it was, the government released over six thousand men before Congress approved the new policy.

Another unanticipated problem threatened to drain National Guard personnel as the summer ended. Parents, university and college officials, public school officers, and Guardsmen themselves asked the War Department if it would release high school and college students in early September. The Chief of the Militia Bureau released a circular letter on 2 August stating the policy for students. All National Guard units composed wholly of students (there were nearly twenty all-student companies or batteries) would be mustered out on 1 September and permanently disbanded. All other students should file individual requests for discharge. Later in August, in a typical bureaucratic afterthought, the War Department surveyed National Guard units to find out the number of student soldiers. In a not-unusual report, Colonel Fraine revealed an estimated 150 students in the 1st North Dakota, both high school and college, and added, "The discharge of these men would break up the regiment." Fraine took an exact head count on 23 August finding 138 students in the regiment (fifteen percent of total strength), with 24 in Company C alone.

Once again, the Army reversed course. Secretary of War Baker announced on 9 September that the War Department would muster out the all-student units. It cancelled individual discharges, however, because "any general release of high school and college students would produce profound disorganization in the regiments which are doing border service," he added. The shift in policy confused the public. Parents and school officials wrote regimental officers throughout August, all with the expectation of having their boys return to school in the fall. But, as Captain James D. Gray replied to Norman C. Koontz, superintendent of city schools in Jamestown, home of Company H, "I am sorry that these boys will have to be disappointed." Gray mistakenly tried to ease the disappointment by telling Koontz, "from rumors going the rounds it looks like we might be home soon." He was wrong, for the boys would even miss the start of the second semester in 1917.

Like most soldiers stuck with an unpleasant assignment, Captain Gray was thinking wishfully when he speculated in early September that the 1st North Dakota "might be home soon." Colonel Fraine, a wiser, more experienced soldier, thought differently, and he told Governor Hanna in late August, "It looks as though we are due for a protracted stay here, probably only to be broken by a southward move," that is, into Mexico. Fraine admitted this was "conjecture, merely." Later, on 6 November, General Tharalson told the colonel, "I hardly believe that the regiment is likely to come home this winter." He, too, thought, "you will have to go across the border before you get home." Governor Hanna wrote Major General Henry P. McCain, adjutant general, United States Army, in November to ask when he could expect the regiment's release. "If the idea of having the militia in Texas is largely one of training," Hanna said, "it would seem that the boys have been there now for several months and ought to be in pretty good shape." The governor went on to say that his men were needed at home. "Those who have been left behind," he added, were ready to accept keeping the regiment "in Texas if there is something to be accomplished by having them there." McCain replied that the Southern Department was sending National Guard units home, replacing them with outfits that had not yet performed border duty. The Southern Department, however, would decide when the 1st North Dakota could return, and it had not yet decided.

In the meantime, Colonel Fraine, the Southern Department, and the War Department allowed officers and men to take leave when necessary to tend to business and family matters. Private Arthur G. Homme, Company C, was allowed thirty days, from mid-September to mid-October, to prepare his farm for winter. When Homme re-enlisted on 1 July, before the muster-in, he explained, "I felt there was need for all to respond." A month at home would allow him to help his mother and sister winterize his farm. Major Dana Wright, 2nd Battalion, asked for leave in October to return to Stutsman County in order to carry out his duties as county sheriff. When he got home, Wright discovered that the county commissioners planned to replace him. "They said they would reappoint me if I would resign from the army but I could not see it," he lamented. Wright lost the position. After the Brownsville District maneuvers ended in late November, several other officers who were county or state officials went on furlough to prepare their annual reports and catch up on office work. Unlike the unfortunate Major Wright, they did not lose their posts.

When the 1st North Dakota Infantry at last left Texas on 23 January 1917, headed for Fort Snelling, Minnesota, and muster-out, it went with a written testimony of thanks from the people of Mercedes. The regiment's brigade commander, Colonel A. P. Blacksom, 3rd United States Cavalry, offered

Colonel Fraine his ''appreciation'' for his ''work in camp, on the march and during maneuvers.'' Blacksom noted, the ''excellent conduct of the regiment in Mercedes is especially commended.'' The Brownsville District Sanitary Inspector praised the 1st North Dakota's health record ''over all other organizations of the 13th Provisional Division.'' Waist-deep snow and below-zero temperatures greeted the regiment on its arrival at Fort Snelling, 28 January. Two weeks of processing followed. The Army gave all officers and enlisted men a thorough physical examination, paid them off, and carefully itemized all property accounts. Attempting to recruit Guardsmen for further duty in Texas, the Army promised new enlistees that they could serve in regular regiments with which they had been affiliated along the border. A recruiting circular, devoid of any sense of irony, stated: ''It has occurred to this office that after they enjoy the temporary popularity and distinction due to their service on the border, there may be some of the returning Guardsmen who will desire enlistment in the Regular Army.'' No record suggests a stampede on the Fort Snelling recruiting office. Instead, the Guardsmen took muster out on 14 February and a day later were back at their home stations after eight months of active service.

Deteriorating German-American relations altered the Mexican border crisis before the 1st Infantry arrived home. When Germany resumed unrestricted submarine warfare at the end of January 1917, President Wilson broke off diplomatic relations. Two days later, 5 February, General Pershing led his Punitive Expedition back into the United States. A possible American intervention in the European war compelled Wilson to find diplomatic means to solve the nation's problems with President Carranza as the border question rapidly took second place to German-American difficulties. National Guard service on the border, however, comprised a crucial event between pre-World War I military planning and war mobilization in 1917. The 1903 Militia Act committed the federal government to aid the National Guard financially and to accept the Guard as part of the nation's land forces. In the ensuing years, the General Staff sought ways to work state military forces into its mobilization and contingency plans, but it grew increasingly skeptical of the Guard's ability to provide sufficient trained troops, properly organized and led by knowledgeable officers. Their skepticism ran as strong as ever when President Wilson called the Guard in June 1916.

The mobilization confirmed the General Staff's worst fears. Everywhere they saw chaos, inefficiency, ignorance, and, perhaps worst of all, a grudging reluctance to serve. The Army subjected the National Guard to intense scrutiny throughout 1916, assessing the Guard's performance at mobilization camp, subjecting it to detailed inspections while on the border, and running the state soldiers through exhaustive tactical exercises from battalion to divisional levels. Never had the National Guard been so intensely studied and never had the Army's professionals been so disheartened. In internal memos and published reports, staff officers and department commanders criticized the state soldiers. The Guard's shortcomings seemed evident to all: it failed to provide up-to-strength units; Guard officers barely understood command responsibilities or Army administration; too many Guardsmen were unfit for active duty (eighteen percent of enlisted men failed the Army physical at muster-in); the Guard could not recruit successfully; far too many officers and men sought resignation or discharge.

General T. H. Barry, commanding Central Department, echoed the sentiments of nearly every Army officer commenting on the Guard's performance: "There is but one conclusion to be drawn from what goes before, and that is that the National Guard as now dually organized and administered is not efficient or dependable, cannot be made so in any reasonable time, and it should therefore remain solely as a State force." Barry and his fellow officers agreed that "the only remedy for the defective training of the National Guard is its complete Federalization....A National force if it is to be efficient must be removed from state influences and from state politics," to quote Lieutenant Colonel Eli Helmick. He argued for "some form of compulsory military service" to provide soldiers, another sentiment regular officers repeated. "It is not the men and officers in the militia who are at fault," Major General Leonard Wood, Eastern Department, concluded, "but rather the system." Then he theorized, if the failures of 1916 at last convinced all concerned "of the entire unreliability and workability of our present militia system," and led to the "adoption of a sound, national system...the lesson will be well worth what it cost."

The Guard did exhibit serious defects in 1916. It fell far short of providing the manpower required in both peace and war tables of organization. The 1st North Dakota steadily lost strength while on the border, with an aggregate of 1,011 officers and men at the end of July, and only 850 when the regiment reported to Fort Snelling in January 1917. As Captain Solum's pessimistic reports indicated, North Dakota fared no better than other states in recruiting. In the 1st North Dakota, as in other state units, some were unwilling to accept that part of their enlistment contract or commission included an obligation to serve the federal government. Others, in the words of the Militia Bureau's General Mann, "assumed to judge and to declare that the emergency requiring their presence on the border was past and it was an injustice to retain them longer." A few, notably Captains Daniel Lewis and Thomas MacLachlan, wished to define the terms under which they would serve. Dr. MacLachlan, as had Captain Lewis, maintained he was ready for duty if the Guard "should be called upon for active service in the field in time of war."

Yet for all its imperfections, the Guard's 1916 performance was not the unmitigated disaster Regular Army officers so fervently depicted. The state military systems placed over a hundred thousand officers and men on the border by the end of July, forces relatively well equipped and serving in organized units. The War Department would have had difficulty obtaining such forces in less than six weeks. The Army fared no better in recruiting throughout 1916 than did the National Guard. However unpleasant border duty was, the 1st North Dakota unquestionably returned home a better-trained and organized unit than when it left. Service in Texas forced the regiment to conform to Army organization by forming a headquarters company, to include the band, and a supply company. Brigadier General James Parker, who actually commanded National Guard troops, unlike many of the service's critics, argued that the harsh assessments of July, August, and September were "not fair to the National Guard." Given time to learn, state soldiers

173

performed well. Parker reported in January 1917, as the Guard went home, "these troops are now fit to take the field against a fairly well trained enemy, or to act on the defensive against well-trained troops." While the intent of border mobilization was not to prepare troops for war in Europe, Herman Brocopp's contention that in April 1917 Guardsmen "were really fitted for the field except for technical instruction in modern military methods" bears repeating.

Army critics gave little attention to the peculiar circumstances attending the mobilization. The recent passage of the National Defense Act of 1916, which made explicit the Guardsman's obligation to serve, had not yet been implemented, and confusion unavoidably resulted. More important, the federal government had never called on state troops to serve what amounted to a constabulary function. In some respects, border service took place in the midst of a kind of cold war, where Woodrow Wilson sought to modify Mexican behavior through an American military build-up, rather than with the actual use of force. In the past, militia or National Guard mobilized at the outbreak of war. Guardsmen expected to cross the border, fight Mexicans, end the conflict, and go home. That was the volunteer tradition. Neither President Wilson nor the War Department made much of an effort to inform or educate Guardsmen and their families on the necessity and purpose of the call up. The American people had little experience with a policy where, in General Mann's words, "military ends are frequently attained more by the demonstration than the actual exercise of military force."

Finally, the General Staff's professional soldiers earnestly and ardently desired a single military system under their complete control. They firmly believed in the possibility of the creation of rational, efficient manpower policies, modeled after continental European practice, which would produce a highly trained, easily mobilized Army. If dropping the National Guard and adopting conscription were necessary to achieve that end, the professionals could not see why Congress, the public, or Guardsmen, for that matter, would object. They gave little thought to the serious problems that a conscripted citizen army would pose, as future wartime and peacetime drafts would reveal. Compulsory service would not eliminate the nagging questions of how to treat students, married men, or men with dependent parents. A call to arms of an Army-controlled reserve force would disrupt reservists' civilians lives as had the 1916 call for Guardsmen. Their eagerness to denounce the National Guard as a military failure easily revealed the professional soldiers' myopia and political naivetse. Their criticisms angered Guardsmen and their supporters and made it more difficult to obtain the reforms necessary to improve the state services.

To men like John Fraine, Dana Wright, and Arthur Homme, the Army's denunciations sounded harsh indeed. Colonel Fraine abandoned his campaign for the Republican gubernatorial race at the call to arms, Major Wright lost his sheriff's post, and Private Homme left his farm. Yet Army officers wrote as if they alone had concern for the nation's military system or that only they sacrificed for a higher cause. The majority of officers and enlisted men of the 1st Infantry answered the June call, went to the border, and did their duty. Certainly they complained, for it was often unpleasant duty. For Guardsmen, the 1916 mobilization clearly defined what National Guard service ultimately meant. It made evident what the law implied. To join the Guard no longer only meant a way to spend time with the boys at the armory, or to escape the office for ten days in the summer, or to add another club membership for social or political reasons. It could now mean active duty on the Rio Grande or serving in France. It was a difficult lesson to learn, one not expected by all Guardsmen. The possiblility of a call to active duty, however, remained the essence of National Guard service after 1916.

The state attempted to ameliorate the cost of duty in two bills passed by the legislature during its 1917 session. One appropriated ten thousand dollars to pay for food, clothing, and lodging for enlisted men who had served in Texas but were unemployed after muster-out. The legislature granted the money, partly because "the compensation of the soldier is too small to enable him to save any money," but also because these men "have not only upheld the honor of their Country, but especially the pride, glory and honor of their State." State assistance ended when the men secured employment. Another law provided fifty thousand dollars "in recognition of meritorious military service...and to reimburse such enlisted men for necessary expenses and time lost, not otherwise provided for." Enlisted men received ten dollars for each month served on the border, although those who had taken money from the federal government for dependent relatives were ineligible for this bonus. In this way, the state recognized the extraordinary nature of duty along the Mexican Border.

Notes on Sources

General correspondence and orders for 1916 in Records of the North Dakota National Guard provide detailed coverage of the mobilization. The 1st North Dakota Infantry muster-in rolls, July 1916, the regiment's field and post returns for 1916 and 1917, monthly reports to the Army's adjutant general, and a special "Mobilization and Demobilization File, 1916-1917" were particularly valuable. Sometime in the middle 1930s, Colonel Herman Brocopp, a sergeant in Company A in 1916, wrote a thirty-page history of the North Dakota National Guard. This manuscript covered the Guard from 1898 to World War I. Colonel John Fraine made marginal comments and textual corrections in the manuscript. This short history and a pamphlet Brocopp wrote in the 1950s on Company A's 1916 experience were useful for this chapter.

The National Archives and Records Service, RG94, entry 25, and RG168, entry 12A, offered material on how the Army assessed the mobilization and memoranda written by regular officers suggesting the elimination of the National Guard. RG407, World War I Strength Returns, North Dakota, and World War I Organization Records, National Guard, North Dakota, First Infantry, despite their titles, helped immensely. In the latter, boxes 349 to

352 contained regimental and company reports and correspondence detailing Mexican border training activities, requests for discharges and leaves of absence, and letters between regimental officers and General Thomas Tharalson and Governor Lynn Frazier.

Interviews and questionnaire responses from Leo Dominick and Leroy Goodwater were informative. The Bismarck *Tribune*, Fargo *Forum*, and Walsh County *Record* offered glimpses of events on the home front.

The Militia Bureau's *Report on Mobilization of the Organized Militia and National Guard of the United States, 1916* (Washington, D.C., 1916) was an essential source. Its regular 1916 annual report was also used. The Moses Thisted Papers, held by the United States Military History Institute, Carlisle Barracks, Pennsylvania, helped in understanding the overall border experience. Thisted was National Historian, Mexican Border Veterans, into the 1970s. He collected a wide variety of materials from these veterans, some of which he published in *With the Wisconsin National Guard on the Mexican Border, 1915-1917* (San Jacinto, Calif., 1981). Clarence C. Clendenen, *Blood on the Border: The United States Army and the Mexican Irregulars* (New York, 1969), devotes about half his book to the 1916 intervention and presents the best scholarly study of the military aspects of President Woodrow Wilson's Mexican diplomacy.

[1]Until 1916, all federal legislation and War Department correspondence referred to state troops as "Organized Militia." I have generally avoided the phrase in order to be consistent and limit confusion.

Unidentified company of the First North Dakota Infantry on a field march in Texas during Mexican Border Incident, 1916.

Battalion staff, 2nd Battalion, First North Dakota Infantry (second row includes Gilbert C. Grafton, second from left, and John H. Fraine, third from left.) Date of photograph is unknown.

"Out in the mesquite." Members of the 3rd Battalion, First North Dakota Infantry guarding an irrigation canal during Mexican Border Incident, 1916.

"G.I. humor." Mexican Border Incident, 1916.

☆6☆
World War I: The 164th Infantry
(1st North Dakota, North Dakota National Guard)

A little over a month after the 1st North Dakota Infantry returned home, Colonel John Fraine wrote his regimental adjutant, Captain T. S. Henry, "It looks as tho we are again to take the field. Of course no one can look into the future, but every indication is that we will be going in for a year or more within the next ten days." Germany's unrelenting submarine warfare, which had sunk several American merchant ships by mid-March, sparked Fraine's letter. As early as 28 February 1917, the chief, Militia Bureau, asked the Army's adjutant general to alert the geographic commanders to prepare for full National Guard mobilization and sent a similar notice to state adjutants general. President Woodrow Wilson ordered a partial mobilization in late March, ordering selected National Guard units to federal duty to protect railroad tunnels and bridges, public utilities, and war-related industries from German sabotage. On 26 March 1917, the 2nd Battalion, 1st North Dakota, Major Dana Wright commanding, assembled at home stations. They had been home from Texas just forty days.

Wilson's March call found the North Dakota National Guard in disarray. After eight months on the Mexican border, many enlisted men and some officers decided that state military service demanded greater sacrifices than they were willing to give. Herman Brocopp later wrote sadly on the disintegration of his Company A on its return to North Dakota. The company had gone south in July 1916 with 91 officers and men, and it had returned with a total of 85. On 26 March 1917, 2 officers and 35 enlisted men reported for duty. "It was disheartening that day," Brocopp lamented, "to only be able to muster a few men for duty from that once proud group." Mandan's Company F assembled a pathetic 3 officers and 9 enlisted men while Company K reported with 2 officers and 31 enlisted men. At Jamestown, Company H mustered a more respectable 3 officers and 50 men, but it was still 15 below the federal minimum.

Some enlisted men declined to re-enlist when their contracts expired that spring, a few just disappeared, but the majority took advantage of a War Department decision concerning the dual oath required by the 1916 National Defense Act. A large number of enlisted men and a lesser number of officers who had declined to take the new oath when mobilized in 1916 had remained in the Guard in early 1917. The Militia Bureau's 28 February letter to state adjutants general noted that in future calls "No individual will be accepted who has not taken the oath." Another Militia Bureau memo, to the Army's Chief of Staff on 29 March 1917, re-stated this policy. The President's call

179

was for National Guardsmen only, that is, officers and men who had taken the oath or were willing to take it at the call. Individual Guard units would be accepted "without regard to any limitations as to minimum numbers." The Militia Bureau classified men not taking the oath as Organized Militia, and "this will relegate them to State service only," it said. States were to drop all Militiamen from their rolls when reporting strength returns.

The decision created two state military systems—one composed of men under the dual oath, in the National Guard, and the other, the Organized Militia, made up of men obligated to serve their states until officers resigned and enlisted men's contracts expired. All states had both kinds of soldiers. Some Organized Militia still served along the border in federal service, although the Militia Bureau intended to send them home soon. Deteriorating relations with Germany dictated the War Department's action, for the government could send the National Guard overseas but not the Organized Militia. The National Defense Act gave the War Department far greater authority over the National Guard than previous federal laws had given for the Militia. With war impending and the need to mobilize obvious, the Militia Bureau wanted to dispense with the useless Organized Militia as soon as possible.

In North Dakota, enlisted men who had not yet taken the dual oath used the decision to escape federal service. State and federal records do not make clear who or how many refused to sign the oath. In the rush to mobilize, enlistment records were lost, and Guard officials understandably made little public comment on the low turnout. Estimates can be made, however. The companies composing the 2nd Battalion, A, F, H, K, reported 12 officers and 283 enlisted men at muster-out, 14 February 1917.[1] When mustered in for the March call, the battalion reported 10 officers and 120 enlisted men. According to one government report, the National Guard enlisted strength for the entire 1st Regiment on 1 April came to only 371. The remainder of the 786 enlisted men mustered out in February had left the service or were Organized Militia. The state's delay in adjusting its military code compounded the confusion surrounding the new National Guard obligations. The legislature did not meet until January 1917 and finally amended the military code on 17 March, requiring state enlistment contracts to include federal obligations.

Despite its limited strength, Major Dana R. Wright's 2nd Battalion went on duty immediately, assembling in its armories on 27 March. Company A, Bismarck, and F, Mandan, established guard posts at both ends of the Northern Pacific bridge spanning the Missouri River. At Jamestown, Company H remained at its armory until 1 April. Then, one detachment, an officer and twenty-four men, moved to Fargo to guard bridges crossing the Red River. The rest of the unit went to Valley City to protect railroad bridges over the Sheyenne River. When Dickinson's Company K unexpectedly received orders to report to Fort Missoula, Montana, it left on 2 April, arriving at Missoula two days later under orders to "report to Comdg. Officer thereat as guard for government property." Leaving two men in Dickinson as a recruiting party, Captain Clarence N. Barker led his command of twenty-nine men. On arrival at Missoula, he reported, "A large crowd had gathered to welcome us and I took my *two squads* out to parade them. The people expected a co. of 150 men and were disappointed" (emphasis in the original).

Major Wright set up battalion headquarters, with Lieutenant John W. Murphy as his only staff, at Bismarck's post office. Once on active duty, the battalion was controlled by the Central Department. As Wright told Captain Barker on 30 March, "I have no authority to call the other companies here at present or you would have been here before this." Central Department orders sent the Company H detachments to Fargo and Valley City and Barker's unit to Montana, leaving Wright to command Companies A and F. Throughout April and May, the companies performed guard duty at their assigned places— it was dull, routine work. Although the regiment had recently returned from federal service and Congress had appropriated millions of dollars for the states under the National Defense Act, the 2nd Battalion lacked uniforms and equipment. Barker reported only twenty-three cartridge belts for his unit and the Central Department proved unmercifully slow in meeting supply requisitions.

Company K found itself in a bureaucratic nether world. Although under Central Department orders, the unit actually served in the Western Department, where Fort Missoula was located. Barker had no supplies to equip new recruits arriving from Dickinson. The Central Department ignored him because he was now in the Western Department, and the latter refused to assist him because Company K was from Central Department. Barker tried to get supplies from North Dakota, but he often failed because his unit was in federal service. Finally, Barker wrote Major Wright's new adjutant, Lieutenant Alex Steinbach, in early May, begging for clothes and adding, "Where are we to get the rest of the equipment for this outfit? Have you got any there?" When supplies finally arrived from North Dakota, Barker had to pay the freight bill, as the post commander maintained it was not his responsibility. Too many of his recruits, Barker told Steinbach, "are going around in an assortment of uniforms that would make a rag peddler sit up and take notice." Similar bureaucratic difficulties complicated recruiting for Company K, far removed from its home station in Dickinson. All in all, Barker was fed up. He missed his wife, and, as he wrote Major Wright on 5 May, "I miss the comrad[e]ship of those officers that I got so well acquainted with on the Border and in the various camps that I have attended in the last few years."

Captain James D. Gray, Company H, had even more unpleasant experiences when he provoked the anger of Captain B. F. Ristine, United States Mustering Officer for North Dakota. Central Department headquarters told Ristine that "Any neglect on the part of officers" called to duty in March "will be reported to these headquarters." Ristine quickly followed the orders when Captain Gray took too long to submit enlistment and property account papers. Although North Dakota adjutants general were accustomed to a company officer's delays, the demanding Regular Army officer was not. After he reported Gray's neglect to the Central Department and further charged that Gray tolerated disreputable sanitary conditions at Company H's Valley City quarters, the Central Department sent Ristine's complaints to Major Wright for comment and correction.

When Wright asked Gray to explain, the captain reported that he had been sick and too busy with recruiting to send in the reports. He pointed out that when his detachment came to Valley City, it had to take quarters in an abandoned railroad station frequented by transients. "The windows were boarded and the walls and floors covered with human excreta and dirt"—the building had no toilet or bathing facilities. Gray's men attempted to clean up the old building but, Gray reported, "We had nothing but mud from the time we arrived" owing to heavy rains. Further, he wrote, "the men were new recruits and did not know the meaning of sanitation." At Ristine's request, a North Dakota National Guard medical officer visited the detachment on 15 April and again five days later. On the latter visit, the medical officer reported, "conditions first class in every way and all bad sanitary conditions righted." By the time Major Wright went to Valley City on 13 May, Company H had moved to new quarters and Wright found "all conditions satisfactory." Inadequate quarters and too many untrained recruits partly accounted for Gray's problems, but obviously his officers and noncommissioned officers failed to supervise their men and enforce sanitary practices. Gray found out quickly that the haphazard company administration so common in the peacetime Guard would not be tolerated, or, to use a phrase from another war, he learned that he was in the Army now!

Companies A and F fared better at the Northern Pacific bridge spanning the Missouri River, where the men were close to home and families. Railroad officials, Major Wright wrote Captain Barker, "put up a shelter at each end of the bridge for the men on duty and carry men in uniform back and forth between the bridge and Bismarck and Mandan without tickets." The two companies shared guard assignments, allowing off-duty men to live in their armories. Eventually, the units established a semipermanent camp at the east end of the bridge. Major Wright closely supervised the men's activities, resenting the time he spent in his office. "I'd rather be out on a 12 mile hike than put the same time in an office." He slept at the field camp with his men and went into Bismarck each morning. Wright brought horses from his Jamestown farm, and, he noted, "we have graded up the camp so it is quite level." By late May, over two hundred men occupied the site, sleeping in squad tents with wooden flooring. The city of Bismarck ran a water line to camp. All in all, it was a comfortable place. Wright improvised a firing range for target practice, although, he said, "I have no authority for what I am doing." Unaccountably, while the Army insisted that Guard units in federal service adhere strictly to military procedure and paperwork, neither the Militia Bureau nor any other War Department agency prescribed any training program, even after Congress declared war on Germany on 6 April 1917.

Dana Wright genuinely enjoyed active service. After thirteen years in the Guard, he at last had an independent command. "One delightful thing about this affair," he told Barker, "There is absolutely no one to interfere with me." General Tharalson was busy with mobilization problems and, with Colonel Fraine away, there was "no one to suggest or improve my plans," he commented, adding, "We are as happy as we can be under war threats." At times, Wright practically flaunted his independence. Late in May, "Col. Fraine called on us," he noted, "and went out to the camp." Wright enjoyed the visit "hugely for [Fraine] was bursting to make suggestions but restrained himself with an effort. It's a rare privilege to get the Col. where he cannot give orders and I am making the most of it. I kept telling what I was going to do and how I had done this and that.'' Of course, realizing his independence would not last, the major went on, ''Never mind, he will soon have a chance to even up when the reg. is together again.''

The 2nd Battalion's mobilization brought to the surface frustrations Guardsmen had suppressed during the border call-up. Coming so soon after the Texas duty, the 1917 call caused many state soldiers innumerable problems. Wright told Captain Barker, ''I am sorry that it was necessary to call the Guard out. It makes me sad to think of the trouble it is causing all these fellows. The penalty of patriotism.'' Barker agreed as he hurried to organize business affairs before leaving Dickinson. ''One thing is certain,'' he pointed out, ''and that [is] private business and the National Guard were never meant to go together.'' These frustrations turned to resentment when 2nd Battalion officers learned that non-Guardsmen were seeking, and sometimes obtaining, commissions. Major Wright wrote that some people in Bismarck were talking of raising a second Guard regiment. ''The country is full of patriots,'' he complained to Barker, ''who will save the country if they can have a commission or prescribe the conditions under which the nation is to be led out of the wilderness.'' The War Department, on the authority of the National Defense Act, opened officer training camps in early May. ''All the fellows that want to,'' Barker griped to Alex Steinbach, ''can get anything from Capt. to Major in the Officers Reserve Corps....In three weeks training those men can get a higher command than a Guard officer could get in twelve years service.'' (Actually, reserve officer candidates took three months' training.) Steinbach shared Barker's dislike for the reserve officers. ''Some mob, if they let them all in,'' he carped. The Guardsmen were understandably angry, for they had spent years in the National Guard with limited promotion opportunities. Many hung on with only the hope of taking their commands to war and, at best, earning a higher rank.

Barker and Wright, in particular, resented Organized Militiamen who refused to become National Guardsmen. The captain told Wright, on 23 April, ''I wish that the state would get every one of those men who would not take the dual oath, take them up to Devils Lake and put them to work and good hard work too.'' Major Wright presented the idea to General Tharalson, who approved it. Wright wrote Barker a week later: ''One man of the H bunch which we sent to Devils Lake has kicked in and I anticipate that the others will.'' He wanted a list of Company K men refusing to sign on as Guardsmen ''to take a trip to D.L. for their health,'' he said, adding, ''I will be glad to make the necessary arrangements.'' He put the men at Devils Lake to work chopping wood, in effect a form of hard labor. Barker happily named candidates for the major's woodpile. ''With your coarse fare and the active exercise which we know you will give them...they will be in a fine state physically if not mentally by the time that they decide to join their comrades in Missoula,'' Barker gloated. According to Alex Steinbach, Wright was still sending men to ''the Devils Lake woodpile'' well into May. Certainly no one could be expected to have sympathy for the Militiamen, but Wright's coercive policy, illustrative of a near-hysterical superpatriotism across the nation in 1917, was both mean spirited and hardly likely to gain him enthusiastic National Guardsmen.

Near the end of May, the Central Department ordered the 2nd Battalion to concentrate at Fort Lincoln. Wright moved his headquarters there on 24 May and Company K left Fort Missoula on the 26th. After a twenty-four-hour layover in Dickinson, courtesy of the battalion commander, Company K went into quarters at Fort Lincoln on the 28th. Companies A and F reported on 4 June. While the Fort Lincoln units rotated guard duty at the Northern Pacific bridge near Bismarck, Company H's detachments remained at Valley City and Fargo. By the end of May, the battalion's strength had tripled, from 120 men on 1 April to 364. Company F, which went on duty with 9 enlisted men, totaled 92.

Through no fault of its own, the 2nd Battalion achieved little distinction guarding railroad bridges in North Dakota and protecting Fort Missoula. The fear of German saboteurs, another example of early wartime hysteria, proved to be unfounded. The battalion at Fort Lincoln from June through August carried out routine duties and close-order drill. On 3 May, Clarence Barker bemoaned to Alex Steinbach, "Don't it beat the Devil that they do not order the rest of the Regiment out. It seems as though they did not want the Guard." "They," that is, the War Department, were not at the present time ready for the National Guard. Just over eighty thousand National Guard officers and enlisted men had been in federal service when the United States declared war in early April, but the War Department had not thus far devised training plans for the state forces, nor did it yet know the exact military role the United States would play in the European war. Barker did not miss the mark too far when he wrote to a Regular Army friend back at Fort Missoula, "If the War Department is doing anything it is not evident from this place."

Barker's complaint reflected the frequent confusion of a soldier at the lower end of the chain of command who rarely knew or understood what his superiors were doing. This rang particularly true in 1917, when the United States was as unprepared for war as at any time in its history. German-American relations steadily deteriorated from the summer of 1916 onward, and the theme of military preparedness had played a prominent part in the presidential campaign. Still, even when President Wilson broke diplomatic relations with Germany in early February, he hoped to avoid war. Wilson kept military planners from developing specific mobilization and strategic plans in the event the nation might enter the conflict. The President generally ignored military matters, was uncomfortable with military men, and sincerely believed that contingency planning at worst provoked war and at best prejudiced decision makers' thinking. Even after opting for intervention in April, Wilson and his advisers had little idea how many American soldiers might go "over there." The Army had no means to train, arm, and equip millions of men, and the country lacked manufacturing facilities for the major weapons, machine guns and heavy artillery, which dominated the Western Front. Few in the Wilson administration or the War Department understood the enormous logistical appetites of modern combat. April, May, and June 1917 were months of learning. The War Department sent American military missions to Britain and France to study the strategy, tactics, and logistics of trench warfare. In turn, British and French missions came to the United States, loaded with information and desperate pleas for millions of American soldiers.

World War I posed major problems of a kind the United States had never faced before. As history's first truly mass, industrial war, the conflict consumed men and materiel at a rate that surprised and dismayed even Europe's professional military men. American military planners, both soldiers and civilians, learned quickly in the spring of 1917 that the war's demands necessitated a huge organizational effort. The nation needed to mobilize and organize not only its military manpower but its economy and public opinion as well. Thus, while Clarence Barker and his fellow North Dakota Guardsmen grumbled about the pointlessness of routine duty at Fort Lincoln, the War Department worked on plans that would guide the nation's war effort through 1918. Using provisions in the 1916 National Defense Act, and subsequent authority given in the Selective Service Act of 18 May 1917, the War Department set out to create a large infantry army able to take a major role on the Western Front.

America's war army of 1917-1918 did not compare with any the nation had fielded. Originally, Major General John J. Pershing, commanding the American Expeditionary Force, recommended that the United States send over twenty combat divisions and support troops totaling just over one million men. He later revised his recommendation to sixty-six divisions, or three million men. Eventually the United States sent two million men in forty-two divisions from the nearly four million taken into the Army. This was no volunteer force hurriedly put together at state camps and rushed to the front as soon as they were equipped. Thirteen percent of them joined the Army, another ten percent enlisted in the National Guard, but the vast majority of American soldiers, seventy-seven percent, were drafted. The War Department developed systematic plans to organize, equip, and provide officers for the combat divisions bound for France. Professional officers dominated the American Expeditionary Force. Gone were the days when volunteer military entrepreneurs started their own companies, battalions, and regiments, and then used political influence to acquire commissions. The Army ultimately determined the fitness of National Guard officers and shaped thousands of reserve officers in their image at the Officer Training Camps Clarence Barker and Alex Steinbach so despised.

The War Department moved slowly in implementing its mobilization and training programs. Draftees could not be called until federal and state governments established local draft boards, which were not fully prepared until the first draft took place on 20 July. Army and National Guard volunteers and draftees could not begin training until the government built training camps. The adjutant general, United States Army, sent a program for organizing troops to department commanders on 22 May. His memo revealed the desperate shortage of equipment, noting that "Non-essentials should not be permitted to delay...putting a large army into training....Even the lack of uniforms for a week or two should not delay organization." The program called for all Regular Army divisions to be in training by the end of June, the Guard in camp by early August, and 500,000 National Army troops (draftees) at work by 1 September. It based National Guard mobilization on a 1916 plan to field sixteen National Guard divisions. The 1st Infantry, North Dakota National Guard, was slated to report for training on 1 August 1917 at an as-yet unbuilt and unspecified camp in the Southern Department.

After 2nd Battalion's call in March, the rest of the regiment anticipated active duty. Colonel Fraine thought the government intended to raise a large volunteer army, taking from the 1st North Dakota "enough men of training to officer and train such other troops as are necessary." General Tharalson sent a memorandum to all unit commanders not on active duty, dated 31 March 1917, requesting them to prepare their companies for federal service. No immediate call came, of course, but the 6 April declaration of war made it evident that the 1st Infantry would eventually serve. Fraine encouraged company commanders to recruit to war strength, 150 enlisted men for rifle companies, but enlistees appeared slowly, especially in the inactive units. Captain T. S. Henry, regimental adjutant, fretted, "People do not realize that we are at war...there appears to be rather a lack of interest in the country's affairs, especially among the young men who are coming forward very slowly." Henry said, if Congress approved a draft law, "in that event we can get the men." One correspondent from Bismarck told Captain Henry on 30 April, "All the young men here are trying to beat conscription by enlisting in their home organizations." According to Alex Steinbach, the rush to volunteer in face of the pending draft allowed Guard recruiters to be "more careful of the men selected than ever before, and the difference in personnel is startling."

The Guard had to compete with the regular services as some North Dakota boys, eager to join the fray, enlisted in the Army, Navy, or Marine Corps. Others, particularly young college men avidly recruited by the Army, volunteered for Officer Training Camp, including National Guardsmen. Captain Henry lamented the loss of the latter, although he felt "proud," he said, "that a few of our boys will better themselves." In the interim between the declaration of war and the call to active duty, "The regiment itself, without financial aid or other assistance either from the government or the War Department," recruited to near war strength, Herman Brocopp later wrote. When called on 15 July the 1st Regiment had 150 men in eight of the twelve infantry companies. Only Company L, at 61 men, was far off the mark.

Prospects of lengthy federal service led to numerous company officer changes from March to July. By the latter month, eight captains serving in February 1917 were no longer with their companies. Guard officers had learned during the Mexican border mobilization that the War Department refused to accept officer resignations once it called the Guard, so those who believed it necessary to leave the service resigned before the 15 July call. Captains E. W. Jeffery, Company K, and Calvin H. Smith, Company H, submitted resignations. Company A's Captain A. B. Welch requested and received transfer to the supernumerary list. Interestingly, 2nd Battalion officers who criticized Organized Militiamen for refusing to take the dual oath had little to say about officers who resigned in the face of mobilization. Why they saw Militiamen as slackers trying to avoid their obligations but apparently did not view resigning officers in the same light poses an interesting puzzle.

It is impossible to determine why the officers left the service. Undoubtedly family and business responsibilities were paramount, but enlisted men had the same responsibilities, although not the option to resign. Sergeant Major Oscar B. Treumann probably typifies both enlisted men and officers who did not feel they could remain in the Guard. When Treumann decided not to re-enlist in April 1917, Captain Manville Sprague told regimental adjutant T. S. Henry, "He is married and his wife dependent upon him." Sprague and Treumann worked at the First National Bank of Grafton. If both went to war, "we would have no one to run our business here—for that reason it was simply a question of which one of us quit—all things considered I decided it would be better for me to stick," Sprague explained. Henry was pleased that Sprague decided to remain with the North Dakota National Guard. "There are very few resigning, and the regiment, even with a big bunch of recruits, will be in as good condition as before with a few months training."

While Captain G. A. M. Anderson, Company B, resigned to accept a second lieutenancy in the Regular Army, other captains left their companies to take transfers or promotions. Company C's Captain Sprague transferred to the Supply Company to replace Baird. Barney C. Boyd, of Hillsboro's Company L and the regiment's company commander of longest tenure, sixteen years, took promotion to major, 3rd Battalion, replacing Major G. Angus Fraser when the latter became adjutant general in July. The captain of Company D, Frank Wheelon, resigned to become major and regimental surgeon, 2nd North Dakota Infantry, when it was organized in late June. Finally, Captain Guttrom I. Solum, Company F, failed the physical examination when his unit entered service.

Resignations, transfers, and promotions necessitated other promotions and transfers. The realignment of the officer corps revealed the difference that continued to exist between the National Guard and the Army despite the new militia laws. Company B, for example, elected its second lieutenant, Reginald F. E. Colley, to captain over its incumbent first lieutenant. In Company L, Second Lieutenant Henry Halverson also jumped his first lieutenant to take the captaincy. Major Dana Wright did not want First Lieutenant Vincent J. Melarvie to take command of Company F. With support from state headquarters, "We put the skids under him," Wright told Clarence Barker, and "asked him to retire." The major "felt sorry" for Melarvie but added, "There was no hope for the company as long as he stood in the way." Wright managed to have his battalion adjutant, Robert Wilson, promoted to captain to lead Company F. Melarvie transferred to Company H so Alex Steinbach could then become battalion adjutant. John W. Murphy, adjutant for the 1st Battalion, took command of Company A, which lost all of its officers before the end of June. Other companies, C, D, and M, promoted their first lieutenants to company commander. The different ways in which the new captains obtained their promotions indicated an informality in officer selection which would have dismayed any officer in the seniority-bound Regular Army. All the new captains, however, shared one common trait—and an important one: they all came from the Guard with several years of service.

Personnel changes always disrupt and sometimes leave bad feelings—this was the case for the 1st Regiment. Dana Wright and Alex Steinbach did not like at least one consequence of the April-June changes in the 2nd Battalion. They both wanted to see Vincent Melarvie retired, and they also resented the transfer of a certain young second lieutenant from Grafton's Company C to Jamestown's Company H. He was John R. Fraine, the colonel's son. Wright told Captain Barker, "It was suggested that Johnnie transfer back to 'C' but that was not very cordially received by any of the Grafton bunch." Although Steinbach reluctantly admitted, "Young Fraine is doing better this time and Melarvie is holding down the fort at Fargo" with the bridge guard, he still thought it was "a shame to be stuck with both Fraine and Melarvie" in Company H. "Both halves of the company would do far better with their own officers," that is, with men from Jamestown, said Steinbach. Steinbach had served previously with Company H, before he went to battalion headquarters, and the insertion of "outsiders" from Mandan and Grafton was too much for him.

Regimental jealousies and the interests of local groups were probably unavoidable, given the Guard's decentralized nature. Major Wright worried that a vacancy in Company A "will probably be filled by some sprout from Grafton," he said, but did not specify which sprout. By July 1917, however, a young "Johnnie" Fraine served as a second lieutenant in Company A. Other changes created a sense of sadness. Clarence Barker regretted that Captain Guttrom Solum, Company F, failed his physical, commenting, "He was a very faithful fellow." Barker worried, noting, "I may get plucked myself on account of that hernia," a problem that nearly kept him from serving on the border. "If I do," he added, "I don't think that much money will be wasted on telegrams trying to get the War Dept. to reconsider their action."

Some Guardsmen no longer in service wanted to rejoin with prospects of war service assured. B. D. Cloud, Mandan, formerly sergeant major, 1st Battalion, wrote Captain T. S. Henry, "Have discussed the war situation frequently...with my wife and she has consented to let me go back in, so will reenlist at once." He wanted his old job back, and Henry assured Cloud he could have it. James A. Soules, a sergeant in Headquarters Company, also wrote Henry asking for sergeant major's stripes. His enlistment expired on 15 June, and, he said, "I had just about decided to enter the navy or aviation corps." Soules would remain in the Guard if he could become a sergeant major. "I have a reasonable amount of ambition, so of course would like to get along as fast as possible," he added. Henry got Soules the promotion.

State headquarters also experienced a major change. Adjutant General Thomas H. Tharalson retired on 1 July, having remained in office beyond the January retirement date set by law to oversee demobilization of the 1st North Dakota from border duty. Major G. Angus Fraser took the adjutant generalcy after Colonel Fraine, Lieutenant Colonel Gilbert C. Grafton, and Dana Wright, all senior to Fraser, turned down the appointment. Fraser, who proved effective in preparing the North Dakota National Guard for mobilization, also assumed responsibility for administering North Dakota's selective service system. Serving as an active duty captain in the Army for draft purposes, he supervised fifty-three local draft boards. These boards registered over 160,000 men and inducted nearly 19,000. Overall, including National Guard and regular service volunteers, North Dakota provided 27,253 men for the war effort. The various changes in North Dakota National Guard personnel, inevitable in any military organization moving from peacetime status to a war footing, fortunately took place in the quiet months from April to July, before the entire Guard entered active duty.

Approximately 3,700 North Dakota men went to war as National Guardsmen, with the 2,051 from the 1st Regiment and the remainder from the newly organized 2nd Infantry Regiment. In many respects, the 2nd Regiment was a final expression of the nineteenth-century volunteer spirit. The Fargo *Forum* first mentioned the new outfit on 23 May, erroneously reporting that the War Department had asked the state to organize it. This was not the case, for the Department intended to form National Guard divisions from existing state units. From conception to organization, the 2nd Infantry was a private effort, gladly accepted by the state, but only reluctantly approved by the federal government. Former National Guard officers no longer active or on the supernumerary list, and staff officers not eligible to serve with the 1st Regiment, concocted the idea. Though eager to go to war in a state unit, they were denied the opportunity.

Former governor, and major in the 1898 1st North Dakota Volunteers, Frank White, General Thomas Tharalson, and District Judge James M. Hanley, recently retired major, 3rd Battalion, North Dakota National Guard, figured prominently among those organizing the 2nd Regiment. Governor Lynn Frazier supported the proposition, as would have any nineteenth-century governor, because sending a second regiment enhanced his reputation as well as North Dakota's. Frazier's endorsement was no backroom payoff to long-time political associates. A maverick in state politics representing the first significant victory of the reformist Nonpartisan League, the governor owed no debts to these Republican stalwarts, particularly Frank White. As one correspondent told Secretary of War Newton D. Baker, "White is not a political adherent of the governor." North Dakotans pressuring the War Department to accept the regiment used the obvious political differences between Frazier and the 2nd Regiment's organizers as proof of the enterprise's purity. In this instance, the ambitions of the regiment's proponents and Governor Frazier neatly coincided, overriding political rivalries.

It was one thing to propose a new unit and quite another to convince the War Department to accept it within the strict federal laws now governing the National Guard. General Tharalson first suggested the new regiment to Washington on 18 June. Surprisingly, the Militia Bureau immediately approved the project, but its regulations were not going to make organization easy. First, North Dakota had to ensure that "the regiment already organized is first raised as far as practicable to maximum strength." Second, the Militia Bureau stipulated that the new unit had to be recruited to minimum strength, inspected, and recognized by 10 July, giving the state only three weeks to raise it. When General Tharalson and Governor Frazier attempted to have the deadline extended to 20 July, the War Department refused to budge. Even pressure from Senator P. J. McCumber failed. The Militia Bureau explained that granting an extension would "derange" the pending National Guard mobilization. Military planners had to know exactly how many men and units would mobilize on 15 July. Furthermore, any delay in organizing the 2nd Regiment would likely "upset the calculations on selective service...on account of voluntary enlistments."

Recruitment for the 2nd Regiment followed the old, free-style volunteer system, as men of local prominence worked to raise companies and anticipated winning election to a captaincy. The Fargo *Forum* reported on 3 July: at least "sixteen companies are now in course of organization over the state," when only twelve infantry companies would be accepted. Meanwhile, the originators of the regimental idea met privately, without Governor Frazier's participation, to select regimental field and staff officers. James Hanley in his World War I diary gives information on the final selections. From 24 June to 7 July, Hanley, Tharalson, White, and others met almost daily to consider regimental officers. At a meeting in Hanley's Mandan home on the 24th, White not present, the judge "suggested as Colonel some Regular Army officer," preferably one of the men who had served as inspector-instructor with the North Dakota National Guard. Leaving the colonelcy aside for a time, the men discussed a "proposed 'line-up' of officers," with Tharalson as lieutenant colonel, White and Hanley as majors, and several of the old 1st North Dakota Volunteers as company commanders.

In the ensuing days, Hanley's daily entries indicate he offered commissions to nearly every man to whom he talked. (His sense of importance in the project may have been an exaggerated one.) On 26 June, while in court "hearing equity cases, I could, in imagination," he recalled, "see the battlefields of France and a charge with much loss of life." The regiment's organizers met again four days later in Bismarck at the McKenzie Hotel to go "over the list of officers," Frank White, Charles Mudgett, A. B. Welch (recently of Company A, 1st North Dakota), Tharalson, and Hanley taking part in the discussion. General Tharalson reported that the War Department refused to allow regular officers to accept National Guard commissions. The rather sensitive question of whom, among this ambitious group, should take the colonelcy they apparently settled without rancor, when someone suggested "that White should be the man for Col., to which I agreed," Hanley wrote. Just before Governor Frazier announced the regiment's formation, the group reached agreement on all officers, with White as colonel, Tharalson as lieutenant colonel, and Hanley, Mudgett, and Edward C. Gearey, Jr., as majors. According to the diary, "Adj. Gen. Frazier [*sic*] probably suggested Gearey."

Governor Frazier announced the 2nd Regiment's organization on 30 June, released the field and staff officers' names on 3 July, and published the unit's entire list of officers and home stations in a 12 July general order. (See Table 6.1.) The regiment's officers comprised an amalgam of Philippine Insurrection veterans, former National Guard commissioned and noncommissioned officers, and men with no military experience. Field grade officers were men long active in state politics and military affairs. The captains were a more mixed lot, ranging from old-timers like Thomas Lonnevik and Frank Ross, both veterans of 1898-1899 and both fifty years old in 1917, to Captain Charles L. Rouse, a mere twenty-two years old with no military experience. Of the latter, Captain T. S. Henry later wrote, "he would make a good platoon leader with the grade of second lieutenant" if given three months training. "His present grade of captain is too high for his age, qualifications and experience." Captain John Rock, Supply Company, a nine-year enlisted veteran of the Regular Army, had served a two year stint as sergeant-instructor with the National Guard, 1911-1913. Most of the lieutenants had once served as noncommissioned officers in the 1st Regiment and, as a group, had more National Guard experience than the captains.

TABLE 6.1

Roster, 2nd Infantry,
North Dakota National Guard, 1917

Field and Staff

Name and Rank	NDNG Service/ Highest Rank	Service, 1898-1899
Colonel Frank White	1892-1900, Major	1st ND, Major
Lieutenant Colonel T.H. Tharalson	1889-1917, Brigadier General	1st ND, 2nd Lieutenant
Major Charles F. Mudgett	1890-1912, Major	1st ND, Captain
Major James M. Hanley	1906-1916, Major	12th Minn., Private
Major Edward C. Gearey, Jr	1890-1914, Lieutenant Colonel	1st ND, Captain
Captain Henry T. Murphy, Headquarters Company	1898-1912, Captain	1st ND, Private
Captain John W. Rock Supply Company	1914-1917, Captain	None
Major Frank E. Wheelon Medical Detachment	1909-1917, Captain (Infantry)	None

Company Commanders

Unit	Home Station	NDNG Service/ Name	Highest Rank
A	Minot	Millard C. Lawson	None
B	New Rockford	Charles L. Wheeler	None
C	Crosby	Charles L. Rouse	None
D	Devils Lake	Thomas Lonnevik	1892-1907, Capt.; in 1st ND, 1898-1899
E	Langdon	Frank Ross	1894-1906, Capt.; in 1st ND, 1898-1899
F	Carrington*		
G	Rolla	John W. Grant	None
H	Harvey	George Crawford	1901-1910, Sergeant
I	Bismarck	A. B. Welch	1913-1917, Capt.; in 1st ND, 1898-1899
K	Ellendale	Harry E. Thomas	1899-1906, Captain
L	Hankinson*		
M	Beach	Charles I. Cook	None
Machine Gun	Dickinson (Lieutenant)	Fred J. Flury	1907-1915, 1st Lieutenant

*No captain as of 1 July 1917.

Several captains and lieutenants, following the volunteer tradition, earned selection as a consequence of their efforts to organize companies. General Fraser supported commissioning all three officers in Company A, Minot, despite their lack of military experience, largely because "through their efforts this company was recruited in three days." He gave similar endorsements to Captains John Grant, Company G, and George Crawford, Company H. Fraser praised Lieutenant Fred J. Flury of Dickinson's Machine Gun Company as "a very active young man of excellent standing" who had "organized a fine company," impressing the adjutant general because he did not ask for a captaincy. Rather, the young man hoped the state could find a candidate for captain "who had received instruction in machine gun work." Nothing better illustrated how outdated the volunteer tradition was in 1917, or the naivetse of these otherwise well-intentioned men. The machine gun dominated daily life on the Western Front, yet the 2nd North Dakota's Machine Gun Company did not have a single man able to instruct his comrades in using the weapon. In any event, the company had no guns and most likely no one in the unit had ever seen one.

With field-grade and company officers commissioned in early July, the 2nd Regiment faced the daunting task of recruiting to minimum strength before the 10 July deadline. It would have difficulty accomplishing this, for the long-established 1st Regiment had not yet filled up to war strength. The Militia Bureau informed Governor Frazier that on 20 June the older unit fell short of the maximum by over 880 men. State officials knew by mid-June that President Wilson would call the National Guard in July for initial service at home stations and then shipment to divisional training camps. Wilson made this official on 3 July in a proclamation to state governors. On 15 or 25 July, the President would *call* the Guard into United States service "for proper protection against possible interference with the execution of the laws of the union by agents of the enemy." Similar in legal terms to the 1916 mobilization, the call was for traditional constitutional militia use. Under authority given in the Selective Service Act of 18 May 1917, Wilson would "*draft* into the military service of the United States...all members of the National Guard" on 5 August (emphasis in the original). The call made the Guard subject to War Department orders and put it on the federal payroll and Army supply list, but only for service within the United States. The draft, on the other hand, took Guardsmen as individuals into the Army and automatically discharged them from state service. Initially, the drafted Guard would enter the Army in units under officers commissioned by the states. The Army, however, had no legal obligation to maintain state units once they were drafted.

North Dakota's two regiments were slated for the 15 July call and, after a two- to three-week organization period at home station, would move to training camps. An initial Militia Bureau memo of 4 July mentioned sending the 13th National Guard Division, of which the North Dakota National Guard was a part, to Fort Sill, Oklahoma, but later the bureau decided to send the division to New Mexico. Another bureau decision two weeks later removed North Dakota's regiments from the 13th Division and assigned them to the 20th, because the former had too many infantry regiments. The 20th Division would go for training to Palo Alto, California, according to planning memos written at the end of July. These plans, too, would change, as would the actual dates when the 1st and 2nd regiments finally left the state. Equipment shortages, difficulties in completing training camps, and major changes in divisional tables of organization caused many delays. A harried War Department moved slowly in informing states of mobilization alterations and rarely took the time to explain why it made changes. The regiments remained in North Dakota until late September, biding their time and attempting to fill in their ranks.

The 1st Regiment had an easier time finding recruits and meeting the mobilization deadline than did the newly organized 2nd. General Fraser issued a general order to 1st North Dakota units not yet on active duty asking company commanders to check their rolls for men who had taken the dual oath, particularly in July and August 1916, and remind them that they were National Guardsmen "subject to the call during the unexpired portion of [their] enlistment contract." A private in Headquarters Company wrote Captain T. S. Henry requesting release from his oath because he was a farmer. "At the present time I do not see how you can be excused," Henry told the man. "Even the conscript men are not excused from serving tho they claim farming as an exemption."

Despite the 1st Regiment's lengthy history and the state's efforts since the government activated the 2nd Battalion in March, recruiting went slowly. When the regiment mobilized on 15 July, several companies had not attained war strength and Companies I and L lacked half the required men. Fargo's Company B, fifty men short on mobilization day, launched a vigorous recruiting campaign. A parade through downtown Fargo, plus bands and speeches, on 16 July failed to produce recruits. Captain Reginald Colley issued an appeal to Fargo citizens to lend automobiles to his unit as a part of "a campaign for recruits from the cities and villages within a radius of 50 miles of Fargo." That the state's largest municipality had to scour the countryside for new men suggested the difficulties all Guard units faced in reaching war strength. Colley told the Fargo *Forum* that his recruiters would use the pending draft to win over young men. He said he advised them that the effort was the "last chance to join a company in which they have friends instead of waiting for the draft which will place them in ranks where they are strangers." By the end of July, Company B finally reported an enrollment of 156 enlisted men, just over war strength. The rest of the regiment, except for Company L at 61 enlisted men, approached or exceeded the required number by the end of July. The regiment needed to meet that strength by 5 August when the Guard entered the Army, for, after that, state forces could only enlist men not eligible for the draft, that is, men under twenty-one or over thirty. Wesley Johnson, a sophomore at the University of North Dakota, enlisted at Grand Forks on 17 August. Although underage at seventeen and underweight, only 126 pounds at six feet in height, he managed to become a private in Company M. The 1st Regiment lacked 100 men on 31 August, a far better recruiting success than it achieved during the Mexican border mobilization.

On 15 July 1917, 1st Regiment units mobilized at their home stations' armories. Colonel Fraine established regimental headquarters at Grafton, his hometown, with Lieutenant Colonel Gilbert C. Grafton, and Majors Frank S. Henry, 1st Battalion, and Barney C. Boyd, 3rd Battalion, present. Headquarters Company under Captain T. S. Henry and Supply Company, Captain Manville Sprague commanding, also reported to Grafton. Under the Army's awkward decentralized command system, the infantry and machine gun companies reported to Central Department headquarters in Chicago, not to Colonel Fraine. Company commanders submitted supply requisitions to the Central Department, which in turn directed company training activities. General Fraser advised his captains, "Care of your men for the next fifteen days will demand...much executive and resourceful capacity." Captains had to feed and quarter their men and see to their health and moral welfare. Since local armories did not suffice to house the large wartime companies, Fraser urged commanders, "Interest your citizens in this subject" and house extra men in public buildings or private homes. "Your success in this respect will mark your ability as a commander and a provider."

Expectations that the regiment would leave North Dakota by early August were soon dashed as War Department efforts to prepare divisional training camps fell behind schedule. Although the large number of green recruits needed basic training and the isolation of a military camp, they idled their time away in their hometowns, unable to work or live at home. All units had desperate shortages of equipment. Captain Thomas Thomsen, Company I, reported on mobilization day, "This Company short knives, forks, spoons, meat cans, haversacks, canteens, cartridge belts, entrenching tools, cook stove and utensils, also tentage and rifles, bayonets and bayonet scabbards, in fact all ordnance." Supply deficits persisted into September. When Company H's Fargo and Valley City detachments returned to Fort Lincoln in early August, the 2nd Battalion had four war-strength companies under a single command on a military post. The battalion lived more comfortably in barracks than did the separate companies crowded into their armories. As early as 10 August, the Fargo *Forum* reported that in Company B "The monotony of constant drill with none of the excitement of camp life is beginning to tell on the morale of the soldiers."

The soldiers rightfully complained as the dull weeks dragged on. Morale and training would have greatly improved had the regiment concentrated at either Devils Lake or Fort Lincoln, but the War Department did not order a concentration because it wanted all training conducted by the Army at divisional camps. It expected to order the Guard to such a camp soon. Too much time and money would be wasted in establishing a temporary training camp in North Dakota. As a result of delays in opening training camps, however, the 1st Regiment idled away two and a half months in their armories to no particular purpose. Wesley Johnson recalled, after joining Company M, "During the stay of our unit in Grand Forks, preparatory to leaving for camp, we had a few guards, a few inspections, light drill during which poker occupied a good part, and a few maneuvers." Inevitably, during the waiting period, rumors filled the armories and newspapers as to the Guard's ultimate destination. The Fargo *Forum* reported every rumor related to the regiment's possible training sites, and suggested first Russia, then the Philippine Islands as the Guard's final overseas assignment. The regiment's long waiting period from mid-July to the end of September was a particularly unpleasant example of the military's "hurry up and wait" syndrome, but unavoidable given the nation's unpreparedness in 1917. As the War Department struggled to do everything at once—build training camps, acquire clothing and equipment, determine divisional organization, implement the draft, and innumerable other things—the 1st Regiment waited, though not necessarily patiently.

Compared to the 2nd Regiment's numerous difficulties, the 1st fared fairly well. The new unit had little to build on except its originators' enthusiasm and the initial burst of pride in the small towns designated as home stations. Neither enthusiasm nor pride, however, could manufacture able-bodied enlistees. Companies A and I, Minot and Bismarck respectively, and the Machine Gun Company at Dickinson competed with established 1st Regiment units for recruits. The 2nd's Company L, home station Hankinson in the state's southeast corner, failed miserably in recruiting. As late as 12 August, it reported only thirty-three enlisted men. Company I, 1st North Dakota, Wahpeton, less than thirty miles from Hankinson, had already recruited the area thoroughly. The upcoming 20 July draft also threatened to take away potential enlistees. The 2nd North Dakota needed to bring all units to minimum strength by 10 July. If it failed to field twelve infantry companies and a machine gun unit at minimum strength, the War Department would not grant the regiment federal recognition and would deny recognition to individual companies also.

By the eve of the 15 July call it had become obvious that the new regiment would not succeed in mobilizing all units at minimum strength. An overworked Central Department had been unable to send mustering officers to examine officers and inspect new companies. General Fraser asked the Militia Bureau if the 2nd North Dakota should answer the call. The bureau replied, "Enlisted personnel duly sworn in are included in the call." Finally it extended recognition to eight 2nd Regiment units "as separate companies" on 4 August. The bureau refused to recognize Companies B, F, K, L, Headquarters, and Supply companies unless the units reached a strength of one hundred enlisted men each by midnight 4 August, as the Guard was to be drafted into federal service the next day. And, it added, all enlisted men of the unrecognized companies "will respond to draft as individuals." The Militia Bureau offered what seemed a false hope. If the companies and the regiment "comply with requirements as of date midnight tonight they will be accepted." Failing that, enlisted men taken individually "will be formed into companies under orders of the Department after the draft."

Governor Frazier and General Fraser, then Senators Asle J. Gronna and Porter J. McCumber, telegraphed appeals to the Militia Bureau and Secretary of War Newton Baker in a last effort to save the regiment. Senator Gronna assured Baker that Governor Frazier had "selected good clean men of merit and military ability" to lead the regiments. "The men are largely farmer boys," he emphasized, "inured to outdoor life." Former Governor John Burke, now Treasurer of the United States, added his voice to the pleas in a letter to the Army's adjutant general. He pointed out the "great disappointment if they are not mustered in," and added that accepting the outfit "will dispense with the expense of conscription...and while conscription is necessary, I think the volunteer is always a little bit more willing, and makes a better soldier." Burke's last point was a fitting endorsement to the volunteer spirit which animated the 2nd Regiment from its beginning. The Militia Bureau agreed to recognize the understrength companies, although not owing to sympathy for the volunteer argument. In a 6 August telegram to Governor Frazier, Brigadier General William Mann, chief, Militia Bureau, reported that his office had committed a serious error. Someone in the bureau inadvertently told North Dakota officials back in June that sixty-five men comprised the minimum for infantry companies seeking federal recognition, when actually, General Mann went on, the bureau's "fixed rule" stipulated a one-hundred-man minimum. He added, however, "in order to keep faith with your officials who were acting on what they believed was the authorized minimum," the Militia Bureau had granted recognition to all understrength units except Company L. The latter never exceeded forty-four men, although it accompanied the 2nd Regiment to training camp.

In the nineteenth century, particularly during the Civil War and the Spanish-American War, governors eager to enhance their individual states' role in the war effort successfully forced incomplete, understrength units on the federal government. State congressional delegations and other politically prominent men joined the lobbying effort. North Dakota's attempts to save the 2nd Regiment mirrored the old pattern. Despite the flow of telegrams to Washington, the regiment was clearly doomed until General Mann discovered the bureaucratic mistake concerning minimum strength. The War Department resisted with far greater success than in the past demands to accept hastily formed state units in 1917. Federal law specified in detail the procedures for starting a National Guard regiment. If states failed to comply with the law, the federal government had no obligation to accept their units. Furthermore, detailed General Staff mobilization plans gave the War Department a bureaucratic argument to use in rejecting new state organizations. Taking them might disrupt mobilization planning. The 2nd North Dakota Infantry was National Guard in name only, its rank and file composed of raw, untrained troops and at least half its company officers just as unprepared. The outfit lacked sufficient training to ensure cohesion. In all but its National Guard title, the regiment was a volunteer unit, nineteenth-century style, and one of the few hastily organized Guard units to gain War Department recognition.

The 2nd Regiment's failure to comply with both the spirit and the letter of the National Defense Act became evident when the Militia Bureau examined its officers. Sections 74 and 75 of the 1916 law enumerated National Guard officers' qualifications for federal recognition. Officer candidates had to have military experience (enlisted service was acceptable), ideally be graduates of colleges and universities where Regular Army officers taught military science, and pass physical, moral, and professional examinations. The Militia Bureau reluctantly recognized the 2nd Regiment's companies, because it had made a mistake, but refused to recognize eighteen of the unit's company officers because they did not comply with Sections 74 and 75. Traditionally, from the Revolutionary War to 1898, state governors held the right to appoint all officers in state units, from the colonel down to the last second lieutenant. Governors could use any method they desired for selecting officers and the law bound the federal government to accept them. But in 1917, federal law gave the War Department final authority to accept or reject National Guard officers entering United States service.

The War Department turned down officers for a variety of reasons. Some were too young and others too old for their assigned rank. The Army's mustering officer rejected one lieutenant "because of lack of education and no military training and experience whatever." Milton Thompson lost his second lieutenant's position in Company G, 2nd Regiment, explaining, "I failed a physical because of underweight and was...separated."[2] Most officers failed to meet the requirements for military experience, an inevitable consequence of allowing private individuals to recruit companies. When the regiment entered service in early August, Companies A, F, G, and M had no officers at all, forcing the Central Department to place four first lieutenants from the 1st Regiment in temporary command. With the mix-up on minimum strength, followed by rejection of company officers, according to the Fargo *Forum* on 10 August, "a generally confused condition exists in the unit."

State officials again protested War Department actions. On 28 July, General Fraser sent a lengthy letter, moderate in tone, to Major Douglas Settle, Mustering Officer, reviewing the regimental and company officers' backgrounds. He admitted that several of the latter failed to comply with Section 74 but hoped Settle would approve them anyway because they all had ability. Governor Frazier sent a much stronger telegram to Secretary of War Baker, asserting that it was "unfair to state to accept men without officers commissioned by me." Frazier's ultimate argument resounded in nineteenth-century tones, "People of state very anxious that these boys be sent [to the] front under their own officers." Members of Company C, Crosby, petitioned the War Department "to waive the technicalities...preventing muster" of their lieutenants and, invoking the volunteer tradition, argued, "We enlisted voluntarily and with the understanding that we could go with our own officers."

In his letter to Major Settle, General Fraser incidentally noted: all 1st Regiment officers "qualified under Section 74. All of them has been a member *[sic]* of the National Guard for over one enlistment and none of them were commissioned until after having served at least one year as an enlisted man, the state laws requires this, and the Colonel insisted upon it." If state officials had applied the law and 1st Regiment practice to the 2nd, they would have avoided much confusion and resentment. From 6 August to 27 September Companies A, F, and G remained under the command of 1st Regiment lieutenants with no officers of their own, and Companies C, H, K, and M operated with only one officer each. Almost literally at the last hour, on 27 September, the War Department relented and accepted fifteen of the eighteen rejected men. Still, when the 2nd left for divisional training, it remained short nine officers.

Under these conditions, the newly formed companies encountered difficulty in carrying on minimal training. Other factors limited training in any event. The companies in the 2nd Regiment had no armories, little or no equipment, not even uniforms. Although clothing allotments began to arrive in the second week of August, the outfit never had the opportunity to drill with rifles. Rolf Glerum recalled that Company D, Devils Lake, received "excellent outside parade ground training" but little else. Of necessity, 2nd Regiment enlistees lived a casual, nonmilitary life. Since the companies lacked field kitchens and other messing equipment, they ate at local hotels and restaurants. In many home stations, the Fargo *Forum* reported, the men were "quartered in school houses, and other public buildings, while many hospitable citizens have opened their homes to the soldier boys."

Rolla's Company G suffered the most. Lieutenant Berto Olson, Company L, 1st Regiment, took temporary command of Company G on 10 August. He found ninety-three enlisted men, commanded by the first sergeant, "quartered upstairs in the City Fire Hall, an old frame building, in a room 32 feet by 48 feet in size." The building was poorly ventilated, "with no water...or latrines of any sort." Many of the men slept on the floor without mattresses and took their meals at a local hotel at thirty-five cents per meal per man. Olson discovered company records scattered around the room, some on a table, others in boxes or loose on the floor. Company G had no accounting system for the few quartermaster supplies available, and these too were scattered around the fire hall. He found "the enlisted men and private citizens in and around the home station of Company G...in a hostile frame of mind on account of the loss of 'their captain,'" John W. Grant. Olson met with Grant and Rolla's businessmen, explaining his responsibility and the federal law. Thereafter, "they became enthusiastic in support of the organization and a big help to me," he noted. Grant also "used his best efforts and influence" to assist Olson. The lieutenant asked Major Settle if Company G could move to Devils Lake and take quarters at the Chautauqua grounds near the state military reservation. When Settle agreed, the Company moved to Devils Lake on 18 August, where living conditions improved greatly.

Orders to report to divisional training camp finally arrived on 19 September. The War Department assigned the two regiments to the 41st Division, then organizing at Camp Greene, Charlotte, North Carolina. Rolf Glerum and the men of Company D, 2nd North Dakota, attended "Many going away parties, picnics, dances, farewells," and state newspapers focused increased attention on the units in their last days at home. With an aggregate of 2,051 officers and men, the 1st Regiment left on 29 September. The 2nd Battalion entrained at Fort Lincoln, while the remaining companies boarded trains at home stations. In Grand Forks, Wesley Johnson reported, "We took our leave amid some confusion and considerable sadness; nevertheless we held our heads high in expectation of what was ahead." The 2nd Regiment took trains at their home stations two days later, each of the three battalions making up a troop train. Major James Hanley's train stopped at Devils Lake to pick up Companies D and G, where two thousand people "packed the railroad yards." No one made a speech, but the two companies paraded "before entraining. It was a sad sight to see the mothers, wives, and fathers in tears as the train left." Hanley's train rendezvoused in Minneapolis on 1 October with battalion trains commanded by Majors Charles Mudgett and Edward Gearey. Colonel Frank White also joined the regiment at that point. All of North Dakota's Guardsmen were then en route to Camp Greene.

General Staff planning emphasized the infantry division as the American Expeditionary Force's focal point. Infantry divisions and their support troops served as training units and building blocks for higher tactical groupings. The General Staff had experimented with divisional tables of organization for years and developed several plans to form Regular Army and National Guard regiments into combat divisions in the event of war. A lack of funds and shortage of regular troops prevented the Army from forming its own divisions in peacetime, except for an experimental 1911 Maneuver Division fielded along the Texas-Mexican border. Numerous problems worked against creating active National Guard divisions before 1917. Many states were reluctant to establish auxiliary forces (field artillery, cavalry, and engineer units) needed to complete divisional tables because these were more expensive than infantry. The Militia Bureau found it difficult to organize Guard divisions that included more than one state. As with the Army, insufficient funds prevented the War Department from forming temporary Guard divisions during summer maneuvers to see how they might function. When war came in 1917, the War Department faced the problem of giving life to the long-dormant paper plans. Inevitably, confusion, misunderstanding, and dramatic changes occurred in the hectic months following the declaration of war.

First, the War Department needed to adjust the old plans to the tactical and strategic conditions of Western Front warfare. The military missions Secretary of War Newton Baker sent to Europe reported in July 1917 that the Army's divisional tables needed drastic alteration, so the American Expeditionary Forces could effectively handle trench warfare. Baker accepted the recommendations. The Army had published divisional tables on 3 May which provided for the so-called triangular division, made up of three infantry brigades, each containing three infantry regiments. Regimental tables provided a total of 2,002 enlisted men and 54 officers in fifteen companies. Twelve rifle companies, each with 150 men and 3 officers, formed the heart of the infantry regiment. Including artillery, cavalry, and logistical troops, the triangular division totalled 28,256 officers and enlisted men. From May to September 1917 National Guard regiments recruited on the basis of these tables.

The new system, called the square division, differed little in aggregate strength, but it expanded regimental manpower and reduced the number of regiments. A square division included two infantry brigades with two regiments each. Regimental strength totaled 104 officers and 3,768 enlisted men with the rifle company now at 250 men led by 6 officers. The new tables, adopted in mid-July, necessitated a complete reorganization of National Guard divisions, for they had too many infantry regiments and too few artillery, cavalry, and support troops. This rearrangement removed North Dakota from the 34th Division and reassigned it to the 41st and also accounted in part for the long delays in moving to training camp. The 41st contained National Guard troops from Idaho, Montana, Oregon, Washington, and Wyoming, with Palo Alto, California, originally set as its training site. Later, the War Department named Camp Greene the divisional camp. Activated early in September, the 41st received its first unit, the 3rd District of Columbia Infantry, another surplus outfit, on 3 September. A 19 September division general order implemented reorganization under square division tables, noting, "The for[e]going reorganization applies at once to organizations present in camp; to those not present reorganization applies on date of arrival at these headquarters." Two more weeks would pass before the North Dakota Guard left for Camp Greene, but neither the War Department nor the 41st Division informed the two regiments of the pending changes.

Divisional authorities did not wait long to tell North Dakota Guardsmen once they reached North Carolina. The 2nd Regiment's trains arrived in Charlotte at 9:00 A.M., 5 October. "We were met at the depot by a staff officer," Major Hanley wrote, "who told us the regiment had been broken up and that the different companies would be assigned to different organizations." Reorganization was a blow to the unit's founders. Confused and disappointed, Colonel White, with Majors Mudgett, Gearey, and Hanley, "Went to what was supposed to be a camp of 2nd N.D." to await orders. White's son Edwin, serving in the Navy, reflected the sadness of the regiment's supporters in a letter to his mother: "I do hope that something may be done and the regiment may yet exist as a whole for it doesn't seem fair to the men to say nothing of Dad." Hanley was particularly irked because, he said, "We seemed to get no sympathy from the officers of the 1st N.D." His adjutant, Lieutenant Frederick Neumeier, "reported to me," he added, "that they were all laughing up their sleeves and that Captain Ritchie [David Ritchie, Company G, 1st North Dakota] seemed to glory in the fact that we were broken up." Some rivalry had occurred between the two outfits, as a few men in the older regiment saw the 2nd as a Johnny-come-lately bunch who stole their recruits. Hanley thought it proper that his old comrades should visit 2nd North Dakota officers, but only Lieutenant Colonel Gilbert Grafton made the effort. While Hanley was out of camp, "Col. Fraine called and asked for me," wrote Hanley, "and left word for me to call." That was not enough for the major. He then added: "I noticed an entire absence of invitation to go over to their camp to eat and sleep, which is only ordinary courtesy. I got a room downtown and spent most of my time in camp waiting orders."

Division headquarters reassigned 2nd Regiment officers and men, as well as personnel from other state units which were broken up, to the 41st's auxiliary units. Colonel White took command of Headquarters, 116th Train and Military Police, the administrative unit for divisional trains, or support units. Lieutenant Colonel Thomas Tharalson became commanding officer of the 116th Ammunition Train; regimental surgeon and Major Frank Wheelon went to the 116th Sanitary Train [Medical Corps]; and Majors Gearey and Hanley took command of the 147th and 148th Machine Gun Battalions, respectively. Major Charles Mudgett transferred to the division's 81st Infantry Brigade as brigade adjutant. Most of the 2nd Regiment's captains, some lieutenants, and about half its enlisted men were distributed to the auxiliary units. The entire 2nd Battalion and Headquarters Company, for example, entered the 116th Engineer Battalion. Reorganization under square division tables broke up scores of National Guard regiments in other training camps. Many Guardsmen resented the action, for it destroyed state units and cost many officers combat commands. Moreover, as in the case of a raw unit like the 2nd North Dakota, which had not even received adequate training as infantry, it put Guard personnel into military assignments for which they totally lacked preparation.

Of the nine infantry regiments assigned to the 41st Division, four remained intact; the 2nd Washington, 3rd Oregon, 2nd Montana, and 1st North Dakota. In order to give the American Expeditionary Force uniformity, the Army adopted a numbering system for use throughout the service, regardless of a unit's origin. It numbered Regular Army infantry regiments 1 to 100 inclusive; National Guard regiments, 101 through 300; and National Army (draftees) outfits numbers over 300. This new system eliminated all state regimental names, another source of resentment for Guardsmen. The four infantry regiments of the 41st became: 161st (2nd Washington), 162nd (3rd Oregon), 163rd (2nd Montana), and 164th (1st North Dakota).

Under reorganization, the 164th retained all its field, staff, and company officers, but it now fell well understrength for enlisted men and short two first lieutenants and a second lieutenant in each rifle company. All the enlisted men from Companies A, B, C, D, and Machine Gun Company, 2nd North Dakota, transferred to the 164th, as did a number of the regiment's first and second lieutenants. The entire Medical Detachment, 3rd District of Columbia Infantry, was also assigned to the 164th.

Although War Department plans called for each division to spend at least four months, preferably six, in basic training before movement overseas, the desperate need to get American troops to France prevented the 41st from following this schedule. Even before the last National Guard troops reached Camp Greene on 25 October, divisional teams were moving north to ports of embarkation for shipment to France. Consequently, the division never underwent a full training cycle. The 164th put in nine days' target practice soon after it arrived, but Wesley Johnson wrote that each man only shot two hours during the entire time on the rifle range. One 164th veteran recalled ''Basic close order drills and physical conditioning'' as the only Camp Greene training activities. Lack of equipment, particularly machine guns and trench mortars, further hampered training, as did a shortage of uniforms. The division's War Diary noted that ''instruction was somewhat interfered with by the lack of adequate space for drilling, also by time lost in readjusting the old units to the new organization and in the securing of equipment.'' The auxiliary units did not have time to learn anything about their new specialities.

The men of the 41st barely adjusted to Camp Greene before they began to move to Camp Mills, Long Island. Some National Guard units joined the division at Camp Mills without ever going to North Carolina. The first outfits left Charlotte on 22 October, the 164th being the last out, on 16 November. ''Charlotte has been very pleasant and we have enjoyed the camp,'' Major Hanley noted. ''The move means, however, one step nearer to France and, of course, that is what we all want.'' Manville Sprague, Captain, Supply Company, also found North Carolina ''very pleasant but...expensive.'' Enlisted men had little time to discover the delights of southern hospitality, although Boyd Cormany later remembered that ''the Band gave a lovely and formal party at the old Selwyn Hotel...in the nature of a dance. Our Colonel Fraine and other officers were there,'' he added. Just before leaving for Long Island, the 164th football team played and defeated the regulars of the 39th United States Infantry.

While the bulk of the 41st moved north, some units with horses went to Newport News, Virginia, including the 116th Ammunition Train and the 148th Field Artillery Regiment. Colonel Frank White took charge of these "casuals," as the Army called them. Newport News became a kind of purgatory for these 41st Division orphans awaiting ships to transport their horses overseas. Their pay and health records went with the division, causing the men to receive no pay for months. Mrs. White accompanied her husband to Virginia and, according to an enlisted man's letter, became "a mother to us all." She even organized a Christmas Day party for the homesick men. "If it hadn't been for Mrs. White I don't know how it would have turned out, God bless her," the enlistee added. When the War Department at last remembered these lost souls, in March 1918, the men petitioned the department to allow Mrs. White to accompany them to France, pointing out, "She has demonstrated by her kindliness and care of our men that her presence with us would be very useful." There was, of course, no place for Mrs. White in Pershing's American Expeditionary Force, and she remained in the United States.

For the rest of the division, Camp Mills proved to be more miserable than Newport News. No one remembered the camp with any fondness. "It was a hell hole," Boyd Cormany wrote. They arrived in mid-November "and the weather was really cold." The 41st's War Diary recorded: "The Division was under canvas at this camp and suffered from the severe cold weather, all water pipes being frozen at times." Tents were old, full of holes, and rotting. The bandsmen stuffed the holes "with our campaign hats and rags," Cormany wrote. To keep warm, the men tore down every wooden building in sight to fuel "those miserable little camp stoves-one to a tent." Twelve to sixteen men lived in eight-man tents. Latrines, Cormany went on, "were merely burlap sides hung on wood poles." Due to the bad weather, "We drilled spasmodically," Wesley Johnson remembered, adding that one morning Company M awoke "to find a flood of water over all our section of the camp. That meant that all of our clothes were soaked or had floated away."

A War Department inspection found the division, just prior to shipment overseas, careless "as to dress and appearance among both officers and men," as if it were possible to keep neat and clean at Camp Mills. The 41st remained short of "practically all kinds of equipment." The report concluded: "The progress of instruction and discipline in this division has not been satisfactory. Commanding officers have not accomplished all that the War Department had reason to expect of them." The division did not deserve such harsh criticism. It had never stayed in one place long enough with its full complement of twenty-eight thousand officers and men to complete even basic training. Soon after arriving at Camp Mills, the 41st absorbed eight thousand drafted men from Fort Lewis, Washington, yet another disruption. Through no fault of its own, the division did not receive needed clothing and equipment. On 30 September the War Department selected the 41st to go overseas before the end of 1917, when less than half the division had arrived at Camp Greene. Its commanding officer, Major General Hunter Liggett, spent less than a week in command before going to France and never rejoined the division. A second Inspector General's report, submitted in January 1918, concluded that the

41st's failures resulted from its late, disorganized mobilization, supply problems beyond its control, and the War Department's haste to move it overseas. Its woeful condition in December 1917 clearly indicated the nation had not yet overcome its unpreparedness for war.

For the 164th, the influx of drafted men to bring it to war strength disrupted unit cohesion. Boyd Cormany remembered them as "a tough and motley crowd. They did not like the country, the army or us," he noted, "and there was a lot of trouble which continued after we hit France." The Guardsmen viewed these men as outsiders, and many drafted men were aliens in the legal sense of the word. Captain Thomas Thomsen reported thirteen new men in Company I, all with Italian surnames, who, he said, "Cannot read, write, speak or understand English." All units reported draftees of German, Turkish, Austrian, and Bulgarian nationality with relatives fighting for the Central Powers. This was the new army, raised by mass conscription to fight a mass war. The camaraderie, neighborliness, and local flavor of the 1898 1st North Dakota Volunteers had gone, because the nature of World War I dictated conscription. When the 164th left Camp Greene, it had a strength of 78 officers and 2,602 men, almost all of them from the two North Dakota Regiments. On leaving the United States, the regiment totaled 107 officers and 3,563 men. The majority of additional officers were first and second lieutenants transferred from Officers Reserve Corps training camps and the new draftees.

The 41st Division at last escaped Camp Mills on 6 December, moving to Camp Merritt, Tenafly, New Jersey, where it took refuge from the winter in wooden barracks. On the 14th it shifted to Port of Embarkation, Hoboken, New Jersey, and set sail for Europe on the SS *Leviathan* a day later. The 164th left an old friend behind on its departure. Captain Clarence Barker, Company K, Dickinson, took discharge for a physical disability, his hernia finally costing him his command. The regiment's officers gave Barker a gold watch and chain, "a small token of the friendship and best wishes we hold for you," they said. Lieutenant Colonel Thomas Tharalson, commanding 116th Ammunition Train and second only to John Fraine in seniority of service in the Guard, did not go overseas either. James Hanley recorded that Tharalson's discharge "was the result of the claim that he was incompetent to command the 116th Ammunition Train." Colonel Fraine, sitting on Tharalson's review board, "came to me...and explained the hard situation that Tharalson was up against," he continued. The former adjutant general managed to secure a discharge for physical disability, but clearly he had become a victim of the volunteer tradition which had organized the 2nd North Dakota Infantry and put him in a command beyond his knowledge and capacity.

As had mobilization, movement overseas proceeded in bits and pieces. Shipping shortages and continued German submarine threats slowed transport of the American Expeditionary Force to Europe until the spring of 1918. Division advance parties left the United States on 26 November, the 81st and 82nd Infantry brigades departed in mid-December, but divisional artillery did not go until the first week of January. One artillery regiment remained at Camp Merritt under a scarlet fever quarantine. Major Hanley's 148th Machine Gun Battalion, also quarantined due to a measles outbreak, at last got away on 11 January. "In some ways it seems strange," he pondered, "because for over 20 years I have been off and on in the military, always looking forward to the time when orders would come that would mean service and action." While in the 12th Minnesota Volunteers in 1898, Hanley never left the United States. He served on the Mexican border in 1916, but again he saw no combat. "Now the orders expected for 20 years have come and I approach it with satisfaction," he wrote. The last division personnel to leave, of course, were the "casuals" under Frank White at Newport News who sailed in early April.

The 41st; the 1st and 2nd divisions, Regular Army; the 26th, Yankee Division, New England National Guard; and the 42nd, Rainbow Division, composed of surplus National Guard units unable to fit into other reorganized square divisions, were the first five American combat divisions to go to France. The 1st, 26th, and 42nd were already engaged in trench warfare training when the 2nd and 41st reached France. Except for the men from Newport News, all elements of the 41st passed through England on their way to the French port of Le Havre. After landing at Liverpool, on England's west coast, they took trains across the island to rest camps near the port of Southampton. The 164th entered Liverpool on 24 December 1917 and arrived at Camp Winnall-Down, Winchester, on Christmas Day, six days later beginning movement across the English Channel. The North Dakotans expressed little liking for England or the British. To Wesley Johnson, Liverpool was a "dismal port." Camp Winnall-Down was cold and wet, and many in Johnson's Company M contracted measles and scarlet fever. The British troops in camp, according to Boyd Cormany, "had no use for us....We were damn glad to leave Merry Old England." When Hanley's battalion passed through the same places a month later, he complained that "The food was poor," and he found most British officers unpleasant. "As a rule I did not like the English officers very much. They seem cads," he added.

Fortunately for Allied relations, American troops soon left for France, crossing the channel in a variety of uncomfortable seacraft. Cormany recalled that the band went over on "a cattle ship" that "smelled like a pig pen." Most of the North Dakota landlubbers suffered during the short trip to Le Havre, Johnson recounting that most of his comrades spent the voyage "dismissing their meals on every side below deck." The 164th moved to France in five separate detachments from 31 December to 9 January 1918, each detachment spending time near Le Havre in a French rest camp that made Camp Winnall-Down seem like a pleasant place. "We lived uncomfortably there for about two weeks," Johnson wrote. It rained all the time, and Company M lost more men to disease. They lived in conical tents built for six but holding twelve to fourteen doughboys. They had no cots or blankets, Boyd Cormany remembered, and "The rations we received before leaving the cattle ship was [sic] raw bacon and ground coffee. How we were supposed to cook it will forever remain a mystery." Although Major Hanley's men went to a British camp when they reached Le Havre on 22 January, they had no better accommodations. "The men are formed and marched to a common kitchen for grub which was very poor," he observed, "The mess being a hunk of bread and bad coffee and a little jam!" Clearly the Americans, thrust into foreign countries about which most of them knew little, had no appreciation for the enormous costs the war had exacted from the British and French nations. Already, disillusionment could be sensed among the North Dakotans as they first met the ugly signs of war.

Confusion and unhappiness deepened as the 164th left Le Havre at one- or two-day intervals, bound for the 41st Division camp at La Courtine, two hundred miles south of Paris. On this "cold, miserable trip" the men sat crammed into third-class day coaches or the famous French "40 and 8" railroad wagons, large enough to carry forty men or eight horses. Tired, dirty, hungry, with nothing but hardtack and canned meat to eat, "we were ready to mutiny or lick the whole German Army," Cormany recalled. Unfortunately, the men took out their anger on innocent Frenchmen at stops along the way. According to W. J. Peters, "Stoves were picked up to heat cars," that is, they were stolen, and soldiers swiped chocolate and wine at another stop. Division headquarters later billed the regiment for the stolen goods. "We all swore we would never pay it," Cormany remembered, "but we did. Colonel Fraine changed our minds about that affair."

After arriving at La Courtine, the regiment took quarters in nearly uninhabitable stone barracks once occupied by Russian troops. Cormany wrote, "There was about 3 inches of Russian human filth all over the floor and we had to get boards and water to scrape it out." He found a skull under his rough lumber bunk and though "I did not care too much for the under bed ornament," he recalled, he "was too tired and sick to think about it." Morale in the 164th remained low, due to the unit's lengthy transiency from Hoboken to La Courtine and away from Colonel Fraine's well-known insistence on discipline. The adjutant, 41st Division, sent Fraine a memo on 9 January 1918, charging the regiment with indiscriminate destruction of its barracks and widespread uncleanliness. "It is with great regret that the Division Commander informs you, through me, that the general condition of your regiment during the few days he has seen it, has been disgraceful," the adjutant wrote. Fraine later reported that they had arrested a man for destroying barracks property and that the regiment had cleaned up its quarters.

General Headquarters, American Expeditionary Force, intended to put each division in France through a thorough training program, beginning with basic training in rear-area camps. Later, infantry and artillery brigades would take position in trenches in quiet sectors, brigaded with veteran French units for instruction. Once each brigade had spent time on the front line, the entire division would reassemble in the rear for full field maneuvers. At the end of a four- to five-month instruction cycle, General Pershing intended to place trained American divisions on the line in an active sector with the American Expeditionary Force holding a full section of the Western Front. The 41st, however, never went through the divisional training program. The planners at General Staff and General Headquarters had failed to consider the combat divisions' needs for replacements. Even in training, units were bound to lose men to accidents, sickness, and transfer, and combat would inevitably generate additional losses. Furthermore, the divisions in France in early 1918 fell short of war strength. The 1st Division had come over in June 1917, before the War Department adopted square division tables. In January, General

Headquarters selected the 41st Division to provide replacements for other combat divisions.

The 164th's January strength return tersely recounted the consequences of this decision: "Arrived in France first part of January, transferred all available privates to First Division." Within days after its arrival at La Courtine, between 9 and 20 January, the regiment sent approximately eighteen hundred privates to the 16th, 18th, and 26th Infantry Regiments, 1st Division, and over one hundred men to the unit's machine gun battalions. Other infantry regiments in the 41st also lost their privates, as did most of the auxiliary and support units. For example, the 116th Engineer Battalion, which had taken in an entire battalion from the 2nd North Dakota back at Camp Greene, forwarded twelve hundred men to other units. Later, toward the end of January, when James Hanley's 148th Machine Gun Battalion rejoined the 41st, it too provided 1st Division replacements.

The breakup of the 164th "was a demoralizing blow to everyone," Boyd Cormany recalled. Some of his comrades believed General Pershing's staff picked the 41st for replacements "due to the fact that we were a National Guard Division and a lot of Top Brass did not care for the National Guard and thought they were no good." Other divisions, both Regular Army and National Army, however, later suffered the same treatment. Perhaps because he had not joined Company M until August 1917 Wesley Johnson did not understand "the so-called tragedy of the breaking up" of the 164th. The expressions of grief and sadness shown by many of his comrades when privates said goodbye to their officers and noncoms "puzzled and annoyed" him. Yet even James Hanley, who had some reason to resent men in the 164th, displayed great sympathy for his former friends: "I learned that the 1st ND had been almost completely broken up," he recalled when his battalion reported to the 41st in late January. "This seems hard when one thinks of the fine personnel of those North Dakota boys who were all volunteers and had been in the militia for years...to have all those fine boys thrown into the regulars without their officers or the men from their own state or town with them."

The volunteer spirit died hard in the face of the brutal, anonymous Western Front. Guardsmen focused most of their anger at the Regular Army, not the war itself. "One of our officers," Johnson remembered, "told us that if we believed any of the delightful fancies of justice and equality and democracy, we should get them out of our system." Under American Expeditionary Force control, "over here they did not exist." Hanley resented the regulars also. For years, he explained, "there has been so much distinction between the Militia and Regulars," and many "promises on the part of the Government to keep the services separate." Now, the Army was breaking those promises, though the necessities of war, not an Army plot, dictated splitting up the 41st Division. War Department errors in manpower policy, as well as earlier mistakes and changes in divisional tables, did, however, intensify Guard resentments. It appeared that the professional soldiers did not know what they were doing, as they broke up and reorganized National Guard units back in the United States, only to repeat the process when the reorganized divisions came to France. Of course, the regulars did not always understand the situation as they adjusted the antiquated, unprepared American military system to the demands of modern war. Awareness of that did not lessen the bitterness or sense of betrayal.

Most 164th privates left the regiment on 9-10 January, with others to follow on the 14th and 20th. "These men were loaded in open cattle cars in the depth of winter, the country covered in snow, in bitter weather," Herman Brocopp, a sergeant in Company A, later wrote. Boyd Cormany would "never forget the sights," he recalled, "as we marched the men to the station" when the Band played for each departing detachment. "There were brothers who were parted and men who had been friends in the guard for years. There was a lot of crying and men openly and without shame threw their arms about each other and kissed as they said goodbye." Earle H. Tostevin, a member of the regiment and former newspaperman, later wrote that Colonel Fraine, silent tears on his face, paced the railroad platform, bidding farewell to his men. "Hardboiled birds glared at each other as though challenging a smile at tears; as though daring anyone to speak of the 'Old Man's' display of feeling, or their own."

Boyd Cormany and his fellow bandsmen heard rumors that the band would be broken up and its members reassigned to combat divisions as stretcher bearers or infantry. "So—we did everything possible to justify our position as a band and musicians," he said. They played all routine military formations, "for every one of the departures," and jazz and concert music at the barracks in the evening "to try to cheer up the boys. We could hardly play outside it was so cold but," he added, "we played on the slightest provocation." The band managed to remain together. The men sent to the 1st Division at last received intensive training. One private, who went from Company C, 164th, to Company E, 18th United States Infantry, remembered, "We were billeted for several days in a little woods and drilled, close order, on the side of a little hill facing the German Army five kilometers away." Wesley Johnson left Company M to report to Company F, 26th Infantry. His new outfit went through the full training cycle and entered a quiet trench on 26 March. He later saw action at Cantigny and Soissons and in the St. Mihiel and Meuse-Argonne offensives. In July 1918, a private from Company A, Frank Last, fell wounded at Soissons, as a member of the 18th Infantry. Captured there, he spent the rest of the war as a prisoner of the Germans. Milton Thompson and other men from the 164th's Company L reported to Headquarters Company, 26th Infantry. Thompson first entered trench duty on 24 February, his unit serving in the same battles as Johnson's. The hundreds of 164th privates serving in the 1st Division shared similar experiences, for that outfit was one of the first American Expeditionary Force units to enter combat.

Soon after General Headquarters stripped the 41st Division of its privates, it redesignated the unit Base and Training Division, I Corps. It would later carry other names, including Depot Division, I Corps, and First Depot Division, American Expeditionary Force, but its functions remained the same. From 15 January to 26 December 1918, when it was reconstituted as the 41st Division, the unit provided officers and noncommissioned officers to operate a replacement center, training camp, and several specialty schools. For the

164th, this meant temporary assignment to the Services of Supply, the American Expeditionary Force's logistical arm, while the remainder of the division moved from La Courtine to St. Aignan-Noyers to establish its replacement center and training camp. The regiment left La Courtine on 18 January, in three detachments, to provide administrative personnel as follows: Regimental Headquarters, Headquarters and Supply Companies, and 1st Battalion, to 1st Corps School, Gondrecourt; 2nd and 3rd battalions (less one company) to 2nd Corps School, Chuatillon-sur-Seine; and Company M and Machine Gun Company to Headquarters Army Schools, Langres. All three villages lay within a few miles of General Headquarters at Chaumont, about 125 miles east of Paris. The regiment then totaled 103 officers and 953 enlisted men, the majority of the latter noncommissioned officers.

In March, Companies I, K, and L, 3rd Battalion, moved from Chuatillon-sur-Seine to join Company M at Headquarters Army Schools, at Langres, with Major Barney C. Boyd in command. Regimental officers sometimes served on detached duty with the American Expeditionary Force. Captain David Ritchie, Company G, served as assistant to the Chief of Staff, 41st Division and Depot Division, from mid-January through March. On two separate occasions, Colonel Fraine took temporary command of the 82nd Infantry Brigade, but only for a few days. Captain L. L. Eckman, Machine Gun Company, performed detached duty as an instructor with the 2nd Brigade, 1st Division machine gun battalions for several weeks. In June, Major Boyd took the 3rd Battalion and Machine Gun Company to St. Aignan-Noyers to assist Headquarters, Depot Division, I Corps, in operating the replacement center. The battalion's strength for five companies totaled 147 men. Regimental Headquarters moved to Headquarters, Army Schools, Langres, the same month.

North Dakota Guardsmen transferred to noncombat organizations attempted to return to their old units. Private First Class John Nelson, serving with Ordnance Department, 164th, requested a move to Company A because, he pointed out, "Co. A is from my home town in North Dakota and I am well acquainted with most of the members so I would be among friends." Colonel Fraine approved the move, but I Army Corps had no interest in getting old friends back together and disapproved it. Left behind at Camp Greene to care for horses, Edward J. Owen and Kenneth C. Gray sought to return to Supply Company once they finally reached France in April. They were currently serving in the 161st Ambulance Company, 116th Sanitary Train, and, as Gray wrote, "We know nothing about Medicine so would like to get back" to Supply Company. They were back with the regiment by the end of the month.

School duty, essentially ordinary administrative work, meant a daily life that differed little from the routine of a peacetime Army post. The band adjusted to life at I Corps school, Gondrecourt, rapidly. Here they finally found their captain, John Grant, formerly of the 2nd North Dakota, commanding Headquarters Company. Grant warmly greeted the bandsmen, who had received no pay in months, and gave each man twenty-five francs. "He asked us to take this money and buy a clean pair of socks and a bottle of rum," Cormany remembered. The band obtained a room at the local Y.M.C.A. for rehearsal and played concerts and dances as well as performed their military duties. A friendly place only twenty miles to the rear of the front line, Gondrecourt had few French men, a large female population, and an excess of bars. Cormany remembered that at times bandsmen talked to frontline troops passing through the village. "It all sounded very exciting and the Band life was boring." Several asked for transfer to line units, but Captain Grant always said no. "He said none of us was in our right mind and that he was not transferring any of us as we might lose a limb or an eye or be killed," Cormany remembered, and added he was "very glad that [Grant] had more judgment than" he did. In May, after the band heard they were destined to go to the front as stretcher bearers, they went on one last trip to play for the 164th detachments at Chuatillon-sur-Seine and Langres before breaking up. When the major general commanding Army Schools at Langres heard them play, he transferred the band to his command. "Prior to our move to Langres, we had experienced some rather rough living," Cormany complained. "Lots of rain, cold, poor quarters, and really lousy food." Now they had a permanent barracks, a full-time cook, and easy duty. "Everything was lovely and we lived high on the hog," he added.

Other North Dakota Guardsmen had essentially the same kind of life. Captain Manville Sprague, Supply Company, at Gondrecourt, told a friend, "we now and then easily hear the rumbling of the big guns," but that does not mean "we are in any danger of suffering casualties." Sprague kept busy "doing odds and ends, though not accomplishing any great amount of work." He attempted to keep his company up to military standards, requesting in a special order, "let's not have any one bring down its name by poor saluting, dirty clothes, drunkenness, shirking duty." As a letter from Major Dana Wright to Sprague suggested, lost freight seemed to be the 2nd Battalion's biggest problem. Neither Wright's outfit nor Major Boyd's 3rd Battalion had received their mess chests and were eating on rented dishes. "There is little news here," Wright went on, although several of his captains and lieutenants had "just left on a two week's observation tour on the French front." In June, Captain Sprague wrote to a friend in Grafton, briefly describing the regiment's school duties, clearly implying that few of them liked it: "We are all hoping of course that some day, sooner or later, the Governemnt will see fit to give us the opportunity of active service." Until that time, he continued, "All we can do is to perform the labor laid out for us with a cheerful and smiling face."

Other North Dakota officers in the 41st Division, but not in the 164th, performed similar noncombat duties. When James Hanley's 148th Machine Gun Battalion reached its assigned post, the village of Selles-sur-Cher near St. Aignan, on 27 January, he wrote proudly, "The troops marched fine and it was some satisfaction to lead a force of some 700 American soldiers up through a city in France, realizing the mission we came on and feeling that we were indeed welcome." Major Hanley would not lead his troops in battle, and four days later he was sending off his privates to combat units. The gregarious Hanley roamed about the 41st Division area, encountering several North Dakota Guardsmen, mostly from the 2nd Regiment. He visited Major Charles Gearey of the 147th Machine Gun Battalion and found him "almost in tears." Gearey's commanding officer, an embittered regular serving rear-area duty, eagerly harassed National Guardsmen. Major Gearey seriously considered resigning, and "The only reason he stayed was the thought that he might be able to help his men some by staying." Hanley worked to cheer Gearey up and, he recalled, "I argued with him not to resign. That he could never explain it at home and that all the service could not be as bad as that." Gearey remained.

Colonel Frank White reached the 41st Division at St. Aignan on 27 April, and with "the trains...all scattered and performing other duty there was little for me to do," he noted. He had time to look up friends, including Major Hanley, Captain Thomas Lonnevik, and an old Philippines comrade, Charles Gearey, with whom he spent much off-duty time. In May, White told his wife, "On account of my age I will not likely be called to the front for active service. I can see plenty to do back of the lines. The handling of the large amount of supplies will require a great many men and need a lot of organizing." Headquarters, Depot Division, gave White one of those organizational assignments when it made him Division Billeting Officer, a job that required him to visit the towns and villages surrounding St. Aignan to buy or rent barns, warehouses, and other buildings suitable for quartering troops in the replacement and training centers. In July the position received a new title, Commanding Officer, Renting, Requisitions, and Claims Service. Chiefly, Colonel White dealt with French property owners, to set rental agreements and settle claims on property damage complaints. Although an essential service, it involved endless detail and negotiation. "My insurance experience is valuable in settling claims," he told his wife, but, as he noted earlier, "If I had a job that any one wanted they would probably find some excuse to go after me."

Frank White did not feel completely comfortable with his military assignment, expressing his frustrations, held by many North Dakota Guardsmen pushed into the administrative backwater of the war, in frequent letters to his wife. He recognized the great complexity of the war and the necessity for the complex logistical organization the American Expeditionary Force created. Someone had to perform those important but often mundane tasks. Still, he told Mrs. White in June, "It is evident there is no absolutely safe place in this war except where we are." And two weeks later, "May not get up on the firing line but will be able to help even if [I] don't get much glory." He ate well, exercised by walking, and slept in a clean bed every night. With the rents, requisitions, and claims assignment, he pointed out, "I won't have a chance to get up to the front line. This will probably please you and I haven't any great ambition 'to go over the top.' I want to get up there once on a tour of inspection and at least smell gunpowder." When wounded men from the front passed through St. Aignan, White could not help but recall, "All of my old regiment is up there and a great many will never come out." When the American Expeditionary Force at last launched offensive action independent of the British or French in early September, he wrote home, "Well my love I feel like I was hardly doing my full duty back here where all is calm and peaceful." Finally, on 1 October, a year since the 2nd Regiment left for Camp Greene, he lamented: "We were full of enthusiasm expecting to get into the game at the head of a fine regiment of men. Our plans went all aglee and my principal job now is holding down a desk....Perhaps it is a lot better to be a live colonel than a dead hero.'' None of White's letters home suggests he really believed that.

"The 164th is expected down here soon," White wrote on 30 June, "so will probably see all the old bunch for long." He told his wife how the regiment lost its enlisted men. "Well, I had my grief all at once and am well over it." He met Colonel Fraine in early July for the first time since arriving in France, "and," he wrote, "have had several visits with him. His organization has been scattered and he feels worse than I do. He has been doing nothing for sometime and is feeling restless." Later, in September, White recounted the success stories he had heard about several 2nd North Dakota men, officers who had won promotions and received combat assignments. With just a touch of sweet revenge, he added, "None of the 1st N.D. have been specially mentioned that any one has heard of." As the war neared its end, most of the rancor from the two regiments' rivalry evaporated. When White heard the 164th would be reunited at St. Aignan, on 1 October, he wrote sympathetically, "Col. Fraine will at last get his regiment together. The first since coming over."

Some of Fraine's and White's subordinates escaped the Depot Division's humdrum duty. Charles Mudgett, orginally major, 1st Battalion, 2nd North Dakota, then adjutant, 81st Infantry Brigade, 41st Division, finally served out the war in the Adjutant General's Office, General Headquarters, American Expeditionary Force. Promoted to lieutenant colonel in September 1918, he was decorated for his contribution to the demobilization. Another 2nd Regiment officer, Second Lieutenant Werner Goerner, Company D, won a silver star for gallantry in action with the 18th Infantry. Charles Rouse, the youthful captain of the 2nd's Company C, also received the silver star as an officer in the 16th Infantry. From the 1st Regiment, Captains T. S. Henry, Headquarters Company, and L. L. Eckman, Machine Gun Company, earned the same medal. Eckman fought with the 3rd Machine Gun Battalion, 1st Division, and Henry with the 28th Infantry. Leaving the Depot Division was important to them all. When Manville Sprague at last escaped Gondrecourt and the Supply Company, he wrote back gleefully, "Hain't had a day's rest since we started things four weeks ago....Give my regards to all the supply co.—wish I had them here right now." And, Frank White told his wife late in November, after the armistice, "Col. Fraine finally got up to the front just before the close," although only on a tour of observation.

The 164th lost 278 men in the war. One hundred seventy-six died in battle, 62 died of wounds, and the remainder succumbed to disease. Nearly 650 men suffered battle wounds. None of the casualties, of course, were attributed to the regiment since the men served in the 1st Division. Lieutenant Colonel Gilbert C. Grafton, a member of the North Dakota National Guard since territorial days, died in France on 5 February 1919 "from an operation for gall stone and adhesions," according to White. He was buried in an American military cemetery at St. Mihiel. Reconstituted with all its original units, the 41st Division left France early in February 1919. "I don't care much about going with them," Frank White told his wife, "as I don't think more than 5% of the original 41st will be among them. Major Gearey and Major [F. S.] Henry will go but mighty few else from N.D." He added, "Col. Fraine is up towards the front and won't go with the 164th."

Departure of the 41st left Colonel White without the comradeship of his North Dakota friends. He wrote Mrs. White, when news arrived that the division would soon ship out, it was "about my bluest day since I came over." White's responsibilities as claims officer grew, rather than diminished, as the American Expeditionary Force closed out billeting contracts and settled claims for damaged property. He faced the probability of remaining overseas for most of 1919 and his attempts to gain permission for Mrs. White to join him failed, leaving him even more melancholy. Once again, Frank White tried to reconcile his concept of soldierly duties with the realities of military desk work. "I am inclined to think it takes as much courage and more loyalty to stay here in the intermediate section and dig to keep things moving forward," he wrote home in January 1919, "than to go over the top on the front line." When politicians and newspapermen began to criticize conditions at St. Aignan, now a demobilization camp, White's frustration burst out again: "I had the feeling, perhaps a mistaken one, that it was the duty of everyone who knew anything about the military game to offer his service to his country," which he did despite his age, sixty-one. He continued: "So I went in and as you know didn't do the things at all I expected to do. We thought of the war only on the firing line....We little realized the small percentage of men actually on the line in this war." Now he only heard complaints after he and many others silently performed wartime chores none of them liked, far from the battlefields where they wished to serve.

White, Colonel Fraine, Major Hanley, and other officers from the North Dakota National Guard regiments perceived war in nineteenth-century terms—a test of personal courage and an opportunity to achieve individual success—not as an organizational conflict between mass societies. Again and again, Frank White used the word "glory" in his letters home, while complaining that his desk assignment denied him the opportunity to win recognition. Officers and men of the Depot Division worked twelve- to fourteen-hour days to send 350,000 replacements to front line units, and "So perhaps we did our part," he commented, but what rankled him, he added, was "we got little of the glory and no promotions to speak of." He restated his disappointment on 14 February 1919: "I have been here at St. Aignan ten months....It don't take much heroism to perform the duties here and I guess we won't get much glory either." Sadly, Frank White seemed ashamed of his wartime service. When he learned he would remain in France well into 1919 and not go home with the 41st Division, he thought that was best: "My story of the war will not be a very exciting one. I hardly feel it was worthwhile. Well the homecoming excitement will all be over before I get back so won't have to tell my experience."

Other officers shared White's romantic view of war. "It is a great and glorious life," Captain Sprague wrote from the front, "and it's full of excitement." He served as a staff officer at Headquarters, I Army Corps, it should be pointed out, not as an infantry officer in the trenches. James Hanley had the opportunity to visit a French infantry regiment in an active sector from 25 to 30 March 1918 and found it an exhilarating experience. "I surely have had one wonderful day," he noted on 25 March. Of all the events of the day, he wrote, the most important was "I have today been under fire

212

of the enemy," when the Germans sporadically shelled the trench and observation posts he visited. He sincerely believed he lived a dangerous life during his tour, although his daily entries noted nightly chess and whist games with French officers and seven-course dinners, including wine, at their mess. For 27 March, he wrote, "I have been in the danger zone since about 10 [o'clock] Monday morning the 25th and seem to be getting used to it. It will probably seem monotonous when I get back to my battalion." Enlisted men viewed the war differently. Wesley Johnson's account of his war experiences contains no romanticism and, although Boyd Cormany saw no combat, his reminiscence deals with the basic issues of a soldier's daily life: food, a decent place to sleep, and the safest duty a man could line up. Few North Dakota officers spent any time in battle, and those who wrote about the war, none at all. Most in the 164th felt cheated when relegated to rear-area work. They never lost their romantic conception of war because, through no fault of their own, they never experienced the shattering realities of trench warfare.

By March 1919, Colonels White and Fraine, with a few other North Dakota Guardsmen, still remained in France. When White traveled to Paris at mid-month to represent the 41st Division at a convention to organize a veteran's group, which would later become the American Legion, he accidentally encountered John Fraine. The men attended the theater and talked a good deal. Fraine "is just out of hospital and on way south for a month" after a severe case of bronchitis, "Col. looks bad and very much older than when I last saw him." White also learned of Lieutenant Colonel Grafton's death. It was time for the old soldiers to go home. Leaving France on 22 May, Frank White arrived at Hoboken on 6 June where his wife met him. Colonel Fraine departed a month later, reaching the United States on 27 June.

The 164th Infantry's return home in 1919 ended a significant period in the North Dakota National Guard's history. World War I closed the active military career of the last man to have served in the territorial National Guard. Symbolically at least, the 1880s to 1920 period may be called the Fraine years, partly because Fraine served continuously during that time in ranks from private to colonel. He did not become a leading figure in the North Dakota National Guard until his promotion to lieutenant colonel in 1910, however. His greater importance stemmed from his ability to adapt to changes which occurred in both the North Dakota National Guard and the National Guard at large. Fraine remained in the service during the difficult 1890s, a period that offered little promise of a bright future for an aspiring citizen-soldier. Having volunteered as a captain in 1898, he went on to earn a major's commission once the regiment reached the Philippines. After proving his value as a disciplinarian and combat leader in the Islands, he remained in the Guard upon returning home. He came into his own during the reform years, indicating a willingness to learn as much as possible about military leadership and administration in the less-than-ideal conditions under which the Guard operated, and adapting far more readily than many of his peers to the Guard's move from a social-military organization to a reserve force for the Army. Fraine led his regiment to Texas in 1916 and then to France a year later, only to see it taken away from him due to the necessities of a faceless, mass war.

John Fraine's career in the National Guard represented the great strength of the service, whatever its deficiencies, and that strength was his persistence. Fraine, and others like him, managed to raise a family, conduct a business, and yet continue a military career valuable to his state and nation. This was not purely selfless and altruistic service, for surely Fraine's military titles aided him in his many political activities, and probably in his real estate dealings as well. Most importantly, though, by contributing years of duty to the National Guard, Fraine and his fellow Guardsmen kept the institution alive during periods when state and national indifference, then professional military hostility, might have killed it. The Guard survived these difficult years because men like John Fraine persisted in keeping it alive. Federal funds and the Guard's contributions in World War I ensured the service a more permanent existence in the 1920s, but the Guard reached that stage of promise through the efforts of men like Fraine who supported the it during the previous three decades.

Notes on Sources

Correspondence, reports, orders, and rosters from the Records of the North Dakota National Guard detail the mobilization of the 2nd Battalion, 1st Infantry, March to July 1917, the mobilization of the remainder of the regiment in July, and organization of the 2nd Infantry. Particularly useful were the following:

1. Field, post, and monthly returns, 1st and 2nd Regiments, North Dakota National Guard, later the 164th Infantry, 1917 and 1918.
2. Official and personal correspondence, orders, and returns, Supply Company, 1st Infantry, later 164th Infantry.
3. Untitled history, North Dakota National Guard, 1898 to 1918, by Herman Brocopp, with comments by John Fraine.
4. Herman Brocopp, "Roster and History Data: Company A, 1st N. Dak. Infantry (164th Infantry), North Dakota National Guard, 1916-1917." Privately printed pamphlet, 1957.
5. Untitled manuscript history of 1st and 2nd Regiments, North Dakota National Guard, and 164th Infantry, in World War I by Earle H. Tostivin. No date, eleven pages.
6. *History 116th Engineers: AEF. Sunset Division (41st)* (Angers, France, 1918). No author listed.

The questionnaire survey produced responses from the following:

1. Anonymous, PFC, Co. C, 1st North Dakota and 164th Infantry. He later served in Co. E, 18th Infantry.
2. Leo H. Dominick, 2nd Lt., Co. I, 1st North Dakota and 164th Infantry.
3. Rolf Glerum, Sgt., Co. D, 2nd North Dakota, and Headquarters Co., 164th Infantry.

4. Leroy W. Goodwater, Co. M, 1st North Dakota and 164th Infantry.
5. Milton Thompson, Pvt., Co. D, 2nd North Dakota and Co. L, 164th Infantry. He later served in Headquarters Co., 26th Infantry.

Dominick and Goodwater also gave information in interviews.

Questionnaires from the World War I Research Project, 41st Division, provided through the courtesy of James Kegel, Archives, United States Army Military History Institute, Carlisle Barracks, Pennsyvlania, included responses from:
1. Raymond F. Heidenreich, Co. E, 164th Infantry.
2. Bernard P. McCusker, Co. I, 164th Infantry.
3. W. J. Peters, Co. B, 164th Infantry.
4. Lewis P. Warren, originally in the 2nd North Dakota Infantry, later in the 147th Machine Gun Battalion, 41st Division.

Two very valuable sources were James M. Hanley, "Diary 1917-1918," held by the State Historical Society of North Dakota, Manuscript Collections, and the Frank White Papers, Orin G. Libby Manuscript Collection, Chester Fritz Library, University of North Dakota. Of lesser importance were the Frank Last Papers (Private, Company A, 1st North Dakota and 164th Infantry, then Company G, 18th Infantry), 1917-1918, held by the State Historical Society, and the Edwin White Papers from the Libby Collection.

Material from the National Archives was essential. Record Group 168, National Guard Bureau, Entry 12A, File 325.4 (E), North Dakota, box 292, offered the fullest details on the 2nd Infantry Regiment's organization. Some mobilization information came from RG94, Entry 25. Of greater merit in tracing the North Dakota regiments from home station to France were the records in RG407, particularly World War I Strength Returns, National Guard, North Dakota, boxes 940 and 941, and World War I Organization Records, National Guard, North Dakota, boxes 350 to 352 for the 1st North Dakota and boxes 354 and 355 for the 2nd North Dakota. Also consulted were Record Group 120, AEF Combat Divisions, 1917-1918, 41st Division, Historical File, and RG391, U.S. Regular Army Mobile Units, 1821-1942, Records of Infantry Regiments, 164th Infantry.

The *Reunion Volume, 164th Infantry, IInd Island Command, 294th AGF Band* (Bismarck, N.D., 1983) reprints a variety of historical materials on the 164th Infantry Band. Particularly informative was Boyd Cormany's twenty-one-page letter to Harry Moore, dated 5 January 1959, recounting the band's World War I experiences. The Bismarck *Tribune* (April-December 1917) and the Fargo *Forum* (April-December 1917) provided background information. The following published material was used: Adjutant General's Office, North Dakota National Guard, *Official Roster of North Dakota Soldiers, Sailors and Marines, Wold War, 1917-1918* (Bismarck, N.D., 1931), four volumes; Leonard P. Ayres, Colonel, General Staff, United States Army, *The War With Germany: A Statistical Summary*, Second Edition, Revised (Washington, D.C., 1919); Luther Birdzell, "North Dakota's Contribution of Men," *North Dakota Quarterly* Vol. 10, No. 1 (October 1919), pp. 3-16; Edward M. Coffman, *The War to End All Wars: The American Military Experience in World War I* (New York, 1968); Historical Section, Army War College, *Order of Battle of the United States Land*

Forces in the World War: American Expeditionary Force: Divisions (Washington, D.C., 1931); Wesley R. Johnson, "War Experiences of a University Student as a Doughboy," *North Dakota Quarterly*, Vol. 10, No. 1 (October 1919), pp. 93-120; Marvin A. Kreidberg and Merton G. Henry, *History of Military Mobilization in the United States Army, 1775-1945* (Washington, D.C., 1955); U.S., Department of the Army, Office of Military History, *United States Army in the World War, 1917-1919* (Washington, D.C., 1948), Volume 1, "Organization of the American Expeditionary Forces."

[1]The North Dakota National Guard did not follow the Army's organizational chart in assigning companies to battalions in strict alphabetical order, that is, Companies A, B, C, D to the 1st Battalion; E, F, G, H to the 2nd; I, K, L, M to the 3rd. North Dakota assigned companies according to geography and location on main railroad lines. 1st Battalion had units from Valley City (G), Fargo (B), Wahpeton (I), and Hillsboro (L). Except for Valley City, these units lay on a north to south line along the Great Northern Railroad, from Hillsboro to Wahpeton. The 2nd Battalion took in towns along the Northern Pacific from Jamestown (H), west through Bismarck (A), Mandan (F), to Dickinson (K). The 3rd Battalion included Company C, at Grafton, on a Great Northern Railroad spur north of Grand Forks, then M at Grand Forks, and west on the Great Northern Railroad to Minot (D) and Williston (E).

[2]Thompson adds: "In Sept. of 1917 I inveigled the Capt. of D Co. 2nd N.D. into recruiting me. He did so without a physical."

Camp Frazier, located near the east side of the Northern Pacific Bridge
on the Missouri River, Bismarck.

Army chow." Camp Frazier, 1917.

164th Infantry bayonet drills in France, 1918.

The 164th Infantry Band during World War I, Langree, France, 1918.

164th Infantry laying barbed wire entanglements at 1st Corps School at Gonrecourt, France, 1918.

☆7☆
The North Dakota National Guard
Between World Wars, 1919-1940

The call to federal service in July 1917 removed North Dakota Guardsmen from state control and placed them under War Department authority. For the next two years, Guardsmen served at the beck and call of the Army. Under the somewhat confusing language of the 1916 National Defense Act, and Congressional legislation authorizing President Woodrow Wilson to mobilize the Guard for war, the War Department "drafted" Guardsmen as individuals, thus terminating their state enlistments. Returning soldiers were likewise discharged as individuals. In any event, the break-up of the 41st Division had so dispersed the officers and men of the 164th Infantry that it was impossible for them to return as a unit. Until Congress passed new legislation, the states no longer had an organized National Guard. Postwar policy would not be determined until the middle of 1920, after which time North Dakota could begin reorganization.

In the interim, during the winter of 1919, Governor Lynn J. Frazier broke precedent in North Dakota history by using his constitutional authority as commander-in-chief of the National Guard to intervene in a labor dispute. Millions of workers went on strike throughout 1919, as the American economy moved rapidly from war to civilian production. Although prices had risen steadily during the war, industrial wages had failed to keep up. Coal miners numbered among the many unhappy workers seeking to improve their wages. Under the leadership of John L. Lewis, the United Mine Workers voted in the fall to strike the bituminous coal industry, beginning on 1 November 1919. Of the multitude of strikes which affected the nation that year, only that of the coal workers directly touched North Dakota. The United Mine Workers represented a majority of miners in the state's lignite mines, scattered west and north of the Missouri River to Montana.

Frazier, the first governor from the reform-minded Nonpartisan League, viewed the pending strike with apprehension. While lignite coal mined in the state provided one-third of the state's fuel for home and business heating needs, North Dakota imported the remaining two-thirds of its coal from the east, chiefly through the lake port of Duluth, Minnesota. A lengthy dock strike in August and September had prevented North Dakota coal wholesalers from stockpiling winter fuel. Frazier later explained that North Dakota not only lacked its normal out-of-state coal in the late fall, but, he added, "We have had snow and winter weather since the 23rd of October." He feared that continued snow would block branch railroad lines to many small towns, leaving them isolated from fuel supplies no matter when the strike ended. To avoid this calamity, Frazier telegraphed John L. Lewis on 30 October, asking him if United Mine Workers miners in North Dakota would work the mines if the state took control of them until the strike was settled. Lewis and Henry D. Drennan, president of District 27, United Mine Workers, which included North Dakota local unions, agreed to Frazier's proposal. The governor went one step further by calling union leaders and mine operators to Bismarck where they met during the first week of November, with Frazier acting as mediator.

The Bismarck conference failed to solve the issue, although it delayed the strike in North Dakota when soft coal miners left their work in other states on 1 November. North Dakota United Mine Workers members went out a week later, halting seventy percent of the state's coal production. On 10 November, Governor Frazier published a proclamation warning mine owners and workers that unless they settled the strike in twenty-four hours, the "state will take over mines and operate them until emergency has passed." Snow and sharply cold weather continued to buffet the state. Individuals, businessmen, and municipal officials deluged the governor with pleas for coal. Mayor J. H. Cook, of Willow City, among many, wired Frazier on 11 November, "Fuel situation very serious. Not a pound in the city to be had." In view of the severe weather, the desperate shortage of coal, and the backlog of coal piled up in Duluth, Frazier deemed state action essential. When neither the miners nor the owners showed any sign of changing bargaining positions, the governor issued a second proclamation on 12 November. "By virtue of the authority vested in me as Governor...and commander in chief of the State Militia," Frazier directed G. Angus Fraser, adjutant general, "to take charge of and assume control over and operate" a total of thirty-three mines. He further authorized the adjutant general to "call to his assistance such male persons between the ages of eighteen and forty-five as he may deem necessary...to carry out the provisions of this order." The proclamation ordered General Fraser to supply the public with coal and to pay coal operators a special twenty-five cent per ton royalty on all coal mined under state control and also said, "This order ends when agreement is reached by miners and operators."

Governor Frazier's most radical provision in the proclamation empowered the adjutant general to call on the entire militia population, that is, all militarily obligated men, if needed to enforce state seizure of the mines. No governor had sanctioned a blanket militia call since the Civil War. Undoubtedly, Frazier included this proviso because North Dakota had no organized National Guard, the only readily available men being Quartermaster Corps personnel on duty at state headquarters in Bismarck. In the event, these few officers and noncommissioned officers sufficed to carry out Frazier's edict. The governor had secured the miners' promise to work the mines, at wages and conditions prevailing in October, before issuing his proclamation. Although many state newspapers, particularly the Fargo *Forum* and the Bismarck *Tribune,* strongly attacked the seizure, branding Frazier as a socialist and Bolshevik and comparing him to Lenin, the public clearly supported him throughout the strike.

Even the Attorney General of the United States, A. Mitchell Palmer, rapidly gaining a reputation as a union buster and all-out enemy of radicalism, assured Governor Frazier on 13 November, "As at present...I see no occasion for action by the Department of Justice." Most mine owners reluctantly cooperated with Frazier, at least to the extent of advising Guardsmen on the intricacies of coal mining. Major resistance to the seizure came from the Dakota Coal Company, a Minnesota corporation with mines at Burlington, and the Washburn Lignite

Coal Company of Wilton. Dakota Coal Company attorneys informed Frazier they viewed the seizure "as a wil[l]ful criminal trespass and a violation of [their] constitutional rights." The company intended to hold the governor "to strict accountability." The Washburn Company condemned seizure as "unwarranted, arbitrary, unconstitutional, illegal and without precedent." Despite their strong objections, the two companies resisted in state and federal courts, not at the mines. P. J. Cahill, superintendent of the Washburn mine, refused to cooperate with Guardsmen sent to operate his mine and ordered his supervisory personnel not to work for the state, but otherwise did nothing to obstruct state soldiers.

In the first days after Frazier's second proclamation, Guardsmen went to Wilton, Williston, Medora, Noonan, Burlington, and other mine sites in the state's western section. They found the miners ready to cooperate and in most instances simply acted as general supervisors. Guardsmen had responsibility for making an inventory of mine property and logging daily coal production as well as for ensuring that work went on every day. In most instances, only one or two Guardsmen, usually sergeants, oversaw mine operations. At the Washburn lignite mine, Captains Laroy Baird and Joe S. Underwood took direct control of mining operations when P. J. Cahill refused to cooperate. In no instance did Guardsmen confront disorder or physical obstruction. In Bismarck, General Fraser oversaw distribution of coal according to requests submitted to his office or to Governor Frazier. Again and again, Frazier sought to make clear that he intended to provide coal to people who needed it, "without involving the state administration with regards to the merits of the miners' demands." As soon as the contending parties reached agreement, the state would leave the coal business. As Frazier advised one Minnesotan attempting to buy coal from North Dakota, during state control, his administration could not "sell this product outside the state" for the state had seized the mines in order to meet an emergency in North Dakota.

The Washburn Coal Company succeeded in obtaining an injunction from the Burleigh County District Court ordering General Fraser and Captain Baird to return the Wilton mine to Washburn's control. Intent on defying the court order, Governor Frazier was relieved of embarrassment when Captain Baird convinced the Washburn Company and the miners to reach agreement, on 22 November, a day after the court issued its decision. Washburn resumed control on the 24th. On another legal front, the Dakota Coal Company failed to win an injunction from Federal District Judge C. F. Amidon, who upheld the governor's right to seize the mines to meet a public emergency. Meanwhile, President Wilson's administration took action to end the nationwide strike, winning a court order enjoining the entire United Mine Workers from continuing the strike. Attorney General Palmer then forced labor and management back to bargaining, with strong threats that the federal government might use war powers still in effect to seize and operate soft coal mines throughout the country. Agreement came on 10 December, with the miners winning a fourteen-percent wage increase. That day, Governor Frazier reported a temperature of thirty degrees below zero, and the Fargo *Forum* headlined "Worst Winter in 30 Years." The weather and the Wilson administration's own threats to take over mines seemed to justify Frazier's unprecedented actions.

By the end of December, all North Dakota mines had reverted to their owners, and the fifteen or so Guardsmen had returned to Bismarck. The

Nonpartisan League-dominated legislature, called to special session by Governor Frazier, had passed emergency measures early in the month which gave the governor statutory power to "commandeer and take over for use...any coal mine or other public utility" when a strike or lockout threatened life and property. It sanctioned as well the use of state military forces in any takeover. Proud of his action, Frazier informed one constituent on 23 December, "the coal situation seems to be getting a little better and we have had no reports of shortages in the last few days." An independent audit ordered by Frazier to ensure that the coal companies received their rightful profits and royalties collected by the state found that Guardsmen had been fair and scrupulous in their management, though the audit reluctantly conceded that Sergeant Ambrose H. Gallagher, who oversaw operations at the Williston Coal and Ice Company mine, had kept poor records, due to his "inexperience in handling business affairs." Although literally not much larger than a corporal's guard, the North Dakota Guardsmen pressed into coal mine management in late 1919 accomplished their assignment with little conflict.

A year would pass after the coal strike before North Dakota organized a single infantry company. On his reappointment to the adjutant generalcy in March 1919, G. Angus Fraser announced he intended to delay the Guard's reorganization until war veterans returned, at which time he would call a convention of Guardsmen to solicit their views. "I am of the opinion," Fraser said, "that North Dakota will want two regiments. A majority of the cities which raised companies for the Second North Dakota will want to retain them." The North Dakota National Guard's future, however, was largely in the War Department's hands. The Militia Bureau allotted the state one infantry regiment for fiscal year 1920, under authority of the 1916 National Defense Act, and available federal funds; but until North Dakotans readjusted to peacetime conditions and Congress acted on military legislation, the North Dakota National Guard remained unorganized.

After months of acrimonious debate, Congress approved the National Defense Act of 1920, and President Wilson signed it on 4 June. A series of lengthy amendments to the 1916 measure, the new law did not significantly alter the National Guard's relationship with the federal government, but it solidified its place in the nation's defense system by making the Guard a permanent component of the Army of the United States, along with the Regular Army and Organized Reserve. It also provided that the chief of the Militia Bureau must be a National Guard officer of at least ten years commissioned service and further stipulated that the Guard should have representation in the War Department and General Staff.

Envisioning a military force substantially larger than pre-1917 strengths, the 1920 statute authorized an Army of 280,000 enlisted men and a National Guard of 435,000 officers and men. It also called for an Organized Reserve of twenty-seven infantry divisions, although it did not provide money or methods to recruit the force. In addition, it continued the Reserve Officers Training Corps from 1916 and created Civilian Military Training Camps to prepare officers for the Guard and Reserves. The law also required Guardsmen to participate in sixty annual armory drills and fifteen days in summer camp, and it said reserve officers must take regular summer training in order to keep their commissions. The Army's major functions were to instruct these citizen-soldiers and keep abreast of modern weapons technology and tactics.

Another feature of the law required all three components to be organized in tactical divisions, distributed in nine corps areas across the United States. The corps replaced the Army's traditional geographic departments as administrative districts and also assumed tactical responsibilities. Each area had one Regular Army, two National Guard, and three Organized Reserve infantry divisions assigned to it. Corps commanders were to direct training and prepare mobilization plans for these units, following policies established by the General Staff. In theory, the nation had fifty-four infantry divisions for defense, organized on a peace basis. Forty-eight divisions would have officers and men who were partially trained citizen-soldiers. The system would work only if money and manpower became available to flesh out these skeleton organizations. In the ensuing two decades neither the men nor the money appeared. The Organized Reserve never attempted to recruit enlisted men, although it counted nearly 100,000 officers enrolled at its peak in the late 1920s. Declining military appropriations steadily eroded the Army's available force. From an aggregate of 230,725 in 1921, the Army dropped to 133,000 in 1923 and averaged 137,000 during the decade. Its numbers climbed slowly thereafter to 190,000 in 1939, with 50,000 officers and men serving overseas.

The National Guard never approached its authorized strength of 430,000 in the two decades between the world wars. Its aggregate rarely exceeded 180,000 in the 1920s, edged up to 192,000 in 1937, and only went over the 200,000 level in 1940 as the nation began to prepare for war. When it became apparent that Congress had no intention of funding the military establishment it had authorized in 1920, the War Department developed a modified program in 1923 to recruit 250,000 Guardsmen by 1926, but this attempt failed for want of funds. The War Department set a new goal of 210,000 in 1928, but Congress did not appropriate funds for that level until 1935 and then required the increase to take place over three years. The recession of 1938 delayed adding the final 5,000 men until fiscal year 1940. Finally, in September 1939, when President Franklin D. Roosevelt declared a limited national emergency, he convinced Congress to increase the Guard's authorized strength to 235,000 in the coming year.

The authorized strength determined the number of Guardsmen the Militia Bureau allocated to each state. Under the 1916 law, as amended in 1920, states received federal monies only for those units the government assigned to them. This allowed the Militia Bureau to ensure that the states formed units of the particular types necessary to create balanced infantry divisions and other organizations needed for forming field armies. Under the original 435,000-man National Guard, for example, the Bureau allocated to North Dakota a full infantry regiment, three hospital units, a field artillery battalion (155 mm howitzer), a horse-drawn artillery battalion, three truck companies, and an Air Service observation squadron. The state's small, rural population probably could not have supported these units, but it became a moot point, for with the limited funding, North Dakota was empowered to form an infantry regiment in 1920 and the field artillery battalion in 1936.

In a series of meetings with VII Corps Area officers and adjutants general from other states in the corps area (Minnesota, South Dakota, Iowa, Nebraska, Kansas, and Missouri) in 1920 and 1921, General Fraser and other officers planned the restructuring. War Department policy allowed states to keep their wartime unit designations whenever feasible. North Dakota retained the 164th Infantry Regiment, even though the War Department allocated its parent division, the 41st, to California. The 164th became an element of the 68th Infantry Brigade, 34th Division, in the postwar divisional arrangement. Minnesota, South Dakota, and Iowa also contributed to the 34th. Other states in the VII Corps Area composed the 35th Division.

Though Governor Frazier directed the adjutant general to reorganize the regiment in an executive order issued 3 January 1920, the process went slowly. General Fraser wrote the Militia Bureau in February that he intended to place companies at the same home stations that had provided units for the 1st North Dakota Infantry in 1917. He would establish those units during the year. Nonetheless, at the end of 1920 only Company M, Grand Forks, was ready and given federal recognition. Captain Heber L. Edwards, a sergeant in the company during World War I and proprietor of a Grand Forks insurance agency, formed the command. The North Dakota National Guard added five companies during the next year. Despite General Fraser's hopes, few veterans came forward to don a doughboy's uniform. One aspiring veteran wrote the general in September 1921, "there is a bunch of us ex-service men here at Cannon Ball and we would like to start a national guard company here if possible." Such offers rarely came, and reorganization continued slowly.

The remaining companies were constituted during 1922, except for Company F and a battalion headquarters. Company F had been stationed at Mandan before the war and had avoided disbandment in 1917 only because of mobilization. General Fraser at last found a home for it at Carrington. Federal recognition came in January 1923. The state could then establish battalion headquarters. With all units completed and recognized, the 164th Infantry itself received federal approval on 16 May 1923. Because of federal regulations, it had taken four years since the war's end to activate the regiment. Each officer now had to meet the requirements of the 1916 law, effectively ending the election of officers, and each company had to enlist a minimum of sixty-four men. Neither the battalions nor the regiment could be acknowledged until their constituent companies were first completed. The 164th Infantry's companies paralleled the old 1st North Dakota, with few exceptions. (See Table 7.1.)

Stability marked the North Dakota National Guard's experience in the interwar years. In contrast to the pre-1917 period, the Guard managed with little difficulty to keep its units intact and at the same home stations. The regiment's organization remained unaltered from 1923 until 1940, except for one minor change: in 1929, owing to lack of recruits, the state disbanded Headquarters Company, 3rd Battalion, at Kenmare, and moved it to the more populous city of Minot. Under the 435,000-man limit, states were to recruit their units to peace strength, roughly fifty percent of wartime manpower needs. Budget limitations necessitated holding the Guard at maintenance strength, or one-third wartime levels. Only then could the War Department afford drill and summer-camp pay as well as meet uniform, arms, and equipment requirements. The North Dakota National Guard performed significantly better after 1922 in keeping up minimum strength levels than it had before World War I. Throughout the two decades, the 164th sustained a force of just under twelve hundred officers and men, averaging sixty enlisted men per line company. It never faced the threat of losing federal recognition for any unit due to under enrollment.

TABLE 7.1
Units of the 164th Infantry, North Dakota National Guard,
1920s and 1930s

Unit	Home Station	Year Unit First Organized	Date of Federal Recognition
Headquarters Company*	Fargo	1922	9 January 1922
Service Company*	Lisbon	1922	4 April 1922
Band	Lisbon	1889	4 April 1922
Medical Detachment	Edgeley	1900	4 May 1922
Howitzer Company*	Devils Lake	1922	4 January 1922
Company A	Bismarck	1883	9 March 1922
Company B	Fargo	1883	9 January 1922
Company C	Grafton	1886	6 January 1922
Company D	Minot	1906	3 January 1922
Company E	Williston	1906	22 January 1921
Company F	Carrington	1922	29 January 1923
Company G	Valley City	1884	9 June 1921
Company H	Jamestown	1883	20 January 1921
Company I	Wahpeton	1897	8 June 1921
Company K	Dickinson	1897	8 June 1921
Company L	Hillsboro	1898	22 January 1922
Company M	Grand Forks	1915	6 December 1920
Battalion Headquarters*			
1st Battalion	Cavalier	1922	9 January 1922
2nd Battalion	Cando	1923	16 March 1923
3rd Battalion	Kenmare	1923	3 April 1923

*These units were not in the 1916 Tables of Organization. In 1939, the Howitzer Company was redesignated as the Antitank Platoon, Headquarters Company, but remained at Devils Lake.

The 3rd Battalion moved to Minot in 1929.

Federal financial support contributed significantly to stability. In 1923, the first year the full regiment was activated, the Militia Bureau disbursed $118,140 to North Dakota. From 1923 to 1937, the years before the Roosevelt administration began its cautious rearmament programs, federal spending on the North Dakota National Guard averaged $149,400 annually, peaking in 1926 with $192,529 and the low coming in 1935 at $105,366. High enlistment rates accounted for the 1926 figure, and in the latter year, depression-era fiscal problems reduced federal spending. The $149,400 annual average contrasted sharply with pre-World War I support. Aid before the war reached its highest in 1908 when North Dakota received $48,000, $20,000 of which the state used to send the Guard to maneuvers at American Lake, Washington.

While federal support increased dramatically after 1920, state spending did not change for years. From 1919 through 1928, North Dakota continued to appropriate $30,000 annually for National Guard maintenance. It raised the amount to $35,000 in 1929, but again the depression intruded, forcing the state to reduce the allotment to $22,500 in 1933 and 1934. Support rose to $30,000 in 1935 and finally again reached the $35,000 figure in 1937. The legislature also provided separate monies for the adjutant general's office to cover salaries and office expenses. This account did not exceed $8,000 until 1939 and varied from $4,500 in 1921 to $7,700 in the late 1920s. The combined maintenance fund and adjutant general's costs, totaling at its highest $42,700 in the late 1920s and early 1930s, represented less than one-third of the average annual federal allotment. Federal expenditures for the entire National Guard during the interwar years, which averaged $32,000,000 from 1921 to 1940, was crucial to Guard success. Estimates vary considerably on the amount all the states allocated to the National Guard units, but at best they provided only half as much as the federal government. North Dakota fell at the lower end, and clearly the North Dakota National Guard could not have carried on at the levels it did without the money sent from Washington.

Armory support, set at $600 a year for each organization in 1923, comprised one-third of the maintenance fund. The military code also provided $1,200 per year to the Service Company "for use only in paying all or parts of the salary of the bandleader of the band." State staff salaries, the development and care of the Devils Lake training camp, and general administrative expenses consumed the remaining state monies. Federal allocations covered all other costs. The War Department, as before the war, supplied uniforms, arms, and equipment. Most materiel given to the Guard, including trucks and automobiles, was World War I vintage but essential. The annual allotment paid Regular Army officers' and sergeant instructors' salaries and expenses as well as those of state-employed caretakers, who looked after government property stored at Devils Lake. The state used federal funds to improve the military reservation and to send North Dakota National Guard officers to Army service schools.

The most important federal contribution went for armory and summer-camp pay. From 1923 through 1939, drill and camp pay took seventy to eighty-five percent of the annual allotment, usually eighty percent. Guard pay regularly brought $100,000 to $125,000 into the state each year, depending on enrollment. The 1916 National Defense Act first approved federal pay (prior to 1916 the government paid Guardsmen in summer camp only if regular troops were in attendance), but World War I intervened before it aided the National Guard. After the war, armory pay solved one of the Guard's major problems, recruiting dependable enlisted men. Privates earned $1.00 each drill, paid quarterly. Noncommissioned officers received somewhat more, a sergeant's weekly pay being $1.60, for example. Though the 1920 National Defense Act called for sixty drills a year, insufficient appropriations forced the War Department to reduce the number to forty-eight. Privates earned another $15.00 at summer camp, a further incentive to remain active in the Guard.

Men joined the North Dakota National Guard in the interwar years for many reasons, but drill pay came first for most of them. A dollar a week may seem, in the 1980s, a small incentive for a man to sign a three-year enlistment. William Johnson of Company H remarked in retrospect, "It's pretty hard to figure out just what the hell you were doing there for a dollar a drill!" Johnson knew, to cite another Company H veteran, however, that fifty years ago "was when a dollar was worth 100+." The few dollars earned from the National Guard each year went a long way in a state wracked by agricultural depression from 1920 to the outbreak of World War II. This held particularly true for the growing number of teen-agers joining the Guard. Charles Norton, a mere fourteen years old when he enlisted at Cavalier in 1931, cherished drill pay. "During the winter months that dollar was what you had for pocket money." James Aipperspach, Company H, aptly summarized the interwar trend: "A great number of youths who enlisted...did so for money." A comrade, Albert Wiest, put it more bluntly: "In the early 1930s the extra pay was a definite factor in joining. Few were motivated by any great desire to serve the country."[1]

Many men used Guard pay to help with their higher education. State colleges charged sixteen dollars a semester for tuition, and the quarterly drill check almost covered that amount. Elmo R. Olson, Headquarters Company, among many, found "money in short supply, so joined for help to go to college." Lawton Osborn of Dickinson, site of a state college, remembered that Company K easily met its strength requirements because "Students were looking for a way to make extra money to enable them to continue in school." Some of the more enterprising company commanders played on their young charges' desire for extra money. Company E's commander "Paid a bonus to recruit," Edward Murphy remembered, "and at that time [1933], money was scarce." The commanders of Company L and Company M offered one dollar for each new recruit. Few veterans could recall any difficulty in finding new men, several noting that their commanders kept a waiting list, as their units were normally at or above allotted strength. Drill pay, above all other factors, accounted for this. As John Holt put it, "During the depression...people enlisted for extra money."

Drill attendance improved significantly with the stimulus of pay. The prewar Guard suffered continually from the failure of enlisted men to show up for weekly drills. Under postwar regulations, irregular attendance hurt both the unit and the individual. Absentees lost their pay for each missed drill, and if an organization failed to maintain an average annual attendance rate set by the War Department, the entire outfit lost its pay and very likely federal recognition. Data is sketchy for the 1920s, but in the thirties the Guard never slipped below a ninety-percent rate at the annual federal inspection, the most crucial one of the year, and company commanders made every effort to have all their men turn out. On a yearly basis, the Guard performed less impressively. National Guard Bureau figures show that, for the thirties, average yearly attendance usually hovered around eighty percent. The highest attendance occurred in 1933, with ninety-two percent; the lowest came in 1937, with seventy-six percent.

Frank Richards, commander of Company K in the mid-1930s, recalled that a state law permitted a captain to send a squad to round up absentees or request the county sheriff to arrest negligent soldiers. He never used these expedients. For a unit, it was a "black mark on you if a unit did not hold drill." Regular attendance for individuals became "a matter of pride." Captain John Kohnen, Battery F, 185th Field Artillery Battalion, Jamestown, wrote Assistant Adjutant General Colonel Herman Brocopp early in 1938, "Several of my men are deliberately staying away from drill without a legitimate excuse and I want to put pressure on them. I've sent out details and brought them in." This stopped the truancy for a few weeks, but not permanently. "I think it would have a good healthy effect on the whole organization if I threw one of the chronic offenders in the jug," Kohnen added. He asked Captain Brocopp for advice on the proposal and for copies of the appropriate state statutes. No record contains Brocopp's reply or Kohnen's further action, but Battery F's problems were an exception. When compared to drill attendance before 1917, the difficulties of the 1930s seemed small. Drill pay made all the difference. The usual punishment for missing drill, in Albert Wiest's words, meant "loss of drill pay (where I should add it hurt the most)."

Summer-camp pay had the same effect. In the twenties, eighty to eighty-five percent of the then-enrolled Guardsmen put in their fifteen days each summer. The rate improved significantly during the 1930s. Camp attendance slipped below ninety percent only once in the decade: in 1937 when the North Dakota National Guard trekked to Camp Ripley, Minnesota, for 34th Division maneuvers, only seventy-eight percent went. In 1932, 1933, and 1935, the Guard put ninety-eight percent of its officers and enlisted men in camp, and ninety-seven percent in 1934. These figures matched or exceeded camp rates for the National Guard as a whole and were far better than anything achieved from 1903 to 1915.

Although a major factor in attracting enlistees to the North Dakota National Guard, federal pay was not the only one. Harold Aarhus, Company B, enlisted in 1934 because of the "Attraction the military held for me," he explained, adding, "I loved it." Another Guardsman shared the same feeling, but not strongly enough to join the Regular Army, so he signed on with Company M. The World War I mobilization so impressed Clarence McClure that, although under the legal enlistment age, he became a soldier in 1921 when Company A reorganized at Bismarck. Others saw in the Guard a chance to further hobbies or favorite pastimes. The band offered Raymond Ellerman dual appeal: he could play his clarinet in a musical organization and "two weeks in camp every summer was better than farming!" Alfred Thomasen "loved music" also and served in the band from 1928 to 1940. The chance to take part in rifle marksmanship competition lured Lawrence Poe, among several. He "was high scorer in the state in 1932." Radio ham operator Charles Welch learned he could use his hobby in Headquarters Battery, 185th Field Artillery, in 1937.

The personal example of one Guardsman motivated Stafford Ordahl to enlist. "My coach in H.S." he said, "was an officer [Major Charles C. Finnegan]... and his character influenced me greatly" to sign up in 1925. Enough of the old social and fraternal appeals remained to affect some men. Albert Wiest recalled that he had enlisted in Jamestown's Company H because "belonging to the NG in a small town in those days was 'the thing to do.'" A fellow Company H man, Richard Hoffman, also thought the unit "a rather exclusive club" not easy to get into. "Its entry was by being asked by a friend and then interviewed by the company commander," he explained. "If you passed [the interview] and the physical you were allowed in."

Effective recruiting brought in many otherwise uninterested men. Survey respondents indicated that next to drill pay, a friend, classmate, or relative had the greatest influence on their decision to enlist. Company K's A. A. Hannel noted his unit's simple recruiting method. "Those of us in the Guard talked our friends into joining." Groups of friends sometimes enlisted together. Edward Dietz went along with "the whole north end" of Grand Forks to become members of Company M in the late 1930s. In Fargo, Captain Albert D. Haven, an engineer with the Northern States Power Company, used his connections at the Agricultural College to recruit engineering students like James Moe for Company B. Some friends tirelessly persisted in their efforts. "I can still remember Bud Murphy leading me by the hand up to the armory," Victor McWilliams recalled. "I didn't really want to join. I was running around town making fifteen dollars a week." Still, Second Lieutenant Francis "Bud" Murphy of Jamestown's Battery F inveigled McWilliams and Murphy's younger brother to sign up. Several former Guardsmen remembered Warrant Officer Gerald E. Wright of the band as "a master of recruiting." Wright taught music in the Lisbon schools, led a dance band which toured the eastern part of the state, and took the 164th Band on concert tours. According to Douglas Campbell, "He used high school musical organizations as a feeder system" and always sought potential Guardsmen at the dances and concerts he conducted.

Social change contributed to the Guard's ability to find new members. A persistent farm depression from 1920 to 1940 drove farmers off the land and either out of the state or into towns and cities. North Dakota's population grew slowly after World War I and declined by six percent during the 1930s. In the devastating depression years, rural areas lost seventeen percent of their people. Meanwhile, the cities and towns grew over the two decades. The state's urban population, fourteen percent in 1920, had grown to twenty-one percent by 1940. The smaller towns, places under twenty-five hundred, also grew, by nine percent in the 1920s and six percent in the next decade. The Guard, always a town and city institution, benefited from the increase in the manpower pool from which it could recruit.

Two other social changes affected the Guard, one being the automobile revolution. As a rural state with a widely dispersed population, North Dakota gained from the mass ownership of cars after 1920. Automobiles broke farm isolation and allowed farm families to trade in the larger towns and cities. By 1930, eighty-seven percent of the state's farmers owned cars or trucks, with motor vehicle ownership per person nearly twice as high in North Dakota as in the rest of the United States. Cars gave farm boys the chance to join the Guard and allowed the service to establish small headquarters units in towns like Cavalier and Cando. Farmers appear in the ranks in much greater numbers during the 1930s than before 1920.

The Guard also gained from changes in education. North Dakota's high school system developed slowly, largely because of the widespread rural population and the need of farmers to use their teen-aged children, especially boys, to work their land. With a mere 570 students in high school in 1890, enrollment edged upward after the turn of the century. Some 9,505 students took secondary education in 1918, and the number reached 20,000 by 1930, distributed among 191 classified high schools. The larger population centers, several of which served as home stations for National Guard units, contained the accredited, classified schools. The state's colleges and university also developed after 1920. Student population more than doubled by 1930, and former two-year normal schools at Dickinson, Mayville, Minot, and Valley City joined the Agricultural College at Fargo and the University of North Dakota at Grand Forks as four-year institutions. A private school, Jamestown College, and the State School of Science at Wahpeton completed the higher education system. The National Guard had units located at all these places except Mayville.

The growth of high schools and colleges had significance because students comprised the largest single group of recruits. Of the 126 survey respondents who indicated occupations at first enlistment, 60 had been students; the next highest number, 16, had been farmers. These responses and other evidence make clear that fifty to sixty percent of all privates were attending high school or college. Frank Richards, commanding officer of Company K in the late thirties and a teacher in the city's high school, reported that sixty-five percent of his enlisted men were students when called to federal service in early 1941. Company H's William Johnson remembered that the majority of his unit's members, including himself, were attending high school in the 1930s.

A large number of high school students joined the Guard before the legal enlistment age of eighteen. (Of the 156 questionnaire respondents, 36 had been under eighteen; another 46 had been eighteen or nineteen.) Thurston Nelson enlisted at Hillsboro in 1938: "I entered the Guard at age 15....When I joined Co. L I went in to see the Capt. He said how old are you? I said fifteen—he said 'You're eighteen, sign here.'" Another veteran, James Aippersbach, recalled his age at enlistment as seventeen. "A great number of us were younger....If one identified himself as being 18 years of age, no one questioned him." Another man admitted he was only sixteen, but "a big sixteen." A few claimed they were only fourteen years old at enlistment. When asked if he had ever enlisted underage boys, Frank Richards paused, then chuckled, but did not answer the question.

Numerous unit activities, similar to prewar practices, attracted young men. Several companies used athletics, a long-standing Guard tradition, to win recruits. Company M, Grand Forks, was perhaps the most sports-minded outfit in North Dakota, Captain Heber L. Edwards having set the tone at reorganization. He wrote Major Harold Sorenson in November 1920, before federal recognition, that his unit recently held a boxing match which "was a brilliant success in every way except financially," and then added, "The main thing is to get boxing back on its feet." Edwards hoped boxing would eventually earn income but also "stimulate recruiting. Since the bout," he explained, "we have had an increase in applications." Company M thereafter established its reputation as the regiment's leading boxing outfit. One veteran recalled that Edwards's successor, Captain Ira Gaulke, managed to recruit most of the University of North Dakota's boxing team in the late 1930s. During the drill year, several Guard basketball, baseball, and softball teams played local civilian teams. Regimental competition came only at summer camp, because "Distances in ND made this very difficult" at other times. Jamestown was one of the few home stations for two units before 1940. Company H, 164th Infantry, and Battery F, 185th Field Artillery, shared the same armory after 1937. According to the battery's Francis Murphy, "We played some basketball games with them—also baseball."

Social events, such as dinner and dance in connection with the annual federal inspection, helped spur recruiting and maintain morale. Albert Wiest's memories of Company H's affair were slightly jaundiced, for, he recollected, "Each year we listened to the same local veterans relate the same stories about the 1916 border incident and WWI. And we always passed the I.G. inspection." Walter Mellem recalled one spectacular Company M event. "As an EM in the 30s I remember at one party 2 .30 cal. M.G.s [machine guns] were placed on the stage for decoration. During one of the dances the lights were dimmed and both guns fired a belt of blanks." Company L sponsored dances and stag poker games "not only for recruiting purposes but to build a mess fund." The band naturally participated in many social functions. One bandsman, Franklin Schoeffler, remembered: "Quite often in the early thirties-164th Inf. Band Sunday concerts, and weekly dances," in Lisbon, and "band concerts [were held] in nearby towns for social and recruiting purposes."

The armories frequently served as social centers for civilians as well as soldiers and provided the Guard another means to reach out to the community. At Lisbon, Douglas Campbell wrote, the armory "was the auditorium of the community and its uses were many and varied," including "Dances, card tournaments, basketball games and tournaments, home talent days, bazaars, meetings, etc." In many North Dakota towns, as Albert Wiest noted for Jamestown, "in those days the armory was the only place large enough to hold a sizeable crowd." Renting the armory for roller skating, conventions, and other events allowed units that still owned their buildings to meet maintenance expenses.

The significance of the armory to civic life as well as to the National Guard suggested to the teen-agers filling the ranks that they belonged to an outstanding community organization. The youngsters discovered that many adults approved of their military service. Walter Abbot's employer, "a former military man, both NDNG and World War I...gave me plenty of encouragement as a young man in the Band," he recalled. "He paid me while away from the job on NG encampments." Francis Murphy's father, who was also his employer, "was very lenient about my attending drills locally and our annual 2 weeks" at camp. "We even used my Dad's big semi to haul all of our own 185th F.A. Btry. equipment to Camp Riley in 1940." Guard membership seemed particularly important to young, unsophisticated farm boys venturing into the urban world for the first time. Wilbur Pierce, Company H, fondly remembers his service, for "it made me more outgoing because of my youth on the small farm north of Jamestown." Another Guardsman learned to overcome the sense of inferiority the isolation of farm life sometimes bred. In the Guard he "found out that a little old farm boy had as much get-together as the big town boys," that he could do his "own thing as well as they." Military life could teach an intelligent but perhaps innocent young man important lessons. To quote Donald Pfiefer, "As a farm boy I did learn to keep my mouth shut, eyes and ears wide open and to mind my own business." Town boys could learn the same thing if they paid attention. In Grand Forks, the state's second largest city, Paul Norman's enlistment in Company M gave him "the chance to do and be myself," he explained, "no help from Mom and Dad. I grew up in a hurry in the National Guard."

Charles Norton first joined the Guard in Headquarters Company, 1st Battalion, Cavalier, in 1931. A strapping 170-pound lad, standing five feet, nine inches tall at fourteen years old, he went to Grafton that fall to attend high school and transferred to Company C. The company's armory, he discovered, was "like a fellowship club." Company C sponsored basketball and volleyball teams for its younger members as well as maintained a canteen which sold soda pop, candy, and cigarettes, which Guardsmen could buy "on the tab" and pay off when their drill checks came. "The guys of high school age...hung around there all the time. It was a hang out for them." While some of Grafton's more worrisome mothers saw the armory as a gathering place for roughnecks, Norton viewed it as a good place for idle young men to go to stay out of trouble.

As in the prewar years, the decentralized Guard's fortunes were determined at the armories. Success in the companies decided the regiment's ultimate performance. The North Dakota National Guard's many connections to home communities contributed to its interwar stability. By the mid-1930s, the older line companies had established a fifty-year tradition with service in two wars. Many local men were Guard veterans with a lasting interest in their old outfits, ready to encourage young men to enlist. Chambers of commerce and other commercial organizations, American Legion posts, civic groups of all sorts, all consistently supported their local units with funds and publicity. Federal aid ensured that existing organizations would not founder as long as community support continued.

School-age boys from the town and countryside provided a steady source of recruits not available in the prewar years, and Guard officials were well aware of this. In a picturebook history of the North Dakota National Guard published in 1940, Colonel Herman Brocopp addressed his last few paragraphs "To the fathers and mothers of North Dakota." He stated that the Guard was dedicated to giving the state's young men quality military training "under officers who know your boy and love him." Guard training was a "fitting supplement to whatever education your boy has had," including teaching the lad "to stand on his two feet like a man...to be obedient, self-reliant, self-respecting and respectful to constituted authority." Under the Guard's tutelage, he added, "He is becoming a better citizen and a better son." No doubt, he intended this appeal to assure parents that the National Guard did not contain rowdy boys looking for a spree.

Cities and towns without a Guard unit sought to obtain one, though some petitions often expected too much or promised more than they would be able to deliver. A group seeking a unit for Rugby in 1925 wrote General Fraser: "We understand that the government furnishes an officer, the necessary uniforms, guns, etc., and also stands a certain amount of the cost of erecting an armory." Officers, of course, had to come from the local population, and the federal government gave no armory assistance, the latter being the largest cost unit supporters had to bear. Ten years later, an ardent Guard aspirant from the small town of Beach informed Frayne Baker, the adjutant general, "The sentiment here is very strong for an armory, and I can conscientiously say that we could get enough men for two companies if necessary." This assertion created doubts, even in light of drill pay, for a town the size of Beach.

When it became evident that North Dakota was going to add a field artillery battalion in 1936, the city of Mandan mounted an effort to become home station for one of the new batteries. The Chamber of Commerce, city council, and American Legion post jointly offered the town's World War Memorial Building as an armory. For a time, when it appeared that the state would split the battery between Mandan and Bismarck, this proposal brought a sharp reply from the city fathers to General Baker. Mandan resented its loss of Company F, 164th, after World War I, and declared that if it could not have a full battery, it would "not go part way with someone else." Baker tartly replied, "there are several cities in the state which are more than anxious to have a National Guard unit, and a part thereof." If Mandan did not want the unit as offered, he would place it somewhere else. Promptly backing down, Mandan's leaders accepted the unit on the state's terms. Municipalities continued to seek units, as Heber L. Edwards, adjutant general, informed a correspondent in 1940: "I only wish that we had National Guard companies to put in all of the cities and towns...that have asked for the same."

All the old problems did not disappear under the post-World War I regime. Finding recruits had become less difficult; keeping them often posed problems. While Guardsmen bound by the dual oath still gained discharges with ease if they moved away from home station, many simply dropped out without legal approval and without punishment. Information from the 1920s is scanty, but a few remarks by General Fraser suggest that keeping all units at minimum strength was still challenging. He informed a friend in 1925 that Company A was on the verge of disbandment due to underenrollment, but he intended to give it one more year to stabilize. Company A survived. Fraser complained to a Rugby man in 1926 "of the lack of interest in some towns where they have National Guard units." The adjutant general resisted breaking them up because of the value and usefulness of their armories, saying: "I have taken the matter up with...commercial clubs of these towns and they have promised to assist in reorganizing their units." During the 1930s, National Guard Bureau inspection reports indicated that the North Dakota National Guard replaced from one-quarter to one-third of its enlisted men every year. Many companies continued to follow the old practice of intense recruiting just before summer camp, on the average taking 128 men with less than two months' training to camp throughout the thirties. Arthur Timboe, who commanded the Howitzer Company at Devils Lake after 1936, remembered that "it was difficult to recruit in a small town....Some businessmen—very few—would wisecrack 'Our man is off playing soldier.'"

National Guard training failed to improve significantly in the interwar years. Before the war, the Division of Militia Affairs worked diligently but unsuccessfully to compel the Guard to develop progressive armory training programs. Ideally, company training would progress from the School of the Soldier (individual training) to squad, platoon, then company instruction. Well-trained companies could then go to summer camp ready for battalion and regimental tactical exercises. Guard companies were rarely prepared for the higher-level camp work, and much time was wasted, in the Division of Militia Affairs's eyes, on rudimentary instruction. Similar conditions too often prevailed in armory and field training up to World War II.

A shortage of modern arms, clothing, and equipment severely hampered training. All veterans who served before 1935 recalled with marked distaste the World War I olive-drab uniform. The men wore the all-wool blouse with high collar, wool knee breeches and wrap leggings, and stiff-felt campaign hat in the armory, on the firing range, in the field at camp, and on parade, winter or summer. They only had a few standard-issue blue-denim fatigue uniforms. The olive drabs were "hotter than hell," especially for camp, which the Guard always held in June. The stiff collars chafed the neck and the leggings shut off circulation to the feet. Most men had only one uniform for all fifteen days of camp, and, as Charles Norton remarked, they wore them "until they walked away." The Guard eventually received khaki uniforms for drill, and brown jackets and slacks, and Pershing-style hat, for parade and dress uniforms in the mid-1930s. Uniforms did not necessarily limit military efficiency, but they did affect morale and influence how new men saw themselves as soldiers. Too often, by the mid-thirties, "Uniforms were badly worn, not always the correct size." One man recalled: "When I joined in '38 they had a hell of a time to find anything that fit me and I was of...standard build." Poor uniforms surely would diminish the recruits' initial enthusiasm.

Weapons and equipment directly affected military efficiency. The Army and National Guard had only World War I infantry and artillery weapons until the eve of the Second World War. Though these were new and in sufficient supply during the 1920s, by the mid-thirties, new men were being issued "hand me downs—and older equipment" which was "generally quite obsolete." One veteran commented that "Most of it was serviceable"; others described weapons as "old but good," or "good, not new, but good." As war surplus stocks dwindled, the quantity of materiel available diminished. The Springfield rifle, model 1903, a bolt-action, magazine piece, remained the standard infantry weapon until 1941. The fourth company in each battalion (D, H, and M) served as a heavy-weapons company and supposedly had heavy and light machine guns and mortars, but they actually had only water-cooled, heavy, .30-caliber guns from 1917-1918. The Army developed new-model light machine guns and mortars in the late 1930s, but it could only provide the Guard with their field manuals. "We trained from the manuals," Richard Hoffman, Company H, recalled, "but did not receive the weaponry until mid-1941." Some enterprising Guardsmen improvised weapons for training purposes. Clarence McClure, a machinist in civil life, fashioned a mock mortar from an automobile drive shaft for Company A. In Company F, the men mounted a fence post between bicycle wheels to represent a mortar. Realistic training inevitably suffered under such limitations.

The 3rd Battalion, 185th Field Artillery Regiment, activated in 1937, suffered greater equipment shortages than did the 164th Infantry. Added to the North Dakota National Guard in the midst of the depression, the artillery received little assistance from the state. Artillery units cost more than infantry organizations, with their large guns, trucks, trailers, and radio equipment. In addition, they needed more storage space, had to employ part-time mechanics to maintain motor vehicles and guns, and required more room for drill. When Battery F was first organized in Jamestown, Francis Murphy noted, "many of our NCOs and EMs did not have basic uniforms (and had to wear civilian clothes). NDNG training funds were short too, very little gasoline was used." The battery had no guns during its first year and "a limited number of .45 caliber pistols, which were rotated among the officers and enlisted men." Battalion personnel worked out firing problems on paper. Overall, Murphy recalled, "Our training was pretty skimpy; we had to simulate a great deal...to train the 155 mm howitzer crews with no guns but pictures."

Artillery pieces came in 1938—French-made Schnieder guns from World War I with solid rubber or steel tires and no brakes. Antiquated, six-wheeled General Motors trucks pulled the guns, but very slowly because the pieces bounced up and down at over five miles per hour. The trucks had so little power, according to Victor McWilliams of Battery F, that the men pulled them up hills with ropes. Lack of a proper firing range, even at the state military reservation, limited practice firing. The only ammunition available was World War I shrapnel, a dangerous and unstable type of ammunition. The Army provided 37 mm tubes for bolting onto the 155 mm guns for firing. Artillerymen sited the guns using standard equipment but fired the cheaper, shorter-range tubes. Equipment was always in short supply, and "it took maneuvering and planning to have all personnel acquainted with at least 'hands on' experience," said George Toman of Mandan's Battery E. The gunners learned more than might be expected, largely because, as Murphy noted, "Our officers...were very good at improvising training equipment."

The internal-combustion engine, military historian Walter Millis has observed, began to transform war in 1914-1918. Planes, tanks, trucks, and other mechanized vehicles would revolutionize combat twenty years later, but in the 1920s and 1930s little evidence of this impending change existed in the North Dakota National Guard, or in the Regular Army for that matter. The Guard routinely took trains to summer camp until late in the period, unloading at the Fort Totten station and marching to camp under full pack. What few trucks the government allotted to the Guard were all made before 1918. North Dakota kept its vintage trucks, equipped with hard rubber tires and unable to go faster than ten miles per hour, at the military reservation. Regimental and battalion officers rode horses during tactical maneuvers and parades. The heavy-weapons companies used mules to pull their ammunition and machine gun carts. Farm boys, many of whom saw camp as a two-week escape from daily chores, invariably received stable duty, which they resented. "That was just taken for granted," Charles Norton remembered, "that they [farm boys] would take care of the commander's horse." Neither the Guard nor individual officers owned horses or mules, and farmers near Devils Lake made a tidy profit renting animals to the state. Even as late as 1938, when William Johnson attended his first camp, horses could prevail over trucks. Johnson, the innocent rookie, volunteered to drive a truck, but he discovered it dated from World War I and had no motor. Two horses pulled the vehicle around camp to pick up garbage.

The Guard began to acquire motor vehicles after 1933 when the National Guard Bureau initiated a drive to motorize its field artillery, most of which was still horse drawn. Bureau figures showed that trucks were easier and cheaper to maintain. At the time of the activation of the 185th in 1937, the War Department provided it with some trucks and station wagons, though not the newest models. In the middle thirties, the federal government used Works Progress Administration and Public Works Administration funds to supply vehicles to the rest of the Guard. The entire service had only 5,900 trucks in 1932, all from the war, and 10,500 vehicles in 1939, all of recent make. At that, the Guard counted only twenty-seven percent of its needs for mobilization strength. One horse-drawn artillery regiment remained in the Guard as late as 1940. The shortage of motor vehicles severely hampered National Guard training, not only because it prevented Guardsmen from learning the tactical possibilities of mobile warfare, but also because it limited the experience officers and men could gain from the enormous logistical demands of mechanized combat.

Armory training suffered in part from the weapons and equipment problem, although the Guard usually had sufficient amounts to equip the infantry, even if the materiel was outdated. The steady influx of new men and unimaginative company commanders more often kept instruction at an elementary level. In some companies "you had to go to recruit school the first week of camp, which consisted of weapons training and school of the soldier." A Company I veteran remembered that upon enlistment he was taken aside and "taught the school of the soldier by a fine corporal," a man demanding enough that he "kept me pretty much scared stiff." Generally, however, recruit training was not systematic throughout the service. New men learned by observation as they joined the rest of their outfit in its weekly work, which did not put many demands on them. Close-order drill, first aid, nomenclature and care of weapons, and military courtesy made up the weekly regimen for most units. For John Vold, Company M, training "Back in 1928" was "very ordinary, very basic." Arthur Timboe served in Devils Lake's Howitzer Company from 1925 to 1940. For him, there was "too much close order drill in squad, platoon, and company formations. Very few had any knowledge of administration or logistics. There was no adequate space for maneuvers or other operations." The routine varied only a little in Company E, according to George Christensen. "During cold weather we had close order drill and instruction in weapons, tactics, and military customs. We also had 'dry firing' of rifle. In warmer weather we had exercises outdoors and on the firing range."

Many veterans, from the perspective of World War II, were not impressed with the quality of training. For one Company K man, it was "not the kind that was needed later on to prepare us for the task ahead....The Guard was too soft on us prior to WWII." One of his comrades also viewed instruction as "All very basic—never saw a lesson plan and very few technical manuals....The 2 hour drill was too short a period to accomplish much more than hello and goodbye." Indeed, one veteran thought "the main objective" of the weekly meeting "was to put in the time required each period." In a few instances, former Guardsmen reported that they did not attend drill at all because they lived too far from home station and "so only attended summer camp." The value of drill instruction, Company C's Sterling Walker commented, was "much affected by the enthusiasm (or lack) of the instructor." Unimaginative company commanders, not aware of teaching techniques, relied too heavily on rote learning, dull lectures, and the endless repetition of close-order drill.

In some units, enthusiasm, imagination, and competence prevailed. Richard Hoffman recollected, for Company H, in the late thirties, "we had a very capable co. commander [Captain Robert K. Hall]. At our weekly meetings we snapped to and from the time we fell in we were expected to work—no beer and skittles—until after drill." Another Company H man, Albert Wiest, believed the "Training was good—conducted by NCOs whom *[sic]* were old hands with a sense of responsibility." Morton McBride served in Company K in the early thirties. "We had 2 WWI officers and the instruction they offered was very good," he said. Time restrictions limited even the best commanders, as future adjutant general LaClair Melhouse pointed out: "In the limited time of a 2 hr. drill the officers and NCOs did a good job." A veteran of Company I also thought "armory training was rather brief but conducted in a good military manner." The Guard also had enthusiastic officers, although at times enthusiasm proved to be dangerous. Alvin Paulson, Company F, related the story of an overly exuberant lieutenant, standing at attention with his sword on his right shoulder. He snapped to with the sword to give a salute. The lieutenant "Went to whip the thing off his shoulder...and holy smoke he pretty near cut his ear off." Not all drills were dull and boring.

Soldiers who took only seventy-six hours of company work a year were not likely to be prepared for battalion and regimental field training. Consequently, summer work tended to follow the same course as armory instruction, with an emphasis on the routine and the simple. One man described work at camp as "Poor—little time...devoted to progressive training—time wasted on marches, close order drill, inspections and parades." With many former World War I officers in command, much of the tactical work stressed trench warfare and sham battles in which "a platoon would rush across the parade ground in waves, bayonets fixed." Work usually ended at 3:00 P.M., and, until the late thirties, Albert Wiest recalled, "it was unheard of to keep troops out over night or in heavy inclement weather." To some, training seemed "somewhat haphazard, not well planned." Arthur Timboe related, "Unit training was stressed up to battalion level, but very little, not enough, training in regimental size field maneuvers, or what to do if attacked or to attack."

The National Guard Bureau chief conceded in his 1941 report, with most of the Guard then in federal service, that interwar training had neglected modern tactics, with too much importance attached to large, fixed formations and individual marksmanship. He noted the need to stress small-unit work, with sergeants and corporals directing teams in fire and maneuver tactics. This was hindsight, for the field manuals of the 1920s and 1930s neglected these tactics, which depended on infantry units equipped with semiautomatic and automatic weapons light enough to be hand carried. Memories of trench warfare unavoidably worked against experimenting with more mobile tactics, as did the weapons Guardsmen used. Once the service acquired trucks, for example, some units drove to camp, gaining experience in moving troops over the road.

Limitations at the military reservation also hampered training. The state had owned the Rock Island Military Reservation since the early 1890s but had never developed it completely. It was renamed Camp Grafton in 1921 in memory of Lieutenant Colonel Gilbert C. Grafton, 164th Infantry, who had died of disease in France. In an effort to better the camp, General G. Angus Fraser directed the construction of permanent kitchen and mess halls, warehouses, and a water and sewage system in the twenties. Other improvements followed in the 1930s with road building, a larger target range, and a full motor repair shop. The Guard used some state funds for the project, but most of the money came from National Guard Bureau allotments or Works Progress Administration funds in the thirties. The latter paid for labor and material costs to build the Governor's House, a commodious lodge used to accommodate important visitors. Captain Philip Christopherson took command as camp superintendent and served in that capacity until after World War II. Despite these improvements, Camp Grafton remained fairly primitive. Since it had no permanent barracks, troops always spent the first day in camp erecting tents in high grass and clearing off the company streets. And, with no electrical connections for the tents, the men used candles in gallon cans.

Most Guardsmen nonetheless saw summer field training as a valuable experience. Some enjoyed the opportunity to meet men from all over the state. For many, to cite Company E's Lawrence Poe, "We put into practice what we learned in armory training. Working as one segment of the entire regiment. It put us in the proper perspective." Summer work not only gave companies their proper perspective, but the men had "more time to do things, and [it was] like being on active duty." Morton McBride liked camp because of the "Field work," he said, "that we learned from the book and put into practice at camp. It made me good after all the dry runs." Riflemen and machine gunners spent as much as a week on the target range. "In my opinion," Albert Wiest wrote, "the weapons training was by far the most beneficial element of summer camp." The field artillery battalion looked forward to camp, for it "allowed marches by vehicles, emplacement of pieces and actual firing over an extended period," according to George Toman. It provided the only opportunity the battalion had to operate with its Headquarters Battery directing the firing batteries.

Camp also offered diversions, high jinks, and much public attention. Governor's Day continued to be a popular event, the Guard giving a dance the night before the governor reviewed the troops. Thousands of civilians came to Camp Grafton on the Sunday dividing the two-week training period to see the governor and his honorary colonels, all uncomfortably mounted on horses, conduct the review and to watch a sham battle. Governor's Day ended with the machine gun companies holding a competitive shoot, firing at helium-filled balloons floating over Devils Lake. In the late afternoons and at nights during the work week, the men participated in regimental sports competitions. Boxing led as the most popular sport, and, as usual, Company M won most of the bouts. Some companies held initiation rites for recruits who had never attended camp. These involved such tricks as walking a plank over a mud hole, wiring a field telephone to a man's testicles, or running the infamous "hot ass line," where nude or seminude men ran down a gauntlet while the old salts slapped at them with bayonet scabbards or belts. One man recalled that initiation was "more or less harassment," and for new men, camp "was bad enough without being harassed." Guardsmen rarely went to Devils Lake while on evening pass because they could not walk that far. Many strolled over to the old Chautauqua grounds to visit the general store or ice cream parlor. Until 1933, when prohibition was repealed, it was easy to find bootleggers close to Camp Grafton.

Richard Hoffman summed up the camp experience for most Guardsmen: "Summer camp was generally hard work except for nights when you didn't have duty. We were well trained and at night the 'natives' were friendly." Bandsmen particularly looked forward to field training. They played for the daily camp routine, provided one of the chief attractions on Governor's Day, and also gave concerts at the Chautauqua grounds and in Devils Lake. Franklin Schoeffler remembered "the joy of looking forward to the encampment with its training and off hours activities." Fellow bandsman Douglas Campbell thought "The Camp Grafton episodes were fun times and made for a good vacation." The infantrymen and artillerymen might not have thought of two weeks at Camp Grafton in the middle of June as a vacation, but annual training, whatever its limits in tactical instruction, was essential to the Guard's sense of purpose and the Guardsman's perception that he was a soldier.

Discipline at home station and in field training was much improved over prewar years. The contractural obligations accompanying drill pay made it easier to impose. So, too, did the legacy of service in the American Expeditionary Forces. Officers and noncommissioned officers with war experience had some familiarity with Regular Army methods and standards. Stripped of some of its social club atmosphere, most notably the election of officers, the Guard followed a mixture of formal and informal punishments which conformed to the Army's general disciplinary system and were imposed "not too formally but very fairly, as must be in a civilian organization," in many companies. In Company M, according to Walter Mellem, "It was not by the book. It depended on the attitude of the Co. Cmdr." In other organizations, former Guardsmen recalled, "Discipline was STRICT," or "Very formal. Most every punishment was read to us from the book." Lawrence Poe of Company E said in his outfit, "A member who didn't comply with regulations was discharged quick." Company punishments, similar to Army practice, included kitchen police, latrine duty, extra guard duty, and, occasionally, demotion. Courts martial were rare.

Discipline at camp was more formal and severe than in the armory. At Camp Grafton, "the 'ground rules' were different." Here, a more military atmosphere prevailed. "You can imagine the endless opportunities at camp," Richard Hoffman wrote. "K.P., guard duty, leave cancellations, other 'joys' of the first sgt." Digging holes, some for functional purposes like latrines, others for educational purposes, frequently provided a form of camp punishment. Camp was no longer quite the lark it had once been, and the stricter discipline imposed there made that evident. Still, the Guard could not easily overcome its essentially civilian, part-time nature. "When everybody knows everybody," Arthur Timboe pointed out, "there is bound to be some informality."

Armory and camp training had limited value and scope, but a seriousness not evident in the past governed the North Dakota National Guard. Duty on the Mexican border in 1916 and, more importantly, mobilization in 1917 served as permanent reminders that enlistment in the National Guard carried with it a well-defined obligation to serve in times of emergency or war. The numerous war veterans in the officer corps and noncommissioned ranks reinforced that fact. While the veterans' reminiscences of the Mexican border and France might have seemed tiresome to the younger men, they nonetheless made clear that a Guardsman might one day find himself on duty somewhere other than Camp Grafton. Drill pay contributed to the Guard's greater efficiency. A man who took the government's dollar was expected to give something in return. Furthermore, in the old days, when a man rendered voluntary but uncompensated service, he believed he retained the right to decline to volunteer if business or family needs loomed larger than the nation's needs. Accepting drill pay not only bound the Guardsman contractually but morally as well.

Legal changes clarified the nature of Guard service and its obligations. Pressured by the National Guard Association, Congress amended the National Defense Act in 1933 to remove confusion concerning the dual oath and the Guard's rights under a federal call. The amendment made the Guard a reserve component of the Army and replaced the dual oath with a dual enlistment. Officers and men now simultaneously joined the National Guard of the United States and the North Dakota National Guard. This provision ensured the calling of state forces to federal duty as units, not as individuals. Another provision changed the Militia Bureau to the National Guard Bureau, the former name long seen by many Guardsmen as historically inaccurate and a description carrying negative connotations. Finally, the law ended the general practice of officers' holding commissions in the National Guard and the Officers Reserve Corps at the same time. Men formerly took Officers Reserve Corps commissions to ensure themselves a place in the next war army in the event the government called the Guard as individuals and not as units. Most importantly, the law made clear to all Guardsmen that as members of the National Guard of the United States they were a part of the Army of the United States, subject to the orders of the President or the War Department.

Interwar mobilization planning by the General Staff assured the Guard a role in any future war and they completed the first such peacetime plan in the nation's history in 1923. Modified, and sometimes completely rewritten, several times in the next fifteen years, it nevertheless retained its essential parts unchanged. In the original concept, Regular Army, National Guard, and Organized Reserve divisions formed the heart of the next war army. The reserves failed to develop, and, after 1932, the General Staff focused its thinking on the forces in being, the Army and the Guard. In 1937, it thoroughly rewrote its plans and produced the Protective Mobilization Plan, which called for the mobilization of all Army and National Guard units at peace strength, with a minimum combined force of 400,000 deemed necessary. These units would serve first as a training cadre for up to a 1.5 million men, then as an initial fighting force while the nation organized a mass army for all-out war. The Protective Mobilization Plan force would contain a total of twenty-six divisions, of which eighteen infantry and two cavalry divisions were National Guard. The Guard had always played a significant part in interwar mobilization planning, but, by the late 1930s, it represented the majority of forces which would bear the first burden of training and fighting should a war come.

The average Guardsman, officer or enlisted man, most likely had no knowledge of the complexities and details of preparing for a call-up or had ever heard of the Protective Mobilization Plan. Planning of this sort was carried on within the War Department bureaucracy, rarely given publicity, and, until the late 1930s, was of a most general kind unconnected to any specific foreign problem. It nonetheless affected the North Dakota National Guard in a variety of ways. The 1920 National Defense Act required the Army, National Guard, and Organized Reserves to maintain tactical divisions in peacetime. Peace-strength tables of organization, on personnel and equipment, were geared to mobilization plans. Commanders of the nine corps areas had the task of overseeing divisional mobilization and planning. For all intents and purposes, this meant overseeing the National Guard, for the Army lacked the manpower to keep up even skeleton divisions, and the Organized Reserve was never funded. Each corps area assigned Army personnel as inspector-instructors to the states, supervised National Guard training, and made sure the states cooperated with each other in creating their divisions. As part of the VII Corps Area, the North Dakota National Guard made up part of the 34th Division. A North Dakota Guardsman, Brigadier General David S. Ritchie, colonel of the 164th Infantry from 1923 to 1928, commanded the division's 68th Infantry Brigade from 1928 to 1940. The 164th Infantry and the 135th Infantry (Minnesota National Guard) comprised the main elements in the brigade. Several other North Dakota National Guard officers held staff positions in the 34th Division.

Mobilization planning affected the Guard in two direct ways. In 1932, Chief of Staff Douglas MacArthur directed that the General Staff arrange Army and Guard divisions into four field armies, under corps area control. MacArthur wanted to create a skeleton organization for higher-level commands and also to advance training beyond the state military reservations. Owing to fiscal shortages, Army and Guard units had not maneuvered together since 1915. Large-scale joint field maneuvers under the four-army scheme began in 1935, preceded by so-called command-post exercises in which regimental and divisional officers conducted war games to learn higher-level administration and strategy. The North Dakota National Guard traveled by truck to Camp Ripley, Minnesota, in 1937 to join troops from Minnesota, Iowa, and South Dakota in the 34th Division's first peacetime maneuver, as part of the Fourth Army. Nearly ten thousand Guardsmen attended. They repeated the exercise in 1940. The field army maneuvers revealed many problems in the Guard, particularly equipment shortages and a low level of training, but they were crucial in teaching Guardsmen that they were part of a larger military system.

The development of the Protective Mobilization Plan, with its strong emphasis that mobilization planning be based on existing forces, led the

General Staff and National Guard Bureau to lobby for an increase in the Guard's strength in order to meet the 400,000-man minimum needed to carry out the plan. The Guard's authorized strength had remained at 190,000 from 1930 to 1935. With congressional approval in 1936, the National Guard Bureau initiated a program to enlarge the Guard to 210,000 by the end of the fiscal year 1940, in increments of 5,000 men. The National Guard Bureau stressed raising units authorized back in 1921 but never created, particularly those organizations that would give the divisions the proper tactical balance. In 1936 and 1937, the National Guard Bureau used the two first 5,000-man increments to activate the third battalions of artillery regiments belonging to infantry divisions. North Dakota acquired the 3rd Battalion, 185th Field Artillery Regiment, a part of the 34th Division. The other two battalions were already part of the Iowa National Guard. The state placed Headquarters Battery at Bismarck, Battery E at Mandan, and Battery F at Jamestown. All were active by the spring of 1937.

Postwar policy and practice significantly improved the officer corps. Provisions in the 1916 National Defense Act requiring minimum educational and professional standards for officers did not take full effect until after World War I. When imposed, they ended the long tradition of electing company officers. Adjutants general could not allow unqualified men to take commissions, for the War Department would withhold federal recognition of both the officers and their units, denying the state its federal funds. According to his aide, Lieutenant Noel Tharalson, General Fraser took the matter in his own hands. From 1921, Tharalson wrote five years later, "it has been the policy of the Adjutant General to make appointments of all officers," and his successors followed that example. General Fraser made some of his selections in a rather casual fashion. Leo Dominick, who served as a lieutenant in the 164th Infantry during the war, did not rejoin the Guard afterward because his hometown did not have a unit. He related how a chance encounter with the adjutant general in Fargo in 1923, at a time when Dominick was a major in the Officers Reserve Corps, led to his return to the Guard. When Fraser asked him if he would accept a commission and appointment as assistant adjutant in the 34th Division, Dominick agreed and, later, took the division's G-3 post, as operations and planning officer, with the rank of lieutenant colonel, serving until 1940.

General Fraser and other adjutants general were usually more systematic. World War I veterans offered the obvious place to seek postwar officers. All the regiment's field-grade officers from 1923 to 1940 came from the prewar North Dakota National Guard roster, and nearly all of them had served in the war. A major when discharged in 1919, David S. Ritchie assumed regimental command in 1923. When he moved to the 68th Brigade in 1928, Lieutenant Colonel Laroy Baird succeeded him. Baird, who had been in the Guard since 1907, resigned in the spring of 1917 but later took a captain's commission in the state Quartermaster Corps to serve as United States Property and Disbursing Officer. He commanded Company K in the early 1920s and followed the regular promotion route thereafter. Earle R. Sarles, a war veteran, assumed the colonelcy in 1940 when Baird succeeded Ritchie in command of the infantry brigade. Manville H. Sprague (1923-1927) and

Barney C. Boyd (1929-1937), among other old hands, served in the regiment as lieutenant colonels. The latter first joined the North Dakota National Guard in 1898 when he enlisted for the Spanish-American War and retired with thirty-nine years of service in 1937. Boyd and Colonel Ritchie were the only line officers with service in 1898-1899.

All but two of the company commanders in the early 1920s were regimental war veterans, four of whom continued to lead the units they took to war in 1917. Emery Jeffrey, Company E, like Baird, resigned before mobilization but resumed command in 1920. Inevitably, time or promotion removed veterans from company command, but as late as 1940 five infantry captains were veterans, four having served as enlisted men. The North Dakota National Guard replaced captains by promotion within the company. Many men served as second, then first lieutenants for ten or fifteen years before moving up to captain. With seniority governing promotion, advancement came slowly, true also in the early twentieth century. Colonel Baird, for example, headed the regiment from 1928 to 1940, and Boyd held the lieutenant colonelcy for eight years. Captains and lieutenants waited patiently or left the service. Many waited. Seven company commanders led their units for ten years or more during the period. Herman Brocopp topped the list with eighteen years in command of Company A (1922-1940). Slow promotion did not drive many officers from the service, even in the junior grades. The low turnover in company officers contrasted remarkably with the prewar years.

Faced with the major challenge of finding able, interested young men to serve as lieutenants for years until they could earn their captain's bars, the Guard found help in John Fraine's legacy, for it followed his practice of seeking candidates from the enlisted ranks. The presence of many students in the Guard reinforced the policy. Although the National Defense Act vaguely referred to minimum educational qualifications for commissions, the War Department interpreted the provision to mean, wherever possible, a college degree. Lacking that, the department extended recognition to men with some college experience or, at the very least, a high school education. College enlistees were encouraged to take the full four-year Reserve Officers Training Corps course, then accept an Officers Reserve Corps commission while serving in the ranks. After 1933, the National Guard Bureau allowed enlisted men to hold reserve National Guard of the United States commissions. When an officer's slot opened up in their unit, these reservists took the commission. Frank Richards proudly related that eight men from his Company K held National Guard of the United States reserve commissions, and all became second lieutenants when the Guard went on active duty in 1941. Company and battalion officers, and sometimes Regular Army instructors, sought out the abler and more enthusiastic enlisted men with high school educations and attempted to convince them to take a correspondence course offered by the War Department. The course, series 10, could lead to a commission if the candidate completed it and then passed an examination before a board of officers at Bismarck.

Ira M. F. Gaulke followed the first method. After enlisting in Company M in 1923, while still a student at the University of North Dakota, following graduation in 1925 he qualified for second lieutenant in the Officers Reserve

Corps. Gaulke was a sergeant at the time. With the support of his company commander, Captain Heber L. Edwards, and Major Earle R. Sarles, 1st Battalion, Gaulke took the second lieutenant's examination in 1926 and received his commission. He eventually succeeded Edwards as company commander in 1935 and went to war in 1941 as a major of artillery. On the other hand, Victor McWilliams, an enlisted man and high school graduate in Battery F, 185th Field Artillery, took the series 10 course at the urging of Lieutenant Colonel John Gross, Regular Army adviser to the battalion. Gross, a tough but fair examiner, graded the course, McWilliams remembered. McWilliams, the battery's supply sergeant, eventually earned his commission on the basis of his series 10 performance. The adjutants general heeded the advice of company and battalion officers on promising officer candidates and often sought background information on them from local friends or prominent people.

Lacking personnel trained in the technicalities of artillery, the state called on Officers Reserve Corps officers to organize the 185th Field Artillery in 1936-1937. It commissioned Percy M. Hansen, editor of the Jamestown *Sun*, a major to lead the unit. Hansen had served in the Coast Artillery in World War I and held a reserve commission in the field artillery from 1919 until he joined the Guard in 1937. Leslie V. Miller, another veteran and Officers Reserve Corps artillery officer, took command first of Mandan's Battery E in 1936 and, after establishing that unit, led Headquarters Battery in Bismarck. Reserve officers like Robert Carlson, Bismarck, a graduate of the Agricultural College's engineering department, and Jamestown's Francis Murphy became junior officers in the battalion.

The officers had similar occupational backgrounds to those serving before 1920. Many owned small business firms or real estate and insurance brokerages, others practiced law and medicine. A growing number of teachers introduced a new trend. Officers had a considerably better education than those who entered service before World War I. In part, this reflected North Dakota's evolution from a frontier state to a more settled community. Jerome Norman, a veteran of Company M, remembered that his officers, and many noncommissioned officers, had attended college. The officers, as he put it, were not "down the line political hacks....They were people you respect[ed]." A better-educated officer corps also mirrored trends in the Army evident since 1900. The service had sought to develop a professional education system beyond the four-year West Point program. A military graduate school system did not develop fully until after World War I when the Army established schools for the combat and support branches, the Infantry School at Fort Benning, Georgia, the best known of these. For high command and strategic studies, the Army continued and expanded the prewar Command and General Staff School at Fort Leavenworth, Kansas, and the Army War College in Washington. As World War II revealed, the Army's educational system was its most significant achievement during the interwar years.

The National Defense Act of 1920 provided for qualified National Guard officers to go to Army service schools at government expense. Although limited funding circumscribed the program, between 1920 and 1941 nearly six thousand Guard officers attended the schools, thirty-four of them from the

North Dakota National Guard. Three North Dakota Guardsmen, Frayne Baker, Heber L. Edwards, and Frank Richards, graduated from the Command and General Staff School, and twenty more graduated from the Infantry School. The National Guard Bureau encouraged officers to take correspondence courses appropriate to their rank and branch and also developed command and staff short courses for regimental and divisional officers, to be given by corps area commanders. At each promotion, before receiving federal recognition, officers had to show they had completed course work fitting them for their next assignment. Neither the residency schools nor correspondence courses guaranteed an officer's tactical skill or leadership qualities, but the complexities of modern war demanded more than simple courage. The Army's emphasis on continuous education forced National Guard officers to demonstrate their willingness to prepare themselves for these responsibilities.

TABLE 7.2
Adjutants General, 1920-1940

Name	Term in Office
G. Angus Fraser	1917-9 January 1933
Herman Brocopp (acting)	9 January-5 June 1933
Earle R. Sarles	6 June 1933-8 February 1935
Frayne Baker	9 February 1935-2 January 1937
Heber L. Edwards	4 February 1937-1940

The adjutants general's administrative abilities contributed greatly to the North Dakota National Guard's stability between the wars. (See Table 7.2.) Prominent in civilian life, they had all had successful business careers yet also had had extensive military experience as well. Except for Frayne Baker, they had followed John Fraine's example, moving from private up through the ranks to a commission and service with the regiment, in peace and war. Baker entered the Army's Quartermaster Corps with a direct appointment to a captaincy in 1917, served overseas with the American Expeditionary Forces, then held an Officers Reserve Corps commission until 1933, when he went active with the Guard as a lieutenant colonel. He received assignment to a staff position with the 34th Division.

General Fraser directed the Guard from 1917 to 1933, his sixteen-year tenure the longest in the Guard's history to that time. Fraser retained office after 1919 because the legislature revised the military code. The new version dropped the provision making the incumbent ineligible for reappointment, and it also eliminated the section that required the adjutant general to be the highest-ranking field or line officer willing to take the appointment. Now, the adjutant general simply had to be a commissioned officer with at least three years' continuous service. The law contributed to slower regimental promotion but permitted leadership continuity, something the Guard had never had.

Active in the Guard since 1891 and a veteran of the Spanish-American War, Fraser earned something of a national reputation in Guard circles. After serving first as president of the National Rifle Association, long closely affiliated with the Guard, he became president of the National Guard Association of the United States in 1927 and 1928. A careful administrator, Fraser maintained good relations with the Militia Bureau and took particular care in selecting officers to lead the reorganized 164th Infantry. He was also instrumental in establishing Camp Grafton as a permanent training ground. As seen during the coal strike, General Fraser knew how to carry out difficult orders and how to get along with governors. His assistant adjutant general, Major Harold Sorenson, who also commanded the state Quartermaster Corps and acted as United States Property and Disbursing Officer, served Fraser well. Sorenson was another veteran from the mid-1890s and the Spanish-American War. The adjutant general selected Colonel John Fraine as paymaster general, largely an honorary post except during camp. Keeping the grand "old man" active was both an act of friendship and a way to retain connections with the Guard's past.

General Fraser left office in 1933 when newly elected Governor William Langer declined to reappoint him. The governor had no particular objection to Fraser; he wished to have his own appointees to head all the executive departments. With Langer's inauguration, North Dakota entered the most turbulent period in its political history. A series of confusing, sometimes bizarre, events kept state politics in a turmoil for four years. William Langer led the revived Nonpartisan League faction of the Republican party to victory in 1932 under a reform platform to combat the depression. Resentful members of the Independent Voters Association, also Republicans, and hostile New Deal agency representatives, all Democrats, went after the abrasive Langer. A federal court convicted the governor of illegally collecting campaign contributions from federal employees in May 1934. Two months later, the state supreme court ordered Langer to vacate the governorship. Finding no means to defy the court, Langer stepped down, and Lieutenant Governor Ole Olson, another Leaguer, assumed office.

Langer attempted to run again in 1934, but, when the state court thwarted the move, the Republican party made Lydia Langer, his wife, their nominee to run against Democrat Thomas Moodie. The latter won but barely served a month, January 1935, before the Langer forces revealed that Moodie did not meet residency requirements to hold office. Court orders ousted him, too, and Lieutenant Governor Walter Welford, the fourth governor in six months, became chief executive. The final spin in the political swirl came in 1936 when Langer, his conviction overturned by a federal appeals court, again won the governorship. Political sanity returned to the state thereafter. The flamboyant Langer's second term proved far less turbulent as he prepared to run for the United States Senate, an office he won in 1940 on his second attempt. John Moses, a Democrat, triumphed in the 1938 gubernatorial race. Moses was a popular governor, and his re-elections in 1940 and 1942 ensured political stability at last.

The Guard unavoidably became involved in Langer's tempestuous governorships. No governor had used the Guard as frequently or for such diverse purposes as William Langer, before or after the 1930s. He had campaigned in 1932 with the promise to deal effectively with the enormous problems depression-ridden farmers faced. Above all, he guaranteed that he would cut state spending, raise farm prices, and save family farms from mortgage foreclosures. To deal with the latter problem, Governor Langer issued a proclamation on 4 March 1933 declaring a moratorium on mortgage foreclosures, "either real estate or chattel." Since he lacked the authority to order judges or sheriffs to stop mortgage sales, Langer relied on his power as commander in chief of the state militia. In his Executive Order No. 3, 16 March 1933, he directed Herman Brocopp, acting adjutant general, "to use as much of the State Militia as in your judgment may be necessary to enforce the above mentioned proclamation."

Captain Brocopp and two enlisted men from Company A stopped the first mortgage sale, that of a personal residence in Bismarck, on 15 April. J. L. Kelley, sheriff of Burleigh County, reported to Justice of the Peace Edward S. Allen that three uniformed Guardsmen armed with pistols averted the sale, and, he continued, "I am unable to physically, without bloodshed, to [sic] execute the said process." In the next three months, Captain Brocopp and other officers prevented another twenty-nine foreclosure sales. Despite Sheriff Kelley's overly dramatic affidavit, the Guard's intervention was never heavy-handed, and no violence accompanied the stoppages. Most sheriffs were pleased to be relieved of the onus of selling family farms and homes. Foreclosures were always unpleasant and likely to cause violence in the desperate 1930s. A system was devised whereby, first, Governor Langer, Captain Brocopp, or Earle R. Sarles, adjutant general, appointed early in June, either wrote or telephoned the sheriff and attorney representing the mortgage holder, informing them of the state's intent to stop a sale. Then, on the day of the sale, a Guard officer and one or two enlisted men would appear at the appropriate county seat at the appointed hour. Alvin Paulson, an enlisted man in Company F, accompanied his company commander, Captain Frank Putnam, on three occasions. Putnam always followed the same procedure, Paulson related, by saying, "Mr. Sheriff we the military are here to prevent you from proceeding further with the foreclosure. That was the end of it." Company C's Charles Norton confirmed the ease with which the Guard enforced Langer's proclamation. "We just went there and took over the auction and said it was over and that was it."

Officers from Company A, with home station in the capital city, went out most frequently, particularly Lieutenant Gilbert Cass. In one instance, Cass received orders to stop sales in two separate places at the same hour and successfully performed the task. He intervened at Linton, Emmons County, at 2:04 P.M., Central Standard Time, then at Fort Yates, Sioux County, at 2:00 P.M. Mountain Time. "To accomplish my mission under this order it was necessary to employ the services of an aeroplane and pilot," Cass reported, "it being physically impossible to do so otherwise." On a few occasions, Guardsmen returned farm machinery or livestock seized to cover indebtedness. They managed the restoration without difficulty, although Lieutenant Cass failed to recover a bull calf which had died "because of faulty casteration [sic]." After Langer left office, his successors relieved the Guard of this duty. When he returned in 1937, however, Langer again directed Adjutant General Heber L. Edwards to intervene in some mortgage sales, though not on the scale of 1933. The last intervention occurred on 3 January 1938.

Guardsmen found this duty "unusual," according to Frank Richards. "They didn't like it, but they were loyal, they would obey the orders if they had to but they weren't too enthused about it." In October 1933, General Sarles cautioned Governor Langer to take care in selecting which foreclosures to stop. Mortgage sales ordered by state district courts, he wrote, differed from those simply advertised in the papers by the mortgage holder. Sarles feared that intervention in court-ordered sales, he explained, "would be placing myself and the officer stopping the sale in contempt of court." He warned Captain R. J. McDonald of Company G not to carry out the governor's order on a sale in Barnes County until, he said, "I find out that it is legal to do so." The same concern appeared again in 1938. Battery F's Captain John Kohnen disliked the foreclosure duty and told General Edwards, "I would prefer not to have anything more to do with the case." Langer also used the Guard to enforce a grain embargo imposed on 19 October 1933, directing the Guardsmen to protect bridges over the Red River at Grand Forks and Fargo to prevent shipment of wheat into Minnesota. This occasioned no problem, largely because farmers were not shipping grain owing to low prices.

Governor Langer used the Guard for other less drastic and less publicized matters. In May 1933 he ordered Captain Brocopp to investigate the residency of men employed in erecting the new capitol building and to utilize "as much of the military forces...as" was "necessary to stop employment of any person not bona fide residents of the State." Brocopp also looked into the matter of construction companies' building of highways with state and federal relief funds to make sure they were paying fair wages and employing North Dakota residents only. Workers at the capitol building site went on strike briefly in early June. Langer declared martial law in Bismarck from 1 to 3 June 1933 and ordered Company A and the Quartermaster detachment on active duty to protect the site as well as the men willing to work. A total of four officers and seventy-five enlisted men served there for three days. In his second term, Langer sent General Edwards with a few men to the State Hospital for the Insane at Jamestown to guard inmates and assist hospital officials in cleaning out infested buildings. He told Edwards, do not "return to Bismarck until you can upon your word as an officer, assure me that not a louse or bed-bug remains in the State Asylum." On another occasion, the governor ordered the Guard to provide cots, bedding, and field kitchens for meetings of the Nonpartisan League, Farmer's Union, and Farmers' Holiday Association, three groups that were ardent Langer supporters.

Except for the latter instances, Langer's ready reliance on the National Guard stemmed from the problems attending the depression. The mortgage moratorium, grain embargo, labor troubles at the capitol, and issues at the insane asylum resulted from economic failures and North Dakota's desperate lack of revenue. As a state agency, the Guard could be expected to serve as the governor's instrument in coping with such extraordinary difficulties. In a move reminiscent of Huey Long's machinations in Louisiana, however, Langer called the Guard out the day the supreme court ordered him to vacate the governorship. Ostensibly, as his order to General Sarles stated, the Guard was to protect "state property from destruction and vandalism and suppress any rioting." Langer's opponents argued he planned to use the military to intimidate the legislature into carrying out his threat to impeach the supreme court justices and to prevent Ole Olson from taking office. Whatever the intention, Langer's Executive Order No. 10, 17 July 1934, which suggested a desperate man no longer thinking clearly, declared martial law throughout the state and called up the entire National Guard "to suspend and prevent the service of Civil Process, and unlawful assemblies, and prevent disorders." He justified his action on the grounds that "mobs" were "beginning to assemble" and that they threatened the capitol building and the people therein. According to most newspaper reports, the largest number of non-Bismarck residents in the city that day were Langer supporters in from the countryside to back their favorite politician.

Fortunately, cooler heads prevailed. Only Company A and the Quartermaster detachment actually reported to the capitol for duty. After wavering for a day, General Sarles decided that Ole Olson was his lawful commander in chief. On July 18, Olson issued an executive order countermanding Order No. 10. It cancelled martial law and directed Sarles to send the Guard home. The new governor changed his mind the next day with yet another executive order directing Sarles to "retain troops on duty as long as he deemed necessary." Company A patrolled the capitol grounds for a week and then went home. The crisis passed, and Langer went into temporary political retirement. His actions moved the Guard dangerously, and unnecessarily, close to involvement in a political issue where it did not belong. They also brought ridicule down on the state. The press from eastern states, the *New York Times, Newsweek Magazine,* and the *Literary Digest,* for example, temporarily shifted their focus from Franklin Roosevelt's recently installed administration to the plains state's political doings. The *Times* featured a two-column picture of Guardsmen, armed with fixed bayonets, protecting the governor's office, erroneously stating that federal troops were on the verge of intervening, while the *Literary Digest* poked big-city fun at the "State Nobody Knows." Whether Langer seriously considered using the Guard to keep the governorship is unclear, but his declaration of martial law, which implied such an intent, was one of the rashest acts of his political career.

Institutionally, the National Guard did not suffer unduly from the political turmoil of the thirties, except for the turnover in adjutants general. Three men, Earle R. Sarles, Frayne Baker, and Heber L. Edwards, held the post in a matter of four years, and Captain Herman Brocopp served as acting adjutant general from January to June 1933. Although Ole Olson suspected that Sarles was sympathetic to Langer, he retained him. Thomas Moodie also kept Sarles upon inauguration in January 1935, but when Moodie left a month later, his successor, Walter Welford, dismissed Sarles and appointed Frayne

Baker. When Sarles protested and asked the state supreme court to permit him to remain adjutant general, arguing that his appointment covered Moodie's full term, even though the latter was no longer governor, the court rejected the argument. After Langer returned in 1937, he selected Edwards, then a major, to replace Baker, for the governor was never a man to keep another's appointees. John Moses, inaugurated in 1939, ended the revolving adjutant generalcy by retaining General Edwards, and the two men developed a warm and effective working relationship. The legislature revised the military code in 1941 and set the adjutant general's term at six years, partially isolating the position from partisan manipulation and ensuring continuity in military leadership.

Despite their short tenures, Generals Sarles and Baker contributed to the Guard's development. Sarles was instrumental in acquiring Works Progress Administration funds to improve Camp Grafton. General Baker played a major role in bringing the 185th Field Artillery battalion to North Dakota. When the National Guard Bureau implemented its plan to expand the Guard to 210,000 men in 1936, it wanted to activate the third battalions of divisional artillery regiments and expand divisional Quartermaster regiments. The 185th was an element of the 34th Division, its two active battalions serving in the Iowa National Guard. Baker oversaw negotiations with Iowa and Minnesota to obtain the 3rd Battalion, while those states divided the Quartermaster regiment. Undoubtedly Baker's biggest disappointment was his failure to win Works Progress Administration funds to construct new armories. Under his direction, the Board of Armory Supervisors developed a plan to construct twenty armories, which could also be "used as community centers." State and local funds, added to Works Progress Administration assistance, would finance the armories. The plan foundered when the agency's administrator in North Dakota raised so many objections that Harry L. Hopkins, head of the agency, refused to approve the plan. The Works Progress Administration's man in North Dakota was Thomas H. Moodie.

While both Sarles and Baker suffered bruised egos as a consequence of their short terms, they managed to keep the Guard and themselves from becoming deeply involved in the complicated political fray of the Langer years. Generals Fraser and Sarles, Major Harold Sorenson, and Lieutenant Colonel Barney Boyd typify the generation of Guardsmen who entered the service in the 1890s, when the Guard began to evolve into its modern form. Each of them invested more than forty years in the Guard and saw it grow from an unstable, underfunded institution with a poorly defined role in military policy to a permanent part of the nation's armed forces. Their service contributed to that change.

Heber L. Edwards represented the next generation. He enlisted in Company M in late 1915, then went to the Mexican border and subsequently to France with the regiment. Discharged as a sergeant in March 1919, Edwards reorganized Company M in 1920. He commanded the company until 1933 when his promotion to major led to assignment as the regiment's S-3 officer, for plans and training. Edwards took the National Guard officers' course at Fort Benning in 1924, received a law degree from the University of North Dakota three years later, and graduated from the Command and General Staff

School in 1939. His career to 1937 reflected post-World War I Guard developments, particularly the growing emphasis on education. At the same time, he managed to build a successful insurance business in Grand Forks.

An adroit recruiter, especially in his ability to attract athletes to Company M, Edwards also early on displayed a sharp sense for public relations. He frequently volunteered his unit for public service in Grand Forks, especially for crowd control during public events. "Captain Edwards was very community minded," one veteran recalled. Food seemed to be his one weakness: throughout the 1920s and 1930s he got himself into trouble with the Militia Bureau and National Guard Bureau because his annual physical showed him to be overweight. Only five feet, seven inches tall, Edwards consistently weighed from 180 to well over 200 pounds. He was forever promising to go on a diet, in letters to the bureau, but the problem persisted. In his evaluation of Edwards, the director of the National Guard class at the Command and General Staff School in 1939, a Regular Army colonel, found him a "very satisfactory" student and "a determined and able officer who has judgment and common sense far above the average." He would display those traits throughout his career as adjutant general, which lasted until 1962.

In the years before World War II, Edwards's main achievement was to obtain a permanent home for state headquarters. In 1937, "The newly built Capitol was already beginning to burst at the seams," Mrs. H. L. Edwards recalled. "The National Guard with its voluminous records was being pushed into a corner." General Edwards, a first-rate scrounger in the best sense of the word, set out to acquire an abandoned Indian school just west of Bismarck, on the banks of the Missouri River. The Bureau of Indian Affairs, Department of the Interior, held the property. The adjutant general vied successfully with the Bismarck city school system, the Civilian Conservation Corps, and other groups to procure the grounds.

Several large buildings, which once held classrooms and dormitories, and five houses where the teaching staff lived offered the Guard spacious accommodations. Though the state had no funds available for the renovation, Edwards wangled Works Progress Administration money, materials, and labor to make the buildings usable. The Edwards family, Major and Mrs. Sorenson, and the families of Army adviser Lieutenant Colonel Thomas Smith and Assistant Adjutant General Herman Brocopp moved into vacant houses. On General Edwards's advice, Governor Langer named the location Fraine Barracks. State headquarters took on the tone of a small military post. Children from the Edwards, Smith, and Brocopp families romped about the grounds. The adjutant general moved Walter and Luella Erickson, caretakers at Camp Grafton, down to Fraine Barracks to care for the grounds and buildings. Mrs. Edwards oversaw the decoration of the "Dugout" in the basement of the main office building, where her husband and his aides could entertain and woo legislators and officers could socialize. Fraine Barracks provided a more-than-adequate headquarters conveniently removed from the political bustle of the capital. Its acquisition also served as a sign of the intentions and abilities of Heber Edwards. He brought to office a foresight, combined with political and administrative skills, never seen in the adjutant generalcy.

General Edwards's administrative and leadership abilities were challenged in the hectic months after 1939, as the nation edged toward war. During the 1930s the world reeled from one international crisis to another while the industrialized countries tried to cope with the worldwide depression. Many, particularly the democracies, were more intent on solving their domestic problems than expending their efforts upon international disputes. In the United States, as in the European democracies, unemployment, low farm prices, and economic stagnation required more attention than international hostilities in distant lands. Japan was the first power to disturb the status quo, first by taking Manchuria from China in 1931, later with a full-scale invasion of that beleaguered nation in 1937. Europe, too, saw the uneasy peace settlement of 1919 slowly unravel. In 1935, Benito Mussolini led Fascist Italy on an invasion and conquest of Ethiopia. After assuming power in January 1933, Adolf Hitler cautiously dismantled the restrictions the victorious Allies placed on Germany, then rebuilt the German army, reoccupied the Rhineland, and annexed Austria and the Sudetenland by the end of 1938.

The turning point for the United States came in September 1939 when Germany attacked and quickly conquered Poland. Hitler erred in this instance, for, unlike his previous land grabs, the invasion of Poland provoked France and Britain to declare war. The American response also differed from earlier reactions to Axis aggression. Until 1939, many Americans, including influential congressmen, believed that the possibility of another big war loomed on the horizon. Congress passed a series of Neutrality Acts to limit American participation in foreign wars. These acts prohibited the United States from exporting arms to any belligerent or making loans to them and warned that citizens who traveled on vessels of belligerent nations did so at their own risk. Senator Gerald Nye of North Dakota, who had led an investigation of the role munitions-makers and bankers played in World War I, was an outspoken supporter of neutrality.

When war came to Europe in 1939, President Roosevelt invoked the Neutrality Acts, including the arms embargo, and proclaimed a state of limited emergency. Unlike Woodrow Wilson in his position on neutrality in 1914, however, Roosevelt did not ask the American people to be neutral in their attitudes. He and most of his fellow Americans opposed the Axis powers, but, above all, they wanted to avoid becoming a participant in the conflict. Roosevelt believed that the best way to aid the Allies and to keep the nation out of the conflict was to repeal the arms embargo so that the United States could sell the tools of war to those resisting aggression. In special session in late 1939, Congress repealed the arms embargo provision, and the United States began to sell munitions to the Allies on a cash-and-carry basis. Since Great Britain had the largest navy and merchant marine, it benefited the most from this new American policy.

At home, the President took tentative steps to prepare for war. He ordered twelve additional armory drills and seven extra field-training days for the Guard as part of his national emergency call, all to be carried out before the end of May 1940. The Guard had nearly completed its expansion to the 210,000 manpower level when Roosevelt called for an increase to 250,000 men. He also added 17,000 men to the Army. For fiscal year 1941, which began in July 1940, he directed the War Department to prepare for sixty drill meetings and a three-week field-training period. National Guard allotments for fiscal year 1940, due largely to increased armory and camp pay, totaled nearly $70 million, compared to $43 million a year earlier. For 1941, Congress appropriated $88.5 million.

These measures hardly led to full mobilization. Neither Roosevelt nor the American people were yet inclined to intervene. Then, in the spring of 1940, lightning struck. Germany invaded Denmark and Norway and won control of both. Next came France, believed to have one of the largest and best-trained armies in the world. The panzer thrusts through the Ardennes caught the French by surprise as the Maginot Line became a trap instead of a fort. In less than two months France fell, and now Britain stood alone. The war in Europe assumed a new dimension for Roosevelt and many Americans. This nation's security, hitherto reliant upon the oceans and the Allies's military capacity, became more precarious. Nominated for a third term, Roosevelt began to concentrate more on the international situation, on efforts for the defense of the nation, and on helping Great Britain.

At the urging of Army Chief of Staff George C. Marshall, the President asked Congress for standby authority to call the National Guard. Marshall directed the General Staff to prepare plans for a partial mobilization, following the outlines of the 1937 Protective Mobilization Plan. Inevitably, the General Staff saw the need for at least a limited draft, and only the Guard offered a sufficient number of officers, noncommissioned officers, and units to train draftees. Congress and Roosevelt were slow to push the recommendation to call up the Guard and draft young men, fearing that a divided, perhaps still isolationist, public might turn on them in the fall elections. In this instance, the usually astute Franklin D. Roosevelt underestimated public opinion. Various civilian preparedness groups pressured Congress to act, and on 27 August 1940 it authorized the President to call the Guard to active duty for one year. Three weeks later, on 16 September, it gave him a Selective Service Act, providing a one-year training period for men twenty-one to twenty-eight. Deteriorating Japanese-American relations that summer gave added force to military legislation.

In North Dakota, federal spending rose nearly fifty-five percent in one year. The 1940 allotment of $338,000 rose to $519,000 a year later, and the latter amount included a special allocation of nearly $148,000 worth of new motor equipment, part of a belated effort to modernize the Guard. State expenditures increased, also, with appropriations for a $25,000 emergency fund and a special $3,000 allotment to expand the artillery. The extra drills kept the Guardsmen busy, and the 1940 field-training season saw an unprecedented number of Guardsmen, nearly 210,000, go into summer camp. All four field armies maneuvered, including Regular Army troops and Officer Reserve Corps members. The North Dakota National Guard again traveled to Camp Ripley as part of the August 1940 Fourth Army maneuvers. Both divisions from the VII Corps Area, the 34th and 35th, trained at Camp Ripley for three weeks.

Upon their return from Minnesota, Guardsmen learned that they would soon go on active duty, although their induction date remained a mystery for months as the War Department scrambled to establish training camps and prepare mobilization schedules. In the meantime, the North Dakota National Guard underwent a series of changes from August 1940 to early 1941. The War Department had already modified the 164th's table of organization in March by rearranging battalion headquarters units, the first step in a major change of the Army's entire divisional organization, which would not be completed until Guard units were mobilized.

More significant was the National Guard Bureau's September 1940 decision, concurred in by General Edwards and the other states in the 34th Division, to return the 3rd Battalion, 185th Field Artillery, to Iowa. The National Guard Bureau authorized North Dakota to establish a full artillery regiment of its own, the 188th, as part of the 43,000-man increase ordered by President Roosevelt in September 1939. The 188th was not part of the 34th Division but an element of the 76th Field Artillery Brigade, a general reserve force not attached to any Guard division. Units of the 185th at Bismarck, Mandan, and Jamestown were redesignated as part of the new 188th, but General Edwards had to find home stations, officers, and hundreds of enlisted men to fill it out.

The need to organize the 188th rapidly in the face of impending induction led in turn to major restructuring of the 164th Infantry. After a careful review of conditions in the infantry and promising sites for new home stations, General Edwards ordered the disbandment and relocation of the Service Company at Lisbon, Company D at Minot, and three smaller outfits. He disbanded the 164th's Medical Detachment at Edgeley, for example, because Major Lee B. Greene, a doctor and founder of the unit in 1922, had recently died. The little town no longer had a physician and would have lost the detachment anyway. Edwards put a small outfit there because, he explained, "Edgeley has always loyally supported their unit. They have built a small armory which would adequately support an infantry Headquarters Detachment." He converted some infantry outfits to artillery. Minot's Company D became Battery B, 188th, and, as Boyd J. Joyer, also of Minot, recalled, "I went to bed one night as commander officer of Hq. Co., 3rd Bn, 164th Infantry, and woke up as commanding officer Hq. Btry., 1st Bn, 188th FA Regiment."

Edwards moved the Service Company from Lisbon to Devils Lake. He had used Works Progress Administration and National Guard Bureau funds to build storage garages and repair shops for the Guard's seventy trucks at Camp Grafton. "The Service Company is supposed to man these" and "to be experts in the care and operations of these trucks," he stated. "It is their duty to go out from Camp Grafton and transport part of the regiment to camp." It only made sense to have Service Company as close to Camp Grafton as possible. Lisbon kept the band, and personnel of the service outfit became artillerymen in Headquarters Battery, 3rd Battalion, 188th. Company D, long stationed at Minot, was moved to Rugby, a town that had never had a Guard unit. The small towns of Bottineau and Oakes also won organizations, the 164th's Medical Detachment going to the former and a headquarters battery of the 188th to the latter. Edwards placed the remaining artillery units in towns and cities that already had infantry outfits but populations large enough to support others—Valley City, Fargo, and Grand Forks.

It took time to establish and recruit the new Guard groups. In some instances, infantry companies provided cadre for the new artillery batteries and, in the case of Company D at Minot, a full complement of officers, noncommissioned officers, and men for Battery B. In Fargo and Grand Forks, Companies B and M respectively, some privates and corporals moved over to the gunners with a step or two up the promotion ladder. Company M's Captain Ira Gaulke became a major, 2nd Battalion, 188th Field Artillery. William Mjogdalen, a teacher at Leeds, a small town near Rugby, moved from the Officers Reserve Corps to become captain of Company D.

Sufficient recruits were readily available because the newly approved draft stimulated volunteering, most men doing so because they preferred to chose when and with whom they served. Edward Puhr, for example, enlisted in Company G, Valley City, because, he explained, I "was single, did not have a job, knew I would be drafted," and "wanted to be with people I knew." Fred Schmisek and three friends enlisted in Battery F at Grand Forks, believing that if they were among the first to put in one year of training, they would find better jobs available twelve months later when other men were drafted. Although off in Alaska, Donald Bell came home to Grand Forks to enlist rather than be drafted. Some young men were attracted by the idea of active service, and "many boys joined to get out of N. Dak.," according to Gordon Holt. Most who volunteered fully expected to put in only one year. Clarence McClure, Company A, decided to re-enlist at age forty, as active duty looked like a "year's paid vacation." An artillery recruit, Harold Henninger, who knew he would be drafted, said, "Well there wasn't nothing around here [Oakes] for us and that was twenty-one dollars a month" private's pay.

New units faced innumerable problems. Although authorized in September, few were sufficiently organized to begin training before November. At Rugby, William Mjogdalen worked to recruit Company D, even though his captain's commission did not arrive until the end of October. When Edwin Kjelstrom signed on in late November, he was only the twelfth man to enlist. He and his comrades knew of the coming induction, and so "It was hurry, hurry, hurry," all the time with drills and meetings nearly every day. With only two or three experienced noncommissioned officers from the old outfit in Minot, Captain Mjogdalen regularly wrote General Edwards seeking advice: "Please excuse the number of questions but I am very anxious to get the right kind of start in my work." He continued to teach at Leeds and commute to Rugby at every chance. Still, Assistant Adjutant General Herman Brocopp had few comforting words for him. "It is customary," Brocopp wrote, "that the company commander and people interested in organizing a unit accomplish the required work and believe this would be a good test of your ability."

General Edwards assigned Captain John Kohnen, of Jamestown's Battery C, to start a battery at Oakes. Originally, this was to be a firing battery, but Kohnen reported that "From the standpoint of officer material" Oakes offered few candidates "that looked at all promising." A similar situation prevailed at Valley City. Kohnen thought it might be necessary to have an "officer nucleus....put out from Jamestown with perhaps [the] two batteries...under-officered." Eventually Oakes established a headquarters battery, smaller than a firing unit. Two of the 2nd Battalion's three firing batteries were inducted without captains. Major Gaulke did not understand his place in the 188th. He wrote Edwards on 23 December 1940, "Just what is my status since the reorganization of the 188th? Am I surplus in grade, transferred to some other battalion, back to Infantry, or still undecided?" Edwards assured Gaulke, "You are the senior major in the artillery, anything might happen whereby you might find yourself even in a higher position."

Inevitably, the hurried restructuring of the infantry and expansion of the artillery created difficulties similar to the hasty recruitment of the 2nd North Dakota Infantry in 1917. Most of the new outfits lacked armories. Rugby's Company D used the county memorial building for drill, although it was hardly fit for such use. At Oakes, E. A. Perkins recalled, "No armory was available," so a "Local schoolhouse was utilized...for drills and storage of equipment." Later the Oakes battery used the "fireman's pavillion located | mile north of the city." In Bismarck, the 188th's Headquarter's Battery was forced to turn to "a small gym for drill floor and classes." The artillery lacked guns and was short of uniforms and other basic equipment. In the infantry, Company D did not have enough rifles for all its men.

War Department intrusion into this already-confusing situation further complicated matters. A National Guard Bureau letter of 4 December 1940 informed General Edwards, "The Bureau has prepared revised tables of organization for the field artillery." They provided two battalions, each with three firing batteries, a service battery, and an antitank battery. Under old tables, an artillery regiment had three battalions of two firing units each and no service or antitank units. The National Guard Bureau wanted North Dakota to carry out the reorganization, if possible, even though it had set the 188th's induction for 3 February 1941. If the state did not do it, the bureau advised, "This reorganization will undoubtedly be made after induction." It was necessary, at this late date, to expand the battalion headquarters units and start and recruit three new outfits and convert a fourth. In the latter case, Headquarters Battery, 3rd Battalion, at Lisbon, which had been Service Company, 164th, as recently as September, now became an antitank battery. General Edwards established the three additional units at Bismarck, Fargo, and Minot. They were not recognized until late January 1941.

The 164th also underwent one final modification, ordered by the National Guard Bureau on 11 December 1940 to comply with the new tables, which required the addition of an antitank company to infantry regiments. Again, the National Guard Bureau hoped the state could complete the unit before induction, tentatively set for 27 January 1941. This alteration was less drastic than that of the 188th, for it only entailed adding three officers to the regiment. Otherwise, the bureau stipulated, "The Antitank Company...will be formed from within the present allotted strength of this regiment."[2] Reorganization meant disrupting the 164th yet again by culling noncommissioned officers and men from existing units. The adjutant general selected Harvey as the Antitank Company's home station, and it received recognition on 15 January

1941. For both regiments these last-minute changes put officers and men into units whose functions and specialties were wholly unfamiliar to them. The regiments already had a large number of untrained men, but even the older hands too often found themselves befuddled by new assignments. It was not an auspicious beginning.

The National Guard had as its major function during the interwar years the training of its rank and file and the educating of its officers for war. To a large extent it failed to meet its training mission, partly because of the service's part-time, decentralized organization, but also owing to other factors beyond the Guard's control which hampered effective training. Insufficient federal funds for drill and camp pay and for modern equipment contributed. The Army suffered the same shortages throughout the period. Just as important, since, until 1939, it did not seem likely that the United States would become involved in another world war, no one saw any urgency in providing the armed forces with the latest equipment or intensifying training. However obvious the nation's involvement in World War II appears in hindsight, it is important to repeat that the vast majority of North Dakota Guardsmen believed they would return home in a year, even as they prepared for induction in early 1941. Their recollections accurately reflect public opinion of the time and mirror as well the expectations of the Roosevelt administration. If the country did not anticipate a war, not surprisingly it did not attempt to keep its military forces trained to a fighting edge. Maintaining a perpetual wartime mentality to meet a war that only might come poses a sociological and psychological impossibility and a danger for a democracy. The test of political leadership requires the ability to discern when a nation can and should prepare for war. The United States nearly failed that test in 1940-1941 and consequently did not have its military forces ready.

Guard veterans, in retrospect, have divided opinions as to the value of their interwar training. While a majority believed that they were adequately prepared to cope with advanced training in 1941 and combat a year later, roughly twenty percent think they were "somewhat" ready, and another twenty percent disagree with both propositions. Byron Gilbertson, Company K, said Guard training "gave us a period to get into combat readiness and improved physical conditioning for what was coming," adding, "although at that time we didn't know that." Those who thought prewar training was effective stressed individual preparedness and knowledge of the Army's way of doing things. For Howard Erickson, "Discipline and command were already bred into the personnel" when they went on active duty. Another Guardsman argued that "Army duty demands discipline. The Guard taught that before being activated." Guard training, a third veteran stressed, "Gave most of the basics needed....Also instilled in the men the spirit of comradeship and cooperation."

Others disagreed. A Company L man commented, state training "helped—but actually the federal training was most necessary." Perhaps, Arthur Timboe conceded, "the troops were well trained but" they lacked "experience as a unit ready for combat." Some were most definite on the Guard's failings. "We were 'green,'" one man wrote, "very little training during 2 hour drills, once a week." Another said, "No. Lack of knowledge of what combat was really like."

Albert Wiest, now a retired colonel after twenty years service in the Army, wrote that the North Dakota National Guard lacked work "in areas of tactical training of large units, e.g., company, battalion, and [was] very limited in small unit tactical training." Combining his perspective as an experienced regular officer with his nine years in the Guard before the war, Wiest conceded that the Guard fell short in 1940-1941. This, he went on to say, was not the service's fault, since it "was guided by pre-WWII training manuals, and by the late '30s was directed by officers, many of whom had no combat experience or, if they did, it was based on WWI tactics." For all those limitations, he continued, "What most NG units *did have* when they were called to active duty were two elements that go a long ways in preparing a unit for success in combat—they are *espirit de corps* and *proficiency* in *weapons*, especially small arms" (emphasis in original). Unfortunately, preinduction reorganizations and an influx of new men weakened even these strengths. There was much yet to be done.

Notes on Sources

Material on the coal strike came from orders and reports in the Records of the North Dakota National Guard; Executive Orders from the Governor of North Dakota to the Adjutant General of the State National Guard, 1919-1950, in the Orin G. Libby Manuscript Collection, Chester Fritz Library, University of North Dakota; and State Historical Society of North Dakota, Series 153, Incoming and Outgoing Correspondence, Governor Lynn J. Frazier, 1919-1920. The Bismarck *Tribune* and the Fargo *Forum* (November 1919 through January 1920) were also used.

For developments in the 1920s and 1930s, orders, reports, and correspondence from National Guard records were most important. The adjutant general's office, for unknown reasons, ceased publishing annual or biennial reports after World War I and did not resume doing so until 1962. A search for manuscript reports proved fruitless. Questionnaires and taped interviews helped fill in the gap, particularly with information on the kind and extent of training, the quantity and quality of uniforms and equipment, and general armory activities. One hundred people returned their questionnaires for the period, chiefly men who had served in the 1930s, mostly in the 164th Infantry. Unless otherwise noted, all interviews were conducted by Chief Warrant Officer Bryan O. Baldwin. Interviews for this chapter were given by the following:

1. Louis Bogan
2. Robert Capes
3. Edward Dietz
4. Arnie Elton
5. Howard V. Erickson
6. John Grabor

7. Harold Henninger
8. James A. Johnson
9. William Johnson
10. Clarence McClure
    Clifford Keller
11. Victor McWilliams
12. Walter Mellem

13. James Moe
14. Francis Murphy
15. Jerome Norman
16. Paul Norman
17. Charles Norton
18. Alvin A. Paulson

19. Frank Richards
   (by Clifford Keller)
20. Fred Schmisek
21. Kenneth Swartz
22. John Vold
23. Bernard Wagner

Dr. Cooper conducted interviews with Mrs. Heber L. Edwards and Mrs. Robert Carlson in Bismarck, North Dakota.

Some information came from RG407, Office of the Adjutant General, Central File, 1926-1939, and RG168, Records of the National Guard Bureau, Entry 12, National Archives. These two sources also supplied general information on the National Guard for the 1920s and 1930s, which was supported by material from the annual reports of the Chief, Military Bureau, 1920 through 1933, and the Chief, National Guard Bureau, for the years 1934 to 1941.

Beyond material from the adjutant general's office, North Dakota National Guard, much was found on William Langer's use of the Guard in Executive Orders from the Governor...to the Adjutant General, in the Libby Collection, cited earlier. The New York *Times*, 19 and 20 July 1934, and *Newsweek Magazine*, 28 July 1934, were perused. Interpretive views on Langer came from Walter C. Anhalt and Glenn H. Smith, "He Saved the Farm? Governor Langer and the Mortgage Moratoria," *North Dakota Quarterly* (Autumn 1979), pp. 5-17, and Glenn H. Smith, "William Langer and the Art of Personal Politics," in Thomas Howard, ed., *The North Dakota Political Tradition* (Ames, Iowa, 1981), pp. 123-150.

The Adjutant General's Office, *NDNG, Official Roster of North Dakota Soldiers, Sailors and Marines, World War, 1917-1918* (Bismarck, N.D., 1931), four volumes, and Army and Navy Publishing Company, *Historical and Pictoral Review: National Guard of the State of North Dakota, 1940* (Baton Rouge, La., 1940) were of use. Marvin A. Kriedberg and Merton G. Henry, *History of Military Mobilization in the United States Army, 1775-1945* (Washington, D.C., 1955) discuss interwar mobilization planning.

---

[1]Quotations from veterans come from the questionnaire survey or oral interviews.
[2]The belated recognition of the need to give American ground forces some means of fighting tanks necessitated both last-minute reorganization.

Company A, 164th Infantry (Bismarck) on parade in Bismarck, 30 May 1926. Captain Herman Brocopp is shown at extreme right (first row) leading the unit.

Machine gun firing at Camp Grafton during the late 1930s.

Aerial view of Camp Grafton 21 June, 1931.

164th Infantry in parade at Camp Grafton during Governor William Langer's visit, 1933.

Typical field gear inspection at Camp Grafton, 1920s.

Left: Unidentified member of the North Dakota National Guard in standard fatigue uniform with full field equipment. (This was the standard field uniform for the U.S. Army until 1935.)

Right: Colonel John H. Fraine at Camp Grafton, 14 June 1925.

Members of Company A and the Quartermaster Detachment, 164th
Infantry (Bismarck) on guard duty at site of the North Dakota State
Capitol during a construction workers' strike, 1933.

☆8☆

The 164th Infantry Regiment in World War II

On 11 December 1940, Adjutant General Heber L. Edwards of the North Dakota National Guard received word that the 164th Infantry Regiment would enter federal service on 27 January 1941. Originally set for 6 January, their entrance had been changed because of "inadequate housing facilities and other factors." Shortly after Christmas, General Edwards learned that the call to federal service would take place on 10 February. The general had doubts about the practicality of the date. The 164th was scheduled to go to Louisiana to a new military installation there called Camp Claiborne, and from reports that he and Governor Moses had received about lack of progress in construction there, Edwards thought April a more realistic time for the movement of the North Dakota Guardsmen. Although Governor Moses had serious concern regarding health, living, and recreational conditions at Camp Claiborne, a post far away in a climate considerably alien to North Dakotans, the United States Army had assured him that troops at Camp Claiborne would experience no health problems. It pointed out that the Red River furnished a good water supply, the camp had a sewage disposal plant comparable to one that would serve a city of sixty thousand, and a two-thousand-bed hospital was under construction and near completion. But, the Army added, the North Dakotans should have rain gear, including slickers, overcoats, and rubber overshoes, because Louisiana had a heavier rainfall (fifty-six inches per annum) than North Dakota. Thus on 17 January 1941, Secretary of War Henry Stimson notified Governor Moses that the 10 February date for calling up the 164th was firm. The men of the regiment prepared to spend their year in the federal service, thus fulfilling their obligation. By the time they reported for duty on 10 February, the German General Staff had started arranging for the invasion of Russia. More to the point, Admiral Isoroku Yamamoto, commander in chief of the Combined Fleet of Japan, had ordered his staff to begin planning a surprise attack on the American naval base at Pearl Harbor.

The men of the 164th spent over two weeks at their armories or other facilities waiting for transportation. During the interlude they were fingerprinted, given physical exams (which over a hundred did not pass), and issued additional equipment. They devoted the days to training, often outdoors in bitter cold, to get themselves in good physical condition. Those men who lived in the town of their companies were allowed to spend their evenings at home. Although the advance party was supposed to leave by truck on 18 February, the bitterly cold weather (-30° F) delayed its departure for two days. The main body of the 164th was scheduled to board four separate troop trains on 25 and 26 February. The many towns that headquartered units of the 164th all gave the men a rousing send-off in spite of the cold weather. "Goodbye Dear, I'll be Back in a Year" were the lyrics of a popular song when the men left their homes. It would be the longest year of their lives.

The Guardsmen reported from almost every city, town, and village in North Dakota. Many of them lived on farms, often several miles from the headquarters of their unit. The actual headquarters of the regiment was Bismarck, though only one of its eight assigned officers listed that city as his residence. Headquarters Company was located at Fargo and the Service Company at Devils Lake. The Antitank Company headquartered at Harvey, the band at Fargo, and the Medical Detachment at Bottineau.

Headquarters of the 1st Battalion was at Bismarck and the detachment at Cavalier. Company A was at Bismarck, Company B at Fargo, Company C at Grafton, and Company D at Rugby.

The 2nd Battalion headquartered at Fargo and its detachment at Cando. Companies E, F, G and H were located at Williston, Carrington, Valley City and Jamestown respectively.

Headquarters of the 3rd Battalion was located at Williston and the detachment at Edgeley. Company H was at Jamestown, I at Wahpeton, K at Dickinson, and M at Grand Forks.

In spite of recent increases in enlistments, practically all units of the 164th had insufficient strength when they departed, the one exception being the regimental band, which was authorized to have twenty-seven men but actually had forty-seven. Colonel Earle R. Sarles from Hillsboro, son of a former governor and commanding officer of the 164th, considered a good, big band essential to the morale of the regiment, and he wanted one that made itself seen and heard easily as it led the regiment in parades. Warrant Officer Gerald Wright, a persuasive man, led the band. Contacting several musicians who had played for or with him in the past, he asked them to join the band, telling them they might just as well enlist and get their year of service out of the way. After pointing out the advantages of spending a year in the "sunny south," he added that if war did come, band members probably would not see combat. Thus, the band was the only unit of the regiment that was considerably overstrength.

With short stops for provisions and periods of exercise for the men, the trip to Camp Claiborne took over four days, during which the men sought occasionally to break the monotony of the long ride with card games, reading, and discussion of the latest rumors. When the 164th climbed into the trucks at Alexandria, Louisiana, to make the final leg of the journey, many of its men were probably ready to get into their quarters and start the drilling and training. They would receive a rude shock.

Camp Claiborne was more of a place name than a training camp. Carpenters had built wooden frames and side walls over which the newly arrived troops placed pyramidal tents. Although natural gas connections for heating stoves were in place, the men had no stoves for the first few days. Generously called streets, the narrow lanes between the rows of tents were intermittently quagmires of red mud or long alleys of blowing dust. The workmen had not completed the latrines or the recreation and training facilities and were still building chapels and the base hospital. The construction of Camp Claiborne simply lagged behind schedule, as did many other preparations for the defense of the nation.

In retrospect, anything else would have been a surprise. The United States had done very little to build up its military strength in the 1930s, except for small increases in appropriations for the Navy and air forces. At the time that President Franklin D. Roosevelt pushed a limited military conscription bill through a reluctant Congress, the nation had few adequate training camps. Since the Army had decided to train troops on a divisional basis, it had to have large camps, and it had to start many of them from scratch. It still had to purchase, survey, clear, and level millions of acres of land before it could erect buildings and training facilities. Also, distribution of new equipment for the men was haphazard at best. Although the president was torn between allotting arms to Great Britain and meeting the nation's own demands and tried to do both, the country lacked enough new material. Clearly, being the "arsenal of democracy" was a bigger job than anticipated. Thus, the men of the 164th began their training with obsolete weapons, such as the 1903 Springfield bolt-action rifle, or with no weapons at all, particularly mortars. They even used pieces of downspout or part of a fence post on a makeshift mount to simulate a 60 mm mortar and attached plyboard slabs to the sides of a jeep to create a tank.

The 164th began its training as one of the four infantry regiments of the 34th Infantry Division, which consisted entirely of units from North Dakota, Iowa, and Minnesota. At full strength, the division resembled those that served in World War I with a complement of over twenty thousand officers and enlisted men. A movement already under way, however, would make the Army infantry division smaller, more self-sufficient in combat, and more maneuverable as a fast, hard-hitting unit on the offensive. Part of this proposal would trim the division to three regiments, each with supporting artillery, engineer, medical, and other units. The regiment, with its assigned supporting units, would become a regimental combat team. But, since reorganization in the Army was a slow process, it did not become reality until early 1942. Throughout the entire period of training at Camp Claiborne, the 164th was one of the four infantry regiments of the 34th Division, a "square" unit, later made a "triangular" division of only three infantry regiments.

Tables and charts of organization had no effect upon the miserable conditions at Camp Claiborne, however. The cold, damp weather made nights a challenge to get a few hours sleep. Because the tents initially had no heat, the men huddled beneath their blankets, overcoats, and anything else they could find to ward off the chill. The high humidity made the cool temperatures more uncomfortable than the dry, sub-zero climate they had left. Although respiratory ailments became common, the medical staff could do little for the men except to give them some medication and advise them to keep as warm and dry as possible. The spring rains made that nearly impossible.

Perhaps the morale of the men posed a more difficult problem. After the theaters and post exchanges opened, they were crowded and the men often had to stand in line for movie tickets or at the post exchange for beer of an unknown brand. Already they had developed an aversion to standing in line. Alexandria, the nearest town of any size, was bulging with construction workers, servicemen's wives, and hucksters out to make some quick dollars from the soldiers. New Orleans lay over a hundred miles away, and even if one could get a weekend pass, transportation was limited. The daily routine of training, drilling, marching, and field exercises soon became monotonous. After rising at about 5:00 A.M., the men made their bunks, washed and shaved, and swept out the tents. Reveille, at 5:40, preceded roll call, calisthenics, and "policing the area." Following a 6:15 breakfast, the men began training at 7:00 and usually finished by 5:00 P.M., in time to stand retreat and have their evening meal. (They called all the meals "chow," regardless of when they came.) From then until taps at 10:00 P.M. the men had free time to clean their rifles, shine their shoes, brush the red mud from their cartridge belts, and take a shower. Few needed encouragement to hit the sack shortly after taps because tomorrow promised another long day with the same routine.

By the end of April 1941, the men had devised some measures of relief from the monotony of training. After some units formed softball teams, they played each other when time and weather permitted. Boxing teams and matches, popular when the units were in the National Guard, continued. Some of the men organized variety shows featuring local talent. The divisional morale officer also arranged truck convoys to take the men on tours of scenic and historic sites in the vicinity, some of the luckier ones going to a newly improvised recreation area on the shores of Lake Pontchartrain near New Orleans. There they found dances, swimming, sightseeing tours, and an amusement park available, though they had to sleep in tents and on bunks like those at Camp Claiborne.

The regiment began to receive selectees, as the government called them (the men themselves said they had been drafted), to fill out the ranks. Understrength when called to federal service, almost all companies of the regiment experienced further depletion as some of their men left for special training schools. The selectees had to learn the basics of close-order drill, military courtesy, and how to handle various weapons. From the Upper-Midwestern states of Minnesota and North and South Dakota, most of those selectees fit in well with the North Dakotans and made friends in their respective units soon after arrival. Their addition to the regiment helped relieve the tedium of training, training, and more training.

As summer came, the 164th went on field exercises more often and for longer periods of time. The men occasionally found themselves besieged by swarms of insects and also encountered snakes, some poisonous. When word of this reached North Dakota, several irate mothers wrote to Governor Moses about the horrible conditions at Camp Claiborne where, they complained, "our boys are continually fighting snakes and insects in swamps." Sympathetic, the governor requested other mothers to communicate to him any legitimate protests about the situation at Claiborne. He promised an investigation of these grievances, adding that he shared "in the views of these others that it would have been better if our men had trained in northern camps." Dr. O. J. Hagen of Moorhead, Minnesota, who had a son at Claiborne, looked into conditions at the camp and reported that the men were in no danger. The Army held its maneuvers near, but not in, the snake-infested swamps, and it had also sprayed the swamps with chemicals to control insects. The temperature was hot, but no worse than the men had experienced at home in the summer. Seeing no signs of the epidemic that some mothers had claimed existed in the camp,

Dr. Hagen expressed the opinion that the biggest problem for the men of the 164th was the long distance between them and their homes. While his estimation of the situation had no official status, it did tend to reduce the complaints about Claiborne. Meanwhile, the "boys" prepared for the biggest maneuver ever held on American soil by Army units.

So that the men and officers could gain extensive training under combat conditions, over 350,000 troops were divided into two forces, a Red army and a Blue army, which would "fight" against each other for a month or more. The general area of the mock battle lay in northern Louisiana, southern Arkansas, and eastern Texas. To prepare for the upcoming conflict, the 34th Division, including the 164th Regiment, had gone on a surprise training exercise in August. The men had only five minutes to pack their personal belongings before loading their equipment on trucks, and officers cancelled all passes and leaves. After traveling over ninety miles, the division engaged in simulated combat against a nonexistent enemy, but this amounted to only a scant rehearsal for a larger exercise involving several divisions.

The maneuvers resembled actual combat as nearly as possible without endangering the lives of the men. While bombers dropped small sacks of flour, sound trucks broadcast explosions of artillery and mortar shells along with the clatter of small-arms fire. Tanks, actually jeeps with plyboard siding, roared about harassing troops. Blank ammunition for rifles and machine guns added realism to the scene. Some men were "wounded" and had to be treated and evacuated. A simulated gas attack gave the men a chance to test their quickness in putting on a gas mask. When referees declared some units captured, the soldiers became prisoners of war. At the end of the maneuvers, most of the commanding officers felt that the whole undertaking merited the effort, although they heard criticisms, especially of some of the commissioned officers, particularly those from National Guard units, probably because the majority of the officers involved in the exercise came from the National Guard. Regular Army and reserve officers also received their share of criticism, however.

Through no fault of their own, many National Guard officers were overage for their rank and undertrained for their responsibilities in combat. Army statistics revealed that while twenty-two percent of the first lieutenants of the National Guard (usually platoon leaders or company executive officers) had reached forty years of age or over, a large percentage of captains (usually company commanders) were over forty-five. Furthermore, less than forty percent of all National Guard officers had had the opportunity to complete a course in one of the service schools. Many National Guard officers did not want to take a chance on losing their jobs by taking time off from them, and military pay was very low owing to paucity of funding. Although they fell short of the demands of combat command, these officers often had talents and abilities that the Army needed. The same situation applied to reserve officers and, to a lesser degree, to Regular Army officers, too. The scant appropriations for military training in the 1920s and 1930s had given them little chance to gain any significant experience in handling units under simulated battle conditions. As the Army saw it, reassigning many of these officers to other duties without lowering their morale offered one solution. Another possibility, though less desirable, was having some of these officers resign their commissions. In any case, many of the older officers of the National Guard units eventually received orders assigning them to less rigorous duties.

The enlisted men of these divisions received both praise and words of caution. Lieutenant General Walter Krueger, commander of one of the armies in the maneuvers, observed that National Guard and selectee enlisted men were better soldiers than those of the Regular Army. Of greater intelligence, the men in these two groups reacted to situations more quickly and displayed a higher degree of ingenuity under combat conditions, although they often had too much enthusiasm in coming to grips with the "enemy." As they moved in large groups on roads toward their objective, they made themselves easy targets for enemy aircraft. Also, they attacked without sufficient reconnaissance of enemy positions, and some platoons and companies became lost because of faulty scouting. Most of these problems reflected their poor leadership and inadequate training.

The overall assessment of the Louisiana maneuvers was positive, however. The soldiers and officers had learned much and they had come to believe that with more training and modern equipment, they could take the measure of any enemy in a real battle. The men of the 34th Division came in for special praise from their commander, Major General E. L. Daley, who cited them for their steady advance against the enemy despite many destroyed bridges and other obstacles. The division was nearing combat readiness, and none too soon.

After the exercise ended, the men of the 164th received furloughs in two-week shifts. Most went home to see friends and family, some men from the same company and town chartering buses for the trip. Now the mothers could see their "boys," who had probably become heavier, stronger, and healthier than when they had left home. While a few of the men took the opportunity to marry, others, already with families, became reacquainted with wives and children. They found life in North Dakota much as they had left it, and this nation was still at peace. Although the war was getting worse, it was still very far away.

Seven weeks passed before the 188th Field Artillery Regiment joined the 164th Infantry on active duty. The artillery, so recently reorganized and expanded, continued to recruit men through the end of March. Several infantrymen, particularly from Company B, Fargo, and Company M, Grand Forks, transferred to the artillery prior to the 164th's 10 February mobilization. In order to prepare the 188th for active duty, the War Department sent fifteen officers to Fort Des Moines, Iowa, for a thirty-day preinduction course, from mid-February to mid-March. A number of enlisted men attended courses at Fort Sill, Oklahoma, home of the Army's Artillery School, during this same period, taking specialist courses in artillery mechanics, auto mechanics, and other technical aspects of artillery work.

Like its sister regiment, the 188th spent its first two weeks on active duty at home station, completing physical examinations and necessary government paper work. The regiment mobilized on 1 April 1941, with orders to leave on 12 April, Easter Sunday. So many parents protested their boys' leaving on such an important family holiday that the government delayed departure until the 14th. Troop trains collected units at home stations that day for the two-day trip to Fort Francis E. Warren, near Cheyenne, Wyoming. Among those leaving with Headquarters Battery, Bismarck, was Private First Class James J. Moses, son of Governor John Moses. Colonel Percy M. Hansen, Jamestown, commanded the unit, with Lieutenant Colonel Leslie V. Miller, Bismarck, as executive officer. The 188th's induction put 3,222 North Dakota Guardsmen in federal service.

TABLE 8.1

188th Field Artillery, April 1941

Unit	Home Station
Headquarters Battery	Bismarck
Band	Bismarck
Medical Detachment	Grand Forks
First Battalion	
Headquarters Battery	Minot
Service Battery	Bismarck
Antitank Battery	Minot
Battery A	Mandan
Battery B	Minot
Battery C	Jamestown
Second Battalion	
Headquarters Battery	Oakes
Service Battery	Fargo
Antitank Battery	Lisbon
Battery D	Valley City
Battery E	Fargo
Battery F	Grand Forks

Note: Strength: 62 officers, 1 warrant officer, 1,274 enlisted men. Aggregate: 1,337.)

    Fort Warren offered much more pleasant surroundings than did Camp Claiborne. In operation since the late 1860s, the fort provided large, comfortable brick barracks and the usual amenities of a permanent military establishment so lacking at Claiborne. In addition, Wyoming had a climate more agreeable and familiar to the North Dakotans than that of Louisiana. The major drawback to Fort Warren was the attitude of the citizens of Cheyenne. Long exposed to the sometimes rowdy behavior of off-duty regular soldiers, Cheyenne did not welcome Guardsmen with open arms and treated them as just another group of soldiers. The frosty welcome and the many off-limits areas in the better parts of Cheyenne offended the citizen-soldiers. Eventually Guardsmen proved their worth to the city as they moved beyond the taverns and honky tonks to attend church, movies, and other respectable places. Still, many veterans never forgot that dogs and soldiers were unwelcome in some sections of

Cheyenne. With most of their weekends free, the men drove or took Army buses to Denver or Fort Collins, Colorado, hiked in the mountains near the fort, or played softball. Many married men, both officers and enlisted men, brought their wives and children to Cheyenne in order to maintain family life, at least on weekends.

In most respects, the artillery's experience at Fort Warren paralleled that of the infantry's at Camp Claiborne. Training consumed their days, which, after all, was the purpose of the mobilization. Major General Lesley J. McNair, Chief of Staff, General Headquarters, Field Forces, directed the Army's 1941 efforts to train the National Guard and draftees. Wholly unimpressed with the Guard, perhaps even hostile to it, McNair, through his training directives, insisted that all National Guard units undergo a minimum of two months of basic training before they accepted any drafted men. Therefore, organizations would follow a progressive training program from basic to small-unit to regimental training, and after that sequence, divisional and field army maneuvers could take place. The Army, in its usual fashion, made little attempt to explain the program or the reasoning behind it. Some Guard leaders resented seeing their men and units treated as raw recruits but could do nothing to alter McNair's approach.

As part of the 76th Field Artillery Brigade, which also included the 183rd Regiment, Idaho National Guard, and headquarters troops from the California National Guard, the North Dakotans spent April, May, and June in close-order drill, rifle-range firing, and physical conditioning. In late June the first draftees arrived from their basic training at Fort Sill. Thereafter, well into the fall, the training program emphasized battery work, including trips to the firing range on Pole Mountain. Throughout this period, according to the unit's history, "there was an acute shortage of equipment, a great deal of it being shipped overseas." Most of the equipment went to the British, then the only Allied power still fighting the Germans. The regiment continued to use its old Schneider guns, although they had air brakes and pneumatic tires which replaced the solid steel tires. Only the 1st Battalion was fully equipped, so it shared its guns when the 2nd Battalion conducted battery work. Because of an acute shortage of small arms, most of the 2nd Battalion was issued British Enfield rifles for range work. "We went with a bunch of junk that the state had," John Grabor recalled, but that "junk," the old guns, trucks, and cars, was all the regiment had to work with until the fall of 1941.

As James Moe remembered, "we felt kind of silly out there training without the primary equipment." Any man would have felt the same way, for, according to John Sullivan, "when we first started there we were drawing pictures on the ground and pretending they were howitzers." Sergeant Peter Schwab, Headquarters Battery, devised a working antitank gun from a 37 mm tube and wheels, tires, and old iron brackets dug out of the Fort Warren garbage dump. Officers underwent a double dose of training. At the end of each day's field work, they took an hour off for dinner, then reported to classrooms. Older, more experienced officers served as teachers, with the younger junior officers, many recently promoted from the ranks, as their students.

A number of junior officers left to attend the Artillery School's three-month battery officer course. Later in the fall, many captains went to Fort Sill for the battalion officer's course. Many who attended Fort Sill were marked for transfer as cadre to newly forming units. Other branches of the Army, particularly the Army Air Corps and paratroopers, sought and won volunteers. A number of men, not all volunteers, were assigned to the 98th Field Artillery Regiment, a Regular Army pack-mule unit which trained at Camp Carson, Colorado. The 98th eventually shipped out for the South Pacific, where the mules proved nearly useless, and where the unit was reorganized into the 6th Ranger Battalion. Begun in the summer of 1941, the process of combing the existing units for officers and men to serve in other branches, which eroded the regiment's National Guard flavor, continued until the North Dakotans moved overseas.

The regiment's largest loss came in July when the Army, in its infinite wisdom, decided to remove the two antitank batteries from all artillery regiments and use them to form tank-destroyer battalions. Antitank batteries had just been added in December 1940, during the final regimental reorganization before mobilization. Although lacking guns and vehicles to equip it, the 76th Brigade was required to organize a provisional battalion on 14 July. The unit traveled to Fort Lewis, Washington, in August to take part in Fourth Army maneuvers, returning to Cheyenne in September. The rest of the brigade remained at Fort Warren. Late in December 1941, the provisional unit became the 776th Tank Destroyer Battalion, with Companies A and B from the 188th. Major Ira M. F. Gaulke was among several North Dakota officers in the battalion, which later saw service in North Africa, Italy, France, and Germany.

The long, repetitious training was more tolerable when the men could tell themselves that it would all be over in April 1942. Whatever reality lay in that dream was smashed in August when Congress reluctantly agreed to President Roosevelt's request for an eighteen-month extension for all Guardsmen and draftees then on duty. Veterans would later describe their time at Fort Warren as "our growing-up days," an insight produced only through the perspective of war. The 188th continued its field work well into the fall, at last completing efficiency tests on basic and battery training required by General McNair's directives in November. Then it was their turn to go home on leave.

As German armies penetrated Russia at an alarming pace, some military and civilian experts predicted Russia's defeat within weeks; then, with the additional resources of the Soviet Union available to Germany, the Nazis would have the most formidable military force the world had ever seen. In Japan, Admiral Yamamoto had threatened to resign unless the Naval Ministry alloted him six aircraft carriers for the planned attack on Pearl Harbor. The ministry had offered four, but realizing the popularity of the admiral, it gave in to his demands. Largely because of the Emperor's pleading, the Japanese government decided to continue conferring with the United States in an attempt to reach a peaceful solution to issues involving Japanese occupation of part of China and French Indo-China. Japan sent Saburo Kurusu, a special envoy to the United States, to help Ambassador Nomura with the negotiations, but the faction in the Japanese government favoring continued talks was losing its influence. Meanwhile, Congress had extended the selective service act by the scant margin of one vote in the House of Representatives, the American destroyer *Greer* had exchanged fire with a German submarine near Iceland, and the war kept coming closer to the United States as the autumn leaves of 1941 were falling.

When the men of the 164th returned from their furloughs, Camp Claiborne was bustling as construction workers put finishing touches on about 200 company recreation halls, 12 new chapels, another tent theater, and new quarters for additional antitank companies and engineer units. Workers had begun erecting a new post exchange building as well as new hospital administration buildings and 160 motor-transport sheds. Bulldozers contoured the bare earth to prevent erosion, and by spring new grass in those areas prevented them from being the quagmires of previous years. Camp Claiborne was nearing completion when the men of the 164th received orders to leave it.

7 December 1941, the "day that will live in infamy," began as most other Sundays at Camp Claiborne: some of the men had invitations to dine with friends off the base, others were going to take in a movie that afternoon, but many had made no plans other than spending a quiet time on base resting after another long week of training. A few of the less fortunate had pulled guard duty or kitchen police (KP). After the Japanese attacked this nation's largest naval base at Pearl Harbor, thousands of miles away, radio reports made it evident that the United States had suffered heavy losses to its Pacific fleet. Each news bulletin seemed to add to the tragedy. For the men of the 164th, the attack changed almost everything. Since the United States was now at war, and they were soldiers with over nine months of training, the men realized that, sooner or later, at a time and place unknown, they were going into combat.

On 8 December 1941, Colonel Earle Sarles received orders that detached the 164th Infantry Regiment from the 34th Infantry Division and directed it to proceed to San Francisco. Events were moving rapidly as the men of the 164th prepared to board the hastily contrived troop trains. Congress declared war on Japan, making official that which was obvious. On 11 December 1941, before the 164th arrived on the West Coast, Germany and Italy lived up to their pledge to their Japanese ally and declared war on the United States. This nation replied in kind; the war had now become global.

When the 164th reached San Francisco, many people on the West Coast were near panic. Rumors, most of them highly implausible, spread like a prairie fire, some suggesting that huge Japanese armadas would disgorge their invading troops within a few days, others advising that hundreds of Japanese planes would soon be bombing the population centers of the West Coast and wreaking havoc upon the shipyards and aircraft factories, just as they had done to the Navy at Pearl Harbor. Normally quiet and passive citizens donned helmets and grabbed guns of any size and shape to repel the invaders. Turning suspicious eyes toward the Japanese people who lived there, Californians suddenly concluded that they were all spies and saboteurs, a fifth column to commit treachery when the invasion came. Prominent public officials, movie actors and actresses, editors, and others began to demand that the nation remove Japanese in their midst to some remote areas where they did not constitute a threat to the country's security.

The regiment had its quarters in the Cow Palace, a livestock exhibition pavilion which required some cleaning before the men could settle down, but only a few days elapsed before most of them found themselves scattered over several states doing guard duty. Since the fear of sabotage prompted the demand for troops to protect vital railroad bridges and junctions, ordnance depots, dams, and communications facilities, the units of the 164th were spread throughout much of the western United States. In some instances, whole companies had one assignment, such as the Ordnance Depot at Umatilla, Oregon, where the men had temporary quarters, a mess hall, and often stood regular formations. In other places, where a platoon or less was stationed, the men had to prepare their own food from rations delivered periodically. While the duty was often monotonous, it was necessary in order to allay the country's fears, given the panic that had gripped much of the western United States after Pearl Harbor. Cordially welcoming the men of the 164th, local civilians often extended them the hospitality of a home-cooked meal. The men often found that someone else was eager to pay for the beer at the local tavern. They all knew, however, that their guard duties were a temporary assignment.

By March 1942 the United States was taking steps to remove all those of Japanese ancestry, citizens and aliens alike, from the West Coast to detention camps located inland, thus eliminating the threats, real or imaginary, of espionage and sabotage. The electric atmosphere in many West Coast cities gradually diminished. Since the guard duty performed by the 164th no longer had great urgency, the men of the regiment received orders to gather at Fort Ord, California, where the addition of other men brought the regiment to full strength as it prepared for going overseas.

Rumors were rife as the men received immunization shots and some new equipment, including new helmets and some antitank guns to replace old World War I gear. The most prominent speculation was that they were headed for the Philippines to reinforce the beleaguered troops at Bataan. Unknown to the men, the American Chiefs of Staff had already written off those islands, the Japanese blockade and air superiority having made reinforcing Luzon a greater risk than our limited armed forces had the capability to undertake successfully. The nation's leaders left the "battling bastards of Bataan" to fight it out with the few men and weapons available, condemning them to suffer eventually the agony of the infamous death march.

On 18 March 1942, the 164th boarded the converted luxury liner *President Coolidge*. Although the ship still had some of its tourist facilities, such as the swimming pool and Continental Lounge, its newly remodeled cabins now contained several small bunks barely wide enough to support a human body. With a small escort, the *President Coolidge* sailed to the Marquesas Islands, where it refueled and joined two more ships. Since the small convoy then headed southwest, it effectively negated the Philippine rumor. Cautiously altering course frequently to avoid presenting an easy target for Japanese submarines, the *President Coolidge* crossed the equator. In an appropriate celebration of the event, Colonel Sarles, majestically holding a makeshift trident, initiated the men into the realm of Neptune. Within a few days the men of the 164th laid eyes on Melbourne, Australia, where they would stay only briefly.

The *President Coolidge* had New Caledonia as its ultimate destination for the troops, but the ship was too big for any harbor facilities there. Thus, the men and equipment were unloaded at Melbourne and then reloaded onto three small Dutch freighters that the harbor of Noumea could handle with ease. While these tasks went on, many of the men took time to enjoy the sights of the city. They also drank their first Australian beer, immediately pronouncing it a quality product. Losing track of time, a few men missed the boats; in retrospect, they were the lucky ones. They later joined the regiment via better transportation.

The Dutch freighters sharply contrasted with the *President Coolidge*. Filthy and rat infested, they were permeated with foul odors. The crewmen, Javanese, knew no English except one phrase—"hot stuff"—which they yelled out whenever they were carrying food. The troops found the food barely edible, and, to add to their woes, a big storm came up in the Tasmanian Sea, tossing the small ships like corks. One ship had something that made these conditions a bit more tolerable. On that vessel the Dutch captain had a considerable cache of beer and liquor aboard. Although the storeroom holding the liquid refreshments was under guard, nevertheless, someone decided the time had come to change that guard.

Obtaining officer's bars, an enlisted man donned the bars and recruited four new "guards." After "relieving" the appointed guards, the fox was in the henhouse. The new guards began systematically to loot the liquor from the hold by filling barracks bags with bottles and passing them along. The voyage became easier for the men in the compartments that enjoyed the fruits of plunder. Not content with petty thievery, the "guards" left the surplus in barracks bags, tied securely to a rope and then hung outside a porthole for future use. Unfortunately, the elements did not cooperate, for the high waves of the storm smashed the bags against the side of the ship, breaking all the bottles. Needless to say, the prank made the ship's captain furious. Although an assessment against the men later paid for the liquor, the captain vowed never again to carry American troops.

When the 164th arrived at New Caledonia, a French colonial possession, it temporarily joined the units sent there to safeguard the island from possible Japanese invasion. American troops were taking up defense positions not only there but also at the Fiji and Samoan islands, to protect supply lines from the United States to Australia. As the Japanese military forces conquered one important stronghold after another, the threat to Australia itself became greater. After Malaya, Singapore, the Dutch East Indies, and other areas fell to the Japanese, it appeared that the Allies had to stop their thrust to the south and east somewhere if they were ever to mount an offensive action. They needed to hold New Caledonia, as well as other important islands, if the Allies were going to have bases from which to attack in the future.

New Caledonia also posed a political problem for the Allies. After France fell in the summer of 1940, it formed a new government, with its capital in Vichy, that collaborated with the Axis. Some French, however, formed a Free French provisional government, headquartered in London, with General Charles DeGaulle as its leader. The allegiance of French fighting forces in Africa was divided, though the United States accepted General Henri Giraud as being the Free French leader there. On New Caledonia, most of the people were loyal to DeGaulle, but after the fall of France, the government of the island was in turmoil as Lieutenant Colonel Denis, commander of the island militia and openly pro-Vichy, took over by ousting Governor Pelicier. Reacting quickly, General DeGaulle appointed a new governor, Henri Sautot, formerly commissioner in France's New Hebrides Islands. It appeared that all was well as Denis relinquished his power, but then DeGaulle sent to New Caledonia a new group of officials as commissioners who succeeded in creating problems again. Admiral Georges d'Argenlieu, head of these new officials, and some of the commissioners soon alienated many natives with their haughty demeanor. Besides confiscating some of the finer residences and automobiles of the island for their personal use, they spent money recklessly and often expressed their contempt for the natives, who, out of respect for DeGaulle, put up with their antics. By the time the 164th arrived, the whole island was seething with resentment toward the commission and especially toward Admiral d'Argenlieu.

Two regiments of infantry and some artillery and quartermaster units had already come to New Caledonia and were under the command of General Alexander M. Patch, Jr., formerly commander of an Infantry Replacement Center at Camp Croft, South Carolina. General Patch took a neutral stand on the problems of the island's governance until events forced his hand. After Admiral d'Argenlieu imprisoned some members of an island committee seeking redress of grievances, the admiral then kidnapped Governor Sautot, who had received orders to report to General DeGaulle. Subsequently a group of islanders retaliated by taking the admiral and other members of the commission hostage, then demanded the release of Governor Sautot and the native committee. The island militia now threw its support behind the governor, and demonstrations by the islanders brought large crowds to Noumea, its capital. While these events were taking place, General Patch learned that a Japanese carrier force was in the waters not far from New Caledonia. (It marked the prelude to the Battle of the Coral Sea.) Because he could not tolerate possible rebellion on the island while a Japanese fleet was threatening, the general ordered the crowds to disperse. Patch now had three regiments of infantry plus other units to back up his order. At first resenting Patch's actions, the New Caledonians later realized that he had wanted to scatter the population in case of aerial attack. The turmoil soon subsided when d'Argenlieu came to the conclusion that opposition to his presence had grown. He then released Governor Sautot and the native committee members, and the governor proceeded on his way to London to meet DeGaulle. D'Argenlieu and his retinue left New Caledonia. After DeGaulle appointed a new governor and commission, political stability returned. For the first months of 1942, however, the situation was precarious; the 164th may possibly have been sent there to bolster Patch's position if he needed to use force.

On New Caledonia, men of the 164th assumed various duties. While some guarded an airfield, others took up positions of defense in case of a Japanese invasion. Many of the men unloaded cargo vessels in the harbor of Noumea, and, of course, training exercises always kept the men busy. Some men regarded the training in New Caledonia as more rigorous than that at Camp Claiborne.

The troops also had a little time for recreation. The band played several concerts before large crowds, and a few of the men did a little fishing, often by tossing a hand grenade into the water, while some hunted deer on the island as a diversion from duty. Fish and deer helped to supplement the evening meal in which mutton, generously called lamb by the Army, often comprised the main course. Although the soldiers also welcomed beef as a relief, obtaining it caused some problems. Several of the farmers on New Caledonia raised cattle, which some men of the 164th called slow elk. When a few of the men occasionally succumbed to temptation by shooting one of them to put some beef on the table, needless to say, the farmers objected. A hasty collection of cash usually, though not always, sufficed to soothe the ruffled feelings.

While on New Caledonia, the 164th came into contact with troops of other units who formed part of Task Force 6814. Sent to New Caledonia via Australia in late January 1942, the task force had as its mission assuring the anti-Vichy people there that the Allies would protect them from Axis forces and prevent Japan from acquiring the island. New Caledonia also played a vital part in guarding the American supply line to Australia. On 24 May 1942, units of this task force, including the 132nd Infantry Regiment from Illinois and the 182nd Infantry Regiment from Massachusetts, joined with the 164th to form the Americal Division, the only unnumbered division in the United States Army and the only division of the United States Army organized overseas. The name resulted from the combination of America and Caledonia, and the shoulder patch of the division contained stars in the form of the Southern Cross constellation, indicating the southern hemisphere. A jerry-built division, it did not always fit the Table of Organization or the Table of Equipment, but it did have three trained infantry regiments, all "orphans" created by reorganizing divisions on the triangular basis. General Patch became its first commander.

Because the Americal Division had too few commissioned officers, the Army created an Officers Candidate School on New Caledonia. Units of the division selected from their enlisted men those who had displayed potential for leadership. Following approval by a screening board, these men then went to the school for about eight weeks. Upon receiving their commissions, the new officers were then assigned to units of their own regiment, though never to their former company. Before some of them completed the course, the 164th received an alert order to depart from New Caledonia.

Other changes took place in the officer ranks. Colonel Sarles relinquished his command of the regiment on 14 September 1942, Colonel Bryant Moore, a West Point graduate, succeeding him. Although no official reason was given for this change, many of the men in the regiment assumed that Colonel Sarles, at fifty-four years of age, was too old for combat command. Colonel Moore became the first of many regular Army officers to command the regiment, and Colonel Sarles was the last National Guardsman to do so, except for short temporary periods. Throughout the war this constant influx of Regular Army officers to head the regiment created some resentment among the National Guardsmen. The change in command was another portent of pending action. Though the men did not know, many suspected that they were going to

Guadalcanal, a small island in the Solomon Island chain that had recently taken on special significance.

The first American offensive action against Japan began on 7 August 1942, as the 1st Marine Division, reinforced with an additional regiment, landed on Guadalcanal. In their first two months there, the Marines had written another chapter in their illustrious history. After they had landed on Guadalcanal, almost unopposed, they had quickly captured an unfinished airstrip which they soon named Henderson Field for one of the many heroes of the Battle of Midway. They established a perimeter around the airstrip as best they could with the scant supplies and equipment available.

The Guadalcanal campaign, in its initial stages, suffered from lack of adequate planning and insufficient experience with island warfare. Furthermore, the American forces had landed in an area where the Japanese could assemble superior air and sea forces. Under these conditions, the commanders of some of the United States naval units assigned to this campaign feared large losses that they could ill afford. Withdrawing many of the transports from the landing area before they had disgorged their cargoes, they left the Marines with inadequate supplies of food, construction equipment, and barbed wire for protecting front-line positions. Fortunately, the Japanese had abandoned large food supplies (including many cases of canned crab) and all of their construction machinery, most of which had come through the preinvasion bombardment unscathed. To a large extent, the Marines continued construction of the airstrip with Japanese equipment, though it would not be completed for some weeks.

Commanding the Marines, General Alexander A. Vandegrift, a soft-spoken Virginian, realized that the Japanese, taken by surprise, were going to retaliate and try to push his men off the island. Orders to do the pushing fell upon General Harukichi Hyakutake, commander of the Japanese Seventeenth Army with headquarters at Rabaul, located on the northern tip of New Britain. The unfortunate victim of faulty intelligence, he thought that the American forces were small, demoralized, and preparing to withdraw at the first sign of Japanese strength on the island. He was also grossly overconfident: the great Japanese victories over the armies of China, the British in Malaya and Singapore, and the combined American-Filipino armies at Corregidor had led Hyakutake to believe that Japanese troops were invincible. Thus he began to send units, piecemeal and no bigger than a regiment, into the fray. When none had any success in denting the small American perimeter, by the middle of September the Japanese committed larger units to the battle. After assuming tactical command of the larger forces on Guadalcanal, General Kiyotaki Kawaguchi devised a plan for a three-pronged attack on the Marines to recapture the airstrip, now operational. Attacking from the south, the main force temporarily dented the Marine line, but the Marines stopped the assault short of its objective at a knoll christened "Bloody Ridge."

By 13 October 1942, when the 164th landed at Kukum Beach on Guadalcanal, the battle had reached a stalemate: the Japanese could not dislodge the Marines, and the Marines lacked sufficient strength to mount an offensive without dangerously stretching their thin perimeter. Yet neither the Japanese nor the Americans had given any thought to quitting.

Guadalcanal had become a battle of attrition as each side poured in reinforcements. Japanese troops came from other areas of the southern Pacific and were transported from Rabaul through Sealark Channel, now commonly referred to as "the slot." Stepping up its activities, this "Tokio Express," another popular appellation, landed Japanese troops, usually at night, on the western shores of the island. Coastwatchers, courageous men and women who daily risked their lives to relay information on Japanese air and naval operations, confirmed the increased movement. General Vandegrift knew something big was going to happen. So did General Hyakutake, who had another scheme, a larger, more complex one designed to bring glorious victory by eliminating all Americans on Guadalcanal.

The Japanese general planned to strike the American perimeter simultaneously from three different directions. The first prong of the attack—a combined infantry, tank, and artillery force under General Tadashi Sumiyoshi—would come from the Matanikau River near the western sector of the American forces. It would be a divided maneuver, part of the force swinging to the south to strike an extension of the perimeter while the other hit from the west. The second prong would come from the east, near Koli Point, but would not take part in the action until the Japanese had captured Henderson Field, which task belonged to the third and main force under General Masao Maruyama. Maruyama's seven thousand troops were to sweep around south of Mt. Austin, attack from the south, and punch a hole through the perimeter in this sector to gain Henderson Field, the objective. Once he arrived at the airstrip, General Maruyama would then destroy the ammunition, fuel, food dumps, and headquarters and communications facilities, the very heart of American capacity to continue the battle. On paper, the plan looked good, especially when the Japanese navy and air force had orders to destroy American aircraft systematically with aerial and naval bombardment for days prior to the land attacks.

The Japanese grand scheme was already under way when the 164th landed, and the men spent their first hours on Guadalcanal unloading supplies and talking with Marines. Because the rest of the Americal Division remained on New Caledonia, the regiment came under the command of General Vandegrift and was temporarily attached to the Marines. Shortly after noon, Japanese planes flew over, as they usually did in good flying weather, to bomb Henderson Field. This bombing phase of the Japanese plan had been expanded, and it caused the first casualty of the regiment: Corporal Kenneth Foubert of Company M, Grand Forks, was killed in this raid, which lasted less than a half hour. After this interruption, the men hastened their activities, and, with the 3rd Battalion in reserve, the 1st and 2nd battalions rushed to the front on the western edge of the line. Japanese activity suggested that the western sector soon would have heavy combat, exactly what General Hyakutake wanted the Americans to believe. The Marines had pushed a vulnerable, finger-shaped extension of the perimeter westward along the coast, and along the inland side of this finger the 1st and 2nd battalions had their first combat with the enemy.

Part of the Japanese campaign called for extensive air and naval attacks on Henderson Field to destroy the American air forces. The bombing of the airstrip on 13 October and before had been a component of their plan. That night, carrying out its role, the Japanese navy blasted Henderson Field with intense bombardment. Two battleships carrying fourteen-inch (360 mm) guns, one heavy cruiser, and several destroyers steamed along the north shore of the island, wreaking havoc on the airstrip with salvo after salvo. Then, turning about, the great fleet with impunity sailed back to shell the installation again. Soldiers and Marines scurried to find shelter from the heavy bombardment, often finding a huge shell hole for protection. Left in shambles, Henderson Field had only a few of its precious aircraft operational the next morning.

As Japanese patrols probed the American positions in preparation for the big strike, the Americans also advanced in order to gain valuable information as to the location of the Japanese forces and to reduce any strong points that might support a Japanese attack or halt an American one. Thus, the 164th became the first unit of the United States Army to take offensive action against the enemy in World War II.

General Maruyama had problems getting his large force into position for the main assault from the south. His soldiers had to carry all their supplies, including mortar and light artillery shells, through the jungle. Lacking trails, the Japanese had to hack their way, torturous step by step, for several miles before getting into their assigned places. Though scheduled for 22 October 1942, the attack had to be postponed for two days. On 24 October the Japanese were still not ready, and Maruyama sent word to delay the coordinated assaults for another day. General Sumiyoshi, in command of the western forces, either did not get the message or, if he did, ignored it. (He was gravely ill with malaria at the time.) He launched his part of the strike one day prematurely.

Sumiyoshi made the attack look like a major offensive. Led by nine medium tanks and supported by 150 mm artillery, the largest caliber on the island, the Japanese infantry struck the American perimeter from the west. Marines and the 2nd Battalion of the 164th took the brunt of the blow and threw the Japanese back, but a few Japanese got through the lines and, as snipers, harassed the Americans the next day. Though not in accord with the overall plan, the Japanese assault tended to make General Vandegrift believe that the main strike was coming from that area. He had not yet discovered the forces of General Maruyama to the south, but his ignorance soon ended.

As an advance scout for a patrol, Corporal Louis Lochner of Ely, Minnesota, came upon five of Sumiyoshi's Japanese combat veterans. Taking them by surprise, he killed all of them. When he realized that many more Japanese were in the area, he took up a position in front of the Browning Automatic Rifles and machine gun placements to protect them from possible grenades. Shortly thereafter the enemy rushed forward and Lochner fired with devastating effectiveness. Then his rifle jammed, and, while he field stripped it in an effort to repair it, the Japanese rushed again. Wounded by rifle fire and a bayonet thrust, Lochner continued to protect the Browning Automatic Rifles and machine guns until the enemy withdrew. Shortly thereafter he collapsed from loss of blood and succumbed to his wounds. For his valor he received the Distinguished Service Cross posthumously. The fury of these events portended the heavy fighting that followed.

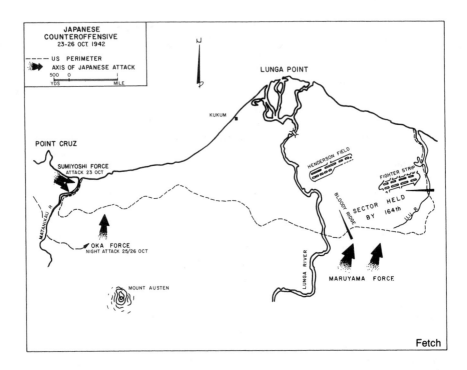

Even though some of his troops with heavy weapons were still straggling into position, thoroughly exhausted by their ordeal, Maruyama decided to launch his attack the next night. He counted heavily on the element of surprise and the superior fighting spirit of his troops, some of Japan's best and all veterans of previous campaigns in China and Java.

The night of 25 October 1942 will live forever in the memories of those who fought in the biggest battle waged on Guadalcanal. The Japanese came from both west and south in numbers hitherto unequaled. As the Sumiyoshi units renewed their assault, Maruyama's men struck with fierce determination to drive the Americans back to the sea. The battle raged incessantly as Japanese pressure from the south mounted. General Vandegrift decided to commit the 3rd Battalion, his only reserve unit, to action: the Marines facing the Maruyama troops needed help and needed it immediately.

Shortly before midnight, the 3rd Battalion received word to advance to the southern front. A heavy tropical rain made movement difficult. Because the black night cut visibility to a few feet, the men followed the Marine escorts to the line by holding the pack of the man in front. When the men got to the perimeter, they took their places in the line piecemeal wherever the Marines needed added firepower—almost everywhere in their sector. In spite of the downpour, slippery mud, and narrow, winding trails, they carried out the reinforcing movement with dispatch.

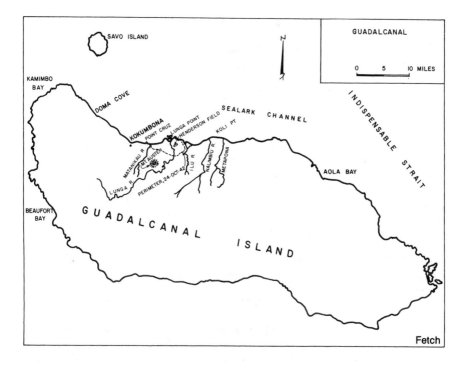

It had taken the entire battalion less than two hours to take up its arms and ammunition and assume its place on the line. Some of the men, the first to arrive at their designated positions with the Marines, had already killed several of the enemy before the last troops arrived. Under most difficult conditions, the 3rd Battalion had become a fighting force that played an important role in saving Henderson Field. Marine commanders, including General Vandegrift, later gave special praise to the battalion and Lieutenant Colonel Robert Hall, its commander from Jamestown, North Dakota. Afterward, Hall received the Navy Cross for the leadership he had displayed in this crucial action.

The Japanese pressed their attack until dawn. While the eerie light of flairs revealed that a major battle was taking place, the men of the 164th poured relentless fire into the continuous waves of oncoming Japanese soldiers. Machine gunners fed ammunition belts into their lethal weapons for so long that some of the guns simply gave out, and riflemen fired hundreds of eight-round clips into the charging hordes. Moving their 37 mm guns up, the antitank company shot canisters, tearing gaping holes in the oncoming Japanese and ripping apart the foliage from which the Japanese rushed. Used in this manner, the antitank guns became huge shotguns, and most North Dakotans knew how shotguns worked. Signaling the end of the night attack, the dawn also revealed fields of fire literally covered by dead Japanese.

During the last hours of darkness, Corporal William A. Clark, from Grand Forks, and two companions crawled out from the line to retrieve two damaged and abandoned machine guns. Although the weapons lay within a few yards of the Japanese, Clark inched his way toward them. The other two men were killed, but Clark persisted, recovered the guns, and, while still under heavy fire, assembled a serviceable machine gun from their parts in time to help repulse a large enemy thrust. He later received the Distinguished Service Cross for extraordinary gallantry in action.

The next day the 3rd Battalion took up its own position in the line and cleared larger fields of fire in the dense jungle. On its flank, the 2nd Battalion, which had also inflicted heavy casualties on the Japanese, prepared for another night of Japanese attacks. Spared much of the heavy fighting, the 1st Battalion received orders to prepare to send some of its units to the south, where it had now become evident the main Japanese force had struck. As for the Japanese, they had failed to dent the line but were still not ready to give up. General Maruyama's force, still formidable and determined, spent the day setting up new mortar and machine gun positions to support the next assault. They were not harassed by heavy artillery as were the Americans. General Sumiyoshi's 150 mm howitzers, the largest artillery on the island, and Japanese mortars fired constantly at the American troops and Henderson Field, giving them no rest throughout the day, which the men came to call "dugout Sunday."

At dusk, the Americans could hear the Japanese coming again, and come they did. By this time many of the stragglers of the Maruyama force had reached the front with added mortar and light artillery. As wave after wave attacked the American positions, once again the Japanese depended heavily upon their superior fighting spirit, their *bushido*. But the men of the 164th now had confidence in themselves. They also had M-1 semiautomatic rifles that used an eight-round clip of ammunition, a weapon that gave them much more firepower than the Marines, still using the 1903 Springfield bolt-action rifle with a five-round clip. As the flares and fire-mines cast their greenish glow upon the battle, they revealed a ghastly sight: the rifles, machine guns, and 37 mm canister of the antitank guns had created grotesque piles of dead Japanese. Yet Maruyama continued to press the attack throughout the night. Behind the lines of the 164th, service personnel and others hastily threw up a perimeter close to Henderson Field in case the Japanese broke through, about 175 cooks, messengers, clerks, and others manning positions and waiting for the worst. Band members served the regiment as litter bearers. Some units of the 1st Battalion reinforced the south line. Every member of the 164th had some role in the battle, the biggest and fiercest of the entire campaign.

Midst the roar of the battle, Sergeant Kevin McCarthy of Jamestown, North Dakota, noticed several Marines at an outpost surrounded by the enemy. Using a Bren gun carrier, a small, lightly armored, open-topped, tracked vehicle, he drove to the beleaguered Marines and loaded them into the vehicle, carrying them to the comparative safety of their own lines. The sergeant made three trips and rescued all eighteen Marines, many of them seriously wounded. For this courageous deed, performed under heavy enemy fire, he received the Distinguished Service Cross.

By dawn, when the Japanese attack began to weaken, everyone realized that Maruyama had suffered a disastrous defeat. Though a few of his troops had penetrated the American lines, they could do little but try to find their way back to their defeated comrades. An estimated seventeen hundred dead Japanese, their bodies already bloating, lay in front of the 164th as mute testimony to the regiment's deadly proficiency with its weapons. Once again the Americans had saved Henderson Field, and its precious aircraft, now increasing almost daily, began to assert themselves against decreasing Japanese opposition.

When the fighting subsided and the Americans had completed the gruesome task of burying the dead Japanese, a wave of relief swept over the Marines and the men of the 164th. General Vandegrift realized that the 164th had played a key role in a significant victory and sent the following message to Colonel Moore and the men of the regiment:

Subject: Congratulations

1. The officers and men of the First Marines salute you for a most wonderful piece of work on the night of 25 and 26 October, 1942. Will you please extend our sincere congratulations to all concerned. We are honored to serve with a unit such as yours.
2. Little did we realized when we turned over our "quiet sector" to you that you would bear the brunt of an attack so soon. I'm sure you are very proud of the fighting ability demonstrated by your unit and our hat is off to you.

Having killed about one-third of Maruyama's entire force and wounded countless hundreds, the regiment deserved this recognition. In return, the regiment had suffered only twenty-six killed in action and fifty-two wounded. It had lived up to its motto *Je Suis Pret*.

But perhaps the men in the ranks of the Marines paid the supreme compliment to the men of the 164th. Marines seldom held Army troops in high regard and often referred to them as "doggies" or "boy scouts." After the big conflict ended, however, those grizzled, battle-worn Marines called the men of the 164th "soldiers" and really meant it.

After the fighting ended, patrols probed the area formerly occupied by the Japanese. A few Japanese stragglers, weary from the long trek and heavy fighting, remained in the vicinity, but the main force, or what remained of it, had returned to the western sector over the same trail it had used to launch its attack. Some of Maruyama's men, however, escaped to the east and joined with a small group of Japanese troops in the Koli Point region.

Koli Point assumed great importance soon after the big fight south of Henderson Field. General Vandegrift received a report that the Japanese planned to land about three thousand troops in the area, thus threatening his eastern flank just when he planned a major offensive to the west. The general had only one understrength regiment of Marines in the Koli Point region, hardly large enough to defeat a force of three thousand determined Japanese. He ordered the 2nd and 3rd battalions to Koli Point to reinforce the Marines already there and prevent the Japanese from establishing a stronghold on his eastern flank. Thus began a controversial and less than commendable campaign.

Although the Koli Point operation began under the false belief that a major Japanese invasion was imminent there, the Japanese actually had no intention of landing three thousand troops in that area. They did land about two hundred troops near Koli Point, along with supplies for the Japanese troops already stranded there. A few collapsible landing craft used by these troops tended to make the Japanese presence at Koli Point look larger than it really was. Those troops were trying to build an airstrip, a hopeless task. Thus the main reason for the operation simply did not exist. Because they did not have enough landing craft available to go by sea, the 2nd and 3rd battalions had to hack their way through dense jungle, while carrying all their own supplies, and ford streams swollen by recent rains. Some of the supplies and equipment fell by the way during the ten-mile or more advance through the steaming jungle.

General William Rupertus, assistant commander of the 1st Marine Division and in command of the maneuver, had only recently arrived at Guadalcanal, having been at Tulagi throughout the campaign. Already very ill with malaria, he had to be relieved of the command shortly after the action began. Though he possessed no previous combat command experience, General Edmund Sebree, assistant commander of the Americal Division and a recent arrival on the island, succeeded him. Colonel Bryant Moore, regimental commander, had only the combat experience of placing his men into an already established perimeter. None of these officers had accurate maps of the area, nor did they know the exact location or purpose of the enemy. Furthermore, although this military action required close and accurate communication among all units involved, Army and Marine, terrain and the corrosive effect of the climate rendered the obsolete radios virtually useless. Field telephones, though more reliable, required wires strung from one unit to another, but Japanese patrols or an errant mortar or artillery shell could easily sever these lines. Under these conditions, along with the possibility of human error, some parts of the campaign could easily go badly, and they did.

As dusk of 6 November approached, the 2nd Battalion took up a position south of the 3rd; but when it came under some mortar fire, Major Arthur Timboe, commanding the 2nd Battalion, decided to move the men nearer to the 3rd Battalion. Although he probably assumed that notice of his movement had reached the 3rd Battalion, it had not. Instead, the 3rd Battalion had received a message informing them that a heavily armed Japanese patrol was in the area and thus opened fire on the men of the 2nd Battalion. Fortunately a machine gun jammed after shooting several rounds and, in the ensuing interlude, men of the 2nd Battalion identified themselves. The firing ceased, but casualties had resulted in what General Sebree later called the "battle of the battalions."

As the two battalions swept toward the beach to envelop the Japanese, they became aware that the large force anticipated was not there. By 8 November General Vandegrift decided to recall the 3rd Battalion to help in the offensive on the western sector, where the 1st Battalion had been attacking enemy positions in an attempt to wrest from the Japanese the ridges in the Matanikau River area. The 2nd Battalion remained near Koli Point and moved toward the main Japanese stronghold, which the Marines had found. Two battalions of Marines had occupied positions to the east and west of the Japanese, while the ocean lay to the north. The 2nd Battalion received orders to take up positions south of the Japanese and hem them into a tight pocket where they could be eliminated, but once again the plans went awry. Because of difficult terrain and the high water of Gavaga Creek, Company F could not close a gap between itself and Company E, and many of the Japanese escaped the trap through this opening. The Marines were irate, as were General Sebree and Colonel Moore. The colonel relieved Major Timboe of his command of the 2nd Battalion after Timboe defended his company commander and refused to relieve him. Nonetheless, the Koli Point operation had some success: the Americans had killed over 450 Japanese and secured the eastern flank. In poor physical condition, the Japanese who had escaped the trap finally found their way to the western sector, but they lacked the capacity to contribute much to the combat effectiveness of the units.

For the 164th the Koli Point campaign had been less than glorious. Considering the effort involved, the men found the results disappointing. Obviously, confusion had been commonplace, and much of it sprang from inexperienced command from the top on down. Later, some of the men referred to the operation as "Moore's march to the sea." Others concluded that "nobody knew what in hell was going on. Nobody!" They may not have been far from the truth.

While their comrades were struggling at Koli Point, the 1st Battalion joined Marine units in a general drive westward from the Matanikau River, in a part of Guadalcanal consisting of many small, spiny ridges, which jutted out of slopes and were bordered by steep ravines. Since the terrain did not lend itself to a frontal assault, the Americans used different tactics. One unit, usually a battalion, moved westward against a ridge but out of small-arms range, while another circled around the ridge and pushed from the south. Artillery fire and strafing by aircraft killed many of the Japanese on the ridge as patrols eliminated outlying positions. The Japanese either remained on the ridge to die or retreated to another, where the Americans employed the same tactics.

The American advance west of the Matanikau was steadily driving the Japanese back as the men of the 1st Battalion reached a point over a mile west of Point Cruz. After receiving word of another impending Japanese attack, which caused him to want to establish a strong defense around the original American perimeter, General Vandegrift called off the operation. As the Americans withdrew, the Japanese reoccupied their former positions, taking advantage of the opportunity and fortifying many of the ridges more intensely. American forces could not advance that far west again until January 1943.

After all battalions had returned to the Henderson Field area, the entire regiment went into reserve for a brief rest. General Vandegrift hoped to begin his plan for a general offensive to the west, where the 1st Battalion and the Marines had been attacking and patrolling for over a week. From these operations, he concluded that a general offensive was possible, providing he had enough troops available. By the middle of November, Vandegrift had the manpower to launch the drive. Though the Marines also played a part, the task of attacking the Japanese and driving them from these ridges fell to the 164th and the newly arrived 182nd Regiment of the Americal Division. General Sebree became tactical commander of these western forces.

Before he launched a general offensive to the west, General Vandegrift needed to know if the southern and eastern parts of the island contained any Japanese troops. A special patrol consisting of First Lieutenant Frederic Flo and thirteen men of the 164th, accompanied by a native policeman and two Marine Indians who were fluent in the Navajo language, received the task of reconnoitering these areas. The men boarded a native schooner, manned by its local crew, and set sail westward to round Cape Esperance and then head south to their first destination, a small village and mission on Beaufort Bay. Upon arrival there, the patrol contacted Father Henry De Klerk, a Roman Catholic missionary, and several local islanders who had gone inland recently. All the reports they received indicated that no Japanese were in the vicinity. The patrol then departed eastward, where other islanders confirmed the absence of Japanese. Each time the men gathered more information, the Marine Navajos sent radio messages in their native tongue back to headquarters, where other Navajos translated them. It made a perfect code, for the Japanese had no knowledge of the Navajo language. The patrol continued its way around the southern and eastern coasts of Guadalcanal collecting valuable intelligence. When they found no reliable native source, the patrol moved inland, carefully searching for signs of Japanese, but discovered none. Vandegrift now knew that the only enemy in strength lay to the west of the Matanikau and he gave orders to begin the assault there.

Geography heavily favored the Japanese defenders. The rocky ridges they occupied were high and steep, and their automatic weapons placed on the elevated ground gave the Japanese a commanding field of fire. The jungle in the ravines at the base of the ridges afforded the Americans some cover, but between the ravines and ridges lay open areas covered only by kunai grass. Although this vegetation often grew to as much as six feet in height, the Japanese could clearly see American troops moving into it. Placed behind the apex of the ridges and thus protected from American artillery, enemy mortars covered this open space and had the capacity to reach targets in the ravines to their front. Using the respite Vandegrift had given them to great advantage, the Japanese had devised a system of mutually supporting machine guns, grenade launchers, and riflemen along the slopes of the ridges. The men of the 164th would soon experience their bloodiest week of World War II.

With the 3rd Battalion still in New Caledonia, the newly arrived 1st and 2nd battalions of the 182nd regiment, the first troops to move west of the Matanikau since the Americans had pulled back from there over a week before, took up their positions on high ground. As they moved in, only a few skirmishes occurred, but by the time each battalion had dug in for possible Japanese counterattacks, a thousand yards separated them, a situation that the Japanese soon exploited. When the Japanese attacked the 1st Battalion on front and flank, the green troops of the 182nd gave ground, although they soon recovered it with help from the 164th, which had closed the space between the two battalions of the 182nd. With the combined strength of the 164th, 182nd, and the 8th Marines, General Sebree planned to dislodge the Japanese with a frontal assault.

Ironically, General Hyakutake, who had come from Rabaul to assume direct command of all Japanese forces on Guadalcanal, had in mind doing the same thing. Amassing a formidable force, he planned to seize the east bank of the Matanikau as a jumping-off area for a direct attack on Henderson Field and a new fighter strip nearing completion. Since the American air power had sunk many of the barges carrying more troops down "the slot" for him, the general delayed his offensive until more men arrived, even though he had an estimated twenty-five thousand at his disposal. He had placed many of his best soldiers in the area facing the Matanikau, the region where the 164th and other units attempted to occupy all the ridges and commanding terrain.

On the night of 20 November 1942, under cover of darkness, the 1st and 3rd battalions of the 164th took up their positions between the battalions of the 182nd in order to launch an all-out attack the following morning. Daylight revealed a ravine directly in front of them about 200 feet deep and 150 to 300 feet wide, beyond which lay an open space of about 150 feet approaching the ridge occupied by the Japanese, who had constructed formidable positions flanking the ravine (and the open space beyond it) with automatic weapons. Thus the attack immediately received a hail of fire, the 164th advancing no more than 150 feet before it had to withdraw. Another assault, this time supported by artillery, took place the following day with results no better. Indeed, the heroism of Corporal Willard Dowsett helped avert a tragedy. In jungle, Company E was about to emerge into a clearing when Dowsett volunteered to reconnoiter the area while the rest of the company remained under cover. He spotted one Japanese machine gun nest, then another, and yet another. When he shot at them, they all returned the fire, giving their location away. Although killed by the machine gun fire, Corporal Dowsett had saved an entire company from moving into a deadly ambush. For his courageous act, Dowsett received the Distinguished Service Cross posthumously.

On 23 November, when the 164th pulled back about three hundred yards, the 8th Marine Regiment, determined to show the Army how to attack successfully, came to the front. Supported by a thirty-minute artillery barrage on the Japanese lines, the 8th Marines moved out. They soon came back under withering small-arms and mortar fire. After deciding that the frontal-assault tactics resulted in mounting casualties that the Americans could ill afford, Generals Sebree and Vandegrift ordered the men of the 164th and 182nd to dig in and hold what high ground they now controlled. The 164th moved to the right flank, along the ocean. From there they were to probe enemy positions with "tiger patrols" and either wipe them out, if they could, or get accurate coordinates for American artillery fire.

Before the 164th took up their new positions, the Japanese zeroed in with heavy mortars and delivered many deadly rounds. Colonel Robert Hall, commanding the 3rd Battalion, was wounded and had to be evacuated. Several others were killed, among them 3rd Battalion surgeon Captain Andrew Panettiere. The Army hospital in Noumea, New Caledonia, bore the name Panettiere Hospital in his honor.

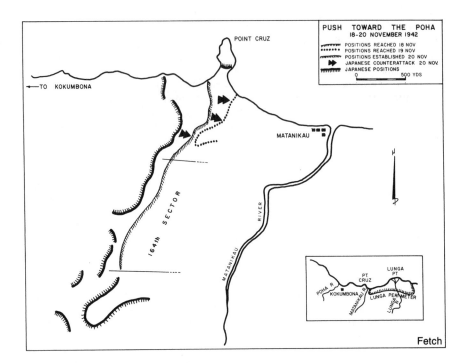

The week of 20-27 November cost the regiment dearly: it had suffered over one hundred men killed in action and over two hundred wounded, many of whom were evacuated. Yet the men had not fought in vain. Although the two forces had reached a stalemate with neither having the capacity to launch a successful attack, the Americans had reached the west side of the Matanikau, this time to stay, and they had thwarted the plan of General Hyakutake for a large offensive east of the Matanikau.

The month of November heralded the big turning point in the battle for Guadalcanal. The dark days of October, when the Japanese had possessed the initiative, had ended. Although victory for the Americans was not yet definite, defeat, a possibility in September and October, was now out of the question. Having grown, the American air forces were now consistently asserting themselves and taking a heavy toll of Japanese planes. The ground troops had swelled to about thirty-five thousand men, approximately ten thousand more than the Japanese had on the island. And, although the American Navy had suffered some humiliation at the hands of the Japanese, it, too, could now prevent the Japanese navy from having its own way. The Americans only needed some fresh troops who could renew the attack west of the Matanikau and drive the Japanese from the island, and they were already on their way.

The 1st Marine Division was spent, having been on Guadalcanal since the initial landing on 7 August 1942. Although it had suffered relatively few battle casualties, malaria, dysentery, dengue fever, and just plain exhaustion had taken a heavy toll. Now the unit was scheduled to leave Guadalcanal in December for a well-deserved rest. The 25th Infantry Division, however, and the remaining units of the Americal Division were on their way. These two Army divisions, the 2nd Marine Division, plus the 147th Regimental Combat Team and other units, gave the Americans the advantage needed to complete the defeat of the Japanese. Thus, during December, a considerable turnover took place in the personnel on the island. After commanding the operation on Guadalcanal since the Americans initially landed, General Vandegrift relinquished his position to General Patch of the Americal Division. The 164th was no longer attached to the Marines. For the men of the regiment, all of these developments meant that they, too, enjoyed some relief from the days of continuous combat.

Throughout the first half of December, the 164th carried on extensive patrol activity west of the Matanikau. The regiment had moved to the right flank of the American position, thus placing itself near the coast. Occasionally engaging the enemy in combat, these patrols most often carefully observed enemy positions and relayed the information to the artillery. Aerial photographs of the western half of Guadalcanal had enabled the Americans to draw accurate maps of the region. Now more and heavier artillery fire (including 155 mm "long toms") was available to the Americans. Closer to the Japanese lines, the mortars of Companies D, H, and M delivered their deadly shells. Slowly the Japanese gave way to the constant pounding and began to abandon some of their positions facing the Americans. Perhaps the Unit Report of 10 December 1942, best describes this type of activity:

Enemy units in contact: A few well placed machine guns supported by riflemen.

Enemy reserves: Possibly a regiment with heavy weapons.

Enemy activity: Limited to securing positions and resisting our patrols. S-2 estimate: Exposed enemy troops were fired upon by artillery with good results. The Japanese positions appear to have been weakened by artillery as the enemy is exposing himself to our observation to move supplies. S-2 conclusion: The enemy's line becomes progressively weakened as the destroyed positions are difficult to rebuild without drawing mortar and artillery fire.

Report of Operations: Patrol activities: 1st Bn. sent out one patrol 100 to 150 yards in front of lines. No enemy seen or heard. 2nd Bn. sent out patrol 150 to 200 yards, patrol shot sniper out of tree and threw hand grenades into enemy dugouts with unknown results.

Ten to fifteen Japs observed along beach road by our Point Cruz OP (observation post). Artillery and mortar fire placed on them. Mortar fire was placed on Jap positions in front of our lines intermittently throughout the day with unknown results.

The terseness of the journal does not readily reveal that the men of the 164th were in daily contact with the enemy. On 2 December 1942, a patrol worked its way about a hundred yards behind enemy lines, charting Japanese mortar and automatic weapon emplacements. When the patrol was ambushed, its leader gave the order to withdraw back to their lines. Private Herbert Witte of Cambridge, Nebraska, came upon a wounded comrade and, disregarding his personal safety, rolled the soldier onto his back and began to crawl toward the American lines. Private Witte collapsed from exhaustion and, when he regained his strength, discovered that his comrade had died. Witte hid the body and made his way to safety. The next day he lead a patrol to recover the fallen soldier, but Japanese mortar fire drove the men back, though they recovered the rifle and identification tags of their comrade. For his selfless deed, Private Witte received the Distinguished Service Cross.

On 15 December 1942, as other units began to take up the positions held by the 164th, the regiment went back east of the Matanikau. Its primary assignment for the next weeks consisted of long-range, company-sized patrols in the area south of the original perimeter and east of Mt. Austin. Often guided by natives, these patrols were hunting for possible Japanese positions or troop movements in this large region and thus spent as many as six days on a single search. Fortunately, they only encountered Japanese stragglers in search of their units and unable to offer any serious threat. It was just as well, for the regiment needed a respite from combat.

The companies that went on these long patrols really consisted of men from two or more companies. Since tropical diseases, particularly malaria, took increasingly large numbers of men out of action, some of the line companies of the regiment had fallen to less than half strength. Other men, simply too weak from exhaustion, could not physically stand the rigors of long patrols. Thus the companies on these patrols were often called composite companies to indicate that they were made up of men from the parent company and others as well.

By January, many of the men not engaged in these patrols were helping unload transports and stockpiling supplies. This afforded them the opportunity for a good night's sleep in an area secure from Japanese attack (save for an occasional air raid) and for hot meals instead of the monotonous field rations. It also gave those inclined to do so a chance to sample the latest batch of jungle juice, though some had less complimentary names for the concoction.

To prepare jungle juice, the soldiers first had to find suitable containers for the ingredients. Sometimes they used one-gallon vinegar jugs, but they were small and available only if the cooks saved them. They next needed some dried fruit, canned fruit being too precious. They could usually locate plenty of raisins, and, on occasion, some dried apricots or apples. A small amount of bread yeast from the company baker, a few pounds of sugar from an understanding cook, and a piece of gauze from the medics completed the requirements. They combined in any order suitable to the makers the fruit, sugar, yeast, and enough water nearly to fill the jug. Next, they tied gauze over the mouth of the jug to keep out insects and to let the brew breathe. The jug then needed only a warm spot to let nature take its course, and that was anywhere on Guadalcanal. For young men born and raised in a dry state, these North Dakotans possessed a remarkable knowledge of the process of fermentation, and in three or four days the batch was ready for consumption. Anything older became vintage.

Those who imbibed showed up at the appointed place with canteen cups in hand to spend an evening with their comrades, their conversation ranging over sundry subjects including the latest rumors, one of the most popular (and least plausible) being that the 164th was going to return to the United States as a unit. Although they also discussed the new regimental commander, Colonel Paul Daly, another Regular Army officer, who succeeded Colonel Moore on 1 January 1943, sooner or later their talk turned homeward to the latest news about home towns, mutual friends, the last harvest, or the recent snowstorm. For a few brief hours they forgot their troubles as their thoughts centered on the small towns, open prairies, and loved ones they had left behind. Then back to the cots and tents for a night's rest, everyone hoping that a Japanese air raid would not interrupt their sleep.

Those who had drunk deeply of the cup had to pay the price, for the next morning usually brought them a throbbing headache, parched mouth, and a rumbling digestive system. Though many swore that they would never partake of that foul drink again, when the next batch was ready, they showed up, canteen cup in hand, and before the evening was over took another brief trip home.

Some troops of the 164th continued patrol activity throughout most of January, but they contacted very few of the enemy. When it became obvious that most of the Japanese were confined to the extreme western part of the island, Company C of the 164th was given a separate mission. Savo Island, only about three miles in diameter and lying several miles north of the western tip of Guadalcanal, was possibly an observation post for the Japanese; if not, it might serve the Americans as such. On 28 January 1943, after landing on Savo without resistence, Company C sent patrols throughout the island for the next four days. Natives cooperated to the fullest extent, and one Mr. Shroeder, a former resident thoroughly familiar with the geography of the island, gave his knowledge freely. No Japanese were on Savo. Some Japanese ammunition, attached to floating devices, had washed up on the shores, but nothing indicated the presence of Japanese. (In the latter stages of the Guadalcanal campaign, Japanese transports unloaded supplies on floats at sea and counted on the waves and tides to take them ashore.) After leaving a squad on Savo to establish an observation post, the company returned to Guadalcanal.

During their final days on Guadalcanal, some of the men of the 164th had an opportunity to see a show put on for their entertainment by Joe E. Brown, a popular film comedian. He cracked jokes, often about his own facial construction (he had a very large mouth) and about the "invincibility" of the Japanese. Brown won the respect of the men on Guadalcanal because he was willing to come and lighten their hearts with a little humor, in spite of the possible danger. The men of the 164th later bestowed on him honorary membership in their Regimental Association in gratitude for his efforts.

In a series of daring night operations by their destroyers, from 1 to 9 February 1943, the Japanese succeeded in evacuating several thousand troops from Guadalcanal. This signaled the closing of the campaign as well as the first big victory by the Americans in the Pacific war. Success came none too soon, for the 164th, as a unit, was no longer combat effective. Over three months on Guadalcanal had taken a heavy toll.

When the Guadalcanal campaign ended, the regiment had less than two-thirds its authorized number, and many of the men still in the unit were not in good physical condition. Almost all of them had lost twenty pounds or more. The extreme heat and high humidity of Guadalcanal had sapped their strength, and, in spite of salt pills available to them, many had suffered from heat exhaustion. Malaria, as well as a multitude of other tropical diseases, infected the men to such an extent that over 2,200 cases had required medical care throughout the battle. During the crucial days of October and November 1942, only those with body temperatures of over 101 degrees were relieved of combat duty. Cases of malaria continued to increase after hostilities ceased. More tragic, however, was the fact that the regiment lost 147 men killed in action and reported 309 wounded by enemy fire. Another 133 were victims of shock, trauma, and neurosis. The men of the 164th buried most of their dead comrades in the 1st Marine Division cemetery on Guadalcanal because the 164th had been attached to that unit throughout much of the campaign. Little wonder that some Marines referred to Guadalcanal as "green hell," but the Japanese had a more appropriate name for it: they called Guadalcanal the "island of death."

The regiment received much recognition for its accomplishments on Guadalcanal, including a Presidential Unit Citation because of its outstanding contribution to the victory. General George Marshall, chairman of the Joint Chiefs of Staff, sent his congratulations to the 164th, as did Admiral William Halsey, who took command of the South Pacific forces on 18 October 1943. Many individual members of the regiment received decorations: one Navy Cross, five Distinguished Service Crosses already mentioned, forty Silver Stars, and many Soldier's Medals and Legions of Merit. Scores of them had been cited for bravery by their regimental or divisional commanders. Over three hundred received the Purple Heart, the most common decoration awarded to members of the regiment.

On 1 March 1943, the 164th left Guadalcanal, not for the United States as the optimistic rumor held, but for the Fiji Islands, another French colonial possession. Although the Fiji Islands did not have the attraction the United States had, they had a lot more to offer than Guadalcanal, with such things as brick buildings, surfaced streets, movies, canned beer, and women. The main island, Viti Levu, with the biggest town, Suva, even had facilities suitable for United Service Organization shows. Perhaps best of all, the Fijis had no malaria.

Malaria had taken and was still taking from duty an alarming number of American servicemen in the Solomons, New Guinea, Burma, and India. Unknown to the 164th, its men became part of an experiment in an attempt by the Medical Department to curb the disease. Although quinine was the recognized preventative of malaria, the Japanese now controlled most of the world's supply, and the Americans reserved theirs for the most serious cases. Also, many men of the 164th who had taken quinine at the beginning of Guadalcanal had suffered an adverse reaction to it. After deciding to try out various dosages of Atabrine, a suppressant of malaria, to determine how much a man needed and how often he should take it in order to keep malaria from rendering him combat ineffective, the Medical Department administered various doses three, five, and six times a week to control groups so that medical teams might test its effectiveness. When the results proved disappointing, the medical teams took the men off Atabrine and left them to build up their own immunity to the disease. But then the number of cases requiring medical attention in the regiment rose sharply, and it was back to Atabrine. Finally the Medical Department recommended a dosage of five grains taken daily, an amount that remained standard for the rest of the war. The incidence of malaria in the regiment dropped considerably in their next campaign.

On Viti Levu, the regiment received 1,088 replacements to bring it back almost to full strength. The 164th had lost many of its original men on Guadalcanal, owing to casualties, disease, and other causes. While on Viti Levu, about fifty of the men volunteered for service in another unit, the 5307th Composite Unit, better known as Merrill's Marauders, which wanted only experienced jungle fighters. The regiment also lost the band, whose members had served as litter bearers and had performed other vital tasks in combat. After a new Table of Organization for the Army Infantry Division came out in the summer of 1943, making the regiments and divisions leaner yet, members of the band left for various other units as part of the reorganization. The Table of Organization added three cannon companies to the division on paper, only because none were yet available. Large cuts in headquarters and service personnel decreased the authorized strength of the regiment by over one hundred men. The composition of the regiment changed little, however.

As reorganized, an infantry regiment still consisted of a headquarters staff and detachment, medical detachment, a headquarters company and a service company. The antitank company and new cannon companies were also considered parts of a regimental group because they were seldom attached to a specific battalion.

Each of the three battalions in a regiment had a headquarters company and four other companies, three rifle companies and a weapons company. Thus 1st Battalion Companies A, B and C were rifle companies while Company D was a weapons company. Each rifle company had a small headquarters including company commander, executive officer, clerical and supply personnel, cooks, bakers, and others. It also included three rifle platoons and a weapons platoon, each about forty men when full strength. The standard weapons of the rifle platoons were the M-1 rifle and the Browning Automatic rifle (BAR), while those of the weapons platoon were the .30-caliber light machine gun and the 60 mm mortar. Company D, often called "heavy weapons," manned the heavy machine guns and 81 mm mortars. At full strength the rifle company had slightly more than two hundred men while the weapons company was smaller in number. The 2nd and 3rd battalions were the same except for the letters designating the various companies. The 2nd Battalion consisted of Companies E, F, and G, with Company H being the weapons company, while the 3rd Battalion was composed of Companies I, K, and L, with Company M as the weapons company. At full strength the infantry regiment was about three thousand enlisted men and officers, though that number was seldom maintained. A regiment that had been in combat for only a short time was short of manpower: as an extreme example, after

Guadalcanal the 164th had less than two thousand men, many of whom were physically unfit for combat. The reorganized infantry regiment had less personnel but more firepower than its antecedent, but except for the changes noted, it was essentially the same as it had been in the National Guard.

During the respite from combat, many commissioned and noncommissioned officers were asked to give their views on how to improve the combat effectiveness of the unit and infantry in general for future operations. Many recommended more thorough training in the use of their weapons, believing that the men had not had enough opportunities to practice with them. Some of the men of the 164th had not even fired their M-1 rifles until they were in combat. They suggested that shooting at moving targets, proper methods of throwing hand grenades, and doing this while explosions took place near the men in simulated combat conditions were more realistic training practices than the men had experienced. They thought they should have more automatic weapons, such as the Browning Automatic Rifle, as part of standard equipment. They complained that although the Army had furnished ample supplies for Guadalcanal, they were often stored in places remote from the troops that needed them. Too often there had been too much dependence put on vehicular transportation where there were no roads, thus requiring a near-superhuman effort on the part of headquarters personnel to get ammunition to the men who needed it. Medical officers criticized their own regulations regarding the placement of aid stations and the roles and assignment of litter bearers. They believed that medical units should locate aid stations nearer areas of combat and recommended that litter bearers carry pistols in the event of harassment by Japanese who had infiltrated the lines. (The litter bearers of the 164th, often members of the band, had already made this change.) Most of the officers agreed, however, that more emphasis had to be placed on the techniques and objectives of patrolling, patrols being the single most effective method of finding the enemy, estimating their strength in men and arms, and gathering important information for future operations in areas held by them. Patrols had to be more thorough in their missions. Some thought that this required more patience, better leadership, and assignments to smaller sectors, while others believed patrols should be smaller in size and have some means of reliable communication with headquarters. When the regiment undertook extensive training late in the summer of 1943, it followed many of these recommendations.

Colonel Moore, formerly commander of the regiment and now assistant divisional commander, found much fault with the junior officers of the 164th. He believed that too many of them were unfit to lead men in combat because they were not themselves leaders, nor did they discipline their men enough. He cited a company commander who was lax in requiring his men to take salt tablets, and as a result, less than one-fourth of the company could carry out its assignment because the rest came down with heat exhaustion. In another example, he said a platoon leader got lost when on patrol. Moore concluded that the regiment needed many junior officers of higher quality and that many of those currently in the 164th should be reassigned to noncombat responsibilties.

With the addition of nearly eleven hundred replacements to the regiment, more unit training became necessary so the new men could learn how to work as members of squads, platoons, and companies. Instead of making units solely out of replacements, the commander filled out the existing ones with the new men, who thus received the benefit of serving with combat veterans. From these experienced soldiers, the green troops learned what to do in combat conditions and how to work together as a whole. In these field exercises the rookies also learned that the men of the 164th were in good physical condition in spite of the hardships they had endured on Guadalcanal. The first days of training were more exhausting to the new men than to the veterans.

The replacements also received some indoctrination to instill in them a pride in the regiment. The 164th had already compiled a very outstanding record of accomplishments, and it expected the new men to help maintain that standard. Those who shirked their duty jeopardized not only their own lives but those of their comrades. Since combat required teamwork, the regiment expected all to carry their load to ensure a maximum rate of survival. Above all, they stressed that the 164th did not abandon its dead and wounded, even when under extreme pressure from the enemy. To allow the enemy to mutilate the bodies of the dead or torture the wounded was unthinkable. The replacements learned that the regiment expected much of them, but no more than the veterans demanded of themselves. When the regiment received orders on 25 November 1943 to prepare to move to Bougainville, it was ready for another campaign.

Bougainville, the top rung in the "Solomons' ladder" and also the largest of this group of islands, had many of the geographical features of Guadalcanal, although it was larger, and had higher mountains and ridges, and, if possible, denser jungles and rain forests. It also had two large, active volcanoes. The establishment of an air base on this island was an essential part of Operation Cartwheel, designed to reduce the Japanese base at Rabaul, New Britain, the center of operations for the whole South Pacific. Only three hundred miles from Bougainville, that bastion lay within easy range of American medium bombers as well as fighter aircraft. If the Americans could establish and protect an area on Bougainville large enough for bombers and fighters to attack Rabaul continuously, Japanese control of the Solomons (what little they retained), the Bismarck Archipelago, the Admiralty Islands, and New Guinea would be in great jeopardy. Realizing this, the Japanese, as early as July 1943, had begun to reinforce the island as much as their limited resources allowed.

During the late summer of 1943, the Japanese had sent large amounts of artillery and heavy mortars to Bougainville, usually landing them at night under cover of darkness. To get these weapons into inland positions where they could defend the island from invasion had proved a monumental task, however. With no roads, as such, on Bougainville, the Japanese could move the heavy guns by truck only a very short distance. Then they had to pull the guns, usually by sheer manpower, up the trails that formed the only arteries of transportation. Reaching their destinations, they had positioned the guns to defend against invasion in the areas General Hyakutake and his superior, General Hitoshi Imamura, believed that the Americans would land. They were both wrong.

On 1 November 1943, the 31st Task Force, which included the 3rd Marine Division, the 37th Infantry Division, and many other units, began coming ashore at Empress Augusta Bay. Initially they encountered the problems of high surf, which destroyed or immobilized many of the landing craft, and Japanese planes from Rabaul, which caused some of the transports carrying supplies to leave the area temporarily. Because the Japanese had expected the Americans to land about sixty miles to the southeast, the Americans met only slight resistance from the enemy. Although he rushed a few hundred troops to the area to repel the invaders, General Hyakutake remained convinced that this American operation was only a feint and that the main invasion would take place elsewhere. The Americans expanded the perimeter over the next weeks until they controlled an area sufficiently large for the construction of three airstrips.

Having other plans for the 3rd Marine Division, Admiral Halsey decided to call in the Americal Division to replace it. Under these conditions the 25 November alert went to the Americal and the men of the 164th. Once again the 164th was to be the first unit of the Americal Division scheduled to make the landing, and it began loading on the assigned transports on 10 December 1943. Leaving the relative peace and security of the Fijis nine days later, the regiment reached Bougainville on Christmas day. It spent the first day on the island preparing to take over perimeter positions held by the 9th Marine Regiment, accomplishing the replacement with dispatch. Some of the men may have witnessed an amusing sight when a battalion of Fijians, who where excellent scouts, marched from their transport while singing their favorite marching song—"Pistol Packin' Mama." By this time, General Hyakutake knew that the American landing at Empress Augusta Bay was the main American operation.

Shortly after the 164th took up its perimeter position, it began to send patrols out from its sector to gather as much intelligence about the enemy as possible. The regiment also needed to fix exact positions of hills, mountains, rivers, and valleys in the area because the maps currently in use contained much inaccurate information. In order to get a better idea of the terrain they had to traverse, patrol leaders flew in light aircraft over the areas to be patrolled. Besides finding some strong enemy positions, many of which the Americans shelled by artillery, the patrols of the 164th noticed increasing movement on the part of the Japanese. Since the jungle and rain forest prevented the Americans from getting much data on Japanese activity, however, aerial observation added little to their knowledge. Although General John R. Hodge, the new commander of the Americal Division, believed that the Japanese were planning something, he had little concrete intelligence upon which he might make decisions. Where was the main body of Japanese forces on the island? What was its strength? Did the enemy have any plans of attack? Since the general wanted some answers to these questions, he offered the troops incentives to bring in Japanese prisoners by issuing the following memorandum:

> The division commander will give one bottle of Scotch liquor and one case of beer for each of the first six prisoners captured.

Additional offers raise the award for the first prisoner to three bottles of Scotch. One bottle of Scotch will also be given for the first officer prisoner, regardless of whether or not he comes within the first six.

The memorandum stipulated that the prisoners must be in good enough physical condition to withstand interrogation and that the offer included only one award per prisoner. Sharers in capture would share in awards.

Although the general was offering an attractive prize, most soldiers in the South Pacific had misgivings about taking Japanese as prisoners of war. Many stories, probably supported by a few incidents, told of how Japanese soldiers, carrying a white flag of surrender, approached American troops only to lob a hand grenade at them. When two or more Japanese surrendered, one might have a light machine gun strapped to his back; when near the Americans, he would bend over so the other could begin firing. Thus most Japanese taken prisoner of war were those physically incapable of resisting. Though the United States had accepted the rules for the treatment of prisoners of war drawn up at the conventions in Geneva during the 1920s, the Japanese had not adopted them. Imbued with the spirit of *bushido*, Japanese soldiers looked upon surrender as an act of supreme cowardice and dishonor. They held in contempt those who did give up, as seen, for example, in their treatment of prisoners during the Bataan death march. Although the Americans and Japanese entered the war with different views about the treatment of prisoners of war, the Americans changed theirs after Bataan. The general rule about taking a Japanese soldier prisoner was not to capture him unless he was absolutely harmless, a situation seldom encountered. Generals might want prisoners for the information they could give, but the front-line soldier had to take the risks. While dead Japanese soldiers told no tales, they also could not harm you.

On 30 January 1944, ten days after the general's memorandum, men of the Americal brought in a Japanese prisoner. By this time the division had a full and efficient intelligence section, and these men extracted from the prisoner valuable data, just as General Hodge had hoped. After telling intelligence officers that the Japanese were preparing for a major strike in early March, the prisoner added that they also had supplies to sustain them only through that month. Shortly thereafter, papers found on a dead Japanese officer revealed the time and place of the attack in such detail that the Americans knew as much about the plans as did the Japanese. They also had learned of the extensive artillery that the Japanese had laboriously placed behind ridges overlooking the American sector. These valuable pieces of information enabled the Americans to make preparations for the assault as their patrols stepped up their reconnaissance in areas in front of the perimeter. Accompanying the patrols, artillery observers called for fire whenever scouts ascertained an exact location of Japanese troops and guns. Because of this harassment, the Japanese had to abandon one of their primary trails and make a new one farther from the American lines.

The Americans made good use of the time available before the anticipated assault by strengthening their positions. Flanked on the left by the 145th Regiment of the 37th Division and on the right by the 182nd of the Americal, the 164th was almost in the middle of the perimeter, a likely spot for an attack, even though the 164th occupied the available high ground of this sector. Clearing fields of fire fifty yards or deeper and stringing double apron wire in their front, the North Dakotans also set booby traps at likely areas of entry and prepared fire pots of sand and gasoline to give illumination at night. Contrary to the official Table of Equipment, each squad now had two Browning Automatic Rifles for additional firepower. If the Japanese were looking for trouble, the position of the 164th was a good place to find it.

Once again General Hyakutake devised a grand strategy, this time to drive the Americans from Bougainville. The plan resembled the ill-fated ones he had drawn up for the recapture of Guadalcanal in that he divided his forces into three prongs to assault the American perimeter. In counting on his artillery to destroy the three airstrips, he planned to negate any advantage of air control the Americans had. He also arranged for an amphibious landing east of the American perimeter to catch the Americans off guard, confuse them, and drive them into artillery range. Rabaul would furnish the usual air support. The Japanese navy did not figure prominently in Hyakutake's scheme, however, as it had on Guadalcanal, for the simple reason that it was no longer an effective force in the region of the Solomons. Consisting of four 150mm, two 105mm, and over one hundred fifty 77mm guns, each of which had about three hundred rounds of ammunition, his artillery had to suffice for the destruction of the airstrips.

Hyakutake's plan had fatal flaws. Although he had estimated the American force at thirty thousand, including only twenty thousand combat troops, it actually had twice that number. To carry out the attack, Hyakutake had slightly over fifteen thousand men, many of whom were exhausted, wracked by malaria, and demoralized. He had diminished their effectiveness by dividing them into three sections, each to strike from a different direction and separated from the others by about two miles. Though the Japanese air forces had bombed the area held by the Americans whenever weather permitted, they had done little damage. Their pilots lacked good training and often approached Empress Augusta Bay across open water, where American radar picked them up in plenty of time for American pilots to intercept them or alert antiaircraft gunners of their altitude and course. Air support for the Japanese assault was virtually nil.

On 8 March 1944, the Japanese struck. Concentrating on the bomber strips, their artillery pounded that general area but in the process often gave away their own positions. When the American pilots took to the air, they bombed these positions heavily while American artillery zeroed in on them. After the Japanese found the range of the airstrips, however, all except six American planes left for the safety of New Georgia. Japanese ground forces began their attack on the American perimeter and the battle was joined. Fortunately for the 164th, none of the three prongs of the assault was at its sector of the defense line. But the 182nd, on its right flank, found itself facing heavy pressure from the enemy.

One particular area of intense combat, a hill shaped like an hourglass, lay about 800 yards out from the main perimeter. Crowned by a huge tree some 150 feet tall, the hill made an excellent observation post for whoever held it. The men of the 182nd had occupied the rise and named it the OP tree, but since the hill, numbered 260, protruded so far beyond the main defenses, it was vulnerable to Japanese attack. A "sore thumb stuck out into the poison ivy," it became the scene of heavy fighting. The newly formed flame thrower platoon and Company G of the 164th were temporarily assigned to the 182nd to give that regiment some help.

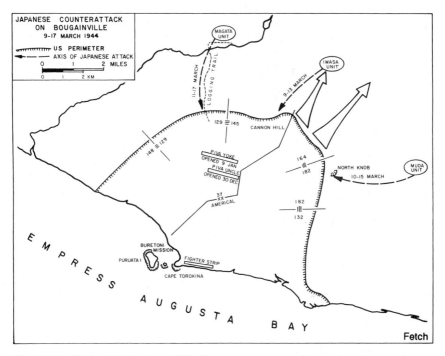

Until 1916, all federal legislation and War Department correspondence referred to state troops as "Organized Militia." I have generally avoided the phrase in order to be consistent and limit confusion.

After the Japanese captured the OP tree, the troops of the 182nd made several valiant efforts to dislodge the enemy but could not do so. American artillery fired directly at the tree in an attempt to topple it, but it also had no success. Digging a tunnel toward the tree with the idea of burning it up with gasoline or blowing it up with dynamite, soldiers unknowingly tunneled into a Japanese pillbox, fortunately unoccupied at the time. They then poured several gallons of gasoline into it, hoping to burn the exposed roots of the tree. Though the first attempt to ignite the gasoline by flame throwers failed, the second succeeded. Smoke and flames poured out of the bunker's holes but, in spite of being shelled above the ground and burned beneath, the mighty tree still stood. After considering a combined tank and infantry assault, the American commanders discarded the idea because the hill was too steep for the tanks. Finally they decided to have patrols harass the Japanese, keeping them hemmed in, while artillery and mortars pounded them into impotence. At the same time, the Japanese withdrew, leaving only a small force to cover the movement. Then, as if to show both sides the futility of the struggle, the OP tree fell with a mighty crash. The provisional flame thrower platoon of the 164th had suffered fifteen casualties, about one-third its strength, in the battle. Perhaps never in the annals of warfare had soldiers spent so much effort, ammunition, and blood for the possession of one tree.

While this battle raged, the 164th continued to send out patrols to gather as much information as possible about Japanese strength and dispositions beyond their sector of the perimeter. Although they found may dead Japanese, killed by American artillery and mortars, and a few small patrols and positions, they discovered nothing of any great strength. Nonetheless, Japanese artillery and mortar fire did cause some casualties in the perimeter of the 164th. Near the end of March 1944, the Japanese assault gave out. After General Hyakutake ordered a systematic withdrawal of his men, the complexion of the campaign on Bougainville changed.

When it became apparent that the Japanese attack had spent itself, the Americans changed their tactics. Up to that time, they had been establishing and defending a perimeter that protected three airstrips as well as patrolling areas in front of the line, though not as part of a coordinated offensive. Now they assumed the initiative and began to pursue the enemy over the vast stretches of jungled mountains and ravines, their new objective being to eliminate all Japanese resistance on Bougainville. Thus began an operation characterized by constant patrolling to find the enemy, the widespread use of mortar and artillery to shell his positions, and, if necessary, the rooting out of the Japanese at close range with rifles, machine guns, and hand grenades. The men of the 164th had trained extensively in operations with tanks on Fiji but to little avail. Although the Americans had plenty of tanks on Bougainville, the terrain did not afford them much opportunity to use them in the offensive. Air support could not contribute much because from the air one jungle ridge looked much like all the others, even on a bright, clear day. The new tactics thus depended primarily upon the infantry and artillery.

Although General Hyakutake had lost the battle of the perimeter, he had not given up hope that he might salvage victory in the long run. The Japanese still held six airfields on Bougainville, though they had been bombed into disrepair. They could get supplies of men, ammunition, and rations from Rabaul, only three hundred miles away, and the Japanese navy had not lost its potency, though it had sought refuge at Truk from American bombers. In his usual optimism, or due to lack of accurate intelligence about the American force on Bougainville (he still believed it numbered about thirty thousand, less than half its strength), Hyakutake decided to prevent the Americans from controlling as much of the island as possible, while awaiting reinforcements. To accomplish this, he ordered the establishment of strongholds at key positions along the native trails, the main transportation arteries on Bougainville. The Americans showed their penchant for exaggerated terminology by calling these positions "roadblocks."

On 1 April 1944, Company F, on patrol in search of possible roadblocks, departed from bivouac with a four-day supply of K rations and a Japanese prisoner who had promised to show them "some interesting places." After climbing ridges all morning, the patrol stopped to eat and rest. Shortly thereafter a torrential rain fell, making the trail so slippery that the men had to pull themselves up the steep grade by hanging onto branches and vines. By late afternoon, although thoroughly exhausted, they had only a short distance to go to reach the top of the highest ridge in the area. The men knew that this offered a likely place for Japanese troops, since it commanded the trail for hundreds of yards in either direction. Sergeant Miles Shelley from Carrington, an experienced scout, and Private First Class Leonard Drabus of Kenmare volunteered to reconnoiter the area before the rest of the company proceeded. Several silent moments later shots rang out. Leading the company, the third platoon rushed forward to form a skirmish line and found that Shelley had been hit close to a Japanese roadblock.

A short but furious battle developed as the Americans fired back, though they could not see the Japanese. After crawling into a slight depression despite being paralyzed from the waist down, Shelley began to direct the fire of his comrades. A man with a Browning Automatic Rifle tried to reach him but had to withdraw under withering fire. A hand grenade had bounced off his back and rolled into the depression where Shelley still directed fire. Although it exploded, it did not silence Sergeant Shelley. Shortly thereafter, the Japanese officer in command decided that the Americans were in disarray. Brandishing his samurai sword, he shouted *banzi* and led a charge into the Americans, he and over a dozen of his men falling to their deaths almost instantly. Then the firing stopped as suddenly as it had started. Though the men of Company F hastily threw up a stronger defense line, the Japanese did not come again. Having had enough, they began to retire. Sergeant Shelley had died, still giving firing directions to his comrades. He became the sixth, and last, member of the 164th to earn the Distinguished Service Cross.

Four of the men of Company F had received serious wounds in the fray, and the medics had done all they could do, which was to administer plasma and morphine. Now the company faced the task of evacuating them. The men knew nothing about the terrain of the shortest route, an area occupied by Japanese in strength. Using the safest route, the way the company had come earlier that day, meant moving the wounded down one steep ridge, up another, and down again before coming to a road large enough for the jeeps. Furthermore, it was humanly impossible for litter bearers to carry the wounded over the long, steep, and slippery trail. Then some unknown hero came up with an idea.

Now reasonably sure that the Japanese had abandoned the roadblock under heavy American artillery, the company formed a human conveyor belt by lining men up on each side of the trail and passing the litters along. As they passed the last litter, the men moved ahead to keep the lines continuous. Fortunately, Company G came to the scene and helped by cutting steps into the sides of the steep slopes and joining in the line. By this time darkness had overtaken the area; though the moon was full, its light seldom penetrated the dense vegetation. The commanding officers radioed a request for the air force to drop flares in the region to give the men some light. It did so—at dawn. When the men reached a reasonably flat area, they caught a few moments of sleep before the litters caught up with them. At dawn, other men of the 164th began to hack a trail wide enough for a jeep toward the direction of the oncoming litter bearers. By midmorning the wounded had reached a battalion aid station. Thoroughly exhausted, the men of companies F and G dragged their weapons, packs, and weary bodies to the water tanks where they gulped down full canteen cups of the refreshing liquid. Later they ate pancakes and coffee, brought to them from a distant field kitchen. Although not fresh off the griddle, the pancakes tasted better than K rations. Some of the men joked about putting in for overtime and others wondered if they had gained any points toward rotation, but not one of them complained. They had saved the lives of four comrades.

When the men of the 164th talked about rotation, they were hoping that a new policy announced by the United States Army might apply to them. First explained in War Department circular number 58, dated 9 February 1944, this policy provided the guidelines for the return to the United States of men who had been in the service and overseas for the longest periods of time. Although the specific guidelines were left to the theater commander, the circular singled out as eligible "those with the longest service in command or those with the longest service overseas." Many in the 164th qualified on both counts. But that rose called rotation had many thorns. The wheels of the Army's bureaucracy turned slowly, if at all, and the circular stated that eligibility constituted only a "basis for selection, the actual relief being dependent upon the personnel situation, exigencies of the service and prosecution of the war." Also, many of the junior officers of the 164th had only recently come to the unit and therefore lacked the knowledge and experience of the hardened veterans. One platoon leader later recalled that when he received orders to patrol an assigned sector, he called the veteran noncommissioned officers together, related the orders to them, and then relied upon their judgment. He admitted: "I would have been a damn fool to tell them what to do. They knew more about it than I did." Thus, many of the veterans were necessary for the "prosecution of the war." Only a few of the men of the 164th enjoyed the fruits of rotation while the regiment was still on Bougainville.

During April and May 1944, when combing their sector in search of the enemy, the patrols of the regiment found only small, isolated groups of Japanese, who had set up roadblocks and ambushes or were simply on the move, probably in search of their unit. The men of the 164th often came upon abandoned artillery and ammunition dumps. In the first week of April Company K destroyed six artillery placements and nearly five hundred rounds of ammunition, mostly 77 mm. The company also captured an unestimated number of small areas, a testimony to the effectiveness of American artillery.

Patrols began to assume a pattern that continued throughout the Bougainville campaign. Ranging from platoon to company in strength, they also had a forward artillery observer, native guides, and pack carriers to accompany them. If the men found an abandoned Japanese position, they examined it for documents that might contain valuable information. Whenever they sighted Japanese soldiers, whether in roadblocks, bivouac, or just moving about, the forward artillery observer called for fire or asked an aerial observer to ascertain the exact position. Aerial observers, flying small Cubs, could flit in and out of ravines or over ridges, thus getting a better view than ground observers, whose sight was hindered by dense vegetation. If artillery could not reach the target, a relatively new weapon, the 4.2 chemical mortar, might be used. Only if the Japanese were out of range of both artillery and mortars did the patrol take action to eliminate them with small-arms fire. If the patrol remained out from its base overnight, it found a suitable place to dig in before darkness and lined the area to its front with bobby traps and other devices to warn the men in case of Japanese attempts to infiltrate the position. Empty cartridge clips hung on wire often sufficed. The men then had to take turns remaining awake and on the alert for enemy movement. At daylight they heated a little water over a portable gas burner, if they had one, for the morning instant coffee, which helped wash down the inevitable K ration. Then "move out—five pace intervals—no talking," the start of another day much like yesterday, to be spent taking one cautious step after another and always looking for danger. Little wonder the average infantryman became a bit surly when ordered to go on a four- or five-day patrol.

Beside patrolling, the men of the 164th also set up their own ambushes and roadblocks. By the middle of 1944 they realized that the Japanese on Bougainville were not gathered in a single, cohesive force, but rather had scattered into many relatively small groups. Often moving about, the Japanese were either patrolling in search of Americans or just looking for other Japanese troops with which to carry on the war. Natives kept the Americans well informed of the movements that took place along their main trails. At key positions, such as the junction of two or more main trails, men of the 164th set up strongholds or ambushes, letting the enemy come to them. Although not many did, these tactics did prevent the Japanese from combining into one strong unit.

The veterans of the regiment noticed that the Japanese on Bougainville did not have the aggressive fighting spirit displayed on Guadalcanal. By the summer of 1944, they seemed content to remain behind their defenses and let the Americans come to them. Some Japanese still capable of fighting offered to surrender, unlike those on Guadalcanal. On almost every front the war was going badly for them, causing morale among many of the Japanese to fall. Their security measures, always lax, became more so on Bougainville, and the men of the 164th took advantage of this condition.

On patrol, the new divisional Intelligence and Reconnaissance Platoon discovered many Japanese living in grass huts. Initially counting only five huts, they later discovered many more, indicating a sizable force. After withdrawing out of sight, the platoon called for help in attacking the area. The nearest available troops were the men of the Antitank Company, for all practical purposes a line unit most of the time, simply because the Japanese had no tanks left on Bougainville. On 3 August 1944, after enveloping the huts, on signal the two units opened fire with rifles, Browning automatics, and light machine guns. After raking the huts for several minutes, they ceased fire and waited to see if any Japanese tried to escape. None did, and, aware of the presence of a large Japanese force in the vicinity, the men of the 164th retired. Later reconnaissance revealed that they had killed over twenty-five enemy officers and enlisted men. Besides illustrating how adept the 164th had become at jungle fighting, this incident also showed that the Japanese were not taking even the most elementary security measures to prevent surprise attack.

By the autumn of 1944, Japanese resistance on Bougainville consisted mainly of small, isolated groups with little means or will to carry on the struggle. Reinforcement was out of the question, for the Japanese had bigger problems elsewhere. Unit reports of the 164th indicate that its patrols ranged far afield without seeing the enemy. By this time, less than half the regiment was patrolling or occupying roadblocks and ambush sites; most of the 164th were in bivouac undergoing unit training exercises, usually in platoon and company strength. While some of the training involved target practice on the firing range, part of it consisted of combined infantry and tank operations. Throughout December the entire regiment took part in bivouac training for the next campaign. Although it had received over three hundred replacements while on Bougainville, the regiment still fell short of full strength by about two hundred men when it left that island.

Considering the length of the campaign, the 164th had not suffered many casualties: 35 members of the regiment had been killed in action and 153 wounded. Throughout the final three months on Bougainville, the 164th had no casualties at all. The number of men who required medical attention for various tropical diseases decreased dramatically, especially those with malaria. This may have been due to what the Medical Department termed "malaria discipline," namely taking regular doses of Atabrine. Perhaps some of the veterans had acquired a degree of immunity to the disease after heavy infestation on Guadalcanal. For whatever reasons, the regiment had suffered less disease in spite of the fact that Bougainville was considered as malarial as other Solomon Islands.

The nature of the campaign did not lend itself to heroism that qualified for major decorations. Sergeant Shelley had earned the Distinguished Service Cross, and the regimental field on Bougainville was named Shelley Field in his honor. The number of decorations received fell considerably short of those awarded for action on Guadalcanal, but the Bougainville campaign had been much less intense. Also, the 164th did not fight in the thick of the big battle on the perimeter as it had on Guadalcanal.

In November 1944, the 164th received orders to begin extensive training for offensive combat "elsewhere in the Pacific area." Although a schedule of exercises, especially company and battalion attacks with close artillery support, began immediately, the regiment did not complete the schedule. On 18 December, after receiving orders to make preparations for a "shore to shore movement," all units began to crate and pack equipment for departure from Bougainville on the first available transportation. By 4 January 1945, the 164th began embarking on vessels anchored in Empress Augusta Bay, completing the task within four days. The first transports left on 8 January, the last, two days later. The ships carrying the 164th rendezvoused at Hollandia, New Guinea, where they joined several cargo ships, destroyers, and other escorts to form a convoy. After sailing from Hollandia, on 21 January they arrived at Leyte, Philippine Islands.

Four Army divisions had invaded Leyte on 20 October 1944, in the first of many engagements to liberate the Philippines from Japanese control. The Japanese again had devised a complicated strategy to repel the Americans by combining air, naval, and ground forces, this plan calling for the Japanese to allow the large American convoy to proceed unmolested to the landing area. After they arrived, the Japanese intended to spring the trap by launching a massive aerial attack accompanied by a large, three-pronged naval operation. Following its success, ground forces would complete the annihilation of the Americans. But the plan had gone awry. Bad weather delayed the air strike for three days, and, though Japanese bombers did inflict damage to American supplies that clogged the beachhead, the material loss was not crucial to the Americans. After meeting total disaster in the Battle of Leyte Gulf, the Japanese navy ceased to be a threat to Leyte or, for that matter, to any future American campaign. Meanwhile, the Americans increased their holdings on Leyte day by day.

The Japanese high command could not agree as to what to do about Leyte. While Imperial Headquarters believed that the decisive battle for all the Philippines was taking place there, area army commanders disagreed. General Tomojuki Yamashita, the "tiger of Malaya" who commanded the Fourteenth Area Army headquartered in Manila, regarded Leyte as a lost cause and thought that the Japanese should concentrate on defending Luzon. Opting for the defense of Leyte, however, his superiors ordered him to send reinforcements there. Yamashita, obedient officer that he was, complied, and more Japanese troops began to join the one division on Leyte. Although many of those sent arrived with limited supplies, others did not reach Leyte at all, owing to an alert United States Navy. Nonetheless, the thousands of reinforcements Yamashita dispatched to Leyte prolonged the battle beyond the date set for completion. Perhaps this condition prompted General Douglas MacArthur to make the statement on 27 December 1944 that Leyte was "secure" and that the "Leyte-Samar campaign can now be regarded as closed except for minor mopping up."

The phrase "mopping up" had different meanings to different people. To General MacArthur, it probably suggested that he could now forget Leyte and proceed with plans to retake the apple of his eye, Luzon. To the war correspondents covering Leyte, it was a message to put away their typewriters and prepare for the main event. To the mothers who had sons on Leyte, it most likely said that they could cease their worries for the time being because their sons were now safe. For many American civilians, mopping up in all likelihood meant that a few soldiers now had to go out and either shoot or capture fewer Japanese, who were completely helpless, and then return in time for the evening meal and the latest movie. But for the infantrymen doing the mopping, it amounted to endless weeks of gut-wrenching combat, exhausting ridges to climb, and day after day of contact with an enemy who often vowed to take as many Americans to their deaths as he possibly could. The vast divergences in interpretation of the meaning of the phrase were vividly portrayed on Leyte. After the general's premature pronouncement, over a thousand Americans died in combat there, about one-fourth of the total killed on that island. Furthermore, the fighting continued for nearly four months thereafter, a longer period of time than the campaign that secured the island. To many infantrymen, the person who first used the phrase "mopping up" had created a cruel hoax.

On 28 January 1945, the men of the 164th began to take up positions at Valencia, Ormoc, and Palompon, relieving troops of the 77th Infantry Division. During the 1st Battalion's first night at Valencia, three Japanese attempted to infiltrate its position. The next day, in a series of combat patrols in front of its sector, the battation killed twenty-four Japanese without suffering a casualty. The other battalions had just taken up their positions when trouble in the Villaba area changed the tactical situation, and Company K, reinforced, boarded four Landing Craft Medium and departed for that town.

The Americans planned to take Villaba and turn it over to Filipino troops, who were still supposed to be there. Company K expected to land at a peaceful village and meet Japanese resistance some distance to the east. The men had a big surprise. The Filipino troops had left Villaba for reasons unknown, not taking the trouble to inform the United States Army of their departure. As the men of Company K began to debark at a pier, a hail of machine gun bullets greeted them. Hastily advancing through the town, they found the Japanese on a small ridge and forced them to withdraw. That night the company built a defensive perimeter around the town, and the Japanese attacked after dark. Not successful in penetrating the defense, the assault cost the Japanese eighteen men. Initial patrols and information gained from natives indicated that many Japanese were east of Villaba, so Company L joined K for operations in that area.

While Company K was having its surprise, the 1st and 2nd battalions patrolled as far as two miles in all directions from Valencia, killing thirty-two Japanese and capturing four more. Some of these Japanese, obviously service troops, were ill trained in the use of small arms, but they chose to die fighting rather than surrender. After nearly two weeks of combat, the men of the 164th became aware that they were fighting against two distinct types of Japanese. One kind, battle-wise and familiar with their weapons, had robbed the countryside of food, gathered ammunition, and taken up positions on terrain to their advantage. In spite of the hopelessness of their situation, they were willing to fight to the death for country and Emperor. The other kind were soldiers lost from their units, confused, weary, and hungry, often men who knew nothing about combat, who had been trained in some technical specialty, and had never heard a shot fired until the Americans came. But the men of the 164th had no way of knowing which sort of troops they faced until the shooting had ended. They still tended not to take prisoners, even though an increasing number of Japanese were willing to quit the fight. That number, however, still amounted to a minute fraction of the Japanese forces on Leyte.

On 8 February 1945, the 164th took up new positions in order to establish bases nearer the enemy. The 1st and 2nd battalions began to operate out of Dipi and Soong respectively, both having as their objectives coastal regions to the west. Thus the two battalions began a coordinated push toward the sea to clear out all enemy in the area. After completion of that phase of the campaign, plans called for the two battalions to swing north while the 3rd Battalion, operating from Villaba, pushed to the east to cut off any attempt by the Japanese to escape in that direction. The 182nd Regiment had the assignment of coming from the east and completing the encirclement of the enemy. At this early stage of the campaign, the men of the 164th had little idea of the number of Japanese in the pocket they were forming. The intelligence sections of the 77th and 7th infantry divisions, both of which had campaigned in that sector prior to turning operations over to the Americal Division, estimated a minimum of three thousand enemy in the region where the 164th and 182nd were carrying out their maneuvers. They probably estimated low, for neither of these divisions had patrolled the area near Villaba extensively.

Although the Japanese had made plans to evacuate most of their troops from Leyte, especially those men still in good health and capable of continuing the fight, their project had run afoul of the United States' air forces after removing only a little over seven hundred men from the island. Thus at least eight thousand Japanese remained on Leyte to offer what resistance they could muster and eventually die. On 19 December 1944, General Yamashita informed Japanese commanders on Leyte that they could no longer expect to receive reinforcements or supplies. General Sosaku Suzuki, commander of the Leyte forces, devised a scheme whereby many of the Japanese would occupy a high plateau located to the southeast of the Villaba area. He had instructed the men staging there to bring as many arms with them as possible. After he had taken measures to ensure adequate food by having his men systematically loot the countryside, he told them to become self-sufficient by planting fields of corn and beans for future sources of food. Then, having made all these plans, General Suzuki departed from Leyte on the first available boat. He had left behind at least three thousand Japanese in northwestern Leyte, where the terrain favored the defenders, and who allegedly had ample supplies for weeks to come. The 164th was headed in their direction.

When they began their push westward, the 1st and 2nd battalions soon found scattered groups of enemy soldiers, most of them probably trying to find their way to the region designated by General Suzuki. In the first three days of this sweep the 2nd Battalion alone killed ninety-eight Japanese while the 1st Battalion killed twenty-nine and captured one. After extending its perimeter, the 3rd Battalion started to probe for Japanese positions, which they soon encountered and upon which they inflicted light casualties, while suffering three men killed and four wounded. Here, in this area near Villaba, the 164th found the first line of defenses planned by Suzuki. Reports indicated that the Japanese soldiers there were well armed, in good health, and some of them even had new uniforms.

On 11 February 1945, two battalions of the 96th Filipino Army Regiment joined the 1st and 2nd battalions on their push to the sea. Moving westward from Valencia, two batteries of artillery gave closer support to the infantry as more isolated groups of Japanese fell victim to the assault. Company E

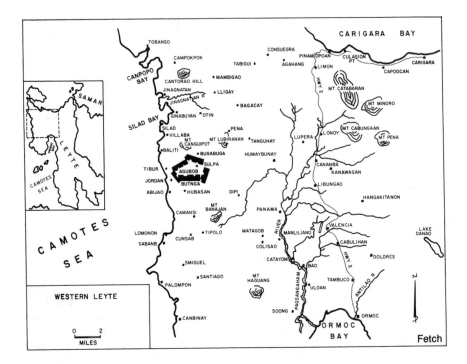

was especially active, its patrols killing over fifty enemy one afternoon while it suffered only one man killed and two wounded. But the 1st Battalion, on the right flank of the sweep, began to run into Japanese who were well dug in and had a variety of weapons, including mortars and machine guns. It, too, had come upon the first line of defenses surrounding the plateau that General Suzuki had selected for the major defense system of the region. The 3rd Battalion continued to patrol its area and awaited the arrival of Company I, which had been patrolling territory around Palompon.

On 16 February 1945, the 1st Battalion reached the sea at Abijao and immediately established a perimeter on high ground around the town. During this action, Company A had two men wounded, one of whom was evacuated by helicopter, at that time an awkward-looking machine with unrealized potential. A forward artillery observer and a cub pilot also sustained wounds, the latter when his plane crashed as he was trying to drop fresh radio batteries to the infantry. A hastily devised patrol rescued him just beyond the perimeter lines. After regrouping near San Miguel, the 2nd Battalion began to push north to meet the 1st Battalion. It ran into several small groups of Japanese, which its records describe as "stragglers and foraging groups." The 3rd Battalion, having come upon enemy defensive positions, began to attack from its Villaba area. Company L hit a well dug-in and armed position to its front, killing four Japanese but suffering one man killed and five wounded in the exchange.

While the 2nd Battalion was continuing its sweep northward toward the 1st Battalion, the latter began to send patrols out to probe for enemy positions. Although these patrols found none, during the night of 17 February 1945, some Japanese did succeed in infiltrating its lines and throwing hand grenades among the men, wounding four. After setting up a machine gun position on a ridge near Company C, another small group of the enemy fired into its perimeter and wounded two men. Once again Company L hit the Japanese northeast of Villaba, and once again it had to withdraw, having been met by a hail of mortar and heavy machine gun fire. Company K, however, patrolled as far as twenty-five hundred yards to the southeast without running into a single enemy position, killing thirty-seven Japanese without suffering one casualty.

By 21 February 1945, after the 2nd Battalion had come abreast of the 1st, the push to the north had begun. A short distance north of Abijao, the 1st Battalion ran into heavy enemy fire from small mortars and light machine guns. Before long the battalion received fire from three sides and retired to establish a perimeter east of Abijao. The sharp fighting caused the Japanese to lose sixty-four killed and an undetermined number wounded while the 1st Battalion lost nine men killed in action and thirty-five wounded. The 3rd Battalion, still in the Villaba area, began to experience enemy attacks on its positions. Japanese using knee mortars, grenade launchers, and automatic weapons attacked both Companies K and L. Although the companies repulsed the assaults, these attacks indicated that at least some of the Japanese troops were not willing to concede Leyte to the enemy, even though the odds overwhelmingly favored the Americans.

Some of the Japanese troops had lost the fighting spirit often displayed in the early part of the war, but they somehow managed to escape the trap formed by the Americal Division and roamed about in areas formerly covered by patrols. Thus the Americans received reports of Japanese troops near Palompon, an area United States troops had combed at least twice. Since the battalions of the 164th and other regiments of the Americal had not yet made contact with one another, the gaps between them allowed some Japanese to avoid being surrounded. Therefore, in these areas the AntiTank, Service, and Cannon companies patrolled daily and often found some stragglers.

Other Japanese tried to break out of the trap by attacking the Americans, probably in the hope that they might get through a patrol or perimeter to relative safety and plentiful supplies of food. Some of these attempts employed night attacks similar to but on a much smaller scale than those the 164th had experienced on Guadalcanal. On the night of 23-24 February, about thirty Japanese, trying to infiltrate the perimeter between Companies E and G, were thrown back with heavy losses after they killed one American and wounded another. At the northern end of the operation, the Japanese, using machine guns, small and large mortars, and rifle fire, assaulted companies I and K shortly after midnight. Although the attack did not succeed in denting the perimeter, five Japanese, all killed, had come within hand grenade range of the lines.

By the end of February, the 1st and 2nd battalions were attempting to make contact with the 3rd along the coast between Abijao and Baliti. Troops of the 3rd Battalion were also trying to reach the men of the 182nd Regiment. But the Japanese did not cooperate. When the 2nd Battalion ran into about two hundred enemy troops, well dug in but rather widely spread, artillery and mortar fire supported its attack on their positions. After suffering many casualties, the Japanese withdrew under cover of darkness; the battalion had lost two men killed and fifteen wounded. By this time the Americans knew that the 164th was reaching some of the inner defensive positions of the enemy, pushing against increasing numbers of Japanese who had more and superior weapons and were better prepared to resist the advancing Americans than the stragglers first encountered in the campaign. As the area they controlled became smaller, the Japanese prepared more elaborate defensive positions to protect themselves from the inevitable mortar and artillery fire. The Americans began to realize that, in spite of having been abandoned and written off by their commanders, the Japanese troops in that area of Leyte had no intention of surrendering. The 164th and other regiments of the Americal continued to tighten the noose.

The men of the 164th never had the chance to take part in the final victory in northwestern Leyte. On 8 March 1945, the 1st and 2nd battalions received orders to move from their respective positions back to Abijao and, from there, redeploy to the Ormoc, Valencia, and Palompon areas. The 3rd Battalion, however, was instructed to return to Villaba (near Baliti), relieve troops of the 182nd Regiment in that region, and wait for further orders. On 10 March 1945, the 164th was released from the command of the Americal Division and was placed under that of the Eighth Army, their mission being that of "continuing offensive operations against and destroying the enemy on Leyte Island." In addition, the regiment was ordered to be prepared by 24 March to move on twenty-four-hour notice to support operations of the Eighth Army. So, awaiting the arrival of other units, the men of the 164th began to get ready for redeployment.

The 164th continued fighting for several days after receiving their orders, however, because the regiment had to wait for its relief and then brief it on the tactical situation after it arrived. In addition, though the relieving unit, the 108th Regimental Combat Team, began to arrive on 12 March, it did not complete taking up the positions of the 164th until 23 March. During that interlude, the 164th continued to send patrols out daily to contact the enemy and, on occasion, to repulse an attack on some sector of its perimeter. By 24 March, the 164th was in bivouac, going over the lessons learned on Leyte and drawing up another training schedule for the next campaign. Meanwhile, the regiment served as the Eighth Army reserve.

Before the Leyte mopping up, the 164th had acquired the reputation of being jungle fighters, having spent nearly four hundred days in jungle combat, perhaps more than any other Army unit in the Pacific. The jungle and terrain of northwestern Leyte fostered the same fighting conditions the men had encountered on Guadalcanal and Bougainville. The wealth of experience they had gained there they put to good use on Leyte. By actual count, the 164th had killed 2,010 Japanese, wounded an unestimated number, and taken 18 prisoners of war, while suffering 86 killed in action and 278 wounded, a few by defective American mortar rounds. The "kill ratio" of the regiment during the Leyte campaign had been twenty-four to one, an unusually high one considering that the 164th fought offensively throughout the entire campaign.

By the beginning of April 1945, the 164th had lost much of its North Dakota character. While at Camp Claiborne, it had absorbed almost one thousand men, mostly from the Upper Midwest, to bring it to full strength. The regiment received some replacements before shipping overseas and about eleven hundred more after Guadalcanal. Over four hundred more replacements came after Bougainville. These two sets of replacements had brought in about half the regiment's full strength from outside North Dakota. Also, more defined but complex criteria of eligibility for rotation qualified most of the original members of the unit for return to the United States. As the war in Europe was rapidly coming to the inevitable surrender of Germany, the military might of the United States began to shift to the Pacific. Since the Army could now afford to send most of the weary, battle-worn veterans of the Pacific home, many of the former Guardsmen of the 164th received the joyous notice that their days in the rotten jungles were drawing to an end. It was now a regiment North Dakotan in its origin but American in its personnel, but it still carried the same pride that it had displayed so well on Guadalcanal.

Before the Leyte campaign ended, the Americal Division received orders to prepare for Operation Victor-2, the conquest of, and the restoration of civil government to, the Philippine Islands of Cebu, Bohol, and Negros Oriental. Of these, according to all intelligence reports, Cebu, defended by the largest Japanese force, ranked first. Because General William H. Arnold, commander of the division, requested that the two regiments designated for the Cebu invasion be at full strength, some of the men of the 164th were assigned to the 132nd and 182nd regiments. The 164th was to remain on Leyte as Eighth Army reserve, which meant a few days rest for the men. The operation called for the Cebu invasion to take place on 26 March 1945, only a few days after the 164th had turned over their Leyte positions to other troops. The men of the regiment probably shed no tears over remaining on Leyte as a reserve unit.

Primarily because of the excellent harbor facilities at Cebu City, the island of Cebu became an important objective in the Philippines. The harbor, the second largest in all the islands (Manila had the largest), could handle up to ten Liberty Ships at one time. Because of its large capacity for cargo, Cebu City made an ideal staging area for future operations and General Headquarters, Southwest Pacific Area, had already selected it as a site from which American troops would leave en route to the first invasion of the main Japanese islands. A corps of three divisions, consisting of the Americal, the 44th, and the 97th, was to take part in the invasion of Honshu, code named Operation Olympic. Thus, although the Americans had no plans for major air bases on Cebu, the island assumed a key role in their plans.

The Cebu invasion nearly met with disaster. The 132nd and 182nd regiments ran into some well-placed mines at their designated landing beaches. Confusion and hesitation overtook the troops in this, their first

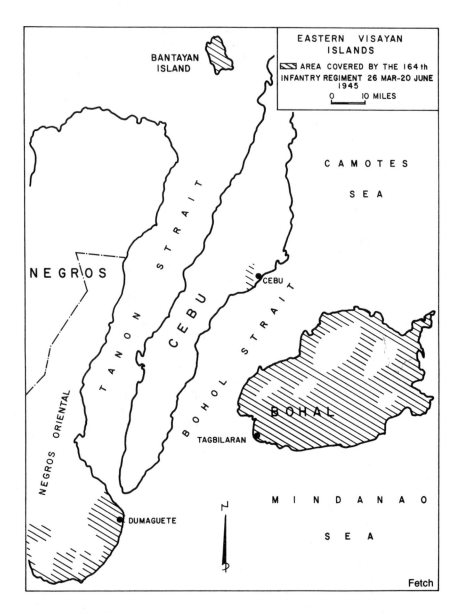

beachhead landing, but fortunately the Japanese had no force in the vicinity large enough to take advantage of the situation. Soon the two regiments established a position on the beaches and proceeded to Cebu City, which they took with little opposition. Intelligence from Filipino guerrillas and sympathetic natives on Cebu revealed that the main force of the Japanese, estimated at 12,500, was located just a few miles to the north and northeast of the city.

Of great concern to General Arnold, the reports also indicated that the Japanese had spent months arranging elaborate defensive positions there. The general had only two regiments at his disposal plus about 8,500 guerrillas, many of whom were still awaiting American arms. General Arnold had little confidence in the untrained guerrillas and did not consider them much of an asset.

As the two Americal regiments probed the Japanese defenses, the general had reason for apprehension about the tactical situation. The Japanese had indeed created extensive defenses. General Suzuki, who had ordered the preparations of the defenses on Leyte and then had departed, did the same on Cebu. After placing General Takeo Manjome in charge of the defenses of the area, Suzuki then departed for Mindanao. Manjome had done an excellent job with the resources available. He had constructed three rings of defensive positions, the inner two with tunnels connecting pillboxes, supply caves, and underground living quarters. He had stockpiled large amounts of ammunition, mostly for small arms, for he lacked artillery except for a few 75 mm guns, and enough food for weeks. Gasoline-powered generators provided electricity to some of the living quarters and supply caves. But Manjome had one very big problem—he lacked men trained for ground combat.

Of the 12,500 people that Manjome commanded, less than 2,000 were really combat troops, of whom some had escaped from Leyte. The rest comprised sailors without ships, air force maintenance men without airplanes, and a conglomeration of service personnel including about 1,500 civilians. Furthermore, their morale was quite low because of the adverse news about Leyte, Luzon, and, after 1 April 1945, the invasion of Okinawa. Undoubtedly the refugees from Leyte brought with them information about the formidable American forces in the Philippines. In spite of the propaganda still coming from the homeland, the realistic Japanese must have known that the Japanese sun was setting.

As the 132nd and 182nd began to penetrate the outer defenses of the enemy, General Arnold reassessed the situation and devised a plan to surround them. The two regiments had formed a front on the southeastern edge of Manjome's positions. If another force could move behind the Japanese to the west and north, General Arnold believed that American artillery, mortars, and bombs would annihilate the entrapped enemy. Thus he called Leyte to have the 164th sent to him immediately. He later recalled that he had pleaded: "Give me the 164th! Give me the 164th and I'll have those babies!" The general was evidently a persuasive man. The Eighth Army released the 164th from reserve and sent the regiment on its way to Cebu.

After landing near Cebu City on 10 April 1945, the 164th bivouacked west of the city. The 3rd Battalion, however, had orders to reload their equipment and themselves for another operation, the invasion of Bohol. The 1st and 2nd battalions got the assignment to proceed up the Mananga River valley, under cover of darkness, and to attack the Japanese from the rear. On the night of 11 April, the two battalions moved out, following the river bank where dense vegetation concealed their position. Although they reached their points of departure the next night, their line was too irregular for a coordinated attack, and they took up a new one twenty-four hours later. On the 14th the

315

164th attacked, as did the other two regiments. Now General Arnold would "have those babies."

But his plans went awry. First, the 164th had lost the element of surprise, and when it attacked, the Japanese were ready. Possibly, the Japanese occupying the high ground in the area detected the movement of the two battalions, even though it had taken place at night. Or a Filipino collaborator

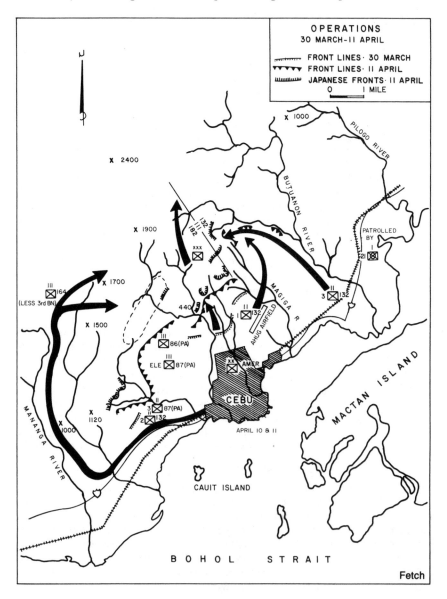

316

may have informed them of the attempted encirclement. Some Filipinos, albeit a small minority, did throw their lot in with the Japanese, even to the extent of fighting with them. Most likely Cebu City, with a population of nearly 150,000, harbored a few of these pro-Japanese natives, any one of whom might have been an informant. Second, and perhaps more important, the American forces never closed the trap envisioned by General Arnold. The 164th was supposed to make contact with the 132nd to seal the Japanese into a pocket, but the 132nd had never located the position that anchored the enemies' left flank. Manjome took advantage of the door left open at that flank. Having devised an evacuation plan before the American invasion, he now began to carry out the plan. The presence of the 164th probably hastened his decision, for it was penetrating his inner defenses.

The attack carried out by the regiment resulted in some bloody fighting, especially in the vicinity of Bagbag Ridge where the Japanese had strong inner defenses. On the afternoon of 15 April, after Company G attacked a hill near the ridge and captured it, a Japanese flare signaled mortar and machine gun crews to fire on the hill. The company had to evacuate after suffering three men killed and forty wounded, but the Antitank Company and the Cannon Company exacted some revenge by destroying most of the mortar and machine gun positions that had fired on Company G. On 17 April, when the company retook the hill and held it, they discovered a network of tunnels and caves and twenty-five dead Japanese who had served as a rear guard.

The 164th pressed the attack, as did the other two regiments, and on 18 April Company F made contact with troops of the 182nd. By this time many of the Japanese had abandoned their strong positions and had left only enough troops on the ridges to protect the withdrawal. As the men of the 164th gained control of the Japanese inner defenses, they came upon caves and tunnels that contained large supplies left behind by the enemy. The regimental S-2 report for 20 April 1945, lists the following captured Japanese arms: an unestimated number of crates of rifles and parts, thirty cases of .30-caliber ammunition, five hundred to a thousand cases of knee mortar ammunition, three hundred to eight hundred cases of 75 mm shells, and seventeen cases of .25-caliber machine gun ammunition. Later discoveries included tons of rice, bundles of new clothing, a phonograph and about a hundred records, and, probably to the amusement of the men, several pieces of women's undergarments. The latter probably belonged to Formosan or Korean women who served in the Japanese "comfort stations" in areas occupied by their troops. The Americans also found several cosmetic kits, bars of soap, and "U.S. issue toiletries."

General Manjome had prepared some of the most formidable positions the men of the 164th had ever seen. One patrol reported discovering a system of tunnels over seven hundred feet long, over five feet high, and four feet wide, with shorter passages off the main tunnel leading to sleeping areas. Heavy timbers reinforced the whole network. A complete telephone system provided communication throughout the entire labrynth. General Robert Eichelberger, commander of the Eighth Army, believed that this defensive stronghold was more formidable than those later encountered on Okinawa.

By 22 April 1945, the two battalions, having helped dislodge the enemy who was now on the run, went into bivouac a short distance from Cebu City and prepared for another operation. They had losses of 19 men killed and 116 wounded in the brief but intense fighting around Bagbag Ridge. The 132nd and 182nd regiments continued the pursuit of the Japanese, who fled northward to join about 2,000 of their countrymen. The men of the 164th had killed 72 Japanese, wounded countless more, and had taken 13 prisoners of war. From them the regimental and divisional intelligence officers learned that Japanese morale was low and that many of the soldiers wanted to surrender but did not do so because they feared reprisals from their officers. Intelligence personnel also learned that the many Korean and Formosan laborers used by the Japanese were becoming a problem because they thought that Japan faced certain defeat in the near future.

After the war, Colonel Satoshi Wada, a divisional chief of staff in the Japanese army who had served on Cebu, ventured the opinion that the Americal Division had tarried too long in attempting encirclement on Cebu. He believed that if the 132nd and 182nd regiments had moved more quickly and shut off the Japanese left flank, they could have wiped out the entire force and spared themselves the weeks of mopping up that followed. He also thought that the movement of the 164th had made little contribution to the campaign, that it had made the wrong move from the wrong direction. But General Arnold had only two regiments to contain the front and encircle the flank until the arrival of the 164th. By then, the Japanese knew they had an escape hatch. This condition probably resulted more from faulty scouting of the Japanese left flank than from poor tactics. Colonel Wada might well have addressed himself to the reason why the Japanese, after constructing such formidable fortifications and stockpiling enough provisions to last for weeks, abandoned the area instead of making a determined stand. The Japanese on Cebu certainly did not show the determination to fight that those on Iwo Jima had in early 1945 or the Japanese were showing on Okinawa, a campaign that began at about the same time as the Cebu invasion.

While the 1st and 2nd battalions were on their way to attack the enemy near Bagbag Ridge, Cebu, the 3rd Battalion received orders to invade the Philippine island of Bohol. Just east of Cebu, Bohol had an area almost as large as Cebu, though it had little strategic value other than its location. Intelligence reports indicated there were probably fewer than 350 Japanese there, of whom less than half were combat troops. Over 4,500 Filipino guerrillas were also on Bohol, but they were untrained and poorly armed. Their assignment had been to harass the Japanese and, in particular, prevent them from obtaining supplies of food. The Americans also counted on them for specific information as to the size and location of the Japanese force. After landing on Bohol on 9 April 1945, a day ahead of schedule, an advance party from division headquarters and the 164th conferred with guerrilla leaders who controlled the landing area. The party learned little about the Japanese at Bohol.

On 10 April the 3rd Battalion made its landing near the only town of the island, Tagbilaran. Artillery, signal, ordnance, engineer, quartermaster, and medical detachments accompanied the battalion. Having encountered no opposition during the landing, the men began to patrol in search of the Japanese. Bohol had a good road system that enabled the fast deployment of troops in the search, but for nearly five frustrating days the battalion found no Japanese. Guerrilla reports did not help, as one said that the enemy was holed up about five miles north of the town while another said that the Japanese had broken up into several small groups seeking cover from the Americans. They were both wrong. On 15 April, a reconnaissance patrol made contact with the enemy near the center of the island. Companies K and L, closest to the area, both hastily made their way to assigned positions in preparation for an attack.

The Japanese had chosen to make their first stand on a ridge that contained some natural caves, but because they lacked strong defenses, the attack of the two companies drove them off the ridge. That night the Japanese launched three counterattacks, all repulsed, and they began to scatter in search of cover. The two companies pursued relentlessly while groups of fifteen or twenty of the enemy took turns fighting rear-guard action. Then, on 20 April, Company I found about 150 more Japanese near the site of the first battle, attacked, and drove the enemy out of their defenses where they abandoned most of their precious supplies. Now the three line companies of the battalion were all in hot pursuit of the harried Japanese. By 25 April, the Americans had destroyed the bulk of the enemy force and the remaining Japanese had scattered throughout the island in an attempt to escape the Americans and guerrillas. On 29 April, the 3rd Battalion, except for Company I, went back to Cebu. After another week of fruitless patrolling in search of the Japanese, Company I also returned to Cebu. The battalion had lost 7 men killed and 14 wounded on Bohol while it had killed at least 104 of the enemy and taken 14 prisoners of war. When the war ended, approximately 50 Japanese on the island surrendered.

The Bohol campaign had turned out to be more of a footrace than other engagements experienced by men of the 164th. But consider the plight of Lieutenant Hadashi Watanabe who commanded the Japanese force there. After having led his men to the center of the island to form as good a defense as possible in the ridges and caves of that area, he then received a radio message that instructed him not to engage the Americans but rather to go to the coast, confiscate native boats, and move his men by water to the island of Negros. Bohol did not offer much cover for moving a company of men from the center to the coast, however, for much of its land was under cultivation and the island had little rain forest or jungle to conceal troop movement. Evidently Watanabe tried to fight and then run, and succeeded in neither, though he did escape to Negros.

Shortly before the 3rd Battalion had finished its assignment on Bohol, the 1st and 2nd battalions received orders to prepare for an amphibious landing on the Philippine Island of Negros. That island had already seen some intensive fighting, the 40th Infantry Division and 503rd Parachute Regiment having fought an enemy force of over 13,500 men in the northern and western sectors. The Americans had the help of about 14,000 guerrillas who, though only half of them were armed, controlled nearly two-thirds of the island. But the guerrillas lacked the training, artillery, and heavy weapons needed to take the offensive, so they often had defensive assignments—to hold areas already taken by the Americans. Approximately one regiment of these guerrillas, over 3,000 in number, was attached to the 164th for the operation in southeastern Negros.

The area of Negros in which the two battalions of the 164th were to engage the enemy was not very large, measuring about twenty miles from east to west and thirty miles from north to south, but it contained some of the most rugged terrain ever encountered by the men. It also had a narrow coastal plain. As the men moved inland, they soon ran into foothills and then mountains, the mountains consisting of a cluster of jagged, forested volcanic peaks culminating in Mt. Cuernos de Negros, over six thousand feet above sea level and only about seven miles from the shore. The dissected nature of the terrain around these mountains made it impossible for the troops to use any type of vehicular transportation. While the men of the 164th had the usual artillery and service units in support, it also had a tank platoon available for its operation. Needless to say, the tank unit saw limited action. Perhaps worse for the infantry, the terrain placed some limitations on the use of the artillery. The advent of the rainy season shortly after the campaign got under way compounded these problems, for the rains caused washouts and small landslides on the few roads the engineers had constructed in the foothills.

Colonel Satoshi Oie, who commanded the Japanese troops in the southeast part of Negros, knew this rugged terrain well and chose to use it to the fullest advantage. Divisional intelligence estimated his force at about eight hundred men, but recent escapees from Cebu, Leyte, and Bohol had swelled these ranks to over thirteen hundred, though less than a thousand of the total had combat training and experience. Making good use of the noncombat soldiers and sailors under his command, the colonel organized them into small units, some of which he ordered to infiltrate American lines and cause whatever damage they could with demolition charges. Still others of these small units served as rear-guard deterrent forces while the main body of Japanese retreated to higher ground farther inland. The journals of the 164th quite accurately referred to these units as "suicide squads."

On 24 and 25 April the men and equipment of the 1st and 2nd battalions boarded the Landing Craft Infantry and Landing Craft Medium. Although the Landing Craft Infantry had about a thirty-five percent overload due to a shortage of these craft, naval officers considered them safe because the Americans had complete mastery of the seas and air, and the voyage was short. On the morning of 26 April 1945, the 1st Battalion, followed by the 2nd, waded ashore not far from Dumaguete, the provincial capitol and a city of over twenty-two thousand. Ironically, it was the first beachhead to be taken by the men of these two battalions and, unknown to them, the beginning of their last operation. The landing took place without casualties, the Japanese having abandoned their positions in the area and moved to higher ground inland. Shortly after coming ashore, officers of the 164th met with those of the guerrillas and of the 40th Infantry Division who had come down the eastern shoreline. From them the 164th learned little about the disposition of the Japanese, so the two battalions began to fan out with patrols to find the enemy.

The 1st Battalion proceeded up the coastal plain toward Dumaguete along a road that the government of Negros had generously designated Highway 1. Guerrillas had informed the Americans of a large number of Japanese pillboxes and land mines in the city, but these reports had been exaggerated. The Japanese had abandoned the pillboxes, and the troops found only four mines, which had been made from bombs and were easily discovered. Dumaguete fell to the Americans without firing a shot, though not without incident. As the men of the 164th approached the far side of the city, shots rang out. The battle-wise veterans could tell from their sound that they had not come from Japanese weapons. Instead they had come from some overly zealous guerrillas who had mistaken the Americans for Japanese but soon recognized their error and ceased firing. Fortunately, because the guerrillas lacked firing skill, no casualties resulted from the error in identity.

The 2nd Battalion began its movement inland along a road and then established a defensive perimeter shortly before darkness set in. It received some machine gun and mortar fire but had no casualties. That night, when about twenty-five of the enemy tried to infiltrate the Americans' line, the alert men placed small-arms fire on them and the next morning the battalion found twelve Japanese and three Filipino dead in their front. (Regimental records refer to Filipino collaborators as "hostile" or "unfriendly.") Continuing its advance up the road the next day, Company E captured one Japanese soldier and two Filipino civilians, whom they interned for future interrogation, and four Japanese trucks. In clearing the area west of Dumaguete, the 1st Battalion discovered no enemy but did find fifteen Japanese vehicles, two generators, a searchlight, and several machine guns. Some of the latter had been stripped from aircraft and modified for use by the infantry.

On the afternoon of their third day on Negros, the men of the 164th began to run into the first of several defensive positions held by Colonel Oie. Making full use of the higher terrain, Colonel Oie had placed men on knobs at the end of steep ridges where they had a good view of the Americans moving parallel to those ridges. Sometimes the Japanese fired on the Americans as soon as they came into sight, but occasionally they waited until the invaders were nearing another knob, at which time both positions opened fire. Since the infantrymen could not scale many of the ridges in the face of enemy fire without sustaining prohibitive casualties, they called upon mortars, artillery, and even light bombers to reduce these positions. As the pressure on the Japanese became too intense, they withdrew on the far side of the ridge to take up or reinforce similar positions farther inland. Company F was the first to experience the difficulties in assaulting one of these positions when, on the afternoon of 28 April, it attacked a ridge and lost five men killed and eight wounded without attaining the objective. The men of the 164th decided to adapt their tactics to this situation by having artillery observers in light aircraft take a close look at the ridges from the air, the engineers having already completed an airstrip for light planes on the coastal plain. The 164th now had the unique experience of looking down upon these light planes as they took off and wound their way upward toward the next ridge, eventually reaching the same altitude as the fighting.

On 30 April 1945, the strong resistance of some of the Japanese defenses prompted the commanding officer, Colonel William J. Mahoney, the sixth consecutive Regular Army man to command the regiment, to try a flanking movement. He redeployed the 1st Battalion so that it could attack the enemy defenses from the north while 2nd Battalion attacked from the east. Thus 1st Battalion left its position, returned to the nearest road, and took vehicles in a route resembling a large U-turn. After that it had a nine-hour trek on foot to arrive at its point of departure, a small mountain village. But when the battalion arrived there, it found no village, even though it had followed the map precisely. A Filipino scout then informed the battalion commander that the village lay nearly two miles away. The explanation for the error was quite simple—the 164th was using inaccurate maps. To compound the problem, a sizable force of Japanese moved in behind the 1st Battalion and cut its supply line. Designed to catch the Japanese by surprise, the flanking movement devised by Colonel Mahoney got off to a ragged beginning. Not all was lost, however, for the 2nd Battalion had continued its push westward and had come upon what it believed was the main enemy force. With some redeployment, it could connect with the 1st Battalion without losing contact with the enemy. The maneuver brought the two battalions abreast approaching a crest that the men christened "rain forest ridge," which was on the northwestern approach to Mt. Cuernos de Negros. They now had the main force of the Japanese to their immediate front, high atop the ridge and well dug in. Colonel Oie and his men had the choice of staying there and taking a pounding by artillery and bombs while starving to death or trying to break out, in which case they would run into the 164th or a reinforced regiment of guerrillas to their rear.

Colonel Oie chose to hold the ridge as long as possible. American artillery, under ordinary conditions, could have pounded the ridge incessantly, but this situation differed. Mt. Cuernos de Negros, which lay to the east of the ridge, actually protected the Japanese from American guns because American artillerymen could only use a very high trajectory and a slight miscalculation meant that the round fell into guerrilla or American lines. The men manning the mortars of the 164th had another, but equally difficult, problem, for they had to fire at a target at a much higher elevation than the mortars. To solve the dilemma, both artillery and mortars fired smoke shells while the aerial artillery observers helped their crews make corrections by observing the smoke and informing the crews of their location. Before long some of the artillery and mortars zeroed in on the ridge as the infantry pressed the attack up the steep slopes. American bombers also lent their support to the operation. In spite of the hopelessness of their position, the Japanese not only hung on but continued to attempt to infiltrate American lines and destroy weapons or kill men with demolition charges. About the middle of May, after Colonel Oie decided to withdraw some of his troops gradually from the ridge, small groups of twenty-five to fifty Japanese left their lines periodically and retreated toward the southwest. The colonel left behind enough men and weapons to hold the ridge, however, and the 164th faced over two weeks of assaulting their positions.

Colonel Mahoney decided to deploy parts of the two battalions to the southern tip of the island to find out if the Japanese had other positions of strength in the mountains. After two companies and one platoon had probed sectors of the area but found only small isolated groups of Japanese, Mahoney concluded that the main force of the enemy was still dug in on "rain forest ridge" and he continued the attacks there. Finally, the Americans took the ridge by the middle of June, enabling the units of the regiment to gather slowly at Dumaguete for return to Cebu. Filipino guerrilla units took over the task of fighting the remaining enemy on the southern end of Negros. Although intelligence officers of the 164th had estimated that about 350 Japanese remained in the vicinity, when the war ended over 800 Japanese laid down their arms. Unfortunately, the end of organized resistance on Negros did not mean the end of hostilities. Filipino guerrillas became undisciplined and began to carry out vendettas against their countrymen, whom the guerrillas often accused, rightly or not, of collaboration. Thus American troops had to occupy the area to control the actions of those who were supposedly allies.

While the 1st and 2nd battalions were completing their campaign on Negros, Company K of the 3rd Battalion received orders to move to Mindanao. American troops were forcing a formidable Japanese force toward the central part of the large island, where the mountainous terrain and jungle afforded the enemy protection. One American regiment had penetrated to the center of Mindanao along a river and road from the north. In doing so, it had stretched its supply line from the north shore inland, thus requiring many men to protect the line and guard the supplies, located at the mouth of the river. Company K was assigned to help guard the supply depot and keep the materiel flowing inland to the area of combat. The company commander later remarked, "I only had an old Standard Oil road map to help me with locations, but we found every place we needed to anyway." The assignment lasted less than a month and the company departed to Cebu to join the other units of the regiment there.

The Negros campaign had cost the 164th only 33 men killed in action while killing 527 Japanese, but 179 of the regiment had sustained wounds and hundreds more had fallen victim to the many tropical diseases common to the area. As rotation continued, it further depleted the combat effectiveness of the regiment. The regiment had fought in four different campaigns in six months, and the strain took a heavy toll. Thus, when the 164th regrouped near Cebu City, it needed hundreds of replacements to bring it up to its authorized strength. By the beginning of August 1945, the 164th had begun unit training exercises in preparation for the invasion of the Japanese island of Kyushu, scheduled for 1 November 1945. Then a series of sudden and dramatic events changed the course of the Pacific war.

On 6 August 1945, the first atomic bomb destroyed the Japanese city of Hiroshima. Two days later Russia, keeping a pledge made to President Roosevelt at Yalta, declared war on Japan, and its armies began an advance over a thousand-mile front into Manchuria and Korea. The next day a second atomic bomb devastated the city of Nagasaki. Japan, now the only Axis power left in the war, reeled from one disaster after another. On 10 August Radio Tokyo announced that Japan was willing to quit the war on condition that the Allies guarantee the future status of the Emperor. The new American President, Harry Truman, in keeping with his predecessor's policies, refused anything but the unconditional surrender of Japan. Russian troops carried on their devastating campaign as American bombers continued to pound Japanese cities. On 14 August, officials of the Japanese government met with the Emperor in a tense, emotional conference. Emperor Hirohito gave his support to those advocating surrender, and it seemed to all except a small minority of officers that Japan had no other logical choice. The next day the radio carried a recorded message from the Emperor to the people of Japan, informing them that the war had ended and marking the first time that millions of Japanese people had ever heard his divine voice. Japan had surrendered unconditionally. When the news reached the many islands where Americans were based, brief, spontaneous celebrations broke out. Many Japanese troops, lacking radio contact with their homeland, however, knew nothing about the sudden turn of events that had led to the decision to quit the war. On Cebu, where the men of the 164th were based, thousands of Japanese had not learned about the ending of hostilities.

General Arnold, commander of the Americal Division, decided to drop leaflets over the jungle and rain forests of the island where many of the Japanese had hidden, the leaflets simply stating that the war had ended and they should surrender. Shortly thereafter, an American patrol found one of the leaflets tacked to a tree. On it, printed in flawless English, appeared the notation, ''We do not believe your propaganda.'' General Arnold then had another leaflet printed, this time inviting the Japanese to send a responsible officer, for whom he assured safe conduct, to American headquarters to hear the news for himself. Shortly thereafter a Japanese officer with a flag of truce came to Arnold's headquarters. After the officer listened to the American radio intercepts for two days, he became convinced that the war had indeed ended. He received safe conduct back to the general area from which he had come and told his commanding officer of the news. Further communication between Arnold and the Japanese set 28 August 1945, as the date for surrender at a site near Cebu City. Arnold then sent a report of these developments to his superior, General MacArthur, in Manila.

Evidently MacArthur did not approve of Arnold's initiative in arranging the surrender on Cebu and told his subordinate not to accept the Japanese surrender before 4 September under any circumstances. General Arnold was now in trouble, for hundreds of Japanese troops were arriving at the surrender site daily, many probably hoping for some American food. How could he tell them that he had made a mistake and that the surrender would not take place until a full week after his designated date? Thus Arnold sent another message to MacArthur, pleading for the original surrender arrangements. MacArthur finally agreed to let the surrender take place on 28 August 1945 under two conditions: first, the surrender had to be informal, though he sent no explanation as to what differentiated an informal surrender from a formal one, and second, Arnold should allow no publicity of the event, no pictures taken, and no news releases. Another directive to Arnold soon followed ordering him to crate all confiscated Japanese material and ship it to Manila. General Arnold acquiesced and on 28 August about ten thousand Japanese laid down their arms at Cebu, though it was an incident not without some apprehension on the part of the men of the 164th who took part in it.

A mixed company, made up of men from every unit of the Americal Division, accepted the surrender of the Japanese. The Americans numbered about two hundred in all, while there were ten thousand Japanese only a short distance away. What if the Japanese decided to stage one final glorious *banzai* attack for the honor of the Emperor and Japan? What could a mere company do to prevent its own annihilation under these circumstances? On the other hand, if the Japanese did surrender peaceably, it would absolutely end the war and all its miseries. These thoughts flashed through the minds of some of the men of the 164th as the two groups of soldiers faced each other. Since Japanese discipline prevailed, the surrender took place in an orderly manner. But very little of the confiscated Japanese material ever found its way to Manila, much of it becoming souvenirs of the men of the Americal Division as General Arnold steadfastly looked the other way.

The men of the Americal had little time for celebration on Cebu because they, including the 164th, were to be part of the forces occupying Japan. Scheduled to leave Cebu on 1 September, the division was heading for Yokohama, or what remained of it. After arriving at the Japanese city, the various units fanned out to their assigned occupation localities to assume a variety of assignments.

The occupation forces in Japan had several tasks to perform, such as taking inventory of the industrial and commercial facilities that had survived American bombing and closing all banks and financial institutions pursuant to orders from General MacArthur on 28 September. Occasionally the Americans had forcibly to prohibit some form of military training of boys attending schools, but, for the most part, the Japanese cooperated with the American forces. The American policy of nonfraternization was probably the most difficult to carry out, more because of American violation than Japanese. Occupation duties for the 164th continued in a routine way until a series of events resembling those of a second-rate detective story began to unfold in early October.

While on their mission of taking inventory of Japanese industry, Americans of another military unit had come across over one hundred bars of silver. Further investigation revealed that much more of the precious metal lay hidden in another prefecture, one of those occupied by the 164th, northwest of Tokyo. Captain Richard Cohen, two lieutenants, and thirty-four enlisted men of I Company received orders to search for the silver in the vicinity of Kasugai, a small town within an hour's drive of company headquarters. Since the silver was allegedly stored in the Kusagai-Mura warehouse, Captain Cohen decided to search there first. Local police and other officials informed him that a warehouse by that specific name did not exist, that there were several storage buildings in and around the town, and that they would cooperate as much as possible with the Americans. The captain had not let the local officials know the purpose of his mission lest they make attempts to remove the metal to another area, so the patrol of the 164th began a systematic search of all the supply depots in the town. They found no silver.

After searching the warehouses in the town, the patrol began to investigate farmers' storage facilities in the vicinity. When it uncovered ten tons of tin, Cohen's suspicions began to rise. The tin had been consigned to Koshiro Haibera, one of the wealthiest farmers of the region, who owned a large estate a short distance from town. Cohen decided to pay Haibera a visit and ask some questions. The Haibera estate also had two large warehouses, as yet unsearched, but the patrol found nothing there except the very cooperative and polite landlord, the essence of Oriental courtesy. Cohen decided to try another approach by questioning the local shipping clerk in charge of freight receipts. When the clerk proved uncooperative, even surly at times, Cohen demanded the complete shipping records of the office for the last six months or, upon failure to produce the records, he would close the office. Now told the specific nature of the investigation, the local police urged the shipping clerk to comply with Cohen's request. By noon of the next day the captain had the records, and after noticing that Haibera had received four shipments of silver, Cohen and some of his men paid the farmer another visit.

Haibera politely received the captain and his men, but a thorough search of the estate warehouses again revealed nothing. Then Cohen noticed a small barn located near the entrance to the estate and ordered the men to search it. Haibera became visibly upset, arousing the American's suspicions. After removing a thin covering of rice straw, the men of the patrol found hundreds of bars of silver. Though Haibera professed his surprise and innocence, Cohen was not convinced and began to question him vigorously. The Japanese farmer started to give answers, revealing that the Mitsubishi Company had contacted him in April about storing some precious metals for the firm. Apparently fearing that American air raids might destroy the silver and other metals, Mitsubishi wanted to remove them to remote parts of Japan. Before the questioning ended, Haibera revealed the location of other shipments consigned to him. All in all, they added up to over one hundred tons of pure silver and smaller amounts of copper, lead, tin, zinc, and antimony. The captain and his men had spent over a week searching, questioning, and going over shipping records before they had completed their assignment. Most of the I Company patrol remained at Kasugai to guard the metals until they were transported elsewhere, but the regimental papers contain no record concerning the final disposition of the silver.

Shortly after Operation Treasure Hunt, the designation given the search for the silver after the fact, the Americal Division received orders to return to the United States where it was to be disbanded. It would not be the Americal Division per se, however, for many of the men recently added to the division did not yet qualify for discharge. Also, many veterans of other units had accumulated enough points to be eligible for separation from the service. Thus the division experienced a massive turnover of personnel, the recent arrivals being transferred to other units while the division absorbed veterans from units throughout Japan. Now a division in name only, it consisted of about fifteen hundred men who had only one thing in common—their eligibility for discharge. As a unit of the division, the 164th shared in the changes. By October 1945, very few North Dakotans remained in the 164th. General

Arnold estimated that fewer than two hundred men still in the division had been members of the division when it was formed on New Caledonia. Most of them were from headquarters and service units. Very few of the original combat infantrymen remained, and the original members of the 164th still in the regiment possibly could not have mustered as much as a squad of twelve. Casualties, disease, and rotation had taken from its ranks almost all of the North Dakotans who had departed from the state during the bitterly cold days of February 1941. On 24 November, at Fort Lawton, Washington, the Americal Division was officially disbanded, and the 164th became designated as inactive. The war was over.

The men of the 164th Infantry took justifiable pride in what they had accomplished in World War II. Yet the record of the regiment does, in some respects, contain irony. When the regiment first landed on Guadalcanal on 13 October 1942, it had arrived as a raw, untested unit that had suddenly been thrust into the limelight. That tiny island became the testing ground of America's will and ability to strike back at a determined and capable enemy. For many weeks it saw the only land operation of American troops in a global war and was the only stage upon which the drama of the war was unfolding. By the time the 164th arrived, the battle had reached a precarious stalemate. In its first six weeks of combat, the regiment had played a major role in turning the tide and assuring eventual victory. It had borne the brunt of the biggest Japanese counteroffensive in the entire campaign and had turned back thousands of Japan's finest soldiers and Imperial Marines. The first Army unit to take the offensive against the enemy in World War II, the 164th had done so with remarkable effectiveness. One officer of the 164th received the Navy Cross and five enlisted men the Distinguished Service Cross for their heroism on Guadalcanal. The regiment had covered itself with glory.

This outstanding record attracted national attention. Several magazines printed pictures and stories about the men of the 164th during and shortly after the battle for Guadalcanal. After the *New York Times* sent a correspondent to the Fijis to interview men of the regiment shortly after those haggard and worn veterans arrived, it published a series of seven lengthy articles about the 164th and the important role it had played in the battle. Several other newspapers reprinted the articles. North Dakota newspapers, not to be outdone, included their own stories about the state's new heroes, some of whom had been sent back to the United States to recover from wounds or illness. Pictures of the men, along with interviews and feature stories, appeared in many daily papers of the state. All in all, the regiment had drawn a great amount of attention and publicity. After Guadalcanal, the operations of the 164th became somewhat anticlimactic, through no fault of the regiment. Bougainville was part of Operation Cartwheel, an overall strategy to reduce the Japanese stronghold at Rabaul on the island of New Britain. By the time the 164th arrived at Empress Augusta Bay, the Americans had invaded New Britain itself. Bougainville then became less important, though the American forces needed to make sure that the Japanese could never use it as an operational base against them. Although the Americans never captured Rabaul throughout the war, the Navy and air forces were already pounding it to such an extent that it was no longer an asset to the Japanese. Also, the invasions of the Marshalls, Marianas, and the Philippines, along with the capture of Hollandia and other bases in New Guinea, overshadowed Bougainville.

When the 164th arrived on Leyte, General MacArthur had already proclaimed that island as secure, only mopping up remaining. Shortly thereafter the Americans invaded Luzon, the main Philippine island where the embattled "bastards of Bataan" had made their heroic stand in early 1942. The men of the regiment carried out their assigned task virtually unnoticed by publicizers. When the 164th played its role in the Cebu battle, the invasion of Okinawa grabbed the headlines in the Pacific. Leyte, Cebu, Bohol, and Negros all became part of the backwash of the war. These campaigns were not the kind that made headlines or led to high military decorations for the 164th. Men of the 164th received six of the highest medals bestowed by the armed forces for their heroism on Guadalcanal, one at Bougainville, and none thereafter. Yet they performed deeds of uncommon valor in all of these operations. History tends to follow the limelight and often neglects those who carry out the dirty but necessary tasks. The United States needed to negate Japanese strength in all these islands so that its forces might prepare for future campaigns in the knowledge that their bases were secure from enemy activity. Lieutenant General Robert Eichelberger, commander of the Eighth Army, which was fighting in the central and southern Philippines, believed that the Japanese were not suffering more casualties in Luzon than they were losing to the action of his army, but his men were getting only "one fiftieth of the publicity." He may have been right, but the lack of publicity changed little as the fighting under his command in the Philippines attracted little notice.

As an infantry regiment, the 164th served in combat for long periods of time during the war. With the exception of the respite it received on the Fijis, the unit was in combat or in transit from December 1943 to the end of the war, receiving only short periods of rest throughout that entire period. Admittedly, the combat on Bougainville during the last three months there was not heavy, but it was not a time of rest and recreation either. From there the regiment went to Leyte where it experienced some fierce fighting for over two months. Although the regiment spent only a few days fighting on Cebu, it immediately left for more combat in Bohol and Negros. All in all, the 164th spent about six hundred days in combat, an unusually large amount of time when one considers the nature of the war in the Pacific.

Considering the long periods in combat for the 164th, its casualty list is not exceedingly high. A total of 325 men were killed in action and another 1,193 were wounded—about fifty percent of the men in the regiment. However, over 3,000 of the men were hospitalized for illness, trauma, accidents, and other causes, a number greater than the regiment at full strength. Although the American divisional records list two men as missing in action, this is in error. The two men, lost on patrol in Guadalcanal, were later found dead and were buried in unmarked graves by another patrol a few days later. Thus the 164th had no one officially missing in action throughout the entire war.

As a unit, the 164th received a presidential citation for its efforts on Guadalcanal, as already noted. Individually, men of the regiment were decorated with 1 Navy Cross, 6 Distinguished Service Crosses, 89 Silver Stars, 199 Bronze Stars (a decoration authorized in February 1944), 6 Legions of Merit, and 10 Soldiers' Medals. Members also received almost 1,200 Purple Hearts and Oak Leaf Clusters. The Navy Cross, 5 of the 6 Distinguished Service Crosses, and almost half the Silver Stars were earned for action on Guadalcanal alone.

Forty years after the Battle of Guadalcanal, one of its former commanding officers reflected on the quality of the regiment. Colonel (later Major General) Crump Garvin, 1920 graduate of West Point and regimental commander of the 164th from May 1943 to June 1944, recalled that he wanted to command the 164th because General Hodge believed it to be the best regiment of the American division. Garvin, confined to staff work until that time, prevailed upon his commanding general to give him the 164th. When Garvin assumed command, it was his first experience with a National Guard unit and he was impressed with the ability and versatility of the men he commanded. He found them superior to the Regular Army units he had commanded in nearly every respect and readily admitted that his command of the 164th had been a big factor in his promotion to brigadier general.

Four decades have now passed since the war in the Pacific came to its sudden and dramatic end. For over three of those decades the veterans of the 164th have met annually to renew old friendships and recall their past experiences. These reunions are held in October, so as to coincide as nearly as possible with the anniversary of the landing on Guadalcanal. It is fitting that they do so, for that tiny island was the site of their first baptism by enemy fire. It was there that the regiment, thrown into the full fury of battle, proved beyond doubt that its motto, *Je Suis Pret*, was well deserved.

Notes on Sources

There are few good general histories of World War II in the Pacific areas, though many excellent books and articles have been published on specific campaigns. One of the best histories of the Pacific war is Ronald Spector, *Eagle Against the Sun* (New York, 1985).

During the war the Office of the Chief of Military History began publication of a series entitled *The U.S. Army in World War II* (Washington, 1944-1981). Rich in detail and remarkably unbiased for an official history, the series is absolutely essential to any historian researching World War II. The specific volumes used for this chapter were John Miller Jr., *Guadalcanal: The First Offensive* and *Cartwheel: The Reduction of Rabaul* by the same author; Greenfield, Palmer and Wiley, *The Organization of Ground Troops*, M. Hamlin Cannon, *Leyte: The Return to the Philippines* and Robert Ross Smith, *Triumph in the Philippines*. The problems involved in medical care for men in the Pacific, especially those afflicted with tropical disease, is treated in the official history of the Medical Department. Volumes V, VI, VII, *Communicable Diseases*, edited by Ebbe Curtis Hoff, were consulted for this chapter.

Army unit records range from sparse to voluminous. The author was most fortunate to have an excellent history of the Americal Division for his research, *Under the Southern Cross: The Saga of the Americal Division* (Washington, 1948) by Francis Cronin. Since the 164th was also once part of the 34th Division and was attached to the First Marine Division for much of the Guadalcanal campaign, the records of these units were also studied. The records of the Americal Division were rather brief until the division was reorganized in the summer of 1943. Evidently its staffs were complete by then and the records become much more informative. This is especially true of the operational and intelligence journals and reports starting with the Bougainville campaign. The papers of the Americal Division, including those of the 164th Infantry Regiment, are in the modern Military Records Branch of the National Archives.

The regimental papers proved to be the most valuable source of information used by the author. Though not well organized, they contain a wealth of information with two notable exceptions. The journal of operations (S-3) is lacking for the Koli Point episode and it is covered only in a very brief historical report. Another shortcoming was the lack of maps from which one might coordinate the movements of the battalions and companies. With these exceptions, the regimental papers proved to be the best source available for the day-to-day operations of the regiment.

As part of this research, over fifty interviews were conducted with former members of the 164th regiment. They helped to fill in many details which have been incorporated. Some of the quotes are from these interviews. This chapter also benefited from interviews conducted by authors of the *U.S. Army in World War II*, particularly John Miller Jr.'s written notes of conversations with General Sebree. Another interview of General William Arnold, Americal Division commander, was interesting but not very revealing. Notes and transcriptions of these interviews, along with copies of General Eichelberger's letters to his wife can be found in the U.S. Army Center of Military History.

After the war, some former members of the 164th began to gather historical information on the regiment. These records are now kept by the regimental association under the care of their historian, Keith Parsons. Some of these papers, especially those gathered by Col. Samuel Baglien, were quite helpful.

Last, and least, were the Japanese monographs consulted by the author. After the war, General MacArthur ordered his historical staff to interview surviving Japanese participants of the many campaigns in the Pacific. From these interviews and the few documents remaining for researchers, a series of monographs emerged. They must be used with caution. Monographs numbers 33 and 34, which dealt with the Japanese in the Solomon Islands, have little information of value except that they reveal that the Japanese had no intention of landing a major force at Koli Point.

[1]Quotations from veterans come from the questionnaire survey or oral interviews.
[2]The belated recognition of the need to give American ground forces some means of fighting tanks necessitated both last-minute reorganizations.

164th Infantry Regiment disembarking from LCIs at Negros Island, the
Philippines.

Filipino stretcher bearers evacuating wounded members of 164th
Infantry near Cebu City, Philippine Islands, April, 1945.

164th Infantry on patrol duty in the Negros Islands.

Left: Display of medals awarded to members of the 164th Infantry during a ceremony in the Fiji Islands, 1943. (Display includes one Distinguished Service Cross, six Silver Stars and eighteen Purple Hearts.)

Right: Colonel Ira M. Gaulke

☆9☆

The 188th Field Artillery Regiment in World War II

The attack on Pearl Harbor affected the 188th Regiment as immediately as it did the 164th. With the end of its efficiency tests in November, the artillery took its ease, sending many men on leave. Fred Schmisek, Battery F, was awaiting his discharge. Having recently turned twenty-nine, and no longer eligible for the draft, Schmisek now qualified for release from active duty. On 7 December 1941, he turned in his equipment and packed his bags to go home. Then word of the Japanese assault came. After immediately unpacking, he went to find his supply sergeant to get his gear back. Jerome Norman, doing his stint on kitchen police (KP), listened to confused soldiers debate the exact location of Pearl Harbor in the Philippine Islands. Military police in Denver rounded up men on weekend pass and hurried them off to Cheyenne. Those on leave needed no special notice to realize they had to return to Fort Warren right away.

Restricted to barracks on the night of the 7th, the men learned the next day they had to pack all equipment and prepare vehicles and guns for a forced motor march to Fort Lewis, Washington, at the southern tip of Puget Sound near Tacoma. It took three days to ready the command, and, on the morning of 11 December 1941, the 188th left Fort Warren on its 1,250-mile drive over the Rocky Mountains. Snow, ice, strong winds, and bitter cold accompanied them through the high country. In military terms, a forced march meant no stops except for the necessities of eating, fueling the vehicles, and resting the men for short periods. Drivers handled the trucks for eight hours, were relieved for eight hours, then again took the wheel. The twisting mountain roads and icy conditions kept the convoy's speed to an average of twenty-five to thirty miles an hour, and made it a particularly challenging job for men driving the five-ton trucks towing the big howitzers. Most of the Guardsmen rode in canvas-covered truck beds, huddled amongst straw bales and bedrolls and wearing overcoats and rubber buckled boots. Since the truck cabs had no heaters, drivers and their companions were little better off. Battery cooks did not have an easy task as they attempted to prepare hot meals on pressurized gasoline stoves carried in the kitchen trucks, and the men found the meals none too palatable. All in all, everyone regarded it as an unpleasant trip, one further clouded by the uncertainty of why they were making it. One veteran stated bluntly, "That was the most stupid thing I think I have ever seen." Remarkably, the regiment reached Fort Lewis at 7:00 A.M. on 15 December without a single major accident, injury, or loss of any of the 450 vehicles in the convoy. Reputedly, no other United States Army unit had made such a lengthy motorized march under wartime conditions.

At this point, the artillerymen began to experience some of the miseries that greeted the 164th at Camp Claiborne. They set up their tents at Camp Murray (known to the men thereafter as "Swamp Murray"), an undeveloped section of the permanent Fort Lewis, on a site that offered them little more than wooden platforms to serve as tent floors. Rain fell for the first twenty-six days the outfit occupied the camp. Rumors inevitably swept up and down the muddy battery streets, convincing some they were marked for duty in Alaska and others that they were heading for the Philippines, particularly after the unit received a full set of vaccination shots. Some of the troops had heard the 76th Brigade was the only outfit on the West Coast supplied with artillery ammunition, but what effect a few hundred rounds of World War I-vintage shrapnel would have on enemy ships and planes was left to their imagination.

They soon found out the purpose for their rapid westward move, when, early in January 1942, all firing batteries were ordered to the north end of the Olympia Peninsula, facing the Strait of Juan de Fuca. A medium artillery regiment was neither trained nor equipped for coastal duty, but despite confusion and doubt, the 188th towed its guns 140 miles up the peninsula to Port Angeles. There, the men hacked their way through brush and woods to clear roads and gun emplacements and positioned their howitzers seaward. Armed with pistols, rifles, and the shrapnel, there they sat in the rain and mud. Though no one ever told them what they were looking for, most assumed, reasonably enough, that those in the know expected a Japanese naval and air attack on the strait. When asked at what he and his comrades were aiming their guns, one veteran replied, only half facetiously, "At the guy who never came, thank Heavens!" With a desperate shortage of battery officers, many of them still off at school, the regiment often used first sergeants as gunnery officers. LaClair Melhouse recalled that once the batteries returned to Camp Murray, after ten days to two weeks on the coast, the first sergeants were reduced to privates because they failed to clean up their gun positions before withdrawing! Though eventually rescinded, this IX Army Corps order suggested that the Army had not yet purged itself of its peacetime garrison mentality where neatness counted most.

After mid-January, the regiment settled into a routine that characterized its life for well over a year. Because of the loss of so many experienced men and the addition of so many new men in the ensuing weeks, the 188th had to repeat the first two training phases, basic and battery, during 1942. It did not pass efficiency tests on those phases until August. With numerous replacements passing through the unit, it maintained a 188th Training Group to introduce men fresh out of recruit camp to the rudiments of artillery work. Charles Hagar of Virginia reported to Fort Lewis in early 1943 with "A bunch of draftees from Va., Maryland, D.C., and Penn." After work in the Training Group, they "were sent to fill the vacancies in the different" batteries. Boyd Joyer, a National Guardsman, wrote, for all intents and purposes, "We were a training unit, the training was not just limited to our units. Instead, the training was to develop personnel, who, when trained, were transferred to other units who were going overseas."

The regiment lost many of its original officers while at Fort Lewis, from 15 December 1941 to April 1943. Lieutenant Colonel Leslie V. Miller, executive officer and one of the first officers in the 185th Battalion formed in 1937, left in February 1942 for training duties elsewhere. Colonel Percy Hansen departed a year later. Because these men, and others, were either too old for their grade or not physically fit for combat, they received administrative assignments commensurate with their rank and experience. In the endless round of schooling, some younger officers failed to return, and welcome promotions removed others because the regiment had no place for them. A large number of promising noncommissioned officers applied for Officers Candidate School, LaClair Melhouse and twenty-one other enlisted men from Minot's Battery B alone earning commissions there, then moving on to new assignments.

Men from various reserve components replaced those who left. Major Hershel Case, a California Guardsman, joined the regiment in December 1942 and remained with it to the end of the war. Reporting just after the forced march, Tom Arnold, a second lieutenant fresh out of Officers Candidate School, would be a major when the artillery went overseas. Other officers from the Officers Reserve Corps, Reserve Officers Training Corps, Officers Candidate School, and National Guard filled the open slots as original members departed. For all these changes, both battalions retained a sufficient number of National Guard officers and men to justify calling them North Dakota units. Replacement of officers and enlisted men would continue, on a lesser scale, until the artillerymen went to Europe.

Many National Guard supporters disputed the War Department's policy of diluting state units with draftees and reserve officers. Guardsmen argued that the service should have been given the opportunity, particularly in the first weeks after mobilization, to recruit at home station to reach full strength, a policy that would have produced Guard units strong in morale and unit pride bolstered by state identification. This nineteenth-century view of manpower procurement contained a clearly implied distaste for conscription. These Guardsmen ignored, and the War Department failed to make clear, the major reason for mobilizing the Guard in 1940-1941—to train men, especially draftees. The United States was not engaged in war at that time and therefore had no intent to rush units to the battlefront, as it had done in 1898 and, to a lesser extent, in 1917. The uneven steps to war, followed by total mobilization, and the inordinate difficulties of placing American units in combat once war came made it nearly impossible to maintain National Guard units made up solely of volunteers from a particular state.

Despite the continual need for basic training, the regiment also worked on combat instruction. It could accomplish some field work at Fort Lewis, but the post grew ever larger in 1942, and it lacked a firing range. The Army acquired a large tract of land in the Saddle Mountains, near Yakima, 160 miles east of Fort Lewis, to use as an artillery firing range. Work at the Yakima range, according to Hershel Case, "covered all phases of artillery including Bn [Battalion] and Battery tactics and line firing." Artillery units at Fort Lewis regularly traveled to Yakima. There, Tom Arnold wrote, the regiment participated in "realistic maneuver/firing exercises to include the Battery and Battalion tests which were the real measures of a unit's ability to perform satisfactorily in the field." The 188th went to Yakima four times between April 1942 and March 1943, for a total of eighteen weeks. It spent six weeks there, beginning on 7

August, during which time it again passed basic and battery tests. Another stint in early November 1942 took the regiment through Phase III tests, "much of this phase" being "completed in heavy snow and extreme cold weather." The men lived in tents at the range, and, though they enjoyed weekend passes in the city of Yakima, few liked the rugged living conditions in the field and the hard work. According to Victor McWilliams, they "Fired time after time, and day after day."

The hectic life at Fort Lewis had its compensations. When not at Yakima, the regiment followed the routine of garrison duty, with occasional nights off and most weekends free. Many families moved to Fort Lewis from Fort Warren or North Dakota when it became apparent that the 188th would be there for some time, and parties at off-base apartments and the officers club made the war seem far away. United Service Organization shows and other on-post recreational facilities offered enlisted men chances to break the training monotony. Newspaper accounts of the brutal fighting on Guadalcanal and brief letters from buddies in the 164th readily convinced the gunners that their lot was not so bad after all. Still, they felt an underlying sense of frustration when watching well-trained officers and men leave the unit, and novices, who had to be taken through all training cycles yet another time, replace them. If the 188th began to think of itself "as a capable combat unit" after its many weeks at Yakima, "At times it looked as though no one else in the Army felt that way."

These frustrations reflected in miniature the enormous difficulties the United States faced in 1942 in fighting a two-front war. The nation had shortages of every kind—shipping, aviation, weapons, manpower. The Army regularly stripped units like the 188th of trained men in order to bolster understrength outfits bound for combat zones. Training at Fort Lewis sometimes fell behind schedule because lack of equipment forced the War Department to ration vehicles, weapons, and ammunition to training units in order to equip those overseas. Until the nation's industrial capacity was fully mobilized, the rationing continued. Strategic problems also slowed the overseas movement of trained units. Prewar planning had emphasized confronting Germany first with the bulk of America's fighting forces, but Japan's surprising advances in the Pacific in late 1941 and early 1942 forced a temporary modification of the Germany-first strategy. As the 164th learned, the War Department scrapped prewar plans to rush available units to the Pacific. By early 1943, the Japanese advance had been stopped, and Allied forces were about to clear the Germans out of North Africa. Strategic pursuit of the war in Europe remained unsettled, however, as the British and Americans argued over where to fight Hitler next, the British favoring an Allied invasion of Italy, and the Americans pushing for a direct attack across the English Channel into France. After agreeing to a compromise strategy, the Allies slated the Italian invasion for the summer of 1943 and the cross-Channel attack for sometime in 1944.

The strategic disputes directly affected the 188th. A 155 mm howitzer unit, with its heavy guns and large motor train, would have little value on the crowded Pacific coral islands, where small-unit infantry tactics predominated. As the build-up at home created more and more armored, artillery, and mechanized organizations for the European area, General George C. Marshall and other planners decided they would commit only a limited number to the Italian campaign. They would hold back the rest for what they saw as the major effort to take Germany out of the war, the invasion of France. Until sufficient shipping became available to move these units to Great Britain, they would remain in the United States. Such was the fate of the 188th.

Meanwhile, the regiment underwent a major restructuring. On 17 February 1943, Army Ground Forces, the Army's training command led by Lesley McNair, directed that all artillery regiments be disbanded and reorganized into independent battalions. McNair believed that modern, mechanized warfare called for structured flexibility. Although it made sense to have permanent organization tables for infantry and armored divisions, higher-level commands, that is, corps and field armies, should not. They should consist of a varying number of divisions, supported by artillery, engineer, and other auxiliary battalions as circumstances dictated. In McNair's scheme, only the infantry would retain the regimental units above the battalion level. All other combat arms were to have battalions only, with the brigade also eliminated. Thereafter, field commanders could create task forces and regimental combat teams according to immediate battlefield needs, using nondivisional battalions as interchangeable parts. To ensure tactical control of these battalions, the restructuring also called for headquarters groups to direct the field activities of up to four battalions at one time.

As a consequence, Regimental Headquarters and Headquarters Battery became the 188th Field Artillery Group, the 1st Battalion became the 188th Field Artillery Battalion, and the 2nd Battalion became the 957th Battalion. Colonel Henry Burr Parker, a regular, replaced Colonel Hansen as group commander. Several National Guard officers served in the 188th Group. At the time, Lieutenant Colonel Lorenzo Belk (a North Dakotan known to some of his men as ''Colonel Goddamn'') led the 188th Battalion, and Lieutenant Colonel John Gross, who had served as Regular Army advisor to the regiment in the late 1930s, the 957th.

A change in the Fort Lewis routine came in mid-April 1943 when the 188th Field Artillery Group left for the Desert Training Center in southeastern California's Mojave Desert. Not surprisingly, all assumed that training in the desert foretold combat in North Africa, although the Germans surrendered there a month later. Actually, the Desert Training Center functioned as the site for units ready to take the last two phases of training, divisional operations and field army maneuvers. General McNair's Army Ground Forces developed a thirteen-week training program in the desert ''to train, maintain and supply troops realistically as in a theater of operations,'' which meant living in the field continuously, using live ammunition, operating with combined arms, both ground and air, and maintaining equipment under combat conditions. This intense work culminated in a large maneuver pitting two field armies against each other. Although the Army failed to explain the purpose of this phase of training to all ranks, many sensed correctly that overseas shipment was coming soon.

The 188th remained at the Desert Training Center for five months, from 14 April to 18 August 1943. Camp Granite, not a pleasant place to live, did not exist until the 188th Group built it. It had no electricity and precious little running water, and rattlesnakes, scorpions, tarantulas, and the ever-present sand constantly plagued the men. Some of the more ambitious men dug deep holes, filled them with ice, and stocked them with beer that had been smuggled in. The southern California location allowed weekend passes to Los Angeles and United Services Organization shows in camp with big bands and Hollywood stars.

The 188th Group left the Mojave on 18 August for Camp Gruber, near Muskogee, Oklahoma. The Army's multistage overseas preparation process, one the 164th Infantry did not go through, culminated at Camp Gruber. Labeled Preparation for Overseas Movement, the final stage included bringing the battalions up to full strength and providing the newest model guns and vehicles. The men, Tom Arnold wrote, found this time "an intense period of both training and administrative preparations." Command of the battalions for the duration of the war was confirmed. Because Lieutenant Colonel Belk had become ill during the time in California, Major Robert Carlson, of Bismarck and a Guardsman since 1937, took command of the 188th. Although Belk reappeared at Camp Gruber to take John Gross's place with the 957th, again poor health forced him to step down. A young regular officer, only twenty-six years of age and a 1939 West Point graduate, Major James L. Collins, Jr., replaced Belk. Many artillerymen had an opportunity to take leave in the fall of 1943. Soon after they returned to Oklahoma, the Group and its battalions left for the East Coast. Boarding ship in New York City on 5 December, they sailed for Great Britain and reached Liverpool on the fifteenth. After nearly three years on active duty, and over a year after their infantry comrades entered combat, the artillerymen were now overseas and less than thirty miles from the enemy.

Upon arrival, the 188th Field Artillery Group entrained for the south of England to be billetted in small towns around Chichester, Sussex, not far from the English Channel and the port cities of Portsmouth and Southampton. Batteries took up residence in hotels, private homes, and on large estates; the 188th quartered in and around the village of Selsey, with the 957th at Barnham. Nearby Walberton housed their Group Headquarters. The men had opportunities to visit Chichester or the resort town of Brighton, but given wartime conditions, Boyd Joyer noted, "Training was the major activity. Do not recall that officers and men had much opportunity to see British Isles." Most of Battery A, 957th, reported to Dumbarton, Scotland, on the River Clyde, in late January for a two-month tour of guard duty at a United States naval installation. The men found this a choice duty, far from battalion headquarters, with plenty of first-rate Navy cooking and even time to hunt deer.

For the first six months of 1944, the battalions spent most of their time training "either in garrison or," according to James L. Collins (now brigadier general, United States Army, retired), "when we could get training areas, in the field." The units traveled to the Royal Artillery firing range at Salisbury for practice firing, but they did not maneuver with British units, although they did exchange officers with equivalent artillery organizations. Major Tom Arnold, operations officer, 188th Battalion, spent two weeks with the 65th Medium Regiment, Royal Artillery, and his counterpart came to Selsey. Arnold had a chance to observe British artillery methods and training, study their administrative procedures, and sit in on staff meetings. He described his hosts as "quite friendly" and recommended that future exchanges "include a number

338

of enlisted men...in order to get a more balanced view of the operations of the two armies," but neither army acted on the suggestion, written in early April 1944, owing to the pending invasion.

Most work concentrated on getting ready for the coming offensive. Though no one knew when or where it would take place, all realized the invasion of France was close at hand. Collins, now a lieutenant colonel, set two goals for the 957th. Tactically, "the emphasis was on quick movement to position and rapid preparation to fire." Rapid movement of a medium howitzer battalion was not easy, for it had twelve guns and over one hundred vehicles, including ten-ton, tracked prime movers to tow the guns, five-ton and two-and-one-half-ton trucks, jeeps, and command cars. This battalion had no tracked vehicles until after it arrived in England. First Sergeant Bernard Clark, Service Battery, 957th, had the task of receiving the vehicles and training drivers. Neither Clark nor anyone else had ever driven tracked vehicles, which, like bulldozers, are steered by manipulating two levers. Many stone fences on the narrow country lanes of Sussex suffered before Clark's men learned the intricacies of driving the M-5 prime movers.

Administratively, Colonel Collins faced a different challenge. "As the only Regular Army officer in the unit, and younger than many," he recalled, "I was on my mettle to prove myself. I think it probably was a little more difficult with a NG unit than an RA or AUS unit because the NG unit had been together longer." Three of his battery commanders and two staff officers, four captains and a major, were Guardsmen, but most of the other officers had joined the unit at Fort Lewis in 1942. Collins kept the men busy with training activities, moved some commanders from one battery to another, and transferred a few noncommissioned officers within the battalion in order to put his own stamp on the 957th. Furthermore, "many new officers and men had joined before I," he recalled, "so it was no longer a 'pure' NG unit and after the initial period of adaptation we all got along well." The 188th Battalion, with Guardsman Lieutenant Colonel Carlson in command, did not have to adjust to a leader from the "outside," although only two of his battery commanders, Captain Charles Welch, Headquarters Battery, and Captain Wilbur Pierce, Battery A, were from North Dakota.

Anticipation of combat heightened in May as more and more American, British, and Canadian troops concentrated in southern England. Everyone knew when the great invasion began on 6 June 1944 because they could hear and see massed Allied bombers heading across the Channel to France. The Field Artillery Group did not immediately enter the fray, being held back until infantry assault teams secured beachheads deep enough to land mechanized units. Colonel Carlson's 188th Battalion left first, departing Selsey on the evening of 6 June for marshaling yards at Weymouth, in Dorset. The battalion anxiously waited orders until it boarded a landing ship tank on the 10th. Here they found "a small hunk of America...American ship, American sailors, good American food." The ship departed Weymouth that afternoon, "destination unknown," according to the 188th's Unit Journal.

The 957th bided its time for two more days, although it had seen evidence of the D-day landings since 7 June. Trainloads of wounded Allied soldiers, followed by German prisoners of war, passed through Barnham until the 957th left. At 10:00 P.M., 10 June, Colonel Collins called his battery commanders to headquarters and told his captains to restrict their men to quarters and double their guards. "It didn't take long to find out that we were alerted for overseas movement," Captain Victor McWilliams recalled. "Most of the guys still thot [*sic*] this was another dry run," Peter Schwab wrote in his diary, but soon found out they were really leaving. "We all felt funny about taking off but there wasn't much we could do about it." After departing for port of embarkation at 5:00 A.M. on 11 June, the battalion boarded a landing ship the next morning and sailed that same evening. "The trip was uneventful," according to Donald Turney, "but most of the boys were pretty nervous."

Both of the battalions were heading for Utah Beach, an American D-day landing spot on the eastern shore of the Contentin Peninsula of Normandy, where they were slated to serve as general artillery support for the VII Corps, First United States Army. Major General J. Lawton Collins, coincidentally the uncle of James L. Collins, Jr., commanded VII Corps. The American Army arranged its field artillery in two echelons. Each infantry or armored division permanently carried four artillery battalions on its table of organization, three of light artillery, with 105 mm guns, and one medium battalion, armed with the 155 mm howitzer. In addition, following General McNair's scheme, each corps included a number of battalions under the tactical control of field artillery groups. Corps artillery command either assigned nondivisional battalions to general firing tasks or attached them temporarily to individual divisions for additional support. The North Dakota battalions served throughout the war as VII Corps artillery and worked with nearly every division in the corps some time during the European campaign. Because their assignments changed frequently, they rarely operated under the direction of the 188th Field Artillery Group.

The standard medium battalion included three firing batteries of four guns each. Firing batteries were organized into sections—four to serve the guns, and one each to man ammunition trucks, wire and radio equipment, motor maintenance, and kitchen. Headquarters Battery carried on unit administration and functioned as the battalion's fire direction center, directing battery fire over radio and telephone communications. A small medical detachment accompanied headquarters. Service Battery met all logistical needs, including ammunition, rations, and clothing supplies, and provided repair facilities for guns and vehicles. An average of thirty officers and five hundred enlisted men composed a full battalion.

Operations for a 155 mm unit were complex. The 155 mm howitzer had a maximum range of fourteen thousand yards (just over eight miles), and its shells weighed ninety-five pounds. The size of the powder charge inserted in the gun to propel the shell determined its range. Medium artillery rarely operated on line with infantry, generally remaining two to five miles behind the fighting line. When a battalion took up a firing position, it had to clear the ground, dig and sandbag gun emplacements, and locate aiming stakes. Service and headquarters batteries almost always remained to the rear of the firing batteries in order to direct operations and serve all positions as necessary.

Firing requests came from a number of places. The battalions assigned a forward observer, usually a lieutenant, to the unit being supported, maybe an infantry regiment or battalion or an armored combat command or squadron. In addition, a captain functioned as liaison officer with the divisional artillery to which a battalion was attached. All artillery battalions included one or two single-engine planes, which carried an air observer to identify targets and report the effect of fire. When a battalion went into a semipermanent position, it established forward observations posts. Finally, a field artillery group or corps artillery might oversee firing. In all cases, firing requests, with map coordinates and target descriptions, came into the fire direction center at headquarters battery by radio or telephone. Fire direction center then phoned or radioed the information to the firing batteries. Gun section chiefs aimed the pieces, determined the powder charge, set fuses, then fired the guns. Forward observers, the liaison officer, or an air observer reported back the result of fire or called for readjustments. Artillerymen rarely saw their targets and practically never saw the destructive effects of their work.

This demanding, technical work required mathematical and map skills, as well as a good deal of mechanical talent, to keep the guns and vehicles in operating condition. It became particularly difficult when the artillery was kept on the move, for the men had to prepare gun emplacements, wire communications, foxholes, and ammunition dumps after every move. Artillery also carried light small arms, .50-caliber machine guns, some antitank rockets, and the M-1 carbine for perimeter defense, although gunners were not expected to defend themselves against enemy infantry. For most of the war, one or two batteries of an antiaircraft artillery battalion were attached to provide air defense. The troops had endlessly practiced technical and tactical aspects of field operations at Fort Lewis and the Desert Training Center. Now, in June 1944, the 188th and 957th would carry them out in the face of the enemy.

When the 188th landed at Utah Beach at midday on 11 June, D-day assault troops had already established a line ten miles inland. After months of stateside training, the men were startled most by "the ever present litter of a tough fight...broken rifles, ammunition cases, packs, mess equipment...shell holes and duds." As soon as it dewaterproofed its vehicles, the unit sent out forward parties to the 101st Airborne Division to select gun emplacements and targets. Late on the 11th, Battery B fired the first round at the Germans. The next day, VII Corps attached the 188th to the 82nd Airborne Division, with which it would serve until 6 July. The 957th arrived off Utah Beach at noon on 13 June, but most of it did not land until after dark, an unsettling time to go ashore, with the sound of guns in the distance. Donald Sathe clearly remembers that, while he knew he was in France, he had no idea exactly where. The noise and confusion of combat also struck these men. "I was just as scared as the rest," Captain McWilliams wrote. "There was some fighting going on ahead of us and some prisoners were being taken toward the beach. The smell of battle was everywhere."

Corps artillery ordered the 957th to support the 9th Infantry Division even before all its equipment landed. While they still had daylight, Colonel Collins led the battery forward parties out to select the battalion's first position. First Sergeant Peter Schwab, part of Battery C's party, wrote: "We go ahead and pick out a gun position so when the btry. gets there everything was all set for them....We have to find a place for the guns—the Capt. does this, a place for the switchboard, the wire corporal does this, and a place for the kitchen and trucks, the 1st Sgt. does this. The Bn is allotted a certain area and then the Bn commander allots each battery.'' They easily located and marked off their position in the daylight, but did not take it up until after midnight. For many, the night move ''was frightening. It was dark. And that's the first time we saw dead,'' McWilliams noted. ''We had one hell of a time to get all the pieces lined up,'' Schwab wrote, ''as everything looked a hell of a lot different in the pitch dark.'' Many men feared the position might have mines. Also, ''Fritz was still firing artillery at us but he was way off the beam. We were plenty scairt *[sic]* though,'' Schwab added. Still, they finally got situated and fired off their first round of the war. ''It took over three and one-half years to get that stuff on its way,'' McWilliams wrote in his diary.

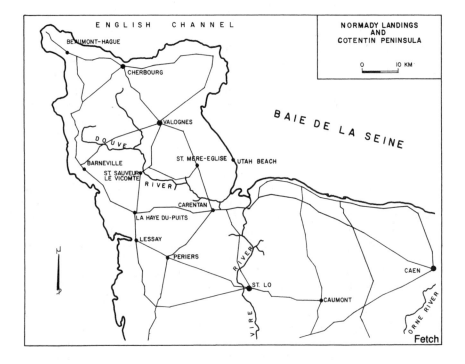

All soldiers, no matter how well trained, naturally experience anxiety and uncertainty when first encountering combat. Normally the case for people at the lower end of the chain of command, few of the artillerymen knew their location or had any knowledge of the tactical or strategic situation. They had little time to contemplate their circumstances or adjust to their new surroundings, for they were included in the VII Corps' westward drive across the Contentin, an operation aimed at cutting the peninsula in half, sealing off German troops to the north, and capturing the port city of Cherbourg. The

188th continued to support the 82nd Airborne, and the 957th worked with the 9th Infantry. After firing 1,160 rounds of preparatory fire on 13 June, the 188th moved westward with the paratroopers the next day. It assisted in the crossing of the Douve River on 19 June, when the drive ended successfully. Neither battalion suffered casualties during the effort. Still, as Donald Turney of the 957th noted, "There was plenty of sniper fire and the boys always rode with their eyes wide open looking for any moving objects." When operations slacked off for a day or two, some of the men in the 188th made tentative steps to make friends with the French. "The civilians are still a little shy," wrote Sergeant Guy Skillman, Battery B, 188th. "But our cigarettes and chocolate are too much to be denied. The eggs and potatoes come to the fore, and each section has its own private cooking utensils."

With the peninsula severed, General Collins turned the 9th Division to the north on 19 June to join the drive on Cherbourg. The 82nd Division, meanwhile, wheeled southward as part of a simultaneous effort to clear the southern portion of the Contentin. Collins and First Army planners hoped to clear all of the peninsula quickly so American troops could mass at its base to launch a breakout from Normandy into the German army's rear, but enemy resistance slowed the effort. The 957th followed the 9th Infantry up the peninsula to Cherbourg during the rest of June. On their second day northward, 21 June, the unit suffered its first losses. In the early morning hours, the antiaircraft battery serving with the battalion shot at an enemy plane, an action that immediately brought down German counterbattery fire, knocking out a gun in Battery C and setting powder cans on fire. Five men were severely burned, and Corporal Marion Green of St. Louis, Missouri, was killed. Green, Captain McWilliams lamented, "was the first man I saw die."

Several days later, as the Cherbourg siege came to an end, the 957th, located at the northern tip of the peninsula near the village of Beaumont, encountered more difficulties. During the night of 30 June and 1 July, the battalion changed positions, although there was little opportunity for forward parties to check out the new location. Batteries B and C pulled into an open field to set up their guns. "We moved in at night," McWilliams wrote, "and it was raining." The field was saturated with small antipersonnel mines, which blew truck and jeep tires and injured several men who unwittingly jumped off their vehicles. The men had a frightening experience as they struggled to remove the wounded while mines continued to explode. Sergeant Peter Schwab turned on his flashlight and "looked around on the ground and you could see them all over. There was 12 of them rite *[sic]* in that small area." With the capture of Cherbourg, the 957th returned south to Carentan on 2 July, where, as Schwab noted with little humor, "mine school was held—a little late, eh?"

At Colonel Collins's direction, the 957th had used a maneuver during the Cherbourg operation to dissuade counterbattery fire. Each night one of the batteries sent out a single gun to a temporary position, the "roving gun," fired a few rounds to draw enemy fire and then quickly moved on. No one liked the roving-gun tactic, for it was hard work all night long, the gun often moving three or four times. More disturbing, the tactic usually had the desired effect of attracting German artillery and sniper fire. Gun crews were always relieved to return to the battalion at daylight, "as you sure feel alone away out there."

one veteran remembered. Although the majority of the unit respected Collins as an officer and artilleryman, the roving-gun policy did not generate affection for him.

During the Cherbourg operation, the First Army activated the VIII Corps to occupy the western half of the peninsula, facing south. With the 188th still attached, the 82nd Airborne temporarily served in the new corps. For the rest of June, VIII Corps attempted unsuccessfully to push southward. When the Cherbourg forces came back to the southern line, the First Army initiated a major offensive using the VII, VIII, and XIX corps, the latter operating to the east of Utah Beach, to oust the Germans from the Cotentin. VIII Corps made the first efforts in the last ten days of June, and the other two corps joined on 1 July. During this time American troops encountered the worst of the bocage country, low, marshy ground crisscrossed with hedgerows and deep country lanes. It offered ideal terrain for troops trained in defensive tactics, skills well known to the Germans. American infantrymen relied heavily on artillery support in the bitter fighting among the hedgerows, too much so in the minds of some critics. Nonetheless, as historian Russell Weigley has observed, in the Cotentin, "Artillery promptly impressed friend and foe alike as the outstanding branch of the American ground forces."

The static fighting of late June left the 188th in the same position for over a week, facing south toward the village of La Haye du Puits and firing support for the airborne troops on a twenty-four-hour basis. For the first time it established forward ground observation posts. Though the unit was not in any direct danger, its on-call status kept the men busy and very tired. Sergeant Guy Skillman described the routine: "Hit the sack, try to sleep, and 'fire mission.' Cuss under your breath, crawl out of the hole (you sleep with your clothes on...shoes and all) and go to work. No lights, everything by touch. Projectile, powder charge, fuze, primer, 'ram,' 'set,' 'ready,' 'fire.'" On 7 July the 82nd Airborne left the line to return to England. The battalion then went into support for the 8th Infantry Division. "The Battalion did some of its heaviest firing of the campaign thus far" on 9 July (1,328 rounds) as the 8th Infantry finally secured La Haye du Puits, an effort begun by the paratroopers on 29 June. It continued this work until 16 July when the infantry captured Lessay. The 188th then returned to VII Corps control and moved to the eastern side of the Cotentin Peninsula, south of Carentan, to rejoin the 957th, in support of the 9th Infantry.

After its move south, the 957th rendered similar support to a number of VII Corps divisions slogging their way through the bocage below Carentan. They were particularly busy on 11 and 12 July, firing 1,137 and 1,377 rounds, respectively, to aid the 9th Infantry. German forces were close enough to harass the battalion with artillery fire and strafing attacks from the air. The 957th lost another man on 19 July when a German ME109 fighter shot down the battalion's observation plane, an unarmed Piper Cub. Lieutenant Fred C. Wallace, Battery C, serving as air observer, died when his plane crashed into some trees.

Stubborn German resistance in the Cotentin, abetted by the bocage, and equally stout defensive efforts in front of the British around Caen seriously delayed the Allies, who had intended a rapid armored advance out of the Normandy beachheads. By late July, after fifty days ashore, Allied troops had barely achieved what the planners had expected they would accomplish in twenty days. The First Army, for example, had hoped to clear the Cotentin in a three- to five-day offensive beginning on 3 July; but from that day to the 18th, the VII, VIII, and XIX corps had advanced only ten miles and the Americans had suffered forty thousand casualties. Lieutenant General Omar N. Bradley, commanding the 12th United States Army Group, sought a way out of the peninsular deadlock in order to make better use of the Americans' greatest advantage, their mechanized mobility.

Bradley and General Collins of the VII Corps devised Operation Cobra, a plan centered on a major drive from the town of St. Lo, south across the Caumont-St. Lo-Periers highway, to the towns of Coutances and Avranches. Such a move would give the Americans control of major highway junctions and access to flatter, more open country ideal for mechanized operations. General Collins's troops were responsible for breaking through German lines in front of St. Lo, and his 1st Infantry Division, fully mechanized, and 2nd and 3rd Armored divisions were assigned to exploit the breakthrough. Operation Cobra plans called for a massive Allied air bombardment and a one-thousand-gun artillery barrage of enemy lines prior to the ground attack.

Operation Cobra began on 25 July 1944, the worst single day of the war for the 957th Battalion. Early that morning, while all American guns were engaged in preparatory fire for the attack, German artillery hit Headquarters Battery, killing one man, wounding two others, and destroying its kitchen truck. The Allied bombing assault began two hours later, its targets lying south of the St. Lo-Periers road. Bombers in the first wave correctly identified the road as their drop line, "but the smoke and dust of these drifted over our lines and later formations dropped their bombs short, apparently mistaking a wrong road for the bomb release line," Colonel Collins wrote. Unfortunately, the 957th was situated between the two roads, and, at 10:05 A.M., an entire stick of bombs hit the Headquarters Battery building. Several men were in line just outside the building, awaiting sick call, while others were standing around watching the awesome air attack. The bombs smashed into the fire direction center and killed or wounded many of those outside. In all, twelve men died and another fifteen received wounds, among them operations officer Major Milton F. Weber, of Jamestown. The enemy would never again inflict such losses on the unit in a single day.

Colonel Collins, although slightly wounded in the hand by shrapnel, Major Hershel Case, executive officer, and others rushed to render first aid and evacuate the wounded. Although buried in rubble, Master Sergeant John W. Benz dug himself out and "assumed control of the men in the area and supervised the aid to the wounded." The battalion lost all communication with 9th Division artillery. For men who had been in combat only six weeks, the gunners overcame the devastating shock quickly. The battalion immediately re-established communication lines, and, "despite the fact that almost half the fire direction personnel were casualties," managed to meet its firing responsibilities before 11:00 A.M. By nightfall, Service Battery had repaired or replaced all damaged equipment, a new fire direction center was in operation, and Staff Sergeant Robert Dudley of Oakes, North Dakota, the only surviving member of Headquarters Battery kitchen section, served a hot evening meal. The 957th fired twenty-four missions totaling 855 rounds after the bombing. All told, bombing shortfalls killed 111 Americans and wounded 500.

If Operation Cobra began ominously, it proved to be far more successful than its planners anticipated. After two days of hard fighting, VII Corps infantry broke through German defenses, opening a breach through which the 1st Infantry and 2nd and 3rd Armored divisions poured southward. Simultaneously, VIII Corps units to the west of General Collins also broke the German line and joined the rush for Avranches. American forces had possession of that important road junction by 30 July, fanning out to their right into Brittany, and to their left into the interior of France during the first week of August. General Bradley activated the Third Army of Lieutenant General George S. Patton, Jr., at this point, sending Patton's units thereafter on their dash to the Seine River south of Paris.

In the weeks since the D-day landings, the Germans in western France, chiefly VII Army, had committed all their forces to containing the Allies within the Normandy lodgment. All available units and equipment had moved close to the battle line running from the Cotentin in the west to the Dives River in the east, in front of Field Marshal Sir Bernard L. Montgomery's 21st Army Group. Lacking any reserve forces west of the Seine, devoid of any significant air power, and forced by Hitler to stand and fight, German commanders by 7 August found themselves facing Allied troops to the north and west, with units south of them as well. Operation Cobra thus not only produced a breakout from the Cotentin Peninsula but, by making the entire German position in Normandy untenable, brought on a desperate German race eastward to the Seine to escape Allied encirclement.

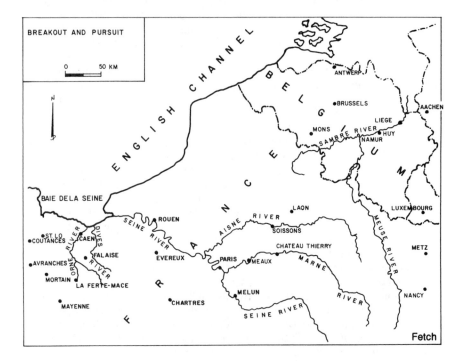

North Dakota's artillerymen soon joined the great pursuit to cut off the enemy. Both battalions were assigned to support the mechanized 1st Division. The 188th joined the 16th Combat Team, composed of the 16th Infantry Regiment, 7th Field Artillery Battalion, and tank elements of the 3rd Armored Division. As a part of the 26th Combat Team, with the 26th Infantry Regiment and the 33rd Field Artillery Battalion, the 957th also moved south, then east as the VII Corps served as the southern flanking force constraining the fleeing Germans. Although the 188th was on the move by 28 July "over roads crowded with heavy traffic," it did not fire for the next three days "since the American Armor and Infantry continued to move forward with great rapidity." German aircraft bombed and strafed the unit on 1 August, killing two men and destroying a Battery B gun and two trucks. The battalion at last went into a firing position on 4 August, with German tanks as targets. Here they saw "More and more signs of a breakdown in the enemy's morale." The 16th Combat Team remained in place near Mayenne from 7 to 11 August to prevent enemy forces from retreating to the south, then went back on the road heading northeast. For the next two weeks the team rarely saw the enemy. The 957th did not leave St. Lo until 30 July and did not join the 26th Combat Team until 1 August. It, too, had casualties soon after entering the pursuit. On 4 August, German shell fire hit Battery A twice, killing four men and wounding five. Thereafter, its experience paralleled the 188th's, with an occasional break from the pursuit. On the 15th, "bathing and swimming was enjoyed in a small creek within the Battalion area. Not often does one find such an attractive and pleasant surrounding to bathe," the Unit Journal commented.

The 1st Division halted temporarily near La Ferte-Mace. From 18 to 23 August, the division and its supporting elements went into a rest, rehabilitation, and maintenance period, the first since all units entered combat. The VII Corps was now within a few miles of Falaise, where units of Patton's Third Army and Montgomery's 21st Army Group were attempting to trap the retreating Germans. The Allies now had to stop the VII Corps in order to lessen traffic jams on the narrow French roads and to prevent American forces from firing into the advancing British. On the 17th, "the day was spent cleaning and washing vehicles, completing necessary maintenance and general policing of all equipment." The battalions also had an opportunity to see movies and United Services Organization shows, and to visit a Red Cross Clubmobile. "For many it was the first taste of doughnuts since leaving the States," and they also had their chance to reap the initial benefits as liberators. "The people here sure are happy that the war is over for them," the 957th's Donald Turney noted, "and have given us anything they had."

Operations resumed on 24 August when the 1st Division leaped ahead almost one hundred miles, from La Ferte-Mace to Chartres, in one day. When the 957th, which moved during the night, awoke to view its new surroundings, the men were surprised by the open country. "This was quite a relief, because it signified that at last the unit was out of the hedgerow country, and the ordeals of fighting in hedgerows was now over." Moves in the next two days brought the battalions up to the Seine River. Increasingly, the French greeted

American troops with enthusiasm. "Now it's getting more like it!" wrote Sergeant Guy Skillman of the 188th. "Pretty girls, pretty frocks. A sun suit or a charming pair of shorts bring whistles and wolf howls" from the men. They crossed the Seine on the 27th, well south of Paris, and headed northeastward toward the Belgian border. "Throughout the march the French people line the roads, both in the country and in the villages," one of the men wrote. French men and women showered Americans with flower bouquets, fresh fruit, and tomatoes. Captain Victor McWilliams noted that one of his sergeants, Robert Gaddie, earned the nickname "Apple Gaddie," because he always sat in the back seat of McWilliams's open command car, "and being in the middle," McWilliams added, "he always gets hit with the hard apples. He always wants to throw them back at the people but the rest won't let him."

Late August brought heady days as VII Corps units moved forward at a rate of twenty-five, thirty, even fifty miles a day. They saw virtually no Germans, and everywhere the jubilant French welcomed the GIs. Everyone enjoyed the pursuit. "It was just kind of go, go, go all the time," one 957th veteran recalled, although it seemed there was "not really any definite strategy." Sergeant Skillman wrote, "we are moving so fast now that we carry infantry with us. A company to a Battalion." As August came to a close, the 1st Division combat teams passed famous World War I battlefields in northeastern France, through Chateau-Thierry on the Marne River, across the Aisne River at Soissons, on toward Mons, Belgium. The rigors of the march began to tell on the equipment. Battery C, 957th, lost first one, then two, then three prime movers as their steel treads broke under the incessant driving. Yet the pursuit continued. The 957th Unit Journal noted for 31 August, "On our marches, maps proved to be quite a problem as the unit moved so fast that we were off them before receiving a new supply."

They found evidence everywhere of a total German rout. Also on the 31st, the 188th "did some spasmodic firing on retreating enemy vehicles and weapons. The enemy continued to withdraw in great disorder, confusion, and without any semblance of organization." Allied forces, with the British 21st Army Group to the west, following the English Channel, and the United States 12th Army Group, including both First and Third United States armies, on the right, flowed northeastward toward Belgium in long, parallel columns. Rarely did artillery units take up position. Rarer still did they need to fire. The 957th, for example, found 2 September "A quiet day, and a typical road march, move forward, halt, and move again. The French" were "always along the road, shaking hands, yelling 'Vive les America[i]ns,' and throwing flowers, apples, pears, tomatoes, and even a kiss now and then." Sergeant Schwab noted in his diary, "A lot of knocked out German stuff was along the road and we were right on their heels."

With no front lines and an extremely fluid strategic situation, the rapidly advancing Allies often had little idea just where the Germans were. Although many enemy units were traveling parallel to, but between, the British and American Army groups, at some point, they would have to make a right turn, to head east for the German border. On 3 September, the 1st Division combat teams crossed into Belgium and took up positions in the dark just south of

Mons. Uncharacteristically, both battalions took German prisoners that night as they set up temporary camps: artillery units were seldom so close to the enemy that they concerned themselves with handling prisoners. Mons, however, happened to be a point where retreating German units decided to make their eastward turn for home. "At 0130 hours," according to the 188th Unit Journal, "two enemy self-propelled 150 mm howitzers and a motorcycle attempted to pass through the battalion position. Btry. C opened fire with small arms and bazookas." While the battery knocked out one of the guns with a rocket, small-arms fire forced the Germans to abandon the other one. Battalion personnel captured 60 prisoners, to add to the 160 taken when they went into position, including a major general. Colonel Carlson saw the incident as valuable experience, for it gave the men "the satisfaction of both visual and material contact with the battle—visual in that they could see the enemy and watch his operations—and material in the capture of both prisoners and equipment."

The 957th found the clash at Mons a more harrowing experience. It, too, went into position late on 3 September, and, because it expected to take to the road right off the next morning, it did not dig in or emplace its guns. At daybreak on the 4th, a large German column, later estimated at the strength of a reinforced regiment, with armored vehicles and artillery approached the battalion on a secondary road in the rear of its position. Immediately, the first platoon, Battery D, 103rd Antiaircraft Artillery Battalion, attached to the 957th, opened fire with its 40 mm Bofors guns. Fortunately, Colonel Collins later remarked, the antiaircraft artillery unit "had been sited around the Bn. where it could perform a close-in security function....The 40 mm to the west initially stopped the German column and gave us time to organize the position and dig a few foxholes." Although untrained in infantry tactics, the artillerymen quickly established a perimeter defense and engaged the Germans in a hot small-arms fight for the next three hours. The big 155 mm howitzers had little value in this fight because, with the enemy as close as three hundred yards, the range "was well below the minimum elevation of the guns."

Three times the Germans attacked to push their way through the battalion. An assault on the east flank at 7:00 A.M., supported by mortar, machine gun, and artillery fire, failed. Then came a frontal strike an hour later. When that, too, collapsed, the Germans came at the west flank. In each case, machine gun fire and hand grenades drove them off. During the second attempt, Colonel Collins requested supporting fire from the 33rd Field Artillery Battalion, a 105 mm unit that was part of the 26th Combat Team. This fire, he recalled, "was adjusted so close to our lines that overs and shorts on our troops were received in the same volleys." The brunt of the German attack fell on Captain McWilliams's Battery C. Private Owen R. Spillum, Grand Forks, set up and manned a .50-caliber machine gun near the battery's exposed position. McWilliams wrote that Spillum "sat right out in the road and fired...until he wore out the barrel." Collins commented that "It was he in large measure who repulsed the initial attack." The colonel praised McWilliams as "the real hero of the action" for effectively organizing Battery C's defensive efforts. At last, just before 11:00 A.M., two platoons of infantry and a platoon each of tanks and tank destroyers came up to relieve the battalion. All batteries except A then left the area. Continued enemy resistance made it "necessary to send an armored car to cover the withdrawal of A Btry....under small arms fire."

"Well, this has been a busy morning, and a noisy one," McWilliams later noted in his diary. The day was certainly unusual for a medium artillery unit, and a costly one as well. Two men died, four suffered severe wounds, and another five took light wounds. Two days later McWilliams experienced delayed shock, with chills and uncontrollable shaking. The battalion doctor wanted to send him to the hospital, but the captain declined and accepted the doctor's second prescription, several shots of Scotch, which solved the problem. In all, the battalion destroyed 7 enemy vehicles, killed or wounded 150 men, and captured 40 prisoners. The next day, 1st Division infantrymen rounded up an additional 2,000 prisoners in the area. McWilliams, Private Spillum, and Private Jack Madden, all of Battery C, later received the Silver Star for their actions that day.

The clash with enemy infantry at Mons resulted from a deliberate VII Corps attempt to prevent remnants of the German VII Army from reaching Germany. In all, the corps captured 25,000 enemy troops near Mons between 3 and 5 September. Thereafter, General Collins's units turned directly east to join other First Army elements and units of General Patton's Third Army in a rush to the German border. General Bradley hoped that American troops could reach and occupy the Siegfried line, a complex of border defenses running from the Netherlands to Switzerland, before the Germans got there. Indeed, there was momentary talk at 12th Army Group headquarters of the opportunity to push through the Siegfried line and continue the advance into the crucial Ruhr industrial complex on the Rhine River. If the Allies succeeded in that, the war would virtually be over.

Few in the line units talked of a quick end to the war when they resumed their march eastward on 6 September. Nonetheless, they encountered no enemy resistance to impede their advance, and the Belgians met American troops with even greater enthusiasm than the French had. Sergeant Skillman of the 188th noted, "Mons is a soldier's paradise." With the military police occupied in handling thousands of prisoners, "They didn't have a chance to put up the 'Off Limits' signs, and the beer was good...yes, real beer! The civilians...couldn't do enough for us." As for the 957th, first the people of Jumet, then Liege, greeted the battalion openly. At the former, McWilliams wrote, "we went into position right in town and it looked like the county fair. The people brought out all the beer we could drink." When they stopped for the night, Belgians offered their homes and beds to the tired soldiers. Younger Belgians beseiged the Americans for autographs and wrote victory slogans on their vehicles, helmets, and jackets. On the road between Jumet and Liege, "The crowd had formed a human chain across the road forcing vehicles to stop." In Liege, Peter Schwab wrote, "People...went crazy when we passed thru town...drinks, women, ice cream, etc." Tragedy marred the 188th's move beyond Liege after it stopped in the village of Herve, east of Liege, on the afternoon of 10 September. Colonel Carlson set up battalion headquarters in a private home in the village, with the firing batteries out of town. When men of Headquarters Battery ran telephone wire from headquarters to the batteries, "the wire truck...struck a Teller mine....The vehicle was blown completely from the road." Two enlisted men died instantly in the explosion, a particularly sad occasion, for no enemy soldiers or enemy fire were within miles of Herve.

In pursuit of the Germans since 20 August, American units in the First and Third armies had made the greatest advances and, since crossing the Seine, had moved "almost without impediment from the enemy," according to historian Russell Weigley. Now the VII Corps approached the German border. On 13 September, while still in Belgium, both battalions fired for the first time into Germany, their target, the city of Aachen. Circumstances, however, were changing rapidly. The 188th discovered that day that "the enemy offered stronger resistance than at any time during the past five weeks. The enemy was beginning to use artillery again." As the 957th neared Germany, it encountered German-speaking Belgians who greeted them with "a cold stare rather than the warm welcome of the French" or French-speaking Belgians. These people did not "display the enthusiasm we have seen in the past," its Unit Journal commented.

The glorious days of pursuit ended when the 12th Army Group units crossed into Germany in mid-September. Though Hitler's apparently short-sighted strategy of compelling the German army to fight to the last in Normandy had wrecked most of those forces, it had allowed his high command to organize new units to man the Siegfried line. These were taking their places in the border defenses and offering strong resistance. At the same time, Allied units faced serious logistical problems. The Americans alone had more than a million men in France, with more coming every day. On 15 August, the Allies opened another front with the Anvil landings in southern France. All these men consumed food, fuel, and ammunition, and the chief problem in supplying them lay in the lack of sufficient ports on the English Channel through which supplies could flow to the front. Most supplies continued to come across the Normandy beaches, whose facilities were barely able to bring in enough to sustain the fighting units and were insufficient to support another major operation. In addition, Allied bombers had damaged much of the French rail system before D-day. Although the damage had worked to the Allies' advantage up to the breakout by hindering German logistics, it now worked against them. With the First and Third armies now in Germany, the Allies had to truck the limited supplies entering France over hundreds of miles to reach line organizations. Logistical shortages and effective German defensive efforts brought the Allied advance to an abrupt halt in mid-September all along the West Wall.

General Omar Bradley's 12th Army Group, composed of the First Army under Courtney Hodges, George Patton's Third Army, and the recently activated Ninth Army, led by Lieutenant General William H. Simpson, held a line from the Netherlands-Belgium border to the French province of Lorraine. Simpson's force stood at the north end of the line, with Patton on the south and Hodges in the center, between the German city of Aachen and the Ardennes Forest in Belgium. J. Lawton Collins's VII Corps was to the First Army's left, in front of Aachen. Planners at all levels hoped that the VII Corps could bypass the Aachen urban-industrial complex, cross the Roer River near Druren, and reach the Rhine before the end of December. If Collins could achieve that, the conquest of the Ruhr industrial region still remained a possibility before 1945. But such hopes were quickly dashed. The penetration of the Siegfried line from 12 to 15 September did not lead to another breakthrough. By the end of 1944, the VII Corps units would be little more than twenty miles beyond the Belgium-German border first crossed in mid-September.

Fall and early winter 1944 caused the most frustration of the entire Allied European campaign, for the weather turned sour soon after Americans entered Germany. According to the 188th's Unit Journal, it rained nearly every day in October and at least half the days in November. Rain, fog, and drizzle prevented air observations for artillery and air support for ground troops. When the battalion changed position in October, a four-mile move occupied eight hours. "Rainfall was heavy....The roads were muddy and traffic was slowed immeasureably [sic]." In the static warfare around Aachen, the battalions remained in place for weeks on end. The constant deluge made gun positions difficult to maintain. The 957th's Peter Schwab noted for 18 October that his "Ammo section had to move...becuz [sic] of the deep mud." All his gun sections "were busy hauling straw and gravel into the sections so they could get around in the mud." Schwab's battery commander, Victor McWilliams, also commented on the need "to move the guns several times because of the heavy rains." In November, he went on, "it rained every day for 17 days."

The battalions experienced the logistics crunch as well. The First Army imposed gasoline and ammunition rationing. To help make up shortages, in late September the 188th turned over all its ammunition trucks to the 1st Infantry Division to haul ammunition from Normandy. They made two 700-mile round trips. "Gasoline is still a difficult problem," the 957th Unit Journal noted at the end of September. "For the past few weeks strong efforts have been made to prevent unnecessary use of vehicles and to conserve present supplies." All American units were beginning to encounter manpower shortages, and the Army lacked sufficient replacements to make up combat losses and a growing sick list. Though artillery units did not suffer casualty rates similar to infantry organizations, their number fell nonetheless. The 188th reported an enlisted strength of 511 at the beginning of August and a strength of 481 in early November. In the 957th, the numbers were 500 and 479, respectively.

The tactical struggle in and around Aachen became a numbing infantry fight reminiscent of World War I. The troops measured their daily progress in hundreds of yards gained. After halting in front of Aachen on 18 September, the First Army spent the rest of the month in reorganization and resupply. It launched a full-scale attack on 1 October, but the assault quickly degenerated into a siege. Day after day the battalions, both supporting 1st Division regiments attacking Aachen, shelled the city. Neither unit moved during all of October. With most of its buildings reduced to rubble, Aachen at last surrendered on 21 October. The city's capture did not open a gateway for the VII Corps into Germany's heartland. To the right of the corps lay the

Huertgen Forest, deeply wooded and lined with ridges and valleys. To its front were a series of suburbs, the largest being Stolberg and Eschweiler, which both had to be taken street by street. The forest and suburbs offered little opportunity for the Americans to utilize their mechanized mobility, and bad weather continued to hamper tactical air strikes. For the remainder of October and all of November, the VII Corps and other First Army elements fought to clear the Huertgen Forest and the Aachen urban corridor in order to reach the Roer River plain.

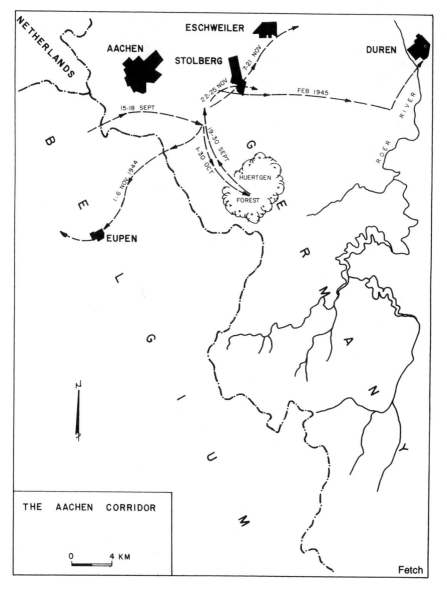

THE AACHEN CORRIDOR

0   4 KM

Fetch

During the first week of November, the battalions pulled out of the line for a seven-day ordnance check. The heavy guns needed recalibration and new bores. Conditions were so bad, said Donald Turney, that "It took three tractors to get my gun out of position as it was so muddy." They traveled back into Belgium where Ordnance Corps technicians could repair the guns. Battalion personnel were responsible for vehicle maintenance and repair, but they found some time for rest and recreation. "A few of the fellows got a little looped on cognac the first night there," Sergeant Skillman commented. Perhaps more importantly, all the men had an opportunity to get inside, out of the rain and muck. In the 957th, billeting officers ensured that "each individual of the Battalion had a warm room, facilities for laundry, bathing, and clean beds with snow white sheets to sleep in. A rather novel experience." All had chances to see movies and United Services Organization shows, and many took passes to Verviers and Liege for a day or two. Chosen by lot from the firing batteries, four lucky men from each battalion got four-day passes to Paris. The week in Belgium, where the Americans remained popular, brought welcome relief. Donald Turney and Donald Bell, Battery C, 957th, were quartered in an apartment with a Belgian family, "and had a good deal. They really treated us good and went out of their way to help and get us anything we wanted," one of them noted.

Then, back to Germany. The VII Corps had another big push planned, aimed at capturing Stolberg and Eschweiler. It assigned the 1st Division (957th in support) and the 104th Infantry Division (aided by the 188th) to a 16 November assault. The attack began in yet more rain with poor visibility. German infantry bitterly contested every American advance with mortars, machine guns, effective artillery barrages, and surprise counterattacks. Although Stolberg fell on 22 November, and Eschweiler the next day, operations continued into December. The VII Corps pushed on to the Roer River until 15 December, when it became evident that the Germans had given up what they held on the west bank. Throughout this month-long operation, the battalions supported the infantry as they had during the drive on Aachen. They maintained observation posts far in front of the firing batteries to report on targets and on the effect of fire, a particularly important task because observation planes could rarely fly.

Artillery supported infantry in a variety of ways. Most commonly, they used preparatory fires, that is, firing on a position just prior to an infantry attack. Cannoneers were often given harassing and interdiction missions. Harassing fire meant shelling manned positions at irregular intervals to keep enemy troops off balance. Interdiction consisted of preplanned fire directed at road junctions, rail lines, and heavily traveled roads and trails to disrupt traffic. Harrassing and interdiction fire sometimes had vague goals, as when the 957th shelled the village of Langerwehe "with the mission of starting fires and blocking roads with debris." Some fire missions were very explicit, as forward observers called for artillery to destroy a barn, pillbox, or tank concentration. Artillery also used devastating tactics, such as the time on target, which called for a concentrated barrage of several battalions on a particular point for a specified time. Time on target barrages invariably demoralized enemy soldiers. During much of the fighting in the Aachen corridor, German artillery was heavy and effective. Americans found it essential to use counterbattery fire, that is, shelling enemy gun positions. On 11 December, for example, VII Corps artillery directed a five-battalion time on target on identified German batteries. The artillery occasionally fired smoke screens to cover infantry attacks or marked targets for air assaults with red smoke shells. The varied fire missions came day and night, and only the worst weather halted artillery work.

Operations around Aachen exposed the artillerymen to frequent enemy artillery fire and occasional air attacks. Since they rarely changed positions, and the Germans had the area well mapped, American batteries came under counterbattery fire. The enemy shelled the 957th several times on 12 and 13 November, though the battalion only lost a radio. On 4 and 5 December, heavy German guns (240 mm) hit the 188th. Battery A lost a gun on the 4th. The next day, "Two howitzers in Battery C and one...in Battery B were damaged. Fifty rounds of ammunition were destroyed. No casualties resulted since the Battalion was not firing...and the personnel were under cover." The 188th lost one-third of its guns from this incident, but they received replacements four days later. Still, for all of November, the battalion suffered only four casualties, all from mine booby traps scattered in buildings in Stolberg.

Compared to the infantry who slogged through the mud, city streets, and the shattered woods of Huertgen Forest for weeks on end, the artillerymen were fortunate. Once a soldier accepted the fact that he would find no women on the firing line and would only infrequently acquire liquor, he thought most of his stomach and of sleep. Unlike infantrymen, the gunners had opportunities to improve on Army food and sleeping facilities. While around Aachen, Colonel Collins wrote, "The men supplemented the ration with game (deer mostly) and maybe even a cow which had gotten wounded, or something." (Battery A treated the colonel to a venison dinner on 17 October.) The 957th had "liberated" several large trailers while in France and fixed them up to serve as mobile dining rooms for the gun crews. Although, to quote Collins, it was "slightly illegal," the battalion used several former Russian prisoners of war to do kitchen police. Being in position at Lichtenbusch for over six weeks, Donald Turney noted, allowed his men to do "a lot of cooking in this position." They must have "made a bushel basket full of shoestring potatoes" while there.

Once into the Aachen corridor, the Allies used the homes, warehouses, and public buildings in the conquered German towns as quarters. Donald Turney recalled, "Had my gun right outside the back door of a house we were staying in. Every time we had a fire mission all that we had to do was run out the door, fire the mission and go back into the house." Battery C's Captain Victor McWilliams conceded, "This has been the best position the Btry has ever had, and every man had some sort of building to live in." Gun crews not so fortunate as Turney's prepared dugout shelters near their guns, "but even there they managed to have small German stoves in their shelters," Collins wrote, "and were reasonably comfortable." Service Battery set itself up in four large houses in Stolberg, three of which had indoor plumbing. "Each Battery has been assigned a day," the Unit Journal noted, "and everyone in the Battalion is enjoying a tub with plenty of hot water. Four bedrooms in the house have been set aside for personnel who return from the front for rest and relaxation.'' The firing batteries tried to send one or two men from each gun crew back to the Service Battery's ''rest camp'' every other day or so.

Since artillery units rarely had direct contact with the enemy, they could release a few men at a time for passes to Liege, Verviers, and even Paris. This policy, begun in the second week of November, gave many men a chance to get away from the line for a short time. The service batteries, 1st Infantry Division, and VII Corps offered movies behind the lines during quiet periods. Even an occasional United Services Organization show came close to the front. Eighty men of the 957th saw Marlene Dietrich in a United Services Organization show in Stolberg on 3 December. The proximity of the two North Dakota battalions in fixed positions allowed Colonels Carlson and Collins to visit each other's command post occasionally during November and December. These small amenities lessened the monotony of endless days of firing, the oppressive rain and mud, and the yearning for home. In the second week of December, the battalions marked their first six months in combat. The next month would bring the greatest challenge they would face in the war.

Enemy behavior changed dramatically in front of the VII Corps after 15 December. All German artillery moved east of the Roer River and ceased firing. On the 16th and 17th, German fighter planes, not seen since late September, reappeared to strafe and bomb. After German paratroopers dropped into the corps's rear area on the night of the 27th, men of the 188th captured two of them. The Germans had planned these small diversions to throw the Americans off balance, for early on 16 December they launched a major counterattack in the Ardennes region of southern Belgium and Luxembourg. They hit the VIII Corps, the last corps on the First United States Army's right flank, with eight panzer divisions and elements of eleven infantry divisions. Only four American divisions held the entire Ardennes front. The attack, both a tactical and strategic surprise, caught American soldiers wholly unprepared. Allied commanders at every level failed to anticipate Hitler's last major effort to stall the war on the Western Front. Stout defensive efforts at St. Vith and Bastogne temporarily stymied the Germans, who then bypassed these villages in their drive for the Meuse River and the rear areas of First and Third United States armies. By Christmas Day 1944 the enemy had punched a bulge fifty miles deep at its furthest into the American line.

Allied reaction to the Ardennes offensive came rapidly. Supreme Commander, Allied Expeditionary Force, Dwight D. Eisenhower directed the 12th Army Group commander, Omar Bradley, to turn units of Hodges's First Army to the south and elements of Patton's Third Army to the north. Eisenhower wanted these forces to stem the German advance, then cut it off from retreat and destroy it. He approved General Montgomery's suggestion that units from his 21st Army Group move to the Meuse River to ensure halting the enemy on that line, then relieve defending American troops so they might reorganize and undertake a counteroffensive. Temporarily reshuffling his forces, Eisenhower gave Montgomery command of all American units on the northeren shoulder of the bulge, while Bradley directed operations on the southern side. Montgomery requested that General Collins and his VII Corps staff direct the counterattack in the north, which Eisenhower quickly approved.

Collins had already sent several units from his corps, notably the 1st Infantry Division and the 3rd Armored, to shore up the northern shoulder before he and his headquarters left the Aachen corridor to head for the bulge. As corps artillery, the 188th and 957th also moved south. The latter departed on 21 December for Belgium, with the 188th under way two days later. They made the ninety-mile trip in one day, though the "weather was very cold. Movement [was] conducted under rigid blackout conditions." Most of the men had only a vague idea of what was happening in the Ardennes, but, as Colonel Collins later wrote, they could understand the basic assignment easily enough: "It was the job of the combat troops to 'head them off at the pass' and push them back." Still, their initial entry into the bulge was confusing. Because of the blackout, the 188th's Sergeant Skillman noted, "It was hard to keep in convoy, and it's a wonder any of us got to the right area." Battery C's kitchen and wire trucks got lost and "wound up in Holland for a few days." They were "kidded unmercifully for taking a furlough at a time like this!"

By the time the VII Corps was in place, 23-24 December, the German onslaught had reached its high-water mark. Elements of the 2nd Panzer Division were at the village of Celles, only four miles from the Meuse. On Christmas Day, the United States 2nd Armored Division, supported in part by the 957th, attacked the 2nd Panzer to stop its advance and in a two-day battle nearly destroyed it. Peter Schwab noted, this was where "we saw the first signs of the German offensive. There were guns and armored vehicles still burning when we got there. It looked like we were pretty close to the Huns." Divisional and corps artillery had a major role in shattering enemy tanks and other vehicles. Elsewhere, to use the professional staff officer's phrase, the situation was fluid, that is, no one knew what was going on. American units on the bulge's shoulders were well in place to prevent any expansion. Those trapped within the bulge continued to fight desperately while awaiting relief. Nonetheless, as a VII Corps situation report bluntly stated, "No organized front line exists." General Montgomery sought to stabilize the bulge as it existed on 25 December. Once it became clear the Germans no longer had the strength to push forward, Montgomery intended to pull the VII Corps out of combat, give it a day or two to reorganize, and then put it on the counterattack.

After British units relieved the VII Corps on 30 December, General Collins's men pulled back ten or fifteen miles. Colonel Collins reminded the 957th, "contrary to what most of you think," the time off the line "will be devoted to the maintenance and servicing of all battery property. It is *not* a rest period." The relief did not enhance Allied relations. With his battalion slated for a difficult move (it was sleeting), the colonel wanted to "travel as much as possible in daylight." The British artillery unit replacing them arrived about 3:30 in the afternoon, but it "decided it was almost time for tea, so everything stopped, personnel got out of their vehicles, built little fires beside the road and made tea." Collins "was furious, because they could have gone into position and then had tea." Tradition overruled military necessity, however. "Despite my remonstrances, a leisurely tea was finished and we didn't get all batteries on the road until after dark," and, he wrote, "It was a miserable evening and a difficult occupation of position."

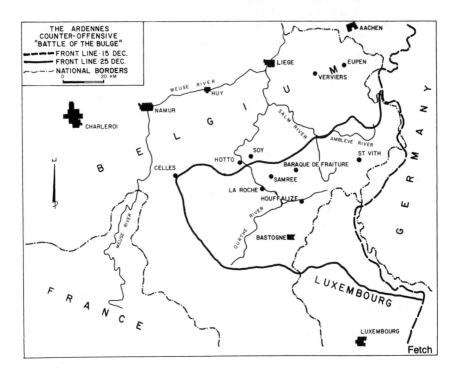

The weather, as great an enemy as the Germans throughout the Ardennes campaign, remained bitterly cold for over a month. Snow and ice greatly hampered movement and made living in the field not only uncomfortable but dangerous. Frostbite and trench foot took their toll as frequently as enemy shells and bullets. The drivers found the battalions' tracked prime movers particularly difficult to handle on icy, snow-covered roads, most of them narrow, winding lanes with no shoulders and sharp drop-offs on each side. Drivers also encountered many hills and unbridged streams. When the 957th moved on 1 January 1945, the liabilities of the tracked vehicles quickly became evident. "The steel tracks of the M-5 when in contact with icy roads" had "a tendency to cause the tractor to react like a box sled and slide down hill and off the road into the ditch." A 188th move early in January, Sergeant Skillman wrote, "took 48 hours of cold, backbreaking work to move the 15 miles to our new spot." A tractor in Battery C overturned, dragging its gun with it into the ditch. Battery B got lost during a night snowstorm and did not reach position until the next morning.

Icy roads forced drivers to attempt various expedients to overcome slipping and sliding. With fairly flat and open terrain, the tractors could leave the road and move cross country. At other times, the men drove them with one track off the road and in the ditch, sometimes a dangerous maneuver. One artillery battalion, not from North Dakota, attempted this method, but its tractor ran over "a 'Daisy Chain' of mines which were laying in the ditch," the resulting explosion destroying the gun and tractor. Most often the drivers wisely abandoned the tractors for the time being and used five-ton Diamond-T trucks to pull the guns. Nothing could eliminate snow, which fell steadily nearly every day. During one particularly difficult move, on 7 January, the 957th's Edward Dietz sat on a truck fender with a flashlight, shouting instructions to his driver who could not see the road.

Despite the weather, VII Corps's counterattack got under way on 3 January, General Collins attacking the bulge from the north, between the villages of Celles and Hotton. He placed the 2nd Armored and 84th Infantry Division on his right, the 957th in support, and the 3rd Armored and 83rd Infantry Division on his left flank, the 188th included there. Collins ultimately desired to pinch off the bulge at the village of Houffalize and meet a similar force directed by General Patton coming up from the south. The Ardennes, a heavily wooded region with hills and ridges, was laced with streams and rivers and dotted by small villages. Regardless of the atrocious weather, the region did not offer ideal country for mobile warfare. The Germans turned every village into a fortress and every ridge into a makeshift fortification, and the weather simply made things worse. According to Colonel Collins, climatic conditions made it "very hard to keep reliable communication, and more reliance had to be placed on radios, which at that time were not all that reliable either."

On the VII Corps's right, the villages of La Roche and Samree became the first objectives, from 3 to 13 January the Americans hammering at these German positions. Weather and terrain prevented the 957th from firing observed fire for most of the campaign. At no other time during the war did the gunners so frequently and literally fire blindly. The unit's daily operations report for 8 January explained "the reason for the quantity of ammunition they have had to fire today." Though "observation" had "been impossible on enemy action," the 2nd Armored Division had been constantly "bothered with pockets of resistance and possible build-up areas." The division artillery commander estimated the map coordinates for these pockets and areas, and "we are 'walking' around the area" with timed volleys. "This is a costly process, but ammunition is more expendable than men's lives." Conditions along the front kept the battalion widely dispersed, with Service Battery remaining far to the rear, and Headquarters Battery split in two sections, one under Colonel Collins and the other under Major Hershel Case, battalion executive officer. The firing batteries were at last reunited on 16 January after "having operated for past several days in a staggered depth formation of several miles."

On at least one occasion, parts of the 957th moved into a town not yet cleared by infantry. As the forward party moved about selecting buildings for quarters, a fire fight broke out at the edge of town. Peter Schwab wrote home, "I never did expect to see an actual infantry and tank battle. I've often complained of how close to the front we were but I never figured out we would see the day that the infantry had to clear out our area for us." Enemy shell fire landed near the party, sending all of them, including Colonel Collins, into a nearby ditch; shell fragments hit Collins's command car. The intensity of combat brought the heaviest firing of the war, the 957th shooting over 1,000 rounds five separate times between 6 and 13 January. On the busiest day, the 9th, it fired 2,430 rounds. Weather complicated the shooting. On the 6th, Battery C had to move two of its guns because "they were going through the frozen crust and sinking way in the mud." During firing on the 9th, "One of the boys slipped" and dropped a shell on Donald Turney's foot. "It swole up like a balloon...I couldn't wear a shoe for about two weeks," he lamented. That same day, a gun in Battery C experienced a hang fire. The primer failed to explode when the lanyard was pulled; but when Private Claude Crabtree stepped behind the gun breech, it went off. The recoil hit Crabtree, and "The blow crushed his chest and knocked him against a pile of shell casings crushing his skull." A few days later the 957th changed positions during another heavy snow. "We had a tank with a dozer on the front clear a place to put the gun," Donald Turney noted. "It was a typical North Dakota blizzard for a couple of days."

Several miles to the east, the left wing of the VII Corps also faced south, its initial objective to take the Samree-Salmchateau road and the road junction at Baraque de Fraiture. The 188th experienced all the vicissitudes of fighting in the Ardennes. Its unit journal noted that 9 January was the "15th day the battalion was unable to register" because it could not see any prominent features upon which to shoot registration fire. Sergeant Skillman reported, "Fraiture was a hot spot. Here for the first time in combat we fired charge two," that is, the powder charge for the shortest range possible for a 155 mm howitzer. "We were so close to the front lines that infantry outposts were on each flank of the guns," he added.

After reaching Houffalize on 16 January, VII Corps units made contact with Patton's men. The Allies had cut the bulge in its center. German forces west of Houffalize broke contact with the VII Corps in their flight to escape entrapment. Units east of the town fought more fiercely to stem the American advance. Consequently, in the 957th's area, action dropped off rapidly, while the 188th remained in contact with the enemy for several more days, firing 1,167 rounds on 17 January. The Allies realized by the 20th that they would soon eliminate the bulge and operations tapered off soon after. The 957th journal recorded on the 23rd that of the fifty miles gained by the Germans, "Today, the American First and Third Armies have regained 44 of those miles and are rapidly recovering the remaining 66 miles."

In retrospect, as Major Milton F. Weber of the 957th wrote to the Jamestown *Sun* in 1945, "We consider that campaign the most strenuous and harrowing of all our combat experiences. Men and officers were called upon to do almost the impossible under the most adverse conditions." The bitter cold, ice, and snow, coupled with the tactical uncertainties of late December and early January, challenged American fighting men as did no other battle of the war. As the 957th moved up to the line to begin the early

January counterattack, Sergeant Schwab wrote in his diary, "Some of the men froze their hands on this trip." He noted soon after that several had fallen ill with colds and dysentery. From 6 to 8 January, perhaps the worst time of all, a severe snowstorm blanketed the Ardennes. The 957th had to move on the 7th, but "only one gun ever got there," according to Schwab. "We had no supper and no breakfast after being out in that blizzard all nite." Schwab's battery hunkered down along the road for the night, surrounded by frozen German corpses and their shattered equipment. Then the "wind came up and...we really had fun," he said. "Part of the men were in one place and the rest back at the other position. Our morale was the lowest right here than it was anytime during the war."

The men had great difficulty finding shelter. "We were 'camping out' in hastily constructed log shelters and tents," the 188th's Guy Skillman wrote. Major Weber recalled "The men using every available cattle-shed, hog-wallow and dugout to protect themselves from the bitter cold." After taking position on the depressing move of 7 January, the gun crews of the 957th "found it necessary to build dugouts and improvise wooden shacks" from lumber taken from a nearby mill. Somehow they found small heating stoves. "These improvised warm up shacks did much to prevent loss of personnel due to exposure."

For all the suffering, the men succeeded in finding small comforts. Despite the weather and the proximity of the enemy, both battalions somehow arranged to eat a traditional Christmas dinner of turkey and trimmings. On 3 January, in one of those inexplicable curiosities of Army logistics, the 957th received a beer ration, which they thoroughly enjoyed, even though it was nearly frozen. The battalion's cooks managed to come up with fresh eggs just a day after the early January blizzard and served them cooked to order. Once the Americans cleared the western end of the bulge, VII Corps divisions established rear-area rest camps. The 957th rotated ten men each from the firing batteries for three days at the 2nd Armored Division rest camp beginning on 13 January. "The camp will provide facilities for bathing, laundry and shelter in homes away from the sound of the guns," the Unit Journal noted.

Relief for all came when the VII Corps was pulled out of combat on 24 January for a rest and rehabilitation period, after just over a month in the Ardennes. Personnel of both battalions found quarters in Belgian homes. To Sergeant Skillman, "It was just like going to visit a country cousin. They shared their fuel, did our laundry, and made evening snacks of waffles, eggs or baked apples." The men, Donald Turney wrote, "spent a lot of time getting our equipment back in shape to go back on the line." They also had time for rest and recreation. "We...saw lots of shows [both live and on film] and had a much needed warm shower," he added. Some of the men even went rabbit and pheasant hunting. Others received twenty-four-hour passes, and several, like Captain Victor McWilliams, enjoyed three-day passes to Paris. The battalions were on stand down for eleven days. All would have agreed with Donald Turney: "It was a really good rest." The VII Corps and its constituent elements returned to their former positions on the west bank of the Roer River in early February. The men found it difficult to generate much enthusiasm at this point. As the 957th's Unit Journal noted, the move back to Germany was "made without incident," but on the trip "the billets consisted chiefly of war torn buildings, some with roofs, some without, all with the usual debris in and about the buildings." And weather continued to plague them. With rain day after day, the gun positions again became muddy swamps. The troops welcomed any small amenity to break the monotony. A great deal of mail finally arrived, for none had been delivered during the hectic weeks in the Ardennes. Scroungers in the 957th used a captured German generator to supply electricity to the men's quarters, "a large air raid shelter," and to operate a radio, "thus furnishing news, music and entertainment...in all sections of the batteries." Reduction of the bulge gave the Americans a continuous front again, permitting a secure rear. Once more, the VII Corps and the First Army sent individual officers and enlisted men off to Paris, Brussels, even the French Riviera, on passes, and two enlisted men from each battalion received seven-day furloughs to England. At every level, however, all knew that until Allied forces crossed the Rhine River the war would drag on. In early March, Sergeant Skillman wrote from the west bank of the Roer, "We resign ourselves to a long wait" before crossing the Rhine.

Allied planners were less pessimistic, hoping to cross the great German river before the end of March. In the north, General Montgomery laid plans for a massive 21st Army Group assault on the Rhine to begin in early February. In the 12th Army Group, Omar Bradley prepared small offensives to break free at last from the West Wall and close up to the Rhine in conjunction with Montgomery's operations. But continued bad weather and flooding along the Roer delayed the attack until the end of February. The VII Corps was the only part of the First United States Army to participate in Montgomery's Operation Veritable. Early on the morning of 23 February the battalions, according to one participant, "with all other arty in the Corps started firing one of the longest and largest preparations we have seen for a long time. There was continuous artillery from 0245 to 0500." During the barrage, the 188th fired 700 rounds and the 957th 864. While British forces to the north made small progress, VII Corps infantry and armor at last jumped the troublesome Roer River and moved eastward toward the Rhine with greater ease than expected. Once American units fought their way through the Roer River defenses, they discovered, as they had back in the August breakthrough, few German units had enough strength to resist. When the artillery units crossed the Roer on the 26th, some VII Corps armored troops were already halfway to the Rhine. During the operation, the 188th supported the 8th Infantry Division, and the 957th the 104th Infantry Division.

The unexpectedly easy VII Corps penetration of Roer River defenses developed into a dash to the Rhine in the hopes of capturing major bridges intact. Viewing the Rhine as a symbolic as well as a military obstacle to the Allies, German troops fought desperately to delay British and American advances until they had destroyed all of the river's bridges. These efforts failed to stop the VII Corps, however. According to one member of the 957th, 28 February was "Reminiscent of our race across France and Belgium last summer" when the unit moved twice in one day, "first to Manheim where we barely had time to register before we packed up and left for our present position.'' At this point, all of the 12th Army Group, Hodges's First Army and Patton's Third Army, joined the advance to the Rhine, but none had the good fortune to secure a bridge. On 5 March the VII Corps closed on Cologne, which straddled the Rhine, but could not clear the west bank before retreating Germans blew the Hohenzollern Bridge at the center of the city. Artillerymen derived some satisfaction in being able to fire across the river at retreating German forces.

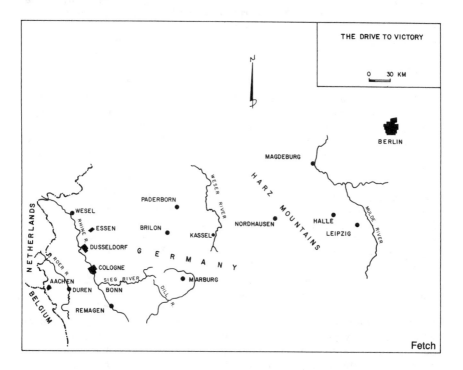

For the next few days, VII Corps forces regrouped and fought to clear suburbs south of Cologne, along the west side of the Rhine. Fortunately they were spared the bitter street fighting that had marked the Aachen urban-industrial complex back in September. Since it appeared they might have a quiet period of two or three days, Colonel Collins ''decided to declare a bn holiday on the 8th of March. We had liberated the wine cellar,'' he explained, ''of a German hotel in Cologne.'' The enterprising artillerymen filled a truck with wine, and, according to Victor McWilliams, ''We brought home enough to get the family plenty drunk.'' Collins rationed out the wine to all batteries and put skeleton crews on duty. ''It was a nice sunshiny day and we had one large picnic...songs and wine and even a softball game or two,'' he remembered. Late that day, VII Corps headquarters told Collins to take his battalion south to Bonn, to go into support for the 1st Infantry. By this time, most of his men were deeply under the influence of the liberated wine. "Fortunately we had enough teetotalers and duty personnel to make the move," Collins recalled, which they did at night, in the rain, and "many of the troops were piled like cordwood on the tractors and in the trucks." They experienced no problems, but McWilliams thought "it was the hardest move of the war....Some of the boys had the most awful hangovers." Collins knew they were lucky to make the move without an accident or any notice on the part of higher commanders. This was "due in large part to luck rather than my planning," he admitted. "I certainly picked the wrong day to declare a holiday!"

The unexpected move south came because troops in the III Corps, to the right of the VII Corps, by sheer luck captured an intact bridge over the Rhine. Located at Remagen, south of Bonn, the bridge had sustained partial damage and could handle only foot troops and light vehicles. American units first crossed the bridge on 7 March and trickled across in growing numbers thereafter. Although it collapsed on the 15th, by that time engineers had put up four pontoon bridges, allowing the American bridgehead to expand. General Bradley exploited this good fortune slowly, in part because he had not expected it and also because he had to redirect troops to Remagen, then funnel them across to the east shore. The Germans also did their part to hinder use of the bridgehead as a jumping off point for the final Allied penetration of the German heartland, their stiff resistance preventing an immediate breakout beyond the Rhine. Still, the Allies became increasingly aware that Germany's ability to keep up the war was fast eroding. More and more Allied forces were leaping the Rhine, as Patton's men got across on 22 March, Montgomery's on the 23rd, and the Ninth United States Army on the next day.

A day later, 25 March, First Army troops began a major attack to break out of the Remagen bridgehead, with simultaneous III, V, and VII corps assaults. The 957th entered the area on the 15th, crossing on a heavy pontoon bridge. For the next few days they were "quartered in a huge hilltop chateau which" was "extravagantly filled with deep rugs, grand piano, and even a billard room. A better than average billet." The 188th came over on 20 March. "For the first time in many months" the sister North Dakota battalions were close together. "Friends in the two units had an opportunity to exchange visits today," the 957th Unit Journal commented on 21 March. The artillery joined in the defense of the position for the next five days, experiencing "the heaviest shelling since the days...in the St. Lo area," although suffering no casualties. The frustrating days on the Cotentin Peninsula, however, did not repeat themselves here. The 25 March breakout effort, involving three infantry and one armored division from VII Corps, quickly got free of the Germans. In two days, General Collins's men were thirty to forty miles east of the Rhine, with practically no enemy in front of them. General Bradley then ordered First Army units to turn to the north for a run to Kassel and Paderborn, a move that would envelop and trap a mass of German forces in the Ruhr industrial region. Montgomery's 21st Army Group and the Ninth United States Army already covered the enemy to the west, north, and south. The First United States Army would serve as the eastern blocking force.

In order to place units at Paderborn as quickly as possible and close the trap, General Collins created three separate task forces from his 3rd Armored Division, assigning the 188th to Task Force Richardson. In three days, 27 to 29 March, the battalion covered 180 miles on the run north. On the first day out, German artillery hit a Battery B truck, killing three men and badly wounding four others. More often than not, as this incident showed, artillery suffered more casualties on the road than in position. The 3rd Armored failed to take Paderborn. Enemy resistance reappeared ten miles south of the city, a training site for SS tank troops. It became evident also that the task forces now had to look west as the first German units attempting to escape the Ruhr pocket began to show up. Infantry combat teams followed behind the armored task forces as rapidly as possible to protect their flanks and rear. The 957th provided support artillery for the 18th Combat Team, 1st Division. On 28 March, the 18th Combat Team traveled thirty miles. In the battalion, "120 infantrymen from C Company of the 18th Infantry 'hooked' a ride with our A&B Batteries," one veteran recalled, "riding wherever there was room on whatever vehicle was available." This signaled a return to the August-September style of war, with rapid movement, little or no firing, and an ill-defined front.

At the end of March, the 957th became part of the 4th Cavalry Group, another ad hoc battlefield task force, which included a mechanized infantry squadron, a tank battalion, an armored field-artillery battalion, and a battalion of regular infantry, as well as the 957th. The 4th Cavalry Group left on 31 March to head for Paderborn to support the 3rd Armored task forces. In the next three days it moved ninety miles, stopping at Brilon on 1 April, some thirty miles south of Paderborn, where it posted road guards. Germans escaping the Ruhr remained the major concern for the 4th Cavalry Group. In the 957th, "The center of our sector of fire," a soldier noted, "is just about directly west." On the move north, the troops saw signs everywhere of a collapsing Germany. The battalion encountered "large groups of liberated people (forced workers)" and prisoners of war from the French, Belgian, and Dutch armies. Both battalions began to take prisoners, a sure sign of a military rout. In the 957th, daily orders stressed the need to keep an eye on German civilians and to remember that they, too, were the enemy.

The arrival of troops at Paderborn and Brilon ensured that no Germans would escape from the Ruhr pocket. After a brief period on hold, the VII Corps turned east to continue its drive into central Germany, General Collins beginning an assault across the Weser River on 8 April. He rearranged his units once again, assigning the 188th to the 26th Combat Team, 1st Infantry, and the 957th to the 104th Infantry Division. Thereafter, Colonel Collins wrote, "We had little fighting the rest of the war. It was mainly a mopping up and pursuit operation." The 188th followed the 1st Division into and through the Harz Mountains, "chasing a mess of Nazis into the forest while the armor went around to complete the pocket," wrote Sergeant Skillman. He then added, "We could see that things were getting pretty strained for the enemy by the number of prisoners who were coming out." The 957th traveled east with the 104th Infantry, dipping south of the Harz Mountains and moving on Leipzig, deep in central Germany. On 13 April, when the battalion passed the Nordhausen concentration camp, Colonel Collins ordered all battery commanders to take their men through the facility. Not all went, but those who did were greatly affected. "It was the most horrible sight that I have ever seen," Donald Turney noted. "Such evidence of brutality of one human being for another has not been believed, scarcely less seen by most members of this command," the Unit Journal commented. "Let this evidence of the ethics of Naziism give further meaning to that cause for which we all are fighting." Battalion personnel watched the male citizens of Nordhausen bury the unfortunate dead, on the orders of General Collins.

By mid-April, the war had effectively ended for the artillerymen. Neither battalion fired after 21 April; they had done little shooting since crossing the Weser River early in the month. American and Russian troops met at the Elbe River, east of Leipzig, on the 25th. The battalions quickly shifted from combat to occupation duty in small towns near the city. Large numbers of refugees and German soldiers, seeking escape from the Russians, flooded west of the Elbe. Civil government practically collapsed, particularly as Nazi officials suddenly lost their desire to hold office and govern. For a time combat units had to aid military police in screening refugees, seeking out Nazi officials, and keeping order. The Americans showed little sympathy for German civilians when they threw them out of their homes so soldiers could make their billets there. The luxury of "living in a home with electric lights and a bed," plus "showers for the first time in weeks," caused no pangs of conscience for Sergeant Skillman when the 188th took over German homes. Donald Turney recorded that late in April, men of the 957th "made a raid on a beer parlor and picked up a guy who was to be a head man of the gestapo. After giving him a little strong arm stuff they turned him over to a PW cage."

The Army, a strong believer in the adage that idle hands and minds were the Devil's playground, quickly established a garrison routine. On 24 April, 957th headquarters announced the new schedule, to include discipline, vehicle and gun maintenance, sanitation, and athletic activity. Soon, "Familiar close order drill commands were heard in the morning and mass athletics in the afternoon. Inspections of howitzers and vehicles were also scheduled." The gunners, citizen-soldiers to a man, received the new routine with limited enthusiasm—they had had more than enough of such activities during the days at Forts Warren and Lewis. Food and alcohol became their main interests, as numerous diary entries indicated. The diaries markedly contained no romantic references to the glory of combat or the desire to grapple with the enemy face to face, which so permeated James Hanley's diary and Frank White's letters of only twenty-five years before. Two world wars had destroyed that conception of war.

Germany officially surrendered on 8 May 1945. In the 188th, wrote Sergeant Skillman, "VE Day came and went without much comment. We're all saving our celebration for home soil." The 957th, where "with notable and marked reserve the officers and men...received the announcement of surrender," exhibited little open jubilation. Since no firing had occurred for nearly three weeks, no one needed an announcement telling them the war had ended. And only half ended at that. A notation in the 957th's Unit Journal for 23 May recorded the topic of the day's lecture to officers: "Japanese

Topographic Maps." Many unanswered questions relating to the Pacific Theater of Operations dampened Victory in Europe Day celebrations. When would the war stop out there? Would the War Department send entire units directly from Germany to the Pacific? Would it pull individuals out to go fight the Japanese? By the end of May, some men knew they would be going home for good when the Army instituted a point system for transfer to the United States. Soldiers earned points for length of service, time in combat, wounds received, family dependents, and other factors. All the high-point men leaving both battalions in early June were Guardsmen who first entered service in April 1941. Both battalions, as units bearing the 188th and 957th number designations, remained in Germany until mid-October. Long before that, Guardsmen, Officer Reserve Corps officers, and draftees who had joined the unit somewhere between the summer of 1941 and the days at Fort Lewis had returned home.

North Dakota's artillerymen came home as individuals, released one by one according to the point system. The state did not prepare a special welcome home for either battalion, as it had done for the 1st North Dakota Volunteer Infantry in 1899. Modern personnel policy prevented repetition of one nineteenth-century practice that deserved preservation. Indeed, not everyone in North Dakota knew that the North Dakota National Guard had two separate artillery units. When Guardsmen in the 957th finally realized this, they began to write state newspapers to inform them of the battalion's existence. Major Milton F. Weber, a Jamestown Guardsman and the 957th's operations officer, led the effort. Kenneth Simons, editor of the Bismarck *Tribune*, answered Weber's letter on 15 March 1945. "Frankly, it was news to us that so many North Dakota boys are in the organization," he wrote. "We are just as proud of the 957th, now that we know about it, as we are of the 188th or 164th Infantry." Other papers then published stories on what the Jamestown *Sun* called North Dakota's "lost battalion."

The story of both battalions deserved a telling, for the men performed their war service in a creditable manner indeed. Continuously in the combat zone, European Theater of Operations, for over 320 days, North Dakota's cannoneers from the 188th fired nearly 71,000 rounds at the enemy, with the 957th shooting 91,000. The former saw twelve of its men die in battle and another thirty suffer wounds. Twenty-four of the 957th lost their lives in combat, fourteen of them at St. Luo on 25 July 1944. Another sixty-one sustained wounds. Seventeen of these received their injuries at St. Luo. In every instance, the artillerymen met their combat assignments with skill and indicated at St. Luo, Mons, and in the Ardennes that citizen-soldiers could handle the unexpected adversities of modern war. They were fortunate enough to be a part of General J. Lawton Collins's VII Corps, First United States Army, conceded by both British and American higher commands to be the best American corps in the European Theater of Operations. Commanders of the best divisions in the VII Corps, the 1st, 9th, and 104th Infantry and the 2nd and 3rd Armored, wrote letters of commendation to Colonels Carlson and Collins praising their battalions.

These regulars did not customarily think highly of National Guard units. Bad feelings between the Guard and the Army, which originated in World

War I, had regenerated in 1941 and 1942 when the Army again reorganized the Guard and purged it of what the Army saw as deadwood in the officer corps. Some ill feeling persisted through World War II. James Moe of the 188th Field Artillery Group said the nature of the group's work, close liaison with corps and divisional artillery commanders, brought him and his fellow Guardsmen into frequent contact with regulars. "I found that there was decided feeling between the NG officers and the regular officers," he recalled. The latter, too, frequently "felt that NG officers were rather incompetent," even before Guardsmen had an opportunity to show their abilities.

Regulars in the VII Corps rarely displayed such prejudices toward the 188th and 957th. Much of their dislike for Guardsmen stemmed from the poor performance of National Guard infantry units during the training days of 1941 and 1942. Often, because of Army policy, artillery and other technical branches had a higher ratio of men with high school educations and acceptable intelligence test scores than did infantry organizations. Also, the artillery battalions retained a higher percentage of their original members than did most Guard infantry units. As seen in the 164th's experience, infantry units sustained more casualties and thus had a high replacement rate. In both the European and Pacific theaters, manpower shortages forced field commanders to keep infantry units on the line and in combat almost without relief. This inevitably wore out units and increased casualty rates. In the European Theater of Operations, the artillery remained on the line a long time but did not suffer the same losses as did infantry. The battalions' efficiency remained high because they retained so many of the men trained so arduously at Fort Lewis and the Desert Training Center.

Essentially, the battalions at V-E Day were the same as when they had left the Desert Training Center in 1943. They had undergone some combat losses and received some replacements in Europe, but neither sufficed to change the units' basic character. The battalions consisted of citizen-soldiers, that is, Guardsmen, reservists, and draftees, almost to a man. Lieutenant Colonel James L. Collins, Jr., was the only regular, commissioned or enlisted, in either organization. By the war's end, he had managed to overcome the initially cool reception the battalion tendered him. Boyd Joyer of Minot said, Collins was "the finest Regular Officer I ever met," a sentiment echoed by Milton Weber. Despite continual changes in personnel since April 1941, both units still had cores composed of men from the National Guard. When the 957th surveyed its personnel at the end of January 1945, it found that its officers and men came from forty-one states and the District of Columbia. A hundred and seventy-one, roughly one-third of the battalion's strength, came from North Dakota, however. The ratio of Guardsmen in the 188th was about the same.

Lieutenant Colonel Robert Carlson personified what an intelligent and dedicated Guardsman could accomplish. In the Guard since 1937, Carlson was a major at mobilization. He, and some other Guardsmen, had benefited the most from Army schooling and active duty training, learning to be an excellent artilleryman when given the right kind of equipment and instruction. Tom Arnold, a major by 1944 and Carlson's operations officer, said, he was "as fine a gentleman as I have ever known." Following a postwar career in the

Army, Arnold evaluated his wartime commander as a soldier "very knowledgeable in artillery tactics and techniques." Although "somewhat reserved (not in a negative way)," Carlson was "highly respected and admired in the Battalion."

The colonel exhibited two characteristics not essential to a military leader but nevertheless valuable in a war fought by coalition armies manned by citizen-soldiers. First, Carlson had an ability to make friends with foreigners; friendships that he made in England, Belgium, and even Germany, lasted long after the war ended. The most enduring was with Ferdinand Bonnet of Herve, Belgium. Bonnet and Carlson first met in September 1944 when the 188th passed through Herve on the way to Aachen and the West Wall. Bonnet welcomed Carlson into his home for two nights. At war's end, Bonnet began a correspondence with Carlson that would last over fifteen years. He told the North Dakotan, "We certainly not forget last Sept. 10 when we had the great joy to have you [in our] home." It was at Herve that two battalion members of the wire section were killed by mines. Bonnet led a successful effort in Herve to place a memorial plaque alongside the road "at the very place where the boys died to enable us to live." The monument was dedicated in October 1946. The Bonnet family assumed the responsibility of visiting American cemeteries yearly to place flowers on the graves of 188th members buried in Belgium.

Second, Colonel Carlson took great pains to write the families of his men who died in combat. Mrs. W. E. Cooper, Seattle, Washington, sister of Lieutenant John Parrott, killed in February 1945, wrote Carlson in July of that year, thanking him for his letter of sympathy: "It is my family's and my hope that you come through this grim war unscathed." Lieutenant Parrott's mother also wrote, saying, "I can understand *now* why John wrote and said he was with the *best* battalion in the world with a leader like you." Carlson took particular care to see that the parents of the men who died in Herve knew of the monument and the special care the Bonnets gave to American graves. With his wife and mother-in-law, Carlson visited Herve in 1962 for a happy reunion with the Bonnets and a rededication of the monument. Robert Carlson's concern for his men, which extended to their families, epitomized the best in the American citizen-soldier tradition, a tradition bolstered in World War II by his 188th Battalion and its sister unit, the 957th.

Notes on Sources

The questionnaire survey produced fifty-six responses, either from men who served in the 188th Field Artillery Regiment from mobilization to some time in 1942, or from men who went overseas with the 188th Field Artillery Battalion, the 957th Field Artillery Battalion, or the 188th Field Artillery Group. Letters to Jerry Cooper from Tom A. Arnold, Hershel O. Case, Brigadier General James L. Collins, Jr., United States Army, Retired, Boyd J. Joyer, and Milton F. Weber helped clarify many important items. Mr. Arnold's lengthy letter gave many insights into the quality of Lieutenant Colonel Robert Carlson's leadership and added details on the 188th Battalion's experiences. He also kindly lent several reports he had written during the war. General Collins wrote extensively on the 957th Battalion's tour in Europe and assisted in answering many questions.

Interviews by Mr. Baldwin with the following veterans provided personal viewpoints not available in the written records:

1. Donald Bell	9. George Fowler	17. Orville Nundahl
2. Louis Bogan	10. John Grabor	18. Stanley Pfau
3. Robert Capes	11. Harold Henninger	19. Donald Sathe
4. Bernard Clark	12. Victor McWilliams	20. Fred Schmisek
5. Edward Dietz	13. James Moe	21. Peter Schwab
6. Howard Erickson	14. Francis Murphy	22. John L. Sullivan
7. Dan Fandrich	15. Jerome Norman	23. Kenneth Swartz
8. Donald Feldman	16. Paul Norman	24. Donald Turney

Dr. Cooper interviewed LaClair Melhouse, Charles Welch, and Mrs. Robert Carlson.

Several veterans lent manuscript or printed materials. James Moe provided a copy of an informally printed report of the tenth anniversary of the 188th Field Artillery Group Association, chich contained recollections and a general outline of the group's war service. Peter J. Schwab, First Sergeant, Battery C, 957th Battalion, lent his combined diary-recollection, covering 5 June 1944 to 22 April 1945, and Battery C's "Daily Report of N.C.O. in Charge of Quarters (C.Q. Book)," covering 26 February to 18 November 1943. Donald Turney's "Record of Events for C Btry 957 FA BN" covered the months from D-day to the end of the war. Donald T. Capes offered a copy of a diary kept by Captain Victor McWilliams, Battery C , 957th, "Battery C, 957th FA Bn, ETO, 1944-1945," and also newspaper clippings. From George Fowler came a copy of the pamphlet "188th Field Artillery Regiment—One Year in Federal Service, 1 April 1942: For Lewis, Washington." These materials were invaluable and greatly appreciated.

The battalions' operations in Europe were followed through their monthly after-action reports, which all field units were required to submit to the Army's adjutant general. The reports contained comments on all movements, firing charts, engagements with the enemy, casualty reports, and other information incidental to campaigning. Mrs. Robert Carlson provided a full set of after-action reports for the 188th Battalion. She also lent many of Colonel Carlson's letters from friends in England, Belgium, and the Army, as well as many of his maps. The Records of the North Dakota National Guard contain copies of most of the 957th war reports, such as its S-2/S-3 periodic reports from November 1944 to May 1945, a variety of operation maps, miscellaneous reports, and newspaper clippings, as well as the June 1944 to May 1945 after-action reports. Also included is the book *End of Mission: 957th Field Artillery Battalion* (Heidelberg, Germany, 1945), which was prepared by battalion personnel and edited by Penn G. Dively. *End of Mission* offers a useful overview of the battalion's operations. Two newsletters written by Sergeant Guy R. Skillman, one in late 1944, the other in the spring of 1945, detailing the experiences of Battery B, 188th Battalion, are available at Fraine Barracks, as is "An Informal History of the 776th Tank Destroyer Battalion," which has no author or date of publication listed. Some general and special orders and correspondence from the Guard's records cover mobilization, but more helpful is Adjutant General's Office, North Dakota National Guard, *Report of Mobilization of the North Dakota National Guard: World War II* (Bismarck, N.D., 1942).

Archival records were not needed in detail because so much material was available at Fraine Barracks. Some came from the Morris Swett Library, United States Army Field Artillery School, Fort Sill, Oklahoma. RG407, Adjutant General's Office, Entry 427, "WWII Operations Reports, Field Artillery," Box 19839, FA Bn 188, and Box 20292, FA Bn 57, essentially duplicated the after-action reports but provided a few additional items. RG337, Headquarters, Army Ground Forces, Adjutant General Section, Records Division, Project Decimal File, 10 March 1942 to 1943, California-Arizona Maneuver Area, Box 1270, File 320.2/1, "Organization and Training, Desert Training Center," also helped. The National Archives holds the latter two works.

Published works included Marvin A. Kriedberg and Merton G. Henry, *History of Military Mobilization in the United States Army, 1775 to 1945* (Washington, D.C., 1945) for the 1940-1941 mobilization; Kent Roberts Greenfield, Robert R. Palmer, and Bell I. Wiley, *The Organization of Ground Combat Troops* (Washington, D.C., 1947); and Robert R. Palmer, Bell I. Wiley, and William R. Keast, *The Procurement and Training of Ground Combat Troops* (Washington, D.C., 1948). The latter two works are part of the series United States Army in World War II: The Army Ground Forces, written and published under the sponsorship of the Department of the Army. They offer details on the reorganization of artillery regiments into battalions and the formation of artillery groups as well as information on artillery training. Two works were used to trace the European campaigns of 1944 and 1945: Simon Goodenough, *War Maps: World War II from September 1939 to August 1945, Air, Sea, and Land, Battle By Battle* (New York, 1982), and Russell F. Weigley, *Eisenhower's Lieutenants: The Campaign of France and Germany 1944-1945* (Bloomington, Ind., 1981).

Typical dugout used by the 957th Field Artillery Battalion in the Ardennes during German counter offensive in Belgium.

"Cats" were often used to pull the 155mm howitzers through heavy snows during the winter campaign.

Another 155mm round on the way, courtesy of a 957th Field Artillery Battalion gun.

Left: A happy 957th Field Artillery gun crew sending the 50,000th round fired by the Battalion.

Right: Lieutenant Colonel J.L. Collins, Jr., Commander 957th Field Artillery Battalion.

155mm howitzer gun crews of the 188th Field Artillery Regiment firing practice round on maneuvers at Pole Mountain, Washington, 1941.

Left: Lieutenant Colonel Robert E. Carlson, Commander 188th Field Artillery Battalion.

Right: Members of 188th Field Artillery Battalion take a break at a Red Cross doughnut wagon.

☆10☆
The North Dakota National Guard in the Cold War, 1946-1962

Two major factors shaped the National Guard for twenty years after 1945. World War II veterans returned to the Guard in far larger numbers than had First World War soldiers. Men who had fought in the South Pacific, North Africa and Italy, France and Germany gave the service a solid corps of experienced officers and noncommissioned officers unlike any it had had in the past or would have in the future. The old timers possessed military skill and knowledge, coupled with a sense of tradition from the 1930s and unit pride from service in the 164th Infantry Regiment and the 188th and 957th Field Artillery Battalions.

Rapidly deteriorating relations between wartime allies, with the United States and Great Britain on one hand and the Soviet Union on the other, evolved by the late 1940s into an undeclared cold war. Thrust into an unaccustomed role as a major global power and faced with a seemingly implacable enemy, the United States drastically revamped its military system. Cold-war military policy affected the National Guard significantly. Federal support increased steadily after 1945, but the Guard lost its pre-eminent place in contingency planning and as the Army's sole source of emergency manpower. The long-term impact of cold-war policies did not become evident until after the Korean War, but they affected the Guard more profoundly than any other factor.

The War Department began formulating postwar policy in 1943, with planners anticipating an increased Regular Army and larger Army Reserve and National Guard forces and assuming that Congress would approve Universal Military Training. When it announced the changes in October 1945, the War Department assured the states, "The National Guard will be considered an integral part of the Army of the United States." States would retain responsibility for recruiting personnel, selecting home stations, and providing "adequate armories and storage facilities," although, in the latter case, the federal government would provide some assistance where "the housing or storage" of heavy equipment "would impose an inequitable burden on the state." It would also continue to provide drill and field training pay, arms, ammunition, and equipment. In 1946, Congress sanctioned twenty-seven National Guard divisions, two of them armored, and twenty-one separate regimental combat teams to be manned at eighty-percent war strength within two years (682,000 officers and enlisted men). The Guard had had eighteen divisions with an average strength of 200,000 during the 1930s.

In early February 1946, Major General Butler B. Miltonberger, chief, National Guard Bureau, informed Governor Fred G. Aandahl that North Dakota was empowered to organize an infantry regiment, a field artillery battalion, a section of a divisional headquarters, a medium maintenance ordnance company, and a fighter squadron with support elements. With one hundred percent officer strength and eighty percent enlisted men, these units would give the state a total force of 4,006, nearly three times the North Dakota National Guard's size in the 1930s. Major General Ellard Walsh, formerly adjutant general of Minnesota and now president of the National Guard Association, privately informed Brigadier General Heber L. Edwards, adjutant general, not to be "overwhelmed with the size or strength" of the allotment. Congress was not likely to fund the eighty-percent level immediately, and, Walsh estimated, Edwards would have ten years in which to bring the Guard to the authorized percentages. The states were to activate all headquarters units first, beginning with state headquarters, followed by divisional, regimental, and battalion commands. Officers and noncommissioned officers were to be signed on before enlisted men were recruited in graduated stages over the next few years.

Governor Aandahl directed General Edwards to conduct a study of conditions in North Dakota before accepting the National Guard Bureau allotment. Edwards selected a board of officers composed both of men who had served during the war but had left the service before the combat units had gone overseas and of men who had gone into combat. Colonel Leslie V. Miller, formerly commanding officer of the 188th Field Artillery Regiment, chaired the committee, which considered War Department policies, tables of organization, prewar locations of units, the conditions of existing armories, and census data for all towns and cities over one thousand people. Their goal was to determine how many units the state's population and economy could support, and what towns and cities could realistically sustain a Guard unit. Postwar strengths were to be higher than those of the 1930s; for example, infantry companies would be kept at 150 enlisted men instead of 81. The new units would need larger armories, and the committee had to estimate if smaller towns could maintain the larger units through volunteering if Congress failed to approve universal military training. Colonel Miller's committee met over several weekends in late February and through March and sent letters to all towns and cities that had served as home stations in 1941, twenty in all, as well as to another twenty places that had never had a unit. The committee asked local officials what civic groups might aid recruiting, and it requested six places (Grand Forks, Fargo, Valley City, Jamestown, Minot, and Bismarck) to accept two organizations of Guardsmen. The committee made it clear that the Guard would need municipal help to construct or expand armories, for neither the state nor the federal government would likely offer armory assistance.

All communities housing the Guard before the war and fifteen of the new places responded positively. Mayors, chambers of commerce, civic clubs, and veterans organizations all promised their cooperation. Many towns emphasized that they would only accept the unit previously stationed there. The president of the Grafton Civic Club wrote General Edwards, "We believe that tradition and sentiment is *[sic]* an important factor in the friendly support and good will of the community in a National Guard unit. 'Company C' is an expression familiar to every resident of this town" and Grafton would welcome only Company C. The mayor of Carrington was even more emphatic. He wanted, he said, "OUR OWN UNIT," and if Carrington could not sustain a full infantry company, "we request and may I say insist upon the return of Company Headquarters and such additional platoons as may be maintained" from Company F. Members of Veterans of Foreign Wars Post No. 3363 at Lisbon assumed that they would have the band again but wanted another unit as well, for "Lisbon has been a National Guard minded town ever since the first units were formed." General Edwards assured towns that had never had a Guard unit that the state was also concerned about them. "I am personally very much interested in getting into the southwestern corner of the State so people may become acquainted with the National Guard," he told a Hettinger petitioner.

One issue engendered community rivalry. Several cities, namely, Fargo, Grand Forks, Jamestown, Minot, Devils Lake, and even Wahpeton with under four thousand people, specifically requested the newly authorized fighter squadron. Jamestown gave Edwards the most difficulty, officials there refusing to make commitments to any other organization "That would hinder" them "from being seriously considered in the award of the Air Unit." When its civic leaders wrote the governor and Senator William Langer to lobby for the squadron, an exasperated Edwards told Governor Aandahl to ask the Jamestown leaders to deal directly with the adjutant general's office. "What they figured the Senator had to do with the allocation of the Squadron I am at a loss to understand," he lamented. General Edwards wanted to keep all Guard decisions under his control and resented it when the overly zealous Jamestown air supporters turned to others for help, even if one of them was a United States senator.

Despite the reorganization committee's work, Edwards controlled the process. He corresponded with civic officials throughout the state, prodded the committee to speed up its work, and shielded it from political interference. Edwards, accompanied by Colonel Eric A. Erickson, Army adviser, and Guardsmen Major Leroy Landom and Captain Waldemar Johnson, drove all over the state visiting potential home stations, meeting with civic groups, and inspecting armory facilities. No other North Dakota adjutant general had given the time or attention to detail in considering the overall Guard organization as General Edwards did in 1946. He was particularly adept at cultivating relations with local civic groups and municipal officials. A quick twenty-four- to thirty-six-hour visit from the Edwards entourage, with the dynamic, gregarious adjutant general dominating affairs, was not soon forgotten.

In late April, Colonel Miller's committee recommended accepting all National Guard Bureau allocations, although it disliked sharing the divisional staff section assigned to North Dakota. The North Dakota National Guard was to be part of the 47th Division, along with the Minnesota National Guard, and the committee suggested giving the headquarters section back to Minnesota in exchange for a company of engineers and a small Signal Corps outfit in order to "form one complete combat team within the state." All prewar units were reassigned to their former home stations. The committee stressed that North Dakota's allotment "far" exceeded "the needs of the State," and therefore the federal government should provide armories for all units organized to meet purely national needs.

The National Guard Bureau responded quickly to the state's acceptance of the allocation and in early May designated the following units for the North Dakota National Guard: the 164th Infantry; the 188th Field Artillery Battalion; the 178th Fighter Squadron (and support units); the 294th Army Ground Forces Band; and the 3662nd Medium Maintenance Ordnance Company. General Edwards secured a combat engineer battalion after negotiating with the National Guard Bureau all summer, and in August 1946 the bureau assigned North Dakota the 231st Engineer Battalion (Combat). This completed the Guard's organization through the Korean War.

Restructuring proceeded slowly. Some prewar officers remained on active duty in 1946 and others had only recently been discharged. All needed time to readjust to civilian life and resume their civil occupations before deciding if they would rejoin the Guard. It took all fall to activate the headquarters units down to battalion level, with the state headquarters detachment the first to receive federal recognition, in early September. General Edwards informed Fifth Army headquarters that at best the Guard would have 30 officers and 250 enlisted men enrolled by the end of 1946, but total strength reached only 118 by late December.

Edwards's first responsibility was to select regimental field and staff officers as well as commanders for the battalions, companies, and batteries. Within the limits of War Department regulations, informality and long personal relations governed his selections. Appointments for higher commands went to men with combat experience, but also those known and trusted by the adjutant general. Edwards made Frank Richards, who first joined the Guard in 1915 and led a battalion of the 164th in the South Pacific, colonel of the infantry regiment. Ira M. F. Gaulke, once the captain of Edwards's old outfit, Company M, and leader of a tank-destroyer battalion during the war, received promotion to lieutenant colonel and accepted command of the 231st Engineers. Edwards logically selected Robert W. Carlson as lieutenant colonel to lead the namesake of his wartime unit, the 188th Field Artillery Battalion. Executive and staff officers of the three organizations went to other prewar Guardsmen with active-duty service.

The adjutant general relied on a network of present and former officers to find company officers, or he turned the job over to regimental and battalion commanders. Again, personal evaluations had as much importance as formal military qualifications. Edwards asked retired Brigadier General Laroy Baird to check out a Dickinson man for a commission, a man who had served in the war but had never been in the Guard. Baird told the general, "I found out nothing but good." He did not know the fellow personally but, he added, "I used to do some work for the father and uncle," and they were reliable people. I "talked with some of the young fellows around town," he continued, "and they all give him a good reputation and they generally know if there is any dirt." Edwards appreciated Baird's efforts and liked what he heard, although, he responded, "I am getting to that age when I consider the sheep are only white on the side I can see." William Mjogdalen, a former Edwards protege just promoted to lieutenant colonel in the 164th, went to Grand Forks to check on a possible commander for Company M. He told Edwards, I talked "with the Chief of Police, with whom I went to school." The chief "personally respected" the candidate and "could not praise him enough." Major Harold Barker of the state staff traveled to Williston to confer with several "old officers of 'E' Company." As a result, he said, "We...picked out three likely prospects" to command the postwar unit and sent the names with general comments on to Bismarck.

Edwards allowed Lieutenant Colonel Gaulke to select all his officers for the 231st Engineers. "It is the policy of our office," he told Gaulke, "to deal through our Commanders wherever possible." When the adjutant general's office did recommend candidates, he explained, "It is only in the interest of conserving our Commanders' time in order that they have an opportunity to make a living." Gaulke had a particularly difficult task because he was organizing an entirely new unit in a branch that had never been active in the National Guard. The Guard planned to establish line companies at Bottineau, Cavalier, and Langdon. The first two had housed small infantry detachments before 1941, but Langdon had never had a unit. The towns had no loyalty to the new units nor any old timers to support them. Gaulke had to find men in these small communities with wartime engineering service or convince former infantry officers to convert to the new branch. The company at Langdon failed to develop and was reassigned to Minot. Despite these difficulties, the National Guard Bureau officially acknowledged battalion headquarters company in Grand Forks and Company A at Cavalier in December 1946. They were the Guard's first line units to win federal recognition.

The second organization to be activated was also new to the service. North Dakota had tried for years to acquire an aviation unit, but its efforts failed in 1922 as did those of Earle R. Sarles, adjutant general, in the mid-1930s. General Edwards told one air supporter in 1940, "Our...drawback is that we do not have a city in the state that can support an air unit." During World War II, the Army Air Corps gained a semiautonomous status within the Army when the War Department created the Army Air Force in 1942. Airmen looked to the postwar years with hopes of seeing a completely separate Air Force standing equal to the older services, the Army and Navy, but this did not occur until Congress approved the National Defense Act of 1947. War Department planners, however, pushed by the National Guard Association, provided for an Air National Guard in its postwar planning on the assumption that Congress would create an independent Air Force. Postwar policy guaranteed each state at least one flying unit.

Traditionally, the states held the right to select home stations for all organizations; but in 1946, the National Guard Bureau stipulated that Fargo, the state's largest city, would serve as the squadron's new home. General Edwards and Governor Aandahl did not disagree. As the adjutant general told a Devils Lake man, "Plainly and frankly....If Fargo, with 32,000 population is able to handle this Air Squadron in the opinion of the War

Department, it is the only city in North Dakota that can." Fargo's Chamber of Commerce nonetheless mounted an impressive campaign, sending a notebook of aerial photographs of Hector Airport and detailed statistics on the city's population and labor force. One segment of the airport contained hangars, barracks, and other buildings manned by an Army Air Force plane-ferrying command during the war. Fargo offered these as the Air National Guard's facilities. The state, the National Guard Bureau, and Fargo's city council then entered a lengthy wrangle over proper compensation to the city for these buildings, the negotiations lasting from June through November 1946 before the city finally signed a contract with the National Guard Bureau.

Meanwhile, former adjutant general G. Angus Fraser wrote Edwards recommending the Fargo Air Force recruiter, Lieutenant Colonel Richard D. Neece, Jr., as the state's first air instructor. Fraser told the adjutant general, "I don't want you to feel that I am butting into things," but he thought Neece was "one who appears to know how to get along with civilian groups." The colonel had an excellent war record, had commanded a combat squadron, and had graduated from the Command and General Staff School in August 1945. When Edwards accepted Fraser's advice, Neece became senior air instructor in July. General Edwards, Major Landom, and Captain Johnson made three trips to Fargo in July and August to recruit pilots and mechanics. Because of the complexities of the air service and the state's unfamiliarity with aviation, Edwards turned over the organizational effort to Colonel Neece. (With tongue in cheek, the adjutant general wrote one correspondent, "It has been said that any resemblance which the Air Corps bears to the Army is coincidental and not intentional.") Fargo's reluctance to sign a contract for Air National Guard facilities at Hector Airport delayed organization. Neece could not begin recruiting until all were assured that the Air National Guard would have a home. He told Edwards men asked him everyday when they could sign up. "The majority of those I have had conversations with are extremely interested in the unit," he explained, "and once the 'go-ahead' is given I am sure we will be able to make rapid progress." On 30 October 1946, General Edwards wrote Neece, "Inclosed please find authority to organize the Squadron and its allied units." He advised the colonel to meet with the Chamber of Commerce and other civic groups and place newspaper advertisements calling for enlistments. "I am of the opinion," Edwards commented, "we are losing valuable time. We should be ready to be federally recognized within 30 days."

The Air National Guard received formal recognition on 16 January 1947 when the 178th Fighter Squadron, the 178th Utility Flight, the 178th Weather Station, and Detachment B, 233rd Air Service Group were activated. The entire command included twenty-three officers and twenty-six enlisted men. Although an active Air Force officer, Colonel Neece, the only regular officer to head a North Dakota National Guard organization during peacetime, received permission to take command of the unit. Captain Homer Goebel led the 233rd Air Service detachment and, as a full-time state employee, acted as base supply officer. The airmen originally held their drills in the basement of Company B's Fargo armory, not moving to Hector Field until April. Though they had no planes in January, in early February they received an AT-6 trainer, and soon thereafter F-51 propeller-driven fighter planes started to arrive. Harsh winter weather prevented flying operations for some time, but the squadron nonetheless was the first full Guard unit to train regularly.

Postwar restructuring essentially took a year to complete. By the spring of 1947, the North Dakota National Guard was intact on paper with all units assigned to home stations and all headquarters organizations activated. Enough prewar officers returned to give the Guard a seasoned leadership. Unlike the first years after World War I, Congress, the War Department, and the National Guard Association readily reached agreement on basic policies. The rapid development of the Air Guard was particularly encouraging. General Edwards displayed effective organizational and political skills throughout the whole effort, guiding the return to peacetime with a sure hand.

Despite the prospects for steady expansion and a stable future, the Guard failed to grow at the expected rate in the late 1940s, largely because Congress reneged on its implied promise to fund a larger force, cutting all military appropriations in 1948 and 1949 and forcing the Guard to halt recruiting. Until 1950, total strength never exceeded 380,000. Although the National Guard Bureau recognized the North Dakota National Guard as fully activated "under the new post-war...reorganization plan" in April 1948, the 164th lacked captains in seven of its twenty companies at the end of the year. The regiment's Service Company at Devils Lake had five different commanders in 1947 and 1948, while the 231st Engineers, supposedly active from December 1946, did not establish Company B at Minot until February 1948. During the years 1947 through 1949, the infantry's line companies averaged only 45 enlisted men, or about twenty-five percent of authorized strength. With an enlisted total of 1,116 in 1950, the 164th needed another 1,500 men. The field artillery and engineer battalions fared somewhat better, standing at fifty percent strength in 1950, while the Air Guard was only 50 men short of their authorized number. (See Table 10.1.)

Table 10.1

Total Strength, Army and Air National Guards, 1946-1950

	Army National Guard				Air National Guard
	Total Strength*	164th Infantry	188th Artillery	231st Engineers	Total Strength
1946	188	49	0	43	0
1947	919	717	69	81	117
1948	1,288	853	156	198	242
1949	1,519	950	259	195	269
1950	1,903	1,211	318	242	298

*Includes state staff, North Dakota's share of Headquarters 47th Division, 294th Army Ground Forces Band, and the 3662nd Ordnance Medium Maintenance Company, as well as the three major ground organizations.

The Guard encountered difficulties in their recruiting efforts in the immediate postwar years. Jerry Wilder, a veteran who returned to Williston's Company E, recalled, "it was very hard to get anyone interested in enlisting" because local people remembered "the tough go E Co. and the rest of the 164th had during WWII." Howard Erickson ran into the same problem in Fargo, where "Many mothers were reluctant after WWII to let their boys join the military." Some veterans signed on to serve as noncommissioned officers, but the Guard had trouble finding privates no matter what their previous service had been.

One provision of the National Security Act of 1947 established full-fledged reserve programs for the Army, Navy, Air Force, Marine Corps, and Coast Guard, in addition to the Army and Air National Guard. All reserve forces competed with the Guard for veterans and new men. The Naval Reserve gave the Guard a difficult time in Fargo in 1947 when it founded a two-hundred-man reserve unit. To the anger of General Edwards, the Navy attempted to take away Company B's armory by offering Fargo a $100,000 renovation plan and a $750 monthly rental fee. "They also stated," Edwards wrote contempuously, "that if it would not interfere with naval operations, the National Guard could remain in the basement." Fortunately, Company B, not the city, owned the armory, but Edwards could not get over the fact that "the officer in charge of Navy affairs in the state makes the statement quite freely that the Navy has plenty of money." A two-hundred-man Naval Reserve and an Army Reserve unit soon to be activated in Fargo meant, Edwards noted in August 1947, "we have been unable to get enough enlistments to organize Company B."

Guard leaders worked hard at recruiting, holding open house at their armories, showing World War II combat films, speaking regularly at local high schools, and using newspaper advertising. They turned increasingly to the radio as a means of spreading the word on the National Guard. When Colonel Neece checked out the first Guard pilot on the F-51, the local radio station transcribed the process and broadcast it several times. "We had quite a few calls from interested parties...due to the broadcast," Neece told Edwards.

The infantry line companies had the greatest difficulty in sustaining membership. At Grafton, home of Company C since the late 1880s, the unit instructor, Army Captain Richard T. St. Sauver, complained in June 1948, "Public support for the unit is far from desirable." The company had only one officer and twenty-eight enlisted men out of a required strength of three and seventy-eight, respectively. Again, reserve units offered some competition, but the old enthusiasm for Company C was missing. Only one unit actually lost federal recognition, a separate detachment of the 164th's Headquarters Company at Bowman. "I do not believe the town of Bowman...has sufficient manpower to maintain the ultimate strength of the unit," Colonel Erickson observed, and General Edwards concurred. The National Guard Bureau withdrew recognition from the outfit.

Lack of proper armory facilities hindered Guard recruiting. General Edwards told the chief of the National Guard Bureau in February 1947, "At present, adequate armory capacity is not in sight for all ground units." Despite the deficiency, the adjutant general intended to activate all authorized units but would keep manpower levels low until the state or federal government solved the armory problem. Few of the prewar armories were in decent shape, most having been built before World War I, and many had stood idle and neglected during the Second World War. Upon returning to Wahpeton in 1947, Earl Holley found Company I's building "cold, damp, and run down." It had "deteriorated" during the war. "The old armory in Grand Forks...was a dump," Lowell Lundberg recalled.

In his explanation to Governor Aandahl, General Edwards said, during the war some cities had used their armories "for other functions...and in many cases the interim tenants are quite reluctant to give up the space." He was referring specifically to Jamestown, where city officials had turned Company H's armory into a Teen Canteen. Captain George Anderson wrote Edwards "That if a choice had to be made whether the Canteen or the National Guard was desired in Jamestown by the citizens, the Canteen would win 'hands down.'" This evident selfishness brought a rare display of anger from the usually careful Edwards, who seldom put his harsher feelings in writing. "It is such statements as that made by well-meaning people that caused a million casualties in World War II," he said. The adjutant general stood firm on the issue and the Teen Canteen moved elsewhere.

"North Dakota is one of the few states wherein the state does not own the armories," Edwards explained to Mayor Harold A. Boe of Grand Forks. While three belonged to infantry company associations, the state leased the other seventeen from city or county governments. Edwards liked the arrangement, he informed Boe, because "The buildings will be used for other purposes than the military when the use does not conflict with military operations." He did not tell the mayor that he also liked the arrangement because it did not tie up National Guard funds in expensive construction and maintenance costs, which the local associations or governments carried. The National Guard Association lobbied vigorously after 1945 to convince Congress to assume armory costs. As Edwards pointed out to Mayor Boe, since the Guard existed primarily to serve as the Army's reserve, it was only right that the federal government pay most of its costs, including armory support. North Dakota had maintained an infantry regiment "since territorial days," and that should "be used as a yard stick for North Dakota needs for local purposes." The field artillery, engineers, and squadron were "troops needed for national defense." Therefore, the federal government should pay for all but the infantry armories. However, Edwards shrewdly argued, it would be unfair to force cities with infantry units only to pay for their armories while other places did not. The only equitable policy, he concluded, would require Congress to share in the expenses of all armories, roughly seventy-five percent, with state and local governments providing the remainder.

The state legislature gave some assistance in 1947 when it allocated $35,000 to construct armories, at $5,000 each, in Bowman, Harvey, Hettinger, Langdon, Linton, Oakes, and Wishek, small towns that were either new home stations or had never received state armory aid. Hardly sufficient for 1947 costs, the allotment equaled the amount given in a 1907 law, and the municipalities had to add to the building funds. Congress did approve federal armory support in 1950, on a seventy-five-percent federal, twenty-five-percent state and local basis. Erecting and maintaining armories was the last major National Guard expense the states had borne, and federal assumption of the major responsibility here placed the Guard even more firmly under federal control. North Dakota's legislature would not appropriate its share of armory costs until after the Korean War.

Adequate training and storage facilities for the Air National Guard posed serious problems as well. The old ferry command had left only one immediately usable building, an unheated hangar neither large enough to store airplanes nor small enough to use for offices and classrooms. During the winter of 1947 and again in winter 1947-1948, icy-handed mechanics struggled to carry out airplane maintenance in below-zero weather. Many of the squadron's F-51s spent the entire winter buried in snow, and airmen dug tunnels from the operations building to the flight line so pilots could get to the few planes that were able to fly. Using all of his persuasive powers to convince the Air Force to build a modern hangar and repair shop for the 178th, General Edwards pointed out that Air National Guard units in other states had received, free of charge, fully developed airfields abandoned by the Air Force after the war. North Dakota did not benefit from the turnover because that service had not built air bases in the state. "In view of the fact that Federal funds were employed to construct the great preponderance of the bases now being used for the Air National Guard, there would be no inequity present if Federal funds were now used to build hangars for North Dakota," he argued. Edwards enlisted the aid of Senator Milton Young in his campaign, but even the senator's efforts failed to move the Air Force. The National Guard Bureau did provide $250,000 in 1948 to heat the existing hangar and construct offices and classrooms and another $150,000 to improve concrete aprons.

In some respects the Guard continued to suffer from the long-term historical developments that had always hindered it. The rural-to-urban trend of the twentieth century continued, with twenty-seven percent of the state's people living in towns and cities in 1950, but overall North Dakota lost population. Approximately one-quarter of its citizens resided in the Red River valley, and, in accepting all units offered to it, the state had to assign some to towns too small to support organizations adequately. Senior Army adviser Colonel Eric Erikson strongly recommended in 1949 that the Guard place the 164th's regimental and battalion headquarters companies in the larger cities so that all commanders and staff officers would live in the same place. As it was, he pointed out, "Some staff officers live at such distances from their headquarters companies that many of them would have to drive over one hundred miles to get to their units." The headquarters companies only functioned during summer camp, and consequently, Erickson added, "Administration and supervision of units by appropriate commanders is very difficult...and as a result training is not making the progress it should." General Edwards did not heed Erickson's advice, for he wanted the Guard represented throughout the state.

Armory training in the late 1940s too frequently resembled that of the 1930s. Earl Holly recalled that training was "extremely limited, 2 hrs. per week. 20% of authorized strength. Facilities poor, lacked equip." Another veteran, Lowell Lundberg, remembered that the "old one night a week was little more than close order drill.'' The Army adviser inspecting the 3662nd Medium Maintenance Ordnance Company in Bismarck found that most of its personnel were veterans, but the company commander's weekly program emphasized basic training. A majority of these former soldiers had joined the unit expecting to receive ''instruction in the technical fields provided by a Medium Maintenance Company.'' But garage facilities and repair equipment were scarce, and, owing to the repetitive basic training, ''morale'' was ''quite low.'' Walter Mellem, who took command of Company M in 1947, experienced the frustrations company commanders had faced in the thirties. Captains had very demanding command responsibilities, Mellem related; ''Many extra hours were spent on administrative duties. At the time my wife said I was working for 10± an hour.'' The infantry and artillery units had one great strength— the presence of combat-experienced officers and noncommissioned officers. Limited equipment and armory facilities, as in the old days, hurt training, but the new men learned the basics from instructors who knew what they were doing.

The late 1940s were difficult but not disastrous years. Both the state and federal governments increased their fiscal aid substantially. North Dakota received $655,000 in federal aid in 1948, for example, and $546,000 two years later, whereas in the 1930s, annual federal allotments had averaged $149,000. The state made a $145,000 biennial appropriation in 1945 and $214,000 in 1947, and it continued to allot over $200,000 biennially through the Korean War. State aid in the twenties and thirties never exceeded $40,000 a year and often dipped below that amount. In June 1948, Congress provided retirement pay for Guardsmen over the age of sixty who had served at least twenty years, although five of those years had to have been on federal active service. The law made it easier to retain experienced officers and noncommissioned officers.

Guardsmen resumed annual field training in 1948, going regularly to Camp Grafton from then through 1950. The 1948 camp, with only 750 in attendance, had limited value, but the 1949 session saw full participation of the infantry, artillery, and engineer organizations in field maneuvers. Governor's Day and the athletic competitions so popular in the 1930s again played prominent parts at camp. The Air National Guard held its first training session at Hector Field in 1948, with the men living in tents. Pilots each day flew from Fargo to Devils Lake, where the state had set up an aerial firing range. In the next two years the airmen took their annual training out of state, going to Casper, Wyoming, in 1949, and to Camp Williams, Wisconsin, a year later.

The 164th Infantry and the 188th Field Artillery Battalion were organic elements of the 47th Division. In 1950, the Army Field Forces command ordered all multistate divisions to train in one place. General Edwards opposed the policy because his men would have to go to Camp Ripley, Minnesota, and lose two training days while going to and from camp. Furthermore, Minnesota always held its camps in August, when grain harvesting peaked. ''To take men from the harvest would cause a serious strain on public relations,'' Edwards pointed out, and would inevitably hurt recruiting. North Dakota always held its camps in early June, the slack time between spring planting and the harvest. The adjutant general wanted his troops to continue training at Camp Grafton in June, and at least for 1950 they were allowed to do so.

Edwards did not like affiliation with the 47th Division. Minnesota men made up seventy percent of its force and dominated its high command. In all major divisional matters, from promotion to the summer camp schedule, Minnesotans made the decisions. Within the 47th, no North Dakota soldier held a rank higher than lieutenant colonel. The North Dakota National Guard had a small share of the divisional staff, headquartered at Fargo and commanded by Lieutenant Colonel Donald Fraser. These assignments included the divisional finance officer, chemical officer, information and education officer, an assistant chaplain, and other noncombat assignments. This element had to go to camp with the 47th at Camp Ripley, and neither Edwards nor Fraser liked the arrangement. The general hoped that the 164th Infantry, 188th Artillery, and the 231st Engineers could be organized as a complete regimental combat team independent of the 47th Division, thus freeing the North Dakota National Guard from Minnesota control and giving North Dakota Guardsmen greater promotion opportunities; but the National Guard Bureau rejected the proposal.

By the end of 1950, the Guard had passed through the uncertainties of reorganization. The Army Guard had grown from 919 officers and enlisted men in 1947 to 1,903 by 1950, and the Air Guard was holding steady at 300. General Edwards gave the service an unprecedented dynamic leadership. Adept at maintaining good relations with the legislature and the governor's office, he was particularly effective in keeping in touch with municipal officials and civic groups in the Guards' home stations. He listened to their complaints and suggestions and often acted on them. With federal aid for armories soon available, the future looked promising.

Then the cold war intervened with North Korea's invasion of South Korea on 25 June 1950. Within a month the United States found itself unprepared but committed to ground operations in an area where it had not expected to act. The Korean conflict revealed some of the inherent contradictions in America's cold-war policy and the intricacies of waging war in the nuclear age. Although poorly defined in 1950, and certainly not explained with any precision to the American public, cold-war policy ultimately aimed, and still does, at the prevention of a Third World War. Conventional mass conflict during the early 1940s revealed the awesome destructive power of industrial, scientific warfare. By 1950, both the United States and the Soviet Union possessed atomic weapons. When coupled with a World War II-style mass conflict, atomic warfare could lead to such devastation as to make meaningless the original purposes for going to war. The United States evolved a complex system of military alliances, most notably the North Atlantic Treaty Organization, and the policy of nuclear deterrence to ensure that the Soviet Union would not succumb to the temptation to launch a total war. The Russians responded in kind with the Warsaw Pact and their own nuclear arsenal.

In 1950 the Truman administration had not yet fully developed or explained the deterrence concept, and this created difficulties. Too frequently the feisty President Truman spoke as if he intended the cold-war policy to prevent the Russians from expanding communist rule, with the clear implication that if they did not stop, the United States would use military force against them. Though containment aimed at halting communism's spread, by force if necessary, that force was not to be used *directly* against the Soviet Union. American money, arms, and military advisers would assist threatened nations to fight communism within their nations. Truman's Republican critics thought containment did not go far enough and that the United States should use its military power to liberate Soviet-dominated countries. Neither Truman's restraining policy nor the Republican's liberation policy, however, envisioned a direct American attack on Russia. When put to the test in Korea, these early, ill-defined versions of cold-war policy were revealed as simplistic and poorly understood. They also bore directly on how Truman and his military advisers in the Joint Chiefs of Staff decided to use the National Guard.

Simply put, Korea forced President Truman and the Joint Chiefs of Staff to decide between limited war there or the likelihood of a mass conflict with China and Russia. They chose to fight in Korea, basing all of their strategic decisions and manpower policies on that option. Truman decided to commit American forces to Korea rather hastily in late June 1950, but from the very start he and his advisers intended to restrict the commitment. With an Army of less than 600,000, the President had few divisions to send immediately to Korea. As America's effort grew, both the total number of troops dispatched to the combat zone and the total number mobilized were well below the nation's war-making potential.

Given this basic decision, the administration adopted a partial mobilization policy in July 1950. Determined to keep the Korean War limited, yet equally determined to show that the West had the manpower to confine aggressive communist expansion, Truman also feared that the Soviet Union might use the war as a means to divert American military strength from Europe. He also had apprehensions that the Soviets might then launch an invasion of Western Europe. Truman's policy, to increase the number of American troops sufficiently to defeat the North Koreans and bolster the North Atlantic Treaty Organization by sending American soldiers to Europe at the same time, would contain communism in Asia and deter war in Europe. Even when China entered the war, however, the President would not call for a full mobilization. He had no intention of threatening Russia with full-scale war. His failure to explain to his fellow citizens why the United States did not propose to seek a World War II-style victory caused Harry Truman endless political difficulties and cost him the support of the American public.

The Army initiated a partial call to arms in July, when it increased monthly draft quotas, then called over sixty thousand reservists in August and ordered a limited National Guard mobilization for September. The Army initially called nondivisional Guard support units such as antiaircraft, artillery, and engineers, as well as Air National Guard squadrons. It also activated four of the twenty-seven Guard divisions in September. As a nondivisional unit, the 231st Engineer Battalion became North Dakota's first outfit to prepare for war. Word of its selection came in early August, with activation set for 1 September. The 231st had a month to recruit and prepare its equipment for transfer to active duty. At less than fifty percent authorized strength, the battalion fell far short of its assigned enlisted men when it left for Fort Lewis, Washington, for twenty-one months of service.

"Once at Fort Lewis, several things occurred," Lowell Lundberg wrote. The battalion reported with "a full complement of engineer equipment," which soon after this "was taken from us," Lundberg added, "and used either to fill out other units which were headed overseas, or were shipped out as replacement items." The 231st underwent a complete basic-training cycle, then was "fleshed out with enlisted reservists who had been called up on an individual basis." After training reservists, Lundberg went on, "The battalion was assigned a lot of draftee recruits...and operated basic training cycles." As a provisional training unit, the 231st grew to over fifteen hundred men, receiving both weapons and combat engineering training. Later in the summer of 1951, the battalion moved to Camp Desert Rock near Las Vegas, Nevada, to aid in the construction of an atomic testing site, then returned to Fort Lewis in early 1952. "The battalion has had about as varied a career as is possible," its commander, Lieutenant Colonel Ira Gaulke, wrote General Edwards. Gaulke continued, "We have gone thru about every cycle that a unit can in training, have trained enough units and men for three battalions, went thru the Desert Rock operations and are now being disintegrated as a working unit by cadres, levies, and normal attrition."

In November 1950, the Army pulled the heavy-equipment operators, the first trained enlisted men from the 231st, and sent them to Korea as individual replacements. Transfers, or levies as the Army called them, reached a peak in summer 1951. Nearly all enlisted Guardsmen with limited or no World War II service went to Korea. After a tour at the Engineering School at Fort Belvoir, Virginia, First Lieutenant Lowell Lundberg returned to Fort Lewis in the spring of 1951. He was immediately slated for duty in the Far East. "At least so far as the officers were concerned," he recalled, "it seemed we went according to length of prior overseas service. Those with little or none were first to leave." By the end of the summer, the 231st had lost most of its captains, lieutenants, and warrant officers. By January 1952, Colonel Gaulke told General Edwards, "Less than 15% of our original personnel are with us and they are fast going out" due to discharge, re-enlistment, or transfer overseas.

The 164th Infantry and the 188th Artillery received their call next, ordered into service along with the rest of the 47th Division on 15 January 1951. When Chinese Communists unexpectedly entered the war late in November 1950 and forced a rapid United Nations retreat south of the 38th parallel, the Joint Chiefs of Staff recommended a second, but also limited, National Guard mobilization. The Department of Defense activated four more Guard divisions, including the 47th. Alerted on 16 December 1950, the infantrymen and artillerymen had a month to recruit and prepare. Although its authorized enlisted strength was 2,671, the 164th had only 913 men and needed 54 more officers. The artillery battalion fell short as well, lacking 159 enlisted men. Limited National Guard Bureau appropriations over the previous three years had created these deficits, but some infantry companies had fewer than 40 men, indicating a continuing difficulty in the older companies to win recruits. At induction, the regiment remained 1,450 enlisted men below strength and needed 40 more officers. The 188th exceeded its quota, reporting 540 enlisted men when it only needed 461. Some of the problems that had attended earlier mobilizations appeared once again, as was inevitable with the National Guard. Six officers resigned and the Army discharged some college students as well as over 60 men under eighteen, men legally enlisted but too young to go into combat according to federal law. All told, 15 officers and 259 enlisted men were separated before induction.

After a few days on duty at home station, the infantry and artillery boarded troop trains for Camp Rucker, Alabama, where they joined the Minnesota segment of the division. The 47th immediately went into training and began receiving draftees by mid-February. It soon became evident that the Army intended to use the 47th as a training division, for it sent nearly all the regimental and battalion officers and half the company commanders of the 164th to the Infantry School at Fort Benning, Georgia, to take either basic or advanced courses. It sent artillery officers to Fort Sill, Oklahoma, for similar schooling. In April 1951, Lieutenant Colonel Robert Carlson reported, "The shortage of officers continues to hamper the training" of the 188th Field Artillery Battalion. Regimental commander Colonel Frank Richards used the constant turnover of his officers, going to and from school, to shift all battalion and company officers from one unit to another. With all these changes, "For a while one didn't know who would be on duty from day to day," Major Robert Baird wrote General Edwards in February 1952, "but it seems that things have quieted down lately."

Like the 231st Engineers, the 164th and 188th served throughout their active duty as training organizations. They, too, began to lose their original members to overseas assignments after the first six months of active duty. For a time, Joseph Walter, commander of the 164th's Headquarters Company, recalled, "We would try to protect our own," but when division headquarters made large requests for men with specific military occupational specialties, he no longer could save the North Dakota men, and "towards the end," he added, "it cleaned us out." The Army particularly needed warrant officers, and nearly all from the regiment went to Korea. Captain Walter just missed being sent over because Colonel Richards gave him the option of remaining with the regiment until the 47th Division completed a field maneuver, Operation Longhorn, in Texas. When given the choice of Texas or Korea, Walter decided on the former because Texas "was a foreign country anyway."

The Air National Guard was the last North Dakota unit activated, neither the 3662nd Medium Maintenance Ordnance Company nor the 294th Army Band serving during the conflict. War first touched the Air National Guard in late 1950 when the Air Force requisitioned eight of its F-52 fighters, but the Army did not call the 178th Squadron to service until April 1951. After a month of duty at Hector Field, the squadron went to Moody Air Force Base, Valdosta, Georgia, with assignment to the 146th Fighter-Bomber Wing, Strategic Air Command. Fifty-one officers and 340 airmen made the transfer. The Air Force and Air Guard had no experience with mobilization, and the move to Georgia was poorly organized. Essentially, Homer Goebel recalled, it was "fall out in Fargo and fall in at Georgia." The Air Force had not well integrated Air National Guard units into its command structure before the war and, as the 178th's commander, Major Robert M. Johnson, reported, "some difficulty was encountered in working into an entirely new wing organization and converting to the Strategic Air Command Fighter Wing structure.'' The 178th stayed at Moody until mid-October 1951, going through an intensive training period. Pilots flew daily, taking gunnery practice, while maintenance crews worked to keep the planes flying. In October, the squadron accompanied the 146th Wing to George Air Force Base, Victorville, California, for reassignment to the Tactical Air Command.

Thereafter, the Air Force selected individual airmen and pilots to go to Korea and other Air Force bases in the United States and Europe. By April 1952, few original members remained, and those who did feared the 178th might not be reconstituted in North Dakota. Captain Marley Swanson wrote General Edwards at that time requesting data on the squadron's future. As one of the few North Dakota officers left, Swanson had airmen coming to him regularly with questions about their chances for pilot training and opportunities for permanent technicians' jobs after the war. "Also, I am vitally interested in the re[-]forming of the unit back in Fargo,'' Swanson noted. The adjutant general's office could not give him much information. Ultimately, the Air Force released the 178th in December 1952 and returned it to North Dakota as a Guard unit, but most Air Guardsmen had finished their duty tour before that and had gone home individually.

The airmen's concern for the squadron's future highlighted the Defense Department's controversial Korean War manpower policy, which had a direct relationship to the larger cold-war policy. Intent on keeping the war limited and also strengthening the North Atlantic Treaty Organization forces in Europe, the Joint Chiefs of Staff used American troops sparingly. The Army organized twenty divisions during the conflict, but the Joint Chiefs of Staff sent only one Marine and eight Army divisions to Korea, shipping the remainder to Europe or holding them in the United States as a strategic reserve. Of the eight National Guard divisions mobilized, two served in Korea, two went to Europe, and four, including the 47th Division, took on the chore of training reservists and draftees. Only thirty-four percent of the 379,000 Army Guardsmen enrolled in 1950 were mobilized, while the regular services called some 800,000 of the 2,000,000 available reservists. Selective service provided the rest of the needed men, but the draft took only one in six from the eligible age groups, and many of those drafted did not go to Korea.

These practices generated resentment and confusion within the Guard and among the general public as well. First of all, they seemed inequitable. Some Guardsmen, many of whom had had their civilian lives disrupted during World War II, served again, but two-thirds did not. Many Guardsmen were separated from their original units and sent to Korea, but again, some were not. Reservists and eligible draftees faced the same inequities, and those called often felt resentment. In order to reduce the imbalance and quiet public indignation, the Defense Department adopted a rotation policy that ensured that any man sent to Korea would serve no more than one year in the combat zone. This decision in turn aroused the hostility of military traditionalists who argued that rotation ruined combat unit integrity.

The Guard organizations mobilized in late 1950 and early 1951 were originally called for twenty-one months, a time period later extended to a full two years. In the summer of 1951 the Joint Chiefs of Staff requested authority to keep the Guard units for four years instead of just two, explaining that they needed the organizations another two years because under the partial mobilization policy they did not want to create more divisions. The National Guard Association protested and asked the Defense Department to demobilize the first units that went and call other Guard divisions to replace them. Defense planners saw this proposal as too complicated, preferring to keep the active units filled with reservists and draftees. In July 1952, Congress gave the President the authority to retain the National Guard units for up to five consecutive years "exclusive of personnel." Though individual Guardsmen would receive their discharges after two years active duty, the states lost their units and equipment until the five years ended. Not surprisingly, the policy deeply angered Guardsmen and state officials.

In the units themselves, the individual transfer practice offended Guardsmen the most. Mobilization upset them less than seeing their comrades transferred piecemeal to overseas duty and their units filled with strangers. "I seriously doubt that the 231st could be rebuilt at state levels on a *volunteer* basis," an angry Colonel Gaulke told General Edwards in January 1952. "Practically every promise and advantage of guard service has been violated or abrogated while this unit has been in service. For myself there will be many difficult and embarrassing questions to answer to the folks back home." Gaulke, an old-time Guardsman, sincerely believed in the fundamental Guard recruiting appeal—serve with your friends in peace and war. One of his officers, Lowell Lundberg, explained that he thought Gaulke felt betrayed by the government because "the battalion didn't stay intact. He was very proud of us." As the only engineer outfit in the state, Lundberg went on, the battalion "was a close bunch back in North Dakota. We were really tight at Fort Lewis." Eventually, practically every 231st company officer went to Korea, and, he added, "I think many of us felt abused when the unit wasn't sent overseas as such." Leo Schwer, a captain in the 188th Field Artillery, recalled that Colonel Carlson, another long-time Guardsman, also was "disgusted when the whole group didn't go" to Korea. The editor of the Bismarck *Tribune* reported similar feelings in the 164th Infantry, where the major complaint concerned "The dismembering of their units to provide Korean War replacements." He quoted one particularly disgruntled officer who said, "When we go back home and they set out recruiting another organization they won't get a man. They won't get me again."

In anticipation that demobilization would not take place easily, General Edwards wanted to start new units, in the absence of the 164th, 188th, and 231st, in order to keep the Guard an active group and also to serve as temporary holding detachments for Guardsmen returning home before the release of their parent units. When Edwards found two unallotted and unorganized truck transportation battalions in the National Guard Bureau force structure, he had them assigned to North Dakota in September 1951. "We are not in a hurry to fill up officer vacancies" in the truck units, he told Colonel Gaulke. "We are holding open spots and only commissioning enough officers to satisfy Federal recognition requirements." The general put the truck units in "The cities," he said, "in which we had the best experience...following World War II," but in 1952, eight companies had only 16 officers and 104 enlisted men.

The law that allowed the President to extend National Guard service from two to five years also permitted the states to establish units "bearing the same designations as the units kept in federal service, with the distinguishing initials 'NGUS.'" That is, there would be a 164th Infantry on duty at Camp Rucker after Guardsmen went home, and a 164th Infantry (NGUS) in North Dakota. The NGUS organizations would be "consolidated with the corresponding units when the latter return to state control." The Army released the Guardsmen at various times, and they came home anywhere from the summer of 1952 to early 1953. They were assigned to the truck companies or holding sections of state headquarters detachments until enough men had returned to start NGUS units. The Air Force followed a more logical and wiser policy. Though it, too, had transferred many Guard personnel out of the 178th Squadron, it returned the squadron to the state in December 1952, permitting rapid postwar restructuring as airmen were being released at the same time.

Guardsmen's frustrations with the Defense Department's treatment of their parent units symbolized the confusion and bitterness attending the Korean War. The longer the war went on, the less most Americans understood the reasons for the conflict. America fought a war against an enemy that its leaders depicted as diabolical, yet it did not fight to defeat him. Healthy young American boys, obviously fit for military duty, played football, went to college, got married, or moved up the career ladder, while their less fortunate contemporaries got drafted and went to Korea. The Army only partially mobilized the National Guard, filled with World War II veterans and manned with volunteers. Despite these contradictions, a rationale did exist behind the Truman administration's conduct of the war. If applied properly, the policymakers hoped, limited war in Korea and deterrence in Europe would simultaneously contain communism and yet avoid World War III. Americans found this a complicated policy, poorly defined and explained, and a first in American history. Korea was not the last time the government would use this policy.

Over twenty-six hundred North Dakota National Guardsmen served during the Korean War. Approximately eight hundred of them went overseas, and sixteen died in combat. Some Guardsmen became embittered by the experience, and most had no positive idea of what was expected of them. A sensitive man like Colonel Gaulke felt responsible to the men he had personally recruited with promises that they would serve with their friends in units organized in their own state. When the last of them went home in late 1952, Gaulke volunteered to extend his service and to go to Korea, as had so many of his men. Only in that way could he show that he had remained true to his belief that Guard membership meant combat service in time of war.

Despite General Edwards's hopes, the partially formed truck companies acquired in 1951 did not ease postwar restructuring. Since personnel received releases individually at various times, those who went to Korea tending to get their discharges later than those remaining in the United States, it was difficult to move the men from assignment in the truck units to the NGUS organization. As the initial unit called, the 231st Engineer Battalion was the first to reorganize and establish NGUS companies, in September 1952. The state organized the 164th Infantry and 188th Artillery as NGUS in January

1953. In the process, Edwards rearranged parts of the infantry and engineers. All home stations for the 231st were placed in the northeast section. Headquarters Company remained at Grand Forks and Company A returned to Cavalier, but Company B moved from Minot to Cando, and Company C from Bottineau to Grafton, the latter a particularly significant change, for Company C was one of the oldest infantry outfits in the North Dakota National Guard, founded in the late 1880s and John Fraine's old unit, and now changed to engineers.

Several other old-time infantry companies changed home stations, largely to place each of the battalions in the same geographic area. The 1st Battalion went to the state's western section and took the oldest company designations with it. Company A, formerly of Bismarck, went as a split unit to Hettinger and Mott, Company B of Fargo to Dickinson, and Grafton's Company C of the 164th Infantry to Williston. Another old line outfit, Wahpeton's Company E, moved to Rugby in the 2nd Battalion, and Company K, formerly of Dickinson, went to Fargo and the 3rd Battalion. All battalion companies were now in much closer proximity to their headquarters companies, as Colonel Erickson had suggested in 1949, and the 164th's Headquarters Company went to Bismarck because of that city's central location. This was only the first of many post-Korea reorganizations, for the Guard would be reshuffled continually in the ensuing decades.

Moving companies around did not put people in them, and finding personnel continued to give difficulty in the next two years. Total strength for the infantry, artillery, engineers, and the 3662nd Ordnance Company reached just under 750 in 1953 and just over 1,000 in 1954. The Guard did not return to its 1950 strength (1,903 officers and enlisted men) until 1956. Once again, as in 1946-1947, rebuilding went slowly. "The first few years after a mobilization are the difficult years," Herbert Mack recalled, and this held true in the middle 1950s, when, as another veteran remembered, "Recruiting...was like pulling teeth. We had to beat the woods after the Korean War." Even the popular Air Guard faced recruiting problems in 1953, particularly in winning back the younger men who had experienced their first mobilization. James Buzick estimated that sixty to seventy percent of nonprior service airmen did not rejoin the Air National Guard. Lowell Lundberg, of the 231st Engineers, did not return until 1955. He explained: "Once I got home, I didn't even inquire...about the Guard....I just sent in a...letter resigning. I was determined that I was not going to active duty again until I got a college degree." Lundberg was not alone. Returning Guardsmen at Devils Lake, who still had time left on their state enlistments, refused to sign up with the 3662nd Ordnance Company. They feared that "the Ordnance Company, being a non-divisional unit, could be activated," Captain Joseph Walter wrote the adjutant general. Walter asked General Edwards to assure men who had already done their twenty-four-month service that they would be exempt if the 3662nd received mobilization orders. Edwards gave that guarantee.

Officers remaining on extended active duty or choosing to make the Army or Air Force a career complicated reorganization. Thirteen of the 37 officers and warrant officers of the 231st Engineers (over one-third) chose extended active duty, including Colonel Gaulke. The Air National Guard lost nearly all its pilots, particularly the captains and lieutenants, to active Air Force duty. (All told, 17 of the 50 officers of the 178th Squadron stayed on extended active duty.) Lesser numbers of infantry (26 of 124) and artillery (9 of 39) officers and warrant officers remained with the active Army. While at Camp Rucker, Colonel Frank Richards had moved from command of the 164th Regiment to Chief of Staff, 47th Division. He liked the Army, and, since he disagreed with the Dickinson school board, he requested a three-year extension of active duty. "Of course I make more money in the army anyway," he told General Edwards, and that "helped me decide too." Edwards liked the idea and used his contacts in the National Guard Association to have Colonel Richards assigned to the National Guard Bureau in May 1953, partly because "The fur bearing Swedes of North Dakota have never had an officer" on duty with the bureau. The loss of these experienced men made it that much more difficult to revive the North Dakota National Guard.

The Air Guard rebounded faster than the Army National Guard, its recovery due partly to the continuing public perception of the Air Force as a more romantic service than the Army, but more importantly to changes in how the regular service itself saw the Air National Guard. Until the Korean War, the Air Force treated the Air Guard as a poor second cousin. Regular airmen had opposed creating a state air arm because it saw no need to share aviation with the states. Fighter and bomber squadrons obviously had only a national mission, and even before the Korean War federal funds accounted for ninety-seven percent of Air National Guard costs. This money came from the Air Force's budget and its leaders resented giving money to the states. They also disliked dealing with state adjutants general through the National Guard Bureau's Air Guard division, for they saw the bureau as merely a tool of the Army. Given these conditions, an unenthusiastic Air Force kept Air National Guard spending as low as possible, made little effort to incorporate it into national contingency planning, and oversaw Guard training indifferently. These practices, to quote a recent study, by 1950 had caused state aviation units to become little more than "glorified flying clubs formed into forty-eight little state Air Forces."

Though the Korean mobilization was a fiasco and the Air Force could not readily use Guard wings and squadrons because they had had such poor training and administration, Air National Guard pilots and ground crews individually carried out their duties effectively. Their performance indicated that Guardsmen could be used to augment active units. Congress would not abolish the Air National Guard; this meant, in any event, that the Air Force had to work with it, and the active service set out to better integrate the Air National Guard into its structure. Cold-war policies aided the Guard's improved post-Korea status. President Dwight D. Eisenhower's "New Look" military policy, aimed at diminishing defense costs, led to cuts in all the regular services and put greater emphasis on reserve components. Although the Air Force took some reductions, it fared better than the other services in the 1950s budget battles. The Air Guard benefited in both instances: its federal budget more than doubled between 1950 and 1960, rising from $114.7 million to $233.4 million over the decade. By 1960, Air National Guard units "were regularly involved in the everyday business of running the Air Force.'' Guard squadrons directly served in fighter and reconnaissance assignments and did reserve duty for troop carrier, airlift, and aeromedical evacuation missions.

These changes became evident in North Dakota after 1953. On 1 January 1953, the National Guard Bureau redesignated the 178th as a figher-interceptor squadron to serve as part of a combined Air Force-Air National Guard air defense program. The Air Force conducted a limited experiment in 1953 in which selected Air National Guard units maintained a runway alert program with planes and pilots on duty several hours a day, prepared to scramble and intercept unidentified aircraft entering United States airspace. During 1953, meanwhile, the North Dakota Air National Guard rebuilt itself. Owing to the scarcity of pilots, North Dakota began participating in the Air Force's Aviation Cadet program. The squadron selected promising young airmen, often students at North Dakota Agricultural College in Fargo, and sent them to pilot training schools. This training was particularly important, for many World War II pilots were too old, by Air Force standards, to fly fighter planes and had to be replaced. Also, the Air National Guard was going to switch to jet fighters soon, and the older men had no experience with them.

North Dakota shifted from propeller-driven F-52 fighters to F-94 Lockheed Starfighter jets late in 1954. It had already joined the runway alert program in August, which required the 178th Squadron to keep two combat-ready planes on the runway for fourteen hours daily. Practice alerts and scrambles allowed plenty of flying time and kept ground crews busy maintaining aircraft. Though the alert program involved only a small portion of the squadron at any one time, pilots shared the duty so all could log flight time throughout the year. In 1958, the Air National Guard's air defense role expanded to a twenty-four-hour alert with two planes at the ready. Most important of all, even if limited to only two planes per squadron, the program was ''the first large-scale effort to integrate reserve units into the regular peacetime operating structure of the armed forces on a continuing basis.'' To that extent, the Air National Guard had become part of the Air Force's daily operations and not merely a partially manned training unit with a reserve role only in wartime.

Participation in air defense with jet aircraft necessitated enlarging and improving Hector Field. The Air National Guard rebuilt and expanded the runways, aprons, and taxiways in 1953 and 1954 and constructed a new hangar in the latter year, for a total of $1,883,600 in improvements. Further runway construction came in 1958, at a cost of nearly $950,000. Additions in 1958 and 1959 included a warehouse and a new operations and training building. By 1961, the Air National Guard held real property at Hector Field valued at $5,000,000, nearly all of it provided by the federal government. Operating expenses at the end of the 1950s exceeded $2,000,000 annually, with drill pay approaching $500,000 yearly and the salaries for permanently employed air technicians over $800,000. In 1957, the Air Guard held $19,460,000 worth of supplies, equipment, and aircraft, and a total of $29,000,000 in 1961. The Air National Guard thus became a substantial government investment in less than ten years after the Korean War at a level John Fraine, Frank White, or Gilbert C. Grafton would have found unimaginable.

After the initial difficulties of reorganization in 1953 and 1954, the Air National Guard had little trouble in maintaining its numbers. It grew from 263 officers and enlisted men in 1953 to 798 in 1961, or ninety-three percent of its authorized strength. The squadron halted its recruiting efforts in 1959 because it had nearly attained its quota of men and had 92 potential recruits on a waiting list, which grew to 150 men a year later. In part, the Guard needed the waiting list because, beginning in 1957, all its enlistees had to take six months of basic and advanced training with the active forces before joining their local units. The Air Force had limited training facilities and could accept only so many new men each year. Post-Korea draft laws also stimulated enlistments, as they required drafted men to serve a total of six years combined active and reserve duty. Many men chose the six months of basic training and completed their remaining time in the Guard. Many men found the Air National Guard attractive because of the skilled jobs available to permanent technicians, all of whom also had to belong to the Guard. By 1960, nearly twenty percent of airmen were permanent employees, a far higher percentage than in the Army Guard. Employment opportunities offered a valuable recruiting tool, and the Air National Guard clearly drew high-quality recruits. In 1958, for example, only four percent of enlisted airmen lacked a high school diploma while thirty-six percent had one or more years of college education.

For several years after the Korean War, the Air National Guard followed the Army pattern of weekly three- to four-hour training drills, but then shifted to weekend training assemblies in 1958. The latter permitted sustained training in a realistic military setting and particularly suited Air National Guard work, which stressed aircraft maintenance and repair. Though Guardsmen did not initially like the once-a-month meetings, they eventually adapted to it. The Air Guard took its annual field training outside the state from 1954 through 1959, traveling each year to Volk Field, Wisconsin. Once again, however, the Air Force broke Army practice, and in 1960 its fighter-interceptor squadrons began holding field training at home station. Air National Guard Chief of Staff Colonel Homer Goebel reported after the 1960 session at Hector Field, "Our field training operation was considered more successful than those of previous years." The men found maintenance easier there, they saved time by not moving, and pilots logged twice the flight time as in 1959. Under the air defense program, a Guard interceptor squadron's home station was also its wartime assignment, and it made sense to take field training there.

For all intents and purposes, Hector Field became a small, permanent air base under continuous operations. The technicians worked daily, carrying out repair and maintenance, and flight operations occurred regularly. In 1956, the Air Force and National Guard Bureau reorganized fighter-interceptor squadrons to conform to this reality. They activated the 119th Fighter Group (Air Defense) in North Dakota, which included the 178th Fighter Interceptor Squadron, the 119th Consolidated Maintenance Squadron, and the 119th Air Base Squadron. The 119th Fighter Group, a self-contained unit, could support the squadron's operations fully, maintain aircraft, buildings, and grounds, provide security for the field, and offer medical care. Lieutenant Colonel

Homer Goebel became group commander, and Major Robert M. Johnson headed the 178th. A year later, when Goebel became a colonel and Chief of Staff, North Dakota Air National Guard, Johnson took over the group. The Air Guard gained equal status with the ground forces at state headquarters during the late 1950s. A complicated supply system and ongoing construction necessitated placing an assistant United States Property and Fiscal Officer on permanent duty at Fargo to administer Air National Guard fiscal affairs, and a 1957 state law created a Department of the Army and a Department of the Air Force, each headed by an assistant adjutant general, within the Adjutant General's Office.

Like their counterparts in the Army Guard, airmen discovered that they seldom received equipment in good condition from the active force, and what they did receive could be called "new" only in the sense that they had never previously had the models sent by the Air Force. Jet fighters assigned from 1954 onward "were in a pretty sorry state when we got them," James Buzick recalled. The men invariably had to overhaul the planes completely, including engines, hydraulic systems, electronic equipment, and even airframes. Every aircraft model change meant a complete turnover in spare parts, which numbered in the thousands. The sad condition of the aircraft compelled the Air National Guard mechanics literally to learn them from the inside out and they became adept at repair and maintenance. The Air National Guard flew the F-94, successively models A through C, from 1954 to 1959, then converted to the F-89D, the latter described by Colonel Goebel as "a larger bulky twin-jet interceptor" and referred to by the pilots as "beasts." Because of the F-89's "protracted take-off roll and subsequent low rate of climb," Goebel reported in 1960, "We have been receiving an increasing number of complaints...regarding low flying jet aircraft." They solved the noise problem by moving and extending the runway.

The Air Guard's overall success after the Korean War had significance, partly because the Air Force came to see it as an integral part of the active service's operations and planning, but also because innovations like the runway alert program and the weekend training assembly offered examples for the Army Guard to adopt. By the early 1960s, the Air Force was evolving a policy that would make the Air National Guard and Air Force Reserve ready reserve forces directly assigned to Air Force tactical and strategic commands with immediate wartime assignments. The Air Force wanted to have reserve components fully equipped, well trained, and near war strength, so if mobilization came, these units could move from home station to war assignment without intermediate training, which they had needed in World War II and the Korean War. Ultimately, that would become a goal for the Army Guard as well.

In 1955, the Army Guard consisted of the 164th Infantry Regiment, the 188th Field Artillery Battalion, and the 231st Engineer Battalion as major elements, and the partial 47th Division Headquarters, the 3662nd Ordnance Company, the 294th Army Band, and the 769th Transportation Company (the only unit left from the 1951 truck battalions) as smaller organizations. Its strength stood at 215 officers and 1,535 enlisted men, still 150 below its 1950 total. Several infantry companies continued to have difficulty recruiting, despite the stimulation of the draft and in contrast to the more successful artillery and engineer battalions. Company K, at Fargo, reported only 29 enlisted men and five others had under 40 men. Competition from other reserve forces, particularly in Fargo and Grand Forks, also made the Army Guard's future appear less bright than the Air Guard's.

A major change came in 1955 which drastically altered the Army Guard's organization and solved its recruiting problems. To the great surprise of most 164th Infantry members, General Edwards announced in April that the regiment would convert to combat engineers and the North Dakota Army Guard would leave the 47th Division. The origins of the conversion stemmed from Edwards's persistent unhappiness with the divisional affiliation. Both the 47th Division command and the National Guard Bureau continued to pressure North Dakota to take its annual field training at Camp Ripley, and the adjutant general just as adamantly resisted. Edwards lost all patience with his Minnesota comrades in 1954 when they refused to give Colonel Frank Richards, still on active duty with the National Guard Bureau, a promotion to brigadier general and assistant division commander. "In all of the 30 years that N.Dak. has been divisioned with Minnesota," Colonel Herman Brocopp wrote, "they have never had a division or assistant division commander." General Edwards demanded that the National Guard Bureau force Minnesota to give up at least one general's appointment, but the National Guard Bureau replied that all divisional assignments had to be "by mutual agreement of N.Dak. and Minn."

Heber Edwards could be a stubborn man when he set his mind on a particular objective. He convinced Colonel Richards to submit his name to the 47th Division for consideration as assistant division commander, regardless of what Minnesota said, but both that state and the National Guard Bureau rejected the application. A high-ranking officer in the National Guard Bureau told Richards to inform Edwards that "He does not believe you will ever be able to arrange with Minnesota so that you will be satisfied." The general again sought ways to organize the North Dakota Army Guard as a nondivisional regimental combat team or to convert it to some other branch, which would make it independent of the 47th Division. Having Richards on duty at the National Guard Bureau helped, and he arranged to have the adjutant general come to Washington in late April 1954 to confer with Major General Edgar C. Erickson, Chief of the National Guard Bureau. Edwards and Erickson reached an agreement that allowed North Dakota to leave the division. The 164th would be converted to armored cavalry, the 188th would become a nondivisional artillery battalion, and North Dakota's segment of the 47th Division Headquarters would revert to Minnesota. Lieutenant Colonel Donald Fraser, the latter unit's commander since 1947, wrote Edwards, "Am glad the battle was finally resolved and that we can go our separate way—the last shenanigan did it for me, I didn't believe they would ever try and by-pass Richards." He added that he was pleased that "we can secede from the Vikings."

North Dakota did not convert to armored cavalry, but the National Guard Bureau did find a sufficient number of engineer battalions to match the 164th's strength and number of companies. If Edwards succeeded in winning independence from the 47th Division, he failed to gain a command large enough to earn the state a general officer. He sought an engineer brigade, normally commanded by a brigadier general, but in the National Guard Bureau's estimation, the state lacked the population to support a brigade. The Army Guard's organization after 15 April 1955 is given in Table 10.2.

Table 10.2

Army National Organization Following Conversion to Engineers

Unit	Home Station
Headquarters/Headquarters Company 164th Engineer Group	Bismarck
Headquarters/Headquarters Company 164th Engineer Battalion	Minot
Company A	Rugby
Company B	Minot
Company C	Williston
Headquarters/Headquarters Battery 188th Field Artillery Battalion	Bismarck
Battery A	Mandan
Battery B	Linton
Battery C	Jamestown
Service Battery	Wishek
Headquarters/Headquarters Company 231st Engineer Battalion	Grand Forks
Company A	Cavalier
Company B	Grand Forks
Company C	Grafton
Headquarters/Headquarters Company 141st Engineer Battalion	Valley City
Company A	Valley City
Company B	Edgeley
Company C	Oakes
Headquarters/Headquarters Company 142nd Engineer Battalion	Jamestown
Company A	Carrington
Company B	Cando
Company C	Harvey
Headquarters/Headquarters Company 957th Infantry Battalion (Heavy Mortar)	Fargo
Company A	Lisbon
Company B	Hillsboro
Company C	Wahpeton

Separate Companies

294th Army Band	Lisbon
3662nd Ordnance Company	Devils Lake
769th Transportation Company	Mott
815th Engineer Company	Dickinson
816th Engineer Company	Mayville
817th Engineer Company	Hettinger
818th Engineer Company	Bottineau

The conversion initiated modifications throughout the Army Guard. Headquarters for the 164th Regiment became headquarters for the 164th Engineer Group, a command unit to coordinate and control the separate engineer battalions. As part of the redesignations, the 188th artillery changed from a 105 mm truck-drawn howitzer unit to an armored field artillery battalion with 155 mm self-propelled guns. Its headquarters battery moved from Mandan to Bismarck, and Battery A, previously at Lisbon, shifted to Mandan. Battery B, formerly stationed in Minot, now served at Linton, which had housed Headquarters Company, 1st Battalion, 164th Infantry. Lieutenant Colonel Donald Fraser's former 47th Division Headquarters unit now formed the new headquarters for the 957th Infantry Battalion (Heavy Mortar), which absorbed two of the old infantry companies, from Hillsboro and Wahpeton, and the Lisbon battery from the 188th. In less than a year, the 957th was redesignated a field artillery battalion, although still armed with the 4.2-inch heavy mortar. The 231st Engineers remained essentially the same, except its Company B was placed in Grand Forks instead of Cando, and the latter became home station for Company B, 142nd Engineer Battalion. All the other infantry companies converted to engineers. Two of the separate engineer companies, the 817th at Hettinger and the 818th at Bottineau, had already undergone redesignation and reorganization in 1953. The Bottineau men, who had been part of the 231st Engineers from 1947 to 1953, converted to the 164th's Heavy Mortar Company after Korea, and then reconverted to engineers in 1955, must have found the new arrangement confusing.

Further changes took place in the next four years. The state added two more separate engineer companies in 1956, the 896th at Bismarck and the 897th at Garrison. Three years later, the Army revamped its triangular division organization and altered all combat arms tables of organization. Many National Guard units were restructured as a consequence, and the Guard overall lost nine hundred units. In 1959, the 188th Armored Field Artillery Battalion converted to the 131st Engineer Battalion, and the 957th Battalion was reorganized into the 957th Engineer Company and the 1050th Transportation Company. The National Guard Bureau allotted North Dakota another engineer group, designated the 188th, with the former 957th Headquarters and Headquarters Company serving the same function for the 188th Engineer Group. This move gave the state two engineer group headquarters, five combat engineer battalions, seven separate engineer companies, two transportation companies, and the 3662nd Ordnance

Company. The 294th Band, which had been at Lisbon since 1891, moved to Fargo "due to failure of minimum levels," according to Franklin Schoeffler, and was redesignated the 188th Army Band.

The conversion took a full year to implement, with no field training as engineers until 1956. Under National Guard Bureau regulations, all officers had to qualify as engineer officers in order to retain their federal recognition. Forty officers began the retraining process when they went to the Engineer School at Fort Belvoir, Virginia, in January 1956 "for the purpose of attending a special Orientation Engineer School." This was only the beginning of special schooling and correspondence work before officers were fully qualified. For some it created problems. Milton Kane remembered that, "As a company commander changing from Inf. to Engrs., going to college, and working nights was especially rough."

Some old-timers, mostly retired officers but some still active, resented the 164th Infantry's disappearance. Seventy years of tradition and service in four wars were lost, in their opinion, when the regiment was inactivated. The retention of the 164th designation for one of the engineer groups and one of the engineer battalions did not placate them. Most active officers liked the change. Though Camp Grafton did not provide adequate space for regimental maneuvers and lacked a safe place for artillery firing, it offered an excellent site for engineer training. It became quickly evident that engineers could furnish far greater assistance than infantry in disaster relief and public works projects. Above all, the change made recruiting easier. One veteran recalled, "We had a lot of new jobs to offer men, such as equip. operators, welders, etc." Another commented that, since farm boys were already familiar with heavy equipment, the easiest recruiting method involved holding an open house and simply letting young men inspect the cranes, bulldozers, and dump trucks at will. While the infantry could only offer close-order drill, small-unit tactics, and repetitive weapons exercises at weekly drills, the engineers gave hands-on work in repair, maintenance, and equipment operation.

Strength returns reflected the engineering appeal. In 1957, the North Dakota Army Guard totaled 2,319 officers and enlisted men, an increase of 539 since 1955. The state discovered that many small towns could not support a full company, even in engineers. In the 1959 reorganization, General Edwards established several split units, with two platoons of the 869th Engineer Company of Bismarck stationed at Linton, for example, or one platoon from Rugby's Company A, 164th Engineers, located at Garrison. All told, five companies had at least one platoon placed in nearby small towns. Although the Guard remained in the same towns and cities that had long served as home stations, split units and frequent restructurings eroded the close identity the old infantry companies once shared with their home towns. Guardsmen found it far easier to identify with a specific company which remained the same for years than with partial units which changed designations every four or five years.

Once General Edwards obtained the engineer assignment and release from the 47th Division, he intensified his efforts to obtain a line brigadier general and outlined his strategy to Governor John Davis in April 1957. Federal law authorized the state a brigadier general as assistant adjutant general, but

Edwards said, I intend "to use the position and the rank for our Commander of Troops. The Commander of Troops is responsible for the training of Engineer and Artillery troops in excess of a brigade." Colonel Ira Gaulke had served as commander of troops since 1954, and, according to Edwards, "should be entitled to the promotion," but the adjutant general wanted Frank Richards, soon to leave active duty, to have the promotion. It would be his "only opportunity to be a general officer." Gaulke was willing to wait since Richards intended to serve only a year, and Governor Davis approved the idea. Frank Richards became the state's first line general officer in May 1957. He held the position longer than planned because the National Guard Bureau denied Gaulke federal recognition as a brigadier general in 1958, and Edwards had to use all his political skills and National Guard contacts to win reconsideration. He finally succeeded, and in January 1959 Richards retired and Ira Gaulke became a brigadier general.

Richards and Gaulke were only two of many World War II veterans who continued to dominate the Guard's major commands well into the 1960s. Veterans commanded all the larger units at the time of the 1955 conversion. Colonel William Mjogdalen, the last commander of the 164th Infantry, took leadership of the 164th Engineer Group, and the lieutenant colonels assuming command of the engineer battalions had all served in World War II. They included Robert P. Miller (164th Battalion), Bernard Lyons (141st Battalion), Alvin A. Paulson (142nd Battalion), and Francis T. Kane (231st Battalion). In 1959, Colonel Mjogdalen moved to the newly formed 188th Engineer Group, and Colonel Robert Carlson, wartime commander of the 188th Field Artillery Battalion, took over the 164th Group. Wartime officers still held the major commands in 1968, with Colonel Alvin A. Paulson leading the 164th Group and Colonel Howard Erickson the 188th Group. All their battalion commanders had served during the war.

The Guard could not count on World War II veterans indefinitely as a source for officers. As time passed and they grew older, these men left the service, and none had been available as junior company officers for some time. Although some Reserve Officers Training Corps graduates joined the Guard, many University of North Dakota and Agricultural College graduates left the state as part of the continuing postwar population drain. In 1957, when the National Guard Bureau phased out its long-standing Series 10 correspondence courses, which enlisted men took to earn commissions, North Dakota established an Officers Candidate School to replace the correspondence series. General Edwards announced an Academic Board in April to set policies and select candidates, and the first class of thirty men began their studies in June. The course totaled 238 hours, with the first 95 hours earned during annual field training. It closely followed that of the Army's Officers Candidate School and used material and tests from the Fort Benning Infantry School. In 1958, several Army advisers serving in North Dakota joined the school's faculty, originally headed by Guard Captain Herbert J. Mack. The addition of a noncommissioned officers school at the same time made an effective recruiting tool which offered enlistees a military education and an opportunity for advancement. When coupled with the required active-duty six-month basic training all privates took, the schools guaranteed a constant source of officers and enlisted men far better trained than any in the Guard's history.

The service's financial position steadily improved after 1953 as both federal and state governments increased their support. Federal spending, spurred by cold-war policies, rose rapidly, with the 1955 allotment topping $1 million and exceeding $2 million for the Army National Guard alone by 1962. In the latter year, federal aid for the entire National Guard accounted for ninety-four percent of all expenditures. The state in the 1930s had supplied one-third of all costs. After 1950, North Dakota's spending varied according to yearly needs. The legislature continued the 1951 annual maintenance appropriation of $94,000 through 1956, then boosted it to $124,000 in 1957, $136,000 in 1959, and $152,000 in 1961. Special appropriations for armory construction represented the state's largest commitment in the 1950s. North Dakota was slow to take advantage of the 1950 federal armory support law because it failed to contribute its twenty-five percent share. Unable to move legislators to action, a frustrated General Edwards took several to Washington to visit the National Guard Bureau in late 1952, explaining, "My main purpose is to acquaint them with the fact that there is an armory construction program in process and the state of North Dakota should participate." His educational efforts paid off as the legislature set aside $100,000 for armories in 1953, followed by $404,000 in 1955, and $176,000 four years later.

General Edwards wasted little time in implementing an extensive construction program which ultimately resulted in the erection of eighteen buildings between 1955 and 1962, the first two completed in 1955. The program peaked in 1958 when seven new armories were dedicated. The Guard was making major improvements with federal funding at Hector Field at the same time. The achievement earned Edwards the title "the builder general." Part of his plan called for sharing state costs with municipal and county governments. He permitted the participating cities and counties to have some say in armory design and location and allowed them to use the buildings for civic purposes when the Guard did not need them. Bismarck located its armory, for example, next to Bismarck Junior College, and it served as the school's gymnasium as well as the city's major armory. Under the arrangement, local governments had to pay all maintenance costs, and total local contributions exceeded state costs, with the latter spending $454,000 and local government $963,000 between 1955 and 1962. In Bismarck, the state put in $49,000 for the armory, but the city and Burleigh County paid $72,216. The disparity was much greater in other places. (See Table 10.3.) Often local costs surpassed the state's because municipalities included an auditorium in the building plans, or they required other special facilities the Guard did not need. With responsibility for only part of the twenty-five-percent share federal law required, General Edwards was able to get much greater value from state appropriated funds.

The adjutant general displayed his managerial and political skills to the maximum as he bargained with the legislature, local officials, and the National Guard Bureau to implement the building program. Constantly on the go, General Edwards flew regularly to Washington and traveled throughout the state, his constant goal to get the most out of every dollar. During negotiations for an armory in Minot, he told Captain LaClair Melhouse, commander of Headquarters Company, 164th Engineer Battalion, to sell the old one to the

Minot School District for $25,000. When the adjutant general learned the city also wanted the building, he asked for $30,000 from them. At the same time, Edwards gave Melhouse a letter to deliver to school Superintendent Paul Miller, also requesting $30,000 from the district. Melhouse, a mathematics teacher at the high school, delivered the letter in his capacity as a Guardsman without knowing its contents. After reading it, Superintendent Miller incredulously demanded of his nervous teacher, ''Who is selling what to whom, and for how much, and what the hell is this, an auction?'' Melhouse ''was dumbfounded, to say the least,'' and also caught between his two bosses. The parties finally resolved the matter without too much damage, but ''you know,'' Melhouse recalled, ''The General sold that property to the School District for $30,000.''

TABLE 10.3

Shared Armory Costs, 1955-1962

Location	State	City/County
Grafton	$20,000	$73,864
Grand Forks	40,000	215,610
Hettinger	20,000	48,748
Rugby	20,000	97,428
Williston	20,000	95,794

SOURCE: 1962 *Adjutant General's Report*

The indefatigable Edwards also pushed for constant improvement and expansion at Camp Grafton. Colonel Victor McWilliams, who became camp superintendent in 1957, remembered that the adjutant general never ran out of ideas for work there, often arriving unannounced and pulling out a sheet of paper with some project roughly sketched out. McWilliams supervised the construction of a field repair shop and a new chapel, renovation of the officers club, and rehabilitation of the camp's water and sewer systems. When they ran short on money and new materiel, Edwards proved to be a shrewd scrounger in finding used materials. In pushing the armory program and Camp Grafton improvements, as in seeking independence from Minnesota and gaining promotion opportunities for his officers, General Edwards could be tireless, even single-minded, once he decided to act. His dynamism permeated the service and he literally devoted his life to the National Guard.

Unexpectedly, the cold war interrupted this busy activity in the fall of 1961. President John F. Kennedy directed a partial National Guard and Army Reserve mobilization as part of his response to the Berlin Crisis. Soviet threats to turn control of Berlin over to the East Germans, followed by construction of the Berlin Wall, heightened Soviet-American tensions. Kennedy, believing it necessary to demonstrate American strength by increasing United States forces in West Germany, sent Army and Air Force units from the stateside strategic reserve and called up Air National Guard and Army National Guard units to take their place. Individual Army and Air Force reservists were ordered to active duty to fill out the Guard organizations. Altogether, 2 Army National Guard divisions and 264 separate units, and 25 Air National Guard squadrons, a total of 66,000 Guardsmen, served during the crisis. Under President Eisenhower, Army National Guard units had been kept at strength levels varying from fifty to seventy percent. In 1961 the Army called up organizations selected from among those maintained at the seventy-percent level.

Table 10.4

Units Mobilized for the Berlin Crisis, 1961-1962

Unit and Home Station	Total Strength	Mobilization Station
Headquarters and Headquarters Company, 164th Engineer Group, Bismarck	65	Fort Leonard Wood, Missouri
164th Engineer Battalion, Headquarters Company, Minot	116	Fort Riley, Kansas
Company A (minus 1st platoon), Rugby	70	Fort Riley, Kansas
1st platoon, Company A, Garrison	23	Fort Riley, Kansas
Company B, Minot	110	Fort Riley, Kansas
Company C, Williston	90	Fort Riley, Kansas
869th Engineer Company (Float Bridge) (minus 1st and 2 nd platoons), Bismarck	64	Fort Riley, Kansas
1st and 2nd platoons, 869th Engineer Company, Linton	49	Fort Riley, Kansas
769th Transportation Company (Light Truck), Mott	74	Fort Riley, Kansas
231st Medical Clearing Company, Grand Forks	57	Fort Riley, Kansas
TOTAL*	784	

*Includes 818th Engineer Company.

First alerted in late August, North Dakota Guardsmen were slated for active duty in October. The 818th Engineer Company of Bottineau, a dump-truck outfit, went active on 1 October at home station and reported for duty at Fort Lewis, Washington, two weeks later with sixty-six officers and enlisted men. Old members of the 188th Field Artillery Regiment in World War II and the 231st Engineer Battalion during the Korean War remembered Fort Lewis well. All other Guard organizations mobilized at home station on 15 October and were at their Army posts by the end of the month. (See Table 10.4.)

A mix-up delayed movement slightly when the Department of the Army sent railroad cars assigned to the 164th Engineer Battalion at Minot to the 164th Engineer Group in Bismarck. Otherwise, the Guard made a smooth transition to active duty, which consisted chiefly of training. The 164th Engineer Battalion and accompanying separate companies served throughout the call-up at Fort Riley, Kansas. The 164th received reserve fillers a week after arrival and spent the first four months successfully completing Army training tests. With seventy-percent strength, according to LaClair Melhouse, then a major, the battalion "had an initial operational capability" which contributed to its performance during the tests. The 164th Engineers "achieved by far the highest degree of combat readiness of all the units I had the privilege of serving with," Melhouse noted. After its training period, the battalion prepared and administered readiness tests for other engineer units at Fort Riley, including active Army battalions from the 1st Division, and carried out post engineer projects. Selected battalion personnel also took training in atomic munitions demolition. Melhouse found the 1st Division's reception of Guardsmen cordial and cooperative, and, unlike any time in the past, he came away thinking, "we really were a part of the one-army concept."

North Dakota Guardsmen returned home in August 1962 after ten months on active duty. The call-up was far more limited than that for Korea, and, unlike 1950-1951, Army Guardsmen stayed within their original units and did not go overseas, although several Air National Guard squadrons went to Europe. Some Guardsmen and reservists protested the call as disruptive and unnecessary, although not in the North Dakota Army Guard, and congressional investigations followed demobilization. President Kennedy saw activation as a means of convincing the Russians that the United States would protect West Berlin, but most citizen-soldiers continued to see themselves as only on call to support regular forces in time of total war. Partial mobilization for a limited war or for a show of strength did not sit well with some of them. The uncertainty attending the implied obligations of Guard membership which first appeared during the 1916 Mexican border mobilization persisted into the 1960s. Not everyone shared the "why me?" attitude, but it was sufficiently strong to cause policymakers after 1961 to question the Guard's usefulness as a cold-war instrument.

Major General Heber L. Edwards died two months after the Guardsmen came home, on 18 October 1962. He had served continuously since his enlistment in Company M in 1915, and as adjutant general for the last twenty-five years, the longest tenure in the Guard's history. Under his supervision, the service had more than doubled in size, acquired new armories and the

Hector Field complex, modernized and expanded Camp Grafton, and gained independence as an engineer organization. Although forces outside Edwards's control contributed significantly to this growth, particularly World War II and the cold war, his active stewardship ensured that the North Dakota National Guard benefited from the opportunities at hand. His political skills and gregarious personality guaranteed cooperation from the governor's office, regardless of the person or party in power. He had just as much effect with legislators, local officials, and the National Guard Bureau. Edwards developed wide contacts through his activities in the Adjutants General Association and the National Guard Association which permitted North Dakota a hearing when Guard policies were discussed. Not a perfect man, General Edwards had a tendency to scheme when he wanted something badly or to use heavy-handed retribution when others stood in his way. As could be expected from a person long in power, he rewarded his favorites frequently, although most of those so favored, men like Frank Richards, Ira Gaulke, and William Mjogdalen, deserved promotion and recognition. His achievements far outweighed his liabilities; and when Heber Edwards died, a significant chapter in the North Dakota National Guard's history ended.

Notes on Sources

Interviews conducted by Chief Warrant Officer Bryan O. Baldwin were of particular value for this chapter. He interviewed the following Army Guardsmen:

1. Howard Erickson	9. Stanley Pfau
2. George Fowler	10. Frank Richards (by Clifford Keller)
3. James P. Grimstad	11. George Sattler
4. James A. Johnson	12. Leo Schwehr
5. Edward Kjelstrom	13. John Vold
6. Victor McWilliams	14. Joseph R. Walter
7. Walter Mellem	15. Bernard Wagner
8. Alvin A. Paulson	16. Ralph Wood

Jerry Cooper interviewed Major General LaClair A. Melhouse (retired), Mrs. Heber L. Edwards, and Mrs. Robert Carlson. Lieutenant Colonel Lowell Lundberg (retired) wrote a detailed letter recalling the 231st Engineer Battalion's mobilization in 1950 and was especially insightful in explaining Colonel Ira Gaulke's disappointment with the Army's individual replacement policy.

Another valuable source was the typescript interview of General Melhouse by Colonel Duane Dehne, a part of the Senior Officer Oral History Program of the Army War College and United States Military History Institute, Carlisle Barracks, Pennsylvania. General Melhouse provided a copy of the interview.

Questionnaires from seventy-six Army Guardsmen and six Air Guardsmen offered details on recruiting, training, equipment, and life in the National Guard.

A variety of different Records of the North Dakota National Guard were used. The personnel records of retired or deceased officers, especially those of Heber L. Edwards, Ira M. F. Gaulke, Leroy Landom, Robert P. Miller, William Mjogdalen, and Frank Richards, furnished important information. General and special orders and general correspondence provided some outlines of Guard affairs, but of more importance were numerous organizational files. Particularly useful were the files ''Allotment 47th Division Staff, 1946-1954,'' ''Reorganization and Redesignation of NG Units, 1946 and 1951,'' ''Redesignation, 1919-1951, Reorganization, National Guard Units, Permanent File,'' and ''Induction 164th Inf. and 188th FA, 1951.'' Similar files from the Air Guard Office, Fraine Barracks, particularly ''Federal Recognition and Organization, 178th Fighter Squadron, Single Engine,'' covered the Air National Guard's development through the 1950s. Historical Bulletin No. 6, 21 July 155, ''Strength of ARNG and ANG, 1946-1955,'' and the Lineage Book, both described in notes for sources in Chapter 1, helped trace the Guard's strength and organization. This was essential, for there were no published annual or biennial adjutant general reports in the 1940s and 1950s.

The adjutant general's office did publish some reports. It issued an annual report of the Chief of Staff, North Dakota Air National Guard, for the fiscal years 1957 through 1961. For a short time, 1955 to 1957, it published a newspaper, the *Nodak Guardsman*, with news on promotions, training, and local unit activities, and several historical pieces by Colonel Herman Brocopp. The *Report of Mobilization of the North Dakota National Guard, Korean Emergency* (no date) and *Report of Mobilization of the North Dakota National Guard, Berlin Crisis* (Bismarck, N.D., 1967) were informative. Two useful items on the Air National Guard, which included historical information, were the 1972 pamphlet ''The North Dakota Air National Guard, Silver Anniversary, 1947-1972,'' and *The Happy Hooligans: North Dakota Air National Guard: Thirtieth Anniversary, 1947-1977* (no date). See also *47th Viking Infantry Division: Pictorial Review, Camp Rucker, Alabama, 1951* (no date). The annual reports of the Chief, National Guard Bureau, for 1946 to 1961 were used selectively.

The following helped in forming ideas on post-World War II foreign and military policy: Stephen Ambrose, *Rise to Globalism: American Foreign Policy 1938-1980*, Second Edition, Revised (New York, 1980); Abbott A. Brayton, ''American Reserve Policies Since World War II,'' *Military Affairs*, Vol. 36, No. 4 (December 1972), pp. 139-144; Joseph C. Goulden, *Korea: The Untold Story of the War* (New York, 1982); Charles J. Gross, ''Prelude to the Total Force: The Origins and Development of the Air National Guard, 1943-1969'' (Unpublished Ph.D. dissertation, Ohio State University, 1979); Walter LaFeber, *America, Russia, and the Cold War, 1945-1980*, Fourth Edition (New York, 1980); and Russell F. Weigley, *History of the United States Army*, Enlarged Edition (Bloomington, Ind., 1984).

Company F, 164th Infantry Regiment passing in review at Camp Rucker (Alabama), 1951.

Company C (Grafton), 164th Infantry starts the day at Camp Rucker (Alabama) with the Army's "daily dozen."

First formation of the 178th Fighter Interceptor Squadron, North Dakota
Air National Guard, Avalon Ballroom, Fargo, 1946.

Left: North Dakota Adjutant General Brigadier General Heber L. Edwards and
Lieutenant Colonel Richard D. Neece, "Organizers of the North Dakota
Air National Guard."

Right: North Dakota Air Guard C-47 transport crews delivering hay during
"Operation Haylift", 1949.

☆11☆

The North Dakota National Guard
and the Total-Force Concept, 1962-1975

The National Guard's place in the military system changed significantly after the 1961 Berlin Crisis. Federal spending for the Army Guard grew dramatically and the Army worked to integrate the Guard more closely into its force structure. After 1975, the Army Guard's relationship to the Army closely approximated that of the Air Guard to the Air Force. Secretary of Defense Robert McNamara had been displeased with the performance of the Army Guard and Reserve during the Berlin Crisis. Too many Guard units had been understrength, and both Guardsmen and Reservists had been poorly trained. Although the Air Guard had performed fairly effectively, with several of its squadrons moving to Europe within weeks of mobilization, most Army organizations had needed six to nine months of training before the Defense Department deemed them ready for deployment.

President John F. Kennedy's administration sought military and foreign policies that would allow a response to overseas crises with conventional forces. Kennedy and McNamara disagreed with President Dwight D. Eisenhower's heavy reliance on strategic nuclear weapons. Believing that conventional forces gave greater flexibility, Kennedy increased defense spending on them. Defense planners were willing also to allocate more to the reserve components, for they saw a larger active role for them in national security policy, but first the reserves would have to be restructured.

McNamara wished to reduce the number of units, cut their overall strength, and ultimately have a smaller but better-equipped and trained reserve. The National Guard had been maintained since 1945 on the Protective Mobilization Plan principle of the late 1930s. The Guard had nearly six thousand separate units until the late 1950s, although manned at fifty-percent strength. Its anticipated role in contingency planning remained as before, to provide a large number of units, with partially trained men, which would be filled out with draftees when mobilized. The experiences of the Korean War and the Berlin Crisis made it clear the system was poorly fitted for limited war in the cold-war era. When an emergency developed, the active forces needed immediate reinforcement by well-equipped, fully organized and manned reserve units. The entire system, not just the Guard, was arranged on the presumption that the Defense Department would use reserves only for total mobilization in a mass conventional war, a highly unlikely prospect in the nuclear age. Throughout the 1960s, McNamara's policies were centered on totally restructuring this system.

North Dakota would have a new adjutant general to guide the Guard through the many changes. Governor William L. Guy astonished many Guardsmen and politicians when he appointed Major LaClair A. Melhouse to the adjutant generalcy in November 1962. A Minot High School mathematics teacher, Melhouse was executive officer of the 164th Engineer Battalion. His selection came as a surprise because of his relative junior rank and limited commissioned service in the Guard. Melhouse had enlisted in 1939 with the 164th Infantry's Company D, which was converted to artillery in 1941. After entering federal service with the 188th Field Artillery Regiment, he remained with the 188th until mid-1942 when he went to Officers Candidate School. Following his commissioning, he went as an artillery officer with the 1st Cavalry Division to the South Pacific. Active in the Army Reserve after 1945, Melhouse again went overseas during the Korean War, but did not return to the Guard until 1955, as a captain, to command Headquarters Company, 164th Engineer Battalion, at Minot.

The law allowed the governor to select any federally recognized officer with three years of continuous service, but no one understood Guy's reasons for selecting Melhouse. Guy, a Democrat, had few fellow party members to choose from among Guard officers. His new appointee at least was not an active Republican. That Melhouse had never been part of the late Major General Heber L. Edwards's circle seemed to attract his attention, and the new man garnered support from senators and representatives from the western part of the state, which had never had an adjutant general.

Melhouse became a brigadier general in state service as soon as he took office, but remained a major under federal recognition. He would not gain a federally recognized brigadier generalcy until 1968. Melhouse later recalled that his selection did "raise a question about the appointment of a junior officer to this position and [it did] make it awkward. It's a matter of being real careful and adjusting," he added. His abrupt rise caused ruffled feathers in Bismarck among the old timers, particularly after he made immediate changes at state headquarters and replaced several of the battalion commanders. These moves added to the short-term unhappiness among veterans who missed the Edwards regime.

A few years later, in 1968, Melhouse removed the Air National Guard base detachment commander and the fighter group commander after the 119th Fighter Group had failed two operation readiness tests. At the request of Governor Guy, the adjutant general sent a retired Air Force general to investigate conditions at Hector Field and make recommendations. When the inspector advised removing the current commanders, both World War II veterans, and replacing them with a younger man who would serve as both base and group commander, Melhouse selected Lieutenant Colonel Alexander P. Macdonald for the dual command. "Initially," Melhouse remembered, "I received much criticism for the change," but Governor Guy shielded him from political attack and Colonel Macdonald rejuvenated the Air National Guard.

Changes were inevitable after twenty-five years of one man's administration, and General Melhouse bore the brunt of criticism for altering long-established policies, which almost surely would have happened no matter who took the adjutant generalcy. Many forgot that Heber Edwards only held the rank of major when he took office, and that he, too, had moved quickly to put his stamp on the Guard. Given Edwards's long and effective tenure, any man who succeeded him would have had difficulties. Melhouse's reserved personality and relatively short tenure as a Guard officer contrasted sharply, however, with the gregarious Edwards who had served over twenty years before he became adjutant general. That he had not been in the inner circle of associates from the 1930s made it that much harder. Melhouse proved to be an effective administrator despite his initial chilly welcome, and, after serving the remainder of Edwards's term, received reappointment in 1965 and again in 1971.

As his first challenge, Melhouse undertook putting the Army Guard through another major restructuring. It had undergone significant changes in 1955 and 1959, and a lesser realignment in 1961, the latter to place battalion units closer together. At the time of the Berlin Crisis, Guard units had been maintained at strength levels ranging from fifty-two to seventy-one percent. Even the latter had proved to be undermanned, insufficiently trained, and generally inefficient. Secretary of Defense McNamara directed a Guard reorganization in 1963 to remedy the deficiencies. This one, Melhouse recalled, raised the manpower percentages and the ''number of units assigned to the Guard structure were decreased in order that units...would be fully manned.'' North Dakota lost six companies in the process, with the 142nd Engineer Battalion as one of the casualties. In 1962, the North Dakota Army National Guard included two engineer groups, five engineer battalions, and eleven separate companies. After that year, under the new arrangement it retained the two group headquarters, but had only four battalions and five separate companies. Total authorized strength, about twenty-seven hundred officers and enlisted men, remained the same in order to meet the new eighty-percent manning requirement.

Inevitably, a major reshuffling took place to fit the new structure to the old one. Melhouse recognized the need to place reorganized units in the same towns where the Guard already existed to make use of currently enrolled Guardsmen and their recently built armories. This resulted in twenty-one redesignations in which personnel remained in their home towns but became members of new units. The men from the lost Guard groups ''were absorbed by the existing units in order that increased unit strength could be maintained.'' Then Melhouse created split units to meet these new levels. Many towns received just one platoon, or, in a few cases, two or three platoons. Indeed, split units became the norm, as only a few towns and cities served as home station for a full company. In several instances, old units had to take on entirely new assignments. That at Bottineau, for example, originally the 818th Engineer Company (Dump Truck) since 1955, now became the Battalion Supply Section, Headquarters Company, 164th Engineer Battalion.

Changes in the Guard continued in the ensuing five years, as McNamara persisted in his attempts to create a smaller reserve maintained at a higher readiness level. This became increasingly important as the war in Vietnam escalated. Defense planners feared that sending more and more Regular Army units to Southeast Asia would ultimately strip the country's strategic reserve of trained men. After President Lyndon Johnson announced in July 1965 that he did not intend to call the Guard and Reserve for duty in Vietnam, McNamara established a Select Reserve Force of 150,000 Army National Guard troops to reinforce the strategic reserve. Manned at one hundred percent, these units would receive high-priority equipment and take extra paid drills beyond the required forty-eight per year. North Dakota's Select Reserve Force contingent consisted of the 188th Engineer Group, the 231st Engineer Battalion, and the 816th Engineer Company (Light Equipment).

The Secretary of Defense remained unhappy with reserve policies and directed yet another major reshuffling in 1967. The Army was altering its basic divisional tables of organization at the time, and the Guard would have had to make some adjustments to conform to those changes in any event, but the 1967 moves went beyond altering the tables of organization. The Defense Department inactivated fifteen National Guard divisions, leaving only eight active ones, and altogether eliminated eleven hundred units. It also made similar Army Reserve reductions. Under the new arrangement, engineer battalions went from three to four line companies and from a total strength of 494 to 738 officers and enlisted men. Furthermore, the Defense Department directed all Guard units to maintain their numbers at either ninety-three or one hundred percent strengths. The changes cost North Dakota the 188th Engineer Group and the 131st Engineer Battalion, although it gained a mobile assault bridge company and a military police company. Once again, total strength remained the same. Another round of redesignations of home stations predictably ensued, to the confusion of both civilians and Guardsmen.

After 1968, the North Dakota Army National Guard's basic structure stabilized with the 164th Engineer Group, the 164th and 141st Combat Engineer Battalions, and the 231st Engineer Battalion, a service and maintenance unit. The two combat battalions included four line companies and a headquarters company each, while the 231st served as administrative control for four separate companies. Group or state headquarters supervised three other companies. (See Table 11.1.) Occasional changes in the number of separate companies and detachments allotted to North Dakota occurred in the fifteen years after 1968, with a major realignment of home stations in 1972, but the basic disposition prevailed. These frequent reorganizations were unpredictable and disruptive, imposing an enormous workload on the state staff and on unit commanders and their administrative aides. Guardsmen were asked to change their occupational and unit assignments every three or four years. Above all, the seemingly endless redesignations eroded home station identity with local units, long the great strength of the National Guard.

National defense policy increasingly determined the Guard's development after World War II, but the trend accelerated in the 1960s. Congress sometimes delayed Robert McNamara's attempts to cut the National Guard and Army Reserves and make them small enough to become truly effective ready reserves, and the growing costs of the Vietnam War left them with only partial funding. As the war wound down under President Richard M. Nixon, Secretary of Defense Melvin Laird continued McNamara's policies. Laird announced his "total force" concept in 1970, which stated that the Guard and Army Reserve, according to General Melhouse, "must be prepared to be the initial and primary source of augmentation of the active forces" in any major emergency.

Table 11.1

North Dakota National Guard, 1968

Unit	Home Station
164th Engineer Group	
Headquarters and Headquarters Company	Bismarck
164th Engineer Battalion	
Headquarters and Headquarters Company	Minot
Company A (less 2nd and 3rd platoons)	Carrington
2nd platoon	Harvey
3rd platoon	Minot
Company B	Jamestown
Company C (less 2nd and 3rd platoons)	Rugby
2nd platoon	Cando
3rd platoon	Bottineau
Company D	Dickinson
1193rd Light Truck Company	Williston
141st Engineer Battalion	
Headquarters and Headquarters Company	Valley City
Company A (less 2nd and 3rd platoons)	Lisbon
2nd and 3rd platoons	Wahpeton
Company B (less 2nd and 3rd platoons)	Mayville
2nd and 3rd platoons	Hillsboro
Company C (less 2nd and 3rd platoons)	Oakes
2nd and 3rd platoons	Edgeley
Company D (less 2nd and 3rd platoons)	Wishek
2nd platoon	Linton
3rd platoon	Valley City
231st Engineer Service Battalion	
Headquarters and Headquarters Detachment	Grand Forks
188th Mobile Assault Bridge Company (less support platoon and 3rd bridge platoon)	Fargo
Support platoon and 3rd bridge platoon	Grand Forks
957th Engineer Company (Float Bridge) (less equipment and maintenance platoon, and 3rd, 4th, and 5th bridge platoons)	Grafton
Equipment and maintenance platoon	Grand Forks
3rd, 4th, and 5th bridge platoons	Cavalier
188th Army Band	Fargo
3662nd Combat Support Company, Heavy Equipment Maintenance	Devils Lake

Separate Companies

816th Engineer Company (Light Equipment) (less maintenance and support platoon)	Mandan
Maintenance and support platoon	Bismarck
818th Engineer Company (Dump Truck) (less maintenance and service section, and 2nd platoon)	Hettinger
Maintenance and service section, and 2nd platoon	Mott
191st Military Police Company	Bismarck

Specifically, the reserves were to be equipped, trained, and manned to reinforce the regular services immediately should war break out in Europe. The Guard and the reserves were hereafter considered active parts of the strategic reserve and not as the building blocks for a wartime force as in World War II or Korea. By the end of the 1970s, the Army National Guard formed thirty percent of the Army's total strength, and Guard and Reserve units totaled fifty percent of all ground combat troops and over sixty percent of the Army's support units. From 1945 to the late 1970s, the Guard had evolved from a peacetime training and wartime mobilization outfit to a part of the forces in being, with immediate wartime assignments. Some Guard units were directly assigned to active Army divisions and brigades for both training and wartime responsibilities. The total-force concept would govern the Guard into the 1980s.

Laird pushed the total-force idea as part of President Nixon's overall goal to reduce the armed forces as the Vietnam War ended, which in turn would allow Nixon to achieve an even more important aim, cutting defense costs. Inclusion of the Guard and reserve in the total force would also permit the administration to end the highly unpopular Vietnam draft. Reservists and Guardsmen, not draftees, were slated to augment the active forces in the next limited cold-war fight. Consequently, spending on reserve components increased dramatically, rising fifty percent between fiscal year 1969 and fiscal year 1972, for example. The trend continued through the 1970s and into the 1980s, particularly as the all-volunteer armed forces program faced difficulty winning recruits. With the ending of conscription in 1972, the nation needed to maintain a viable reserve force.

The Air National Guard had established close cooperation and operational integration with the Air Force by 1961 and had set the model the Army Guard followed in the 1960s. Air Guard units also became part of the Select Reserve Force in 1965, and some Air National Guard units were mobilized in 1968 as a result of the North Korean seizure of the USS. *Pueblo* and the Tet offensive in South Vietnam. The Air National Guard squadrons sent to Vietnam proved the effectiveness of the total-force idea, as they mobilized rapidly and took their place on the combat flight line with regular Air Force units in impressive fashion, their combat records often exceeding those of regular Air Force squadrons. The North Dakota Air National Guard was not called in 1968, and it did not suffer continual reshuffling as did the Army Guard. The type of aircraft it flew determined its yearly numbers and organization. The 119th Fighter Group lost over 100 officers and enlisted men in 1968 when it converted from the F-89J to the F-102A. Though the latter plane was supersonic and "the most sophisticated aircraft in...the unit's history," the changeover to a single-seat plane reduced strength. Two years later, the F-101B, a two-seat aircraft, replaced the F-102A, and the Group's membership jumped by 150. The Air National Guard first exceeded 1,000 officers and enlisted men in 1973 and, thereafter, under the total-force policy, consistently maintained a force of over one hundred percent its authorized number.

Increased federal spending throughout the 1960s and 1970s indicated the fiscal consequences of McNamara's and Laird's policies. Congress appropriated a combined $958,670,000 for the Army and Air National Guard in 1968, allotted $1.2 billion in 1971, and $2.2 billion in 1975. Spending for the entire National Guard reached $3.4 billion by 1980. Table 11.2 illustrates North Dakota's share of that support after 1962.

The North Dakota National Guard's allotment grew four hundred percent between fiscal year 1962 and 1973 and 1,175 percent from 1962 to 1983. Dramatic growth became particularly evident once the total-force concept was implemented in the early 1970s. Although federal support had been slowly increasing since 1920, with greater growth after World War II, the spectacular expansion from 1962 onward indicated the impact of McNamara's decision to make the National Guard a force ready for immediate use.

TABLE 11.2

Federal Support, North Dakota National Guard,
Selected Years, 1962-1983

Fiscal Year	Army National Guard	Air National Guard	Total
1962	$ 2,108,900	$ 1,490,000	$ 3,598,900
1967	3,477,000	3,281,000	6,758,000
1973	6,766,000	7,664,700	14,430,700
1978	11,120,000	11,600,000	22,720,000
1983	20,400,000	21,900,000	42,300,000

For the Army Guard, federal pay accounted for seventy-five to eighty percent of its annual allotments from fiscal year 1963 onward. Technicians' salaries, that is, full-time employees, totaled $871,756 in fiscal year 1963, with drill pay at $621,743 and active-duty training pay $240,649. Both technicians' pay and drill pay exceeded $1 million in 1967, and each went over the $2 million mark by the early 1970s. In fiscal year 1980, technicians earned $4.4 million, and Guardsmen took home $3.5 million from armory pay and another $1.3 million from summer camp. A significant shift appeared in 1982, when drill pay, at $4.6 million, exceeded technicians' pay, at $4.4

million. Salaries also made up the largest single category for federal dollars in the Air National Guard, but not at as high a percentage as in the Army National Guard, generally running from sixty-five to seventy percent until the 1980s and then dropping to fifty to fifty-five percent. In the Air Guard, which had a much higher percentage of full-time technicians in its total strength than did the Army Guard, technicians' pay in fiscal year 1963 totaled $1,150,000 compared to $315,700 in drill pay, while in 1970 technicians earned $2,150,000 and drill pay totaled $516,234. In fiscal year 1978 annual salaries for full-time airmen exceeded $5 million for the first time, but drill pay did not break $2 million until 1981.

After salaries, construction projects for both services generally took the next highest percentage of federal allotments. The Army National Guard continued the armory program begun under General Edwards, with construction going on into the 1970s. Under General Melhouse, the Guard built seven new armories, with the Jamestown armory costing $1,889,698 and the one at Mandan $1,289,948, both completed in 1975. Federal funds also assisted the state in constructing organizational maintenance shops, facilities for routine upkeep of and minor repairs to trucks and engineer equipment, and a combined support maintenance shop at Camp Grafton, for major repair work. Only after the Vietnam War did equipment allotments reach substantial proportions. In 1967, for example, the Army Guard received $169,543 worth of clothing but only $153,839 in equipment. Larger amounts of equipment, supplied after 1973, brought the Guard closer to Army requirements.

The Air National Guard benefited from continued expansion and improvement of its operations and repair buildings, runways, and storage facilities at Hector Field, construction costs running from $500,000 to $1,000,000 annually. Air Guard budgets grew rapidly in the 1970s, partly owing to conversions to high-performance aircraft, but chiefly to rapidly inflating fuel costs caused by the pricing policies of the Organization of Petroleum Exporting Countries. In 1968, for example, fuel accounted for just under ten percent of its allotment, or $326,500. By 1975, fuel took nearly twenty percent, $1.9 million, and, in 1980 thirty-one percent, or $5.3 million.

Given the continued growth of federal spending and the Guard's need for better facilities and a larger number of full-time employees, the state contribution was bound to increase. Biennial expenditures mirrored federal patterns, with slow growth in the 1960s, followed by rapid expansion in the mid-1970s and into the early 1980s. North Dakota made a biennial appropriation of just over $400,000 in 1964, allotted $676,770 in 1968, and in 1973 provided $895,761. Two years later, the military budget went over $1 million biennially for the first time, approached $3 million in 1979, and for 1981 passed $6 million. Throughout the period, only a small portion of the state budget went to the Air Guard, usually about ten percent.

By any measure, from technicians and drill pay, to Camp Grafton, Hector Field, and the armories, or with aircraft, bulldozers, and dump trucks, the North Dakota National Guard depended wholly on the federal government for its well being. Consistently from the early 1960s, federal funds provided ninety-five percent of the Army and Air Guard's support. The Defense

Department gave North Dakota aircraft and engineer equipment valued at close to $100 million and physical plants from the airfield in Fargo to Williston's armory worth at least $50 million. This constituted an immeasurable improvement compared to the years of poverty in the 1890s, but in the historical process of moving from those desperate days to the better times of the recent past, the National Guard's fundamental character changed.

In the late nineteenth century, the Guard was essentially a state and local institution. It relied completely on a voluntary, unpaid membership, and, except for the small amount of outdated equipment it received from the federal government, the Guard prospered or suffered according to what the state appropriated or its own members contributed. It used social and fraternal appeals for its chief enlistment attractions, along with the hopes that a young man might win a commission. Until 1916, Guardsmen did not legally have to answer a call to war. The essence of state military service was the volunteer tradition, in peace and war, in which the amateur citizen-soldier ultimately made his own personal decision as to whether or not he would serve his state and nation. After 1916, the individual Guardsman had to answer a federal call, but, until 1941, most other aspects of National Guard life remained similar to those of the 1890s.

World War II and the cold war altered the basic conditions that governed the Guard. Guardsmen called up in 1941 learned that, when they took government dollars for drill pay, they were obliged to serve and were thereafter subjected to five years of Regular Army tradition, training, and regulations. State officers had to conform to the Army's standards if they wished to remain on active duty and win promotion. Postwar practice led to increased federal requirements for commissioned officers, and, after 1957, all enlisted men had to take their basic training from the regular services on active duty. In both instances, the Department of Defense, not the states, set the minimum requirements for Guard membership, formerly a state prerogative.

When the National Guard Association lobbied for federal armory assistance in the late 1940s, it conceded that the state systems could not survive without nearly total federal support. This overwhelming reliance on an outside funding source subjected the North Dakota National Guard to constant reorganization, particularly after 1955 as the Department of Defense constantly searched for an affordable mix of active and reserve forces capable of meeting the demands of global military responsibilities. As the Guard developed under McNamara and Laird, it was unlikely any adjutant general would have defied the Department of the Army and the National Guard Bureau, as had General Edwards when he refused to have the North Dakota National Guard train at Camp Ripley with the 47th Division just a few years earlier.

National policy, either directly or indirectly, consistently affected recruiting after 1945. The limited mobilizations of 1950-1951 and 1961 imposed unexpected obligations which disrupted Guardsmen's civilian lives and invariably hurt recruiting after demobilization. "As anticipated," General Melhouse commented in his 1964 biennial report, "The Army National Guard suffered a constant decline in strength" after units activated for the Berlin Crisis came home. "The tide reversed in June 1963," he went on, but at the end of fiscal year 1964 the Army National Guard was still ten percent below assigned strength. The escalating war in Vietnam ended any recruiting problems the Guard faced. At the end of fiscal year 1966, the entire Army Guard totaled 466,000, the largest aggregate in its history. The service paid a heavy price for its healthy enrollment figures, however, for, in General Melhouse's words, ''There were those who began to believe that the National Guard and Reserves had become a haven for draft dodgers.''

President Lyndon Johnson never explained his July 1965 decision to leave the Guard and Reserves at home and to fight the war with volunteers and draftees. Some observers noted then and later that Johnson, a politician acutely attuned to public opinion, recalled the protests of unhappy Guardsmen and Reservists called to duty in 1961. Historian Russell Weigley suggests that Secretary of Defense Robert McNamara held lingering doubts about the effectiveness and quality of the reserve components and recommended against a partial mobilization. In any event, Guard enrollment swelled as draft quotas increased in the mid-1960s. Both the Air National Guard and the Army National Guard established waiting lists for the eager recruits, for if long-service Guardsmen did not see the Guard as an escape from the draft, many young men did. Master Sergeant George Sattler, long an administrative assistant in the 231st Engineers and responsible for finding new Guardsmen in Grand Forks, recalled the great pressure put on him by young men hoping to become Guardsmen. All recruiters had received orders to adhere strictly to a first-come, first-served waiting list. The father of one young man placed an open checkbook in front of Sattler and told the sergeant he could fill in the amount if only he would sign up his son immediately. Truly shocked by the attempted bribe, Sattler threw the man out. General Melhouse lost a friend of thirty years when he told the man, after intense pleading, that he could not change the waiting list in order to sign up his son.

Colonel Howard Erickson, who commanded the 188th Engineer Group when it was part of the Select Reserve Force, expected his organization and other Select Reserve units to be called to Vietnam. These outfits met for up to ninety-five armory drills a year, instead of the normal forty-eight, and individuals also took extra duty days. They received a great deal of information on the nature of Vietnam combat. The increased training and emphasis on fighting conditions in Southeast Asia left the clear impression that some or all of North Dakota's Select Reserve Force units, which included the 231st Engineer Battalion and the 816th Engineer Company along with the 188th Group, would surely be mobilized. Guardsmen in the units had given twice the normal time to training, while still holding their civilian jobs, and their families had had to cope with the continuing worry that their men might go to war. The call never came. President Johnson did direct a limited Guard mobilization, after the February Tet offensive, and ordered some nine thousand Air Guardsmen and twelve thousand Army Guardsmen to duty. About half of them served in Vietnam for a year. Though a few of Colonel Erickson's men felt relief when they were not called, most felt disappointment, because it seemed that their intense training and extra work were wasted. Most National Guard leaders had wanted a larger call. According to General Melhouse, ''A great disservice was done the Guard during the Vietnam conflict, for no longer do we have that combat experienced mix,'' as was true after World War II and Korea. More importantly, he added, ''The activation of the Guard and Army Reserve would have eliminated the stigma that the Guard and Reserves are simply a way to evade active duty in time of war.'' Guardsman, however, had no control over the matter.

As in the Korean War, the nature of the Vietnam War and the manpower decisions of the Johnson administration did not necessitate total mobilization. With a much larger manpower pool than was needed, the draft again brought up the question, ''who serves when not all serve?'' Given the irrationalities of deferment policies and the safety in joining the National Guard, General Melhouse commented, ''There were glaring inequities in the burden of service.'' President Nixon defused the highly explosive draft question between 1969 and 1971. First, he began to withdraw American ground troops from Vietnam, lessening the need for large draft quotas. He also implemented a random selection process through a lottery, ended nearly all deferments, and limited draft eligibility to only one year rather than six. Finally, upon the President's recommendation, Congress let the Selective Service Act of 1967 expire in late 1971. Thereafter, volunteers would supply the required forces for all the armed services, including the reserve components.

The elimination of the draft ended one of the nation's major sources of social tension and conflict, but it posed a serious problem for the National Guard. Enlistments in all the armed forces dropped sharply once selective service closed down. Nationwide, Guard enrollment declined by over sixty thousand men from 1974 to 1978, a reflection of the difficulties the active forces faced under the All Volunteer Force practice. Though Guard leaders, from the National Guard Bureau to local unit commanders, had consistently denied that the Guard offered draft dodgers a refuge, none could deny that as soon as the draft ended, voluntary enlistments fell off rapidly. Major General C. Emerson Murry, who succeeded General Melhouse late in 1975, admitted as much in his 1977 biennial report. ''The National Guard...appears to suffer as a result of the all volunteer army,'' he wrote. ''We no longer secure the draft-motivated enlistments.'' Early in the biennium, the North Dakota Army National Guard fell to eighty-nine percent of its authorized strength, its worst recruiting performance since the mid-1950s.

Secretary of Defense Melvin Laird had implemented the total-force program to compensate for the loss of draftees and reduction of defense spending. The nation and the states had to develop successful recruiting procedures during the 1970s to make the All Volunteer Force work, including enlistment and re-enlistment bonuses and significant pay increases. Some programs applied to the reserve components as well, and a few were designed specifically for the reserves. In the latter case, for example, the Civilian Acquired Skills Enlistment Program, implemented in 1975, allowed Guard recruits to enlist at an advanced grade if their civilian work skills matched a military occupational skill. That same year, North Dakota adopted a Work Experience/Career Education Program, which permitted high school seniors to enlist and receive high school credit for physical education and up to two credits for work done in advanced individual training. The state paid a fee to cooperating school districts.

The burden of devising state policies to solve recruiting problems went to Major General C. Emerson Murry after 1975. Under his guidance, the Tuition Assistance Program became by far the most successful state-generated recruiting procedure. In 1977, the legislature approved a plan that waived up to seventy-five percent of tuition fees for Guardsmen enrolled in state-supported post-secondary schools and, in 1979, it added four-year private colleges. The state paid $132,924 in fees in the 1977-1979 biennium and $279,076 in the next two years. General Murry reported in 1979, "It is felt that this program has played a major part in North Dakota's recruiting and retention program."

Local units had had the responsibility for recruiting since the Guard's inception, one of the most important functions carried out by companies. To attract new members, successful units had long used a variety of informal methods, relying chiefly on their social or athletic reputation and the face-to-face efforts of individual Guardsmen. The post-Vietnam manpower crisis, however, necessitated greater central control. General Melhouse had created a Recruiting and Retention Office in July 1971. After 1977, General Murry established a full-time recruiting force, paid with federal funds. The government instituted enlistment and re-enlistment bonuses in 1979 for personnel with skills needed in high-priority units. Total costs for recruiting, including full-time recruiters and the bonus programs, grew rapidly after 1977. Combined state and federal recruiting costs for both the Army National Guard and the Air National Guard more than doubled from fiscal year 1978 to 1983. (See Table 11.3.) Federal funds made up approximately seventy percent of these expenses and represented another federal intrusion into an area once belonging completely to the states. The backlash from the draft forced states to rely on Congress and the Defense Department for assistance in recruiting, and increasingly monetary appeals became the primary means of finding new Guardsmen and keeping experienced ones. National policy, from the partial mobilization in 1961 to the Vietnam draft, and then its termination, affected Guard recruitment far more than anything the state did.

Table 11.3

Annual Recruiting Expenditures, 1978 to 1983

1978	$ 321,760
1979	330,539
1980	402,969
1981	592,974
1982	656,670
1983	763,376

NOTE: Includes both state and federal funds, salaries for full-time recruiters, and enlistment and re-enlistment bonuses.

Ultimately, at least in North Dakota, the combined state and federal recruiting programs paid off. By the end of 1977, the Army National Guard had reached 107 percent of authorized strength, and the Air National Guard stood at 116 percent. Two years later, General Murry reported the Air Guard at 124 percent, making North Dakota "the top state in the nation," and the Army National Guard led the country in 1981 with 127 percent of authorized strength, or a total of 3,302 Army Guardsmen. The entire Guard had only 83 percent of funded strength in 1980 and 90 percent a year later. By the early 1980s, the Air National Guard and Army National Guard exceeded 4,000 officers and enlisted personnel (4,547 in 1983), a remarkable achievement for a state with a population slightly over 600,000 and a far better performance than that of most of the states.

After 1973, the Guard could no longer report strength returns using the term "enlisted men," for, under pressure from the National Guard Bureau, North Dakota began to enlist women in 1973. Females could not be assigned to units with a combat mission, which excluded them from two-thirds of the state's Army organizations. Still, in 1975, 44 women belonged to the Army National Guard and 45 to the Air Guard, and by 1983, 230 women, 17 of them officers and 1 a warrant officer, were serving in the Army National Guard. Some old-timers were highly skeptical of the presence of women in what had always been a male preserve, but women offered a large group of potential recruits and served capably in clerical, medical, communications, and maintenance assignments. In 1975, a four-woman weapons loading crew from the Air National Guard, the first in Air Defense Command history, participated in the Air Defense Command's Weapons Load Competition and placed eleventh. The 1976 Air National Guard team, with two men and two women, won third place in the competition. As was so often true after 1962, federal law and regulation governed state actions in recruiting, regardless of past practice or present intention. The Guard had come a long way from the days when a majority vote of currently enrolled members decided who could or could not enlist, or the personal approval of the company commander alone determined a potential recruit's enlistment.

The Guard changed dramatically in another respect after 1962 as more and more of its personnel became full-time employees. From territorial days until the early 1920s, Guardsmen served without compensation and attended drill sporadically, perhaps at best twenty to twenty-five times a year. The advent of drill pay after World War I required a minimum of forty-eight two-hour drills a year with nominal pay. The Guard employed a few full-time workers, called caretakers, to maintain the armories or care for vehicles and other equipment at Camp Grafton. Poorly compensated officers and senior noncommissioned officers prepared training lessons and did administrative work in their spare time. Until 1945, the vast majority of Guardsmen received nothing for their work but drill and summer-camp pay.

After World War II, the Guard took on more full-time employees. According to one veteran Guard technician, "each unit/detachment was assigned a Permanent Duty Assistant to function as an administrator, supply technician, and equipment maintenance technician. These individuals were paid from federal funds." Most were warrant officers with lengthy service.

Because of its highly technical nature and because it served a much greater national rather than state role, the Air Guard had a higher ratio of full-time technicians to total enrollment than had the Army Guard. During the Berlin Crisis, twenty percent of all Air Guardsmen were regularly employed technicians, while at the same time only three percent of Army Guardsmen were. Many in the Department of Defense and the National Guard recognized this factor as the major difference between the Air National Guard's quality performance in the 1961 mobilization and that of the Army National Guard.

As part of McNamara's reserve improvement policies, the number of North Dakota Army National Guard technicians grew during the 1960s to six percent. They came to be, as General Melhouse commented in 1964, "The Guard's 'professional soldiers.'" Full-time technicians included officers, warrant officers, and enlisted men, many working at state headquarters in a variety of administrative, logistical, and maintenance assignments. Others continued to assist unit commanders, as had the pre-Korean War Permanent Duty Assistants, and took an increasing role in planning and directing training. Technicians manned the Organizational Maintenance Shops and the Combined Support Maintenance Shop at Camp Grafton. Air technicians, who by the end of the 1960s had risen to twenty-five percent of the North Dakota Air National Guard, fulfilled the same jobs, but were particularly important to aircraft repair and maintenance and in managing the Air Guard's complicated supply system. Employment as a technician became more attractive after 1968 when the federal civil service with its pension system started including all Guard employees.

With the manpower problems of the mid-1970s, the National Guard took on a larger number of regularly employed Guardsmen in its Full-Time Manning Program. Many technicians were converted from civil service status to full-time active duty, while other Guardsmen and Army Reservists moved directly to permanent active duty. In 1981, the North Dakota Army National Guard had a total of 284 technicians, of whom 180 came under the civil service and the remainder stayed on active duty. The combined payroll of this full-time force totaled nearly $5.3 million. By 1983, technicians made up ten percent of the Army Guard, receiving just over $7 million in annual salaries. These men and women, General Melhouse noted several years earlier, were "responsible for the daily operations of the National Guard and are relied upon to maintain units in the highest state of readiness."

The full-time employees, a tenth of the Army National Guard and one-quarter of the Air National Guard by 1983, logically owed their growing importance to the great emphasis placed on operational readiness after 1962 and the total-force concept of the 1970s. Part-time Guardsmen could not meet the demands the Defense Department put on the service. In effect, however, the policy created a "standing National Guard" barely distinguishable from the active forces. While regularly employed Guardsmen joined their local units as in the past and served within their home states, at the same time their full-time status made them permanent active-duty soldiers and airmen. Their service differed completely from that of the men who had organized the first territorial units at Bismarck, Fargo, Grafton, and Valley City in the 1880s. The change was not necessarily bad, but the two kinds of service differed so that to call both groups Guardsmen was more a matter of convenience than precise definition.

Full-time employment caused a steady improvement in Guard armory training. Some technicians devoted all their time, after appropriate instruction at Army service schools, to preparation and conduct of training. Training comprised four phases. Guardsmen completed the first two, basic combat and advanced individual, while they were taking their six-month active-duty tour with the Army. Except for refresher training, units no longer had to concern themselves with basic instruction, always the Guard's weak point in the past. The third phase required basic unit training, sometimes called inactive duty training (or armory drill in the old days). Efforts here focused on company work, and the training was usually conducted at the squad, section, or team level. Ideally, companies would receive sufficient training so that, in the event of mobilization, it would be unnecessary to cover company training. In the fourth phase, active-duty training, or field training, split companies functioned as units and companies trained ''as part of battalions and all units [had] to perform normal functional or support roles as a part of a larger force'' during the yearly fifteen days at Camp Grafton. This well-structured training program was a marked improvement over the haphazard, unfocused practices of the past.

As had been the case since the 1890s, good training in the local units, by platoons and companies, resulted in Guard effectiveness. Work at this level improved steadily from the late 1950s onward, partly due to a change in weekly drill time from two to four hours and partly due to the technicians' contributions. Beginning in the late 1950s, the Army National Guard occasionally followed the Air Guard's example and held weekend training assemblies once a month. These became a regular practice in the early 1960s. Men serving from the 1930s into the 1960s considered the move from the once-a-week drill to the weekend meeting as the single greatest training improvement. John Holt recalled that under the new system ''everyone benefitted.'' Mess crews could actually cook and serve meals, and maintenance men could complete repair work at one time. ''It helped training 100%.'' For Herbert J. Mack, the assemblies afforded ''the time to accomplish coverage of full subject matter.'' During weekend drills, ''units had time to organize training and conduct [it] in [a] manner similar to units on AD,'' another Guardsman noted.

With individual basic and advanced training already covered, units on weekend assembly could concentrate on vehicle and equipment maintenance as well as engineering work. During the winter months, Guardsmen saw movies, worked with model bridge sets, and heard lectures. They moved outside in warmer weather for ''More and varied hands[-]on training,'' according to one veteran. From the mid-1960s on, the Guard received more and higher-quality engineering equipment, which allowed the men increased practical experience. Much of the outdoor training involved community-action endeavors where units improved city, county, or state parks or worked on other public projects. These were ''simply training vehicles and are treated as such,'' General Melhouse reported in 1964. The Guard could not compete with private contractors or assume financial responsibility to complete the projects. This kind of work, which continued into the 1980s, abounded and included road grading, installing culverts, and clearing new park areas, would have gone undone had not the Guard taken it up, and it provided ideal hands-on training.

From 1962 to the mid-1970s, for its active-duty training the Army National Guard spent time regularly at Camp Grafton. The training there emphasized carrying out combat engineer assignments and civil engineering to improve the camp. The men strove each summer to pass Army training tests, a new requirement under the McNamara and Laird policies. Annual field training began to change in the mid-1970s in two ways. Increasingly, in order to vary and expand training, some units split their summer's work, with a week at Camp Grafton to take the Army tests and the other week somewhere in the field to carry out community assistance work. By the late 1970s, some companies went to camp during January or February for cold-weather training. Second, breaking a long North Dakota tradition, some units began to travel out of state for their active-duty training. The 3662nd Heavy Equipment Maintenance Company, of Devils Lake, went to the Tooele Army Depot at Salt Lake City in 1977, for example, to learn to repair tanks and artillery guns, which Camp Grafton did not have. In 1978, the North Dakota Army National Guard began a "reciprocal exchange program" with Minnesota. Two companies, Company C of the 141st Engineer Battalion and the 191st Military Police Company, went to Camp Ripley, and two Minnesota companies came to Camp Grafton that June to work with the North Dakota National Guard, thus ending the long-standing breach between the two states. In August of the same year, the 3662nd was airlifted to Kaiserslautern, Germany, as part of a test to see how quickly reserve units could deploy overseas.

These variations in active-duty training, General Murry reported in 1977, offered "a broader scope of training...and enables units to better prepare for wartime contingency missions." The markedly better training of the 1970s, when compared to that of the early 1960s or any other period in the Guard's history, resulted from the millions of federal dollars poured into North Dakota for armory construction, full-time employees, more equipment, increased drill pay, and numerous recruiting incentives. In turn, greater amounts of money had become available because the total-force concept integrated the Guard closely with the Army. Inadequate training at every level had plagued the Guard as did no other problem from the late nineteenth century to the early 1960s. If it had not solved that problem totally by the end of the 1970s, it had made great strides toward doing so. In technical branches like the engineers, Guard units often tested better than active Army organizations because the former had more experienced, better-educated personnel than did the latter. The Guard had achieved success mainly through massive federal assistance and near-total Defense Department control. In training, as in all other aspects of the Army Guard's history after 1962, these conditions changed the fundamental character of state military service.

Air Guard training evolved in a slightly different direction. In 1962 it "saw the beginning of the year-round field training plan which replaced the traditional two week annual summer camp." Since the Air National Guard carried on continuous operations with its higher percentage of full-time technicians and on-duty air alert detachments, it found it more convenient and useful to space annual training throughout the year, with portions of the 119th Fighter Group reporting for fifteen days active-duty training at separate times. Year-round training allowed the group commander to use personnel "for peak workload periods and encourage 100% attendance." Armory training, or the Unit Training Assembly, as the Air Force called it, emphasized individual study in a wide variety of military occupational specialties. Classroom work and correspondence courses served as preparation for the major Unit Training Assembly activity, on-the-job training, a necessity in the highly technical air arm.

The 119th Fighter Group rebounded quickly after 1968 under Colonel Alexander P. Macdonald's leadership. In the early 1970s, the North Dakota Air National Guard won an unprecedented number of Air Force and Air National Guard achievement awards and became the first Air Guard unit ever to win the Aerospace Defense Command's William Tell Meet twice in a row. This biennial competition included Air National Guard, Air Force, and Canadian Air Force fighter- interceptor squadrons in an overall contest for superiority in aerial shooting, aircraft maintenance, and weapons loading. In 1974, the 119th became the first Air Guard outfit to win the Hughes Award, which went to the Air Force or Air National Guard unit with the highest overall efficiency in maintenance and training. It broke precedent again in 1974 when it became the first Air Guard organization to win the Daedalian Maintenance Award for achieving the best weapons system maintenance record. Numerous other Air Force and National Guard Bureau awards won in the 1970s attested to the 119th's successful training program.

North Dakota's airmen left for their first out-of-state field-training deployment in ten years when over four hundred men and unit aircraft flew to Elmendorf Air Force Base, Alaska, in 1969 to participate in an Air Defense Command exercise. On 27 August 1969, the unit's C-54 transport plane was lost on a flight out of Elmendorf. Lieutenant Colonel Donald H. Flesland, commanding officer of the 178th Fighter Interceptor Squadron, Captain Eddie E. Stewart, Master Sergeant Ingvold Nelson, and Master Sergeant Floyd D. Broadland were lost with the aircraft. The wrecked C-54 was found three years later. The remains of Ingvold Nelson were identified and interred separately; the remaining three crewmen were buried in a common grave. More frequent out-of-state deployments came in the 1970s, chiefly for the annual "Combat Pike" weapons-firing exercises, a fifteen-day tour at Tyndall Air Force Base, Florida. Other occasionally scheduled deployments for operational readiness testing and special exercises took airmen on active duty for up to thirty days a year in the late 1970s, yet another consequence of the total-force program.

Preparation for combat dominated training from 1945 to the mid-1960s. Since the Guard's combat-reserve function loomed so large during the cold-war years, both the states and the federal government paid little attention to the service's second major mission, that of assisting state and local governments to quell disorders, enforce the law, and cope with natural disasters. Yet the need to control urban and industrial disturbances was the major reason that had led to the National Guard's development after the Civil

War. Fortunately, because of its rural, agricultural economy, North Dakota did not experience the often bitter conflicts between Guardsmen and industrial workers that occurred in so many states from the 1870s to World War I. The North Dakota National Guard's first exposure to military aid to civil authority came during the depression- ridden 1930s under Governor William Langer.

After World War II, the Guard sporadically assisted civil governments. In February 1949, Governor Fred G. Aandahl ordered the 178th Fighter Squadron to use its C-47 transport planes to conduct relief operations in the state's northwestern section. Heavy snows had isolated ranchers, and airmen dropped food, fuel, and hay during a thirty-one-day operation out of Minot. Major Donald Jones, the squadron commander, lost his life when his F-51 plane crashed as Jones flew from Minot back to Fargo, the only Guardsman to die during disaster relief operations. A devastating tornado at Fargo in June 1957 brought out the Air National Guard for traffic control and security, while the 231st Engineer Battalion made a forced motor march from annual field training at Camp Grafton to Fargo. The battalion served two weeks to prevent looting and to clean up the city. At various times up to 1962, elements of the Guard served short tours of duty to assist families uprooted by spring floods.

The North Dakota National Guard did not become regularly involved in disaster relief and other aid to civil authority until after 1962, due largely, and ironically, to federal policy, even though this traditionally had been a Guard state mission. First, only after the Army Guard had converted fully to engineers did it have the equipment and expertise to deal effectively with the state's most frequent natural disasters, heavy snows and spring floods. More importantly, at the direction of the Department of the Army, adjutants general developed state emergency plans in 1964-1965. The plans, intended to ensure military support of civil defense in the event of a nuclear attack, also included, according to General Melhouse, a "comprehensive guide for the National Guard in responding in the event of natural disasters or a breakdown in law and order." Federal funds and a full-time employee allowed the state to prepare operational plans for a variety of contingencies and regularly revise them.

In 1967, "Following repeated acts of violence, riots, and civil disobedience, and taking cognizance of the impact of natural disasters," the Army renamed the program Military Support to Civil Authority. National directives made it clearer how the President and governors might use military forces in civil upheavals, largely in response to racial disorders and spreading protests to the Vietnam War. State headquarters acquired a Military Support to Civil Authority Section staffed by two officers and a warrant officer on a full-time basis. At the same time, the legislature made the adjutant general director of the State Civil Defense Agency, with full operational and administrative control of all state civil-defense responsibilities.[1] At Melhouse's suggestion, the legislature authorized construction of an Emergency Operation Center at Fraine Barracks. Completed by 1968, this underground facility housed the State Communication Agency, which included the Highway Patrol and Civil Defense radio networks. The Emergency Operation Center provided a central headquarters for the governor and adjutant general to direct all responses to nuclear attack, natural disasters, or civil disorders. With a planning staff and a full set of contingency plans, and a statewide communications network, the state was in a much better position to answer local officials' calls for assistance.

Governor William Guy demonstrated the value of centralized control in February 1965 when he ordered the "organized militia into active service as may be needed in aid to civil authority to protect life and property, and to alleviate hardship and suffering." Severe blizzards and sub-zero weather had paralyzed counties south and west of the Missouri River. Owing to the inability of the state highway department and county road crews to keep roads open, small towns and ranchers were isolated. At the request of many county commissions, Governor Guy ordered General Melhouse to direct Operation Snowbound, and the legislature approved an emergency funding bill to assist counties that had already expended their entire year's snowplowing budgets. In all, fifty-seven officers and enlisted men served from 1 to 21 February clearing roads, opening farm lanes, and plowing access to haystacks and feed lots. More importantly, General Melhouse and his officers coordinated the efforts of state and county road workers, private contractors, and Guardsmen in seventeen counties. The adjutant general oversaw the entire project, and officers sent to each stricken county directed joint civil-military snow clearing. The communications and coordination effort, as much as the work done by Guardsmen, marked the operation, an effort made possible by the civil-defense planning done the year before. Operation Snowbound cost the state $81,415 in labor, equipment, and fuel costs for the Guard alone.

"Fiscal year 1969 proved to be a period in which extreme weather conditions and a rare instance of a law enforcement support requirement tested the responsiveness and adaptability of the North Dakota National Guard," General Melhouse noted in a special report to Governor Guy. Twice in the later summer of 1968, the Guard provided cleanup assistance to small towns hit by tornadoes. Guardsmen on weekend assembly training on July 13 and 14 cleared the Antler Memorial Park after a tornado had wrecked it, then gave similar assistance to the village of Courtenay on 24-25 August. Neither effort cost the state anything, for the troops were used on a federal drill status. Far more demanding and costly was a second Operation Snowbound, in two phases, 28 January to 13 February 1969 and 27 February to 22 March, during which the Guard assisted nineteen counties in snow-removal efforts. Counties in the state's southeast, south central, and north central sections were particularly affected. With calls for aid coming at "An overwhelming rate," Melhouse had developed an explicit set of guidelines to allocate assistance, as "The National Guard," he explained, "cannot possibly accomplish all that has been requested due to equipment limitations." Melhouse allotted two bulldozers to each afflicted county for three days to clear roads, and, as in 1965, coordinated the combined efforts of state, county, and private work crews. Over the entire period, 139 Guardsmen saw duty at a cost of $33,863.

By the end of the winter, the snow cover in North Dakota was 150 percent above normal, and officials expected heavy spring flooding. Acting as director, State Civil Defense Agency, General Melhouse began planning for flood duty in mid-March. As anticipated, flooding was severe and widespread, particularly along the Mouse River at Minot and the entire length of the Red River of the North from Pembina through Grand Forks and Fargo to Wahpeton. Guardsmen first went on duty at Minot on 9 April, and by the 17th, when "Flooding was general throughout the state," were serving at Minot, Jamestown, Valley City, and at nearly every city along the Red River. Minot, where two hundred city blocks were flooded and the disaster "taxed all available government facilities," received the brunt. At the peak, 14 April, 521 Guardsmen were on duty, and 735 served in all. Flood waters did not begin to recede until early May, and the last Guardsmen went home on 9 May. While on duty, they built and patrolled dikes, provided security, evacuated stranded civilians, pumped water, and delivered food. The total effort cost $64,131. During both Operation Snowbound and Operation Flood, contingency plans and the existing Civil Defense communications and control organization ensured a coordinated response and allowed the Guard to mitigate the suffering.

North Dakota's rural economy and homogeneous white population had shielded it from the turbulent and violent racial upheavals that struck many cities during the 1960s. The state's acknowledged conservative social and political nature had also exempted it from the sometimes violent war protests and college campus demonstrations. North Dakotans could look out at an apparently disorderly, riotous nation and take comfort that old values, including patriotism and respect for authority, still prevailed on the northern plains. An unexpected event seriously damaged that sense of assurance in May 1969. It began innocently enough when the student newspaper at North Dakota State University, *The Spectrum*, jokingly suggested that the state's college students gather for a spring happening, on 9 and 10 May, at the little town of Zap, eighty miles northwest of Bismarck. The "Zip to Zap," or "Zap-in," *The Spectrum* impishly implied, would make Zap the "Fort Lauderdale of the North." Initially, Zap residents, led by Mayor Norman Fuchs, welcomed the idea, anticipating that the Zap-in would give the village publicity and its residents the chance to make some extra money. Many state newspapers publicized the idea, generally endorsing it. The Bismarck *Tribune*, on 8 May, said in its editorial, "We hope Zap gets college students from all over the country, and that the boys and girls have a good time."

Second thoughts began to develop even before the *Tribune* published its cheery editorial. With a population of less than three hundred and a small business district with one cafe, two taverns, and two service stations, Zap seemed an unlikely place to host hundreds, possibly thousands, of high-spirited college students. Campus papers across the midwest and the national press began to play up the Zip-to-Zap idea, raising the possibility of an influx of young people from across the country. Although his city lay sixty miles from Zap, David J. Price, president of Dickinson's City Commission, wrote Governor William Guy requesting that Company D, 164th Engineer Battalion, "be alerted...to stand by in case of emergency" because of the expected "movement in this area" of students headed to and from Zap. Law enforcement officials in Mercer County, where Zap was located, also requested assistance from the governor when it became apparent that several thousand young people were going to descend on the village.

Governor Guy called General Melhouse and Superintendent of the State Highway Patrol, Ralph Wood, for a conference on 2 May. Guy decided that the Highway Patrol, with only seventy officers on the entire force, would give direct support to Mercer County authorities, while General Melhouse held the Guard in reserve, ready to respond if necessary. Guy gave Wood, who coincidentally was a Guard lieutenant colonel and commander of the 164th Battalion, authority to ask for the Guard if he needed it, and Melhouse could then commit men at his own discretion. During the next week, the adjutant general and senior Guard commanders met, without publicity, at Fraine Barracks to prepare a plan for possible intervention at Zap, using existing procedures from the current Civil Defense Operation Plan as guidelines. Melhouse rescheduled the 17-18 May weekend drill to 9-11 May for units in the state's western half, these forces to remain on federal drill status unless called to state active duty. He ordered Colonel William Tillotson, commander of the 164th Engineer Group, to ready "an adequate task force organization to cope with a local breakdown in law and order." No one could guess how many young people might show up, and crowd estimates ranged from two thousand to six thousand.

Melhouse gave his commanders a thorough review of aid-to-civil-authority procedures. The National Guard had often reacted badly in civil disorders during the mid-1960s. Following the Michigan National Guard's inadequate performance in the 1967 Detroit riots, the Department of the Army had directed all Army National Guard units to complete thirty-two hours of riot-duty training that year and hold sixteen hours of refresher training each year thereafter. The government also sent riot-control equipment to the states as part of its annual equipment allotments. The Detroit riots had also moved the Army to have states upgrade Civil Defense planning. In the process of meeting Robert McNamara's operational readiness standards, most states had neglected their continuing responsibility to be prepared to quell civil disorders, thus necessitating the Army's belated emphasis on riot training and planning. The North Dakota National Guard had taken its riot-control training in 1967 and was now equipped with riot batons, gas masks, and chemical crowd-control agents. Guard units holding drill on 9 May were to review that training. Melhouse reminded his commanders, "This will be the first time that any of them have actually participated in an exercise of this nature." Though troops would receive tear gas and other "riot control munitions," he added, no "ball ammunition is authorized for issue." During the Zap-in, Army National Guard airplanes would conduct aerial surveillance for the Highway Patrol and the State Emergency Operation Center would be manned on a twenty-four-hour basis from 9 to 11 May to coordinate all local and state police forces, and the Guard, if necessary.

Colonel Tillotson presented his "OpOrd Zap" at another conference on 7 May. Five companies were assigned to the mission, with the 141st Engineer Battalion in reserve. All units would begin a regular four-hour drill on Friday evening, 9 May, at 7:00 P.M., and, if not called, would be dismissed at 11 o'clock. Tillotson selected four assembly areas near Zap to pre-position the troops if necessary. He then cautioned his men: if called, you must use only the minimum force "consistent with mission accomplishment; avoid alienating civilian populace.'' Guardsmen were not to exchange epithets or profane language with civilians. Only police officers could search or detain civilians. Company commanders had the authority to order use of the bayonet or chemical agents, but only Tillotson, as task force commander, could issue live ammunition. All directives echoed General Melhouse's emphasis on ''careful planning and sound, rational judgment.'' If the planning seemed excessive and overly cautious, it was due to the recent Guard failures in other states and General Melhouse's intention to have his men well prepared and properly briefed despite the apparent innocuous nature of the anticipated Zap-in.

Unfortunately, the Zip to Zap turned sour the very first night. Students began arriving late on the afternoon of 9 May, drinking heavily into the early evening. Nearly two thousand of them had reached town by dark. When the temperature dropped below freezing by 9:00 P.M., some youths started a bonfire on Main Street, tearing down an abandoned building for firewood. Drunken youths started fighting, then someone tossed a rock through the front window of one of the taverns. In the ensuing melee, the interior of one of the taverns was destroyed, as was the cafe. Rampaging students threw frozen food and pies from the restaurant into the street. ''Kids danced, sang, embraced and fought,'' the Fargo *Forum* reported, ''but for many more it just meant a loss of control over their actions. They passed out, vomited, urinated in the open and wandered deliriously through the streets and alleys.'' Unable to control the mob, the available fifty highway patrolmen and sheriffs deputies left town. Mayor Fuchs was reluctant to ask for the Guard, which could not be committed unless requested by him. He finally made the request to Superintendent Wood at 11:15 P.M. By that time, some Guardsmen had left their armories, and others had bedded down for the night. In any event, none of them had been sent forward from home station to the nearby assembly areas. Not until 1:07 A.M., Saturday, 10 May, did Wood reach Melhouse asking for the Guard, and it took three more hours for the assigned units to move from their armories at Bismarck, Mandan, Dickinson, Hettinger, Mott, and Williston, to the assembly areas. Colonel Tillotson and Wood decided that safety required them to wait until daylight before entering Zap.

Five hundred Guardsmen surrounded Zap at daybreak, and two hundred of them moved into town at 6:30 A.M. with fixed bayonets. Less than two hundred students were still awake and celebrating when the Guard appeared; most were sleeping in their cars or in sleeping bags on the ground. The soldiers ''systematically routed about 1,000 sacked-in visitors from bushes and ravines about the city,'' the Bismarck *Tribune* reported, and pushed them out of town. By 7:30 most of the youths had gone, and it appeared that the silly affair would end with no further damage and no serious student-Guard confrontation. The students, many hung over and in a surly mood, others still drunk, had other intentions. They caught authorities off stride by heading six miles east on Highway 200 to the village of Beulah (population 1,318), where they roamed the streets chanting, ''Open the bars! Open the bars!'' Though the crowd in Beulah was smaller than the one at Zap, perhaps a thousand, it was in an uglier mood and ready to test the Guard when it arrived from Zap. Students taunted the Guardsmen and threw full beer cans at them. According to the Fargo *Forum*, ''One North Dakota State University drunk produced a logchain and swung it at a Guardsman, knocking him down. Other Guardsmen retaliated by pinning the NDSU student up against a car and pummeling him with their rifle butts.''

With a sense of delight in leading the Guard on a merry chase, the students piled into their cars and headed east another ten miles to Hazen (population 1,222). Now down to five or six hundred people, they again took up chants, yelling, "Where is our National Guard?" and "Bring on the military." About 10:00 A.M., the *Forum* reported, "The olive-green trucks arrived. The drunken students went down to meet them," and again rocks and bottles filled the air, some coming from the rooftops of stores lining the main street. Special Agent John Wrona, Bureau of Criminal Investigation and Apprehension, later wrote General Melhouse, in Hazen "I saw one of your men get hit directly in the face with a full can of beer. He ended up with a bloodied face but did not for one moment slow up or break ranks." One ill-advised student turned his rear end to a line of advancing Guardsmen, unsheathed bayonets on their rifles, and screamed, "Stick it in me, stick it in me!" A soldier obliged him by pricking his buttocks. Later, General Melhouse recalled, an old country doctor at Beulah stitched the young man up. "The doctor chose not to use a pain killer...much to the anguish of the student."

At this point, the Guard and Highway Patrol finally adopted a successful strategy to break up the mob and end the steeplechase from town to town. The Patrol blocked all roads leading east, west, or north out of Hazen, funneling students to the south toward Bismarck. Guardsmen broke the crowd into smaller groups so that sheriffs' deputies could arrest the most obstreperous and obnoxious. The remaining students joined the flight to Bismarck where, by early Saturday afternoon, city police steered them to Riverside Park. The authorities permitted them to hold a beer party in the park as long as they remained there and restrained their behavior. Several found wandering around downtown Bismarck with open beer cans were arrested and jailed. Once the students realized that they had to watch their behavior in the capital city, they remained at Riverside Park. By noon Sunday, 11 May, the exhausted, hung-over students were leaving the city to return to their campuses. The glorious Zap-in had come to a close.

Some Guardsmen had stayed at Zap all Saturday and did not return to home station until Sunday morning. Company D, 164th Engineers, went back to Dickinson late Saturday afternoon after strenuous work at Zap, Beulah, and Hazen, but remained on duty all night and into Sunday morning to assist Dickinson police in watching over students who had escaped the Highway Patrol and had come to that city. When it became evident early Saturday morning that the affair was more trying than the planners had anticipated, General Melhouse called two companies of the 164th Battalion to duty and sent them to Bismarck to join Company D, 141st Battalion, as a reserve force. A platoon of Air Police flew in from Fargo to provide security at Fraine Barracks. Melhouse was concerned that, if the students persisted in roaming the state, his men in the field would tire and need relief, so he had called the extra units not included in the original task force.

Though exhausting and a bit nerve-wracking, the infamous Zip to Zap ended without serious injury, except Jan's Cafe and Lucky's Bar in Zap were thoroughly wrecked. Two Guardsmen received injuries serious enough to require their temporary hospitalization, and at least one student participant would carry a permanent reminder of the affair on his rear end. The newspapers, which had commented so breezily on the happening beforehand, now searched for causes of the turmoil. A Fargo *Forum* reporter explained it best: "The quickest...answer is that these students were drunk out of their minds." Not a political protest, not an organized attack on the establishment, just kids from North Dakota State University, the University of North Dakota, and the Minot and Dickinson state colleges, he noted, jeering and swearing at police and Guardsmen for the hell of it. The spring party cost the state $25,768.58 and 970 Guardsmen a quiet weekend. Governor Guy wrote Mayor Fuchs that after the wild fray, all could be sure that "Zap will not become the Fort Lauderdale of the North." The governor also wrote General Melhouse to congratulate him "for the careful preparations" he "made to respond to any requirement at Zap." Given the provocations at Beulah and Hazen, and the unpredictable movements of the students, the Guard had earned the governor's praise. Overall, Guy concluded, 1969 "seems to be the year for the National Guard." Some portion of the force had been continuously on duty since late January through 11 May. The state had spent $124,768.58 during that time to combat snow, floods, and its overly exuberant young people.

Guardsmen returned to state active duty a year later to face another possible confrontation with college students, an incident preceded by greater apprehension and tension than had been the case before the Zap-in. Faculty and students at the University of North Dakota at Grand Forks had decided to stage a protest against an antiballistic missile site then under construction at Nekoma, ninety-five miles northwest of Grand Forks. Organizers prepared a three-day event for the weekend of 15, 16, and 17 May, 1970, with a rally on the University of North Dakota campus scheduled for Friday evening the 15th, followed by a drive to Nekoma and a demonstration at the antiballistic missile site the next day. Coincidentally, although unrelated to the protest, private entrepreneurs had organized a rock concert for the same weekend at Turtle River State Park near the village of Arvilla, twenty-five miles west of Grand Forks and on the route to Nekoma.

Local, state, and federal officials feared the real possibility of violence and disorder. Initially, Grand Forks County Sheriff Emmons Christopher was most worried about the rock concert, estimating that up to five thousand young people might attend. Christopher and several of his deputies had given assistance during the Zap-in, and he wrote Governor Guy, "I feel obligated...to take necessary precaution to prevent such a reoccurrence as was witnessed at Zap." Arvilla citizens were anxious about property damage and Sheriff Christopher wanted the governor to put the National Guard on alert status, which "would immensely... relieve tension and anxieties" among the people of the little town.

Memories of Zap were only one of several concerns. General Melhouse later recounted that students had attacked Reserve Officers Training Corps campus facilities in Michigan, Wisconsin, and Indiana, and firebombed National Guard armories in Missouri, Minnesota, Wisconsin, and Idaho during the spring of 1970. The antiballistic missile protest obviously represented objections to President Nixon's military policies and could conceivably assume an antimilitary tone with possible threats to National Guard property. Rumors advised that many citizens in and around Nekoma were arming themselves and suggesting that they might attack any unruly college protesters who passed through their vicinity. Also unsettling were the sad events at Kent State University in Ohio and Jackson State College in Mississippi just prior to the antiballistic missile demonstration. At Kent State, on 4 May, Ohio National Guardsmen had fired into a crowd of students who were objecting to the recent American invasion of Cambodia, killing four students. Mississippi State Police had killed two black students at Jackson State during a demonstration on 14 May.

Within this context, the possibilities of violent conflict and injuries or death seemed very real and had public authorities on edge. Governor Guy wrote President Nixon on 13 May, "the volatility of student protests across the country makes" the antiballistic missile protest "one of grave concern to North Dakotans and to me." Given the small size of the Highway Patrol and the necessity of keeping the North Dakota National Guard in reserve for possible use both at the University of North Dakota and at the rock concert, Guy informed Nixon that North Dakota would not accept responsibility for protecting the antiballistic missile site. The federal government would have to assume that task. Governor Guy also released a press statement that same day, announcing that the Highway Patrol and the sheriffs departments of six northeastern counties would be out in full force over the weekend. He went on, "it is necessary for me to place units of the North Dakota National Guard on strategic weekend drill status."

Guy said he regretted calling the Guard "because all too often the Guardsmen and dissenters come from the same group of mutual friends." He had to take action, however, despite the evident maturity and responsibility of the University of North Dakota students, for "too often in recent weeks," he explained, "open anarchy has occurred in other states following legitimate demonstrations." The governor assured the public that the Guard was well trained in riot-control duty and was committed to acting with restraint. He did not expect violence but had to be prepared for it. Guy added, "It must be stressed...that select experienced National Guardsmen assigned to sniper response do carry loaded weapons." This sobering statement indicated the seriousness with which state officials viewed the situation and their underlying fears that major trouble could occur. Unlike the Zap affair, the governor made no attempt to conceal the state's civil disorder preparations.

On 14 May, General Melhouse convened his staff, the 164th Group commander, Colonel Tillotson, and the battalion commanders to plan operations. The Guard had to be ready to quell disorder on the University of North Dakota campus, along the route to and from Nekoma, at the antiballistic missile site, and at Turtle River Park. Melhouse also intended to provide security for Hector Field, Camp Grafton, and the armories at Grand Forks, Grafton, and Devils Lake to prevent sabotage. The planners organized two task forces of 500 men each, a reserve of over 360, and a 200-man security force for the Air National Guard installation. Task Force Nora, commanded by Lieutenant Colonel George Fowler, and Task Force Nancy, under Lieutenant Colonel Bernard Wagner, would go on state active duty at 6:00 P.M., 15 May, while the reserve force and the airmen would remain on federal drill status unless called. The task forces would be prepared to support local civil authority, stop disorders, maintain law and order, control traffic, provide air observation, and render emergency medical aid. Elements of the task forces would take positions at Grand Forks, Langdon, and Lakota, the latter two not far from Nekoma, by early Friday evening. Unlike the Zap incident, the Guard would not wait for civil authorities to request help before moving from home station to their field assembly areas. The Highway Patrol under Ralph Wood also made detailed plans to watch over the demonstration, and, like the Guard, patrol officers would carry loaded weapons, which they had not done at Zap.

Governor Guy had intended that his 13 May press release assure the public that the state would act firmly and keep order, but it generated uneasiness among demonstration organizers because of his statement that some Guardsmen would carry loaded weapons. Late that evening, a Wednesday, Steve Lund, University of North Dakota Student Senate president, made a personal phone call to General Melhouse. The adjutant general knew Lund, who served as chairman of the State Youth Advisory Group on Selective Service. Lund was worried about the impact of Guy's announcement on student protesters and asked Melhouse to come to the campus on the morning of the 14th to talk to students organizing the demonstration. He also requested that the general come alone, in his private car and in civilian clothes, so as to be inconspicuous. Remarkably, given the tenor of the times, with talk of a great generation gap, deep mistrust between youth and older authority figures, and strong antimilitary feelings among many college students, Melhouse agreed to the younger man's request.

Melhouse drove to Grand Forks and slipped into the meeting without notice. "My reception was anything but warm," he recalled, "due in part to the Kent State incident that had occurred just a few days earlier." The general defined his responsibilities for the benefit of the student leaders, giving "a frank explanation of what the Guard would have to do if violence broke out." He noted that in part the Guard would be on duty to protect protesters from some of the less-than-friendly citizens in and around Nekoma. Melhouse told them, "We wanted a peaceful demonstration." After lengthy discussion, they reached an agreement. First, neither the protesters nor the Guard would enter Nekoma. Second, Guardsmen would remain out of contact and out of sight of the demonstrators along the Grand Forks-to-Nekoma route, in order to prevent accidental confrontations. Third, the students accepted the responsibility to keep order, with student marshals scattered throughout the demonstration. It was a noteworthy meeting and a remarkable agreement in those times of distrust and fear. It took courage for Lund to propose to his fellow students that they give a military man a fair hearing, and courage and boldness for General Melhouse to lay aside his uniform, and potentially his dignity, to meet with the students. "I believe that by meeting with" them, he reflected, he was able to make them "aware of the problems that may occur and their own responsibility that no incidents" would take place.

Governor Guy also visited the University of North Dakota campus, on the afternoon of 15 May, just before the evening's opening protest, meeting with faculty members and students "to allay fears that the North Dakota National Guard would be opposing a peaceful demonstration with loaded weapons." The professors were particularly "uptight about the possibility of another Kent State tragedy." Guy explained that only a few selected Guardsmen carried ammunition to deal with snipers, and he too stressed that the Guard would be on duty not only to keep order but also to "protect demonstrators from vigilante action." While on campus, Guy received a telephone call from United States Attorney General John Mitchell demanding that the governor use the Guard to protect contractor's equipment at the antiballistic missile site, but Guy repeated his statement from his 13 May letter to the President that the federal government had to assume that responsibility. The governor believed that the Nixon administration was attempting to maneuver him into suppressing a protest, and, he commented, "I saw no reason why the North Dakota National Guard and the Governor...should be placed in a position that the President and the Attorney General did not wish to be placed in by opposing a demonstration." Guy later argued that the administration sought to embarrass him and also to avoid having United States marshals or federal troops "in a situation where a Kent State type of confrontation could be embarrassing to the Nixon Administration."

Images of Kent State dominated the thoughts of everyone involved. Such thinking seemed unavoidable when anyone reflected on the prospect of Guardsmen and college students coming together that spring. Uncertainty prevailed on the afternoon of 15 May. Authorities had no way to determine how many people might appear at the University of North Dakota rally that evening, participate in Saturday's protest, or attend the rock concert. Estimates for the rally ranged up to eight thousand; for the rock concert, anywhere from five thousand to fifty thousand; and for the march to Nekoma, perhaps as many as five thousand. Everyone knew that caravans from Moorhead State College, in Moorhead, Minnesota, and North Dakota State University in Fargo would travel to the University of North Dakota Friday evening, adding to the crowd. Some police and military intelligence reports predicted that hundreds of out-of-state visitors, any number of whom could be radical agitators, would infiltrate the protest. On Friday evening, before the North Dakota State University group left for Grand Forks, the black comedian and civil rights supporter Dick Gregory thoughtlessly called Guardsmen "misfits." While the ingredients for trouble seemed plentiful, there were positive signs as well. University of North Dakota protest organizers handed out fliers on the afternoon of the 15th urging students to join the march to Nekoma, but asking participants to "Cooperate with the Highway Patrol," adding, "There is no reason to expect violence. The demonstration can be peaceful if we keep the peace."

The protest began on Friday evening at 9:00 P.M. at the University of North Dakota University Center. David Dellinger and John Froines, leaders of the New Mobilization Committee to Stop the War in Vietnam and two of the famous Chicago Seven, charged with inciting riots during the 1968 Democratic convention, gave fiery anti-war, antiestablishment speeches to a crowd of about three thousand. By this time, the Guard and Highway Patrol were in place. General Melhouse established a control headquarters at Camp Grafton to oversee operations in Grand Forks and at the antiballistic missile site. Over five hundred troops had come to Grand Forks, with other units in place at Langdon and Lakota. Brigadier General Earl D. Holly, assistant adjutant general, coordinated communications from the Emergency Operation Center at Fraine Barracks and kept Governor Guy informed. Lieutenant Colonel George Gagnon of the state staff served as intelligence officer in Grand Forks, relaying information regularly to the Camp Grafton control headquarters. Friday, 15 May, passed without incident as the rally at University Center ended at midnight and the crowd dispersed peacefully.

Saturday began for General Melhouse with an unwelcome intrusion from Washington. The National Guard Bureau called to see if the North Dakota National Guard was committed to protecting contractor's equipment at the antiballistic missile site. When Melhouse said no, he was told "that a federalization of the North Dakota National Guard could occur." This came as no surprise, for the adjutant general had been accompanied by an assistant United States attorney general since early Friday morning. The Nixon administration intended, upon the attorney's recommendation, to federalize the Guard and use it to protect the site if the demonstrators attempted to enter federal property or threatened the equipment. Melhouse immediately informed Governor Guy of the call, told him that Task Force Nancy under Lieutenant Colonel Wagner would answer the federal call if necessary, and "that should the Guard be federalized," he "had no recourse" but to obey President Nixon. Guy said he understood.

Despite the fears and concerns, the demonstration came off without incident. Rain had fallen steadily all week, up to Saturday morning, making the dirt access roads to the antiballistic missile site rutted and muddy. Far fewer people than expected, no more than fifteen hundred, perhaps as few as a thousand, made the trek from Grand Forks to Nekoma. Though, due to the mud, they had difficulty reaching the site, which was nothing more than a fifty-foot hole in the ground, protesters arrived around noon, sang songs, planted trees, made a few speeches, and left in small groups until by 4:00 P.M. all had gone. Guardsmen remained in Langdon and Lakota, with General Melhouse at the Camp Grafton control headquarters, receiving information minute by minute as the march proceeded. By 7:00 P.M., General Melhouse released the reserve units on federal drill status and reduced the Hector Field security force by half. At 6:45 Sunday morning, 17 May, "based on reports of no activity," the adjutant general "directed all units to return to home station." The only significant trouble throughout the weekend had occurred at the Turtle River Park concert, which attracted five thousand young people, and where some vandalism and rowdiness led to a few arrests.

In retrospect, the state's response seemed heavy handed. The governor had used the entire Highway Patrol in Grand Forks, Walsh, and Cavalier counties and had mobilized the sheriffs departments of six counties. He had called 1,273 Guardsmen to state active duty, the largest state mobilization in North Dakota history. He had another 363 soldiers held on standby reserve in their armories. The entire effort had cost $57,650, an amount that seemed excessive given the fact that all had turned out peacefully. One veteran of the 231st Battalion recalled, "There never was a time when any serious conditions existed." If the Guy administration's response later appeared excessive, or too attentive to self-appointed critics of the nation's military policies, the context of the times dictated its reactions. General Melhouse issued a press statement on 25 May to explain his moves and justify the cost of the mobilization. Again, Kent State and Jackson State loomed prominently. The adjutant general stressed, "It cannot be presumed in these troubled times that peaceful groups have not been infiltrated by persons intent upon destruction." He explained that he used a large number of Guardsmen because, in any potential civil disturbance, "the force must be adequate to convince the crowd that the crowd will be overpowered. To react with too small a force may serve only to compound the situation." Melhouse emphasized in his conclusion that "It must be recognized that the National Guard has no enthusiasm for such duty." Guardsmen had lost a free weekend, had gotten no drill credit, and "Many came...from the same group as those participating in the demonstration. The members of the Guard," he said, "are reluctant participants."

He had no need to apologize for the state's response. Throughout the 1960s, civil-rights and anti-war demonstrations had too often degenerated into senseless violence when both demonstrators and public officials had indulged in overblown rhetoric and threats of retaliation. Frequently during this time, protesters and politicians alike had made little effort to ensure that peaceful protest could work, and they allowed polarization to intensify. Both Guy and Melhouse, aided in their effort by University of North Dakota protest leaders, had worked carefully and conscientiously to see that students were allowed to use their right to protest while ensuring peace and order. The Guard's presence in the field, but not in contact with the demonstrators, contributed to that outcome. The ultimate irony in the affair was that, although the federal government completed the Nekoma antiballistic missile site in 1975 at a cost of $6 billion, it dismantled and abandoned it a year later.

The North Dakota National Guard did not face another civil disturbance in the decade after 1970, although it continued to assist civil authority regularly. Calls for military assistance varied from year to year, with four in 1970, ten in 1975, and three in 1977. The Guard received only two calls in 1978, one, a major snow-removal operation which ran from 27 January to 14 March and cost $185,000. Governors across the nation increased their use of the Guard in the 1970s, although far less frequently for civil disturbances. In 1970, for example, governors mobilized 60,000 Guardsmen in 157 separate instances, 103 of them for civil disturbances. Four years later, 18,500 troops answered 181 calls, only 24 for disorders, and in 1978 the Guard turned out 278 times with a mere 7 civil disturbances among the calls. Social disorder declined during these years, but evidently governors increasingly saw the service as a useful community-action instrument to be used regularly. This development contained a contradiction, for since 1962 the federal government had committed greater and greater amounts of money to the Guard, and the Army and Air Force included the state services in their operational plans more fully than at any time since the Militia Act of 1903. By the early 1980s, the Guard was more fully manned and better equipped than ever, all at federal expense, yet whether carrying out community-action programs during weekend assemblies or answering the governors' calls to state active duty, Guardsmen served the states more regularly during the decade of the total-force concept than at any time in the years from 1945 to 1962.

The federal government has not called up the Guard during the total-force program, and the full effect of that policy and its impact on the state service will be evident only through the perspective of time. Unquestionably, the Guard's fuller integration into the active services has required much more of Guardsmen in time, education, and training than at any other time in its history. North Dakota has achieved significant success since 1975 in meeting these new demands. Under the leadership of Major General C. Emerson Murry, the state has consistently led the nation in recruiting and retention since 1977. Many other states have adopted General Murry's programs for gaining and keeping Guardsmen. Improvements at Camp Grafton, using ten million dollars from the federal government, now enable a full combat battalion and its support units to remain there on a year-round basis. State units have received training overseas in Germany and Korea and have taken part in training exchanges with other states and the Canadian Army. These achievements are a testament to the legacy of Guardsmen of other eras who struggled to sustain the service despite public indifference and inadequate financial support.

Notes on Sources

All interviews and questionnaires noted for Chapter 10 form an important part of the sources for this chapter. The Lineage Book was essential in keeping track of the numerous post-1962 reorganizations and changes of home stations. Major General LaClair A. Melhouse (retired) provided a variety of orders, reports, press statements, and press clippings pertaining to the Zap-in and the antiballistic missile demonstrations from his personal papers. A letter from Chief Warrant Officer Bryan O. Baldwin explained the part permanent duty assistants and technicians have played since 1946.

The adjutant general's office resumed publishing reports in 1962, with an annual report that year and biennial ones thereafter. Reports from 1962 to 1983 form the core of information in this chapter. They included a separate report on the Air National Guard. Other useful publications were: "Operation Snowbound," 1-21 February 1965: *After Action Report* (Bismarck, N.D., 1965); *Year of the Guard: A Report of Emergency Operations* (Bismarck, N.D., 1970); and *Military Support to Civil Defense: Operation Plans* (Bismarck, N.D., 1972).

In addition to the secondary works noted for Chapter 9, see Roger A. Beaumont, "Constabulatory or Fire Brigade? The Army National Guard," *Parameters: The Journal of the U.S. Army War College,* Vol. 12, No. 1 (March, 1982), pp. 62-69.

Major General Heber L. Edwards,
1937-62.

Major General LeClair A. Melhouse,
1962-75.

Major General C. Emerson Murray,
1975-84.

Major General Alexander P. Macdonald,
1984-present.

North Dakota Adjutants General, 1937-present

North Dakota Air National Guard F-4.

North Dakota Army National Guard riot control operations at Zap, N.D., 1969.

North Dakota Army National Guard helicopter transporting hay to snowbound livestock, 1978.

Some present-day North Dakota Army National Guard equipment during earth-moving operations.

Conclusion

The North Dakota National Guard's history has now passed the century mark. Its heritage lies deeper, however. From the earliest colonial settlements to the last territorial organizations in the 1880s, westward-moving Americans included the militia as one of the institutions they incorporated in their laws and constitutions. The people who settled the Dakota plains were thoroughly familiar with that tradition. When Dakota Territory came into existence in 1861, the universal militia no longer functioned, but the Territory established two companies in 1862 for service in the federal volunteers. The wartime units dissolved after 1865, and organized units did not reappear until the early 1880s, then in the form of the National Guard. Thereafter, the North Dakota National Guard developed haltingly.

In most respects, North Dakota's Guard experience resembled that of other states. Guardsmen continually sought more financial support from their state and the federal government as well as recognition as the Army's first reserve. That struggle waxed and waned until World War I, when the National Defense Act of 1916 guaranteed both money and acceptance. During and after the war, the Guard worked to earn the Army's respect for its military capabilities and unit integrity. Success came in the late 1960s and early 1970s, but at the cost of extensive federal control. The Guard units lost much, although not all, of the social and fraternal nature which had given each state force its distinctive identification.

The history of the North Dakota National Guard differed from that of most of the Guard in that the North Dakota force avoided involvement in industrial disorders. It did not gain a reputation as a union buster because the state had no unions to bust. In North Dakota, unlike the majority of states, the Guard did not face union boycotts or a negative press image, nor did it see its fate held hostage to a legislature divided by industrial strife. If the state's agricultural economy spared the North Dakota National Guard this trauma, it also denied it significant appropriations and strong support from an influential business class. North Dakota's boom-and-bust farm economy and small-town society denied the Guard sufficient funding and an adequate manpower pool. These two shortages left it mired in inefficiency for decades. Only the cold-war draft and substantial federal spending ended these problems.

For all its liabilities, the Guard persisted and displayed an adaptability to changing demands. The American militia initially served to meet the military needs of a widely dispersed population lacking public money and a strong central government. This same institution retained adequate flexibility and support to evolve into a service able to meet national military requirements in the late twentieth century. In 1898, the underfunded, undermanned North Dakota National Guard organized and recruited an eight-

445

company regiment led by its own officers, which gave excellent service in the Philippines. Through no fault of its own, the 164th Infantry wrote no combat record in World War I; its predecessors, the 1st and 2nd North Dakota Infantry Regiments, however, took over three thousand officers and enlisted men, volunteers all, to federal service in 1917.

Another thirty-two hundred North Dakota Guardsmen went to war with the 164th Infantry and the 188th Field Artillery Regiment in 1941. Though constant transfers and large draftee infusions diluted the purely state nature of the units, North Dakota National Guard officers and noncommissioned officers remained at their core. The infantry and artillery outfits made clear that, with proper training and equipment, Guardsmen could meet the demands of highly technical modern war. They showed as well, in 1951, that, however frustrating, they could cope with the vagaries of a limited war policy that ignored one of their greatest strengths, unit cohesion and integrity, and sent Guardsmen off in ones and twos as replacements.

The limited Berlin Crisis mobilization in 1961 caused few hard feelings in North Dakota and came to be seen by many as a turning point. In 1951, one veteran recalled, the Army "had the idea we were second rate." In the Berlin Crisis, however, the 164th Engineer Battalion tested better than many Regular Army units. Attitudes changed, he added, when "they found we could outperform regulars." Another veteran, who served in the call-ups of 1941, 1951, and 1961, saw the 1961 call-up as different, for "On induction in Aug. of '61," he explained, "I felt the regular army attitude was much more sociable. We were accepted much more readily." Based on the perceptions of many veterans who had served from World War II into the 1970s, the total-force policy has at last given the Guard the professional respect it has always sought. As one long-service Air Guardsman put it, "In the beginning of my tour, 1956," Air Force officers "were condescending. By the end of 1969 we were part of the team."

Becoming a "part of the team" after 1962 has tested the Guard's adaptability as much as meeting wartime mobilizations. Despite severe budgetary problems in the 1890s and the pre-World War I years, and the lack of growth in the 1920s and 1930s, the infantry companies have remained intact at their original home stations. This stability allowed them to develop a strong sense of identity and to recruit promising young enlisted men who later earned commissions. The infantry regiment was, in effect, a large family with strong local ties dispersed over the state. Perpetual reorganization and the growing emphasis on compensation as the motive for enlistment have eroded that family feeling, although they have not destroyed it. The Guard has shown remarkable elasticity in absorbing many changes and has drawn on its past by keeping new units in the old home stations.

People, however, have been the major force which has allowed the service to respond to change and to persist. The Guard has always been a voluntary service and has always attracted capable people willing to give the time and effort to keep it alive. They did so when no ready reward was evident, and each generation produced men who invested twenty, thirty, or more years in the service. Their list is long, beginning with John H. Fraine and Gilbert C. Grafton, followed by men such as Barney C. Boyd and G. Angus Fraser, then Heber L. Edwards, Herman Brocopp, Frank Richards, and Ira M. F. Gaulke, and into the postwar years with Robert Carlson, Alvin Paulson, and Howard Erickson. The Air National Guard now has a history long enough to claim persons with thirty-year careers, like Homer Goebel, James Buzick, Willis Muir, and the first Air Guardsman to serve as adjutant general, Major General Alexander P. Macdonald. These men are representative of the hundreds over the past century who have found part-time military service, and its concomitant comraderie, attractive and satisfying. Their efforts, rather than any specific institutional arrangement, has kept the National Guard a viable and honorable part of the nation's dual military tradition.

Index

Note: All enlisted men, officers and units mentioned in the index are affiliated with the North Dakota National Guard unless otherwise noted.

D

Dakota Territorial National Guard, 4, 6-8.
Dakota Territorial Militia, 2-4.
Dakota Territory, 2, 4-5.
Daley, Major General E. L. (U.S. Army), 270.
Daly, Colonel Paul (U.S. Army), 293.
Davis, John, governor, North Dakota (1956-1960), 401.
Day, Lieutenant F. R., 20th U.S. Infantry, 19-20, 22, 24.
Department of Defense. See Joint Chiefs of Staff.
Devine, Joseph, governor, North Dakota (1898), 59, 109-110.
Devoy, William (adjutant general, 1890-1891), 10, 12.
Dietz, Edward, 229, 359.
Dominick, Leo,
as 2nd lieutenant, Company I, First Infantry, Mexican Border Crisis (1916-1917), 165.
as lieutenant colonel, G-3, 34th Division, 1920s and 1930s, 242.
Downs, Willis H., 99.
Dowsett, Willard, 289.
Drabus, Leonard, 303.
Driscoll, Isadore, 92.
Dudley, Robert, 345.

E

Eckman, L. L., 208, 211.
as captain, Machine Gun Company, 164th Infantry, World War I, 208.
as captain, 3rd Machine Gun Battalion First Division, World War I, 211.
Eddy, Wayne G., 138-139.
Edwards, Heber L.,
as captain, Company M, 164th Infantry, in 1920s, 224, 230, 244, 251.
as adjutant general (1937-1962),
in late 1930s, 233, 245, 248, 250-251, 255-256.
during World War II, 265.
in late 1940s through 1962, 376, 377, 378, 379, 380, 382, 383, 384, 385-386, 391, 394, 398-399, 401-402, 403, 404, 410, 412-413, 442.
death, 406-407.
Edwards, Mrs. Heber L., 251.
Eichelberger, Lieutenant General Robert (U.S. Army), 317, 328.
Eisenhower, General Dwight D. (U.S. Army), 356.
as president, 394, 411.
Ellerman, Raymond, 228.
Erickson, Howard, 257, 382, 402, 420.
Erickson, Luella, 251.
Erickson, Walter, 251.

F

Fancher, Fred B., governor, North Dakota (1899-1900), 109-110.
Faulk, Andrew J., governor, Dakota Territory (1866-1869), 3, 4.
First California Volunteer Infantry (1899), 81, 82.
First North Dakota Infantry,
Mexican Border Crisis (1916-1917), Guardsmen's displeasure with call-up, 166-171.
mobilization, 157-162.
on the Border, 162-163.
recruiting, 157, 161, 167-168.
return to North Dakota, 171-172, 175.
strength, 173.
training, 163-165.
First North Dakota Infantry, World War I,
assigned to 41st Division, 198-200.
mobilization on 15 July 1917, 194-195.
officers, 186-188.
Organized Militiamen in, 179-180, 183.
recruiting for, 186, 192-193.
reorganized and converted to 164th Infantry Regiment, 201.
Second Battalion on active duty, 179-184.
Strength, 179, 180.
See also 164th Infantry Regiment, World War I.

Gray, James D.,
  as captain, Company H, First Infantry, Mexican Border Crisis (1916-1917), 171.
  as captain, Company H, First Infantry, 1917, 181-182.
Green, Marion, 343.
Greene, Brigadier General Francis V. (U.S. Army), 54.
Gross, John, 337, 338.
Gruschius, W. J., 89.
Guy, William L., governor, North Dakota (1960-1972), 412, 429, 430, 431, 434, 435-436, 437-438, 439.

H

Hagar, Charles, 334.
Hagen, Dr. O. J., 268-269.
Hall, Robert K., 237, 283, 289.
Halverson, Henry, 187.
Hanley, James M.,
  as captain, Company F, First Infantry, early twentieth century, 137.
  as major, 3rd Battalion, First Infantry, Mexican Border Crisis (1916-1917), 163, 169.
  as organizer, Second Infantry, 1917, 189-190.
  as major, 2nd Battalion, Second Infantry, 1917, 190, 198.
  as major, 148th Machine Gun Battalion, 41st Division, World War I, 200, 201, 203, 204. In France, 206, 209-210, 212-213.
Hanna, Louis B., governor of North Dakota (1912-1916), 157, 159, 160, 161, 162, 171.
Hannel, A. A., 229
Hansen, Percy M., 244, 335, 337.
Harden, James W., (adjutant general, Dakota National Guard, 1888-1889), 14, 16-17.
Harris, William, 98-99.
Haven, Albert D., 229.
Henninger, Harold, 255.
Henry, Frank S.,
  as captain, Company G, First Infantry, early twentieth century, 137.
  as major, 1st Battalion, First Infantry, Mexican Border Crisis (1916-1917), 162.

as major, 1st Battalion, First Infantry, 1917, 194.
Henry, Theodore S.,
  as captain, headquarters staff, First Infantry, Mexican Border Crisis (1916-1917), 162.
  as captain, headquarters staff, First Infantry and 164th Infantry, World War I, 179, 186, 194. In France, 211.
Hildreth, Melvin A.,
  as lieutenant, in First North Dakota Volunteer Infantry (1898-1899), 54, 62, 110.
  as inspector general and colonel, early twentieth century, 123, 125, 136, 138-139, 144.
Hill, Ernest S., 167-168.
Hodge, Major General John R. (U.S. Army), 298, 299, 329.
Hoffman, Richard, 228, 235, 239.
Holly, Earl, 383, 384, 438.
Holt, Gordon, 255.
Holt, John, 227, 425.
Homme, Arthur G., 171.
Howard, William, governor, Dakota Territory (1878-1880), 4.

J

Jayne, William, governor, Dakota Territory (1861-1863), 2.
Jeffrey, E. W.,
  as lieutenant and captain, Company F, First Infantry, Mexican Border Crisis (1916-1917), 169.
  as captain, Company K, First Infantry, 1917, 186.
Johnson, John H., 26, 44, 97.
Johnson, President Lyndon, 413-414, 420-421.
Johnson, Robert M.,
  as major, 178th Fighter Squadron, Korean War, 389.
  as lieutenant colonel, 119th Fighter Group, late 1950s, 397.
Johnson, Waldemar, 377, 380.
Johnson, Wesley,
  as private, Company B, First Infantry and 164th Infantry, World War I, 193, 194, 198, 201, 202, 204, 206.

V

Vandegrift, General Alexander A. (U.S. Marine Corps), 279, 280-283, 285, 286, 288-289, 291.
Vold, John, 236.

W

Wagner, Bernard, 436, 438.
Walker, Sterling, 237.
Wallace, Fred C., 344.
Walter, Joseph, 389, 393.
Wampler, John, 92.
War Department. See General Staff, U.S. Army, and Joint Chiefs of Staff.
Weber, Milton F., 345, 360, 361, 367, 368.
Weigley, Russell, 1, 344, 420.
Weisenberger, Major John J. (First Washington Volunteer Infantry, 1899), 89-90, 91, 92.
Welch, A. B., 158, 160, 166-167, 186, 190.
Welch, Charles, 228.
Welford, Walter, governor, North Dakota (1935), 246, 249.
Wheelon, Frank,
  as captain, Company D, First Infantry, 1917, 187.
  as major and surgeon, Second Infantry, World War I, 187.
  as major, 116th Sanitary Train, 41st Division, 200.
White, Edwin, 200.
White, Frank,
  as captain, Company G, First Regiment, late nineteenth century, 24, 25.
  as major, 1st Battalion, First North Dakota Volunteer Infantry (1898-1899), 40, 41, 43, 49, 50, 52, 54, 56, 57, 59, 60-62, 65, 66, 67, 68, 76, 77, 80, 81, 97, 100, 102, 105, 106, 108, 111, 112.
  in April 1, 1899 skirmish, 85-88.
  as colonel, Second Infantry, World War I, 189-190, 198.
  as colonel, 116th Train, 41st Division, 200, 202.
  as colonel, commanding Rent, Req-

uisitions, and Claims Service, 1st Depot Division, France, 210-211, 212-213.
Wiest, Albert, 227, 228, 231, 237, 238, 258.
Wilder, Jerry, 382.
Williams, Captain Gideon H., 28th U.S. Infantry, 139-140, 142, 147.
Wilson, Robert, 187.
Wilson, President Woodrow,
  policy during Mexican Border Crisis (1916-1917), 156-157, 160, 174.
  policy during World War I, 164, 172, 179, 184.
Wineman, A. G., 168.
Witte, Herbert, 291-292.
Women, in North Dakota National Guard, 423.
Wood, Major General Leonard (U.S. Army), 154, 173.
Wood, Ralph, 431, 432, 436.
World War I. See First North Dakota Infantry, Second North Dakota Infantry, 164th Infantry, World War I.
World War II, 252-254, 267, 273. See also 164th Infantry, 188th Field Artillery Battalion, 188th Field Artillery Group, 188th Field Artillery Regiment, 957th Field Artillery Battalion.
Wright, Dana,
  as captain, Company H, early twentieth century, 40, 60, 141.
  as major, 2nd Battalion, First Infantry, Mexican Border Crisis (1916-1917), 162, 171, 174.
  as major, 2nd Battalion, First Infantry and 164th Infantry, World War I, 179-183, 187, 188. In France 209.
Wright, Gerald E., 229, 266.

Y

Young, William H., 97-99.
Young's Scouts, 97-100, 115.

Z

Zip to Zap, 430-434, 443.